Conflicts in Feminism

Conflicts in Feminism

edited by

Marianne Hirsch & Evelyn Fox Keller

Routledge · New York & London

Published in 1990 by

Routledge
An imprint of Routledge, Chapman and Hall, Inc.
29 West 35 Street
New York, NY 10001

Published in Great Britain by

Routledge
11 New Fetter Lane
London EC4P 4EE

Library of Congress Cataloging-in-Publication Data

Conflicts in feminism / edited by Marianne Hirsch and Evelyn Fox
   Keller.
     p. cm.
    ISBN 0-415-90177-4 : — ISBN 0-415-90178-2 (pbk.)
    1. Feminism—United States. 2. Feminist criticism—United States.
 I. Hirsch, Marianne, 1949– II. Keller, Evelyn Fox, 1936–
HQ1426.C634 1990
305.42′0973—dc20   90-34999

British Library Cataloguing in Publication Data

Conflicts in feminism.
  1. Feminism
 I. Hirsch, Marianne II. Keller, Evelyn Fox, 1936–
305.42
ISBN 0-415-90177-4

for our women friends

Contents

Introduction: January 4, 1990
Marianne Hirsch and Evelyn Fox Keller
1

I.   Producing Theory / Thinking History

1.   A Gender Diary
Ann Snitow
9

2.   Historical Perspectives:
The Equal Rights Amendment
Conflict in the 1920s
Nancy F. Cott
44

3.   A Conversation about Race and Class
Mary Childers and Bell Hooks
60

4.   Producing Sex, Theory, and Culture:
Gay/Straight Remappings in
Contemporary Feminism
Katie King
82

II.   In Dialogue With

5.   Replacing Feminist Criticism
Peggy Kamuf
105

6.   The Text's Heroine:
A Feminist Critic and Her Fictions
Nancy K. Miller
112

7. Parisian Letters:
Between Feminism and Deconstruction
Peggy Kamuf and Nancy K. Miller
121

8. Deconstructing Equality-Versus-Difference:
Or, the Uses of Poststructuralist Theory for Feminism
Joan W. Scott
134

9. Adjudicating Differences:
Conflicts Among Feminist Lawyers
Martha Minow
149

10. Conflicts and Tensions in the
Feminist Study of Gender and Science
Helen E. Longino and Evelynn Hammonds
164

11. Race, Class, and Psychoanalysis?
Opening Questions
Elizabeth Abel
184

12. The Facts of Fatherhood
Thomas W. Laqueur
205

13. Thinking About Fathers
Sara Ruddick
222

14. The Woman Warrior versus The Chinaman Pacific:
Must a Chinese American Critic Choose between
Feminism and Heroism?
King-Kok Cheung
234

III. Contested Sites

15. Upping the Anti (sic) in Feminist Theory
Teresa de Lauretis
255

16. Split Affinities: The Case of Interracial Rape
Valerie Smith
271

17. Birth Pangs: Conceptive Technologies
and the Threat to Motherhood
Michelle Stanworth
288

18. Notes of a Post-Sex Wars Theorizer
Carla Freccero
305

19. Feminism and Difference: The Perils of
Writing as a Woman on Women in Algeria
Marnia Lazreg
326

20. Criticizing Feminist Criticism
Jane Gallop, Marianne Hirsch, and Nancy K. Miller
349

21. Conclusion: Practicing Conflict in Feminist Theory
Marianne Hirsch and Evelyn Fox Keller
370

Index
387

Notes on Contributors
395

Acknowledgments

We want first to thank our authors, both for what they have taught us, and for their patient cooperation and endurance through the many demands for revisions we made in trying to understand their complex visions. In addition, we have a special debt to those authors, especially Mary Childers, Carla Freccero, and Sara Ruddick for the helpful readings of our own and others' contributions. Gail Reimer's incisive comments have marked this book through its many stages; her friendship is vital to us both. We want to thank Vanessa Schwartz for her sophisticated criticism, her sensitive editorial suggestions, and her boundless good humor. Jane Coppock has spent a great deal of time with this book and we are grateful for the clarity and precision she has brought to it. Finally, we want to thank Bill Germano for his unflagging and unstinting support, and Wanda Bachmann for her invaluable administrative assistance.

Introduction: January 4, 1990

Marianne Hirsch and Evelyn Fox Keller

The very date of this entry seems to compel thinking in terms of decades. For the two of us—though different in field and academic affiliation (not to mention age, temperament, and marital status), still both white/middle-class/heterosexual/ Jewish/American/academic women who came to feminist theory in the late seventies—the comparison cannot help but be painful. A decade ago, we thought of ourselves as part of—even in the vanguard of—a movement that then seemed capable of changing the world. We thought of feminist theory as an arm of that movement, as providing a radically new, and potentially revolutionary wedge for rethinking, and accordingly, for reshaping the social, political, and economic world in which we lived. A decade ago, there was no professional or indexical category called "feminist theory"; rather there were (a few) people who were "doing theory," and doing it as feminists. And loving the sheer headiness of it all.

To say that the economic and political realities of the eighties were unconducive to such idealisms and enthusiasms is not only to say the obvious, but egregiously to understate that obvious. Even though the focus of this book is on conflicts in feminist theory, rather than on the extensive erosion visited by Reagonomics on the hopes and accomplishments of 1970s U.S. feminism, no discussion of either feminism or feminist theory in the 1980s can begin without at least acknowledging the hostility of the larger political, economic, and cultural climate which we have had to endure. Thus, if many of us are wiser and more sober as we enter the 1990s, and considerably sadder and more troubled, it is undoubtedly that larger climate that is in the first place responsible.

Yet, not also, nor in addition to, but as part of that larger climate—more visible to us precisely because more proximal—is a decade of intense mutual criticism and internal divisiveness; a decade in which the feminist illusion of "sisterhood" and the "dream of a common language" gave way to the realities of fractured discourses. Struggle and conflict have emerged as the salient marks of contemporary feminism's contestation for "the practical as well as the theoretical meanings of feminism"—marks, one might add, that are conspicuously available for appropriation and exploitation by the media. But an even greater concern to us than the risks of this exploitation is the danger that our internal conflicts and struggles obscure the commitment to radical transformation that had been so conspicuous a feature of our earlier efforts. Although we are living amidst dramatic political changes, few of these have directly or indirectly been shaped by feminism. As the eighties turn into the nineties, it may well be that the threat to prohibit abortion offers the only uncontested issue around which most if not all feminists can rally.

To be sure, feminism—either as a political movement or as a theoretical venture—has no special claim to conflict: conflict is as inherent in the intellectual endeavor as it is endemic to the political endeavor. Indeed, although we have been trained to think of the two as separable and in fact separate, it was—and for the most part remains—a fundamental tenet of feminism, that theory is always coextensive with practice. As editors of this volume, we choose the singular form for the term "theory," as we do for the term "feminism," precisely in order to emphasize the generic and transitive nature of both efforts. We would like to encourage the reader to think of both "theory" and "feminism" more in the sense of ongoing movement (in Bell Hooks's use of the term) than as specific forms, products, among which one is necessarily obliged to choose. In particular, we think of "theory" as a vector, deriving from many different possible origins, needs, and pressures, and aiming at the fulfillment of many different kinds of ambitions and desires. Sometimes theories are in direct competition with each other. To the extent that people share the same starting points in which the doing of theory begins, and also desire the same goals toward which that effort aims, then they may well have to choose between alternative theories. For the most part, however, the activity of "doing theory"—in feminism as elsewhere—reflects many different starting points, and many different goals: and in relation to these differences, it is not obvious that consensus is either necessary, desirable, or even possible. Different starting points, and different goals of the general venture we call "theory" may bespeak conflicts that neither require nor permit "resolution."

Thus, our intention in focusing on "conflicts in feminism" is not to suggest the possibility of feminism either as a unitary entity, lacking conflict, or as a place (to paraphrase Peggy Kamuf in this volume) into which disagreements can be gathered back, and *in* which conflicts can or should be contained. Rather, it is our assumption that feminism, like theory, is an activity that would only be imagined as unified and seamless under the illusion of a unitary governing ideal: in the first case, of "woman," or in the second, of "truth." But it is no improvement to displace one governing ideal by several disparate ideals of "woman" or "truth," or to disperse and multiply these very notions. What we think would be more useful is a shift in attention from the meanings of "truth," "woman" to the process of "truth-making," "woman/women-making." Nouns in the plural are still nouns, and multiplication is no escape from reification. For this reason, we reject the notion of "feminisms" and choose instead to speak of "feminism." Similarly, without claiming to speak for all feminists, we have chosen to use a pronoun many feminists have discarded as exclusionary, at worst, or confusing, at best. Preempted from the authorial "I" by the collaborative nature of this project, we have come to a shifting and fluctuating "we" which we try to use carefully, referring at times specifically to the two of us, at other times more generally to a proximal and permeable group of feminists for whom we felt, at least provisionally and in specific instances, we could speak. Although this is an imperfect solution, we felt it to be preferable to the only other available option—a passive voice that elides agency from the endeavor of thinking and writing. In experimenting with forms of "we," we share also Ann Snitow's conviction (in this volume) that the "we" "remains politically important . . . in spite of its false promise of unity."

From the very beginning of our attempt to "do" theory as feminists, it was already evident not only that there were major differences, and conflicts, among us, which we needed not only to recognize but to deal with; it was also clear that these internal differences and conflicts had the potential capability of disrupting the collective effort of gender analysis. So that, even if conflict is peculiar neither to feminism in general, nor to the particular forms it has taken in the U.S. in the late 1980s, the motivation for this particular book, at this particular moment in time, *is* quite specific.

As the 1980s drew to a close, both of us—even as we came to this issue from different directions—found ourselves confronting, at the heart of the venture of doing feminist theory, the realization of the disruptive potential of the conflicts with which we had been living and struggling as feminists. Differences within feminist theory had now become sources of acute pain for ourselves and for many around us. That the cumulative effect of debates over race and class, pornography, the "Sears" Case, the "Baby M" Case (to mention only the most notorious sites of contestation) had so intensified already existing divisions that discussion threatened to stall altogether. Somewhere at the intersection between our dreams, our illusions, and our fears, we felt that our thinking had reached a point of critical implosion. In what emerged as a painful irony, and despite our best efforts, we found ourselves repeatedly caught in oppositions that derived directly from the very dichotomous structures our theoretical efforts had aimed to dismantle. Accordingly, it seemed necessary to us, if the entire endeavor of doing theory as feminists was to survive as a progressive force in the world, to understand more fully the nature of our divisions and conflicts, as well as how these divisions and conflicts were working (or not working) for and against feminism. Most importantly, we felt a certain urgency about identifying better strategies for practicing conflict, for restoring dialogue where it had broken down, and perhaps especially, for reviving the joys and pleasures of working together as feminists, for making productive our multiple and manifold differences. Given that this necessary understanding eluded us as individuals, even in small groups, we sought to elicit the help of a larger and ever more diverse feminist community, conflicted and divided though it now seemed.

In the summer of 1988, we formulated a plan: in conversation with many friends, we drew up a list of those issues that seemed to be most critically divisive at that particular moment, with the idea that we would seek out individuals so situated that they might be able to identify and articulate the interests, hopes, fears, and anxieties that fueled the different and often opposing positions that various feminists were taking. We were not so naive as to think possible, or even wish for, "objective," neutral, or comprehensive accounts; it was sympathy rather than objectivity for which we hoped. Often this meant finding contributors not obviously identified with one position or another. We assumed, of course, that each contributor would nevertheless have positions, investments, hopes, and anxieties of her own; we asked only that she make the effort to inhabit other positions long enough to find out what would be required to restore and renew conversation and dialogue. As we proceeded, we made many adjustments—to the list of issues, to the list of contributors, and to the actual essays finally written. But in order to give the reader a sense of how this collection actually came into being—the "assignment" we gave our authors—we include the proposal we sent to our prospective contributors and publisher:

> Discussions within feminist theory today are racked by intense conflicts. While feminists have in principle tended to agree that difference is a more productive theoretical and political category than either universalizing consensus or divisive oppositions, in practice, actual differences within feminist discourse have tended to erupt into separate camps. At this moment in time, some of these conflicts have proven so divisive that they seem to foreclose rather than stimulate debate, even at times appearing to threaten the very viability of contemporary feminism as a political and theoretical venture. The need for a probing and reflective analysis of divisive issues in feminism today has come to assume urgent proportions.
>
> In this book we propose to explore the general problematic of difference and division by inviting contributors to examine several of the most critically divisive issues in contemporary U.S. feminist theory. We have chosen contributors who seem best able to perceive and articulate the interests of opposing perspectives. We ask them both to map the particular territory of their respective debates in their historical specificity, and to focus on such general questions as: What drives feminist discussions from a recognition of differences to the explosion of polarizing conflicts? What is at stake in the particular debate you are discussing? Can you make specific recommendations for productive ways of dealing with unreconcilable differences? Is it possible to name our disagreements, accept their unresolvability, and still move forward? Do our choices in dealing with conflict need to be confined to resolution or eruption?

Inevitably, both our choice and definition of topics reflect the idiosyncracy of our personal perspectives; equally inevitably, they reflect the interests and availability of contributing authors. Above all, we wished to avoid schematic divisions— e.g., socialist/liberal/radical; French/American; essentialist/post-modernist/psychoanalytic; empiricist/standpoint/post-structuralist—that in our view had already grown stale. Many conflicts surface, and resurface, under a number of different rubrics; some conflicts (of equal if not greater significance) are not represented.

In the end, however, despite lapses and redundancies, we had a list with which we were content. It includes discussion of the most conspicuous debates (e.g., the "Sex Wars"; the "Baby M" and "Sears" cases); of those themes and issues that both cut across and underlie these (and other) debates: most notably, that of the relation of gender to other prominent social demarcations of race, class, and sexual preference; it includes an interrogation of the meaning of "motherhood" (and "fatherhood"), as well as of "rights" and "responsibilities," both individual and collective; it includes, finally, a questioning of the meaning(s) of feminism: does feminism have an epistemological, ethical, or otherwise "essential" core? Each of the topics we identified is represented by one or more essays, almost all of which were written in direct response to the proposal we sent out.

Our organization of the resulting essays is surely idiosyncratic. Roughly, we divided them into three groups: Part I includes those essays that offer, albeit from very different perspectives, broad narratives of our collective history of producing theory as feminists; Part II includes explicit discussions of feminist concerns with major institutional and philosophical structures "outside of," but in dialogue with feminism; and lastly, Part III includes those essays that focus primarily on contested sites within feminism.[1]

Finally, at the very end, we turn to our own hopes and expectations for this volume. As we wrote to prospective contributors in the concluding paragraph of our original proposal, "it is our hope that out of these essays will emerge new models for a discourse of difference—models that would preserve the dynamic possibilities but defuse the explosive potential of enduring disagreements." Accordingly, in a conclusion to this volume, we attempt, as we promised, "to review this hope in the light of the contributed essays." In a final coda, we offer our own, more personal perspectives on the legacy this past decade of conflicts in feminism has left.

Note

1. At the same time, we join Teresa de Lauretis (in this volume) in her questioning of the very distinction between "inside" and "outside." See also the discussion of this false divide in "Criticizing Feminist Criticism" (Part III, this volume).

I
Producing Theory/Thinking History

1

A Gender Diary

Ann Snitow

In the early days of this wave of the women's movement, I sat in a weekly consciousness raising group with my friend A. We compared notes recently: What did you think was happening? How did you think our own lives were going to change? A. said she had felt, "Now I can be a woman; it's no longer so humiliating. I can stop fantasizing that secretly I am a man, as I used to, before I had children. Now I can value what was once my shame." Her answer amazed me. Sitting in the same meetings during those years, my thoughts were roughly the reverse: "Now I don't have to be a woman anymore. I need never become a mother. Being a woman has always been humiliating, but I used to assume there was no exit. Now the very idea 'woman' is up for grabs. 'Woman' is my slave name; feminism will give me freedom to seek some other identity altogether."

On its face this clash of theoretical and practical positions may seem absurd, but it is my goal to explore such contradictions, to show why they are not absurd at all. Feminism is inevitably a mixed form, requiring in its very nature such inconsistencies. In what follows I try to show first, that a common divide keeps forming in both feminist thought and action between the need to build the identity "woman" and give it solid political meaning and the need to tear down the very category "woman" and dismantle its all-too-solid history. Feminists often split along the lines of some version of this argument, and that splitting is my subject. Second, I argue that though a settled compromise between these positions is currently impossible, and though a constant choosing of sides is tactically unavoidable, feminists—and indeed most women—live in a complex relationship to this central feminist divide. From moment to moment we perform subtle psychological and social negotiations about just how gendered we choose to be.

This tension—between needing to act as women and needing an identity not overdetermined by our gender—is as old as Western feminism. It is at the core of what feminism is. The divide runs, twisting and turning, right through movement history. The problem of identity it poses was barely conceivable before the eighteenth century, when almost everyone saw women as a separate species.

Since then absolute definitions of gender difference have fundamentally eroded, and the idea "woman" has become a question rather than a given.

In the current wave of the movement, the divide is more urgent and central a part of feminism than ever before. On the one hand, many women moved by feminism are engaged by its promise of solidarity, the poetry of a retrieved worth. It feels glorious to "reclaim an identity they taught [us] to despise." (The line is Michelle Cliff's.) Movement passion rescues women-only groups from contempt; female intimacy acquires new meanings and becomes more threatening to the male exclusiveness so long considered "the world."

On the other hand, other feminists, often equally stirred by solidarity, rebel against having to be "women" at all. They argue that whenever we uncritically accept the monolith "woman," we run the risk of merely relocating ourselves inside the old closed ring of an unchanging feminine nature. But is there any such reliable nature? These feminists question the eternal sisterhood. It may be a pleasure to be "we," and it may be strategically imperative to struggle as "we," but who, they ask, are "we"?[1]

This diary was begun to sort out my own thoughts about the divide. I have asked myself, is the image of a divide too rigid, will it only help to build higher the very boundaries I seek to wear down? Yet I keep stumbling on this figure in my descriptions of daily movement life. Perhaps the problem is my own. But others certainly have shared the experience of "division." Maybe the image works best as a place to start, not as a conclusion. A recurring difference inside feminism seems to lie deep, but it is also mobile, changing in emphasis, not (I'm happy to say) very orderly.

Take as an example my checkered entries about the women's peace movement. A number of feminists, myself included, felt uneasy about the new wave of women-only peace groups of the early 1980s. As feminist peace activist Ynestra King characterized the new spirit: "A feminist peace sensibility is forming; it includes new women's culture and traditional women's culture."[2] Some saw such a fusion between traditional female solidarity and new women's forms of protest as particularly powerful. Others felt that the two were at cross-purposes. Might blurring them actually lead to a watering down of feminism? The idea that women are by definition more nurturant, life giving, and less belligerent than men is very old; the idea that such gender distinctions are social, hence subject to change, is much more recent, fragile, counterintuitive, and contested. Can the old idea of female specialness and the newer idea of a female outlook forged in social oppression join in a movement? And just how?

A study group met for a time in 1983 to talk about women's peace politics.[3] *I was the irritating one in our group, always anxious about the nature of our project. I was the one who always nagged, "Why a* women's *peace movement?"*
I argued with a patient Amy Swerdlow that women asking men to protect the

*children (as Women Strike for Peace asked Congress in 1961) was a repetition
of an old, impotent, suppliant's gesture. Men had waged wars in the name of
just such protection. And besides, did we want a world where only women worried
about the children?*[4] *"So what's* your *solution?," the good-tempered group
wanted to know. "Should women stop worrying about the children? Who trusts
men to fill the gap?" Amy described how the loving women, going off to Washington to protest against nuclear testing, filled their suburban freezers with dinners
so their families would miss them less.*

*I tried to explain the source of my resistance to the motherly rhetoric of the
women's peace movement. During the 1960s, some of us had angrily offered to
poison men's private peace, abort men's children. We proposed a bad girl's
exchange: We'd give up protection for freedom, give up the approval we got for
nurturance in exchange for the energy we'd get from open anger.*

*Of course, I knew what the group would ask me next, and rightly, too: "Whose
freedom? Which rage? Isn't abandoning men's project of war rage enough? And
is women's powerlessness really mother's fault?" Although I reminded the group
that the new wave of feminists never blamed motherhood as much as the media
claimed, we did run from it, like the young who scrawled the slogan on Paris
walls in 1968: "Cours, camarade, le vieux monde est derrière toi." (Run,
comrade, the past is just behind you.)*

This scene is caricature, but it begins to get at the mood of our group. Fractious,
I was always asking the others if they didn't agree that peace is assumed to be
a women's issue for all the wrong reasons. I argued that if there is to be no more
"women-only" when it comes to emotional generosity or trips to the laundry,
why "women-only" in the peace movement? Maybe the most radical thing we
could do would be to refuse the ancient women-peace connection? The army is
a dense locale of male symbols, actions, and forms of association, so let men sit
in the drizzle with us at the gates of military installations. Even if theorists
emphasize the contingent and the historical and say that peace is an issue that
affects women *differently* from men because of our different social position, we
are trapped again in an inevitably oversimplified idea of "women." Are *all* women
affected the same way by war? Or is class or age or race or nationality as important
a variable? What do we gain, I asked the group, when we name the way we suffer
from war as a specifically *women's* suffering? And so it went.

Until one day Ynestra King tactfully suggested that perhaps I was seeking a
mixed group to do my peace activism. (Mixed is a code word for men and women
working together.) I was horrified. We were laughing, I'm pleased to recall, as
I confessed myself reluctant to do political work in mixed groups. The clichés
about women in the male left making the coffee and doing the xeroxing were all
literally true in my case. (I blame myself as well; often I chose those tasks, afraid
of others.) Only by working with women had I managed to develop an intense

and active relationship to politics at all. Not only had my political identity been forged in the women-only mold, but the rich networks I had formed inside feminism were the daily source of continued activism. My experience of the women-only peace camp at Greenham Common, England was to become a source of continued political energy and inspiration. Women-only (the abstraction) was full of problems; women-only (the political reality in my life) was full of fascination, social pleasure, debates about meaning in the midst of actions taken, even sometimes, victories won.

The political meaning of these sides changes, as does the place they hold in each woman's life. But no matter where each feminist finds herself in the argument about the meaning of women-only, all agree that in practical political work, separate women's groups are necessary. Whatever the issue, feminists have gained a great deal by saying, "We are 'women,' and this is what 'women' want." This belief in some ground of shared experience is the social basis from which any sustained political struggle must come.

Even feminists like myself, anxious about any restatement of a female ideal— of peacefulness or nurturance or light—are constantly forced in practice to consider what activists lose if we choose to say peace is *not* a women's issue. We keep rediscovering the necessity to speak specifically as women when we speak of peace because the female citizen has almost no representation in the places where decisions about war and peace are made—the Congress, the corporation, the army.

In 1979, President Jimmy Carter fired former congresswoman Bella Abzug from her special position as co-chair of his National Advisory Commission for Women because the women on the commission insisted on using that platform to talk about war and the economy. These, said the President, were not women's issues; women's role was to support the President. Carter was saying in effect that women have no place in general social debate, that women, as we learned from the subsequent presidential campaign, are a "special interest group."

What a conundrum for feminists: Because women have little general representation in Congress, our demand to be citizens—gender unspecified—can be made only through gender solidarity; but when we declare ourselves separate, succeed, for example, in getting our own government commission, the President turns around and tries to make that power base into a ghetto where only certain stereotypically female issues can be named. So, however separate we may choose to be, our "separate" has to be different from his "separate," a distinction it's hard to keep clear in our own and other minds, but one we must keep trying to make.

This case may seem beside the point to radicals who never vested any hope in the federal government in the first place. But the firing of Bella Abzug was a perfect public embodiment of the puzzle of women's situation. The idea that "women" can speak about war is itself the unsettled question, requiring constant public tests. It is no coincidence that Bella Abzug was one of the organizers of Women Strike for Peace in 1961. She must have observed the strengths and weaknesses in the public image of mothers for peace; then, on the coattails of feminism, she tried to be an insider, a congresswoman presumably empowered to speak—as a woman, or for women, or for herself—on any public topic. People with social memory were able to witness the problem that arises for the public woman, no matter what her stance. Feminism is potentially radical in almost all its guises precisely because it interprets this injustice, makes the Abzug impasse visible. Once visible, it begins to feel intolerable.[5]

By traveling along the twisted track of this argument, I have made what I think is a representative journey, what feminist historians such as Joan Kelly and Denise Riley have called an "oscillation," which is typical of both feminist theory and practice.[6] Such oscillations are inevitable for the foreseeable future. In a cruel irony that is one mark of women's oppression, when women speak *as women* they run a special risk of not being heard because the female voice is by our culture's definition that-voice-you-can-ignore. But the alternative is to pretend that public men speak for women or that women who speak inside male-female forums are heard and heeded as much as similarly placed men. Few women feel satisfied that this neutral (almost always male) public voice reflects the particulars of women's experience, however varied and indeterminate that experience may be.

Caught between not being heard because we are different and not being heard because we are invisible, feminists face a necessary strategic leap of nerve every time we shape a political action. We weigh the kinds of powerlessness women habitually face; we choose our strategy—as women, as citizens—always sacrificing some part of what we know.

Because "separate" keeps changing its meaning depending on how it is achieved and in what larger context its political forms unfold, there is no fixed progressive position, no final theoretical or practical resting place for feminists attempting to find a social voice for women. Often our special womanness turns into a narrow space only a moment after we celebrate it; at other times, our difference becomes a refuge and source of new work, just when it looked most like a prison in which we are powerless. And finally, although women differ fundamentally about the meaning and value of "woman," we all live partly in, partly out of this identity by social necessity. Or as Denise Riley puts it, "Women are not women in all aspects of their lives."[7]

Peace is *not* a women's issue; at the same time, if women don't claim a special relationship to general political struggles, we will experience that other, more common specialness reserved for those named women: We will be excluded from talking about and acting on the life and death questions that face our species.

Names for a Recurring Feminist Divide

In every case, the specialness of women has this double face, though often, in the heat of new confrontations, feminists suffer a harmful amnesia; we forget about this paradox we live with. Feminist theorists keep renaming this tension, as if new names could advance feminist political work. But at this point new names are likely to tempt us to forget that we have named this split before. In the service of trying to help us recognize what we are fated—for some time—to repeat, here is a reminder of past taxonomies.

Minimizers and Maximizers

The divide so central as to be feminism's defining characteristic goes by many names. Catharine Stimpson cleverly called it the feminist debate between the "minimizers" and the "maximizers."[8] Briefly, the minimizers are feminists who want to undermine the category "woman," to minimize the meaning of sex difference. (As we shall see, this stance can have surprisingly different political faces.) The maximizers want to keep the category (or feel they can't do otherwise), but they want to change its meaning, to reclaim and elaborate the social being "woman," and to empower her.

Radical Feminists and Cultural Feminists

In *Daring to Be Bad: A History of the Radical Feminist Movement in America, 1967–1975,* Alice Echols sees this divide on a time line of the current women's movement, with "radical feminism" more typical of the initial feminist impulse in this wave succeeded by "cultural feminism." Echols's definition of the initial bursts of "radical feminism" shows that it also included "cultural feminism" in embryo. She argues that both strains were present from the first—contradictory elements that soon proclaimed themselves as tensions in sisterhood. Nonetheless, the earlier groups usually defined the commonality of "women" as the shared fact of their oppression by "men." Women were to work separately from men not as a structural ideal but because such separation was necessary to escape a domination that only a specifically feminist (rather than mixed, left) politics could change. Echols gives as an example Kathie Sarachild, who disliked the women's contingents at peace marches against the Vietnam War: "Only if the *stated* purpose of a women's group is to fight *against* the relegation of women to a separate position and status, in other words, to fight for women's liberation, only then does a separate women's group acquire a revolutionary character. Then separation becomes a base for power rather than a symbol of powerlessness.[9]

On the other side stands Echols's category, "cultural feminism." In her depiction of the divide, the cultural feminist celebration of being female was a retreat from "radical feminism": "[I]t was easier to rehabilitate femininity than to abolish gender.[10] She offers as a prime example of the growth of cultural feminism the popularity of Jane Alpert's "new feminist theory," published in *Ms.* magazine in 1973 as "Mother Right":

> [F]eminists have asserted that the essential difference between women and men does not lie in biology but rather in the roles that patriarchal societies (men) have required each sex to play . . . . However, a flaw in this feminist argument has persisted: *it contradicts our felt experience of the biological difference between the sexes as one of immense significance* . . . . The unique consciousness or sensibility of women, the particular attributes that set feminist art apart, and a compelling line of research now being pursued by feminist anthropologists all point to the idea that *female biology is the basis of women's powers*. Biology is hence the source and not the enemy of feminist revolution.[11]

Echols concludes that by 1973, "Alpert's contention that women were united by their common biology was enormously tempting, given the factionalism within the movement."[12]

Ironically, then, the pressure of differences that quickly surfaced in the women's movement between lesbians and straight women, between white and black, between classes, was a key source of the new pressure towards unity. The female body offered a permanence and an immediately rich identity that radical feminism, with its call to a long, often negative struggle of resistance, could not.

As her tone reveals, in Echols's account, "radical feminism" is a relatively positive term and "cultural feminism" an almost entirely negative one. As I'll explain later, I have a number of reasons for sharing this judgment. Finally, though, it won't help us to understand recurring feminist oppositions if we simply sort them into progressive versus reactionary alignments. The divide is nothing so simple as a split between truly radical activists and benighted conservative ones, or between real agents for change and liberal reformers, or between practical fighters and sophisticated theorists. The sides in this debate don't line up neatly in these ways. Maximizers and minimizers have political histories that converge and diverge. But a pretense of neutrality won't get us anywhere either. I'm describing a struggle here, and every account of it contains its overt or covert tropism toward one side or the other.

Essentialists and Social Constructionists

We have only to move from an account of movement politics to one of feminist theory in order to reverse Echols's scenario of decline. In academic feminist discussion, the divide between the "essentialists" and the "social constructionists" has been a rout for the essentialists. Briefly, essentialists (like Alpert, above) see gender as rooted in biological sex differences. Hardly anyone of any camp will now admit to being an essentialist, since the term has become associated with a naive claim to an eternal female nature. All the same, essentialism, like its counterpart, cultural feminism, is abundantly present in current movement work. When Barbara Deming writes that "the capacity to bear and nurture children gives women a special consciousness, a spiritual advantage rather than a disadvantage," she is assigning an enduring meaning to anatomical sex differences. When Andrea Dworkin describes how through sex a woman's "insides are worn away over time, and she, possessed, becomes weak, depleted, usurped in all her physical and mental energies . . . by the one who occupies her," she is asserting that in sex women are immolated as a matter of course, in the nature of things.[13]

Social construction—the idea that the meaning of the body is changeable—is far harder to embrace with confidence. As Ellen Willis once put it, culture may shape the body, but we feel that the body has ways of pushing back.[14] To assert that the body has no enduring, natural language often seems like a rejection of common sense. Where can a woman stand—embodied or disembodied—in the flow of this argument?

Writing not about gender in general but about that more focused issue of bodies and essences, sexuality, Carole Vance has raised questions about the strengths and vicissitudes of social construction theory. She observes that the social constructionists who try to discuss sexuality differ about just what is constructed. Few would go so far as to say that the body plays no part at all as a material condition on which we build desire and sexual mores. But even for those social constructionists who try to escape entirely from any a priori ideas about the body, essentialism makes a sly comeback through unexamined assumptions. For example, how can social constructionists confidently say they are studying "sexuality"? If there is no essential, transhistorical biology of arousal, then there is no unitary subject, "sexuality," to discuss: "If sexuality is constructed differently at each time and place, can we use the term in a comparatively meaningful way? . . . [H]ave constructionists undermined their own categories? Is there an 'it' to study?"[15]

In the essentialist-versus-social constructionist version of the divide, one can see that one term in the argument is far more stable than the other. Essentialism such as Jane Alpert's in "Mother Right" assumes a relatively stable social identity in "male" and "female," while as Carole Vance argues, social construction is at its best as a source of destabilizing questions. By definition social construction theory cannot offer a securely bounded area for the study of gender; instead it initiates an inspiring collapse of gender verities.

Cultural Feminists and Poststructuralists

The contrast between more and less stable categories suggests yet another recent vocabulary for the feminist divide. In "Cultural Feminism versus Post-Structuralism: The Identity Crisis in Feminist Theory," Linda Alcoff puts Echols's definition of "cultural feminism" up against what she sees as a more recent counterdevelopment: feminist poststructural theory. By speaking only of "the last ten years," Alcoff lops off the phase of "radical feminism" that preceded "cultural feminism" in movement history, leaving the revisionist image of extreme essentialism (such as Mary Daly's in *Gyn/Ecology*) as the basic matrix of feminist thought from which a radical "nominalism" has more recently and heroically departed, calling all categories into doubt.[16] It is no accident that with attention to detail, Alice Echols can trace a political decline from "radical feminism" to "cultural feminism" between 1967 and 1975 while Linda Alcoff can persuasively trace a gain in theoretical understanding from "cultural feminism" to "poststructuralism" between 1978 and 1988. Put them together and both narratives change: Instead of collapse or progress, we see one typical oscillation in the historical life of the divide.

These two accounts are also at odds because they survey very different political locations: Echols is writing about radical feminist activism, Alcoff about developments in academic feminist theory. Though political activism has developed a different version of the central debate from that of the more recent academic feminism, both confront the multiple problems posed by the divide. Nor will a model that goes like this work: *thesis* (essentialism, cultural feminism), *antithesis* (poststructuralism, deconstruction, Lacanian psychoanalysis), *synthesis* (some stable amalgam of women's solidarity that includes radical doubts about the formation, cohesion, and potential power of the group).

Instead, the divide keeps forming *inside* each of these categories. It is fundamental at any level one cares to meet it: material, psychological, linguistic. For example, U.S. feminist theorists don't agree about whether poststructuralism tends more often toward its own version of essentialism (strengthening the arguments of maximizers by recognizing an enduring position of female Other) or whether poststructuralism is instead the best tool minimalists have (weakening any universalized, permanent concept such as Woman).[17] Certainly poststructuralists disagree among themselves, and this debate around and inside poststructuralism should be no surprise. In feminist discourse a tension keeps forming between finding a useful lever in female identity and seeing that identity as hopelessly compromised.

I'm not regressing here to the good old days of an undifferentiated, undertheorized sisterhood, trying to blur distinctions others have usefully struggled to establish, but I do want to explore a configuration—the divide—that repeats in very different circumstances. For example, in an earlier oscillation, both radical feminism and liberal feminism offered their own versions of doubt about cultural feminism and essentialism. Liberal feminists refused the idea that biology should structure women's public and sometimes even their private roles. Radical feminists saw the creation and maintenance of gender difference as the means by which patriarchs controlled women.[18] Though neither group had the powerful theoretical tools later developed by the poststructuralists, both intimated basic elements in poststructuralist work: that the category "woman" was a construction, a discourse over which there had been an ongoing struggle; and that the self, the "subject," was as much the issue as were social institutions. To be sure, these early activists often foolishly ignored Freud; they invoked an unproblematic "self" that could be rescued from the dark male tower of oppression; and they hourly expected the radical deconstruction of gender, as if the deconstruction of what had been constructed was relatively easy. Nonetheless, radical, philosophical doubts about the cohesion of "woman" have roots that go all the way down in the history of both liberal and radical feminism.

Recently I asked feminist critic Marianne DeKoven for a piece she and Linda Bamber wrote about the divide for the Modern Language Association in 1982. "Feminists have refined our thinking a great deal since then," she said. Yes, no doubt; but there is not much from the recent past that we can confidently discard. In fact, the Bamber-DeKoven depiction of the divide remains useful because we are nowhere near a synthesis that would make these positions relics of a completed phase. One side of the divide, Bamber says in her half of the paper, "has been loosely identified with American feminism, the other with French feminism."

But in fact these labels are inadequate, as both responses can be found in the work of both French and American feminists. Instead of debating French vs. American feminism, then, I want to define the two poles of our responses nonjudgmentally and simply list their characteristics under Column A and Column B.

Column A feminism is political, empirical, historical. A Column A feminist rebels against the marginalization of women and demands access to "positions that require knowledge and confer power." A Column A feminist insists on woman as subject, on equal pay for equal work, on the necessity for women to be better represented in political life, the media, history books, etc. Column A feminism assumes, as Marks and de Courtivron put it, "that women have (always) been present but invisible and if they look they will find themselves."

The Column B feminist, on the other hand, is not particularly interested in the woman as subject. Instead of claiming power, knowledge and high culture for women, Column B feminism attacks these privileged quantities as "phallogocentric." . . . The feminine in Column B is part of the challenge to God, money, the phallus, origins and ends, philosophical privilege, the transcendent author, representation, the Descartian cogito, transparent language, and so on. The feminine is valorized as fragment, absence, scandal . . . . Whereas the Column A feminist means to occupy the center on equal terms with men, the Column B feminist, sometimes aided by Derrida, Lacan, Althusser, Levi-Strauss, and Foucault, subverts the center and endorses her own marginality.[19]

No doubt Bamber and DeKoven would restate these terms now in the light of eight more years of good, collective feminist work, but I am trying to write against the grain of that usually excellent impulse here, trying to suggest a more distant perspective in which eight years become a dot.

Alcoff is only the latest in a long line of frustrated feminists who want to push beyond the divide, to be done with it. She writes typically: "We cannot simply embrace the paradox. In order to avoid the serious disadvantages of cultural feminism and post-structuralism, feminism needs to transcend the dilemma by developing a third course . . . ."[20] But "embracing the paradox" is just what feminism cannot choose but do. There is no transcendence, no third course. The urgent contradiction women constantly experience between the pressure to be a woman and the pressure not to be one will change only through a historical process; it cannot be dissolved through thought alone.

This is not to undervalue theory in the name of some more solid material reality but to emphasize that the dualism of the divide requires constant work; it resists us. It's not that we can't interrupt current patterns, not that trying to imagine our way beyond them isn't valuable, but that such work is continual.[21] What is more, activists trying to make fundamental changes, trying to push forward the feminist discourse and alter its material context, don't agree about what sort of synthesis they want. Nor can activists turn to theorists in any direct way for a resolution of these differences. Activism and scholarship have called forth different readings of the divide, but neither of these locations remains innocent of the primary contradiction. There is no marriage of theoretical mind and activist brawn to give us New Feminist Woman. The recognition that binary thinking is a problem doesn't offer us any immediate solution.

In other words, neither cultural feminism nor poststructuralism suggests a clear course when the time comes to discuss political strategy. Though we have learned much, we are still faced with the continuing strategic difficulty of *what to do*. As Michèle Barrett puts it: "It does not need remarking that the postmodernist point of view is explicitly hostile to any political project behind the ephemeral."[22] The virtue of the ephemeral action is its way of evading ossification of image or meaning. Ephemerally, we can recognize a possibility we cannot live out, imagine a journey we cannot yet take. We begin: The category "woman" is a fiction; then, poststructuralism suggests ways in which human beings live by fictions; then, in its turn, activism requires of feminists that we elaborate the fiction "woman" as if she were not a provisional invention at all but a person we know well, one in need of obvious rights and powers. Activism and theory weave together here, working on what remains the same basic cloth, the stuff of feminism.

Some theorists like Alcoff reach for a synthesis, a third way, beyond the divide, while others like Bamber and DeKoven choose instead the metaphor of an inescapable, irreducible "doubleness"—a word that crops up everywhere in feminist discussion. To me, the metaphor of doubleness is the more useful: it is a reminder of the unresolved tension on which feminism continues to be built. As Alice Walker puts it in her formal definition of a "womanist" (her word for a black feminist): "Appreciates and prefers women's culture, women's emotional flexibility . . . committed to survival and wholeness of entire people, male and female. Not a separatist, except periodically, for health."[23]

This is not to deny change but to give a different estimate of its rate. Mass feminist consciousness has made a great difference; we have created not only new expectations but also new institutions. Yet, inevitably, the optimism of activism has given way to the academic second thoughts that tell us why our work is so hard. For even straightforward, liberal changes—like equal pay or day care—are proving far more elusive than feminists dreamed in 1970. We are moving more slowly than Western women of the late twentieth century can easily accept—or are even likely to imagine.

Motherists and Feminists

If the long view has a virtue beyond the questionable one of inducing calm, it can help feminists include women to whom a rapid political or theoretical movement forward has usually seemed beside the point—poor women, peasant women, and women who for any number of reasons identify themselves not as feminists but as militant mothers, fighting together for survival. In a study group convened by Temma Kaplan since 1985, Grass Roots Movements of Women, feminists who do research about such movements in different parts of the world, past and present, have been meeting to discuss the relationship among revolutionary action, women, and feminist political consciousness. As Meredith Tax described this activism:

> There is a crux in women's history/women's studies, a knot and a blurry place where various things converge. This place has no name and there is no established methodology for studying it. The things that converge there are variously called: community organizations, working-class women's organizations, consumer movements, popular mass organizations, housewives' organizations, mothers' movements, strike support movements, bread strikes, revolutions at the base, women's peace movements. Some feminist or protofeminist groups and united front organizations of women may be part of this crux. Or they may be different. There is very little theory, either feminist or Marxist, regarding this crux.[24]

The group has been asking: Under what class circumstances do women decide to band together as women, break out of domestic space, and publicly protest? What part have these actions actually played in gaining fundamental political changes? How do women define what they have done and why? Does it make any sense to name feminist thinking as part of this female solidarity? Is there reason to think some kind of feminist consciousness is likely to emerge from this kind of political experience? Is the general marginality of these groups a strength or a weakness?

Almost all the women we have been studying present themselves to the world as mothers (hence, "motherists") acting for the survival of their children. Their groups almost always arise when men are forced to be absent (because they are migrant workers or soldiers) or in times of crisis, when the role of nurturance assigned to women has been rendered impossible. Faced with the imperatives of their traditional work (to feed the children, to keep the family together) and with the loss of bread, or mobility, or whatever they need to do that work, women can turn into a military force, breaking the shop windows of the baker or the butcher, burning the pass cards, assembling to confront the police state, sitting-in where normally they would never go—on the steps of the governor's house, at the gates of the cruise missile base.

As feminists, it interested us to speculate about whether the women in these groups felt any kind of criticism of the social role of mother itself, or of the structural ghettoization of women, or of the sexism that greets women's political efforts. As Marysa Navarro said of the women she studies, the Mothers of the Plaza de Mayo, who march to make the Argentine government give them news of their kidnapped, murdered children: "They can only consider ends that are mothers' ends."[25] The surfacing of political issues beyond the family weakened the Mothers of the Plaza de Mayo. Some wished to claim that party politics don't matter and that their murdered children were innocent of any interest in political struggle. Others felt political activism had been their children's right, one they now wished to share. These argued that their bereavement was not only a moral witnessing of crime and a demand for justice but also a specific intervention with immediate and threatening political implications to the state.

This kind of difference has split the mothers of the Plaza de Mayo along the feminist divide. To what extent is motherhood a powerful identity, a word to conjure with? To what extent is it a patriarchal construction that inevitably places mothers outside the realm of the social, the changing, the active? What power can women who weep, yell, mourn in the street have? Surely a mother's grief and rage removed from the home, suddenly exposed to publicity, are powerful, shocking. Yet as Navarro also points out, the unity of this image was misleading; its force was eventually undermined by differences a group structured around the monolith "mother" was unable to confront.

But, finally, to give the argument one more turn, many Plaza de Mayo women experienced a political transformation through their mothers' network. No group can resolve all political tensions through some ideal formation. The mothers of the disappeared, with their cross-party unity, have been able to convene big demonstrations, drawing new people into the political process. Women can move when a political vacuum develops; by being women who have accepted their lot, they can face the soldiers who have taken their children with a sense of righteous indignation that even a usually murderous police find it hard to dispute. On whatever terms, they have changed the political climate, invented new ways to resist state terrorism.

Using examples like these, the Grass Roots study group gave rise to a particularly poignant exploration of the feminist divide. In each member's work we saw a different version of how women have managed the mixed blessing of their female specialness. Actions like bread riots are desperate and ephemeral, but also effective. With these street eruptions, women put a government on notice; they signal that the poor can be pushed no further. It is finally women who know when the line has been crossed to starvation. But what then? Prices go down; the women go home—until the next time.

Women's movements for survival are like fire storms, changing and dissolving, resistant to political definition. We asked: Would a feminist critique of the traditional role of women keep these groups going longer? Or might feminist insights themselves contribute to the splits that quickly break down the unity shared during crisis? Or, in yet another shift of our assumed values, why *shouldn't* such groups end when the crisis ends, perhaps leaving behind them politicized people, active networks, even community organizations capable of future action when called for? If the left were to expand its definition of political culture beyond the state and the workplace more often, wouldn't the political consciousness of women consumers, mothers, and community activists begin to look enduring in its own way, an important potential source of political energy? Perhaps, our group theorized, we are wrong to wish the women to have formed ongoing political groups growing out of bread riots or meat strikes. Maybe we would see more if we redefined political life to include usually invisible female networks.

The more we talked, the more we saw the ramifications of the fact that the traditional movements were collectivist, the feminist ones more individualistic. Women's local activism draws on a long history of women's culture in which mutual support is essential to life, not (as it often is with contemporary urban feminists) a rare or fragile achievement. The community of peasant women (or working women, or colonized women, or concerned mothers) was a given for the motherists; crisis made the idea of a separate, private identity beyond the daily struggle for survival unimportant. Here was another face of the divide: Collectivist movements are powerful but they usually don't raise questions about women's work. Feminism has raised the questions, and claimed an individual destiny for each woman, but remains ambivalent toward older traditions of female solidarity. Surely our group was ambivalent. We worried that mothers' social networks can rarely redefine the *terms* of their needs. And rich as traditional forms of female association may be, we kept coming on instances in which the power of societies organized for internal support along gender lines was undermined by the sexism of that very organization.

For example, historian Mrinalini Sinha's research describes how the Bengali middle class of nineteenth-century India used its tradition of marrying and bedding child brides as a way of defining itself against a racist, colonial government.[26] The English hypocritically criticized Bengali men as effeminate because they could not wait. Bengali men answered that it was their women who couldn't wait: The way to control unbounded female sexuality–in which, of course, the English disbelieved—was to marry women at first menstruation.

In Sinha's account one rarely hears the voices of Bengali women themselves, but the question of which sexism would control them—the English marriages of restraint or the Bengali marriages of children—raged around these women. Neither side in the quarrel had women's autonomy or power at heart. Both wanted to wage the colonial fight using women as the symbolic representatives of their rivalry. Because Bengali men wanted control of their women just as much as the English wanted control of Bengali men, the anticolonial struggle had less to offer women than men. In general, our group found that sexism inside an oppressed or impoverished community—such as rigidity about gender roles, or about male authority over women, or about female chastity—has cost revolutionary movements a great deal. Too often, gender politics goes unrecognized as an element in class defeat.[27]

Our group disagreed about the women's solidarity we were studying: Was it a part of the long effort to change women's position and to criticize hierarchy in general, or did motherist goals pull in an essentially different direction from feminist ones? And no matter where each one of us found herself on the spectrum of the group's responses to motherist movements, no resolution emerged of the paradox between mothers' goals and the goals of female individuals no longer defined primarily by reproduction and its attendant tasks. We saw this tension in some of the groups we studied, and we kept discovering it in ourselves. (Indeed, some of us were part of groups that used motherist rhetoric, as Ynestra King and I were of women's peace networks, or Amy Swerdlow had been of Women Strike for Peace.)

Drawing hard lines between the traditional women's movements and modern Western feminist consciousness never worked, not because the distinction doesn't exist but because it is woven inside our movement itself. A motherist is in some definitions a feminist, in others not. And these differing feminisms are yoked together by the range of difficulties to be found in women's current situation. Our scholarly distance from the motherists kept collapsing. The children's toy-exchange network that Julie Wells described as one of the political groupings that build black women's solidarity in South Africa couldn't help striking us urban women in the United States as a good idea.[28] We, too, are in charge of the children and need each other to get by. We, too, are likely to act politically along the lines of association our female tasks have shaped. We sometimes long for the community the women we were studying took more for granted, although we couldn't help remarking on the ways those sustaining communities—say of union workers, or peasants, or ghettoized racial groups—used women's energy, loyalty, and passion as by right, while usually denying them a say in the group's public life, its historical consciousness.

Culture offers a variety of rewards to women for always giving attention to others first. Love is a special female responsibility. Some feminists see this female giving as fulfilling and morally powerful. Others see it as a mark of oppression and argue that women are given the job of "life," but that any job relegated to the powerless is one undervalued by the society as a whole. Yet in

[handwritten margin notes:] good Q / I think / I think this / give this tension

[handwritten margin notes:] Is it poss. to critique & be aware & still do the work

[handwritten note at bottom:] I used to think that to stand back meant someone else had to pick up the slack - that didn't occur. ANS, what about the value in the work.

[handwritten note at bottom right:] & what do we do if we get rid of this " job" - what happens to it

our group there was one area of agreement: Traditional women's concerns—for life, for the children, for peace,—*should* be everyone's. Beyond that agreement the question that recreates the feminist divide remained: *How* can the caring that belongs to "mother" travel out to become the responsibility of everyone? Women's backs hold up the world, and we ached for the way women's passionate caring is usually taken for granted, even by women themselves. Some Western feminists, aching like this, want above all to recognize and honor these mothers who, as Adrienne Rich writes, "age after age, perversely, with no extraordinary power, reconstitute the world."[29] Others, also aching, start on what can seem an impossible search for ways to break the ancient, tireless mother's promise to be the mule of the world.

Equality and Difference

By now anyone who has spent time wrangling with feminist issues has recognized the divide and is no doubt waiting for me to produce the name for it that is probably the oldest, certainly the most all-encompassing: "equality" versus "difference." Most feminist thought grapples unavoidably with some aspect of the equality-difference problem at both the level of theory and of strategy. In theory, this version of the divide might be stated: Do women want to be equal to men (with the meaning of "equal" hotly contested),[30] or do women see biology as establishing a difference that will always require a strong recognition and that might ultimately define quite separate possibilities inside "the human?"

Some difference-feminists would argue that women have a special morality, or aesthetic, or capacity for community that it is feminism's responsibility to maximize. Others would put the theoretical case for difference more neutrally and would argue that woman, no matter *what* she is like, is unassimilable. Because she is biologically and therefore psychologically separable from man, she is enduring proof that there is no universally representative human being, no "human wholeness."[31] In contrast, the equality-feminists would argue that it is possible for the biological difference to wither away as a basis for social organization, either by moving men and women toward some shared center (androgyny) or toward some experience of human variety in which biology is but one small variable.

Difference theory tends to emphasize the body (and more recently the unconscious where the body's psychic meaning develops); equality theory tends to deemphasize the body and to place faith in each individual's capacity to develop a self not ultimately circumscribed by a collective law of gender. For difference theorists the body can be either the site of pain and oppression or the site of orgasmic ecstasy and maternal joy. For equality theorists neither extreme is as compelling as the overriding idea that the difference between male and female bodies is a problem in need of solution. In this view, therefore, sexual hierarchy and sexual oppression are bound to continue unless the body is transcended or displaced as the center of female identity.

At the level of practical strategy, the equality-difference divide is just as ubiquitous as it is in theory. Willingly or not, activist lawyers find themselves pitted against each other because they disagree about whether "equal treatment" before the law is better or worse for women than "special treatment," for example, in cases about pregnancy benefits or child custody. (Should pregnancy be defined as unique, requiring special legal provisions, or will pregnant women get more actual economic support if pregnancy, when incapacitating, is grouped with other temporary conditions that keep people from work? Should women who give birth and are almost always the ones who care for children therefore get an automatic preference in custody battles, or will women gain more ultimately if men are defined by law as equally responsible for children, hence equally eligible to be awarded custody?)[32] Sometimes activists find themselves pressured by events to pit the mainstreaming of information about women in the school curriculum against the need for separate programs for women's studies. Or they find themselves having to choose between working to get traditionally male jobs (for example in construction) and working to get fair pay in the women-only jobs they are already doing.

One rushes to respond that these strategic alternatives should not be mutually exclusive, but often, in the heat of local struggles, they temporarily become so. No matter what their theoretical position on the divide, activists find themselves having to make painfully unsatisfactory short-term decisions about the rival claims of equality and difference.[33]

Regrettably, these definitions, these examples flatten out the oscillations of the equality-difference debate; they obscure the class struggles that have shaped the development of the argument; they offer neat parallels where there should be asymmetries. Viewed historically, the oscillation between a feminism of equality and one of difference is a bitter disagreement about which path is more progressive, more able to change women's basic condition of subordination.

In this history each side has taken more than one turn at calling the other reactionary and each has had its genuine vanguard moments. "Difference" gained some working women protection at a time when any social legislation to regulate work was rare, while "equality" lay behind middle-class women's demand for the vote, a drive Ellen DuBois has called "the most radical program for women's emancipation possible in the nineteenth century." At the same time, bourgeois women's demands that men should have to be as sexually pure as women finessed the divide between difference and equality and gave rise to interesting cross-class alliances of women seeking ways to make men conform to women's standard, rather than the usual way round—a notion of equality with a difference.[34] As Du Bois points out, it is difficult to decide which of these varied political constructions gave nineteenth-century women the most real leverage to make change:

> My hypothesis is that the significance of the woman suffrage movement rested precisely on the fact that it bypassed women's oppression within the family, or private sphere, and demanded instead her admission to citizenship, and through it admission to the public arena.[35]

In other words, at a time when criticism of women's separate family role was still unthinkable, imagining a place outside the family where such a role would make no difference was—for a time— a most radical act.

Equality and difference are broad ideas and have included a range of definitions and political expressions. Equality, for example, can mean anything from the mildest liberal reform (this is piece-of-the-pie feminism, in which women are merely to be included in the world as it is) to the most radical reduction of gender to insignificance. Difference can mean anything from Mary Daly's belief in the natural superiority of women to psychoanalytic theories of how women are inevitably cast as "the Other" because they lack penises.[36]

Just now equality—fresh from recent defeats at the polls and in the courts— is under attack by British and U.S. theorists who are developing a powerful critique of the eighteenth- and nineteenth-century roots of feminism in liberalism. In what is a growing body of work, feminists are exploring the serious limitations of a tradition based on an ideal of equality for separate, independent individuals acting in a free, public sphere—either the market or the state. This liberalism, which runs as an essential thread through Anglo-American feminism, has caused much disappointment. Feminists have become increasingly aware of its basic flaws, of the ways it splits off public and private, leaves sexual differences entirely out of its narrative of the world, and pretends to a neutrality that is nullified by the realities of gender, class, and race. A feminism that honors individual rights has grown leery of the liberal tradition that always puts those rights before community and before any caring for general needs. Liberalism promises an equal right to compete, but as Bell Hooks puts it: "Since men are not equals in white supremacist, capitalist, patriarchal class structure, which men do women want to be equal to?"[37]

These arguments against the origins and tendencies of equality feminism are cogent and useful. They have uncovered unexamined assumptions and the essential weakness in a demand for a passive neutrality of opportunity. But there are cracks in the critique of equality-feminism that lead me back to my general assertion that neither side of the divide can easily be transcended. The biggest complaint against a feminist demand of "equality" is that this construction means women must become conceptual men, or rather that to have equal rights they will have to repress their biological difference, to subordinate themselves in still new ways under an unchanged male hegemony.[38] In this argument the norm is assumed to be male and women's entry into public space is assumed to be a loss of the aspects of experience they formerly embodied—privacy, feeling, nurturance, dailiness. Surely, though, this argument entails a monolithic and eternal view both of public space and of the category "male." How successfully does public space maintain its male gender markers, how totally exclude the private side of life? (The city street is male, yet it can at times be not only physically but also conceptually invaded, say, by a sense of neighborhood or by a demonstration of mass solidarity.)[39] Does male space sometimes dramatically reveal the fact of women's absence? How well does the taboo on public women hold up under the multiple pressures of modernity? Even if public and private are conceptually absolutes, to what extent do individual men and women experience moments in both positions?

Or, if one rejects these hopeful efforts to find loopholes in the iron laws of gender difference, the fear that women will become men still deserves double scrutiny. Is the collapse of gender difference into maleness really the problem women face? Or are we perhaps quite close to men already at the moment when we fear absorption into the other?

None of this is meant as a refutation of the important current work that brings skepticism to the construction of our demands. When health activist Wendy Chavkin notes that making pregnancy disappear by calling it a "disability" is one more way of letting business and government evade sharing responsibility for reproduction, she is right to worry about the invisibility of women's bodies and of our work of reproduction of which our bodies are one small part. When philosopher Alison Jaggar gives examples of how male norms have buried the often separate needs of women, she is sounding a valuable warning. When critic Myra Jehlen describes how hard it is for the concept of a person to include the particular when that particular is female, she is identifying the depth of our difficulty, men's phobic resistance to the inclusion of women into any neutral or public equation.[40]

Nonetheless, I want to reanimate the problem of the divide, to show the potential vigor on both sides. On the one hand, an abstract promise of equality is not enough for people living in capitalism, where everyone is free both to vote and to starve. On the other, as Zillah Eisenstein has pointed out in *The Radical Future of Liberal Feminism,* the demand for equality has a radical meaning in a capitalist society that claims to offer it but structurally often denies it. Feminism asks for many things the patriarchal state cannot give without radical change. Juliet Mitchell's rethinking of the value of equality-feminism reaches a related conclusion: When basic rights are under attack, liberalism feels necessary again. At best, liberalism sometimes tips in action and becomes more radical than its root conceptions promise. Certainly, no matter which strategy we choose— based on a model of equality or of difference—we are constantly forced to compromise.[41]

It's not that we haven't gotten beyond classical liberalism in theory but that in practice we cannot *live* beyond it. In their very structure, contemporary court cases about sex and gender dramatize the fact of the divide, and media questions demand the short, one-sided answer. Each "case," each "story" in which we act is different, and we are only at moments able to shape that difference, make it into the kind of "difference" we want.[42]

The Divide is Not a Universal

After having said so much about how deep the divide goes in feminism, how completely it defines what feminism *is,* I run the risk of seeming to say that the divide has some timeless essence. In fact, I want to argue the opposite, to place Western feminism inside its two-hundred-year history as a specific possibility for thought and action that arose as one of the possibilities of modernity.

When Mary Wollstonecraft wrote one of the founding books of feminism in 1792, *A Vindication of the Rights of Women,* she said what was new then and remains fresh, shocking, and doubtful to many now: that sex hierarchy—like ranks in the church and the army or like the then newly contested ascendancy of kings—was social, not natural. Though women before her had named injustices and taken sides in several episodes of an ancient *quarrelle des femmes,* Wollstonecraft's generation experienced the divide in ways related to how feminists experience it now. At one and the same time she could see gender as a solid wall barring her way into liberty, citizenship, and a male dignity she envied, and could see how porous the wall was, how many ways she herself could imagine stepping through into an identity less absolute and more chaotic.

Modern feminists often criticize her unhappy compromise with bourgeois revolution and liberal political goals, but if Wollstonecraft was often an equality-feminist in the narrowest sense, eager to speak of absolute rights, of an idealized male individualism, and to ignore the body, this narrowness was in part a measure of her desperation.[43] The body, she felt, could be counted on to assert its ever-present and dreary pull; the enlightenment promised her a mind that might escape. She acknowledged difference as an absolute—men are stronger—and then with cunning, she offered men a deal:

> Avoiding, as I have hitherto done, any direct comparison of the two sexes collectively, or frankly acknowledging the inferiority of women, according to the present appearance of things, I shall only insist that men have increased that inferiority till women are almost sunk below the standard of rational creatures. Let their faculties have room to unfold, and their virtues to gain strength, and then determine where the whole sex must stand in the intellectual scale.[44]

Wheedling a bit, Wollstonecraft made men the modest proposal that if women are inferior, men have nothing to fear; they can generously afford to give women their little chance at the light. This is a sly, agnostic treatment of the issue of equality versus difference. Experimental and groping spirit, Wollstonecraft *didn't know* how much biological difference might come to mean; but that she suffered humiliation and loss through being a woman she did know, and all she asked was to be let out of the prison house of gender identity for long enough to judge what men had and what part of that she might want.

When Wollstonecraft wrote, difference was the prevailing wind, equality the incipient revolutionary storm. She feared that if women could not partake in the new civil and political rights of democracy, they would "remain immured in their families groping in the dark." To be sure this rejection of the private sphere made no sense to many feminists who came after her and left modern feminists the task of recognizing the importance of the private and women's different life there, yet it is a rejection that was absolutely necessary as one of feminism's first moves. We in turn have rejected Wollstonecraft's call for chastity, for the end of the passionate emotions "which disturb the order of society";[45] we have rejected her confidence in objective reason and her desire to live as a disembodied self (and a very understandable desire, too, for one whose best friend died in childbirth and who was to die of childbed fever herself), but we have not gotten beyond needing to make the basic demands she made—for civil rights, education, autonomy.

Finally, what is extraordinary in *A Vindication* is its chaos. Multivalent, driven, ambivalent, the text races over most of feminism's main roads. It constantly goes back on itself in tone, thrilling with self-hatred, rage, disappointment, and hope—the very sort of emotions it explains are the mark of women's inferiority, triviality, and lascivious abandon. Though its appeals to God and virtue are a dead letter to feminists now, the anger and passion with which Wollstonecraft made those appeals—and out of which she imagined the depth of women's otherness, our forced incapacity, the injustice of our situation—feel thoroughly modern. Her structural disorganization derives in part from a circular motion through now familiar stages of protest, reasoning, fury, despair, contempt, desire.[46] She makes demands for women, then doubles back to say that womanhood should be beside the point. Her book is one of those that mark the start of an avalanche of mass self-consciousness about gender injustice. So, in the midst of the hopeful excitement, the divide is there, at the beginning of our history.

If the divide is central to feminist history, feminists need to recognize it with more suppleness, but this enlarged perspective doesn't let one out of having to choose a position in the divide. On the contrary, by arguing that there is no imminent resolution, I hope to throw each reader back on the necessity of finding where her own work falls and of assessing how powerful that political decision is as a tool for undermining the dense, deeply embedded oppression of women.

By writing of the varied vocabularies and constructions feminists have used to describe the divide, I do not mean to intimate that they are all one, but to emphasize their difference. Each issue calls forth a new configuration, a new version of the spectrum of feminist opinion, and most require an internal as well as external struggle about goals and tactics. Though it is understandable that we dream of peace among feminists, that we resist in sisterhood the factionalism that has so often disappointed us in brotherhood, still we must carry on the argument among ourselves. Better, we must actively embrace it. The tension in the divide, far from being our enemy, is a dynamic force that links very different women. Feminism encompasses central dilemmas in modern experience, mysteries of identity that get full expression in its debates. The electricity of its internal disagreements is part of feminism's continuing power to shock and involve large numbers of people in a public conversation far beyond the movement itself. The dynamic feminist divide is about difference; it dramatizes women's differences from each other—and the necessity of our sometimes making common cause.

A Gender Diary: Some Stories, Some Dialogues

If, as I've said, the divide offers no third way, no high ground of neutrality, I certainly have not been able to present this overview so far without a constant humming theme beneath, my own eagerness to break the category "woman" down, to find a definition of difference that pushes so far beyond a settled identity that "being a woman" breaks apart.

Though sometimes I have found the theoretical equality arguments I have described blinkered and reactive, when it comes to strategy, I almost always choose that side, fearing the romance of femaleness even more than the flatness and pretense of undifferentiated, gender-free public space.

I suspect that each one's emphasis—equality or difference—arises alongside and not after the reasons. We criticize Wollstonecraft's worship of rationality, but how willing are we modern ones to look at the unconscious, the idiosyncratic, the temperamental histories of our own politics? It is in these histories—private, intellectual, and social—that we can find why some women feel safer with the equality model as the rock of their practice (with difference as a necessary condition imposed on it), while other women feel more true to themselves, more fully expressed, by difference as their rock (with equality a sort of bottom-line call for basic reforms that cannot ultimately satisfy).

Why do I decide (again and again) that being a woman is a liability, while others I know decide (again and again) that a separate female culture is more exciting, more in their interests, more promising as a strategic stance for now than my idea of slipping the noose of gender, living for precious moments of the imagination outside it? An obvious first answer is that class, race, and sexual preference determine my choices, and surely these play their central part. Yet in my experience of splits in the women's movement, I keep joining with women who share my feminist preferences but who have arrived at these conclusions from very different starting points.

This is not to understate the importance of class, race, and sexual preference but merely to observe that these important variables don't segment feminism along the divide; they don't provide direct keys to each one's sense of self-interest or desire nor do they yield clear directions for the most useful strategic moves.

For example, lesbian and straight women are likely to bring very different understandings and needs to discussions of whether or not women's communities work, whether or not the concept is constricting. Yet in my own experience, trust of women's communities does not fall out along the lines of sexual preference. Instead, up close, the variables proliferate. What was the texture of childhood for each one of us? What face did the world beyond home present?

In the fifties, when an earlier, roiled life of gender and politics had subsided and the gender messages seemed monolithic again, I lived with my parents in the suburbs. My mother's class and generation had lived through repeated, basic changes of direction about women, family, and work, and my own engaged and curious mother passed on her ambivalent reception of the world's mixed messages to me in the food. With hindsight, I can see that of course gender, family, and class weren't the settled issues they seemed then. But the times put a convincing cover over continuing change. Deborah Rosenfelt and Judith Stacey describe this precise historical moment and the particular feminist politics born from it:

> [T]he ultradomestic nineteen fifties [was] an aberrant decade in the history of U.S. family and gender relations and one that has set the unfortunate terms for waves of personal and political reaction to family issues ever since. Viewed in this perspective, the attack on the breadwinner/homemaker nuclear family by the women's liberation movement may have been an overreaction to an aberrant and highly fragile cultural form, a family system that, for other reasons, was already passing from the scene. Our devastating critiques of the vulnerability and cultural devaluation of dependent wives and mothers helped millions of women to leave or avoid these domestic traps, and this is to our everlasting credit. But, with hindsight, it seems to us that these critiques had some negative consequences as well . . . . [F]eminism's overreaction to the fifties was an antinatalist, antimaternalist moment . . . .[47]

I am the child of this moment, and some of the atmosphere of rage generated by that hysterically domestic ideology of the fifties can now feel callow, young, or ignorant. Yet I have many more kind words to say for the reaction of which I was a part in the early seventies than Rosenfelt and Stacey seem to: I don't think the feminism of this phase would have spoken so powerfully to so many without this churlish outbreak of indignation. Nothing we have learned since about the fragility of the nuclear family alters the fundamental problems it continues to pose for women. It is not really gone, though it is changing. And although feminism seeks to preside over the changes, other forces are at work, half the time threatening us with loneliness, half the time promising us rich emotional lives if we will but stay home—a vicious double punch combination. In this climate, feminist resistance to pronatalism—of either the fifties *or* the nineties—continues to make sense.

It's hard to remember now what the initial feminist moves in this wave felt like, the heady but alarming atmosphere of female revolt. As one anxious friend wondered back then, "Can I be in this and stay married?" The answer was often "no," the upheaval terrifying. Some of us early ones were too afraid of the lives of our mothers to recognize ourselves in them. But I remember that this emotional throwing off of the mother's life felt like the only way to begin. Black women whose ties to their mothers were more often a mutual struggle for survival rarely shared this particular emotion. As Audre Lorde has said, "[B]lack children were not meant to survive,"[48] so parents and children saw a lifeline in each other that was harder for the prosperous or the white to discern. The usually white and middle-class women who were typical members of early women's consciousness raising groups often saw their mothers as desperate or depressed in the midst of their relative privilege. Many had been educated like men and had then been expected to become . . . men's wives. We used to agree in those meetings that motherhood was the divide: Before it, you could pretend you were just like everyone else; afterward, you were a species apart—invisible and despised.

But if motherhood was despised, it was also festooned—then as now—with roses. Either way, in 1970, motherhood seemed an inevitable part of my future, and the qualities some feminists now praise as uniquely women's were taken for granted as female necessities: Everyone wanted the nice one, the sweet one, the good one, the nurturant one, the pretty one. No one wanted the women who didn't want to be women. It's hard to recover how frightening it was to step out of those ideas, to resist continuing on as expected; it's hard to get back how very naked it made us feel. Some of the vociferousness of our rhetoric, which now seems unshaded or raw, came partly from the anxiety we felt when we made this proclamation, that we didn't want to be women. A great wave of misogyny rose to greet us. So we said it even more. Hindsight has brought in its necessary wisdom, its temporizing reaction. We have gotten beyond the complaint of the daughters, have come to respect the realities, the worries, and the work of the mothers. But to me "difference" will always represent a necessary modification of the initial impulse, a reminder of complexity, a brake on precipitate hopes. It can never feel like the primary insight felt, the first breaking with the gender bargain. The immediate reward was immense, the thrill of separating from authority.

Conversation with E. She recalls that the new women's movement meant to her: You don't have to struggle to be attractive to men anymore. You can stop working so hard on that side of things. I was impressed by this liberation so much beyond my own. I felt the opposite. Oppressed and depressed before the movement, I found sexual power unthinkable, the privilege of a very few women. Now angry and awake, I felt for the first time what the active eroticism of men might be like. What men thought of me no longer blocked out the parallel question of what I thought of them, which made sexual encounters far more interesting than they had once been. Like E., I worried about men's approval less, but (without much tangible reason) my hopes for the whole business of men and women rose. For a brief time in the early seventies, I had an emotional intimation of what some men must feel: free to rub up against the world, take space, make judgments. With all its hazards, this confidence also offered its delight—but only for a moment of course. The necessary reaction followed at once: Women aren't men in public space. There is no safety. Besides, I had romanticized male experience; men are not as free as I imagined. Still, I remember that wild if deluded time—not wanting to be a man but wanting the freedom of the street. The feminist rallying cry "Take Back the Night" has always struck me as a fine piece of movement poetry. We don't have the night, but we want it, we want it.

Another memory of the early seventies: An academic woman sympathetic to the movement but not active asked what motivated me to spend all this time organizing, marching, meeting. (Subtext: Why wasn't I finishing my book? Why did I keep flinging myself around?)

I tried to explain the excitement I felt at the idea that I didn't have to be a woman. She was shocked, confused. This was the motor of my activism? She asked, "How can someone who doesn't like being a woman be a feminist?" To which I could only answer, "Why would anyone who likes being a woman need to be a feminist?"

Quite properly my colleague feared woman-hating. She assumed that feminism must be working to restore respect and dignity to women. Feminism would revalue what had been debased, women's contribution to human history. I, on the other hand, had to confess: I could never have made myself lick all those stamps for a better idea of what womanhood means. Was this, as my colleague thought, just a new kind of misogyny? I wouldn't dare say self-hatred played no part in what I wanted from feminism from the first. But even back then, for me, woman-hating—or loving—felt beside the point. It was the idea of breaking the law of the category itself that made me delirious.

The first time I heard "women" mentioned as a potentially political contemporary category I was already in graduate school. It was the mid-sixties and a bright young woman of the New Left was saying how important it was to enlist the separate support of women workers in our organizing against the Vietnam War. I remember arguing with her, flushed with a secret humiliation. What good was she doing these workers, I asked her, by addressing them and categorizing them separately? Who was she to speak so condescendingly of "them"? Didn't she know that the inferior category she had named would creep up in the night and grab her, too?

I'm ashamed now to admit that gender solidarity—which I lived inside happily, richly every day in those years—first obtruded itself on my conscious mind as a threat and a betrayal. So entirely was I trapped in negative feelings about what women are and can do that I had repressed any knowledge of femaleness as a defining characteristic of my being.

I can see now that women very different from me came to feminist conclusions much like my own. But this is later knowledge. My feminism came from the suburbs, where I knew no white, middle-class woman with children who had a job or any major activities beyond the family. Yet, though a girl, I was promised education, offered the pretense of gender neutrality. This island of illusions was a small world, but if I seek the source for why cultural feminism has so little power to draw me, it is to this world I return in thought. During the day, it was safe, carefully limited, and female. The idea that this was all made me frantic.

S. reads the gender diary with consternation. In Puerto Rico, where she grew up, this fear of the mother's life would be an obscenity. She can't recognize the desire I write of—to escape scot free from the role I was born to. Latina feminists she knows feel rage, but what is this shame, she wants to know. In her childhood both sexes believed being a woman was magic.

S. means it about the magic, hard as it is for me to take this in. She means sexual power, primal allure, even social dignity. S. became a feminist later, by a different route, and now she is as agnostic about the meaning of gender as I am. But when she was young, she had no qualms about being a woman.

After listening to S., I add another piece to my story of the suburbs. Jews who weren't spending much of our time being Jewish, we lived where ethnicity was easy to miss. (Of course it was there; but I didn't know it.) In the suburbs, Motherhood was white bread, with no powerful ethnic graininess. For better and worse, I was brought up on this stripped, denatured product. Magical women seemed laughably remote. No doubt this flatness in local myth made girls believe less in their own special self, but at the same time it gave them less faith in the beckoning ideal of mother. My gifted mother taught me not the richness of home but the necessity of feminism. Feminism was her conscious as well as unconscious gift.

It is not enough for the diary to tell how one woman, myself, came to choose—again and again—a feminism on the minimalizers' side of the divide. Somehow the diary must also tell how this decision can never feel solid or final. No one gets to stay firmly on her side; no one gets to rest in a reliably clear position. Mothers who believe their daughters should roam as free as men find themselves giving those daughters taxi fare, telling them not to talk to strangers, filling them with the lore of danger. Activists who want women to be very naughty (as the women in a little zap group we call No More Nice Girls want women to be) nonetheless warn them there's a price to pay for daring to defy men in public space.[49] Even when a woman chooses which shoes she'll wear today—is it to be the running shoes, the flats, the spikes?—she's deciding where to place herself for the moment on the current possible spectrum of images of "woman." Whatever our habitual position on the divide, in daily life we travel back and forth, or, to change metaphors, we scramble for whatever toehold we can.

Living with the divide: In a room full of feminists, everyone is saying that a so-called surrogate mother, one who bears a child for others, should have the right to change her mind for a time (several weeks? months?) after the baby is born. This looks like agreement. Women who have been on opposite sides of the divide in many struggles converge here, outraged at the insulting way one Mary Beth Whitehead has been treated by fertility clinics, law courts, and press. She is not a "surrogate," we say, but a "mother" indeed.

The debate seems richer than it's been lately. Nobody knows how to sort out the contradictions of the new reproductive technologies yet, so for a fertile moment there's a freedom, an expressiveness in all that's said. Charged words like "birth" and "mothering" and "the kids" are spilling all around, but no one yet dares to draw the ideological line defining which possibilities belong inside feminism, which are antithetical to it. Some sing a song of pregnancy and birth while others offer contrapuntal motifs of child-free lesbian youth, of infertility, all in different keys of doubt about how much feminists may want to make motherhood special, different from parenting, different from caring—a unique and absolute relation to a child.

But just as we're settling in for an evening that promises to be fraught, surprising, suggestive, my warning system, sensitive after twenty years of feminist activism, gives a familiar twitch and tug. Over by the door, one woman has decided: Surrogacy is baby-selling and ought to be outlawed. All mothering will be debased if motherhood can be bought. Over by the couch, another woman is anxiously responding: Why should motherhood be the sacred place we keep clean from money, while men sell the work of their bodies every day? Do we want women to be the special representatives of the moral and spiritual things that can't be bought, with the inevitable result that women's work is once again done without pay?

Here it is then. The metaconversation that has hovered over my political life since 1970, when I joined one of the first women's consciousness raising groups. On the one hand, sacred motherhood. On the other, a wish—variously expressed—for this special identity to wither away.

Only a little later in the brief, eventful history of this ad hoc Mary Beth Whitehead support group, a cleverly worded petition was circulated. It quoted the grounds the court used to disqualify Whitehead from motherhood—from the way she dyed her hair to the way she played pattycake—and ended: "By these standards, we are all unfit mothers." I wanted to sign the petition, but someone told me, "Only mothers are signing." I was amazed. Did one have to be literally *a mother in order to speak authentically in support of Whitehead? Whether I'm a mother or not, the always obvious fact that I am from the mother half of humanity conditions my life.*

But after this initial flash of outrage at exclusion, I had second thoughts:

Maybe I should be glad not to sign. Why should I have to be assumed to be a mother if I am not? Instead of accepting that all women are mothers in essence if not in fact, don't I prefer a world in which some are mothers—and can speak as mothers—while others are decidedly not?

To make a complicated situation more so: While I was struggling with the rights and wrongs of my being allowed to sign, several other women refused to sign. Why? Because the petition quoted Whitehead's remark that she knew what was best for her child because she was the mother. The nonsigners saw this claim as once again imputing some magic biological essence to motherhood. They didn't want to be caught signing a document that implied that mother always knows best. They supported Whitehead's right to dye her hair but not her claim to maternal infallibility.

I saw the purity of this position, recognized these nonsigners as my closest political sisters, the ones who run fast because the old world of mother-right is just behind them. But in this case I didn't feel quite as they felt. I was too angry at the double standard, the unfair response to Whitehead's attempts to extricate herself from disaster. I thought that given the circumstances of here, of now, Mary Beth Whitehead was as good an authority about her still-nursing baby as we could find anywhere in the situation. It didn't bother me at all to sign a petition that included her claim to a uniquely privileged place. The press and the court seemed to hate her for that very specialness; yet they all relegated her to it, execrating her for her unacceptable ambivalence. Under such conditions she was embracing with an understandable vengeance the very role the world named as hers. Who could blame her?

Eventually, I signed the petition, which was also signed by a number of celebrities and was much reported in the press. It is well to remember how quickly such public moments flatten out internal feminist debates. After much feminist work, the newspapers—formerly silent about feminism's stake in surrogacy questions—began speaking of "the feminist position." But nothing they ever wrote about us or our petition came close to the dilemma as we had debated it during the few intense weeks we met. Prosurrogacy and antisurrogacy positions coexist inside feminism. They each require expression, because neither alone can respond fully to the class, race, and gender issues raised when a poor woman carries a child for a rich man for money.

Over time I've stopped being depressed by the lack of feminist accord. I see feminists as stuck with the very indeterminacy I say I long for. This is it then, the life part way in, part way out. One can be recalled to "woman" anytime—by things as terrible as rape, as trivial as a rude shout on the street—but one can never stay inside "woman," because it keeps moving. We constantly find ourselves beyond its familiar cover.

Gender markers are being hotly reasserted these days—U.S. defense is called "standing tough" while the Pope's letter on women calls motherhood woman's true vocation. Yet this very heat is a sign of gender's instabilities. We can clutch aspects of the identity we like, but they often slip away. Modern women experience moments of free fall. How is it for you, there, out in space near me? Different, I know. Yet we share—some with more pleasure, some with more pain—this uncertainty.

Notes

I am indebted to the hard-working readers of an earlier draft, who are nevertheless not to blame for the times I have failed to profit from their excellent advice: Nancy Davidson, Adrienne Harris, Temma Kaplan, Mim Kelber, Ynestra King, Susana Leval, Eunice Lipton, Alix Kates Shulman, Alan Snitow, Nadine Taub, Meredith Tax, Sharon Thompson, and Carole Vance.

A shorter version of this article ("Pages from a Gender Diary") appeared in *Dissent* (Spring 1989); a longer version ("A Gender Diary") is in *Rocking the Ship of State: Toward a Feminist Peace Politics,* ed. Adrienne Harris and Ynestra King (Boulder, Colorado: Westview Press, 1989).

1. The "we" problem has no more simple solution than does the divide itself, but in spite of its false promise of unity the "we" remains politically important. In this piece, "we" includes anyone who calls herself a feminist, anyone who is actively engaged with the struggles described here.

2. MARHO Forum, John Jay College, New York, March 2, 1984. For feminist critiques of the new peace activism see *Breaching the Peace: a collection of radical feminist papers* (London: Onlywomen Press, 1983) and Ann Snitow, "Holding the Line at Greenham," in *Mother Jones,* February/March 1985, pp. 30—47.

3. Lourdes Beneria and Phyllis Mack began the study group, which was initially funded by the Institute for Research on Women at Rutgers University. Other members were: Dorothy Dinnerstein, Zala Chandler, Carol Cohn, Adrienne Harris, Ynestra King, Rhoda Linton, Sara Ruddick, Amy Swerdlow.

4. See Amy Swerdlow, "Pure Milk, Not Poison: Women Strike for Peace and the Test Ban Treaty of 1963," in *Rocking the Ship of State,* pp. 225—237. (This book grew from the study group above.)

5. Bella Abzug and Mim Kelber, *Gender Gap* (Boston: Houghton Mifflin, 1984). According to Kelber, Carter was outraged that the women of the commission were criticizing his social priorities; they were supposed to be on his side. Most of the commission resigned when Carter fired Abzug. When he reconstituted the commission somewhat later, the adjective national had been dropped from its name and it became the President's Advisory Commission for Women, with restricted powers and no lobbying function.

6. "In the United States, we oscillate between participating in, and separating from, organizations and institutions that remain alienating and stubbornly male dominant," (Joan Kelly, "The Doubled Vision of Feminist Theory," in Joan Kelly, *Women, History and Theory: The Essays of Joan Kelly* [Chicago: University of Chicago

Press, 1984], p. 55). Also see Denise Riley, *War in the Nursery: Theories of the Child and Mother* (London: Virago, 1983).

7.   Denise Riley, talk at the Barnard Women's Center, New York, April 11, 1985.

8.   Catharine R. Stimpson, "The New Scholarship About Women: The State of the Art," *Ann. Scholarship* 1, no. 2 (1980), pp. 2—14.

9.   Alice Echols, *Daring to Be Bad: A History of the Radical Feminist Movement in America, 1967–1975* (Minneapolis: University of Minnesota Press, forthcoming), typescript, p. 81 (Chap. 2).

10.   Ibid., p. 273 (Chap. 6).

11.   Ibid., p. 270 (Chap. 6).

12.   Ibid., p. 273 (Chap. 6).

13.   Barbara Deming, "To Those Who Would Start a People's Party," *Liberation* 18, no. 4 (December 1973), p. 24, cited in Echols, *Daring,* typescript, p. 272 (Chap. 6); Andrea Dworkin, *Intercourse* (New York: The Free Press, 1987), p. 67. Dworkin is not a biological determinist in *Intercourse* but she sees culture as so saturated with misogyny that the victimization of women is seamless, total, as eternal in its own way as "mother right."

14.   Ellen Willis, remarks at the NYU Symposium on the publication of *Power of Desire: The Politics of Sexuality,* New York, December 2, 1983.

15.   Carole S. Vance, "Social Construction Theory: Problems in the History of Sexuality," in Anja van Kooten Niekerk and Theo van der Meer, eds., *Homosexuality, Which Homosexuality?* (Amsterdam: An Dekker, Imprint Schorer, 1989).

16.   Linda Alcoff, "Cultural Feminism Versus Post-Structuralism: The Identity Crisis in Feminist Theory," *Signs* 13, no. 3 (Spring 1988), especially page 406.

17.   Linda Alcoff sees poststructuralism as anti-essentialist; in contrast, in *Feminist Studies* 14, no. 1 (Spring 1988), the editors Judith Newton and Nancy Hoffman introduce a collection of essays on deconstruction by describing differences *among* deconstructionists on the question of essentialism as on other matters.

18.   See New York Radical Feminists, "Politics of the Ego: A Manifesto for N.Y. Radical Feminists," in Anne Koedt, Ellen Levine, and Anita Rapone, eds., *Radical Feminism* (New York: Quadrangle, 1973), pp. 379–383. The vocabulary of the manifesto, adopted in December 1969, seems crude now, its emphasis on "psychology" jejune; but the document begins with the task feminists have taken up since—the analysis of the interlocking ways in which culture organizes subordination.

19.   Linda Bamber and Marianne DeKoven, "Metacriticism and the Value of Difference," (Paper presented at the MLA panel "Feminist Criticism: Theories and Directions," Los Angeles, December 28, 1982), pp. 1–2.

20.   Alcoff, "Cultural Feminism," p. 421.

21.   One might make a separate study of third-course thinking. Sometimes this work is an important and urgent effort to see the limiting terms of a current contradiction, to recognize from which quarter new contradictions are likely to develop. Third-course writing at its best tries to reinterpret the present and offer clues to the future.

(English theorists have called this prefigurative thinking.) But often this work runs the risk of pretending that new terms resolve difficulties, and, more insidiously, it often falls back covertly into the divide it claims to have transcended. I admire, although I am not always persuaded by, the third-course thinking in such pieces as Angela Miles, "The Integrative Feminine Principle in North American Radicalism: Value Basis of a New Feminism," *Women's Studies International Quarterly* 4, no. 4 (1981), pp. 481–495. I have more doubts about pieces such as Ann Ferguson, "Sex War: The Debate Between Radical and Libertarian Feminists," and Ilene Philipson, "The Repression of History and Gender: A Critical Perspective on the Feminist Sexuality Debate," *Signs* 10, no. 1 (Autumn 1984), pp. 106–118. These essays claim a higher ground, "a third perspective," (Ferguson, p. 108) that is extremely difficult to construct; their classifications of the sides of the divide reveal a tropism more unavoidable than they recognize.

22. Michèle Barrett, "The Concept of 'Difference'," *Feminist Review* 26 (Summer 1987), p. 34.

23. Alice Walker, *In Search of Our Mother's Gardens* (San Diego: Harcourt Brace Jovanovich, 1983), p. xi (epigraph). Also see, for example, Kelly, "The Doubled Vision of Feminist Theory"; and Adrienne Rich, "Compulsory Heterosexuality and Lesbian Existence," in Adrienne Rich, *Blood, Bread and Poetry* (New York: Norton, 1986), p. 60ff. Rich also uses the metaphor of the continuum to describe the range in women's lives among different levels of female community. In *The Daughter's Seduction: Feminism and Psychoanalysis* (Ithaca, N.Y.: Cornell University Press, 1982), Jane Gallop describes Julia Kristeva's effort to think beyond dualism: "A constantly double discourse is necessary, one that asserts and then questions," (p. 122).

24. Meredith Tax, "Agenda for Meeting at Barnard, May 3, 1986," p. 1. Members of the study group, convened at the Barnard Women's Center: Margorie Agosin, Amrita Basu, Dana Frank, Temma Kaplan, Ynestra King, Marysa Navarro, Ann Snitow, Amy Swerdlow, Meredith Tax, Julie Wells, Marilyn Young.

25. Marysa Navarro, Grass Roots Meeting, May 3, 1986. Also see Shirley Christian, "Mothers March, but to 2 Drummers," *New York Times,* February 21, 1987.

26. Mrinalini Sinha, "The Age of Consent Act: The Ideal of Masculinity and Colonial Ideology in 19th Century Bengal," *Proceedings,* Eighth International Symposium on Asian Studies (1986), pp. 1199–1214; and Mrinalini Sinha, "Gender and Imperialism: Colonial Policy and the Ideology of Moral Imperialism in Late 19th Century Bengal," in Michael S. Kimmel, ed., *Changing Men: New Directions in Research on Men and Masculinity* (Newbury Park, Calif.: Sage, 1987), pp. 217–231.

27. At the Grass Roots study group, Julie Wells and Anne McClintock offered the example of Crossroads in South Africa, a squatter community of blacks largely maintained by women but finally undermined by, among other things, a colonialism that placed paid black men in charge. Also see descriptions of ways in which women become connected with revolutionary movements in Maxine Molyneux, "Mobilization Without Emancipation? Women's Interests, the State, and Revolution in Nicaragua," *Feminist Studies* 11, no. 2 (Summer 1985), pp. 227–253; Temma Kaplan, "Women and Communal Strikes in the Crises of 1917–1922," in Renate

Bridenthal, Claudia Koonz, and Susan Stuard, eds., *Becoming Visible: Women in European History*, 2nd ed. (Boston: Houghton Mifflin, 1987), pp. 429–449; and Temma Kaplan, "Female Consciousness and Collective Action: The Case of Barcelona, 1910–1918," *Signs* 7, no. 3 (1982), pp. 545–566.

28. Julie Wells, "The Impact of Motherist Movements on South African Women's Political Participation," (Paper presented at the Seventh Berkshire Conference on the History of Women, June 19, 1987).

29. Adrienne Rich, "Natural Resources," in Adrienne Rich, *The Dream of a Common Language: Poems, 1974–1977* (New York: Norton, 1978), p. 67.

30. Alison M. Jaggar gives an account of the contemporary feminist debate about the meaning and value of the demand for "equality" in "Sexual Difference and Sexual Equality," in Deborah L. Rhode, ed., *Theoretical Perspectives on Sexual Differences* (New Haven: Yale University Press, forthcoming). For some general accounts of the debate, also see Josephine Donovan, *Feminist Theory* (New York: Frederick Ungar, 1985); Hester Eisenstein, *Contemporary Feminist Thought* (Boston: G. K. Hall, 1983); Hester Eisenstein and Alice Jardine, eds., *The Future of Difference* (Boston: G. K. Hall, 1980); Zillah R. Eisenstein, *Feminism and Sexual Equality: Crisis in Liberal America* (New York: Monthly Review Press, 1984); Juliet Mitchell, *Women's Estate* (New York: Pantheon, 1971); Juliet Mitchell and Ann Oakley, eds., *What is Feminism?* (New York: Pantheon, 1986). The debates about Carol Gilligan's *In a Different Voice: Psychological Theory and Women's Development* (Cambridge, Mass.: Harvard University Press, 1982), often turn on the equality/difference problem. See John Broughton, "Women's Rationality and Men's Virtues: A Critique of Gender Dualism in Gilligan's Theory of Moral Development," *Social Research* 50, no. 3 (Autumn 1983), pp. 597–624; Linda K. Kerber, Catherine G. Greeno, and Eleanor E. Maccoby, Zella Luria, Carol B. Stack, and Carol Gilligan, "On *In a Different Voice:* An Interdisciplinary Forum," *Signs* 11, no. 2 (Winter 1986), pp. 304–333; *New Ideas in Psychology* (Special Issue on Women and Moral Development) 5, no. 2 (1987); and Seyla Benhabib, "The Generalized and the Concrete Other: The Kohlberg-Gilligan Controversy and Feminist Theory," in Seyla Benhabib and Drucilla Cornell, eds., *Feminism as Critique* (Minneapolis: University of Minnesota Press, 1987), pp 77–95. Similarly, the feminist response to Ivan Illich, *Gender* (New York: Pantheon, 1982), has tended to raise these issues. See, for example, Lourdes Benería, "Meditations on Ivan Illich's *Gender,*" in B. Gustavsson, J. C. Karlsson, and C. Rafregard, eds., *Work in the 1980s* (London: Gower Publishing, 1985).

31. The phrase "human wholeness" comes from Betty Friedan, *The Second Stage* (New York: Summit Books, 1981), and the concept receives a valuable and devastating critique in Myra Jehlen, "Against Human Wholeness: A Suggestion for a Feminist Epistemology" (manuscript).

32. For the pregnancy issue, see "Brief of the American Civil Liberties Union et al." amici curiae, *California Federal Savings and Loan Association et al. v. Mark Guerra et al.,* Supreme Court of the United States, October Term, 1985, Joan E. Bertin, Counsel of record; Wendy Chavkin, "Walking a Tightrope: Pregnancy, Parenting, and Work," in Wendy Chavkin, ed., *Double Exposure: Women's Health Hazards*

on the Job and at Home (New York: Monthly Review Press, 1984); Lise Vogel, "Debating Difference: The Problem of Special Treatment of Pregnancy in the Workplace," (Paper presented at the Women and Society Seminar of Columbia University, New York, January 24, 1988); Kai Bird and Max Holland, "Capitol Letter: The Garland Case," *The Nation*, July 5–12, 1986, p. 8; Wendy Williams, "Equality's Riddle: Pregnancy and the Equal Treatment/Special Treatment Debate," *N.Y.U. Review of Law and Social Change* 13 (1984–1985); Herma Hill Kay, "Equality and Difference: The Case of Pregnancy," *Berkeley Women's Law Journal* 1 (1985). For the custody issue, see Katharine T. Bartlett and Carol B. Stack, "Joint Custody, Feminism and the Dependency Dilemma," *Berkeley Women's Law Journal* (Winter 1986–1987), pp. 501–533; Phyllis Chesler, *Mothers on Trial: The Battle for Children and Custody* (Seattle: Seal Press, 1986); Lenore J. Weitzman, *The Divorce Revolution: The Unexpected Social and Economic Consequences for Women and Children in America* (New York: Macmillan, 1985). The work of Nadine Taub, director of the Women's Rights Litigation Clinic, School of Law, Rutgers/Newark, has frequent bearing on both issues and on the larger questions in equality/difference debates. See Nadine Taub, "Defining and Combatting Sexual Harassment," in Amy Swerdlow and Hannah Lessinger, eds., *Class, Race and Sex: The Dynamics of Control* (Boston: G. K. Hall, 1983): pp. 263–275; Nadine Taub, "Feminist Tensions: Concepts of Motherhood and Reproductive Choice," *Gender and Transition* (forthcoming); Nadine Taub, "A Public Policy of Private Caring," *The Nation*, May 31, 1986, pp. 756–758; Nadine Taub and Wendy Williams, "Will Equality Require More Than Assimilation, Accommodation or Separation from the Existing Social Structure?" *Rutgers Law Review* 37, no. 4 (Summer 1985), pp. 825–844. The burgeoning feminist work on the new reproductive technologies also reproduces the divide. For complete references to all aspects of these debates, see Nadine Taub and Sherrill Cohen, *Reproductive Laws for the 1990s* (Clifton, N.J.: Humana Press, 1989).

33. If I had to come up with an example of a feminist strategy that faced the power of the divide squarely yet at the same time undermined the oppression the divide represents, I'd choose recent feminist comparable worth legislation. Humble and earthshaking, comparable worth asserts two things: First, because women and men do different work, the concept "equal pay" has little effect on raising women's low wages; and, second, if work were to be judged by standards of difficulty, educational preparation, experience, and so on (standards preferably developed by workers themselves), then antidiscrimination laws might enforce that men and women doing work of comparable worth be paid the same. (Perhaps nurses and automechanics? Or teachers and middle managers?) The activists who have proposed comparable worth have singularly few pretentions. They are the first to point out that on its face, the proposal ignores the work women do in the family, ignores the non-economic reasons why women and men have different kinds of jobs, ignores what's wrong with job hierarchies and with "worth" as the sole basis for determining pay. Yet this little brown mouse of a liberal reform, narrow in its present political potential and limited by its nature, has a touch of deconstructive genius. Without hoping to get women doing men's work tomorrow, the comparable worth model erodes the economic advantages to employers of consistently undervaluing women's work and channeling women into stigmatized work ghettoes where pay is always lower. With

comparable worth, the stigma might well continue to haunt women's work, but women would be better paid. Men might start wanting a "woman's" job that paid well, while women might have new psychological incentives to cross gender work categories. Who knows, perhaps stigma might not catch up as categories of work got rethought and their gender markers moved around. And if the stigma clung to women's work, if men refused to be nurses even if nurses were paid as well as construction workers, a woman earning money is an independent woman. She can change the family; she can consider leaving it. Comparable worth asserts the divide, yet, slyly, it goes to work on the basic economic and psychological underpinnings of the divide; it undermines the idea that all work has a natural gender. See Sara M. Evans and Barbara J. Nelson, *Wage Justice: Comparable Worth and the Paradox of Technocratic Reform* (Chicago: University of Chicago Press, 1989). The mixtures of progressive and conservative impulses that have characterized both sides of the divide at different moments get a nuanced reading from Nancy F. Cott in her historical study of American feminism, *The Grounding of Modern Feminism* (New Haven, Conn.: Yale University Press, 1987).

34. See, for example, Judy R. Walkowitz, *Prostitution and Victorian Society: Women, Class, and the State* (Cambridge: Cambridge University Press, 1980).

35. Ellen DuBois: "The Radicalism of the Women Suffrage Movement: Notes Toward the Reconstruction of Nineteenth-Century Feminism," in Anne Phillips, ed., *Feminism and Equality* (New York: New York University Press, 1987), p. 128.

36. See Mary Daly, *Gyn/Ecology: The Metaethics of Radical Feminism* (Boston: Beacon Press, 1978). Maggie McFadden gives an account of this range in her useful taxonomy piece, "Anatomy of Difference: Toward a Classification of Feminist Theory," *Women's Studies International Forum* 7, no. 6 (1984), pp. 495–504. Adrienne Harris has pointed out to me that essentialism comes and goes in feminist psychoanalytic discussions of the penis: "The concept slips, moves and breaks apart."

37. Bell Hooks, "Feminism: A Movement to End Sexist Oppression," in Phillips, *Feminism and Equality*, p. 62.

38. Taken together, Alison Jaggar's essays on the equality/difference debate offer a poignant (and I think continuingly ambivalent) personal account of how one feminist theorist developed doubts about the equality position. See Jaggar, "Sexual Difference and Sexual Equality"; Alison Jaggar, "Towards a More Integrated World: Feminist Reconstructions of the Self and Society," (Talk at Douglass College, New Brunswick, N.J., Spring 1985); Alison Jaggar, "Sex Inequality and Bias in Sex Differences in Research," (Paper for the symposium of Bias in Sex Differences Research, American Association for the Advancement of Science Annual Meeting, Chicago, February 14–18, 1987).

39. See, for example, Christine Stansell, *City of Women: Sex and Class in New York, 1789–1860* (New York: Knopf, 1986).

40. For Chavkin, Jaggar, and Jehlen see notes 30, 31, 32 and 38 above.

41. Eisenstein (New York: Longman, 1981); Mitchell, "Women and Equality" (1976), reprinted in Phillips.

42. The feminist scandal of the Sears case offers a particularly disturbing example of the divide as it can get played out within the exigencies of a court case. See Ruth Milkman, "Women's History and the Sears Case," *Feminist Studies* 12 (Summer 1986), pp. 375–400; and Joan W. Scott, "Deconstructing Equality-Versus-Difference: Or the Uses of Poststructuralist Theory for Feminism," *Feminist Studies* 14, no. 1 (Spring 1988), pp. 33–50 (reprinted in this volume). In her introduction to *Feminism and Equality,* Anne Phillips offers a useful instance of how, in different contexts, the feminist ambivalence about liberalism emerges; she observes that in the United States, feminism began with equality models that revealed their inadequacy in practice, while in Britain, feminists began with a socialist critique of liberal goals that their own disappointments have modified in the equality direction.

43. See the now classic restoration of Mary Wollstonecraft by Juliet Mitchell, "Women and Equality." Also see two more recent, subtle readings of Wollstonecraft: Patricia Yeager, "Writing as Action: *A Vindication of the Rights of Woman,*" *The Minnesota Review,* no. 29 (Winter 1987), pp 67–80; Cora Kaplan "Wild nights: pleasure/sexuality/feminism," (1983), reprinted in Nancy Armstrong and Leonard Tennenhouse, eds., *The Ideology of Conduct: Essays on Literature and the History of Sexuality* (New York: Methuen, 1987), pp. 160–184. An instance of Wollstonecraft's contemporaneity: Linda Nochlin makes precisely her arguments about gender; Nochlin sees it as a variable changeable as class or vocation in her ground-breaking essay, "Why Have There Been No Great Women Artists?" (1971), reprinted in Thomas B. Hess and Elizabeth C. Baker, eds., *Art and Sexual Politics: Why Have There Been No Great Women Artists?* (New York: Macmillan, 1971), pp. 1–39.

44. Mary Wollstonecraft, *A Vindication of the Rights of Woman,* ed. Carol H. Poston (New York: Norton, 1975), p. 35.

45. Ibid., pp. 5, 30.

46. Shulamith Firestone, *The Dialectic of Sex: The Case for Feminist Revolution* (New York: William Morrow, 1970), strikes me as offering the best instance of this mixture of tones in contemporary feminism. Firestone dedicates her book to de Beauvoir, but her political fervor comes much closer to Wollstonecraft's.

47. Rosenfelt and Stacy, "Second Thoughts on the Second Wave," *Feminist Studies* 13, no. 2 (Summer 1987), pp 350–351.

48. Audre Lorde, talk at the MLA.

49. Since the Hyde Amendment restricting Medicaid abortions in 1979, No More Nice Girls has done occasional, ad hoc street events in New York City to dramatize new threats to women's sexual autonomy.

2

Historical Perspectives:
The Equal Rights Amendment
Conflict in the 1920s

Nancy F. Cott

Campaigning for ratification of the Equal Rights Amendment during the 1970s, feminists who found it painful to be opposed by other groups of women were often unaware that the first proposal of that amendment in the 1920s had caused a bitter split between women's groups claiming, on both sides, to represent women's interests. The 1920s conflict itself echoed some earlier ideological and tactical controversies. One central strategic question for the women's rights movement in the late nineteenth century had concerned alliances: should proponents of "the cause of woman" ally with advocates for the rights for freed slaves, with temperance workers, or labor reformers, or a political party, or none of them? At various times different women leaders felt passionately for and against such alliances, not agreeing on what they meant for the breadth of the women's movement and for the priority assigned to women's issues.[1] The 1920s contest over the equal rights amendment reiterated that debate insofar as the National Women's Party, which proposed the ERA, took a "single-issue" approach, and the opposing women's organizations were committed to maintaining multiple alliances. But in even more striking ways than it recapitulated nineteenth-century struggles the 1920s equal rights conflict also predicted lines of fracture of the later twentieth-century women's movement. The advantages or compromises involved in "multi-issue" organizing are matters of contemporary concern, of course. Perhaps more important, the 1920s debate brought into sharp focus (and left for us generations later to resolve) the question whether "equal rights"—a concept adopted, after all, from the male political tradition—matched women's needs. The initial conflict between women over the ERA set the goal of enabling women to have the same opportunities and situations as men *against* the goal of enabling women freely to be different from men without adverse consequences. As never before in nineteenth-century controversies, these two were seen as competing, even mutually exclusive alternatives.

The equal rights amendment was proposed as a legal or civic innovation but the intrafeminist controversy it caused focused on the economic arena. Indeed, the connection between economic and political subordination in women's relation to men has been central in women's rights advocacy since the latter part of the nineteenth century. In the Western political tradition, women were historically excluded from political initiatives because they were defined as dependent—like children and slaves—and their dependence was read as fundamentally economic. Nineteenth-century advocates, along with the vote, claimed woman's "right to labor," by which they meant the right for women to have their labor recognized, and diversified. They emphasized that women, as human individuals no less than men, had the right and need to use their talents to serve society and themselves and to gain fair compensation. Influential voices such as Charlotte Perkins Gilman's at the turn of the century stressed not only women's service but the necessity and warrant for women's economic independence. Gilman argued simultaneously that social evolution made women's move "from fireside to factory" inevitable, and also that the move ought to be spurred by conscious renovation of outworn tradition.

By the 1910s suffragists linked political and economic rights, and connected the vote with economic leverage, whether appealing to industrial workers, career women, or housewives. They insisted on women's economic independence in principle and defense of wage-earning women in fact. Since the vast majority of wage-earning women were paid too little to become economically independent, however, the two commitments were not identical and might in practice be entirely at odds.[2] The purpose to validate women's existing economic roles might openly conflict with the purpose to throw open economic horizons for women to declare their own self-definition. These tensions introduced by the feminist and suffrage agitation of the 1910s flashed into controversy over the equal rights amendment in the 1920s.

The ERA was the baby of the National Women's Party, yet not its brainchild alone. As early as 1914, a shortlived N.Y.C. group called the Feminist Alliance had suggested a constitutional amendment barring sex discrimination of all sorts. Like the later NWP, the Feminist Alliance was dominated by highly educated and ambitious women in the arts and professions, women who believed that "equal rights" were their due while they also aimed to rejuvenate and reorient thinking about "rights" around female rather than only male definition. Some members of the Feminist Alliance surely joined the NWP, which emerged as the agent of militant and political action during the final decade of the suffrage campaign.[3]

A small group (engaging perhaps five percent of all suffragists), the NWP grew from the Congressional Union founded by Alice Paul and Lucy Burns in 1913 to work on the federal rather than the state-by-state route to woman suffrage. Through the 'teens it came to stand for partisan tactics (opposing all Democrats because the Democratic administration had not passed woman suffrage) and for flamboyant, symbolic, publicity-generating actions—large parades, pickets in front of the White House, placards in the Congress, hunger-striking in jail, and more. It gained much of its energy from leftwing radical women who were attracted to its wholesale condemnation of gender inequality and to its tactical adaptations from the labor movement; at the same time, its imperious tendency to work from the top down attracted crucial financial and moral support from some very rich women. When the much larger group, the National American Woman Suffrage Association, moved its focus to a constitutional amendment in 1916, that was due in no little part (although certainly not solely), to the impact of the NWP. Yet while imitating its aim, NAWSA's leaders always hated and resented the NWP for the way it had horned in on the same pro-suffrage turf while scorning the NAWSA's traditional nonpartisan, educative strategy. These resentments festered into deep and longlasting personal conflicts between leaders of the two groups.

Just after the 19th Amendment was ratified in August of 1930, the NWP began planning a large convention at which its members would decide whether to continue as a group and, if so, what to work for. The convention, held six months later and tightly orchestrated by chairman Alice Paul, brushed aside all other suggestions and endorsed an ongoing program to "remove all remaining forms of the subjection of women," by means of the elimination of sex discrimination in law.[4] At the outset, NWP leaders seemed unaware that this program of "equal rights" would be much thornier to define and implement than "equal suffrage" had been. They began surveying state legal codes, conferring with lawyers, and drafting numerous versions of equal rights legislation and amendments at the state and federal levels.

Yet the "clean sweep" of such an approach immediately raised a problem: would it invalidate sex-based labor legislation—the laws regulating women's hours, wages, and conditions of work—that women trade unionists and reformers had worked to establish over the past thirty years? The doctrine of "liberty of contract" between employer and employed had ruled court interpretations of labor legislation in the early twentieth century, stymying state regulation of the wages and hours of male workers. State regulation for women workers, espoused and furthered by many women in the NWP, had been made possible only by differentiating female from male wage-earners on the basis of physiology and reproductive functions. Now members of the NWP had to grapple with the question whether such legislation was sex "discrimination," hampering women workers in the labor market. Initially, there was a great deal of sentiment within the NWP, even voiced by Alice Paul herself, that efforts at equal rights legislation should not impair existing sex-based protective labor legislation. However, there was also contrary opinion, which Paul increasingly heeded; by late November 1921 she had come to believe firmly that "enacting labor laws along sex lines is erecting another handicap for women in the economic struggle." Some NWP affiliates were still trying to draft an amendment that would preserve special labor legislation, nonetheless, and continued to introduce equal rights bills with "safeguards" in some states through the following spring.[5]

Meanwhile women leaders in other organizations were becoming nervous and distrustful of the NWP's intentions. Led by the League of Women Voters (successor to the NAWSA), major women's organizations in 1920 formed a national lobbying group called the Women's Joint Congressional Committee. The LWV was interested in eliminating sex discrimination in the law, but more immediately concerned with the extension of sex-based labor legislation. Moreover, the LWV had inherited NAWSA's hostility to Alice Paul. The first president of the LWV, Maud Wood Park, still smarted from the discomfiture that NWP picketing tactics had caused her when she headed the NAWSA's Congressional Committee from 1916 to 1920.[6] Other leading groups in the Women's Joint Congressional Committee were no less suspicious of the NWP. The National Women's Trade Union League since the mid-1910s had concentrated its efforts on labor legislation to protect women workers. Florence Kelley, director of the National Consumers' League, had been part of the inner circle of the NWP during the suffrage campaign, but on the question of protective labor laws her priorities diverged. She had spent three decades trying to get state regulation of workers' hours and conditions, and was not about to abandon the gains achieved for women.[7]

In December 1921, at Kelley's behest, Paul and three other NWP members met for discussion with her and leaders of the League of Women Voters, the National Women's Trade Union League, the Woman's Christian Temperance Union, and the General Federation of Women's Clubs. All the latter objected to the new constitutional amendment now formulated by the NWP: "No political, civil or legal disabilities or inequalities on account of sex, or on account of marriage unless applying alike to both sexes, shall exist within the United States or any place subject to their jurisdiction." Paul gave away no ground, and all left feeling that compromise was unlikely. Each side already thought the other intransigent, though in fact debate was still going on within the NWP.[8]

By mid-1922 the National Consumers' League, the LWV, and the Women's Trade Union League went on record opposing "blanket" equal rights bills, as the NWP formulations at both state and federal levels were called. About the same time, the tide turned in the NWP. The top leadership accepted as definitive the views of Gail Laughlin, a lawyer from Maine, who contended that sex-based labor legislation was not a lamented loss but a positive harm. "If women can be segregated as a class for special legislation," she warned, "the same classification can be used for special restrictions along any other line which may, at any time, appeal to the caprice or prejudice of our legislatures." In her opinion, if "protective" laws affecting women were not abolished and prohibited, "the advancement of women in business and industry will be stopped and women relegated to the lowest, worst paid labor."[9] Since NWP lobbyists working at the state level were making little headway, a federal constitutional amendment appeared all the more appealing. In November 1923, at a grand conference staged in Seneca Falls, New York, commemorating the seventy-fifth anniversary of Elizabeth Cady Stanton's Declaration of Sentiments, the NWP announced new language: "Men and women shall have equal rights throughout the United States and every place subject to its jurisdiction." The constitutional amendment was introduced into Congress on December 10, 1923.[10]

In the NWP view, this was the logical sequel to the 19th Amendment. There were so many different sex discriminations in state codes and legal practices—in family law, labor law, jury privileges, contract rights—that only a constitutional amendment seemed effective to remove them. The NWP took the language of liberal individualism, enshrined the catch-phrase of "equal rights," to express its feminism. As Alice Paul saw it, what women as a gender group shared was their subordination and inequality to men as a whole; the legal structure most clearly expressed this subordination and inequality, and therefore was the logical point of attack. The NWP construed this agenda as "purely feminist," that is, appealing to women as women, uniting women around a concern common to them regardless of the other ways in which they might differ. Indeed, at its founding postsuffrage convention the NWP leadership purposely bypassed issues it saw as less "pure," including birth control, the defense of black women's voting rights in the South, and pacifism, which were predictably controversial among women themselves.

The NWP posited that women could and would perceive self-interest in "purely" gender terms. Faced by female opponents, its leaders imagined a fictive or abstract unity among women rather than attempt to encompass women's real diversity. They separated the proposal of equal rights from other social and political issues and effects. Although the campaign for equal rights was initiated in a vision of inclusiveness—envisioned as a stand that all women could take—it devolved into a practice of exclusiveness. The NWP's "appeal for conscious sex loyalty" (as a member once put it) went out to members of the sex who could subordinate identifications and loyalties of class, ethnicity, race, religion, politics, or whatever else to a "pure" sense of themselves as women differentiated from men. That meant principally women privileged by the dominant culture in every way except that they were female.[11]

In tandem with its lobbying for an equal rights amendment, the NWP presented its opposition to sex-based labor legislation as a positive program of "industrial equality." It championed women wage-earners who complained of "protective" legislation as restrictive, such as printers, railroad conductors, or waitresses hampered by hours limitation, or cleaning women fired and replaced by men after the passage of minimum-wage laws. Only a handful of working-class women rose to support for the ERA, however.[12] Mary Anderson, former factory worker herself and since 1919 the director of the U.S. Women's Bureau which was founded to guide and assist women workers, threw her weight into the fight against the amendment. Male trade unionists—namely leaders of the American Federation of Labor—also voiced immediate opposition to the NWP aims, appearing at the very first U.S. Senate subcommittee hearings on the equal rights amendment. Male unionists or class-conscious workers in this period put their faith in collective bargaining and did not seek labor legislation for themselves, but endorsed it for women and child workers. This differentiation derived partly from male workers' belief in women's physical weakness and veneration of women's "place" in the home, partly from presumptions about women workers being difficult to organize, and also from the aim to keep women from competing for men's jobs. Male unionists tended to view wage-earning women first as women—potential or actual wives and mothers—and only secondarily as workers. For differing reasons women and men in the labor movement converged in their support of sex-based legislation: women because they saw special protection necessary to defend their stake in industry and in union organizations, limited as it was; men to hold at bay women's demands for equal entry into male-controlled union jobs and organizations.[13]

The arguments against the equal rights amendment offered by trade unionists and by such women's organizations as the League of Women Voters overlapped. They assumed that an equal rights amendment would invalidate sex-based labor laws or, at least, destine them for protracted argument in the courts, where judges had shown hostility to any state regulation of employer prerogatives. They insisted that the greatest good for the greatest number was served by protective labor laws. If sex-based legislation hampered some—as the NWP claimed, and could be shown true, for instance, in the case of women linotypists, who needed to work at night—then the proper tactic was to exempt some occupations, not to eliminate protective laws whole. They feared that state welfare legislation in place, such as widows' pensions, would also be at risk. They contended that a constitutional amendment was too undiscriminating an instrument: objectionable sex discriminations such as those concerning jury duty, inheritance rights, nationality, or child custody would be more efficiently and accurately eliminated by specific bills for specific instances. Sometimes, opponents claimed that the ERA took an unnecessarily federal approach, overriding states' rights, although here they were hardly consistent for many of them were at the same time advocating a constitutional amendment to prohibit child labor.

Against the ERA, spokeswomen cited evidence that wage-earning women wanted and valued labor legislation and that male workers, too, benefitted from limits on women's hours in factories where men and women worked at interdependent tasks. Before hours were legally limited, "we were 'free' and 'equal' to work long hours for starvation wages, or free to leave the job and starve!" WTUL leader Pauline Newman bitterly recalled. Dr. Alice Hamilton, pioneer of industrial medicine, saw the NWP as maintaining "a purely negative program, . . . holding down in their present condition of industrial slavery hundreds of thousands of women without doing anything to alleviate their lot."[14] Trade-unionist and Women's Bureau colleagues attacked the NWP's vision as callously class-biased, the thoughtless outlook of rich women, at best relevant to the experience of exceptional skilled workers or professionals. They regularly accused the NWP of being the unwitting tool (at best) or the paid servant of rapacious employers, although no proof of the latter was ever brought forward.

They heard in the NWP program the voice of the ruling class, and denounced the equal rights amendment as "class" legislation, by and for the bourgeoisie.[15]

Indeed, at the Women's Bureau Conference on Women in Industry in 1926, the NWP's opposition to sex-based labor legislation was echoed by the President of the National Association of Manufacturers, who declared that the "handful" of women in industry could take care of themselves, and were not served by legislative "poultices." In this controversy, the positions also lent themselves to, and inevitably were colored by, male "allies" whose principal concerns dealt less with women's economic or legal protection or advancement than political priorities of their own. At the same conference the U.S. Secretary of Labor appointed by President Coolidge took the side of sex-based protective legislation, proclaiming that "the place fixed for women by God and Nature is a great place," and "wherever we see women at work we must see them in terms of motherhood." What he saw as the great danger of the age was the "increasing loss of the distinction between manliness and true femininity."[16]

Often, ERA opponents who supported sex-based labor legislation—including civic-minded middle-class women, social welfare reformers, government officials, and trade union men—appeared more concerned with working women's motherhood than with economic justice. "Women who are wage earners, with one job in the factory and another in the home have little time and energy left to carry on the fight to better their economic status. They need the help of other women and they need labor laws," announced Mary Anderson. Dr. Hamilton declared that "the great inarticulate body of working women . . . are largely helpless, . . . [and] have very special needs which unaided they cannot attain . . . ."[17] Where NWP advocates saw before their eyes women who were eager and robust, supporters of protective legislation saw women overburdened and vulnerable. The former claimed that protective laws penalized the strong; the latter claimed that the ERA would sacrifice the weak. The NWP looked at women as individuals, and wanted to dislodge gender differentiation from the labor market. Their opponents looked at women as members of families—daughters, wives, mothers, and widows with family responsibilities—and believed that the promise of "mere equality" did not sufficiently take those relationships into account. The one side tacitly positing the independent professional woman as the paradigm, the other presuming the doubly-burdened mother in industry or service; neither side distinguished nor addressed directly the situation of the fastest-growing sector of employed women, in white-collar jobs. At least half of the female labor force—those in manufacturing and in domestic and personal service—worked in taxing, menial jobs with long hours, unpleasant and often unhealthy conditions, very low pay, and rare opportunities for advancement. But in overall pattern women's employment was leaving these sectors and swelling in clerical, managerial, sales, and professional areas. In 1900, women in white-collar work constituted under 18 percent of all women employed. But by 1920 that proportion had doubled, and by 1930 was 44 percent.[18]

The relation of sex-based legislation to women workers' welfare was more ambiguous and complicated than either side acknowledged. Such laws immediately benefitted far larger numbers of employed women than they hindered, but the laws also had a negative impact on women's overall economic opportunities, both immediately and in the long term. Sex segregation of the labor market was a very significant factor. In industries monopolizing women workers, where wages, conditions, and hours were more likely to be substandard, protective legislation helped to bring things up to standard. It was in more desirable crafts and trades more unusual for women workers, where skill levels and pay were likely to be higher—that is, where women needed to enter in order to improve their earnings and economic advancement—that sex-based protective legislation held women back. There, as a contemporary inquiry into the issue said, "the practice of enacting laws covering women alone appears to discourage their employment, and therefore fosters the prejudice against them." The segregation of women into low-paid, dead-end jobs that made protective laws for women workers necessary, was thus abetted by the legislation itself.[19]

By 1925, all but four states limited working women's hours; eighteen states prescribed rest periods and meal hours; sixteen states prohibited night work in certain occupations; and thirteen had minimum wage regulations. Such regulation was passed not only because it served women workers, but also because employers, especially large corporate employers, began to see benefits in its stabilization of the labor market and control of unscrupulous competition. Although the National Association of Manufacturers, fixed on "liberty of contract," remained opposed, large employers of women accepted sex-based labor legislation on reasoning about "protection of the race," or could see advantages for themselves in it, or both. A vice-president of Filene's, a large department store in Boston, for instance, approved laws regulating the hours, wages, and conditions of women employees because "economies have been effected by the reduction of labor turnover; by reduction of the number of days lost through illness and accidents; and by increase in the efficiency of the working force as well as in the efficiency of management." He appreciated the legislation's maintaining standards as to hours, wages, and working conditions "throughout industry as a *whole,* thus preventing selfish interests from indulging in unfair competition by the exploitation of women . . . ."[20]

While the anti-ERA side was right in the utilitarian contention that protective laws meant the greatest good to the greatest number of women workers (at least in the short run), the pro-ERA side was also right that such laws hampered women's scope in the labor market and sustained the assumption that employment advantage was not of primary concern to women. Those who advocated sex-based laws were looking at the labor market as it was, trying to protect women in it, but thereby contributing to the perpetuation of existing inequalities. They envisaged wage-earning women as veritable beasts of burden. That group portrait supplanted the prior feminist image of wage-earning women as a vanguard of independent female personalities, as equal producers of the world's wealth. Its advocates did not see that their conception of women's needs helped to confirm women's second-class position in the economy. On the other hand, the ERA advocate who opposed sex-based "protections" were envisioning the labor market as it might be, trying to insure women the widest opportunities in that imagined arena, and thereby blinking at existing exploitation. They did not admit to the vulnerabilities that sex-based legislation addressed, while they overestimated what legal equality might do to unchain women from the economic stranglehold of the domestic stereotype.

Women on both sides of the controversy, however, saw themselves as legatees of suffragism and feminism, intending to defend the value of women's economic roles, to prevent economic exploitation of women, and to open the doors to economic opportunity. A struggle over the very word feminism, which the NWP had embraced, became part of the controversy. For "us even to use the word feminist," contended Women's Trade Union League leader Ethel Smith, "is to invite from the extremists a challenge to our authenticity." Detractors in the WTUL and Women's Bureau called the NWP "ultra" or "extreme" feminists. Mary Anderson considered herself "a good feminist" but objected that "over-articulate theorists were attempting to solve the working women's problems on a purely feministic basis with the working women's own voice far less adequately heard." Her own type of feminist was moderate and practical, Anderson declared; the others, putting the "woman question" above all other questions, were extreme and abstract. The bitterness was compounded by a conflict of personalities and tactics dragged on from the suffrage years. Opponents of the ERA, deeply resenting having to oppose something called equal rights, maligned the NWP as "pernicious," women who "discard[ed] all ethics and fair play," an "insane crowd" who espoused "a kind of hysterical feminism with a slogan for a program."[21] Their critiques fostered public perception of feminism as a sectarian and impracticable doctrine unrelated to real life and blind to injustices besides sex inequality. By the end of the 1920s women outside the NWP rarely made efforts to reclaim the term feminist for themselves, and the meaning of the term was depleted.

Forced into theorizing by this controversy, not prepared as philosophers or legal theorists, spokeswomen on either side in the 1920s were grappling with definitions of women's rights as compared to men's that neither the legal nor economic system was designed to accommodate. The question whether equality required women to have the same rights as men, or different rights, could not be answered without delving into definitions. Did "equality" pertain to opportunity, treatment, or outcome?[22] Should "difference" be construed to mean separation, discrimination, protection, privilege—or assault on the very standard that the male was the human norm?[23]

Opponents of the ERA believed that sex-based legislation was necessary because of women's biological and social roles as mothers. They claimed that "The inherent differences are permanent. Women will always need many laws different from those needed by men"; "Women as such, whether or not they are mothers present or prospective, will always need protective legislation"; "The working mother is handicapped by her own nature."[24] Their approach stressed maternal nature and inclination as well as conditioning, and implied that the sexual division of labor was eternal.

The NWP's approach, on the other hand, presupposed that women's differentiation from men in the law and the labor market was a particular, social-historical, and not necessary or inevitable construction. The sexual division of labor arose from archaic custom, enshrined in employer and employee attitudes and written in the law. The NWP approach assumed that wives and mothers as well as unencumbered women would want and should have open access to jobs and professions. NWP proponents imagined that the sexual division of labor (in the family and the marketplace) would change, if women would secure the same rights as men and have free access to wage-earning. Their view made a fragile potential into a necessary fact. They assumed that women's wage-earning would, by its very existence, challenge the sexual division of labor, and that it would provide the means for women's economic independence—although neither of these tenets was necessarily being realized.

Wage-earning women's experience in the 1910s and 1920s, as documented by the Women's Bureau, showed that the sexual division of labor was budged only very selectively and marginally by women's gainful employment. Most women's wages did not bring them economic independence; women earned as part of a plan for family support (as men did, though that was rarely stressed). Contrary to the NWP's feminist visions, in those places in the nation where the highest proportions of wives and mothers worked for pay, the sexual division of labor was most oppressively in place. To every child growing up in the region of Southern textile and tobacco mills, where wives and mothers worked more "jobs" at home and in the factory than any other age or status group—and earned less— the sexual division of labor appeared no less prescriptive and burdensome than it had before women earned wages.[25]

Critiques of the NWP and its ERA as "abstract" or "extreme" or "fanatical" represented the gap between feminist tenets and harsh social reality as an oversight of the NWP, a failure to adjust their sights. Even more sympathetic critics, such as one Southern academic, asked rhetorically, "Do the feminists see in the tired and haggard faces of young waitresses, who spend seventy hours a week of hard work in exchange for a few dollars to pay for food and clothing, a deceptive mask of the noble spirit within?" She answered herself, "Surely it is not an increasing army of jaded girls and spent women that pours every day from factory and shop that the leaders of the feminist movement seek. But the call for women to make all labor their province can mean nothing more. They would free women from the rule of men only to make them greater slaves to the machines of industry."[26] Indeed, the exploitation of female service and industrial workers at "cheap" wages cruelly parodied the feminist notion that gainful employment represented an assertion of independence (just as the wifely duties required of a secretary parodied the feminist expectation that wage-earning would challenge the sexual division of labor and reopen definitions of femininity). What such critics were observing was the distance between the potential for women's wage-earning to challenge the sexual division of labor, and the social facts of gender and class hierarchy that clamped down on that challenge.

Defenders of sex-based protective legislation, trying to acknowledge women's unique reproductive endowments and social obligations, were grappling with problems so difficult they would still be present more than half a century later. Their immediate resolution was to portray women's "difference" in merely customary terms. "Average American women prefer to make a home for husbands and children to anything else," Mary Anderson asserted in defense of her position. "They would rather fulfill this normal function than go into the business world."[27] Keeping alive a critique of the class division of wealth, protective legislation advocates lost sight of the need to challenge the very sexual division of labor that was the root of women's "handicap" or "helplessness." As compared to the NWP's emphasis on the historical and social construction of gender roles, advocates of sex-based protective legislation echoed customary public opinion in proposing that motherhood and wage-earning should be mutually exclusive. They easily found allies among such social conservatives as the National Council of Catholic Women, whose representatives testified against the ERA because it "seriously menaced . . . the unity of the home and family life" and contravened the "essential differences in rights and duties" of the two sexes which were the "result of natural law." Edging into plain disapproval of mothers of young children who earned, protective legislation supporters became more prescriptive, less flexible, than wage-earning mothers themselves, for whom cash recognition of their labor was very welcome. "Why should not a married woman work [for pay], if a single one does?" demanded a mill worker who came to the Southern Summer School for Women Workers. "What would men think if they were told that a married man should not work? If we women would not be so submissive and take everything for granted, if we would awake and stand up for our rights, this world would be a better place to live in, at least it would be better for the women. . . ."[28]

The onset of the Depression in many ways worsened the ERA controversy, for the one side thought protective legislation all the more crucial when need drove women to take any jobs available, and the other side argued that protective legislation prevented women from competing for what jobs there were. In the 1930s it became clear that the labor movement's and League of Women Voters' opposition to the equal rights amendment ran deeper than concern for sex-based legislation as an "entering wedge." The Fair Labor Standards Act of 1938 mandated wages and hours regulation for all workers, and the U.S. Supreme Court upheld it in 1941; but the labor movement and the LWV still opposed the ERA. Other major women's organizations, however—most importantly the National Federation of Business and Professional Women's Clubs and the General Federation of Women's Clubs—and the national platforms of both the Republican and the Democratic Party endorsed the ERA by 1944.[29]

We generally learn "winners' " history—not the history of lost causes. If the ERA passed by Congress in 1972 had achieved ratification by 1982, perhaps historians of women would read the trajectory of the women's movement from 1923 to the present as a steady upward curve, and award the NWP unqualified original insight. The failure of the ERA this time around (on new, but not unrelated grounds) compels us to see the longer history of equal rights in its true complexity.[30] The ERA battle of the 1920s seared into memory the fact of warring outlooks among women while it illustrated the inevitable intermeshing of women's legal and political rights with their economic situations. If the controversy testified to the difficulty of protecting women in the economic arena while opening opportunities to them, even more fundamentally the debate brought into question the NWP's premise that the articulation of sex discrimination—or the call for equal rights—would arouse all women to mobilize as a group. What kind of a group were women, when their occupational and social and other loyalties were varied, when not all women viewed "women's" interests, or what constituted sex "discrimination," the same way? The ideological dimensions of that problem cross-cut both class consciousness and gender identity. The debate's intensity, both then and now, measured how fundamental was the re-vision needed if policies and practices of economic and civic life deriving from a male norm were to give full scope to women—and to women of all sorts.

Notes

1. A good introduction to the issue of alliances in the 19th-century women's movement, and an essential text on the mid-19th-century split is Ellen Carol Dubois, *Feminism and Suffrage: The Emergence of an Independent Women's Movement, 1848–1869* (Ithaca, N.Y.: Cornell, 1978).

2. See Leslie Woodcock Tentler, *Wage-Earning Women: Industrial Work and Family Life in the U.S., 1900–1930* (N.Y.: Oxford, 1979), chapter 1, on industrially employed women's wages, keyed below subsistence.

3. On feminists in the final decade of the suffrage campaign, see Nancy F. Cott, *The Grounding of Modern Feminism* (New Haven: Yale, 1987), 23–66.

4. For more detailed discussion of the February 1921 convention, see Nancy F. Cott, "Feminist Politics in the 1920s: The National Women's Party," *Journal of American History,* 71:1 (June 1984).

5. Paul to Jane Norman Smith, Nov. 29, 1921, folder 110, J. N. Smith Coll., Schlesinger Library (hereafter SL). See NWP correspondence of Feb.–Mar. 1921 in the microfilm collection, "The National Woman's Party, 1913–1974" (Microfilm Corp.

of America), reels #5–7 (hereafter NWP with reel#), and Cott, *Grounding*, 66–74, 120–25, for more detail.

In Wisconsin, prominent NWP suffragist Mabel Raef Putnam put together a coalition which successfully lobbied through the first state equal rights bill early in 1921. This legislation granted women the same rights and privileges as men *except for* "the special protection and privileges which they now enjoy for the general welfare." See Edwin E. Witte, "History and Purposes of the Wisconsin Equal Rights Law," typescript, Dec. 1929, Mabel Raef Putnam Collection, SL; and Peter Geidel, "The National Women's Party and the Origins of the Equal Rights Amendment" (M.A. thesis, Columbia University, 1977), chapter 3.

6. Maud Wood Park, *Front Door Lobby*, ed. Edna Stantial (Boston: Beacon, 1960), 23.

7. Historians' treatments of women's organizations' differing views on the ERA in the 1920s include William N. O'Neill, *Everyone Was Brave* (Chicago: Quadrangle, 1969), 274–94; J. Stanley Lemons, *The Woman Citizen: Social Feminism in the 1920s* (Urbana: Univ. of Illinois, 1973), 184–99; William Chafe, *The American Woman: Her Changing Social, Economic and Political Roles* (N.Y.: Oxford, 1972), 112–32; Sheila M. Rothman, *Woman's Proper Place: A History of Changing Ideals and Practices, 1870 to the Present* (N.Y.: Basic, 1978), 153–65; Susan Becker, *Origins of the Equal Rights Amendment: American Feminism between the Wars* (Westport, Conn.: Greenwood, 1981), 121–51; Alice Kessler-Harris, *Out to Work: A History of Wage-Earning Women in the U.S.* (N.Y.: Oxford, 1982), 194–95, 205–12; Judith Sealander, *As Minority Becomes Majority* (Westport, Conn.: Greenwood, 1983). Fuller documentation of my reading of both sides can be found in Cott, *Grounding*, 122–29 and accompanying notes.

8. "Conference on So-called 'Equal Rights' Amendment Proposed by the National Women's Party Dec. 4, 1921," ts. NWTUL Papers, microfilm reel 2; "Conference Held December 4, 1921," ts., NWP #116; Kelley to Hill, Mar. 23, 1921, NWP #7; Ethel Smith to Members and Friends, Dec. 12, 1921, folder 378, Consumers League of Massachusetts Collection, SL.

9. NWP National Council minutes, Dec. 17, 1921, Feb. 14, 1922, Apr. 11, 1922, NWP #114. To the NWP inner circle Laughlin's point was borne out by a 1923 ruling in Wisconsin, where, despite the Equal Rights Bill, the attorney-general declined to strike down a 1905 law which prohibited women from being employed in the state legislature. He likened the prohibition to an hours-limitation law, because legislative service required "very long and often unreasonable hours." Alice Paul read his decision as "an extremely effective argument against" drafting equal rights bills with exemptions for sex-based protective legislation. Anita L. Pollitzer to Mrs. Jane Norman Smith, Jan. 5, 1922, folder 110, and Paul to Jane Norman Smith, Feb. 20, 1923, folder 111, Smith Coll.

10. National Council Minutes, June 19, 1923, NWP #114. Before 1923 the ERA went through scores of drafts, recorded in part F, NWP #116. Versions akin to the suffrage amendment—e.g. "Equal rights with men shall not be denied to women or abridged on account of sex or marriage . . ."—were considered in 1922, but not until 1943 was the amendment introduced into Congress in the form "Equality of

rights under the law shall not be denied or abridged by the U.S. or by any state on account of sex," modeled on the 19th Amendment, which in turn was modeled on the 15th Amendment.

11. Quotation from Edith Houghton Hooker, Editor's Note, *Equal Rights* (the NWP monthly publication), Dec. 22, 1928, p. 365. See *Grounding*, 75–82.

12. The two most seen on NWP platforms were Josephine Casey, a former ILGWU organizer, suffrage activist, later a bookbinder, and Mary Murray, a Brooklyn Railway employee who had resigned from her union in 1920 to protest its acceptance of laws prohibiting night work for women.

13. Kessler-Harris, *Out to Work*, 200–05, and "Problems of Coalition-Building: Women and Trade Unions in the 1920s," in *Women, Work and Protest*, ed. Ruth Milkman (Boston: Routledge and Kegan Paul, 1985), esp. 132.

14. Pauline Newman, ts. debate with Heywood Broun, c. 1931, folder 130, Pauline Newman Coll., SL; Alice Hamilton to Alice Paul, May 7, 1926, folder 19, Alice Hamilton Coll., SL. More extensive documentation of the debate can be found in the notes in *Grounding*, 325–26.

15. Kessler-Harris, *Out to Work*, 189–94, reveals ambivalent assessments of labor legislation by ordinary wage-earning women.

16. Printed release from the National Association of Manufacturers, "Defend American Womanhood by Protecting their Homes, Edgerton Tells Women in Industry," Jan. 19, 1926, in folder 1118, and ts. speech by James Davis, U.S. Sec. of Labor, Jan. 18, 1926, in folder 1117, Box 71, Mary Van Kleeck Coll., Sophia Smith Collection, Smith College.

17. Mary Anderson, "Shall There Be Labor Laws for Women? Yes," *Good Housekeeping*, Sept. 1925, 16 (reprint, June 1927), folder 60, Mary Anderson Coll., SL; Alice Hamilton, "The Blanket Amendment–A Debate," *Forum*, 72 (Aug. 1924), 156.

18. See Oppenheimer, *Female Labor Force*, 3, 149; Lois Scharf, *To Work and to Wed* (Westport, Conn., 1981) 15–16; Winifred Wandersee, *Women's Work, and Family Values, 1920–1940* (Cambridge, Harvard, 1981) 85, 89.

19. Elizabeth F. Baker, "At the Crossroads in the Legal Protection of Women in Industry," *Annals of the American Academy of Political and Social Science*, 143 (May 1929), 277. Summary of protective legislation in 1925 in Edward Clark Lukens, "Shall Women Throw Away their Advantages," reprint from the *Amer. Bar Assoc. Journal*, Oct. 1925, folder 744, SL.

   Recently historians have stressed the regressive potential of sex-based protective laws. See Rothman, *Woman's Proper Place*, 162–64; Nancy Schrom Dye, *As Equals and as Sisters: Feminism, Unionism and the Women's Trade Union League of New York* (Columbia, Missouri: Univ. of Missouri, 1980), 159–60; Olive Banks, *Faces of Feminism: A Study of Feminism as a Social Movement* (N.Y.: St. Martin's, 1981), 115; Judith A. Baer, *The Chains of Protection: The Judicial Response to Women's Labor Legislation* (Westport, Conn.: 1978), and Kessler-Harris, *Out to Work*, esp. 212.

20. T. K. Cory to Mary Wiggins, Nov. 10, 1922, folder 378, Consumer's League of Mass. Coll., SL. See n. 16, above.

21. Ethel M. Smith, "What is Sex Equality and What Are the Feminists Trying to Accomplish," *Century Monthly Magazine,* 118 (May 1929), 96; Mary Anderson, "Shall There Be Labor Laws for Women? Yes"; Alice Stone Blackwell to Carrie Chapman Catt, May 16, 1927, Catt Papers (Library of Congress), microfilm reel 2; Mary Anderson to Mrs. [Margaret Dreier] Robins, Feb. 4, 1926, folder 67, Mary Anderson Coll., SL; Mary Anderson, *Woman at Work: The Autobiography of Mary Anderson as told to Mary N. Winslow* (Minneapolis: Univ. of Minnesota, 1951), 168.

22. There is a valuable discussion of differing meanings for "equality" between the sexes in Jean Bethke Elshtain, "The Feminist Movement and the Question of Equality," *Polity* 7 (Summer 1975), 452–77.

23. This is, of course, the set of issues that has preoccupied feminist lawyers in the 1980s. For a sense of the recent debate, see, e.g., Wendy Williams, "The Equality Crisis: Some Reflections on Culture, Courts, and Feminism" *Women's Rights Law Reporter,* 7:3 (Spring 1982), 175–200; Nadine Taub, "Will Equality Require More than Assimilation, Accommodation or Separation from the Existing Social Structure?" *Rutgers Law Review,* 37 (1985), 825–44; Lucinda Finley, "Transcending Equality Theory: A Way Out of the Maternity and the Workplace Debate," *Columbia Law Review,* 86:6 (Oct. 1986), 1118–82; and Joan Willams, "Deconstructing Gender," *Michigan Law Review,* 87:4 (Feb. 1989), 797–845.

24. Florence Kelley, "Shall Women Be Equal before the Law?" (debate with Elsie Hill), *Nation,* 114 (Apr. 12, 1922), 421; NLWV pamphlet [1922], 10, in folder 744, Woman's Rights Collection, SL; Alice Hamilton, "The Blanket Amendment—A Debate," *Forum,* 72 (Aug. 1924), 156; Florence Kelley, "The New Woman's Party," *Survey,* 47 (Mar. 5, 1921), 828.

25. Dolores Janiewski, *Sisterhood Denied: Race, Gender and Class in a New South Community* (Phila.: Temple, 1985), 30–32, 127–50; Table 26 (134) shows less than 40% of Durham women above age 12 engaged only in unpaid housework.

26. Guion G. Johnson, "Feminism and the Economic Independence of Woman," *Journal of Social Forces,* 3 (May 4, 1925), 615; cf. Tentler, *Wage-Earning Women,* esp. 25, 45–46, and Wandersee, *Women's Work,* on motivations and psychological results of women's wage-earning.

27. Mary Anderson quoted in unidentified newspaper clipping, Nov. 25, 1925, in folder 349, Bureau of Vocational Information Collection, SL. Cf. Ethel Smith's objection that the NWP's feminism required that "men and women must have exactly the same things, and be treated in all respects as if they were alike," as distinguished from her own view that "men and women must each have the things best suited to their respective needs, which are not all the time, nor in all things, alike." Ethel M. Smith, "What Is Sex Equality . . . ?," 96.

28. National Council of Catholic Women testimony at U.S. Congress (House of Representatives) subcommittee of Committee on the Judiciary, hearings, 1925, quoted in Robin Whittemore, "Equality vs. Protection: Debate on the Equal Rights Amendment, 1923–1937" (M.A. thesis, Boston Univ., 1981), 19; mill worker quoted in Mary Frederickson, "The Southern Summer School for Women Workers," *Southern Exposure,* 4 (Winter 1977), 73. See also Maurine Greenwald, "Working-Class

Feminism and the Family Wage Ideal: The Seattle Debate on Married Women's Right to Work, 1914–1920," *Journal of American History,* 76:1 (June 1989), 118–49.

29. For the history of the NWP in the 1930s and 1940s see Becker, *Origins of the Equal Rights Amendment.* On the initiatives of the National Federation of Business and Professional Women's Clubs and other groups to forward the equal rights amendment, see Lemons, *Woman Citizen,* 202–04, and the papers of Lena Madesin Phillips and Florence Kitchelt at SL.

30. Jane L. Mansbridge's astute analysis, *Why We Lost the ERA* (Chicago: Univ. of Chicago, 1986) is essential reading on the failed 1970s campaign for ratification.

3

A Conversation about Race and Class

Mary Childers and Bell Hooks

As new members of the Oberlin College English Department, we began talking several months ago. From the beginning, our conversation had an edge, an edge that has become an intimacy. We are both fundamentally alienated from many aspects of white middle-class male institutions and even from white middle-class feminism. We both use a yardstick whittled from early experience of poverty to measure definitions of oppression and claims of universality. We both also grew up conscious of and having our consciousness shaped by racism: Bell because she is black, Mary because she is white. We wanted to think together about racism and classism in feminist movement, with which we have been involved for close to two decades now.

In part because of the circumstances of our conversations, we have ended up concentrating here on language, the development of feminist theory, and the role of the autobiographical and interpersonal, more than on political activity. Ultimately, it is political activity that challenges hierarchies of race, class, and gender and that is the solution to the persistent problems raised here. The issues on which we focus may be necessary preliminaries to concerted, mass political activity.

As we talked to each other on a tape one Saturday, working from an outline, we were deliberately anecdotal and personal. We wanted both to continue the style in which we talk to one another as friends and colleagues and to enact some of the points we make about language in feminist movement. However, both the carefully devised outline and the limited number of pages we could fill mean that the dialogue as presented here is not a faithful replica of a spontaneous conversation. Though we have maintained some of the informality and repetition that mark this as a conversation, the text is, in fact, substantially edited. This process, ironically, may be most faithful to cross-race dialogue, which is, at best, a combination of the spontaneous and the strained. It is perhaps in the welcoming of conflict within friendship that we can hope to learn and to accomplish the most with one another.

While we know that some of that conflict surfaced in this conversation, the typed transcript may not carry the tone of tension. Even more importantly, the written version of our conversation may not indicate fully enough our own wariness of repeating the very category errors we critique in others. We neither mean to imply homogeneity in such large groups as "working-class women," "black women," and "middle-class white women" nor to ignore the possibility that our bonding may in part be forged by shared anger at some projected monolithic "Others." We have tried, through self-exposure and disagreement, to demonstrate the self-consciousness that has to accompany criticism of others if that criticism is to avoid scapegoating. We hope readers hear that struggle as well as our conviction. At the same time, we invite readers to listen for our silences and to commit themselves to exploring more of the unknown terrain on which truly multi-racial politics can be developed.

We began by introducing ourselves:

Bell: I think of Bell Hooks as a writer identity and as a part of who I am. I talk in my new book *Talking Back* about what that pen name has to do with race and class, with what it means to come from a working-class experience and a Southern black background while trying to develop what we call authorial voice, a voice of power.

Mary: I write as a scholar of 19th- and 20th-century British literature and culture, as someone who has a Ph.D., but not as a white person from a family in which several generations of women have ended up raising children on welfare, not as someone who remains connected to the "underclass" through family and a few "friends from the neighborhood," as we say. That compartmentalization means that I cannot introduce myself as actually being what I would like to be: someone whose thinking benefits women of a class usually not remembered even by oppositional cultural activists.

B: That is interesting because one of the race/class dynamics I confront is that people often presume that I don't have a Ph.D. Even when I was teaching at Yale, students and colleagues would often ask me, do you have a Ph.D.? I never met anybody teaching there who just had a M.A. However, the perception of black women was that we had come in on some kind of new ticket that didn't require us to meet the same standards. They probably would not have assumed that a black man didn't have a Ph.D. This is about class, race, and gender, because basically in the media black women are presented as being part of an uneducated underclass, with these few exceptional black women writers who are somehow intuitively writers and not people who are highly literate, often highly educated, etc. etc.

M: Another part of that media representation of all black women as poor and uneducated is that the number of poor and uneducated white women in this country is often not acknowledged—to the detriment of both groups and of our collective sense of reality.

B: It is telling that we should begin this discussion identifying the powerful connection in this culture between class and literacy, class and education. Undoubtedly these issues will inform our discussion of feminism and the production of feminist theory.

Let us begin by talking about how we experienced the struggle to challenge and expand the category of gender. What I most remember and carry a lot of pain about today is the enormous threat I posed as an undergraduate and a graduate student trying to raise the question of racial difference to white student peers and professors. I critically examine now why it is that I do not rejoice when I see people who taught me in graduate school who were deeply hurting to me when I tried to talk about race, now writing about race. My skepticism is shared by many black women who were very active in the struggle to challenge the feminist movement to confront racism politically. We feel that many white women have not considered the issue of accountability for this persecution and racial harassment, nor have they adequately called attention to the process by which their thinking changed. For some, talking about race is merely a way to enhance academic status. I think it crucial for us to remember that expanding the category of gender is a new direction in feminist thinking which emerges from profound internal political struggle within feminism, from the political confrontation of black women and other women of color confronting white women about racism.

At that time we also evoked class. Ironically, it is currently cool for some white women to say that feminism is not a middle-class movement, that somehow when black women, or women of color, evoke the idea of the white middle-class feminist movement, that is a cliché and a stereotype. But in fact, through all my years of being involved with feminism, the most articulated theories of feminism and the people that I have met who name those theories, have been privileged white women. It is interesting that people do not want to accept that reality. No matter how many working-class white women have participated in the feminist movement, when we look at the production of theory and who has reaped the rewards of voice and articulation, they have rarely been working-class white women.

M: Many white women who are middle class and struggle against gender oppression think that they are free of class bias because they always compare themselves to women and men who have more privilege instead of comparing themselves to those who have less. So they feel as though they are on the bottom and are being entirely just and brave when they speak up over everyone else. When they experience gender as the clearly dominant source of their own suffering, it is hard for them to realize that for other women the acquisition of gender may be inseparable from the discovery of themselves as economically and physically vulnerable people by virtue of poverty and/or race. This difficulty continues to inhibit cross-class dialogue and, thus, the establishment of political priorities that include a broad range of women.[1]

B: Even though we have clearly named the racism of some privileged white women, we have not talked about the fact that a large part of their inability to deal with race and class had to do with not having a language to articulate what it means to be pained via gender even as you are privileged via race and class. After all these years since the whole question of race came into feminism, we still do not have the language paradigms for white women to be able to express, "this is how I am privileged" and yet "this is how I am exploited."

M: It is very hard to pay attention to the realms in which we feel powerless and at the same time remember the people over whom we have power and perhaps make feel powerless. We would have to change the way we think to remember these patterns simultaneously.

B: One of the things that we would have to change is how we think about oppression. A lot of white women were very upset when I raised the issue in *Feminist Theory: From Margin to Center* that we cannot speak of all women as being oppressed, because to do that is to negate the reality that there is a difference in my life as a black woman intellectual who makes a good salary, who has no kids, no concrete unchosen responsibilities to anybody other than myself, primarily in a certain material sense, and my mother, who never went to college, who never completed high school. To try to act like our social circumstance is the same would not make sense, even though we have both been victimized by men. It is important to remember that victimization by men has been the primary category of oppression in feminism.

M: Though I certainly don't want to let men off the hook, it is worthwhile to look out for examples of how often an exclusive focus on male/female conflict serves as a distraction from other kinds of conflict. It is also worthwhile to look our for the ways that some white feminists are now responding to the demand that oppression be more carefully defined. Carolyn Heilbrun, for instance, seems to me to bristle with recognition at your criticism of the idea that all women are oppressed. So in a recent article about the autobiographical writing of some middle-class women, she puts "privileged" in quotes; her tone distinctly, to my ear, registers resentment at having to qualify their pain so much even as she resigns herself to the necessity. The beginning of her article sounds more like a defense against the accusation of exclusion than an acceptance of your idea—as though your critique is objected to but the reasons for that objection cannot or will not be spoken. Too bad, because until white women speak whatever anger they feel toward black women for pointing out racism, racism will continue to simmer below the surface of any angry acquiescence. We will feel as though we are submitting instead of just doing the right thing and we will be unable to distinguish confidently between fair and unfair accusations of racism, fair and unfair distinctions between who is oppressed by dominant social structures and who might more appropriately be described as alienated, harassed, restricted, etc.

I suspect that it may be easier for women positioned as I am, through no virtue of our own, to recognize racism, even our own, as a huge problem. I cannot avoid seeing that I was raised to be a racist. If you grow up poor and white in urban America, you grow up around a lot of people of color, you see racism, you hear it all the time, often in your own family. People have their ways of getting along, but they also have their ways of speaking and acting when not around one another. If you grow up privileged as a white person, you also are likely to grow up in segregated neighborhoods; you are able to deny you have been raised racist especially if you come from the type of genteel family that would never use the words "nigger" or "spik." Racism is more invisible on the personal level, more sanitized.

B: Your comment Mary just made me think about the fact that so much of black life and underclass black life is determined by race that race is very much talked about. When we were interrupted awhile ago by my friend coming over, one of the things you may have noticed in our conversation (which was certainly in our very black style together as two women coming from working-class backgrounds) was that when we talked about men and the women they were with, we talked about them in terms of race. I was very conscious of your presence as a white woman, because when she would refer to certain men she would say, is he with a sister? I know that if you had not been here what she would have said is, is she black? But the fact is that that question was not being raised because of your presence. Had you not been present the question of race would have been just as casual a part of our conversation. Part of the great gap separating a lot of white women from women of color and specifically from black women early on is the fact that black women do not see race as a taboo topic and are comfortable with just bringing it into the conversation. Whereas for white women it has been such a silenced discourse in many aspects of white life. And you are saying that the most powerless group of white women—poor and uneducated—were often able to talk about race, so those women who were more comfortable talking about race were not the white women we were confronting and meeting.

M: I certainly cannot idealize and do not want to overgeneralize about white, urban, working-class women. I can say that they are more likely to know they are racist—I cannot say that it would be any easier to speak honestly with them across race lines or to convince them to fight racism as part of the fight to improve their own lives. But I do think there is substantial shared experience to work with.[3]

B: What you have just said reminds me that we have to talk about the impact of psychological dilemmas on our capacity as women to deal with race and class, to talk about these subjects that are in a sense suppressed subjects among us. Historically most women were kept out of political discussion. Feminism brings to contemporary women and contemporary white women particularly a whole discursive practice that allows entrance into the realm of politics and political discussion in a new and interesting way. But it cannot open itself up to include race and class because in some ways those are still taboo political areas, for men as well. In a way gender, however much women have been oppressed and exploited, has always been a category that is acknowledged and talked about. Let's face it, though his analysis was often biased, Freud was talking about women. Whereas in a sense discourse about race and class has been suppressed in this culture. Lately I have been thinking about how the construction of psycho-analysis in the West erases race while privileging sexual identity and experience as that which is subject to repression and denial.

M: An increasing number of social historians are starting to look at the ways in which gender and male/female opposition were cultivated in public discourse in the 19th century in England in a way that displaces class as a category—that analysis might be extended to include race, especially now that more people are looking at the role of imperialism in constituting post-colonial and colonizing societies. In relation to what you say about psychoanalysis, it's interesting that Freud is Jewish but not concerned with the psychological implications of race and ethnicity.

B: I want to respond to both of your responses. The importance of Zillah Eisenstein's book *The Radical Future of Liberal Feminism* was to show that feminism grew out of certain liberal cultural practices, as you were just identify-ing. It was within that cultural framework that race was erased and obscured. It is not surprising then that white women who are coming out of that philosophical, ideological, and social experience were not able to talk about race. It is almost more surprising that Freud could build his analysis dealing with quote "the psyche," foregrounding sexual identity, even though his own lived experience must have foregrounded the reality of ethnic, racial difference. It would be interesting to think about his suppression of race given the fact that Judaism is so often seen racially.

M: That suppression fits interestingly with some of the work on how Freud's theories come out of a representation of the family that leaves out a crucial aspect of that experience. The nursemaid was often a continual presence in the lives of children of his class, though it is only the mother who is foregrounded in his sexualizing theories. So the woman of the different class is also suppressed in the tale of identity and development. The simple triangle of mommy, daddy, and child has to take another shape to explain development in the hands of a nurse-maid.[4] What is mentioned much less that also challenges the Freudian model is that many poor people of all colors come from large families in which there is less parental individual attention to the child. Siblings provide primary care for one another in ways that may lead to a kind of subjectivity that experiences community differently. Given the importance of psychoanalysis in contemporary feminist dis-cussion, a critique from the perspectives of race and class seems crucial.

B: When we were discussing race and psychoanalysis at a recent conference in New York on difference, some people said you can't "blame" these white people who invented psychoanalysis for not including the category of race. My point was that we don't have to see white people as inventing psychoanalysis—many processes that we name as psychoanalytic we can find in other cultures, so-called archaic or primitive cultures, that use the same processes in therapeutic rituals. Is not to name something as psychoanalysis therefore not to have invented it? I was trying to say we have to try to disrupt the whole discourse on psychoanalysis by saying that in fact racism determines the fact that we see psychoanalysis as white, as something not coming from people of color. We foster an illusion that white people own this particular discourse in a way that people of color do not, because most of the people we would name as being important in the field of psychoanalysis would be white, with the exception of Jewish white people in the field. Reconstructing categories and allowing for race and class have to include challenging that notion of white authority and origin, which is so crucial to the history of white supremacy and intellectual hegemonic domination. We have to explode the assumption that nobody else on the planet is smart enough to have invented explanatory systems like psychoanalysis.

M: I would like to hear more of your thinking about this issue, though I think it makes sense to see "psychoanalysis" as having an historical specificity in the Freudian heritage and to use "psychology" as the general word for a variety of practices and understandings of human behavior. I am thinking, for instance, of working-class involvement in such practices as mesmerism and the oral tradition of ghost stories that metaphorize psychological knowledge.

B: The problem I have with that idea is that a lot of black women would say something similar about feminism: feminism belongs to white women, they originated it, it is a form of analysis that only takes into account their experience. Therefore we shouldn't be involved with it; we should come up with our own terms, like womanist, that allow us to name specifically what we are doing. I would argue that it makes more sense to expand categories, which is exactly what we have been talking about with the idea of gender. I am excited by the idea that as a black woman who is very interested in psychotherapy and psychoanalysis I don't have to see myself as nonblack or as entering a purely white Western tradition in order to participate. Instead, I can see the construction of psychoanalysis in the white West as a particular historical expression of a more inclusive category of psychoanalysis in the same way that I can see white women's articulation, and particularly privileged white women's articulation, of feminism as one component of feminism but not all that feminism is or can be. As long as we stay within the notion of a kind of private property or ownership of certain categories, we end up being confined in a discourse that always makes the powerless subordinate. Even if you use terms that come from other cultures, it would always make those working-class experiences somehow subordinate to this other experience called psychoanalysis, that would be called the privileged experience and the privileged voice.

M: I am persuaded by much of what you have said, but what I would say is the difference is that feminism defines itself as about women and has then elaborated that definition in an inadequate way. Psychoanalysis seems to me to be a specific form of psychology; psychology is the umbrella term I would want to use.

B: That is acceptable to me too. I hadn't thought of it that way, mainly because I am so concerned about how these words are themselves used as instruments of exclusion.

To return to where we started. In some ways we are talking about the question of standpoint; how can we locate ourselves from standpoints that allow us to be inclusive of difference while also appreciating similarities of experience? How can we displace paradigms of domination that in fact establish authority through exclusion through asserting one people as having knowledge and the other people as not having something? Which takes us back to the whole question of what it meant to try to expand the category of gender. 'Cause I know I felt my heart beating faster just then when you said "feminism has defined itself as being about women." Growing up I never thought of feminism as being about women, solely. The way I grew up conceptualizing what it means to resist male authority was not about women. One of the things I remember was feeling how much my father repressed and hurt my brother, so that I saw him as being just as included in this domination by this male figure as us girls and my mom. We were all in it together against him. So the conceptualization was not "this is about females" and "males represent power," but it was very clear that some males have power and other males do not, depending on their status. As a boy my brother had no power in relation to my father as man.

When we talk about race and class in convergence and conjunction with gender, we really struggle for a new language. Part of race, class, and gender oppression is that we have not been given a discursive practice that is oppositional, so that even in this conversation we are trying to invent one. This same difficulty arises when we try to move feminist discussion of race and class beyond simplistic acknowledgment; you know, how everybody nowadays mentions race and class without then revising substantially their notion of gender. We still struggle with language.

M: I feel caught here. I do not want to relinquish the idea of feminism having specific reference to women. At the same time I wonder about my reluctance because I know that partial definitions can exclude certain conceptual and political possibilities. The degree to which so many feminists have not noticed that "white" is a qualifying category as much as "black" when women are being discussed haunts me whenever I resist changing my language. I know that the persistence of this language habit of referring to white women as women and black women as black women—what Adrienne Rich calls "white solipsism"—is what forces you to function at times as a composition teacher for white women, always reminding us to add the word white to "women" instead of appropriating the universal. So, I guess I am obliged to ask: How could we redo the simple definition of feminism I proposed so that it does not leave out the specificity of your response to all autocratic male behavior, whoever the victim? Perhaps we feminists, however we define feminism, should decide to spend more time encouraging writerly behavior that can help us find words we can agree to use.

Otherwise, we will keep coming back to the same questions. Your phrase, "feminist movement" is an example of the refinement of language of interest here. The emphasis isn't on an established entity. The phrase allows for a possibility of various kinds of movement, parallel and colliding, for instance.

B: I drop the definite article rather than speaking of "the" feminist movement. When we do not have a definite article, we are saying that feminist movement can be located in multiple places, in multiple languages and experiences. Future feminist movement will necessarily focus more on the ways we use language. We will need to be more daring—to shape feminist theory in ways that will make it an act of political resistance for larger groups of women.

M: The question of terminology is one academics frequently raise of course. But I am afraid that when we come up with new terms, they are often very exclusive: we develop these academic categories many people cannot use. We develop all these critiques of the words we are already using and substitute them with more complicated words or structures. I suspect that academic comfort with hyphenated and Latinate terms may be a part of living in a world of language that isolates those of us who use it from the larger community for which we think and write. So we have to find words or phrases that seem critically incisive and precise but also sufficiently general and accessible to encourage participation. Patriarchy is one of those words that moved a lot of people, but now, out of a desire for academic precision and historical specificity, we have critiqued it out of existence. People are afraid to use it now because it is not subtle, but in fact for a lot of people who know what it is to have a daddy who beats everybody in the family, patriarchy is a great word (Bell comes in with heh!). And for all of us who work in institutions where there are inaccessible, controlling men at the top, patriarchy is a damned good word. How is it that we are going to get to some kind of agreement that some of the words we use have recognized inadequacies but we are going to go ahead and use them because they work in some environments? Of course, we do not have to wait for inspiration to specify race and class in discussions of gender more often. Even if it means continuously using extra adjectives, as in poor Latinas, black middle-class women, white working-class women, it is worth it so that people don't feel excluded or robbed of an ability to identify with the category "women" because they feel appropriated rather than addressed by feminism. Having said all this, I still want to hold on to a notion of feminism as focusing on women while at the same time recognizing that race, class, and sexual preference determine various political and theoretical priorities.

B: Your point takes us right into consideration of attitude and behavior. We were talking earlier about the way in which our lived realities already expand the category of gender. Working on our language is an attempt to give expression to the expansion that is already our lived reality. None of us experiences ourselves solely as gendered subjects. We experience ourselves everyday as subjects of race, class, and gender.

But we were going to talk more specifically about ways within feminism we change our attitudes and behaviors as we talk about race. A lot of black women I know feel that it is one of the tragic ironies that we forced recognition of quote "race" and "racism" and now a lot of white women are appropriating this discussion to serve opportunistic ends, to serve the projection of themselves as politically correct, cool, or to engage in a kind of sterile discourse that is not connected to behavioral change. I told you about going to a women's studies pot luck at a white woman scholar's house where her black maid or, in fact (Bell catches herself), I want to critique my own language there: "her black maid" is language that suggests she owns this person. I should say "the black woman who works for her as a maid," which allows this person an identity outside this job.

One of the things that I noted was that all of us black women who were also scholars and theorists invited there as guests sat off in a corner and said passive/ aggressive things like, Here are these white women who think they have changed, but the very fact that she has invited us here, exhibiting a maid, shows that her racism has not changed and that she is flaunting her status over us. None of us considered trying to transform that social environment where we might share with one another as black and white women what we were experiencing. Perhaps some of the white women there felt uncomfortable with the presence of a maid, irrespective of her color, and felt that it called into question certain things about feminism. But we didn't confront or address the issue of either the color of the maid or what it means to have in a room of feminists someone who serves but does not speak. Therefore we were able to take away a lot of assumptions about our white woman host that may or may not be correct. The anti-feminism and anti-white feeling of many black women there was reinforced. This is one of the problems we face when we try to address race and class within feminism; we do not know how to create a space where we can confront some of the differences that are now playing themselves out on this new feminist terrain.

M: We are stuck constantly with all these problems about cleaning our houses and what we do with our money, if we have any; we have to look at the fact that some of us actually benefit from inequalities in the society. Some white people who are feminist and act as though they are conscientious about race privilege hire black women and pay them a minimal amount. What if the decision were made that instead of getting a new rug, one pays that woman—who often has no choice but to do that kind of work—real money, above the market value. I will never forget the shock of hearing a white feminist who had just gone on a very special vacation complain about "the fortune" she was paying the Chicana who cleaned her house once a week. In that situation, someone white such as myself has an obligation to ask another white woman exactly how much she is paying the Chicana, so that it is not always the woman of color who has to take on that task. I am suggesting I guess that among white women varying consciousness about race and class should make us dwell on *our* differences. Some of us should be able to ask, what is a fortune? who defines it? why is it more important for you to have vacations than for this woman to have good shoes for her children?

We have to be able to do that, even at a dinner party where we are all supposed to be having fun together, celebrating our community in opposition to the often alienating institutions that make us need our fragile communities so badly. I like the title of this book, "Conflicts in Feminism," but also want to talk about feminism *within* conflict, so that we realize that we can get together and learn that practicing conflict is also practicing feminism as well as learn that we can recognize someone's virtues at the same time that we wonder how she can *not* speak about hiring a black maid as problematic.

B: We live in a culture that makes it seem as though having contradictions is bad—most of us try to represent ourselves in ways that suggest we are without contradictions. Contradictions are perceived as chaos and not orderly, not rational, everything doesn't follow. Coming out of academe, many of us want to present ourselves as just that: orderly, rational. We also then must struggle for a language that allows us to say: we have contradictions and those contradictions do not necessarily make us quote "bad people" or politically unsound people. We have to be willing as women and as feminists and as other groups of people, including as men who enter feminist discussion, to work with those contradictions and almost to celebrate their existence because they mean we are in a process of change and transformation. I think it has been very hard to do that.

M: In a way the denial of contradiction is what produces so much irresolvable conflict. It might be more helpful to begin with an expectation of conflict and division.

B: You and I have talked about bonding as two women who have known each other now for six months. On the one hand, we have many shared working-class experiences that help us to feel close, but we also experience race as well as status as something that disrupts that feeling of bondedness. All of these feelings exist simultaneously. Sometimes we have shared perceptions of classist events and sometimes we have felt race and status disrupting our bonding. It is because we have something in common and because we started off confronting differences with one another, that we can now talk about it.

M: There is a hidden benefit to finding bonding at around the same time as conflict with one another. It prevents the development of problems of merging and expectations of sameness that so many women have seen backfire in feminist movement. Even women who fit into the same sociological categories have many differences. By imagining ourselves as the same, we almost guarantee devastating disappointment with one another. Perhaps in knowing we are different from one another we can avoid the fear of disagreement that keeps us from sorting out divisive issues.

B: Part of our process is that we are both people who have a high level commitment to honesty and openness. Which means that we start off expecting from one another that we will both be forthcoming and forthright. We have talked before about how we see loudness and directness as cherished parts of our backgrounds. But when we confront middle-class and upper-class culture in this society, it is so often anti-directness. That has stood in the way of confrontation between women across class, because so many people of privileged backgrounds experience directness as threatening rather than refreshing. You and I mutually experience it as a sign that: "Oh, I can relax; I can just be loud, be straightforward, and demand that you tell me the truth." In this discussion of directness we have identified something important: skills and dispositions that come out of working-class and certain ethnic experiences that can be useful to feminist movement. All feminists could study strategies of talking and ways of using language common among working-class people that could help in the reconceptualizing of feminist theory. We are saying that one of those strategies could be talking directly and not feeling threatened by directness.

One relationship that seems never to be characterized by directness is that in which black women and white women historically have most often met, the servant/served relation. Reciprocity is necessary to changing that relationship. As long as white women within feminism still ask black women to teach them about race, we are still being put in a servant/served relationship. The same holds as long as privileged white women ask working-class women to teach them about class. Part of what makes me feel that you and I are subjects together is reciprocity and the sense that you have something to give me as well as me having something to give you.

M: An important part of that reciprocity for me is that I rarely meet other people in academia whose early lives resemble mine enough so that certain things do not have to be explained, such as why I started working as a servant at an early age. Perhaps it is because of those important shared experiences that we do not feel threatened when we run up against the difference that race made. One of the ways I have learned to understand some of the specificity of black women's continuing experience is through my own experience as a servant. When I was 11, I started cleaning up homes and taking care of children of white people living in the suburbs outside of New York. These people pretended that they were doing me a big favor taking this welfare kid out of the ghetto. The first time anyone paid me decently for babysitting was a black woman in my own neighborhood who had much less money but paid me the legal minimum wage; the white folks with money paid $15 a week for about 60 hours' work, and then would give a surprise bonus at the end of the summer. My obedience was purchased by the arbitrariness of the surprise payment at the end. Knowing what it is to serve under oppressive white women taught me a great deal.

B: This raises a theoretical question that I wouldn't presume to answer today that came up yesterday in a discussion of domestic workers and their employers. Can there be a nondehumanizing servant/served relationship or do those categories automatically mean dehumanizing relationships? When I worked as a maid growing up, I worked for another black woman. There again we get into the politics of class; I didn't feel any more humanized in that setting by that black woman than I would have been by a white woman. What is interesting is that class is the thing that made me feel put down, whereas if I was with a white woman the issues that would have made me feel put down would have been a combination of race and class.

M: I always described those white women who gave me orders as "white women," not having any vocabulary for describing white people in my position and thus having to experience myself as racially undetermined in a weird way. Which says something about my own racism as well as something about certain types of categories. It reminds me of white maids-of-all-work in England in the 19th century being called "slaveys." I wonder if this move signals the unnaturalness to white people of white people being that oppressed and may naturalize the oppression of black people. It helps white people to say "I am not a slave," but not necessarily "no one should be a slave."

B: This goes back to the young white working-class woman student we have talked about on occasion who feels somehow that to highlight black women's experience erases her own. She feels the pain of lacking a category for the experience of poor white women. You as a young woman had to, in a sense, empathetically identify with blackness in order to articulate your pain. We have got to come up with a way to talk about different experiences of pain, which means that there is a lot of weight on privileged white women to give up some of their space so that working-class white women can contribute to the articulation of white women's experience.

M: We both have been in situations where feminist story telling has broken down as a cultural mode when women who have been victimized by race and class as well as gender speak. Many privileged women are made uncomfortable by stories of the abuse rather than the help doled out by middle-class teachers, preachers, social workers, store owners, classmates, etc. They don't want to realize that their class has been a sphere of trauma for others or to remember the ways in which they participated in mocking poor kids in the second grade. So much of feminist activity includes the informal exchange of stories, but if a working-class woman intervenes with her stories, people often react in two unhelpful ways. One is to say, you are trying to make me feel bad; they assimilate that experience as an attack on themselves because they are afraid it makes it seem that their experience hasn't been difficult. Or they think we are holding on to little details and refusing to let go, so they need to correct our obsession. There is resistance to recognition that what is described is as important as when women of a certain class who could dare to aspire were denied entrance into medical school. I do not want to deny that people such as myself can be unhealthily tuned in to slights and deformed by envy of those who have not had to struggle for basics like food, shelter, health care and education. We all have to be cautious about what Florence Kennedy has labeled as "horizontal violence." I know there are privileged women who do not defensively silence women from poverty and I also think it is important to remember that even privileged women need more institutional resources. Still, I think privileged women as a group have to work harder at understanding women who do not identify gender as the primary source of oppression in their lives.

I should add a qualification here. Though the culture of story telling in order to understand one another is a base for political action, of course it is important to remember Barbara Smith's criticism of people thinking that oppression is only a matter of how we treat one another.[5] Nonetheless, how we treat one another socially and in our theories about the world affects political life. Feminist theory which tries to characterize all women as slaves or servants or members of one class indicates on the conceptual level the same tendencies I've just outlined in the social realm.

B: For me this raises questions about what it means for us to feel allied with the working-class experience of our childhoods and move into situations of privilege. In my case there has always been the struggle to cope with language. Being raised in a working-class household with a particular regional patois, a particular kind of black speech, it was difficult when I went to Stanford where that speech was not appreciated. So I spoke primarily in other ways, but when I went home my parents and sisters would say, what's wrong with you, why are you talking so funny? So language becomes a source of estrangement. I've given considerable thought to why a lot of black working-class people who enter the academy end up largely forsaking their working-class past. It becomes very hard to know how to "talk" in that past if we spend a lot of time talking with privileged white people and in fact develop that particular kind of speech. I know that I work very hard to keep my bi-lingualness. I have to go where other black working-class people are and cultivate friendship and ties in order to maintain that authentic sense of myself so that it is not some kind of affectation or nostalgia but is in fact part of my everyday lived experience.

M: I have tried unsuccessfully for nine years to get a job at a state university where I might be able to teach students whose accents approximate the voices I grew up with, as though I could then go back to speaking in some way that feels less alienated, less learned, less like an imitation of middle-class people and as though I could save other students from enduring the humiliation I went through as an undergraduate student. Though, of course, there are many causes of people feeling alienated by their own public voices and obliged to speak artificially in order to secure respect for the content of what they say, many causes cannot be limited to individual psychological difficulty. One of the options for those of us who want to resist the homogenized, professional voice that is so alienating to students whose parents never talk that way is to value the performative and experimentation with voice. But I know that can make some folks hostile. Instead of people feeling as though they are learning something about a variety of voices, as though there are things to learn that have to be embodied rather than abstractly referred to, people recoil. I think this reflects fear of embodiment—which is connected to fear of directness—and an unwillingness to realize that we have been trained not to associate certain attitudes and accents with authoritative intelligence.

B: Also that language is about empathic identification and that you can use language to connect with people. Since academia has not privileged our discourse as one that connects us, our verbal use of language to connect has been devalued. And in fact, often the work we do that is most valued is the work that will make the least connections across class. The work that we do that is most valued is the work that not only reinforces class hierarchies, but establishes new ones. We certainly see that happening now with the production of feminist theory. It is not only interesting that a lot of privileged white women have appropriated the discourse on race, but in fact they are writing about it in ways that even the average academic woman cannot necessarily understand. So we are not even talking about a distinction between non-educated and educated; we are talking about different status hierarchies within people of the same class background.

M: What is so weird about that is that we have so many students who are being bored to death in the classroom by

B: PREACH

M: by professors talking in controlled, often monotone voices. We all know what it is like to be bored to tears and yet there is no recognition that maybe we ought to develop alternative styles. We are not encouraged to appreciate that intelligence might be interactive and hit different registers.

B: This question of spoken voice is very much connected to location and standpoint (in terms of race and class) in feminist theorizing. Thinking about examples of feminist theory that is moving us in the right direction, I was impressed in reading Elizabeth Spelman's book, *Inessential Woman*. Even so, I was troubled by the fact that she appropriated ideas from women of color without dwelling on their particular perceptions enough. Joking with a number of women of color lately, we have been saying that we are increasingly confined to the footnotes, which reproduces, in a sense, the servant/served relation, since footnotes support. An excellent part of Spelman's book was her critique of Nancy Chodorow's exclusion of race and class in *The Reproduction of Mothering*. This is an exciting way for white women to utilize new knowledge and skill about race and gender, to look at one another's work critically as opposed to appropriating a discourse on race where black women are discussed in ways that erase the importance of our own voices and thoughts.

M: I appreciate the way you have just made it clear that you don't think of this category of "privileged white women" as monolithic or even of one book as a monolithic example of the best or the worst tendencies. Some white women, regardless of class background, have listened actively to what has been said and have given substantive time to taking black women seriously. Remembering who does that and finding the examples of when something other than appropriation is going on seems to be a productive way of finding some solutions to the conflicts that keep re-arising in feminism and in our discussion. Let's acknowledge that some people are doing a good job, at the same time that we have to acknowledge how hard black women in particular have had to work to get that little bit of progress.

B: Progress will happen much faster if we stop hesitating about acknowledging privilege as a class issue. I do not have trouble naming myself as a "privileged" black woman. It is important for me not to pretend that I am completely representative of oppressed black women. I try to make a distinction between what it means to be from an oppressed group and yet be privileged—while still sharing in the collective reality of black women. What I think we really need to emphasize is that we have choices about how we respond to privilege. Feminists need to recognize that naming yourself as privileged is not to name yourself as oppressive or dominating, because we have choices as to how we exercise privilege.

M: In *Landscape for a Good Woman* by Carolyn Steedman, a very powerful theoretical autobiography about working-class life in England, she notes that when she goes to parties now as a feminist and meets another woman she remembers that, because of her class background, a hundred years ago she would have been cleaning that woman's shoes and can assume that the other woman does not remember that. It is not always the difference itself that feels most raw in feminist encounters, it is the sense that some women have a continued self-interest in refusing to acknowledge inherited inequalities that other women are not in a position to forget.

B: Women seem to be particularly threatened when our differences are marked by class privilege. What do you do when you are not privileged and have contact with a privileged woman of any race? Or when there is race and class difference? What gives us a space to bond? These are questions we have had trouble answering. I want to privilege political commitment because in this culture we do not emphasize enough that you can choose to be politically committed in ways that change your behavior and action. We need to do more work examining the reasons white women and black women of all classes view one another with suspicion, thinking we are trying to take something from each other (whether it is the privileged white woman thinking that a black woman is trying to take some power from her to make herself more powerful or it is black women feeling like there are these white women who have everything and want more). I don't think we really understand either historically or in terms of contemporary circumstances why we view each other in such incredibly negative terms. Certainly as a group white males have been more oppressive to black women, yet black women don't unequivocally view white males in the hostile, suspicious ways that we often view white women. And I would say vice versa as well. Feminist theory needs to study historically, sociologically, and anthropologically how we see one another and why it has been so hard for us to change how we see one another.

M: I am persuaded by some of the analyses of conflict between black and white women that I've come across. As you argue in *From Margin to Center*, when white women with relative material privilege inflate the significance of their own psychological victimization, women who suffer racial and other material oppressions can dismiss them as self-indulgent, or unaware, or victimizing others with unearned martyrdom. Certainly pervasive images of white women as the standard of beauty have posed a threat to black women who see not the white men designing and buying the billboards but the faces of white women. Even more important is the servant/served relation you have mentioned and which Judith Rollins has written about so compellingly.[6] So many black women have themselves or have close relatives who had to clean homes for white women, while entering white homes under few other circumstances. Few white women are aware of how images of their sexuality are designed in opposition to images (and uses) of black women's sexuality; some buy the myth that black women are more sexually free than themselves, sort of like upper-class feminists in England in the 1890s envying working-class women their liberty to work. We will not get very far with one another without more of an analysis of the relationship between our various privileges and deprivations, the history of our relations with and fantasies of one another.

It would also be instructive to scrutinize some of the heated and anguished exchanges between white women and women of color, not just for their content but also for how we align ourselves in the process of reading. For instance, the publication in *Feminist Review* of the responses of various women of color to an article by two prominent white theorists trying to correct what they called the "ethnocentrism" of their earlier work.[7] I read that exchange with great confusion and a sense of being threatened because I admired the effort of the white women to challenge their own work and then was shocked by the seriousness of the inadequacies the respondents pointed out. But even as I learned from the respondents, I was aware that as a white woman I felt very defensive: "How can we take any risks in expanding the way we think if we are going to be jumped on in this way?" The "we" in my mind is white women; I identify with their exposure more than with the intellectual vigor and just anger of the women of color. I have to *work* on myself to remember that the women of color are participating in critical debate in the same vigorous and vituperative way that white women do among themselves across lines of theoretical difference. My defensive identification with the vulnerability of the white women who are making an effort to change their thinking is something I think many white women feel but haven't worked through to the point where we can distinguish unfair and fair critiques, critiques that leave room for heated dialogue and critiques that turn a cold shoulder on solidarity.

B: Sorting through questions such as those is related to seeing how race and class determine which feminists are listened to. Certainly the early feminist movement had a lot of important feminist spokespeople like Charlotte Bunch, who just recently published *Passionate Politics*, and like Celestine Ware, who didn't have Ph.D.s, who were doing incredibly inclusive feminist theory, reaching out to a variety of groups of people. This is happening less now that feminist theory comes almost solely out of academe.

M: We are back now to our earlier concern about the controlling effects of academic standards on feminist theory. Bunch is a terrific example because her writing comes out of her working with a wide range of women. It is accessible without being simplistic, but I suspect that a similar style of writing would be unacceptable in feminist academia. Now that we have our high-powered theorists identifying with the standards of elite schools, it is harder and harder to develop a language that includes everyone. Even as I speak it occurs to me that many feminists, regardless of race and class, complain about this problem—as do other academics. Distinguishing between complaints about theory itself and about obfuscating language is too much for me to take on right now however.

B: Piggybacking off that, let's name what we have lost in this shift in directions. One positive feature of contemporary feminism was insistence on experience as a location for the construction of theory. Across class, women were encouraged to see critical analysis of personal experience (not mere confession) as a ground on which to construct theory. Lately there is a tendency in feminist theoretical writing to be contemptuous of the personal. An example that comes to mind is Meaghan Morris's "Introduction" to *The Pirate's Fiancé: Feminism, Reading, Postmodernism*.

M: We especially have to hold on to valuing the analysis of experience because story telling is a primary mode of discussion for many people and because, as Carolyn Heilbrun has argued, the range of narratives about the lives of women will exceed the plots we have inherited only if many different women tell the truth about their lives.[8] In academia now there seems to be an odd refusal to respect the ways in which the confessional can lead to the conceptual and the political, as though people cannot distinguish between personal discourse that is self-absorbed rather than community building. Ironically, what is more self-absorbed than a certain kind of theoretical performance which only a small cadre of people can possibly understand? I am talking about impersonally articulated narcissism, which is much worse than confessional discourse as far as I am concerned.

B: I have gone back to "confession" not as a need to tell my story in public or to be narcissistic, but because I now realize that people really learn from the sharing of experience.

M: I wonder about the particular danger of you being, as a consequence, perceived as an essentialist black woman who speaks an atheoretical personal discourse. But what you do in your latest book is talk about aspects of your life others may know in their own but do not have the resources to think about. You bring to bear everything you know in speaking about your life and thus try to integrate intellectual, political, and personal experience—a primary goal of the women's movement. This too is theory, and it is the kind of theory my sisters who dropped out of high school can read. We certainly need a variety of different types of theory: you doing what you are doing in *Talking Back* and other women, including women of color, perhaps choosing to speak more abstractly. I am thinking now of the fine example of Chandra Mohanty's highly abstract writing.

B: Of course, when more abstract writing is seen as more important, the language of underclass women is a speech that then has no relevance. When black women confronted feminist movement, urging inclusion of race and racism, this was revolutionary. Yet now the new terms of this discussion suggest that words like race and racism are inappropriate, not sophisticated, too simplistic. Currently the discussion of race takes place within the framework of "colonial discourse." How many women and men know what that means? This shift tends to deflect attention away from works by women of color who are not from privileged groups, or who have not had a ruling class education. Currently, we hear more the voices of third world elites, brown women and men. Though their perspectives greatly enhance our understanding of third world feminism, of race and racism, it is crucial that they be heard in conjunction with the theoretical voices of other women of color. At times it seems the category "women of color" works to erase class and other differences among us, so that to have any woman of color at a conference means that certain experiences are taken care of when, in fact, they are avoided or merged with others.

M: Maybe it is time to stress the importance of people being bi-lingual, with bi-lingual being broadly defined to refer to different speech communities, and of academic acceptance of enacting a variety of different modes of speech on the stages of our classrooms and conferences. Otherwise, I'm afraid that the discourse that dominates these days will be very discouraging to working-class women who want to be intellectual without giving up their home-bases. Don't you wonder who is dropping out of graduate school these days?

B: Oh absolutely. I think that if people are truly committed to radical cultural praxis, then whether you come from the working class or not, whether you are black or white, if you really want to communicate, you will learn varieties of presentation. I will tell a story I heard recently about a white woman theorist who teaches in an ivy league institution. I overheard a group of white women putting her down for singing a song in class. Singing was a sign that she was less theoretical or was a spectacle. I felt as though I was listening in on a conversation that was also downgrading me, because I have often sung spirituals in class. Here again we have the question of the performative. This is another aspect of working-class and underclass experience that is devalued in academia but valued in black culture. To perform with "style" is a sign of value, uniqueness, and seriousness, because in a sense you have to be like "down," like serious, to cultivate something. What academia does is try to erase our uniquenesses; in a sense to make us all homogenized members of a privileged class group. When people break away from that, using the subversion of style, we are often condemned. This is certainly happening in feminist theory. It is very frightening to see women of color who fear that if they do not use certain kinds of convoluted language their work will not be seen as legitimate or meaningful and they will not be heard.

M: Participating in theoretical language is one thing; feeling as though you have to imitate it even at the cost of feeling committed to what you are saying is another. But, getting back to your anecdote, the only way we are going to handle all this conflict in feminism is if we have pleasure together. We are going to have more pleasure if we can sing than if we can talk in convoluted sentences.

B: I agree, shared pleasure is very important. In most encounters between white women and black women or other women of color, if there is confrontation, all pleasure ends and total disintegration takes place. So that we also have to conceptualize how we can deal with difference in a way that allows for the experience in a given setting of both pain and pleasure. It is possible to remember what provides a connection even as you deal with what makes you different, with what you vehemently don't agree about. But it is very hard to be frank in a culture in which friendship is so constructed around a notion of shared sentiment.

M: It was, in part, the alternative definitions of friendship offered by Lugones and Spelman that made us want to write something together. As we were suggesting earlier, friendship is typically constructed by the same ideas that construct the couple: seamless harmony.

B: And when one does not have that, we often do not know what to do. This has been one of the central issues that has kept feminists from dealing with race and class. What do you do with having a hostile confrontation? We go back, you and I, to a discussion of the importance of honesty and facing differences, as opposed to trying to erase them, transcend them, or getting stuck in them. The idea of talking through them means process, which is a crucial act. The very kind of conversation we are having today and the many conversations that we have had leading up to being able to have this conversation is the kind of gesture of process that we are talking about. I think it is important for us to emphasize the need to confront and criticize one another even when there is holding back and fear. We cannot expect always to be casual and completely at ease. We will tangle, as you and I did, over definitions of psychoanalysis and feminism. It is this kind of interaction multiplied in many neighborhoods and among different types of people that has the power to help us encourage inclusive and revitalized feminist movement.

M: Do you think we have a vital feminist movement outside of academia at this point in this country?

B: There are important, concrete manifestations of the power of contemporary feminist movement. Some of those concrete manifestations are battered women's shelters and rape crisis centers, but we don't have what I think of as a mass-based political movement, like the civil rights movement. One of the things that really sticks out in my mind is that that movement did not take place in the academy. It is true that a lot of the theories behind that movement were developed by black nationalists who were privileged people; Angela Davis and others were not coming from underclass backgrounds. And yet they left spaces of privilege and went into spaces of nonprivilege in order to build a movement.

M: Many feminists have been distracted by the toil of building careers instead of the toil of building a movement. It is so much easier for privileged people to change their individual lives and careers than to remain engaged in the long term struggle against inequalities from which they individually benefit in a secondary way.

B: Feminism has been completely incorporated into the market economy of the academy. There is an elite group of feminist theorists who are paid way above scale and who benefit from the production of feminist theory in a way that allows them to lead *more* privileged life styles. How do we encourage those women to interrogate their class alliance, their "radical" commitment to feminist movement? Co-optation divides us. It does not enable us to address a mass-based group of women.

M: In certain disciplinary homes within academia we speak such rarefied language we can barely speak with colleagues in other disciplines. How many of us could actually go door to door encouraging less educated women to fight for even a limited intervention such as affirmative action? What is the relationship between theory and developing the habits of being that allow one to learn new vocabularies?

B: The most exciting political and theoretical implication of expanding the category of gender so that it gives expression to reality—of the ways race and class converge—is that understanding this link has the potential to give us the base to begin to work towards inclusive feminist movement.

Notes

1. An invigorating discussion of how the class and race of Women's Studies faculties affect research opportunities and development occurs in Maxine Baca Zinn, Lynn Weber Cannon, Elizabeth Higginbotham, and Bonnie Thornton Dill, "The Costs of Exclusionary Practices in Women's Studies," in *Reconstructing the Academy: Women's Education and Women's Studies*, ed. Elizabeth Minnich, Jean O'Barr, and Rachel Rosenfeld (Chicago: University of Chicago Press, 1988), pp. 125–138.

2. Heilbrun, "Non-Autobiographies of 'Privileged' Women: England and America," in *Life/Lines: Theorizing Women's Autobiography*, ed. Bella Brodzki and Celeste Schenck (Ithaca, NY: Cornell University Press, 1988), pp. 62–64. *Mary*: I am criticizing Heilbrun here. Later on in the conversation when Bell and I talk about the importance of the autobiographical in feminist theory, I acknowledge the contribution Heilbrun continues to make to feminist literary criticism. I want to anticipate that moment in this footnote and thus criticize negatively and positively at once because contradiction is so crucial to what we try to suggest in this essay.

3. *Mary*: reading my comments months later, after many white working-class women as well as men in Bensonhurst, NY marched against primarily black activists, I want

to qualify my comments about the reverberation of shared working-class white and black experience; they seem more like fantasies now. Many white working-class people are raised openly speaking racism, which is not the same thing as having a discourse about race, a discourse that would allow for the examination of fears of black people and the national compulsion to blame African-American folks for violence, drugs, and crime. Shared experience alone does not prompt people to learn that the mostly white men behind the savings and loans scandal and behind monetary manipulation of real estate have done violence to the lives of so many Americans of different races and classes.

4. See Leonore Davidoff, "Class and Gender in Victorian England: the Diaries of Arthur J. Munby and Hannah Cullwick," in *Feminist Studies* 5, 1 (Spring, 1979), 89–141; and Peter Stallybrass and Allon White, "The Maid and the Family Romance," in *The Politics and Poetics of Transgression* (Ithaca, NY: Cornell University Press, 1986).

5. Smith, "Between a Rock and a Hard Place: Relationships between Black and Jewish Women," in *Yours in Struggle: Three Feminist Perspectives on Anti-Semitism and Racism*, also authored by Elly Bulkin and Minnie Bruce Pratt (Brooklyn, NY: Long Haul Press, 1984). Because political objectives can often be obstructed by group dynamics, we benefit from thinking about various ways of interpreting, making, and receiving accusations of being silenced. Some challenging suggestions occur in Eve Kosofsky Sedgwick, "Tide and Trust," in *Critical Inquiry* 15 (Summer 1989), 745–747.

6. See Rollins, *Between Women: Domestics and Their Employers* (Philadelphia: Temple University, 1985). It is very illuminating to read this sociological study alongside a fiction by Alice Childress, *Like One of the Family* (Boston: Beacon Press, 1986). Also see the sections on domestic work in Jacqueline Jones, *Labor of Love, Labor of Sorrow: Black Women, Work, and the Family from Slavery to the Present* (NY: Basic Books, 1985). Many of the issues at stake are mapped out by Phyllis Palmer, "Housewife and Household Worker: Employer-Employee Relationships in the Home, 1928–1941," in *"To Toil the Livelong Day": America's Women at Work, 1780–1980*, ed. Carol Groneman and Mary Beth Norton (Ithaca, NY: Cornell University Press, 1987).

   For a symptomatically inadequate version of privileged white feminists thinking about "nanny-employer relationships," see Pat Bradshaw-Camball and Rina Cohen, "Feminists: Explorers or Exploiters," in *Women and Environments*, 10, 4 (Fall 1988), 8–10 (Thanks to a former student, Emily Wilcox, for giving me a copy of this article).

   A primarily empirical comparison of issues in addition to that of service differentiating black and white women is offered by Gloria I. Joseph and Jill Lewis, *Common Differences: Conflicts in Black & White Feminist Perspectives* (Boston: South End Press, 1986).

7. The exemplary exchange referred to "started" with Michèle Barrett and Mary McIntosh, "Ethnocentrism and Socialist-Feminist Theory," *Feminist Review*, no. 20 (1985), 23–47. Four separate responses were written by Caroline Ramazanoglu, Hamida Kazi, Sue Lees, and Heidi Safia Mirza, "Feedback: Feminism and Racism— Responses to Michèle Barrett and Mary McIntosh," *Feminist Review*, no. 22 (1986), 83–105. Further comment was offered by Kum-Kum Bhavnani and Margaret Coulson, "Transforming Socialist-Feminism: The Challenge of Racism," *Feminist Review*, no. 23 (1986), 81–92.

8. Heilbrun, *Writing a Woman's Life* (NY: W.W. Norton & Co., 1988).

4

Producing Sex, Theory, and Culture: Gay/Straight Remappings in Contemporary Feminism

Katie King

Introduction

This essay explores the shifting feminist politics of sexual preference from three directions; the first—the Sex Debates—historically situating some of the issues at stake and redrawing the map of what was once called "the gay/straight split," the second and third—Theory in Press and the Apparatus for the Production of Feminist Culture—constructing an argument for how these issues look currently, and suggesting some ironic and hopeful interconnections across differences.

The term "gay/straight split" marks out, specifies, and layers together several historical moments in gay liberation, feminism, lesbian feminism, and feminist lesbianisms. In one meaning it refers to a time when homosexual women and men shared the term "gay," when "lesbian" and "gay woman" were used interchangeably, when gay women and men were alike recruited from the bar scene, the homophile movement, and new gay liberation. Inside feminism, the first gay/straight splits revolved around passionate worries over the stigmatizing of feminism by the presence of a lesbian minority and passionate affirmations of the importance of resisting dyke-baiting and examining homophobia as central feminist projects, engaging in the critique of the institution of heterosexuality.

In another meaning it refers to a time when U.S. lesbians were increasingly recruited inside the "women's movement" itself, with investments in specifying non-parallel experiences of homosexual women and men, constructing sometime alliances and oftentimes distinctions across the categories of "lesbians and gay men." Inside feminism, lesbianism was constructed as privileged signifier, as magical sign: a vanguardism retreating as lesbianism became more and more acceptable in feminism, an avant-garde activism and theory ranging from lesbian as outside the collaborating categories of male and female to the lesbian continuum defining woman. The gay/straight splits quieted as lesbian vanguardism quieted and as homophobia and heterosexism were successfully challenged, though hardly eradicated; still resentments smoldered under this magical sign.

In yet a third meaning it refers to a time when gay has a new salience among some lesbians, who see gay men bashed on the streets, denounced by other lesbian feminists as perverts, increasingly caught up in state repression, and dying from and living with AIDS. Inside feminism, the term gay/straight split marks a kind of mistake: the assumption that differences among women are only bipolar. Instead differences come to be seen as simultaneously creating and created, strategically positioned. Situationally other differences that cannot be imagined as opposites may be as salient or more salient: race, class, nationality, language, religion, ability. All suggest that sexualities are too plural, too politically granulated to be named in a gay/straight division, as women have too many genders, sexes to be seen simply across such a "gay/straight" divide; indeed, any such centering of a gay/straight divide is in itself deeply divisive: mystifying the power dynamics feminists play with each other, and our accountabilities to each other.[1]

My own moment of coming out: in 1970 when the homophile movement, feminism, gay liberation, children's liberation, and mental patients' liberation seemed very closely pulled together for gay youth; harassed by and also protected in the academy in Santa Cruz, California. My own first feminist mentor was a gay man running a women's bookstore in Berkeley and doing feminist theory, convinced and convincing that only feminist theory could provide the theoretical grounding for understanding gay oppression and for mobilizing against it.

Time and space are deliberately problematized in the production of multiple stories in this essay. Feminists too easily believe "we" already know the "history" or even histories of feminism, even in the U.S. What is taken as history are some privileged and published histories of feminism, which have been all too quickly naturalized. What I've just produced here is a series of overlapping—in time and space—historical "moments," what I've sometimes called conversations in feminism. I've located myself a bit because I believe this to account for my own place in time and space, to describe some of my political origins. These three "meanings" of "gay/straight split" are roughly successive historically. One can locate examples documenting each statement I've made in a place and time, but as periods in feminism they actually overlap, since they also describe different realities for slightly different political unities shifting over time. Also they describe *kinds* of events which might have happened in some places in different times than at other places. This may not be *your* historical memory, but maybe that means you are overhearing, eavesdropping on a recentered history.

The essay connects and separates two threads of argument in a kind of weaving together and apart: each section begins with a dense set of summary statements, which sometimes summarizes issues of that section, sometimes contextualizes issues of that section, sometimes generalizes from examples offered in that section. I've made some of my arguments out of seemingly "local" issues and conversations precisely because I can be accountable to my own political communities for my stories about events and meanings. I consider these stories exempla illustrating large structural issues of general importance to feminist theory, and thus a form in which theorizing takes place.

At the same time, the essay as a whole has a rather sweeping agenda. I've tried to give a sense of dynamic play among differing historical moments and feminist conversations, sometimes engaging each other, sometimes not, changing in the middle into something else, and turning out to be right and wrong in unexpected forms. So, while sometimes the argument may seem too local and detailed, at other times it may seem too global and sketchy. Given the space I can occupy in this book this is the best way I know how to tell the stories I think are important.

Shifting the Ground of the "Gay/Straight Split": Sex Wars

1st direction—The Sex Debates, in which divergent investments in "the lesbian" and her meanings and political activism in feminism fractured, and alliances (between some lesbians, heterosexual women, and gay men) reformed along the lines of a critique of the anti-pornography movement, the reperiodization of "radical feminism," and the indictment of cultural feminism.[2]

The scope of the so-called "Sex Debates"—or my favorite term (lifted from Gayle Rubin and Ruby Rich) "Sex Wars"—currently is too narrowly drawn around the April 1982 Barnard conference[3] and its synecdochic expansion, the academy. The Barnard conference and its products identify only one range of activity and activism. Some of the very feminists who appropriately pointed out how white-centered these "Sex Debates" are, are also among those responsible for reconceptualizing sexual politics, indeed sexualities, the meanings of race/sex identities, and the blurred boundaries between these, the site of proliferations of both.[4]

So right from the beginning we need to expand what's going to count as these "Sex Wars," seeing as not the whole but only a *part* of this field the critique of the anti-porn movement, the reduction of cultural feminism (which unfortunately contributed to an invisibility of the work of some women of color, some lesbians), and the valorization of lesbian s/m and proliferated perversions. I begin with Ruby Rich's troubled descriptions and questions at the end of her insightful 1986 review essay in *Feminist Studies*. I begin with it in order to examine and reconfigure that formative intertwining of sex and theory drawn in her essay in a generic economy constructed in the academy; sex and theory in production, distribution, and reception: that is, sex and theory in the apparatus for the production of feminist culture.

Rich herself calls for such a reconfiguration, insisting on the significance of the contributions of women of color to feminist concerns in sexuality; she demonstrates in her questions the very premises on which their exclusion depends, but her questions actually reproduce these problematic premises in her critique.[5] Rich names the generic politics: women of color contributing *"outside* the nonfiction books that constitute the official discourse, in texts that exist on the margins of the debate, as currently constituted." Here, as she herself constitutes one version of the debate for *Feminist Studies,* she helplessly, but critically "discovers" an "official discourse," a set of "certified theorists" and a reign of "polemicists" who are *not* these women of color. She critically names but also continues to establish a generic hierarchy: academic polemics and histories vs. non-academic autobiographical testimonies, each differently valued "currency in this theoretical economy." She laments the "inevitable dominance" of "theorized issues" "within feminist debates." Why is such dominance "inevitable?" Certainly it is currently powerful, and I think she means here to emphasize and problematize it. Here too, the term "feminist" ranges from a specific group of women physically present at the Barnard Conference and/or represented in publication in Vance's collection of papers and in the books centered in Rich's review article, to a larger group of feminists (who yet do not exhaust the category "feminist") writing and discussing these materials. The local/global shift assumed here in the ranges of "feminist debates" matters in examining these "Sex Wars."

The problem is how to criticize a white-centered discussion of sexuality, without making visible only white women's participation in the large feminist interweaving conversations about sex. What's called for is similar to the historical reappropriation which draws a tension between critical histories of "the white women's movement," on the one hand, and reconceptualizations of simultaneous women's movements, on the other. It must be possible to critique the formation in the U.S. of a "white women's movement" without simultaneously constructing a bogus history that makes invisible the contributions to feminist social justice which actually center in the political work of women of color, in the U.S. and elsewhere. In other words, the critique of the "white women's movement" doesn't mean relinquishing "ownership" of feminism in the U.S. to white women. Chicana theorist Chela Sandoval puts it this way: ". . . the U.S. women's movement of the seventies was officially renamed the 'white women's movement' by U.S. feminists of color, a re-naming which insisted on the recognition of other, simultaneously existing women's movements." Notice how the agents doing the "official" naming in Sandoval's description differ from those in Rich's.[6]

A similar refiguration redraws the map of what counts as "sex," "theory," and these "Sex Wars." Compare these shifts also to Bell Hooks's distinction between "the feminist movement" as an object, and "feminist movement" as an action. Note also the power of publication to center and make visible particular histories of feminism, and particular mappings of the current "Sex Wars."[7] Any gay/ straight split is numerously fragmented in these new mappings which the sex wars demand, confounded with other markings. White heterosexual socialist feminists find themselves aligning with white lesbian s/m people to critique the anti-porn movement, and a consolidated radical/cultural feminism.[8] Black feminist lesbians find themselves aligning with white self-proclaimed radical feminists to critique the symbolic and erotic uses of the paraphernalia of domination/"domination."[9]

A different group of white self-proclaimed radical feminists align with the anti-porn critique and draw distinctions between an early feminist radical feminism, and a later developing cultural feminism.[10] Lesbian s/m people point out that they have most in common in terms of legal criminalization and on the street bashing with gay men, especially s/m gay men, and s/m heterosexuals, and with other visible and/or ostracized sex perverts.[11]

The renewed salience of the term "gay" among some lesbians invites both a revision of an early radical feminism, and a continuity across gender in alliances with gay men, as it makes visible lesbian homophobia against gay men and corrosive judgments about gay male sexuality. Heterosexual women's fascination with gay men meets/overlaps with the possibly sexually specific perversions of fag-hagging.[12] Butch and femme roles conflate/separate in erotic dances with s/m, with the roles of top/bottom. An erotic analysis of power among black and white lesbians, shifting across time, across the historical meanings of butch and femme contributes to an examination of what counts as "sex" in these "Sex Wars".[13] Women of color working as artists, writers, and theorists produce breathtaking new analyses of the "race of sex"/"sex of race"—gender and sexuality and sex acts and sex meanings and memories; for example, Moraga's "My brother's sex was white. Mine, brown."[14]

Women in several countries continue and begin analyses of sex tourism in the context of an emerging interconnected international sexual division of labor. The sex industry (domestic and international) becomes the site of more writing, identity-making; producing personal stories, films, and continuing moves for decriminalization.[15] Anti-porn activisms are sometimes distinguished from a critical, but academic theoreticism.

Some shifts have been in the making a while, some are old allegiances newly refreshed, some are momentary and fleeting, some emerge from old wounds of the early gay/straight splits, and are fueled by still smoldering resentments. Long-standing resentments against the formation of lesbianism as if at the center, the very heart of feminism, fan homophobia, internalized and external, as groups struggle for both vanguard perversion and gatekeeping sexuality, for political centrality, for new political identities, for new strategies of activism. The work, the labor, active and written, of lesbians of color is central. Such work creates new critiques of homophobia in various separated and connected communities, new critiques of racism among feminists, and most powerfully insists on the specificity and overlapping necessities of political positioning—not simply a simultaneity of oppressions, but the complex interdefining, interacting movements of power, for change and against it.

Gayle Rubin's Foucauldian historical proliferation of perversions under attack by the Reagan New Right contrasts here with the old Norman O. Brown celebration of polymorphous perversity that colored the beginnings of gay liberation in the late sixties, early seventies. Sexual identities and sexual acts merge and pull apart. The moments of reidentification, of the consolidation of new identities is deeply distressing when unmanaged.[16] Polymorphous perversity suggested that sex was another set of hallucinogenic drugs, each to be savored for their specific reconstitutions of reality, for their special insights and truths. Proliferated perversions suggest that people can orchestrate, stage, contract for sex acts regardless of sexual identity, or in complex dances with sexual identities, just offering even more senses of variation, variety, and especially specificity. The struggle over the givenness or the choice: the possible subtleties within, the psychic subtleties of sexual identity, are heightened. Personally I've begun to wonder if the dualist distinction here isn't rather between those who are erotic specialists and those who are erotic generalists.

Some subtle and not so subtle reinterpretations of events are evident in my stories, all pointing toward my own investments in challenging the ways that most participants in these debates use the term "cultural feminism." I contend that at this moment cultural feminism is best seen as the very apparatus for the production of feminist culture and thus the important political site in which race, sexuality, art activism, and new forms of gay culture are being interconnected. Understanding such connections requires us to not separate away from one another debates about sexuality and race from sex radical debates, for example, about s/m. I want to focus less on the contents of these debates—summaries now often ritualized—and more on the political terrain, and how it's sculpted, textured, crafted by all of us involved in these conversations, specific and momentary, but strategically important. I also agree with Gayle Rubin, we don't need a "middle ground" in analysis of our "Sex Wars"—a reconciliation of the contents of debate, the conservative answer to conflict and struggle—but I think we need to do some mapping, some rehistoricizing, some understanding of our multiple mediations, a term I use in Lata Mani's meaning, as the analysis of the political receptions of feminist theory and its products.[17]

Theory in Press

2nd—*Redefinitions of feminist "theory,"* especially as influenced by the powerful explanatory systems of poststructuralist practice in the academy, or by Euro-centered philosophical traditions. In 1979 Barbara Smith and Lorraine Bethel could recommend *conditions: the black women's issue* (later expanded and reprinted as *Home Girls: A Black Feminist Anthology*) as a text for feminist theory courses, (implicitly) including as theoretical genres poetry, prose poems, fiction and autobiography, journals, essays, song lyrics and reviews. In 1989 "theory" is more narrowly defined from a number of disciplinary and political perspectives. The academic and commercial success of feminist publication vs. movement, small-press publication has effectively recreated both a straight/gay split and a white/women of color split sometimes now coded as "theory" vs. "experience."

So, it's deeply important to understand that what was once called the "gay/straight" split, has been irrecoverably altered, now positioned on many axes of meaning and political investment. This doesn't mean that gay people have no interests in common: we do. But our coalitions and identities are in flux and appropriately so.

The second site of the reconstitution of such meanings is the academy: for feminism in the U.S., that vexed and valued sometimes "home"—in that desiring and subjecting sense brought out by Bernice Reagon. It is only home for some, and even for them, only sometimes; yet it is one center for the proselytizing of feminism, within the academy, and beyond.[18] A new gay/straight:women of color/white split emerges in the academy, in the late eighties. The commercial success of feminist work, the new interests of university presses in trade books, and of commercial houses in feminist academic work, combine in a visibility of feminist "theory" unstably and tensely inside and outside of literary theory, shading into cultural theory. Disciplines are mined for and mired in commercially successful appeals to the niches of reading and writing markets of the academy. Feminists laughingly and ruefully say to each other that they have sold their souls to some trade house with a feminist line, generating reviews and reports, anthologies and collections, and texts for classes (but not textbooks).[19]

Lesbian theory, fiction, scholarship, activist writing, once occupying a center (if not the center) of feminist "thought," has now been displaced in the academy. One might chart who is publishing, and who is reading lesbian writing, that proliferating work in mixed genres, creating new forms of intertextuality and abstraction. Such work may call for a vigorous reinvention of reading protocols on the parts of academic theorists. Especially now, in that context, note what counts as theory and for whom. How is that assessment affected by the genres in which theory is written? Consider which bookstores carry which kinds of writing, and what clientele they attract. These questions of distribution are part of the apparatus in which theory is produced for feminist consumption.

As mixed genres emerging from and theorizing mixed complex identities are produced in the feminist press, genres of academic feminist writing are increasingly compartmentalized in production, distribution, consumption in the academic and commercial presses. Political meanings are assigned to all these activities, redrawing political communities. "Theory" here has shifted from an activity possibly (though not without exception) embodied in many written genres to a genre of writing itself. The precedence of the rationalist essay becomes murky in these generic valuations. The hierarchies of value produced, as suggested by Ruby Rich in her discussion of the sex debates, complexly crosses the race and sex exclusions of the academy.[20] These are indications about how theory travels and in what forms, the local/global structures theory repositions, and which structures get to count as object-language and which as meta-language. Theory finds different uses in different locations.[21]

Some of the categorizing feminist work has been subjected to is indeed the fallout of the "Sex Wars" (and of commercial constraints). The equation of cultural feminism with a naturalizing, unself-consciously universalizing, theoretically naive anti-porn activism—or in the case of Catherine MacKinnon, a theoretically sophisticated but essentializing anti-porn activism—has certainly deflated the value of a much broader segment of work for a range of academic feminist theorists. The big three—essentializing, universalizing, naturalizing, the "sins" of feminist theory—are currently powerful gatekeepers among a particular grouping of feminists.[22] Non-academic lesbian writing has been assumed to and is sometimes insensitively read as simply replicating these sins.[23] Reconstructions of the history of feminist theory have facilitated these sometimes correct and sometimes incorrect readings of lesbian materials. The work of women of color, lesbians, and heterosexuals, has also been marked by these practices.[24]

These histories and gatekeeping practices—although only having currency inside the feminist academy, and even there only among a relatively small grouping of feminist intellectuals—are currently disproportionately powerful in visible university and trade publications. They reify a division of labor which is sometimes characterized as the "theory" of white women, built on the "experience" of women of color; or in a move that keeps these ranges inappropriately separated—the "theory" of heterosexual academics, built on the "experience" of lesbians. Gatekeeping works both ways across these divides: see for example the increasing code terms for "accessible language and style" in feminist journals and among editors and publishers; once meant to encourage interdisciplinary submissions, now they are also often meant to transform, discourage, or admonish "theorists," especially deconstructionists.

An error feminists make over and over is to mistake the *part* of a particular theoretical reading, especially a published reading, for the *whole* of the many forms theorizing takes: active thinking, speaking, conversation, action grounded in theory, action producing theory, action suggesting theory, drafts, letters, unpublished manuscripts, stories in writing and not, poems said and written, art events like shows, readings, enactments, zap actions such as ACT UP does:[25] or for that matter, incomplete theorizing, sporadic suggestiveness, generalizations correct and incorrect, inadequate theory, images and actions inciting theoretical interventions, and so on. It's not that all human actions are equivalent to theorizing, but rather that a particular product of many forms of theorizing should not be mistaken for the processes of production themselves. Theorizing can find its embodiments in a variety of forms, written or not, published or not, academic or not, individual or not. Like the other forms of cultural production I look at—the poem, the art work, art activism—the exchangeable product with a single, valorized author/actor is the visible and venerated metonym oversimplifying the intersecting systems of production and reception.[26] Issues of the production and reception of theoretical work are meaningful, and feminists are now struggling over these meanings. These issues of the production and reception of theory become visible as sharply disciplinized, colored by race and racial privilege in the academy, strangely fixed by sexual identity, defined by a division of labor and a generic hierarchy, and consumed within politicized systems of publication and distribution.[27]

Barbara Christian's "The Race for Theory" attempts an intervention into some of the statuses accorded a particular reified product called "theory" in the academy. The title of her article plays on the commodification of theory in a factory sped-up university system where publication defines a particular "fast-track"; similarly it also plays on the theorizing activities of black people, seeing theorizing-as-a-verb as a necessity for survival by oppressed people.[28] The passion of Christian's work, and the passion it provokes in reaction reflects on the struggles over "theory" in U.S. feminism today. It is one of the areas in which the so-called "gay/straight split" might be said to appear in reconstituted forms.[29] Christian and others contesting the spoils system in the academy, especially in relation to literary and cultural studies, may be surprised to discover that those seen as the standard bearers of high theory themselves feel embattled and devalued. The "stars" rewarded by the academy for the practice of "high theory" may benefit from this spoils system, but most practitioners of these specific schools of theoretical practice, especially in literature (sometimes the only ones perceived as, or perceiving themselves as, the "theorists"), find themselves solitary workers in departments of hostile "non-theorist" critics.[30]

Chicana theorist Chela Sandoval has spent many years working out a theory of what she calls "oppositional consciousness," a theory of the production of theory, and specifically of a descriptive but also utopian form of it, "differential consciousness," which she sees as pointing and contributing to alternative theoretical paradigms, ones already and potentially departing from "hegemonic feminist theory."[31] Sandoval is a theorist influential in specific circles, who, in the manner of some other feminist workers—Gayle Rubin and Alice Echols come immediately to mind—has been a graduate student working on a long-awaited doctoral thesis. Sandoval has been published only sporadically and eccentrically, yet her circulating unpublished manuscripts are much cited and often appropriated, even while the range of her influence is rarely understood. Belonging to several national networks of women of color, she has described, helped to develop, and herself been influenced by the feminist theoretical work of lesbians of color. Sandoval has deeply influenced what might be a nascent "school of feminist theory" housed in the History of Consciousness program at the University of California at Santa Cruz. (This names one of my own formative intellectual communities; one among many such places of feminist academic theorizing.) A story of the uses of Sandoval's work offers a kind of parable about the apparatus that reifies theory in the academy, and the abilities of this apparatus to hide the race-consolidated structures of power in which knowledge is produced.

Sandoval has described some processes in which the theory produced by U.S. third world women has been appropriated by white academic feminism. She, like many other women of color, have seen this first hand: where her own work on "oppositional consciousness" is attributed to her teacher Donna Haraway in Sandra Harding's insightful and sometimes surprising book *The Science Question in Feminism*. Haraway is a powerful contributor to, and an imaginative as well as an astonishingly broad-ranging synthesizer of the theorizing ocfcurring at the History of Consciousness. She scrupulously attempts acknowledgment in her publications of her own indebtedness to this active work, thus making some of these systems of production within the program visible, as in the notes to her "Cyborg Manifesto." "Cyborg" is presumably the work from which Harding extracts the idea of "oppositional consciousness," but without reproducing Haraway's acknowledgment of Sandoval. More recently Teresa de Lauretis, a prolific thinker producing exacting and absorbing theory and description, has moved to, been influenced by, and has influenced this HistCon theorizing. The footnotes to her essay on "Sexual Indifference and Lesbian Representation," follow a different strategy for acknowledgment and authorization than Haraway's, and her recent "Eccentric Subjects" is also clearly indebted to Sandoval's work.[32] Haraway and de Lauretis are more visible in terms of publishing and career trajectories than Sandoval (and other HistCon feminist theorists), and so may acquire cultural capital in the work they actively mentor but are also imaginatively indebted to. The processes that institutionalize Sandoval's work as Haraway's through publication and citation, exemplify processes in which reified "theory" in the academy depends upon communities *theorizing*.

These processes—despite the intentions of individual authors—are not simply not innocent of racism and heterosexism. In fact, they are constituted in structures which depend upon wide-and-on-going theorizing work done by whole communities, but most prized when decontextualized, exchangeable, race- and sex-consolidated in their published forms, forms mystifying their own processes of production. Thus, this term "theory" has to be bracketed in feminist thinking now, used ironically and proudly, shamefacedly and shrewdly, gloriously and preposterously, if it is really to convey anything like what feminists are doing, in the academy and elsewhere.

The Apparatus for the Production of Feminist Culture

3rd—*Proliferations of lesbian sexualities/ethnicities* (both in the plural). The powerful critique of cultural feminism emerging from the sex debates was especially helpful in drawing attention to the homophobia among lesbians practiced against gay men and against other sexual minorities among lesbians. However the reduction of cultural feminism to the anti-pornography movement was premature and narrow. In the 1980s cultural feminism (that is, the apparatus for the production of feminist "culture") also becomes the site for political art activism and for art-theoretical elaborations of multiple identities and the anti-racist critique of "the white women's movement." Mixed literary/theoretical genres connect women's lived experience with the shiftings of what Chela Sandoval calls "differential consciousness." Lesbianism is remade in this continuing "cultural" blossoming of art activism, intertwined now with race, ethnicity, religion, national origin, decolonization, language, region, ability, and so on. Multiple identities refigure and make more complex any simple "gay/straight" split now, since coalitions among many differences may be profound while historically momentary.

The zealous narrowing of cultural feminism to the movement arm of anti-pornography activisms led to challenges redirecting feminist energies and calling us to accountability. The challenges to lesbianism as magical sign were profound and largely successful. The challenges to a coalition with the New Right around pornography and violence against women have been cautionary: they have split apart groups within "cultural feminism," and decentered anti-porn practice. The challenges to the equation of fantasy with violence against women have made such an equation harder and harder to sustain. The challenges to unexamined assumptions about s/m and other proliferating sexualities have opened up new paths of inquiry about heterosexualities and homosexualities supplanting simple dichotomies when it comes to thinking about sex. The challenges to an international feminism founded in ahistorical, acultural "crimes against women" have required U.S. feminists to examine some of their cultural hubris, and feminism itself as a kind of cultural imperialism.[33]

The zealous narrowing of cultural feminism to the movement arm of anti-pornography activisms was also premature and problematic. It solidified a particular form of U.S. socialist feminism expensively writing a taxonomic history of the women's movements, pedagogically powerful but historically mystifying.[34] Beyond that it overgeneralized—or perhaps better, *intervened* in—the ubiquity of the anti-porn imperative in lesbian politics and in current U.S. feminism, though undoubtedly *not* overgeneralizing its power in national politics. Its critique of lesbianism as magical sign revealed homophobia among some heterosexual feminists who mistakenly equated cultural feminism with lesbian feminism (a shift the critique of femin*in*ism made all too easy). It downplayed the tremendous pleasures provided for all feminists in the often lesbian-centered but not exclusively lesbian alternative institutions in its cautioning against entrepreneurial capitalism. Many alternative cultural institutions and much cultural activism in feminism became tarred with the brush of this narrowed pejorative vision of "cultural feminism."[35]

Bernice Reagon's "Coalition Politics" offered a critique of cultural feminism from the angle of identity politics. Cultural feminism and identity politics may be shifting and overlapping terms, may be historically successive as centers of feminist practice. Despite some early fears that its political strategies might deflect attention *away* from an analysis of racism, identity politics has often turned out to be the site of anti-racist work in current U.S. feminism.[36] Much powerful anti-racist work has been in what might be called the "cultural" camp of feminism, or among those who sometimes call themselves "cultural workers." (A term with a powerful history in nationalist movements around the world.) Early on, lesbian-centered alternative institutions were figured in women's music, women's book-stores and coffeehouses, women's buildings: sites of the production, distribution, and consumption of feminist "culture."

Cultural analysis, critique, even theory in agit prop and other art activist forms similarly and strikingly marks AIDS political interventions, sex radical productions of gay culture.[37] Within a range of forms of art activism, one might see a coming together of cultural feminism, anti-imperialist work, AIDS activism combined with sex radicalism, and anti-racist cultural products and strategies. Some of the politics and possibilities overlapping with this cultural analysis/activism have altered the terrain of what counts as the "gay and lesbian community," and "cultural feminism." AIDS activism combined with sex radicalism produces "sex-positive" political demands for respect for gay male sex practices and "liberated heterosexuality," while at the same time challenging reformist gay politics.[38] Successful coalitions in urban communities, such as San Francisco, make for pockets of support, even public documentation of the history of gay activism.[39]

Lesbian interest in AIDS activism produce new community with gay men; lesbian interests in safe sex offer opportunities for redefinitions of lesbian sex practices and meanings, forms of public lesbian sex.[40] A backlash, or troubled sense of priorities incites some lesbians to challenge involvement in AIDS work or policy priorities for AIDS, while other lesbians and heterosexual women, women of color, prostitutes, drug users make new coalitions to describe AIDS as a "women's disease."[41] Calls are made by sex radicals for a return to, but at the same time a revision of the consciousness-raising group as a site for the production of theory about sex, while anti-essentialist anti-autobiographical individual and collective writing and film projects re-structure/re-vision bodies and body parts.[42]

AIDS activism domestically and internationally draws upon Foucauldian histories and anthropologies of sexuality, literalizing such theory in interventions into forms of global gay organization and local homosexualities.[43] The cultural and historical appropriations that create homosexual continuities across time and space are in tension with the imperatives of transnational influences and realities creating some kinds of gay organization globally. The flows of capital that appear to be linked to the possibilities of gay urban formations, intervening into family forms of organization, intersect with flows of sexual repressions and license. Lesbianisms in specific cultural locations are subject to multi-national receptions.[44]

Meanwhile feminist presses become the site for the production of proliferating lesbian sexualities/ethnicities: new genders, new sex, restatements and mixtures of sexuality and identity, colonialisms and decolonizations, essentialisms and anti-essentialisms, sex and language, sex and diverse bodies.[45] Not simply are the contents of recent materials about such mixing (Sandoval notes "U.S. third world feminists are 'new mestizas' " describing "this in-between space, this third category"), but the written genres themselves mix life stories—autobiographical and anti-biographical—letters, journals, poems, short stories; many are theoretical interventions, origins, and supplements in "white hegemonic feminist theory." It is no accident that academic high theorists discover/convert to feminism, or that academic feminists turn to the powerful destabilizing theoretical tools of poststructuralist thought at the same time in the U.S. that identity politics and cultural feminism elaborate issues of "difference." Our theorizing communities across feminisms have produced intersecting conversations, mutually influencing. Sandoval connects these ranges of production, sometimes differentiated in a division of labor: "such contemporary theoretical spaces as post-structuralism, dominant feminism, ethnic studies, and the critique of colonial discourse meet and intersect in the analytic space represented by U.S. third world feminism." Sandoval points out that "this other kind of feminist theoretical activity" caused "a rupture," "a crisis in the terms of dominant feminist theory and activity." "[A] theory of difference—imported from Europe—could subsume, if not solve it." "This recognition but concomitant deflection or sublimation of U.S. third world feminism can be tracked throughout the text of hegemonic feminist theory."[46]

Conclusion: Hopeful Ironies

An emphasis on multiple identities and non-unified subjects brings together political investments across several "divides" here. Ironically, academic feminism is deeply indebted theoretically to this proliferation of lesbian identities, even though this influence is not always understood or acknowledged. I think drawing upon this interconnection is hopeful, pointing to the possibilities of *conscious and appreciated* mutual influences. Current academic work "theorizing lesbianism" shifts the "theory" vs. "experience" divide in the "straight/lesbian" split, as does current work on race, but challenges to what counts as theory are still needed.

Notes

When I first considered this essay I talked with some colleagues about making it fully collaborative, but practical time constraints enforced more single authorial responsibility, and it ends up being written in my style and with my special concerns centered. Still, quite a few people were involved in the thinking and writing of this essay. Biddy Martin and Evelyn Fox Keller urged me to undertake it; and Lata Mani, Ruth Frankenberg, and Harriet Mullen all spent many hours both talking about it and reading pieces while we still mulled over the possibilities of making it a collective effort. Caren Kaplan and Donna Haraway were enCOURAGEing readers during the processes of writing and Chela Sandoval was inspirational in the midst of life's traumas. Marianne Hirsch, Carla Freccero, and Juliana Schiesari were suggestive readers and editors, and Eve Sedgwick and her Duke graduate students in "Literature and the 'Invention of Homosexuality' " gave me a chance to argue my conclusions here and see new connections with graduate student experiences in making theory today. Chandra Mohanty has helped in final revisions. A Mellon Fellowship from Cornell University has given me more time to work and write.

1. Some of these formulations I've already argued in "The Situation of Lesbianism as Feminism's Magical Sign: Contests for Meaning and the U.S. Women's Movement, 1968–1972," *Communication* 9 (1986): 65–92. For some specific purges of lesbians and lesbian zap actions in 1968–1972 see Sidney Abbott and Barbara Love, *Sappho Was a Right-On Woman: A Liberated View of Lesbianism* (New York: Stein & Day, 1973). For the political locations of gay recruitment see John D'Emilio, *Sexual Politics, Sexual Communities: The Making of a Homosexual Minority in the United States, 1940–1970* (Chicago: Univ. of Chicago Press, 1983). Contemplating and analyzing lesbian repositionings and new coalitions are: Gayle Rubin, "The Leather Menace: Comments on Politics and S/M," in *Coming to Power: Writings and Graphics on Lesbian S/M*, eds. Samois (Palo Alto: Up Press, 1982), 192–225; Combahee River Collective, "A Black Feminist Statement" (April 1977), in *Capitalist Patriarchy and the Case for Socialist Revolution,* ed. Zillah Eisenstein (New York: Monthly Review Press, 1978); Chela Sandoval, "Chapter Two: Toward a Theory of Oppositional Consciousness: U.S. Third World Feminism and the U.S. Women's Movement" (14 March 1988 draft unpublished diss., History of Consciousness, University of California, Santa Cruz). Compare with Donna Landry, "Beat Me! Beat Me! Feminist Appropriations of Sade" (ms. 1984).

2. In previous work I've suggested how "lesbianism as magical sign"—the formation fractured in these "Sex Wars"—was historically constructed; I've also suggested that the polarization of the sex radicals from identity politics is currently in flux. See King, "Magical Sign," and Katie King, "Audre Lorde's Lacquered Layerings: The Lesbian Bar as a Site of Literary Production," *Cultural Studies* 2 (1988): 321–342.

3. The controversial Scholar and The Feminist IX Conference, "Towards a Politics of Sexuality," held on 24 April 1982 at Barnard College, New York City.

4. Rubin, "The Leather Menace"; B. Ruby Rich, "Review Essay: Feminism and Sexuality in the 1980's," *Feminist Studies* 12 (1986): 525–561; Cherríe Moraga, "Played between White Hands: A Response to the Barnard Sexuality Conference Coverage," *off our backs* (July 1982); Barbara Smith, *Home Girls: A Black Feminist Anthology* (New York: Kitchen Table: Women of Color Press, 1983); Hortense Spillers, "Interstices: A Small Drama of Words," in *Pleasure and Danger: Exploring Female Sexuality,* ed. Carole S. Vance (Boston: Routledge, 1984), 73–100: see comments about proliferations of gender in Sandoval, "Oppositional Consciousness"; Barbara Smith, "Toward a Black Feminist Criticism," *conditions: two* (1977): 25–44; and the reading of Smith in Teresa de Lauretis, "Eccentric Subjects: Feminist Theory and Historical Consciousness," *Feminist Studies,* 16, 2 (1990), 115–150.

5. Forming, as they do, the ground of much feminist theory in the academy, I too find it difficult to extricate thinking from them.

6. Sandoval, "Oppositional Consciousness."

7. B. Ruby Rich, "Review Essay"; Sandoval, "Oppositional Consciousness"; Bell Hooks [Gloria Watkins], *Feminist Theory: From Margin to Center* (Boston: South End, 1984); King, "Magical Sign"; Katie King, "Feminism and Writing Technologies" (paper delivered at Modern Language Association, New Orleans, 28 December 1988).

8. Ellen Willis, "Feminism, Moralism and Pornography," *The Village Voice* (15 October 1979); Vance, *Pleasure and Danger*.

9. Audre Lorde, *Zami: a new spelling of my name* (Watertown, MA: Persephone, 1982); Alice Walker, "A Letter of the Times, or Should This Sado-Masochism Be Saved?" in *Against Sadomasochism: A Radical Feminist Analysis,* eds. Robin Ruth Linden, Darlene R. Pagano, Diana E. H. Russell, Susan Leigh Star (East Palo Alto, CA: Frog in the Well, 1982), 205–209; Linden et al., *Against Sadomasochism.*

10. Alice Echols, "The Taming of the Id: Feminist Sexual Politics, 1968–1983," in Vance, *Pleasure and Danger,* 50–72; cf. Hester Eisenstein, *Contemporary Feminist Thought* (Boston: G.K. Hall, 1983).

11. Rubin, "The Leather Menace," and "Thinking Sex: Notes for a Radical Theory of the Politics of Sexuality," in Vance, *Pleasure and Danger,* 267–319; Pat Califia, "Feminism and Sadomasochism," *Heresies* 12 (1981).

12. Camilla Decarnin, "Interview with Five Fag-Hagging Women," *Heresies* 12 (1981): 10–14.

13. Joan Nestle, *A Restricted Country* (Ithaca, NY: Firebrand, 1987); Lorde, *Zami;* King, "Audre Lorde's Lacquered Layerings."

14. B. Smith, *Home Girls;* Aurora Levins Morales and Rosario Morales, *Getting Home Alive* (Ithaca, NY: Firebrand, 1986); Cherríe Moraga, *Loving in the War Years: lo que nunca paso por sus labios* (Boston: South End, 1983); Cherríe Moraga, "The Shadow of a Man"; and "An Interview with Cherríe Moraga" by Dorothy Allison, Tomas Almaguer, and Jackie Goldsby, *Outlook* 4 (1989): 46–57; Oliva M. Espin, "Cultural and Historical Influences on Sexuality in Hispanic/Latin Women: Implications for Psychotherapy," in Vance, *Pleasure and Danger,* 149–164; Gloria Hull, *Color, Sex, and Poetry: Three Women Writers of the Harlem Renaissance* (Bloomington: Indiana University Press, 1987); Cherríe Moraga and Gloria Anzaldúa, *This Bridge Called My Back: Writings by Radical Women of Color* (Watertown, MA: Persephone, 1981); see comments by Chela Sandoval, "Oppositional Consciousness." See also white women commenting on the race of sex: Mab Segrest, *My Mama's Dead Squirrel: Lesbian Essays on Southern Culture* (Ithaca, NY: Firebrand, 1985); Minnie Bruce Pratt, "Identity: Skin Blood Heart," in *Yours in Struggle: Feminist Perspectives on Racism and Anti-Semitism* by Elly Bulkin, Minnie Bruce Pratt, and Barbara Smith (New York: Long Haul, 1984); Nestle, *Restricted Country;* Ruth Frankenberg, "The Social Construction of Whiteness" (paper delivered at "Feminisms and Cultural Imperialism: Politics of Difference" conference, Cornell University, 23 April 1989).

15. The sex you do for money and the sex you do for yourself may be the same or different, may situate one in terms of personal/political identities or may not. Swasti

Mitter, *Common Fate, Common Bond: Women in the Global Economy* (London: Pluto Press, 1986); Gail Pheterson, ed., *A Vindication of the Rights of Whores* (Seattle: Seal, 1989); *Sex Work: Writings by Women in the Sex Industry,* Frederique Delacoste and Priscilla Alexander, eds. (Pittsburgh: Cleis, 1987); Laurie Bell, ed., *Good Girls, Bad Girls: Feminism and Sex Trade Workers Face to Face* (Seattle: Seal, 1987; Toronto: Women's, 1987) [Conference in Toronto on Politics of Prostitution and Pornography, 22–24 November 1985].

16. Rubin, "Thinking Sex"; cf. Teresa de Lauretis, "Sexual Indifference and Lesbian Representation," *Theatre Journal* 40 (1988): 155–177.

17. Rubin, "Thinking Sex"; Lata Mani, "Multiple Mediations: Feminist Scholarship in the Age of Multi-National Reception," *Inscriptions,* special issue on Predicaments of Theory Conference, University of California, Santa Cruz, Summer 1989, forthcoming.

18. Bernice Johnson Reagon, "Coalition Politics: Turning the Century," in Smith, *Home Girls,* 356–368; Biddy Martin and Chandra Mohanty, "Feminist Politics: What's Home Got To Do With It?" in *Feminist Studies/Critical Studies,* ed. Teresa de Lauretis (Bloomington: Indiana University Press, 1986), 191–212; Caren Kaplan, "Deterritorializations: The Rewriting of Home and Exile in Western Feminist Discourse," *Cultural Critique* 9 (1987): 187–198.

19. Todd Jailer, "The Widening Orbit of the University Press," *Small Press* 7 (1989): 10–23; Tonya Bolden Davis, "Publish or Perish," *Small Press* 7 (1989): 31–33.

20. For example, in *Pleasure and Danger* Hortense Spillers eloquently hungers for a particular naming of sex by black women, in a particular non-fiction discursive theory. Spillers, "Interstices."

21. See Caren Kaplan's feminist appropriation of Edward Said's "traveling theory" in "Questions of Travel: The Limits of Exile and the Poetics of Displacement" (paper delivered at Modern Language Association, New Orleans, 30 December 1988) and her analysis of mixed genres of de-essentialized writing as poetics of displacement in "The politics of signification in the poetics of displacement: historical and literary dislocation in *Dictee*" (MLA paper, New Orleans, 28 December 1988). See also Sharon Willis, "Feminism's Interrupted Genealogies," *Diacritics* (1988): 29–41. One might also note who is being published in which journals. Now that feminists are published in, for example, *Critical Inquiry, Representations, Diacritics* (examples of cultural analysis), in the major journals of specific disciplines, and with some exciting new academic feminist journals representing new political interests and theoretical investments, what has changed in the status of those gatekeeping, brave, academic standbys, *Signs* and *Feminist Studies?* Which academic feminists are in each of these locations? Not to mention who is not reading (has never read?) *Sinister Wisdom, Conditions, Calyx, Sage, Trivia, Zeta, Outlook,* for immediate examples; which of these movement journals has narrowed the range of genres they publish, and for what political reasons?

22. Donna Haraway, "The Promises of Monsters: A Reproductive Politics of the Inappropriate/d Other" (talk at Rochester University, April 20, 1989); Faith Beckett, "Notes on Reading Ogunyemi and Anzaldua," *HisCon/HerScam: the HistCon fanzine,* forthcoming.

23. Biddy Martin, "Lesbian Identity and Autobiographical Difference[s]," in *Life/Lines: Theorizing Women's Autobiography*, eds. Bella Brodski and Celeste Schenck (Ithaca, NY: Cornell University Press, 1988), 77–103.

24. On radical feminism see Alison Jagger, *Feminist Politics and Human Nature* (Totowa, NJ: Rowman & Allanheld, 1983); Alice Echols, "The New Feminism of Yin and Yang," in *Powers of Desire: The Politics of Sexuality*, eds. Ann Snitow, Christine Stansell, and Sharon Thompson (New York: Monthly Review Press/New Feminist Library, 1983), 439–459. On U.S. feminism, and black and lesbian writing see Toril Moi, *Sexual/Textual Politics: Feminist Literary Theory* (New York: Methuen, 1985). For an example of a rehistoricized intervention inscribing a specific definition of feminist theory see Teresa de Lauretis, "Displacing Hegemonic Discourses: Reflections on Feminist Theory in the 1980's," *Inscriptions* 3/4 (1988): 127–144. For an alternative history of radical feminist theory see Alice Echols, "Cultural Feminism: Feminist Capitalism and the Anti-Pornography Movement," *Social Text* 7 (1983): 34–53. Cf. Pamela Allen, *Free Space: a perspective on the small group in women's liberation* (Washington, NJ: Times Change Press, 1970) and Celestine Ware, *Woman Power: The Movement for Women's Liberation* (New York: Tower, 1970); for my alternative analysis see King, "Magical Sign." For an analysis distinguishing the work of women of color from feminist essentialisms and suggesting a poststructuralist location see Linda Alcoff, "Cultural Feminism vs. Post-structuralism: the identity crisis in feminist theory, "*Feminist Theory in Practice and Process*, eds. Micheline R. Malson, Jean F. O'Barr, Sarah Westpahl-Wihe, and Mary Wye. (Chicago: Univ. of Chicago Press, 1988), 295–326; cf. Sandoval, "Oppositional Consciousness." Socialist feminism and its "others": radical feminism, cultural feminism, black feminism; its variants: British and U.S. versions, object-relations or standpoint theorists and psychoanalytic versions are implicated in these repositionings, and redrawn commonalities.

25. Zap actions, as Celestine Ware points out, are indebted to "elements of Yippie language and psychology," a kind of anarchist protest, sometimes spontaneous, sometimes planned. Here I'm suggesting a genealogy of one strategy in art activism. See Ware, *Woman Power*, 33; compare Douglas Crimp, "AIDS: Cultural Analysis/ Cultural Activism," *October* 43 (Winter 1987): 3–16 (look especially at the illustrations documenting various ACT UP actions).

26. Katie King, "Feminism and Writing Technologies" (paper delivered at Modern Language Association, New Orleans, 28 December 1988); King, "Bibliographic Practice and a Feminist Apparatus of Literary Production" (paper delivered at the Society for Textual Scholarship, CUNY, 7 April 1989); Richard A. Peterson, "Six Constraints on the Production of Literary Works," *Poetics* 14 (1985): 45–68; Robert Escarpit, *Sociology of Literature*, trans. Ernest Pick (London: Frank Cass, 1971; 1st French ed., 1958; 1st English ed. 1965); Mark Schulman, "Gender and Typographic Culture: Beginning to Unravel the 500-year Mystery," in *Technology and Women's Voices: Keeping in Touch*, ed. Cheris Kramarae (New York: Routledge, 1988) 98–115. See also Bruce Robbins, "The Politics of Theory," *Social Text* 21 (1987/8).

27. Cf. Donna Haraway, "Situated Knowledges: The Science Question in Feminism and the Privilege of Partial Perspective," *Feminist Studies* 14 (1988): 575–599.

28. A use that might borrow from and revamp the marxist notion of the proletarian "standpoint." Barbara Christian, "The Race for Theory," *Cultural Critique* 6 (1987): 51–63. See Jagger, *Feminist Politics* and Nancy Hartsock, *Money, Sex, and Power: Toward a Feminist Historical Materialism* (New York: Longman, 1983), and critiques by King, "Canons without Innocence: Academic Practices and Feminist Practices Making the Poem in the Work of Emily Dickinson and Audre Lorde" (diss. History of Consciousness, University of California, Santa Cruz, 1987) and Sandoval "Oppositional Consciousness." Cf. Bell Hooks, *Talking Back: thinking feminist, thinking black* (Boston: South End, 1989).

29. Christian's also belongs to a body of work that indicates that no gay/straight split can ever again be simply divided over sexual preference, as if outside race or as if white; parallel alliances, coalitions, and shifting momentary commonalities mark political struggles in feminism today. (And presumably always did.) See also Lorraine Bethel and Barbara Smith, eds., "Introduction," *conditions five: the black women's issue* (1979): 11–15; Smith, *Home Girls*.

30. For some acute institutional analysis see June Howard, "Feminist Differings: Recent Surveys of Feminist Literary Theory and Criticism," *Feminist Studies* 14 (1988): 167–190. Christian's work is also, perhaps a little less obviously, an intervention into the narrowing definition of cultural feminism produced in the Sexuality Debates. Christian shifts from her analysis of "theory" the product and "theorizing" the activity to a specifically literary-critical critique of the devalued status of the authors of fiction and poetry and the aggrandizement of the authors of criticism and theory. I would differ with her recuperation of the valorized author (either of fiction or criticism) myself, but my own work on the status of "poetry" (parallel to Christian's investment in fiction) as a particular political object suggests that debates about "poetry" and the value of "authors rather than critics" are often contents that signal struggles about cultural feminism in the eighties. The construction of value of literary forms has been politicized in feminist literary criticism. Not only do feminist literary critics challenge the traditional values of women's writing, but they themselves participate in valuing some forms of writing over others. Genres of writing are highly important in these debates, as objects of knowledge, as producers of knowledge, as the very kinds of knowledge themselves. King, "Canons without Innocence."

31. "Hegemonic feminist theory" is a term pervasive within the debates which critique an unself-conscious feminist theory functioning as a colonial discourse. (See for example, Gayatri Chakravorty Spivak, *In Other Worlds: Essays in Cultural Politics* [New York: Routledge, 1988.]) Chandra Mohanty has pointed out to me that hegemonic feminist theory defines all feminist positions in relation to itself such that its centrality then necessitates that all feminisms must in turn define themselves in relation to it. In this essay I quote "hegemonic feminist theory" from Sandoval's "Oppositional Consciousness." See the section entitled "Hegemonic Feminism."

32. Sandra Harding, *The Science Question in Feminism* (Ithaca, NY: Cornell University Press, 1986); Donna Haraway, "A Manifesto for Cyborgs: Science, Technology, and Socialist Feminism in the 1980's," *Socialist Review* 80 (1985): 65–107; de Lauretis, "Sexual Indifference," and "Eccentric Subjects."

33. See Diana Russell and Nicole Van de Ven, *The Proceedings of the International Tribunal on Crimes Against Women* (East Palo Alto, CA: Frog in the Well, 1984);

Kathleen Barry, *Female Sexual Slavery* (New York: New York University Press, 1985). Robin Morgan, *Sisterhood is Global: The International Women's Movement Anthology* (New York: Anchor, 1984) and a critique by Chandra Talpade Mohanty, "Feminist Encounters: Locating the Politics of Experience," *Copyright* 1 (1987): 30–44. Joni Seager and Ann Olson, *Women in the World Atlas* (New York: Simon & Schuster/Touchstone/Pluto Press Project, 1986); New Internationalist, *Women: A World Report* (New York: Oxford, 1985). Pheterson, *Rights of Whores;* Bell, *Good Girls, Bad Girls.* Aihwa Ong, "Colonialism and Modernity: Feminist Re-Presentations of Women in Non-Western Societies," *Inscriptions* 3/4 (1988): 79–93; Rey Chow, "Uses of Feminism in a Non-Western Context" (paper delivered at "Feminisms and Cultural Imperialism: Politics of Difference" conference, Cornell University, 22 April 1989); Kaplan, "Deterritorializations."

34. Jagger, *Feminist Politics;* King, "Canons without Innocence"; Sandoval, "Oppositional Consciousness."

35. Rubin, "The Leather Menace"; Echols, "Cultural Feminism"; cf. Kathleen M. Weston and Lisa B. Rofel, "Sexuality, Class, and Conflict in a Lesbian Workplace," *Signs* 9 (1984): 623–646.

36. Rubin, "The Leather Menace"; Combahee River Collective, "A Black Feminist Statement."

37. ACT UP, see for example *October* 43 (1987), "Issue on AIDS: Cultural Analysis/ Cultural Activism." Cf. Simon Watney, *Policing Desire: Pornography, AIDS and the Media* (Minneapolis: University of Minnesota, 1987). Also The NAMES Project, for example Cindy Ruskin, Matt Herron, and Deborah Zemke, *The Quilt: Stories From The NAMES Project* (New York: Pocket, 1988).

38. Cindy Patton, *Sex and Germs: the Politics of AIDS* (Boston: South End, 1985); cf. Hunter Madsen and Marshall Kirk, *After the Ball: How America Will Conquer Its Fear and Hatred of Gays in the 90s* (New York: Doubleday, 1989).

39. See landmark series in *San Francisco Examiner* 4 June–25 June 1989, "Gay in America: 16-Part Report."

40. Women's AIDS Network, *Lesbians and AIDS: What's the Connection?* (San Francisco: SF AIDS Foundation and the SF Department of Public Health, July 1986; Rev. October 1987); Cindy Patton and Janis Kelly, *Making It: A Woman's Guide to Sex in the Age of AIDS,* Spanish translation by Papusa Molina (Ithaca, NY: Firebrand Sparks Pamphlet #2, 1987); Santa Cruz AIDS Project, "Feeling the Heat: An Evening of Erotic Entertainment, For Women Only" (program from benefit performance, Kuumbwa Jazz Center, Santa Cruz, CA, 27 February 1988).

41. Sonia Johnson, *Going Out of Our Minds* (Trumansburg: Crossing Press, 1987); Jackie Winnow, "Lesbians Working on AIDS: Assessing the Impact on Health Care for Women," *Outlook* 5 (1989): 10–18 [adapted and shortened from her speech at the Conference of Lesbian Caregivers & the AIDS Epidemic, San Francisco, January 1989]. "PWA Coalition Portfolio," *October* 43 (1987): 147–168; Suki Ports, "Needed (For Women and Children)," *October* 43 (1987): 169–176; Carol Leigh, "Further Violations of Our Rights," *October* 43 (1987): 177–182.

42. Amber Hollibaugh and Cherríe Moraga, "What We're Rollin Around in Bed With—
     Sexual Silences in Feminism: A Conversation toward Ending Them" *Heresies* 12
     (1981); Frigga Haug et al., *Female Sexualization: A Collective Work of Memory*,
     trans. Erica Carter (London: Verso, 1987). Trinh T. Minh-ha, "Not You/Like You:
     Post-Colonial Women and the Interlocking Questions of Identity and Difference,"
     Inscriptions 3/4 (1988): 71–77; *Woman, Native, Other: Writing Postcoloniality and
     Feminism* (Bloomington: Indiana University Press, 1989); dir. *Reassemblage*, Idera,
     1982; dir. *Naked Spaces—Living is Round*, Idera, 1985; dir. *Surname Viet Given
     Name Nam*, Idera, 1989.

43. Barry D. Adam, "Homosexuality Without a Gay World: Pasivos y Activos en
     Nicaragua." *Outlook* 4 (1989): 74–82; Tatiana Schreiber and Lynn Stephen, "AIDS
     Education—Nicaraguan Style," *Outlook* 4 (1989): 78–80; Ramon A. Gutierrez,
     "Must We Deracinate Indians to Find Gay Roots?" *Outlook* 4 (1989): 61–67. For a
     model that might be adapted for imagining gay organization in transnational terms,
     see The University Museum, University of Pennsylvania, *Public Culture: Bulletin
     of the Project for Transnational Cultural Studies* 1:1 (1988) and 1:2 (1989).

44. Cf. Lourdes Arguelles and B. Ruby Rich, "Homosexuality, Homophobia, and
     Revolution: Notes toward an Understanding of the Cuban Lesbian and Gay Male
     Experience, Part 1," *Signs* 9 (1984): 683–699; John D'Emilio, "Capitalism and Gay
     Identity," in *Powers of Desire,* 100–113; and D'Emilio, *Sexual Politics.* For a set
     of imperatives through which to read emerging lesbianisms in specific global loca-
     tions see Lata Mani, "Multiple Mediations," for a possible model for how to read:
     Anu, "Sexuality, Lesbianism and South Asian Feminism," "Who Is A Lesbian?"
     "Who Are We?" and "Life in the Interstices," in *Between the Lines: An Anthology
     by Pacific/Asian Lesbians of Santa Cruz, California,* eds. C. Chung, A. Kim, A.K.
     Lemeshewsky (Santa Cruz: Dancing Bird Press, 1987), pp. 10–13; 26–7; 35–6; 42,
     and *Connexions* 3 (1982), "Global Lesbianism I"; 10 (1983), "Global Lesbianism II";
     29 (1989), "Lesbian Activism issue." Also modeling issues of multiple receptions/
     agencies Aihwa Ong, *Spirits of Resistance and Capitalist Discipline, Factory Women
     in Malaysia* (New York: SUNY, 1987).

45. See current catalogues from Kitchen Table: Women of Color Press (New York City)
     and Firebrand Press (Ithaca, New York) for examples, and notice roles in distribution
     as well as in publication.

46. Sandoval, "Oppositional Consciousness"; see also Sharon Willis, "Feminism's Inter-
     rupted Genealogies."

II
In Dialogue With

5

Replacing Feminist Criticism

Peggy Kamuf

What is the place of feminist critical practice in the institution, in particular, the university? Like many invitations to debate, this question seems destined to elicit answers in the form of paired oppositions. It can function, that is, to define potential relative positions as in formal argument. And for this reason, it is unlikely that this particular inquiry will ever lead beyond the limits of its own form and toward a response that is not already constrained by those limits. How can a question be posed here without reverting to the very terms of opposition which feminist theory has sought to undo?

In one sense, the remarks which follow attempt to unravel the logic of relative positions. If there is an answer to the question with which I began, it will not be found in some theoretical stand called for here but rather in the erosion of the very ground on which to take a stand. In another sense, by going over again, so as to erode, some old ground, I hope to leave open the possibility of reframing another question in the necessary terms of a feminist critique of institutions. This other question attempts to articulate the object with the place of critical activity.[1]

In a recent article which argues that feminist scholars cannot continue to study exclusively literature by women, the author suggests as one reason the increased pressures to streamline university curricula, thereby possibly endangering any activity which locates itself too singularly in the margins of a central academic tradition.[2] This view would seem to be part of a growing consensus among those involved in women's studies in general, that they must prepare to respond to an imminent re-centralization of the university. I refer you, for another example, to the debate about "mainstreaming" women's studies in *Women's Studies Quarterly* (Spring/Summer 1981).

In very general terms, such proposals to resituate feminist critical activity appear to rest on a number of unexamined political or theoretical judgments. For example, one finds there a surprising degree of assent to the notion that a recentralized university economy is the inevitable solution to an academic recession, even though this view may also entail subscribing to the principle—which has a certain currency right now—that whatever is good for business is good for the rest of social institutions. This uncritical acceptance of the principle of centrality would relocate at the center of the human enterprise a feminist criticism which has been redefined to reflect, as this same critic writes, "something more in line with what life is really like" [Spector, ibid.]. In this fashion, humanist metaphors of centrality work to coordinate a model of the efficient (i.e., cost-effective) institution with the notion of literature as mimetic representation. What I want to outline briefly is how a recentering of feminist theory can be seen to derive from a dominant pattern of ideological assumptions. I will be suggesting that by delimiting as the object of criticism literature by but also about, for and against women, this central form of feminist theory has already made certain assumptions about the place of critical activity within socio-political structures and their institutions. As one consequence, the attempt to redefine that object and relocate that activity may not be able to acknowledge how it risks getting misplaced.

The feminist critique of cultural institutions (including literature) has, in large part, proceeded from the evidence of woman's traditional exclusion and has therefore implied either that those institutions must be expanded to include what has been excluded (for example, by "mainstreaming" women's literature) or that they must be abandoned in favor of distinctly feminine-centered cultural models. These opposing strategies, in other words, both rest on the same analysis of phallocentrism's most readily evident feature—the order of women's exclusion—and proceed in practice to attempt to correct or reverse that feature at the same level at which it appears. What is thus left intact, perhaps, are the regions where the logic of exclusion disguises its operations more completely. One result may have been a feminist theory that accepts a determination of its place within the larger structure that anchors phallocentrism in culture. I take as an example of this limitation a feminist theory which accepts the place assigned to it by the disciplinary traditions of humanism; in this I am following, up to a certain point, a road which has already been mapped by Michel Foucault in his analysis of humanistic thought and its institutions. I will be looking for the possible extensions that could lead us beyond a too-narrowly defined field of feminist practice. To do so, however, may mean to invite a question about that "us" just offered, the pronoun which signals a common and thus, in a sense, singular subject—or object—of feminist theory.

There are two axes to Foucault's critique of what, in a French institutional context, are called the human sciences, or, less formally but perhaps more accurately, the sciences of man, which include both humanities and social sciences. The first axis concerns the object of humanistic inquiry—what it is that is studied—and the second concerns the aim—what it is that is gained (or simply produced) by that study. Briefly, this critique sets out from the commonplace notion that the human sciences take as their object "man," considered from the several angles of the conditions of his existence and his symbolic capacities. Yet, whereas traditional (i.e., humanistic) history of science tends to extend this model of inquiry back to the renaissance (and even before) as well as forward indefinitely into the future, Foucault's archaeology contends that the objectification of "man"—its appearance within the field of knowable objects—has a much more recent history, only since about the end of the eighteenth century in Europe. It is, then, as a rather novel epistemological invention that "man"—in his social, psychological, and linguistic manifestations—occupies the center stage of inquiry. This view is eccentric in the sense that it does not take up the humanistic assumption of a trans-historical and universal center of thought and, as such, it can theorize about what may lie outside the self-reflecting circle of that thought. In historical terms, for example, Foucault is able to posit both 1) that the human sciences and their object displaced another epistemological domain in which "man" stood at the limit of the represented field, organizing its procedures but not himself interrogated; and 2) that the modern epistemological construct may itself have been brought to the brink of another displacement that would efface "man" as either the hidden or the all-too-visible center of thought. On the last page of *Les Mots et les choses* [*The Order of Things*], one reads: "Man is an invention which the archaeology of our thought can easily show to be of recent date. And perhaps to be nearing its end" [my translation]. This process of ending has begun when thought moves beyond the limits of what has made it possible to think "man" as an autonomous whole, a circumscribable object, and into those regions surrounding the humanistic homeland, what one might call the no-man's land of the unconscious, the autonomous structures of language and the dynamics of history.

Although this particular evaluation of "man-centered" tradition has only been sketched here in its most general outline, it may be possible at least to conjecture along what lines it could intersect with a reflection about an effective feminist practice of criticism. One might conclude, for example, that Foucault's careful excavation of the consolidated image of man on the face of modern Western society's knowledge of itself confirms the exclusion which is a hidden consequence of the identification of human with masculine. Isn't it precisely this exclusion which feminist scholars in all the disciplines of the human sciences have set out to expose and to rectify? Foucault's own conclusion, however, about the necessary displacement of a man-centered or (in less exclusive terms) human-centered epistemology might also give feminist scholars reason to pause and to wonder to what extent their efforts must remain caught as a reflection of the same form of nineteenth-century humanism from which we have inherited our pervasively androcentric modes of thought. In other words, if one can accept the major part of this analysis of how and why Western thought about human forms has taken the shape it has, then can one also conclude that modifying that shape to include its feminine contours will result in something fundamentally different? If, on the other hand, the empirical rectification of an empirical error can only result in yet another form of that error which is the possibility of a totalizing reference to an object—whether masculine, feminine, or somehow both—then what is put in question here is perhaps the idea that feminist criticism can seek to define its object and still practice an effective critique of power structures. To put it yet another way: if feminist theory lets itself be guided by questions such as what is women's language, literature, style, or experience from where does it get its faith in the form of these questions to get at truth, if not from the same central store that supplies humanism with its faith in the universal truth of man? And what if notions such as "getting-at-the-truth-of-the-object" represented a principal means by which the power of power structures are sustained and even extended?

This, in effect, is the question which Foucault has been asking in *Surveiller et punir* [*Discipline and Punish*] and *La Volonté de savoir* [*The Will to Knowledge*]. Reviewing the institutional development of the human sciences in the nineteenth century, he discerns behind the codified procedures for increasing knowledge about "man" in all his many aspects a growing technology of control and a proliferation of instruments of power. It is not so much that the human sciences do not produce knowledge, but rather that the codification of human experience and the investigation of human interaction, at the same time as they extend the empirical base of a given discipline, also open up new and previously uncharted regions for the control (or the *discipline* in another, less ivory-tower sense) of that experience and that interaction. This, together with the fact that the empirical human sciences necessarily operate with the concept of a norm rather than physical or a priori law, goes a long way towards explaining why these disciplines have historically been active partners in institutions which execute social norms by means of exclusion and internment—asylums, prisons, juvenile homes, hospitals, and, not least, schools.

Once again, this is hardly an adequate summary of consistently intricate analyses, but it will suffice if it indicates what must interest feminist theory in those analyses, to wit: that power has pursued its aim of social control through proliferating institutions and that these institutions may be understood in many cases as the spatial realizations of the principles of humanistic knowledge. To put it more simply and with still less justice to Foucault's analyses: power and knowledge maintain highly ambiguous relations which get articulated in institutions.

Returning now to the question of the place of feminist criticism, which is also the question of its relation to an institution, one might at least hesitate before replying that the criticism should aim to rectify an omission from the institutional mainstream, producing a knowledge about women which has been excluded there by a masculine-dominated ideology disguised as universal humanism. To expose and dismantle this disguise, in order to reach, as one feminist critic has described it, the authentic and essential human (as opposed to masculine) truths of literature may have an appeal as a theoretical program precisely because it replicates the familiar dream of humanism: a single center of truth to which all representation refers.[3] In its articulation with and within an institution, what is to prevent such a program from taking the form which that articulation has historically assumed, in Foucault's estimate at least—a centrally defined space of power? If feminist theory can be content to propose cosmetic modifications on the face of humanism and its institutions, will it have done anything more than reproduce the structure of woman's exclusion in the same code which has been extended to include her?

This would seem to be one of the primary limitations of an assumption guiding much current feminist scholarship: an unshaken faith in the ultimate arrival at essential truth through the empirical method of accumulation of knowledge, knowledge about women. Consider for example the following passage from an anthology of essays on feminist literary theory in which the author proposes a revision of aesthetic models to include specifically feminine components:

> Through information gleaned from research in women's studies, I see a gradual falling together of truths and probabilities about women—their experience, their history, their wisdom, their culture—and this constellation will provide the basis for a feminine aesthetic. . . . Until we have had a chance to study women's art, history and culture more extensively, so as to begin to *codify the patterns of consciousness* delineated therein, I believe we will be unable to develop a more substantial feminine aesthetic.[4]

What is striking about this passage, I think, is first the combined appeal to a specific "we" and to a certain method of defining who that "we" is. The "we," in other words, is constituted by a shared faith in its eventual consolidation at the end of an empirical process which will have codified its patterns of consciousness. Secondly, there is an implicit assumption in such programs that this knowledge about women can be produced in and of itself without seeking any support within those very structures of power which—or so it is implied—have prevented knowledge of the feminine in the past. Yet what is it about those structures which could have succeeded until now in excluding such knowledge if it is not a similar appeal to a "we" that has had a similar faith in its own eventual constitution as a delimited and totalizable object?

I earlier pointed to two contrary feminist strategies which share a humanist determination of woman's exclusion: on the one hand an expansion of institutions to include at their center what has been historically excluded; on the other hand, the installing of a counter-institution based on feminine-centered cultural models. By way of indicating another, yet-to-be-determined level of feminist critical practice, I am going to conclude by a strategic shift within the outlines of Foucault's archaeology. That analysis, you recall, ends with the end of man as the central object of thought. What I have suggested above is that to the extent that feminist thought assumes the limits of humanism, it may be reproducing itself as but an extension of those limits and reinventing the institutional structures that it set out to dismantle. By stepping back now from the field which opposes a certain feminist centrality to Foucauldian eccentricity, it may be possible to imagine for a moment that when one or the other speaks of the end of man in Western thought, they are referring *essentially* to the same thing. What one may too easily overlook is the odd relation that can pertain between a discourse which, like most feminist discourse, situates itself at the center of the humanist enterprise and perhaps supplies a new impetus for the totalizing quest of that enterprise, and a discourse which, like Foucault's, situates itself frankly outside this center from where it may envision the approaching end of humanistic goals. What one and the other position may be said to share is the fixity of their situation in relation to an enclosing limit. Each discourse may be seeking to consolidate, by accumulating evidence, its right to speak on one side or the other of this limit. Thus whether one speaks from inside about an end of man and the beginning of *authentic* non-sexist humanism, or from outside about the end of humanism and the beginning of humanity's unthinkable other, it is finally the metaphor of inside and outside which dominates in one direction and the other. And it is at least questionable whether this opposition can ever be simply separated from the long and potent series of other oppositions which it organizes and commands, including inclusion and exclusion, the same and the different, self and other, "us" and "them."[5] That this list underwrites and is underwritten by gender opposition no doubt needs no further elaboration here. Having understood that, however, can a feminist practice on this cultural text stop there, leaving oppositional logic in place and in the place it has always occupied as the unquestioned ground and limit of thought?

One will, of course, continue to find oneself engaged on this ground by a political-social distribution of effects that shapes our institutions and that itself remains an oppressive application of oppositional determinations. Yet through the practice of literature one can understand how every meaning structure attempts to conceal its own contradiction, how logical oppositions rest on an aporia, on undecidability. Thus an engagement of patriarchal meaning structures which does not keep in view its own contradictory disengagement of that meaning can have little interest, finally, for feminist theory. That theory has more to learn from the shifts that affect a discourse on women and fiction which also situates itself in the institutional context. For example, the author of *A Room of One's Own* (the text of lectures read to two newly founded women's colleges) can read the history of woman's silence as a patriarchal invention, can acknowledge many of the structures which must be overcome to undo that silence, and yet can still write that "it is fatal for any one who writes to think of their sex. . . . It is fatal for a woman . . . in any way to speak consciously as a woman."[6] In the more than fifty years since Virginia Woolf gave her lectures, the institutional organization of woman's silence has changed its face. What still remains, however, is that lever of contradiction with which to disengage meaning from patterns of sexual opposition.

That feminist thought has yet to decide where to situate itself on the map of the known world's divisions—either in a canonical mainstream with its centers of learning and culture, or in an outlying and unexplored region—may be the clue that such generic distinctions cannot contain it. To pursue this analogy still further (and at the risk of leaving even further behind or below the solid ground of a more quotidian tread), what feminist thought can and has put in question is the capacity of any map to represent more than a fiction of the world's contours. The line traced along the eastern edge of North America, for example, the line following the extreme border of an American context, for all its inlets and protrusions, its islands and peninsulas, still can only demarcate with the fiction of an arbitrarily traced line the point at which land moves out to sea and the ground slips from beneath us.

At these limits, traced and then retraced, always in view of a greater accuracy of representation, a feminist practice can have its greatest force if, at the same time as it shifts the sands of an historical sedimentation, it leaves its own undecidable margins of indeterminacy visible, readable on the surface of the newly contoured landscape. That is, its own inevitable inaccuracy and lack of finality which must always show up wherever lines are drawn for the purpose of theoretical argument or for the more solid purpose of re-mapping an institution. It is tempting, of course, to assume that, once drawn, the lines of a representation can resist the eroding movement of a fluid element, and can keep the sea of fictions from wetting feet planted firmly in the ground. But that would be to deny a necessary plurivocality and plurilocality which even here, for example, press on the edge of these remarks. I am left, then, with room enough only to conclude from necessity: the necessity of replacing this discourse with another and of finding always another place from which to begin again.

Notes

This article formed part of an exchange between Kamuf and Nancy K. Miller which took place during a Symposium on Feminist Criticism held at Cornell University in October 1981.

1. It is here that these remarks will reflect what they owe to Elaine Marks, director of the Women's Studies Research Center at the University of Wisconsin-Madison.

2. Judith Spector, "Gender Studies: New Directions for Feminist Criticism," *College English* (April 1981), p. 376.

3. Marcia Holly, "Consciousness and Authenticity: Toward a Feminist Aesthetic," in *Feminist Literary Criticism: Explorations in Theory,* Donovan, ed. (Lexington: The University Press of Kentucky, 1975), p. 42.

4. Josephine Donovan, "Afterward: Critical Re-vision," in Donovan, pp. 77–79; emphasis added.

5. A critique of the project to put an end to "man" has been outlined by Jacques Derrida in "Les Fins de l'homme" ("The Ends of Man," Marges de la philosophie [Paris: Minuit, 1972]) where he writes: "What is difficult to think today is an end of man which is not organized by a dialectic of truth and negativity, an end of man which is not a teleology in the first person plural" (p. 144).

6. Virginia Woolf, *A Room of One's Own* (New York: Harcourt, Brace and World, 1957), p. 108.

6

The Text's Heroine: A Feminist Critic and Her Fictions

Nancy K. Miller

I will go so far as to risk this hypothesis: The sex of the addressor awaits its determination by or from the other. It is the other who will perhaps decide who I am—man or woman. Nor is this decided once and for all. It may go one way one time and another way another time.

Jacques Derrida, The Ear of the Other

Man has been raised in order to function, in order to address the world like a text destined to find its readers, while woman was elected to constitute a metaphorical other-world, a repose of thought which steps aside in order to dream for an instant.

Claudine Herrmann, Les Voleuses de langue

When the feminist critic institutionalizes the woman writer, what story authorizes her to do so? As I begin to answer that question, I will be locating myself in a discursively polemical (but personally irenic) relation to Peggy Kamuf's questions about what might constitute an "effective feminist practice of criticism,"[1] particularly in relation to the epistemological mapping and Foucauldian paradigms she so elegantly outlines. I want to say at the start, however, that I foresee no real agreement on this matter here or elsewhere, because I think that the question of an effective feminist practice is *insoluble*. Or rather, while there indeed exist effective practices—written documents or strategies which by their analyses and accounts move, persuade, even transform—I do not believe it is possible to theorize, to think aloud, the grounds of such a practice in a way that transcends powerful internal contradiction. (This may always be the case when practice and its demands precede theory, which historically has been the case with feminism.)

Before addressing the question of the woman writer—the woman who signs "woman" and the feminist critic who places her in the institution—I want now to map out the territory of the dilemma. It is characterized by the polarities of what might be thought of as metonymies as opposed to metaphors; psychohistorical needs as opposed to epistemological claims; material contingencies as opposed to theoretical urgencies. Those oppositions have also been named by Elaine Marks—in a presentation she described as existing in a zone somewhere between a working paper and a position paper at a Barnard College Women's Issues Luncheon (spring 1981)—as the American, empirical, and social science model of Women's Studies vs. the French ludic endeavor; the latter emerging from the more speculative operations of "les sciences de l'homme" engaged in by decentered subjects of the "feminine" (rather than "feminist") persuasion. This problematic may also be understood in relation to *shoes*: as in the sturdy, sensible sort worn by "American" feminists, and the more frivolous, elegant type worn by Cixous herself. This is in fact a Cixousian exemplum. In the course of an informal presentation, also at Barnard, in the fall of 1979, Hélène Cixous figured the same (American/French) paradigm in shoes in order to make a point about difference and recuperation: the danger of a feminist identification too readily perceived; and the distinction as well between lesbian and "homosexuelle."

I think that these polarizations are unfortunate, if all too accurate, when they separate *effectively* women who (ideally) might otherwise collaborate within a single institution or (more realistically) within the larger project of feminist scholarship, but they do not seem about to go away. And they are not going away, I think, because of a larger problem in the women's movement itself, a problem currently reflected in the debates on the proper place of Women's Studies—in the margins or in the mainstream—that Kamuf alludes to in her paper. The problem has everything to do with sexual identity and the ways in which those two terms should be understood, separately and conjoined. For the purposes of argument, but also because of the scene of my enunciation, I will align myself with those on the side of what Peggy Kamuf in these pages calls "correction"; with those who wish to "rectify or reverse women's exclusion" without, apparently (or at least sufficiently), taking the proper measure of the *epistemological* dangers implicit in such a position.

I will speak as one who believes that "we women" must continue to work for the woman who has been writing, because not to do so will reauthorize our oblivion. Perhaps I can expand upon my conviction that it matters who writes and *signs* woman by an example that in many ways works against me. It is the case of the *Portuguese Letters*. These are five letters published anonymously in Paris, in 1669, as being the translation of letters written in Portuguese. They were enormously popular, and for some the debate over their origins and authenticity is not over. (Indeed, in a 1979 paperback edition of the *Letters* [*Lettres de la religieuse portugaise*], Yves Florenne rehearses the "evidence" yet again, arguing for the true sound of "a woman's voice,"[2] the pained cries of a woman in love; or at least for the possibility that anonymous was a woman.) I believe—as ultimately Kamuf seems to—that the letters were probably written by a man, a

Frenchman and literary type (a hack, some say) named Guilleragues, though thought for centuries (by many) to have been written by a *real* Portuguese nun.

Why bother with this slight text, written (perhaps) in the final analysis, by a man? It serves in the French history of the novel not as *the* first novel, as opposed to other forms of prose fiction—for that place is occupied by the anonymously published *Princess of Clèves*—but literally as its pre-text. It prefigures—one might also say, it engenders or at least generates—the production of an epistolary fiction whose fundamental trope, I have argued in "I's' in Drag," is that of a "*penultimate* masochism, the always renewable figure of feminine suffering."[3] The nun's last words in the face of her fickle lover's persistent silence are these: "But I wish nothing more of you; I am mad to repeat the same things so often: I must give you up and think no more of you; I even think I will no longer write to you. Am I obliged to give you an exact account of all my various movements?" The *Portuguese Letters* are a rewriting of Ovid's *Heroides*. Ovid famously feminized the epic model of female suffering by scaling it down, casting it in elegiac verses: the imagined love letters, primarily written by abandoned women to their lovers, of which the exemplary case is Virgil's Dido, who made the fatal error of believing the man would stay and respect her in the morning.

It matters to me that the letters from a "Portuguese nun," as the case in point, situate their line of descent in a patrilineal fashion, because I think that the textualization—hence glamorization—of female suffering around the male is an important issue for women, though less simple than some feminists want to imagine, before and after the epistemological rupture Foucault diagnoses.[4] Indeed, society did not wait for the invention of man to repress "woman" or oppress women, and the "end of man" in no way precludes the reinscription of woman as Other. What bothers me about the metalogically "correct" position is what I take to be its necessary implications for practice: that by glossing "woman" as an archaic signifier, it glosses over the *referential* suffering of women. Moreover, and implicitly, to code as "cosmetic," and to foreclose as untimely, discussions of the author as sexually gendered subject in a socially gendered exchange—who produced, for example, *this* masochistic discourse and for whose benefit?—is to be too confident that nondiscursive practices will respond correctly to the correct theory of discursive practice. It may also be the case that having been killed off along with "man," the author can now be rethought beyond traditional notions of biography, now that through the feminist rewritings of literary history the adequacy of a masculine identity to represent the universal has been radically questioned.

In "Writing Like a Woman," Kamuf, preparing to review the debates over the origins and authorship of the *Portuguese Letters*—written by a man or by a woman—declares (arguing with Patricia Meyer Spacks in *The Female Imagination*):

> If the inaugural gesture of this feminist criticism is the reduction of the literary work
> to its signature and to the tautological assumption that the feminine "identity" is one

which signs itself with a feminine name, then it will be able to produce only tautological statements of dubious value: women's writing is writing signed by women. . . . If these . . . are the grounds of a practice of feminist criticism, then that practice must be prepared to ally itself with the fundamental assumptions of patriarchy which relies on the same principles. If, on the other hand, by "feminist" one understands a way of reading texts that points to the masks of truth with which phallocentrism hides its fictions, then one place to begin such a reading is by looking behind the mask of the proper name, the sign that secures our patriarchal heritage: the father's name and the index of sexual identity.[5]

Kamuf concludes, after applying deconstructive pressures to the terms of the debate, that by refusing the tautological and empirical definition of identity (writing as a woman is to be a woman writing) in favor of an attention to the figuration of resemblance (writing as a woman) one has at least staged another kind of *reading:* a reading that by refusing the metaphors of a hegemonic paternity—the signature—allows for the emergence of a less stable rhetoric of maternity; "reading a text . . . *as if,* in other words, it were illegitimate, recognized by its mother who can only give it a borrowed name."[6] But Kamuf—like Kristeva, whose interest in a female practice is related primarily to a more general concern with an avant-garde, dissident, and marginal work in language—would prefer to see "feminist" criticism address itself not to the productions signed by biological woman alone but to all productions that put the "feminine" into play—the feminine then being a modality or process accessible to both men and women. (This might also be said to be the case of Cixous in "The Laugh of the Medusa," where in one of her famous footnotes she lists Genet along with Colette and Marguerite Duras as examples of French writers who have produced inscriptions of femininity.)[7]

More locally, it doesn't matter to Kamuf's reading whether the *Portuguese Letters* were written by a woman or by a man, but it does to mine. Just as I care if *The Story of O* was written by "Pauline Réage" or Jean Paulhan, which is in fact the same example (though for me the pornographics of female submission is no more than—surely no worse than—the rhetoric of sentimental masochism). I prefer to think that this positioning of woman is the writing of a masculine desire attached to the male body. Just as I like to know that the Brontëan writing of female anger, desire, and selfhood issues from a female pen. This preference, as I indicated earlier, is not without its vulnerabilities. It could, I suppose, one day be proven definitively that the heroines of the *Letters* and *The Story of O* were female creations after all. I would then have to start over again. But it would be a different story, since the story of the woman who writes is *always* another story.[8] In "Ad/d Feminam" Catharine Stimpson astutely assesses the political implications of these bodily identities:

. . . male writers—a Genet—can appropriate the feminine as a stance for the male through which to express receptive subordination before God or a god-like phallus.

. . . Still other male writers, like a Henry James, write about women, particularly lovely victims. Self-consciously empathetic, they speak of and for the feminine.

Each of these strategies is limited, if only because of the obvious anatomical differences. . . . A male writer may speak of, for, to and from the feminine. He cannot speak, except fictively, of, for, to and from the female. This inability hardly has the dignity of a tragic fact, but it does have the grittiness of simple fact.[9]

This "grittiness of simple fact" has everything to do with the ways in which the signature of women has functioned historically: in terms of the body, the sexual ideologies that define it; in terms of civil status, the legal restrictions that construct it. I want to invoke briefly Virginia Woolf's speculation about Judith Shakespeare:

And undoubtedly . . . *her work would have gone unsigned.* That refuge she would have sought certainly. It was the relic of the sense of chastity that dictated anonymity to women even so late as the nineteenth century. Currer Bell, George Eliot, George Sand, all the victims of inner strife as their writings prove, sought ineffectively to veil themselves by using the name of a man. . . . *Anonymity runs in their blood.* The desire to be veiled still possesses them.[10]

The desire to be veiled that unveils the anxiety of a genderized and sexualized body, I would argue, is *not* what runs in the blood of the "Portuguese nun." What is at work there instead, I think, is a male (at least masculine) desire to paper over an anxiety about destination and reception: a sense of powerlessness about writing in a new genre addressed to an unknown "destinataire" that takes the abandoned woman's body—the next best thing to a female corpse—as its pretext. The woman-in-love figured here is the masochist Simone de Beauvoir analyzed in *The Second Sex,* whose passion turns to self-mutilation when it turns out that "no man really is God."[11]

In other words, what I read in the *Portuguese Letters* is an ideology of desire that allows woman to become a subject only upon the condition of her "subordination before . . . a god-like phallus." Just as we read of O:

O was happy that René had had her whipped and had prostituted her, because her impassioned submission would furnish her lover with the proof that she belonged to him, but also because the pain and shame of the lash, and the outrage inflicted on her by those who compelled her to pleasure when they took her, and at the same time delighted in their own without paying the slightest heed to hers, seemed to be the very redemption of her sins.[12]

"Mariane" the "nun" writes her third letter: "I saw you leave, I can't hope to ever see you return and yet I'm still alive: I've betrayed you, I beg your forgiveness. But don't grant it! Treat me severely! Don't judge that my feelings are violent enough! Be more difficult to satisfy! Tell me that you want me to die of love for you! And I beg you to give me this help so that I can overcome the weakness of my sex . . . . "[13] If "dying of love is a trope," as Kamuf queried during the round table, what is it a trope of? Kate Millett has interrogated the psycho-logics of these feminine investments in pain: "It is ingenious," she writes of Freud's "Femininity," "to describe masochism and suffering as inherently feminine. . . . [I]t justifies any conceivable domination or humiliation forced upon the female as mere food for her nature. To carry such a notion to its logical conclusion, abuse is not only good for woman but the very thing she craves."[14]

I arrive here, however, at the end of my "American" posture. For the next step in that agenda typically is to establish reading lists that reflect orthodox feminist positions, and to call for the production of literature with positive role models. To be fair, this prescriptive esthetics represents only one strain of criticism; it does not tell the whole story.[15] Nevertheless, hortatory formulations of this sort, "But women's literature must go beyond the scenarios of compromise, madness, and death. Although the reclamation of suffering is the beginning, its purpose is to discover the new world," threaten to erase the ambiguities of the feminist project, unless they are at the same time reproblematized, as is the case here with Elaine Showalter, who goes on, in her review of feminist tropologies, to cite literature, like Adrienne Rich's poetry, that has "gone beyond reclaiming suffering to its re-investment".[16] Nor would I argue that reading works by women because of the signature is an activity *ethically* superior—*because marginal*—to that of reading works by men; or works by women alongside those of men, though I myself *feel* it to be an absolutely compelling project. Indeed, I think that "intersextuality" (to borrow a coinage from Naomi Schor), has much to teach us.[17] Sand's reading and rewriting of Rousseau is as important as her reading of Staël; and what would James have done without Eliot? Nevertheless, I do believe in books and courses based on the signature even if, as in the case of the *Portuguese Letters, The Story of O,* and the novels of the Brontës, the signature was not at the time of reception a reliable index of sexual identity. (The exceptions in the final analysis only point to the rules.) Even though such lists and such courses may betray a naïve faith in origins, humanism, and centrality, because they also make visible the marginality, eccentricity, and vulnerability of women, they concretely challenge the confidence of humanistic discourse as *universality*.

Let us turn to Foucault before closing; to Foucault perhaps against Foucault at the end of "What Is an Author?" He imagines what would happen in a society "without need for an author":

No longer the tiresome repetitions:
"Who is the real author?"
"Have we proof of his authenticity and originality?"
"What has he revealed of his most profound self in his language?"
   New questions will be heard:
"What are the modes of existence of this discourse?"
"Where does it come from; how is it circulated; who controls it?"

"What placements are determined for possible subjects?"

"Who can fulfill these diverse functions of the subject?"

Behind all these questions we would hear little more than the murmur of indifference:

"What matter who's speaking?"[18]

This sovereign indifference, I would argue, is one of the "masks . . . behind which phallocentrism hides its fictions" (138); the authorizing function of its own discourse authorized the "end of woman" without consulting her. What matter who's speaking? I would answer it matters, for example, to women who have lost and still routinely lose their proper name in marriage, and whose signature— not merely their voice—has not been worth the paper it was written on; women for whom the signature—by virtue of its power in the world of circulation—in *not* immaterial. Only those who have it can play with not having it. We might want to remind ourselves of the status of women's signatures in France before the law of 1965:

> since 1965, a woman can exercise any profession without her husband's permission. She can alone establish a contract which concerns the maintenance of the home and open a personal bank account. Hereafter dual consent is necessary in order to buy, sell, mortgage a building . . . finalize a commercial lease . . . or make purchases on credit.[19]

In the place of proper closure, and in the face of insolubility: let us retain a "modern," posthumanistic reading of "literature" that has indeed begun to rethink the very locations of the center and the periphery, and within that fragile topology, the stability of the subject. But at the same time, we must live out (the hortatory always returns) a practical politics within the institution grounded in regional specificities. This is to call for, then, a decentered vision (*theoria*) but a centered action that will not result in a renewed invisibility. If feminists decide that the signature is a matter of indifference, if Women's Studies becomes gender studies, the *real* end of women in the institution will not be far off. The text's heroine will become again no more than a fiction.

What we might wish for instead, perhaps, is a female materialism attentive to the needs of the body as well as the luxuries of the mind. Can we imagine, or should we, a position that speaks in tropes and walks in sensible shoes?[20]

Notes

1. Peggy Kamuf, "Replacing Feminist Criticism," *Diacritics* (Summer 1982), 2 (12): 42–47, reprinted in this volume.

2. Yves Florenne, ed., *Lettres de la religieuse portugaise* (Paris: Librairie Générale Française, 1979), 77.

3. Nancy K. Miller, "'I's' in Drag: The Sex of Recollection," *The Eighteenth Century* (1981), 22 (1): 56.

4. Kamuf, "Replacing Feminist Criticism," pp. 106–107.

5. Kamuf, "Writing Like a Woman," *Women and Language in Literature and Society* eds. Sally McConnell-Ginet, Ruth Borker, and Nelly Furman (New York: Praeger, 1980), 285–86.

6. Kamuf, "Writing Like a Woman," 298.

7. Hélène Cixous, "The Laugh of the Medusa," trans. Keith Cohen and Paula Cohen, *Signs* (1976), 1(4): 875–94. Elsewhere in the essay, and in subsequent work as well, Cixous also makes claims for a feminine specificity, attached to a female body and libido.

8. Kaja Silverman, in a complexly argued essay on *The Story of O,* puts the matter well: "I do not intend to enter here into the general speculation about the identity of Pauline Réage. To some degree that speculation is irrelevant, since regardless of who actually wrote the novel, the subjectivity designated by the name 'Pauline Réage' is a pornographic construction." *"Histoire d'O:* The Construction of a Female Subject," *Pleasure and Danger,* ed. Carole B. Vance, (Boston and London: Routledge and Kegan Paul, 1984), 348.
   In this sense, perhaps, the pornographic signature, is always terminally conventional in the gendering of its positions. In *O m'a dit,* a book of "interviews" that Régine Deforges conducts with Pauline Réage, "Réage" describes the context of authorship: "I would never have been tempted to write [the book] if I hadn't met someone who wanted to read it. I would never have written it if there hadn't been this need to write a letter. It's a letter" [*O m'a dit* (Paris: Pauvert, 1975), 100]. In an interview with Germaine Brée about erotic writing, Alain Robbe-Grillet talks about men's and women's fantasies, and speculates about Dominique Aury ("Pauline Réage") and Jean Paulhan: "She wrote it for Paulhan. Or perhaps they wrote it together; I don't really know, I'm not familiar enough with it. Perhaps they really did both write it; no one has any idea how it was done. From the start, she's been the one who has collected the royalties, but what was Paulhan's role? *It's a couple's fantasy,* it's not necessarily someone's solitary fantasy" [Germaine Brée, "An Interview with Alain Robbe-Grillet," "What Interests Me is Eroticism," *Homosexualities and French Literature: Cultural Contexts/Critical Texts,* eds. George Stambolian and Elaine Marks (Ithaca: Cornell University Press, 1979), 91; emphasis added.]

9. Catharine Stimpson, "Ad/d Feminam: Women, Literature and Society," *Selected Papers from the English Institute,* ed. Edward Said (Baltimore: Johns Hopkins University Press, 1978), 179.

10. Virginia Woolf, *A Room of One's Own* (New York: Harcourt, Brace, and World, 1957), 52; emphasis added.

11. Simone de Beauvoir, *The Second Sex,* trans. H.M. Parshley (New York: Bantam, 1970), 612.

12. Pauline Réage, *The Story of O,* trans. Sabine d'Estrée (New York: Grove Press, 1967), 93.

13. Florenne, "Lettres de la religieuse portugaise," 80.

14. Kate Millett, *Sexual Politics* (New York: Doubleday, 1970), 194–95.

15. The position is laid out clearly enough in Cherri Register's "American Feminist Literary Criticism: A Bibliographical Introduction" in the Donovan volume Kamuf refers to. But it really seems an easy and early target. *Feminist Literary Criticism: Explanations and Theory,* ed. Josephine Donovan (Lexington: University of Kentucky Press, 1975).

16. Elaine Showalter, "Towards a Feminist Poetics," *The New Feminist Criticism: Women, Literature, Theory* (New York: Pantheon, 1985), 134. In a later overview, "Feminist Criticism in the Wilderness," Showalter takes a nonprescriptive position which is much closer to my own: "feminist critics," she concludes, must address themselves "to what women actually write, not in relation to a theoretical, political, metaphoric, or visionary ideal of what women ought to write." *The New Feminist Criticism,* 205.

17. Naomi Schor, "La Pérodie: Superposition dans 'Lorenzaccio'," *Michigan Romance Studies* (1982), 2: 85.

18. Michel Foucault, "What is an Author?" *Language, Counter-Memory, Practice,* ed. Donald F. Bouchard (Ithaca: Cornell University Press, 1980), 138.

19. Maité Albistur and Daniel Armogathe, eds., *Histoire du féminisme français* (Paris: Editions des femmes, 1957), 641–42.

20. I would like to thank Sandy Petrey and Christie V. McDonald for their help at several key moments in the development of this essay.

7

Parisian Letters:
Between Feminism and Deconstruction

Peggy Kamuf and Nancy K. Miller

July 26, 1989

Dear Peggy:

I'm sitting on the terrace of a stone house in Provence, looking out at a valley of vineyards and fruit trees, and to the insistent accompaniment of the local cicadas, trying to figure out what an "update" to our "debate" would be: the editors of *Diacritics* called it a "dialogue" when they published it, but no one seems to have taken note. I've known since I came here for the month of July that I wanted to begin our correspondence—physically—from this place: from the terrace. Writing from the terrace is a trope I associate with you, or rather by association, with the scene of writing in which, in your earlier work (*Fictions of Feminine Desire*), you imagined the Portuguese nun: a problematic female subject, writing from the balcony, from her abandonment. The authorship of that (letter) writing woman has already been a question between us. More precisely, I began my exchange with you in Ithaca in 1981 over the question of her gender and identity, invoking then your essay "Writing Like a Woman." A decade later, depending how you count, authorship is still a matter that engages us and locates us differently in the field of literary theory in which we both work. Whether this constitutes a "conflict in feminism" is perhaps what this exchange will decide.

We had agreed by phone in the States that we would write to each other in France and see what happened. (I should probably explain that it was just by chance that we both turned out to be in France this summer and fall, but probably not completely irrelevant either to where we are, so to speak, in our current—or past—thinking: being "in French.") So I send you this first installment to your address in Paris with the sensation of being in a slight genre warp (resuscitating the epistolary): writing to you not only *for* publication, which arguably was the case of many female letter writers of the past, but for publication as something else, notably *as* (or in) feminist theory; writing not as *confidantes,* the canonical female letter writer, but as the academic equivalent of *femmes de lettres* about a theoretical conflict between us; between us but also constituted by those who have read us together. Although this appropriation of the epistolary is not unheard of at the end of the 20th century, by its exhibitionism—appearing to be anachronistic—it runs the risk of being received as irretrievably precious (in the French sense), hence ridiculous. On the other hand, it seemed like a good way to reopen the dialogue, since a correspondence will allow us to exchange views without recourse to the rhetorical constraints of formal debate. As we also agreed at the outset, we were not so much interested in *explicating* our 1981 texts as in looking to see how we would begin to *extricate* ourselves from them in order to address whatever issues in a discussion of "conflicts in feminisms" seem alive to us now.

I brought your new book *Signature Pieces* with me to read here. Since the notion of signature is one of the problems that I struggle with both in "The Text's Heroine" and more recently, *Subject to Change,* I was curious to see what you were doing with it. It seemed to me somehow both predictable and unnerving (to borrow a verb you favor in your introduction) that you begin as I do in my introduction (in your case after the few pages on Stendhal) with Barthes and "The Death of the Author." Although my enlistment of that essay receives fuller scope in the chapter "Changing the Subject," Barthes and the Dead Author appear in my introduction as they do in yours as a way of embodying the debate about authorship. Given Barthes's own insistence on the erasure of "the very identity of the body writing" the choice of verb might seem perverse or falsifying, but I don't think it is.

So one sense I had about what would happen if we were to start over in 1989, is that we would again find ourselves positioned if not on opposite sides, at least not on the same side in a discussion of the politics of authorship (the effects of signature, feminist literary history and hermeneutics, etc.). I know from an earlier exchange of letters with you in which I was trying to reconstruct the terms of our "debate" as they were posed to us, that you didn't recall our presentations being paired before the fact as a set of oppositions; and you remark that the concern with positions seems to be a concern of mine: notably my concern with your position, or your defining "your position." This is true—I do think in terms of position and oppositions. But I think now, as I did then, that you do too. According to the terms of the correspondence from Cornell at least, the general charge to the conference speakers was to produce "short position-papers." The problem of our debate recast today, then, would have in part to do with the difference between position and opposition.

For instance, when you write as you do in your new book [*Signature Pieces: On the Institution of Authorship* (Ithaca: Cornell UP, 1988)] about the loss of that writing identity in Barthes's analysis of authorship

> Whatever the stakes of a polemic about "death of the author," however welcome may seem a "return to the subject" (even a "changed subject") or to history, the loss is not to be remedied, just more or less buried beneath appeals to a radical break or to a return (11)

aren't you positioning yourself against those who like me take up the "changed subject" polemic? Distancing yourself from those who fail to learn the lesson of the failure of oppositional thinking; who fail to apply the "deconstructive strategy . . . called for?" I see this move as the same positioning you adopt in your critique of "a central form of feminist theory" ("Replacing," 43).

In other words, asked again today to talk about feminist criticism . . . and deconstruction, or "theory" or the institutions in which feminist criticism is practiced and theorized—the terms more or less of the original discussion—we have already, in our books continued ourselves (to pick up a thread of Woolfian poetics). Having gotten this far, which is not very far, but perhaps the real beginning, I find myself wondering what beyond what we have already said, we would say now that would constitute a significant change in the ways in which we formulate "our" questions.

One thing that has shifted for me in the matter of positions since 1981, though I think that its effects still shape my arguments, is that I am no longer by my title placed *in* Women's Studies: responsible, as the Director of a vulnerable Women's Studies Program, for assuring the survival in the institution of feminist work. It is also the case that I wrote "The Text's Heroine" months after getting tenure *in* Women's Studies at Barnard; eight years later I'm more likely to worry about other people's tenure than my own and I'm housed in an English department. Looking back now, as I write to you, I've wondered whether my perception of the opposition "us" and "them," and the rhetorical solidarity of the feminist "we" has begun to be eroded for me (in a direction that you—in "Replacing"—code as positive, but that I confess to missing) *because* of those differences in location. I no longer do the daily battle with administration over resources that used to wear me down; I also no longer share in the daily and buoyant sense of community—whatever its internal conflicts—that comes from the collective struggle for—I'll use the word: identity. Visibility, viability, in an institutional setting. Because of my "signature," I am of course still asked to speak "as a feminist"— which I do gladly, but I don't go on the road feeling personally compelled to represent and defend Women's Studies to a hostile world; what this has meant for my writing and its reception is perhaps for others to say. I in no way want to suggest, however, that I take my own "de-institutionalization" either as especially desirable, or as the symptom of a trend, or that the world, in any serious sense, has become less hostile to the real implications of women's studies, upper or lower case.

So let me move on to end this piece of the installment by speaking more generally about positionings in the fields of feminist labor. My sense of the development of feminist theory since 1981, and in particular since 1985, is that it has been one of intense dislocation. I pick 1985, which I see as a kind of radical turning point, because of two events, two conferences on feminist theory that took place within months of each other that year; both of which have now become books edited by their organizers: *Feminist Studies/Critical Studies*, Teresa de Lauretis (1986) and *Coming to Terms: Feminism, Theory, Politics*, by Elizabeth Weed (1989). At both conferences, but most dramatically at the first in Milwaukee, where the effects of polarization were intense and explicit, the splits and fractures within feminisms, and the violence with which they are *lived*, especially around issues of race were painfully in evidence. Since then—though I take this moment as an archival mark, rather than an originary occasion, because the elements of the struggle had been in place for at least a decade—feminism has been traversed by currents of conflict impossible to elude. The blindness of a feminist "we" to its own exclusions has continued to complicate and deeply trouble the relations within feminism—manifested by an acute self-consciousness about the deployment of pronouns; and tempered, if not transformed by the grounding assumptions of feminist theory. (I'm thinking in particular of the powerful fiction of universal female subject.)

This is not to say that I think "we" should give up on feminism, or its institutionalization as a project for cultural and social change. But it does mean that the moment of a certain jubilation about "identity politics" has passed. Where we are to go *from here,* and *in what language,* however, is a lot less clear.

In a related manner, though the analogy may not be immediately obvious, the feminism/deconstruction paradigm—oppositional or not—now seems to me in urgent need of replanting, to try another metaphor: it seems root-bound. Given the current revitalized attacks of the New Right, specifically on women's rights to abortion, I'm wondering whether it wouldn't be more fruitful to rethink strategies together (the eternal, canonical feminist belief in coalition, a term more bandied about than enacted, however). What is there beyond the oppositional logic you find so inadequate that could provide leverage into those arenas of the world?

I really will stop here. I look forward to hearing from you.

All best,
Nancy

Paris 31 July 1989

Dear Nancy,

Thank you for your letter and, most of all, for taking the first, most difficult step of our "correspondence." When we agreed to write letters to one another, I must admit that I was not thinking about the feminine epistolary tradition of which you are reminded. My idea was just, as you put it, to "see what happened" if we wrote in installments and without knowing altogether what to expect. We would write to each other, but also for "publication"—and I won't deny that we may thus be doing something ridiculous. Is it, however, preciosity or immodesty that risks showing up when others read our mail? If one worries (in print) about appearing ridiculously immodest (in print), might that not be just another ruse of immodesty? And if writing for publication, publishing one's signature, is always a fundamentally immodest (ridiculous) enterprise (but perhaps you do not agree with that assertion), then at some point the calculation with the risk will be overrun. What we are doing here at some point escapes our accounting. Letters may dramatize better the effect of this unaccountable otherness on the discourse assumed by a subject presumed to know what she is doing, but finally I think all writing is in the same situation. One is always addressing letters to an unknown address.

A gesture we would both like to avoid, however, is any attempt to reappropriate the texts we wrote nine years ago—what you call explication. Given the reception of our earlier exchange, its treatment as an emblem (or symptom) by its readers, we, as the authors, have no privileged insight into this process of conflictual interpretation. I won't say that the process has not interested me, it has, but from a certain distance, almost as if the polemic concerned anonymous third parties. I take this to be an effect of the expropriation that, in this case, determined our exchange from its conception with the invitation which you recall to write "position papers." We were asked to speak and write anonymously, as representatives of "positions." Our signatures on that exchange have been read as virtually generic. Now we have an invitation to "update" these position papers. Perhaps our way of responding to this invitation arose from the wish to resist, with signed letters, the process of expropriation of signatures by yet another exercise in position-taking. A futile wish, of course (precisely because of what Barthes calls the erasure of "the very identity of the body writing" in the passage you cite) and besides, as you point out, like you and everyone else, I think in terms of positions and oppositions. But I also think this kind of thinking (which is that of a subject) cannot exhaust the possibilities for thought. Fortunately.

So obviously I agree with you that there is no opposing opposition. One cannot take up a position against positions. I have never argued for the contrary (or the opposite). And yes, certain disagreements do need to be staged openly, polemically. Although much has been written about the opposition as represented by our exchange in 1981, I think there is still room for some clarification (not explication), specifically as regards the disagreement between us, or at least a misunderstanding, on the question of "positions," "oppositions," and so forth. I will try to set it out as I see it and with reference not only to our most recent publications, but also to our former "debate."

First of all, we disagree, it seems to me, about the conclusions to be drawn from the fact that "there is no opposing opposition" (I am struck now by the ambiguity of that syntax, but I am not going to try to fix it). If one concludes that this means there is nothing beyond oppositional modes of thought and being, no outside from which something else can intervene which is not already programmed by the dialectical machine, then indeed one's oppositional strategy must fully espouse the logic of change (of history) made possible there and in those terms. I think this is in fact the logic you propose for "changing the subject," and which you see already at work in the feminist theory you align with your own writings. What if, however, one could point up traces of an outside-of-opposition, marks left on the structure of opposition which could only have come from a space exceeding that structure? Such a mark or trace would signal its provenance by being non-opposable within the terms of that structure, that is, it would not fit simply on one side or the other of the line thought to divide the poles of the opposition. Instead, the dividing line would itself have to pass through it, dividing it within itself, making it thereby non-self-identical. These non-opposable non-identities would make available a certain amount of room within the structure for the displacement, or dislocation, of the division organizing it. For example, when you write of your sense of an "intense dislocation" within feminism, the growing awareness of the "blindness of a feminist 'we' to its own exclusions," I would argue that the pronoun's construction (but also the construction of a noun, "feminism") within a certain opposition (the "us" and "them" you speak of) has undergone a deconstruction whose force or energy is that of an outside which is non-identifiable in terms of that opposition. Without such a force, if, in other words, the oppositional structure were totalizable, it would also be utterly immobilized and immobilizing. It would spell the death of any possibility for political (or other kind of) change. It remains, nevertheless, true and a truism that "there is no opposing opposition," but one must beware understanding that in a resigned or, worse, cynical manner. It does not mean that there is nothing other than being-in-opposition (i.e., for us post-Cartesians and post-Hegelians, the being of subjects and objects). Rather, it assigns to every kind of practice that must necessarily employ oppositional tactics the task of keeping open a space for possible dislocation, of giving the traces of the non-opposable other a chance to make their mark before they are too quickly reduced to recognizable positions and thereby made available to dialectical reason and its institutions. It means also perhaps, as feminists have had to learn, exercising a vigilant restraint with regard to not only the collective subject pronoun, but as well other forms of self-naming whose exclusionary effects begin closest to home by excluding the marks of the other on the name of the self.

This brings me, secondly, to the question of signatures and how to read them which was already at issue in our exchange in 1981. We disagree, basically, about how much attention to pay to the ways in which a signature is a non-opposable, non-self-identical mark of the sort I have just quickly outlined. I would say that you advise we give this fact little or no attention; consequently, you tend to consider the signature only insofar as it is opposable within a system of already instituted signs, principally those of gender. It may be that you enforce this limitation out of the sense that, beyond a certain realm of recognizable oppositions, there where the signature points to a non-generalizable singularity, the political benefit for women *in general* is less predictable. I believe my calculation concerning the political effects of "theory" (which, precisely because it does have political effects, cannot be simply opposed to practice) is different, more consonant with what I described above as the task assigned to such practice. Put simply, I'm interested in the point at which a calculation of these effects according to a +/- binarism becomes impossible. In fact, I believe it's the only thing I find interesting.

Thirdly, like you, I think "the feminism/deconstruction paradigm," some of whose terms are implied in what I've just outlined, ought to be allowed to outgrow its restrictive container. But how did it get stuck in that pot? And what is the "pot" if not the logocentrism that confuses the names "feminism" or "deconstruction" with what each is supposed to name? That retains, as a result of this confusion, the notion of undifferentiated and therefore opposable entities? This logocentric operation is predictable, but no less perverse, particularly as regards "deconstruction" since that word forges both poles of an opposition (it is thus non-self-identical) and ought therefore to present more resistance. But this just confirms that any name can and will be expropriated. (Because the word "feminism" inscribes itself clearly in an oppositional logic, it is even more vulnerable to these logocentric totalizations and recuperations, which is one reason I have always had trouble with that name.) Far from concluding from this, as some may be tempted to do, that the "feminism/deconstruction paradigm" has been exhausted, I wonder whether the "debate" ever really got started or whether it was not almost immediately hijacked into this shadow arena of opposed names and positions to be taken or rejected. This is how I explain to myself the "success" of our debate in *Diacritics,* which offered a pair of hooks on which to hang the positioning impulses that traverse and, indeed, largely determine an institution like the American university and its adjunct enterprises. An immense program was already in place dictating certain reading effects. And yet, who knows? There is always the possibility of the incalculable or the unprogrammed, I say to myself, banishing any regret.

It is time to close this letter. Will I have answered your last question about the "beyond" of oppositional logic? Perhaps not as clearly as you would have liked, so I'll add just a few more words. I cannot consider "the world" into which you seek leverage to be a space of confrontation and conflict *essentially* removed or different from the space in which we work and write. That is, while there are disjunctions and fractures everywhere and of all sorts, even borders and walls (I think of the campus where I teach which is located in a poorer, largely Hispanic neighborhood of Los Angeles), there are no sealed-off cells, which means there is the possibility of passage, of transference—but also, therefore, of transgression, of conflict, of contamination, of violence. Strategies of opposition remain indispensable, as the abortion rights movement has had to rediscover. But these strategies also must be played out on a field without definitive and immutable limits. Contamination between opposing forces or camps is always possible. (Perhaps this is more evident in an age when a virus, HIV, can produce symptoms all across the sociopolitical field.) And this is why, if you are asking me to produce a *prescription* for a new politics "beyond the oppositional logic [I] find so inadequate," I cannot do so. (To be sure, I spoke of a certain task, but there are no general rules as to how best to pursue that task in any given situation. And there are so many different, heterogeneous situations each of us must confront even in the course of a day!) However, does that demonstrate the irrelevance of any questions such as I and many others might want to pose to this "oppositional logic"? If I answer "no" to that question, it is because I share your belief in "coalition," indeed I think it is the constant, irrevocable condition of the political and its effects (no sealed-off cells). And it is precisely because the political cannot be reduced to positions taken, but is constantly traversed by this conditioning possibility of coalition (or transference or contamination), that "oppositional logic" will never be enough.

Best regards,
Peggy

August 5, 1989

Dear Peggy:

We have both, it turns out, written at some length, and in a manner finally that is more reminiscent of the reply-structure of critical response that you analyze in "Floating Authorship" than the epistolary tradition in which I somewhat fancifully located our exchange in order to have a point of departure. (The example of *Critical Inquiry* comes to mind of course, and I've been trying to think if I've ever seen an exchange *between* women in its pages.) In any event, I thought I would just pick up on a couple of the points you make in your letter, though to be sure, much will be left hanging—not to say floating, when I'm done at this end.

No, I don't think you avoid polemic; on the contrary. In my reference to your discussion of the "The Death of the Author," I was trying to identify a move of yours I can't quite work out but that seems to distinguish between on the one hand "oppositional modes of thought" and what you name here "positioning impulses"—both of which you see as reductive and in that sense dangerous (I don't entirely disagree with that)—and, on the other, polemic (which would be politically productive). (Is that right?) Perhaps what interests me is the way in which you take on (the better to recast—polemically) a polemics already in place: feminism and Foucault, intentionalism (which includes, without being coterminus with, feminist literary criticism) and literary theory (forgive the shorthand): but from what place? Unless it is the town called Aporia (on the relations you wittily pose between Aporia and Peoria, I refer readers to "Resistance Theories," 180). And for the purposes of this exchange, that is, for inclusion in a volume called "Conflicts in Feminism," I wonder what the indeterminacy of that location may turn out to mean.

More pointedly (without asking you to produce a "prescription for a *new* politics"): if, as you suggest, the feminism/deconstruction paradigm has not been exhausted, if it is merely pot-bound, then what do you see as the conditions for new growth?

The remarks you make toward the end of your first letter about my belief in a clear geography of confrontation pose a problem for me. I take them all the more seriously since I have been criticized elsewhere for seeing a separation between, as you put it, "the space in which we work and write" and another space that I refer to as the "world"; I seem to you—and others—not sufficiently to take the measure of a contamination, a mode of passage between places that does not respect border lines (I gather that this mistaken belief in the inside/outside opposition is now called "the discourse of boundaries"). (The language of contamination you use here reminds me of the differences Donna Haraway describes as distinguishing the organism from the virus and the conceptual fallout that distinction entails.) This critique makes me unhappy because it suggests that I fail to understand the way the university functions: its interests and powers. In that sense, I guess I put my question (about a lever into other spaces in the world) badly earlier: wherever we may be located in relation to "theory," as academics we are of course always in the world. I fully appreciate your remarks about campus locations as an instance of this (one can't teach in New York and miss the point). And there is also a lot that could be said about the university and real estate that would usefully expand the discussion of signature and literary property.

But I seem to persist, at the risk of appearing naive (or worse) in wanting to distinguish between the work performed within the institution of the university and the work, say, of the Supreme Court; and wanting modestly (?) to preserve distinctions within our understanding of "the political." (If only, and this is not nothing, to avoid making claims one cannot sustain about one's political work.) Put another way, if the defenders of the canon, say, and the forces of anti-abortion are in one sense locatable on a continuum of reactionary thought, there is another and for me more powerful sense in which their effects—and resistances to them—are radically incommensurate.

Does this sound familiar?

My best,
Nancy

12 August 1989

Dear Nancy,

I have been casting about for a way to respond to your last letter in the very little space that is left to us. Your questions ought to be answered patiently and at length; instead we must go quickly and use shorthand, as you put it. The risk of misunderstanding, always very high, will be increased. Nevertheless, I am going to try compressing what I want to say into the minimal number of words, as if I were writing a telegram rather than a letter.

Puzzlement about your question: "from what place?" "Place" obviously a metaphor. For what? Institutional place? Not in the sense of "affiliation" (public record, no question there), but place on a map drawn up as guide to literary studies in American university? At center, something called " 'theory' " (you write: "wherever we may be located in relation to 'theory' "). Quotation marks signal distrust (thoroughly appropriate) of term as sure marker "in relation to" which location of anything else can be fixed. " 'Theory' ": shorthand for non-place and non-thing which has gotten out of hand; unlike you, most drop quotation marks, forget they are using shorthand, even start believing word has a localizable referent "in the world" (or at least in the university), some "school" or other, and that relative proximities to it can be measured. Movement of forgetting, and in its wake: logocentric trivializing, institutional closure. Shorthand shortchanges thinking. Effects can be quite perverse. (But also inevitable as the very condition of any language.)

Hence, no answer to "from what place?" if question concerns "theoretical" map. (In "Replacing Feminist Criticism," also talked about map as metaphor.) What I might say, in common shorthand, would mean *almost* nothing.

Are we talking about something or this "nothing"? That is the puzzle because "nothing," made up of markers of institutional self-reference, produces very real effects, something. Not enough to denounce the effects; point would be to try for other effects that displace markers and send mapmakers back to drawing board.

All the same, your question: "from what place?" Sense that you have suppressed mention of other marker, beside " 'theory,' " the marker "feminism." (Doubt you would put it in quotes.) Do you not ask "from what place" from the place of feminism? Am asked to answer to that place, in relation to that place. Question prompted, perhaps, by declared reluctance to assume feminism *in and by that name* (or that signature) as place from which to take part in discussions or polemics of all sorts, but particularly those already so named ("feminism and Foucault," "feminism and deconstruction," "men in feminism," "conflicts in feminism," just to take as guide titles of recent anthologies or special journal issues). Thus, I translate your question to me as follows: "Well, since you will not say you take the 'feminist' position in these different debates, by that name, then are you not assuming a position outside of, perhaps even antagonistic to feminism? And if that's the case, why not say so?" Sumoned to "say so" in writing will I respond with an aporia, or "Aporia" (but never imagined latter as possible place; joked about "Peorias of the American literary academy" and glossed phrase as denegation of aporia)? That possibility causes you to "wonder what the indeterminacy of that location may turn out to mean." Me too, I wonder—I wonder about your wonder. Are you worrying that "conflict" staged here over question of place (or "position") will turn out to be *neither* simply inside *nor* outside "space" of feminism as constituted for the occasion by volume titled "Conflicts *in* Feminism," therefore not entirely appropriate for inclusion there? Hope, frankly, that's true. Our only chance. This neither/nor neither aporia nor indeterminacy. Everything (or almost everything) we're saying is quite determined, even overdetermined—as shorthand.

You ask "from what place" *about written texts* (for example, ours of 8 years ago or present correspondence). Is not that place more or less coextensive with the writing itself, with what is written? (Which is not in the least to assert that the only "places" are written ones, "texts" in the trivial sense.) Is it not being determined on every line, with every move? Up to the reader to figure out where s/he has landed, in what kind of strange or familiar territory (and that goes for this "update," which may not correspond at all to expectations about our respective positions). Have always been irked when reading something that tells me how, in effect, to evaluate it, which frequently means no more than what label to affix on it. An impatience by no means only with texts that come pre-labeled "feminist" by their author, but latter label is very often self-addressed. Experience of reading something that has (emphatically) told its reader from the outset it is feminist— or deconstructionist!—and which, nevertheless, I find to hold out almost no promise for thinking in productive tension with phallogocentrism (more short-hand). Self-labeling gesture and collapse of tension can frequently be seen to go together, to imply each other. Times I wonder if text comes self-addressed so as to prevent readers, certain readers, from looking too closely at what's inside the envelope.

Here approaching (at last!) possible core of conflicts-in-feminism issue. Question of what is or is not "feminist," deserving of the name. After all, if conflicts are all safely "in" feminism, belong there together under same title, if it is agreed in advance that that designation will gather all disagreements back into itself, then the outcome of these conflicts is predictable and contained. Possible scenarios here are very familiar: the (usually self-interested) largesse of liberalism and laisser-faire, or the exclusionary *diktats* of dogmatism. Feminism in the American academy seems to have opted primarily for former, avoiding latter as much as possible, with notable exception of what has become litany of dogmatists who denounce pretensions of "theory," and particularly "deconstruction," to have anything of interest to say to feminists (methinks they really do protest too much). Reading across this conflictual field, one might conclude as follows: term "feminism" operates largely as accepted marker by self-designation, except wherever latter operation is itself put in question as of possibly dubious worth or origin. Thus, a closed system. Is feminist what calls itself feminist? Not only and not always, fortunately there is still plenty of room for active reading, but self-proclaiming seems too little aware of how it may be closing itself within a system of empty self-reference without any leverage, to use your term, on anything beyond that limited enclosure. Too content with the apparent effects produced there (the "success" of academic feminism?) to see the ways in which the name "feminism" can also become just another institutional marker.

Is there room "in" feminism's conflicts for a questioning of institutionalized signature that declares itself in advance self-evident, self-explanatory, and therefore does not need to be read? Is there a place here for reading signatures as non-self-identical marks, and thus a place for readers, for other-than-authors, or does feminism, must feminism sign itself "return to sender unopened"? Approaching your other question about conditions for "new growth" in the "feminism/deconstruction paradigm." Prescription here would be utterly superfluous because, fact is, this is not and never has been an opposition; feminism, to the extent it tries to erect its own name as a closed system, as a properly proper name, is already *in* deconstruction, that is, it is engaged in a denied recognition of that name's otherness, its irreducible metaphoricity; only a brittle benefit to be gained from denouncing or excluding signs of this. It is the lesson of what you call the "intense dislocation" of feminism. So my prescription (all the same) would be: drop the name *as a form of self-address there where it risks functioning solely to reinforce the institutionalized signature*. Then see what happens, what effects get produced in unexpected places, what different energies are tapped that as yet have no name, what new signatures make their way. No more return to sender labels which just keep everything moving in a circle, but signatures that have a chance to be opened by (and to) the other. (I fear this will sound to many—beginning with you?— like a preposterous, perhaps even hostile suggestion, at the very least out of place in this place; nonetheless, I swear I know at present no better way of *affirming* future of, yes, feminism.)

Forces displacing phallocentrism are not systematically opposed to it, but connive with what ruins it from within. Is connivence with ruin possible as a project? Doubtless no. What is called feminism at present seems to me poised on the edge of that impossibility: as the last project of phallocentrism, it is headed for ruin; as the ruin of all phallocentric projects, it alone has a future, but on the condition it let the future come as other than a projected present. No longer question of place or position; rather, of *rhythm* with which one ruin advances on and heads off the other.

Despite the shorthand, my "telegram" will have been too long and, I fear, once again too "abstract." My apologies.

My best,
Peggy

August 22, 1989

Dear Peggy,

I've been hoping to find a way to construct a telegram: a brief text that would acknowledge receipt of yours of August 12, make a point in reply, and end: "letter follows" (in which I would take up on the one hand, the great uncharted space of ruin that you describe; the edge of a possibility that I would be tempted to code as an abyss; cliffhangers also come to mind; and on the other, a condition of exchange—correspondence—which you introduce by a metaphorics of *rhythm*). But maybe it's hard to write telegrams in the age of fax.

In any event, what I wanted to say was this—by way of an anecdotal return to the epistolary tradition. When Françoise de Graffigny published her (in my terms feminist) novel the *Peruvian Letters* (*Lettres d'une péruvienne*) in 1747 she left the author's name blank; and at the place on the title page where one would normally expect a place name—Paris, Amsterdam, The Hague—she wrote instead: "A Peine": At Difficulty (or taking the translation in another direction, barely). Also, as I read it, from the place of feminism.

It is true that I write to you, as though that weren't a site subject to scrutiny; from that place; a marker I do not place between quote marks, even though one now speaks more correctly of feminisms, at the very least in the plural, and with positional distinctions—French, first world, etc. Knowing this, and understanding, I think, why for you and others this kind of self-labeling seems both to gloss over important differences crudely and foreclose a certain element of surprise—like the *New Yorker's* column "Letters We Never Finished Reading" (or something along those lines)—I still feel the need to sign, on the map of inclination, from the place called feminism.

But as I said, for the rest: letter follows.

Amitiés.
Nancy

29 August 1989

Dear Nancy,

Not sure that *rhythm* is a metaphor, at least not in classical sense. No proper or literal designation here, no first meaning from which others derive and deviate. Topological language is *hardly* less "metaphoric"; feminism is hardly a "place." And I am not thinking only of the necessary plurality of different feminisms, of "positional distinctions," as you put it. But also of an unplaceable otherness that traverses and divides any proper place, dislocates it. This interval of difference—metaphor without proper meaning or place—is what I was calling rhythm.

But I will take your hint that, without a leap into fiction, our telegrams will go on turning about the abyss and leave everything hanging. So to shore up the fiction, I'll say: I look forward to your letter.

With all my best regards,
Peggy

8

Deconstructing Equality-Versus-Difference: Or, the Uses of Poststructuralist Theory for Feminism

Joan W. Scott

That feminism needs theory goes without saying (perhaps because it has been said so often). What is not always clear is what that theory will do, although there are certain common assumptions I think we can find in a wide range of feminist writings. We need theory that can analyze the workings of patriarchy in all its manifestations—ideological, institutional, organizational, subjective—accounting not only for continuities but also for change over time. We need theory that will let us think in terms of pluralities and diversities rather than of unities and universals. We need theory that will break the conceptual hold, at least, of those long traditions of (Western) philosophy that have systematically and repeatedly construed the world hierarchically in terms of masculine universals and feminine specificities. We need theory that will enable us to articulate alternative ways of thinking about (and thus acting upon) gender without either simply reversing the old hierarchies or confirming them. And we need theory that will be useful and relevant for political practice.

It seems to me that the body of theory referred to as poststructuralism best meets all these requirements. It is not by any means the only theory nor are its positions and formulations unique. In my own case, however, it was reading poststructuralist theory and arguing with literary scholars that provided the elements of clarification for which I was looking. I found a new way of analyzing constructions of meaning and relationships of power that called unitary, universal categories into question and historicized concepts otherwise treated as natural (such as man/woman) or absolute (such as equality or justice). In addition, what attracted me was the historical connection between the two movements. Poststructuralism and contemporary feminism are late-twentieth-century movements that share a certain self-conscious critical relationship to established philosophical and political traditions. It thus seemed worthwhile for feminist scholars to exploit that relationship for their own ends.[1]

This article will not discuss the history of these various "exploitations" or elaborate on all the reasons a historian might look to this theory to organize her inquiry.[2] What seems most useful here is to give a short list of some major theoretical points and then devote most of my effort to a specific illustration. The first part of this article is a brief discussion of concepts used by poststructuralists that are also useful for feminists. The second part applies some of these concepts to one of the hotly contested issues among contemporary (U.S.) feminists—the "equality-versus-difference" debate.

Among the useful terms feminists have appropriated from poststructuralism are language, discourse, difference, and deconstruction.

Language. Following the work of structuralist linguistics and anthropology, the term is used to mean not simply words or even a vocabulary and set of grammatical rules but, rather, a meaning-constituting system: that is, any system—strictly verbal or other—through which meaning is constructed and cultural practices organized and by which, accordingly, people represent and understand their world, including who they are and how they relate to others. "Language," so conceived, is a central focus of poststructuralist analysis.

Language is not assumed to be a representation of ideas that either cause material relations or from which such relations follow; indeed, the idealist/materialist opposition is a false one to impose on this approach. Rather, the analysis of language provides a crucial point of entry, a starting point for understanding how social relations are conceived, and therefore—because understanding how they are conceived means understanding how they work—how institutions are organized, how relations of production are experienced, and how collective identity is established. Without attention to language and the processes by which meaning and categories are constituted, one only imposes oversimplified models on the world, models that perpetuate conventional understanding rather than open up new interpretive possibilities.

The point is to find ways to analyze specific "texts"—not only books and documents but also utterances of any kind and in any medium, including cultural practices—in terms of specific historical and contextual meanings. Poststructuralists insist that words and texts have no fixed or intrinsic meanings, that there is no transparent or self-evident relationship between them and either ideas or things, no basic or ultimate correspondence between language and the world. The questions that must be answered in such an analysis, then, are how, in what specific contexts, among which specific communities of people, and by what textual and social processes has meaning been acquired? More generally, the questions are: How do meanings change? How have some meanings emerged as normative and others have been eclipsed or disappeared? What do these processes reveal about how power is constituted and operates?

Discourse. Some of the answers to these questions are offered in the concept of discourse, especially as it has been developed in the work of Michel Foucault. A discourse is not a language or a text but a historically, socially, and institutionally specific structure of statements, terms, categories, and beliefs. Foucault suggests that the elaboration of meaning involves conflict and power, that meanings are locally contested within discursive "fields of force," that (at least since the Enlightenment) the power to control a particular field resides in claims to (scientific) knowledge embodied not only in writing but also in disciplinary and professional organizations, in institutions (hospitals, prisons, schools, factories), and in social relationships (doctor/patient, teacher/student, employer/worker, parent/child, husband/wife). Discourse is thus contained or expressed in organizations and institutions as well as in words; all of these constitute texts or documents to be read.[3]

 Discursive fields overlap, influence, and compete with one another; they appeal to one another's "truths" for authority and legitimation. These truths are assumed to be outside human invention, either already known and self-evident or discoverable through scientific inquiry. Precisely because they are assigned the status of objective knowledge, they seem to be beyond dispute and thus serve a powerful legitimating function. Darwinian theories of natural selection are one example of such legitimating truths; biological theories about sexual difference are another. The power of these "truths" comes from the way they function as givens or first premises for both sides in an argument, so that conflicts within discursive fields are framed to follow from rather than question them. The brilliance of so much of Foucault's work has been to illuminate the shared assumptions of what seemed to be sharply different arguments, thus exposing the limits of radical criticism and the extent of the power of dominant ideologies or epistemologies.

In addition, Foucault has shown how badly even challenges to fundamental assumptions often fared. They have been marginalized or silenced, forced to underplay their most radical claims in order to win a short-term goal, or completely absorbed into an existing framework. Yet the fact of change is crucial to Foucault's notion of "archaeology," to the way in which he uses contrasts from different historical periods to present his arguments. Exactly how the process happens is not spelled out to the satisfaction of many historians, some of whom want a more explicit causal model. But when causal theories are highly general, we are often drawn into the assumptions of the very discourse we ought to question. (If we are to question those assumptions, it may be necessary to forgo existing standards of historical inquiry.) Although some have read Foucault as an argument about the futility of human agency in the struggle for social change, I think that he is more appropriately taken as warning against simple solutions to difficult problems, as advising human actors to think strategically and more self-consciously about the philosophical and political implications and meanings of the programs they endorse. From this perspective, Foucault's work provides an important way of thinking differently (and perhaps more creatively) about the politics of the contextual construction of social meanings, about such organizing principles for political action as "equality" and "difference."

Difference. An important dimension of poststructuralist analyses of language has to do with the concept of difference, the notion (following Ferdinand de

Saussure's structuralist linguistics) that meaning is made through implicit or explicit contrast, that a positive definition rests on the negation or repression of something represented as antithetical to it. Thus, any unitary concept in fact contains repressed or negated material; it is established in explicit opposition to another term. Any analysis of meaning involves teasing out these negations and oppositions, figuring out how (and whether) they are operating in specific contexts. Oppositions rest on metaphors and cross-references, and often in patriarchal discourse, sexual difference (the contrast masculine/feminine) serves to encode or establish meanings that are literally unrelated to gender or the body. In that way, the meanings of gender become tied to many kinds of cultural representations, and these in turn establish terms by which relations between women and men are organized and understood. The possibilities of this kind of analysis have, for obvious reasons, drawn the interest and attention of feminist scholars.

Fixed oppositions conceal the extent to which things presented as oppositional are, in fact, interdependent—that is, they derive their meaning from a particularly established contrast rather than from some inherent or pure antithesis. Furthermore, according to Jacques Derrida, the interdependence is hierarchical with one term dominant or prior, the opposite term subordinate and secondary. The Western philosophical tradition, he argues, rests on binary oppositions: unity/diversity, identity/difference, presence/absence, and universality/specificity. The leading terms are accorded primacy; their partners are represented as weaker or derivative. Yet the first terms depend on and derive their meaning from the second to such an extent that the secondary terms can be seen as generative of the definition of the first terms.[4] If binary oppositions provide insight into the way meaning is constructed, and if they operate as Derrida suggests, then analyses of meaning cannot take binary oppositions at face value but rather must "deconstruct" them for the processes they embody.

Deconstruction. Although this term is used loosely among scholars—often to refer to a dismantling or destructive enterprise—it also has a precise definition in the work of Derrida and his followers. Deconstruction involves analyzing the operations of difference in texts, the ways in which meanings are made to work. The method consists of two related steps: the reversal and displacement of binary oppositions. This double process reveals the interdependence of seemingly dichotomous terms and their meaning relative to a particular history. It shows them to be not natural but constructed oppositions, constructed for particular purposes in particular contexts.[5] The literary critic Barbara Johnson describes deconstruction as crucially dependent on difference.

The starting point is often a binary difference that is subsequently shown to be an illusion created by the working of differences much harder to pin down. The differences *between* entities . . . are shown to be based on a repression of differences *within* entities, ways in which an entity differs from itself . . . . The "deconstruction" of a binary opposition is thus not an annihilation of all values or differences; it is an attempt to follow the subtle, powerful effects of differences already at work within the illusion of a binary opposition.[6]

Deconstruction is, then, an important exercise, for it allows us to be critical of the way in which ideas we want to use are ordinarily expressed, exhibited in patterns of meaning that may undercut the ends we seek to attain. A case in point—of meaning expressed in a politically self-defeating way—is the "equality-versus-difference" debate among feminists. Here a binary opposition has been created to offer a choice to feminists, of either endorsing "equality" or its presumed antithesis "difference." In fact, the antithesis itself hides the interdependence of the two terms, for equality is not the elimination of difference, and difference does not preclude equality.

In the past few years, "equality-versus-difference" has been used as a shorthand to characterize conflicting feminist positions and political strategies.[7] Those who argue that sexual difference ought to be an irrelevant consideration in schools, employment, the courts, and the legislature are put in the equality category. Those who insist that appeals on behalf of women ought to be made in terms of the needs, interests, and characteristics common to women as a group are placed in the difference category. In the clashes over the superiority of one or another of these strategies, feminists have invoked history, philosophy, and morality and have devised new classificatory labels: cultural feminism, liberal feminism, feminist separatism, and so on.[8] Most recently, the debate about equality and difference has been used to analyze the Sears case, the sex discrimination suit brought against the retailing giant by the Equal Employment Opportunities Commission (EEOC) in 1979, in which historians Alice Kessler-Harris and Rosalind Rosenberg testified on opposite sides.

There have been many articles written on the Sears case, among them a recent one by Ruth Milkman. Milkman insists that we attend to the political context of seemingly timeless principles: "We ignore the political dimensions of the equality-versus-difference debate at our peril, especially in a period of conservative resurgence like the present." She concludes:

> As long as this is the political context in which we find ourselves, feminist scholars must be aware of the real danger that arguments about "difference" or "women's culture" will be put to uses other than those for which they were originally developed. That does not mean we must abandon these arguments or the intellectual terrain they have opened up; it does mean that we must be self-conscious in our formulations, keeping firmly in view the ways in which our work can be exploited politically.[9]

Milkman's carefully nuanced formulation implies that equality is our safest course, but she is also reluctant to reject difference entirely. She feels a need to choose a side, but which side is the problem. Milkman's ambivalence is an example of what the legal theorist Martha Minow has labeled in another context "the difference dilemma." Ignoring difference in the case of subordinated groups, Minow points out, "leaves in place a faulty neutrality," but focusing on difference can underscore the stigma of deviance. "Both focusing on and ignoring difference risk recreating it. This is the dilemma of difference."[10] What is required, Minow suggests, is a new way of thinking about difference, and this involves rejecting the idea that equality-versus-difference constitutes an opposition. Instead of framing analyses and strategies as if such binary pairs were timeless and true, we need to ask how the dichotomous pairing of equality and difference itself works. Instead of remaining within the terms of existing political discourse, we need to subject those terms to critical examination. Until we understand how the concepts work to constrain and construct specific meanings, we cannot make them work for us.

A close look at the evidence in the Sears case suggests that equality-versus-difference may not accurately depict the opposing sides in the Sears case. During testimony, most of the arguments against equality and for difference were, in fact, made by the Sears lawyers or by Rosalind Rosenberg. They constructed an opponent against whom they asserted that women and men differed, that "fundamental differences"—the result of culture or long-standing patterns of socialization—led to women's presumed lack of interest in commission sales jobs. In order to make their own claim that sexual difference and not discrimination could explain the hiring patterns of Sears, the Sears defense attributed to EEOC an assumption that no one had made in those terms—that women and men had identical interests.[11] Alice Kessler-Harris did not argue that women were the same as men; instead, she used a variety of strategies to challenge Rosenberg's assertions. First, she argued that historical evidence suggested far more variety in the jobs women actually took than Rosenberg assumed. Second, she maintained that economic considerations usually offset the effects of socialization in women's attitudes to employment. And, third, she pointed out that, historically, job segregation by sex was the consequence of employer preferences, not employee choices. The question of women's choices could not be resolved, Kessler-Harris maintained, when the hiring process itself predetermined the outcome, imposing generalized gendered criteria that were not necessarily relevant to the work at hand. The debate joined then not around equality-versus-difference but around the relevance of general ideas of sexual difference in a specific context.[12]

To make the case for employer discrimination, EEOC lawyers cited obviously biased job applicant questionnaires and statements by personnel officers, but they had no individuals to testify that they had experienced discrimination. Kessler-Harris referred to past patterns of sexual segregation in the job market as the product of employer choices, but mostly she invoked history to break down Rosenberg's contention that women as a group differed consistently in the details of their behavior from men, instead insisting that variety characterized female job choices (as it did male job choices), that it made no sense in this case to talk about women as a uniform group. She defined equality to mean a presumption that women and men might have an equal interest in sales commission jobs. She did not claim that women and men, by definition, had such an equal interest. Rather, Kessler-Harris and the EEOC called into question the relevance for hiring decisions of generalizations about the necessarily antithetical behaviors of women and men. EEOC argued that Sears's hiring practices reflected inaccurate and inapplicable notions of sexual difference; Sears argued that "fundamental" differences between the sexes (and not its own actions) explained the gender imbalances in its labor force.

The Sears case was complicated by the fact that almost all the evidence offered was statistical. The testimony of the historians, therefore, could only be inferential at best. Each of them sought to explain small statistical disparities by reference to gross generalizations about the entire history of working women; furthermore, neither historian had much information about what had actually happened at Sears. They were forced, instead, to swear to the truth or falsehood of interpretive generalizations developed for purposes other than legal contestation, and they were forced to treat their interpretive premises as matters of fact. Reading the cross-examination of Kessler-Harris is revealing in this respect. Each of her carefully nuanced explanations of women's work history was forced into a reductive assertion by the Sears lawyers' insistence that she answer questions only by saying yes or no. Similarly, Rosalind Rosenberg's rebuttal to Alice Kessler-Harris eschewed the historian's subtle contextual reading of evidence and sought instead to impose a test of absolute consistency. She juxtaposed Kessler-Harris's testimony in the trial to her earlier published work (in which Kessler-Harris stressed differences between female and male workers in their approaches to work, arguing that women were more domestically oriented and less individualistic than men) in an effort to show that Kessler-Harris had misled the court.[13] Outside the courtroom, however, the disparities of the Kessler-Harris argument could also be explained in other ways. In relationship to a labor history that had typically excluded women, it might make sense to overgeneralize about women's experience, emphasizing difference in order to demonstrate that the universal term "worker" was really a male reference that could not account for all aspects of women's job experiences. In relationship to an employer who sought to justify discrimination by reference to sexual difference, it made more sense to deny the totalizing effects of difference by stressing instead the diversity and complexity of women's behavior and motivation. In the first case, difference served a positive function, unveiling the inequity hidden in a presumably neutral term; in the second case, difference served a negative purpose, justifying what Kessler-Harris believed to be unequal treatment. Although the inconsistency might have been avoided with a more self-conscious analysis of the "difference dilemma," Kessler-Harris's different positions were quite legitimately different emphases for different contexts; only in a courtroom could they be taken as proof of bad faith.[14]

The exacting demands of the courtroom for consistency and "truth" also point out the profound difficulties of arguing about difference. Although the testimony of the historians had to explain only a relatively small statistical disparity in the numbers of women and men hired for full-time commission sales jobs, the explanations that were preferred were totalizing and categorical.[15] In cross-examination, Kessler-Harris's multiple interpretations were found to be contradictory and confusing, although the judge praised Rosenberg for her coherence and lucidity.[16] In part, that was because Rosenberg held to a tight model that unproblematically linked socialization to individual choice; in part it was because her descriptions of gender differences accorded with prevailing normative views. In contrast, Kessler-Harris had trouble finding a simple model that would at once acknowledge difference and refuse it as an acceptable explanation for the employment pattern of Sears. So she fell into great difficulty maintaining her case in the face of hostile questioning. On the one hand, she was accused of assuming that economic opportunism equally affected women and men (and thus of believing that women and men were the same). How, then, could she explain the differences her own work had identified? On the other hand, she was tarred (by Rosenberg) with the brush of subversion, for implying that all employers might have some interest in sex typing the labor force, for deducing from her own (presumably Marxist) theory, a "conspiratorial" conclusion about the behavior of Sears.[17] If the patterns of discrimination that Kessler-Harris alluded to were real, after all, one of their effects might well be the kind of difference Rosenberg pointed out. Caught within the framework of Rosenberg's use of historical evidence, Kessler-Harris and her lawyers relied on an essentially negative strategy, offering details designed to complicate and undercut Rosenberg's assertions. Kessler-Harris did not directly challenge the theoretical shortcomings of Rosenberg's socialization model, nor did she offer an alternative model of her own. That would have required, I think, either fully developing the case for employer discrimination or insisting more completely on the "differences" line of argument by exposing the "equality-versus-difference" formulation as an illusion.

In the end, the most nuanced arguments of Kessler-Harris were rejected as contradictory or inapplicable, and the judge decided in Sears's favor, repeating the defense argument that an assumption of equal interest was "unfounded" because of the differences between women and men.[18] Not only was EEOC's position rejected, but the hiring policies of Sears were implicitly endorsed. According to the judge, because difference was real and fundamental, it could explain statistical variations in Sears's hiring. Discrimination was redefined as simply the recognition of "natural" difference (however culturally or historically produced), fitting in nicely with the logic of Reagan conservatism. Difference was substituted for inequality, the appropriate antithesis of equality, becoming inequality's explanation and legitimation. The judge's decision illustrates a process literary scholar Naomi Schor has described in another context: it "essentializes difference and naturalizes social inequity."[19]

The Sears case offers a sobering lesson in the operation of a discursive, that is, a political field. Analysis of language here provides insight not only into the manipulation of concepts and definitions but also into the implementation and justification of institutional and political power. References to categorical differences between women and men set the terms within which Sears defended its policies *and* EEOC challenged them. Equality-versus-difference was the intellectual trap within which historians argued not about tiny disparities in Sears's employment practices, but about the normative behaviors of women and men. Although we might conclude that the balance of power was against EEOC by the time the case was heard and that, therefore, its outcome was inevitable (part of the Reagan plan to reverse affirmative action programs of the 1970s), we still need to articulate a critique of what happened that can inform the next round of political encounter. How should that position be conceptualized?

When equality and difference are paired dichotomously, they structure an impossible choice. If one opts for equality, one is forced to accept the notion that difference is antithetical to it. If one opts for difference, one admits that equality is unattainable. That, in a sense, is the dilemma apparent in Milkman's conclusion cited above. Feminists cannot give up "difference"; it has been our most creative analytic tool. We cannot give up equality, at least as long as we want to speak to the principles and values of our political system. But it makes no sense for the feminist movement to let its arguments be forced into preexisting categories and its political disputes to be characterized by a dichotomy we did not invent. How then do we recognize and use notions of sexual difference and yet make arguments for equality? The only response is a double one: the unmasking of the power relationship constructed by posing equality as the antithesis of difference and the refusal of its consequent dichotomous construction of political choices.

Equality-versus-difference cannot structure choices for feminist politics; the oppositional pairing misrepresents the relationship of both terms. Equality, in the political theory of rights that lies behind the claims of excluded groups for justice, means the ignoring of differences between individuals for a particular purpose or in a particular context. Michael Walzer puts it this way: "The root meaning of equality is negative; egalitarianism in its origins is an abolitionist politics. It aims at eliminating not all differences, but a particular set of differences, and a different set in different times and places."[20] This presumes a social agreement to consider obviously different people as equivalent (not identical) for a stated purpose. In this usage, the opposite of equality is inequality or inequivalence, the noncommensurability of individuals or groups in certain circumstances, for certain purposes. Thus, for purposes of democratic citizenship, the measure of equivalence has been, at different times, independence or ownership of property or race or sex. The political notion of equality thus includes, indeed depends on, an acknowledgment of the existence of difference. Demands for equality have rested on implicit and usually unrecognized arguments from difference; if individuals or groups were identical or the same there would be no need to ask for equality. Equality might well be defined as deliberate indifference to specified differences.

The antithesis of difference in most usages is sameness or identity. But even here the contrast and the context must be specified. There is nothing self-evident or transcendent about difference, even if the fact of difference—sexual difference, for example—seems apparent to the naked eye. The questions always ought to be, What qualities or aspects are being compared? What is the nature of the comparison? How is the meaning of difference being constructed? Yet in the Sears testimony and in some debates among feminists (sexual) difference is assumed to be an immutable fact, its meaning inherent in the categories female and male. The lawyers for Sears put it this way: "The reasonableness of the EEOC's *a priori* assumptions of male/female sameness with respect to preferences, interests, and qualifications is . . . the crux of the issue."[21] The point of the EEOC challenge, however, was never sameness but the irrelevance of categorical differences.

The opposition men/women, as Rosenberg employed it, asserted the incomparability of the sexes, and although history and socialization were the explanatory factors, these resonated with categorical distinctions inferred from the facts of bodily difference. When the opposition men/women is invoked, as it was in the Sears case, it refers a specific issue (the small statistical discrepancy between women and men hired for commission sales jobs) back to a general principle (the "fundamental" differences between women and men). The differences within each group that might apply to this particular situation—the fact, for example, that some women might choose "aggressive" or "risk-taking" jobs or that some women might prefer high- to low-paying positions—were excluded by definition in the antithesis between the groups. The irony is, of course, that the statistical case required only a small percentage of women's behaviors to be explained. Yet the historical testimony argued categorically about "women." It thus became impossible to argue (as EEOC and Kessler-Harris tried to) that within the female category, women typically exhibit and participate in all sorts of "male" behaviors, that socialization is a complex process that does not yield uniform choices. To make the argument would have required a direct attack on categorical thinking about gender. For the generalized opposition male/female serves to obscure the differences among women in behavior, character, desire, subjectivity, sexuality, gender identification, and historical experience. In the light of Rosenberg's insistence on the primacy of sexual difference, Kessler-Harris's insistence on the specificity (and historically variable aspect) of women's actions could be dismissed as an unreasonable and trivial claim.

The alternative to the binary construction of sexual difference is not sameness, identity, or androgyny. By subsuming women into a general "human" identity, we lose the specificity of female diversity and women's experiences; we are back, in other words, to the days when "Man's" story was supposed to be everyone's story, when women were "hidden from history," when the feminine served as the negative counterpoint, the "Other," for the construction of positive masculine identity. It is not sameness *or* identity between women and men that we want to claim but a more complicated historically variable diversity than is permitted by the opposition male/female, a diversity that is also differently expressed for different purposes in different contexts. In effect, the duality this opposition creates draws one line of difference, invests it with biological explanations, and then treats each side of the opposition as a unitary phenomenon. Everything in each category (male/female) is assumed to be the same; hence, differences within either category are suppressed. In contrast, our goal is to see not only differences between the sexes but also the way these work to repress differences within gender groups. The sameness constructed on each side of the binary opposition hides the multiple play of differences and maintains their irrelevance and invisibility.

Placing equality and difference in antithetical relationship has, then, a double effect. It denies the way in which difference has long figured in political notions of equality and it suggests that sameness is the only ground on which equality can be claimed. It thus puts feminists in an impossible position, for as long as we argue within the terms of a discourse set up by this opposition we grant the current conservative premise that because women cannot be identical to men in all respects, we cannot expect to be equal to them. The only alternative, it seems to me, is to refuse to oppose equality to difference and insist continually on differences—differences as the condition of individual and collective identities, differences as the constant challenge to the fixing of those identities, history as the repeated illustration of the play of differences, differences as the very meaning of equality itself.

Alice Kessler-Harris's experience in the Sears case shows, however, that the assertion of differences in the face of gender categories is not a sufficient strategy. What is required in addition is an analysis of fixed gender categories as normative statements that organize cultural understandings of sexual difference. This means that we must open to scrutiny the terms women and men as they are used to define one another in particular contexts—workplaces, for example. The history of women's work needs to be retold from this perspective as part of the story of the creation of a gendered workforce. In the nineteenth century, for example, certain concepts of male skill rested on a contrast with female labor (by definition unskilled). The organization and reorganization of work processes was accomplished by reference to the gender attributes of workers, rather than to issues of training, education, or social class. And wage differentials between the sexes were attributed to fundamentally different family roles that preceded (rather than followed from) employment arrangements. In all these processes the meaning of "worker" was established through a contrast between the presumably natural qualities of women and men. If we write the history of women's work by gathering data that describes the activities, needs, interests, and culture of "women workers," we leave in place the naturalized contrast and reify a fixed categorical difference between women and men. We start the story, in other words, too late, by uncritically accepting a gendered category (the "woman worker") that itself needs investigation because its meaning is relative to its history.

If in our histories we relativize the categories woman and man, it means, of course, that we must also recognize the contingent and specific nature of our political claims. Political strategies then will rest on analyses of the utility of certain arguments in certain discursive contexts, without, however, invoking absolute qualities for women or men. There are moments when it makes sense for mothers to demand consideration for their social role, and contexts within which motherhood is irrelevant to women's behavior; but to maintain that woman-hood is motherhood is to obscure the differences that make choice possible. There are moments when it makes sense to demand a reevaluation of the status of what has been socially constructed as women's work ("comparable worth" strategies are the current example) and contexts within which it makes much more sense to prepare women for entry into "non-traditional" jobs. But to maintain that feminin-ity predisposes women to certain (nurturing) jobs or (collaborative) styles of work is to naturalize complex economic and social processes and, once, again, to obscure the differences that have characterized women's occupational histories. An insistence on differences undercuts the tendency to absolutist, and in the case of sexual difference, essentialist categories. It does not deny the existence of gender difference, but it does suggest that its meanings are always relative to particular constructions in specified contexts. In contrast, absolutist categoriza-tions of difference end up always enforcing normative rules.

It is surely not easy to formulate a "deconstructive" political strategy in the face of powerful tendencies that construct the world in binary terms. Yet there seems to me no other choice. Perhaps as we learn to think this way solutions will become more readily apparent. Perhaps the theoretical and historical work we do can prepare the ground. Certainly we can take heart from the history of feminism, which is full of illustrations of refusals of simple dichotomies and attempts instead to demonstrate that equality requires the recognition and inclusion of differences. Indeed, one way historians could contribute to a genuine rethinking of these concepts, is to stop writing the history of feminisms as a story of oscillations between demands for equality and affirmations of difference. This approach inadvertently strengthens the hold of the binary construction, establishing it as inevitable by giving it a long history. When looked at closely, in fact, the historical arguments of feminists do not usually fall into these neat compartments; they are instead attempts to reconcile theories of equal rights with cultural con-cepts of sexual difference, to question the validity of normative constructions of gender in the light of the existence of behaviors and qualities that contradict the rules, to point up rather than resolve conditions of contradiction, to articulate a political identity for women without conforming to existing stereotypes about them.

In histories of feminism and in feminist political strategies there needs to be at once attention to the operations of difference and an insistence on differences, but not a simple substitution of multiple for binary difference for it is not a happy pluralism we ought to invoke. The resolution of the "difference dilemma" comes neither from ignoring nor embracing difference as it is normatively constituted. Instead, it seems to me that the critical feminist position must always involve *two* moves. The first is the systematic criticism of the operations of categorical difference, the exposure of the kinds of exclusions and inclusions—the hierarchies—it constructs, and a refusal of their ultimate "truth." A refusal, however, not in the name of an equality that implies sameness or identity, but rather (and this is the second move) in the name of an equality that rests on differences—differences that confound, disrupt, and render ambiguous the meaning of any fixed binary opposition. To do anything else is to buy into the political argument that sameness is a requirement for equality, an untenable position for feminists (and historians) who know that power is constructed on and so must be challenged from the ground of difference.

Notes

I am extremely grateful to William Connolly, Sanford Levinson, Andrew Pickering, Barbara Herrnstein Smith, and Elizabeth Weed for their thoughtful suggestions, which sharpened and improved my argument. This essay originally appeared in *Feminist Studies* 14, no. 1 (Spring 1988).

1. On the problem of appropriating poststructuralism for feminism, see Biddy Martin, "Feminism, Criticism, Foucault," *New German Critique* 27 (Fall 1982): 3–30.

2. Joan W. Scott, "Gender: A Useful Category of Historical Analysis," *American Historical Review* 91 (December 1986): 1053–75; Donna Haraway, "A Manifesto for Cyborgs: Science, Technology, and Socialist Feminism in the 1980s," *Socialist Review* 15 (March–April 1985): 65–107.

3. Examples of Michel Foucault's work include *The Archaeology of Knowledge* (New York: Harper & Row, 1976), *The History of Sexuality*, vol. 1, *An Introduction* (New York: Vintage, 1980), and *Power/Knowledge: Selected Interviews and Other Writings, 1972–1977* (New York: Pantheon, 1980). See also Hubert L. Dreyfus and Paul Rabinow, *Michel Foucault: Beyond Structuralism and Hermeneutics* (Chicago: University of Chicago Press, 1983).

4. The Australian philosopher Elizabeth Gross puts it this way: "What Derrida attempts to show is that within these binary couples, the primary or dominant term derives its privilege from a curtailment or suppression of its opposite. Sameness or identity, presence, speech, the origin, mind, etc. are all privileged in relation to their opposites, which are regarded as debased, impure variants of the primary term. Difference, for example, is the lack of identity or sameness; absence is the lack of presence; writing is the supplement of speech, and so on." See her "Derrida, Irigaray, and Deconstruction," *Left-wright, Intervention* (Sydney, Australia) 20 (1986): 73. See also Jacques Derrida, *Of Grammatology* (Baltimore: Johns Hopkins University Press, 1976); and Jonathan Culler, *On Deconstruction: Theory and Criticism after Structuralism* (Ithaca: Cornell University Press, 1982).

5. Again, to cite Elizabeth Gross's formulation: "Taken together, reversal and its useful displacement show the necessary but unfounded function of these terms in Western thought. One must both reverse the dichotomy and the values attached to the two terms, as well as displace the excluded term, placing it beyond its oppositional role, as the internal condition of the dominant term. This move makes clear the violence of the hierarchy and the debt the dominant term owes to the subordinate one. It also demonstrates that there are other ways of conceiving these terms than dichotomously. If these terms were only or necessarily dichotomies, the process of displacement would not be possible. Although historically necessary, the terms are not logically necessary." See Gross, 74.

6. Barbara Johnson, *The Critical Difference: Essays in the Contemporary Rhetoric of Reading* (Baltimore: Johns Hopkins University Press, 1980): x–xi.

7. Most recently, attention has been focused on the issue of pregnancy benefits. See, for example, Lucinda M. Finley, "Transcending Equality Theory: A Way Out of the Maternity and the Workplace Debate," *Columbia Law Review* 86 (October 1986): 1118–83. See Sylvia A. Law, "Rethinking Sex and the Constitution," *University of Pennsylvania Law Review* 132 (June 1984): 955–1040.

8. Recently, historians have begun to cast feminist history in terms of the equality-versus-difference debate. Rather than accept it as an accurate characterization of antithetical positions, however, I think we need to look more closely at how feminists used these arguments. A close reading of nineteenth-century French feminist texts, for example, leads me to conclude that they are far less easily categorized into difference or equality positions than one would have supposed. I think it is a mistake for feminist historians to write this debate uncritically into history for it reifies an "antithesis" that may not actually have existed. We need instead to "deconstruct" feminist arguments and read them in their discursive contexts, all as explorations of "the difference dilemma."

9. Ruth Milkman, "Women's History and the Sears Case," *Feminist Studies* 12 (Summer 1986): 394–95. In my discussion of the Sears case, I have drawn heavily on this careful and intelligent article, the best so far of the many that have been written on the subject.

10. Martha Minow, "Learning to Live with the Dilemma of Difference: Bilingual and Special Education," *Law and Contemporary Problems* 48, no. 2 (1984): 157–211; quotation is from p. 160; see also pp. 202–6.

11. There is a difference, it seems to me, between arguing that women and men have identical interests and arguing that one should presume such identity in all aspects of the hiring process. The second position is the only strategic way of not building into the hiring process prejudice or the wrong presumptions about differences of interest.

12. Rosenberg's "Offer of Proof" and Kessler-Harris's "Written Testimony" appeared in *Signs* 11 (Summer 1986): 757–79. The "Written Rebuttal Testimony of Dr. Rosalind Rosenberg" is part of the official transcript of the case, U.S. District Court for the Northern District of Illinois, Eastern Division, *EEOC vs Sears,* Civil Action

No. 79-C–4373. (I am grateful to Sanford Levinson for sharing the trial documents with me and for our many conversations about them.)

13. Appendix to the "Written Rebuttal Testimony of Dr. Rosalind Rosenberg," 1–12.

14. On the limits imposed by courtrooms and the pitfalls expert witnesses may encounter, see Nadine Taub, "Thinking about Testifying," *Perspectives* (American Historical Association Newsletter) 24 (November 1986): 10–11.

15. On this point, Taub asks a useful question: "Is there a danger in discrimination cases that historical or other expert testimony not grounded in the particular facts of the case will reinforce the idea that it is acceptable to make generalizations about particular groups?" (p. 11).

16. See the cross-examination of Kessler-Harris, *EEOC vs Sears*, 16376–619.

17. The Rosenberg "Rebuttal" is particularly vehement on this question: "This assumption that all employers discriminate is prominent in her [Kessler-Harris's] work. . . . In a 1979 article, she wrote hopefully that women harbor values, attitudes, and behavior patterns potentially subversive to capitalism" (p. 11). "There are, of course, documented instances of employers limiting the opportunities of women. But the fact that some employers have discriminated does not prove that all do" (p. 19). The rebuttal raises another issue about the political and ideological limits of a courtroom or, perhaps it is better to say, about the way the courtroom reproduces dominant ideologies. The general notion that employers discriminate was unacceptable (but the general notion that women prefer certain jobs was not). This unacceptability was underscored by linking it to subversion and Marxism, positions intolerable in U.S. political discourse. Rosenberg's innuendos attempted to discredit Kessler-Harris on two counts—first, by suggesting she was making a ridiculous generalization and, second, by suggesting that only people outside acceptable politics could even entertain that generalization.

18. Milkman, 391.

19. Naomi Schor, "Reading Double: Sand's Difference," in *The Poetics of Gender*, ed. Nancy K. Miller (New York: Columbia University Press, 1986), 256.

20. Michael Walzer, *Spheres of Justice: A Defense of Pluralism and Equality* (New York: Basic Books, 1983), xii. See also Minow, 202–3.

21. Milkman, 384.

9

Adjudicating Differences: Conflicts Among Feminist Lawyers

Martha Minow

Like the "first-wave" woman's movement of the 19th and early 20th century, the "second-wave" women's movement has brought many women's issues to legislatures and courts.[1] New during this second phase, especially since 1970, is the fact that many of the women in the movement are themselves lawyers.[2] Women lawyers have worked to frame persuasive arguments for equality and for the emancipation of women. Yet, by working from within the profession, these women lawyers must struggle with institutional and conceptual constraints beyond their control. Recent disagreements among feminist lawyers stem from the legal structures created without the participation of women.

The disagreements I mean to address are not the highly visible ones between pro-choice and pro-life advocates in the abortion context,[3] or other disputes that divide those who call themselves feminists from those who do not. Instead, I am interested in the divisions among those who together claim the name, feminist. Erupting in both private planning sessions and in the public settings of courts and legislatures, two notable disputes have centered, respectively, on pregnancy and maternity leave policies, and on the regulation of pornography. One might argue that, given the ambitious range of feminist reforms in the legal treatments of rape, contraception, reproduction, abortion, domestic violence, divorce, employment, commercial credit, and torts, the vast areas of agreement deserve more attention than these two disputed areas. Yet, for feminist lawyers in recent years, fights within the movement have been draining and, at times, disturbing.

Two risks—partisanship and facile optimism—confront anyone who writes as a participant in politics and history; I confront them here in the hope that we can begin to move on.

Pregnancy and Maternity Leave Policies

Which rule better serves the goals of equality and freedom for women: one that requires employers to provide for pregnancy and maternity leaves or one that requires employers to provide the same treatment for women and men, pregnant and nonpregnant employees? In some ways, this debate among feminist lawyers in the 1970s and 1980s recapitulates the Progressive-era divide between those who advocated wage and hour labor laws to protect women and those who sought an Equal Rights Amendment to assure women and men the same treatment in employment.[4] It would be wrong to attribute the conflicts during either era to clashing goals. In the 1920s, ERA-supporters and proponents of protective legislation alike sought equality for women and men, and also hoped to reform the workplace so that all workers would have fair wages as well as safe and humane working hours and conditions. They disagreed about the means, timing, and priorities.

In the 1970s and 1980s, the shared goals among feminists who seem to disagree about workplace reforms are even more salient. One group ostensibly favors and defends pregnancy and maternity leaves both as proper recognition of women's special needs and as a first step toward changing the workplace for everyone. Another opposes those sex-specific leaves because they recreate stereotypes, but this group favors medical and family-related leaves as ways to accommodate both women and men, and to promote changes in traditionally gendered parental roles. Both groups seek to alter a workplace which fails to accommodate the experiences of people with family-related needs and obligations. Again, the groups differ chiefly about means, timing, and priorities. Yet, against the backdrop of the established legal rules, these modest differences about means became heated disagreements, producing scholarly fights and opposing briefs in court.

Controversies Arising from Supreme Court Actions

In the mid-1970s, the Supreme Court considered whether a constitutional or statutory problem arose when employers excluded pregnancy benefits from the health care insurance they otherwise provided employees. The Court reasoned that neither the constitutional guarantee of equal protection nor the statutory ban against sex discrimination forbade this exclusion.[5]

Since the employer did not draw a forbidden distinction on the basis of sex, only on the basis of pregnancy, and since women could be both pregnant and not pregnant, these exclusions, it was argued, did not amount to discrimination on the basis of sex. Perhaps only a Court with no women members could view pregnancy as so unrelated to sex. Congress responded to the blatant inequity of the Court's statutory ruling by adopting the Pregnancy Discrimination Act which forbids discrimination on the basis of pregnancy.[6]

Yet, in perhaps unimagined ways, the new legislation merely multiplied difficulties in conceiving of and implementing equality. If differentiation on the basis of pregnancy is forbidden by the federal government, does this mean that individual states may not require their employers to provide pregnancy and maternity leaves, even if this differentiation, or discrimination, benefits women? When California adopted a pregnancy and maternity leave requirement, one employer sought relief on the grounds that this state law conflicted with the federal prohibition against discrimination on the basis of pregnancy. Thus, the courts had to consider whether the federal requirement permits special treatment for pregnant persons, or instead mandates the same treatment for pregnant and nonpregnant persons. What made this formulation of the problem especially difficult for feminist lawyers was that the alternatives seemed to demand a choice between upholding the state's special treatment of women and striking down the state law—thereby eliminating any leave—in the name of the federal law's nondiscrimination policy.

Advocates for women's rights argued about this question with intensity.[7] Friends and allies worked on briefs taking contrasting and conflicting approaches. The lawyers at Equal Rights Advocates, pioneers in the fight against sex discrimination, filed a brief with the Supreme Court defending special treatment for pregnancy because it recognizes "real differences in the procreative roles of men and women."[8] The sex discrimination and reproductive rights staff of the American Civil Liberties Union (ACLU) argued in contrast that pregnancy justified no special treatment which would only perpetuate negative stereotypes of women and justify denying rights to women.[9] The ACLU brief also argued that pregnancy could and should be treated as one of many kinds of temporary physical disabilities warranting accommodation by employers. Indeed, the brief argued, both the state and federal laws could be satisfied if the employers in California simply provided comparable leaves for men, thereby preserving both the state's commitment to accommodating women and the federal government's commitment to ending distinctions along the lines of sex differences.

The disagreement in part reflected different tactical choices about the same goal: integrating pregnancy in the workplace. Yet, they also showed different views, or hopes, about creating a workplace flexible enough to accommodate dependents at home, a workplace in which care-taking responsibility could be shared by women and men. Perhaps tactical concerns also explain the contrast between widely held views defending, or denying, the "specialness" of pregnancy. Whether characterized as deep or tactical, the differences among feminists in the pregnancy and maternity leave debates fit within longstanding disputes over "sameness" and "difference": which comparative term is more useful to characterize men and women?

The Sameness and Difference Conundrum

The debate over the Cal/Fed case resurrects the historic question about whether women are sufficiently the same as men to warrant similar legal treatment. Even that grande dame of advocates for women's rights, Elizabeth Cady Stanton, fluctuated between arguments for women's rights based on their resemblance to men, and for women's rights based on their differences.[10] The choice between arguments about sameness or differences is a conundrum for at least two reasons: if women claim they are the same as men in order to secure the rights of man, any sign of difference can be used to deny those rights; and if women claim they are different from men in order to secure special rights, those very differences can be cited to exclude women from the rights that men enjoy. The difficulties are especially pronounced when women argue they are like men in order to be granted rights that men themselves never claimed or wanted—such as rights to pregnancy and maternity leave.

Yet the conundrum is not really about women. It arises because men have been made the benchmark for social and political institutions. For example, in workplaces designed without women in mind, there may be no bathrooms for women, and women's demands for inclusion can be rejected on the grounds that there are no facilities to accommodate them.[11] This rejection stems from the omission of bathrooms for women, not from the women themselves; this rejection also neglects the possibility of designing bathrooms that can be shared by both men and women, or used, like bathrooms in a private home, by one person at a time. The attribution of some inherent difference between women and men, then, is just that: a cultural decision about how to design a building and about how to conceive of morals and manners, rather than a natural and inherent biological distinction.

Arguments about sexual sameness and difference occur beyond the contexts of bathrooms and pregnancy leaves. For example, questions about gender similarities and differences often stymie analysis of equal treatment in divorce disputes over property division and alimony. Some claim that for women to be treated like men, property after divorce should be split 50/50 and there should be either no alimony payments from an ex-husband to an ex-wife or else such alimony payments should be temporary, until the woman can be trained to earn her own living outside the home. Especially if the goal is to work for a world in which both spouses may have comparable paid employment and participation in childrearing, retaining sex-based distinctions for allocating resources after divorce seems a self-defeating incentive promoting stereotyped gender roles. Others argue that efforts to secure gender-neutral, "formal" equality pretend that all women have the same economic opportunities as men and neglect the greater expenses incurred by a woman who continues to play the traditional role of primary caretaker for the children.[12]

Behind these arguments is the faulty assumption that one answer about sex differences or similarities can work for all couples. Some couples may have shared housework and childrearing tasks before the divorce; many others did not. Some marriages end after 20 years, some after six months. Some women divorce when they are over fifty years old and face large barriers to entering new kinds of paid employment. A small number of women are well-launched in well-paying jobs before divorce. The category of sex or gender is insufficient by itself to respond to these differences.

Even more faulty, though, is the idea that husbands and wives are in the same positions vis-a-vis both their children and their paid employment options, and therefore that "fairness" is achieved by an equal division of the resources. Since most women retain physical custody and primary responsibility for the children after divorce, a policy of dividing the resources equally between two new households neglects the disparate costs entailed by the differences between their households. It is not "fair" to treat people differently when their situations are the same, but nor is it "fair" to treat people the same when their situations are different. Particularized inquiries into the actual situations of the family members are essential to devising fair results.

When important legal questions are posed in terms of sex differences, the variety of human circumstances is hidden under the weight of public policy choices. Historians Alice Kessler-Harris and Rosalind Rosenberg became caught in the crudely legal question "are women like men?" when they testified in the employment discrimination suit filed against Sears, Roebuck and Co.[13] Sears defended against charges that it had discriminated against women in its hiring practices for commission sales jobs by maintaining that women did not want these traditionally "male" jobs. In the Sears case, the court fixed on the question: were the differences between men and women as potential employees sufficient to explain the absence of women from commission sales jobs? This too crude question prevented the district court judge from comprehending the more nuanced attempts to describe the contrasts between cultural ideals and the great variety of actual practices. Despite normative differences between the jobs of men and women, historically, many women have happily served in "men's jobs" when allowed to do so.

The sameness/difference framework calls for simple yes or no answers that require suppressing counter-examples. It seeks one set of rules to govern a range of experience too varied to be so subsumed. Rather than placing the burden for the moral and political choices on the cultural construction of gender, we could, and should, debate the policy choices directly.[14]

The women lawyers who try to persuade reluctant courts to respond to new claims about sex equality know well the judicial demands for precedents, for rationales that comport with the judges' own perspectives, and for arguments that seem familiar and uncontroversial. The court context narrows a potentially broad interrogation of workplace and gender relations into a specific controversy about whether a given practice is permitted or prohibited in light of the legal rules already in place. When the legal rules ban discrimination on the basis of sex or pregnancy, courts are supposed to consider only whether a given practice distinguishes on these grounds, and if so, whether there is a strong justification for such a distinction.

Accordingly, some may argue, courts must use the sameness/difference analysis. I would like to suggest that the inquiry into sameness and difference wrongly constricts analysis even in the context of court-based challenges to sex discrimination. The policies against sex discrimination may represent a commitment to alter the historic assumption that men are the norm against which all are to be treated.

However, the very phrase, "special treatment," when used to describe pregnancy or maternity leave, treats men as the norm and women as different or deviant from that norm. The question, therefore, is not whether the ban against pregnancy discrimination also forbids special accommodation for women, but instead, whether a workplace rule satisfies the ban against pregnancy discrimination if it uses as the norm the experiences of both women and men, people who become pregnant on occasion and people who do not.[15]

Justice Thurgood Marshall's opinion for the Supreme Court in California Federal Savings & Loan Ass'n v. Guerra endorsed this construction and thereby pointed to a way out of the sameness/difference debate. While the employer asked the Court to consider whether California's law violated the requirement of nondiscrimination because it called for special treatment for pregnancy and maternity, Justice Marshall reframed the question for the Court, asking whether the California law violated federal law when it allowed women and men to have the same chance to combine work and family obligations.[16] In this way, the Court accepted a version of the argument advanced by the ACLU attorneys: employers could comply with state law and thereby afford women the same chance to have families and to hold jobs that men enjoyed; any conflict with federal law could be resolved by making comparable leaves available to men.

A similar approach could inform legal treatment of other disputes that have been frustrated by the focus on differences and similarities. In the context of divorce, rules about distributing property and alimony can be drafted in sex neutral terms, such as primary caretaker for minor children and primary wage-earner, or combinations of these roles. Then the roles could respect actual roles filled by particular spouses. Functional descriptions of the roles actually played by the parties, rather than sex-linked rules, avoid re-inscribing sex differences and this can help to promote long-range equality.[17]

I suggest that we resist the temptation to deflect largely political judgments onto historical constructions of sexual differences, that we reject simplistic either/or questions in favor of nuanced assessments of actual social roles and experiences, and that we demand elucidation of the underlying norms for acceptable legal treatment in light of the varieties of human experiences. Conformity with the experiences of only half the species cannot be the meaning of equality. Exploring the variety of human experiences and debating how social arrangements in the future can prevent inequalities on the basis of sex (or race or disability) will not eliminate conflict. Instead, it will allow people to express disagreements about social purposes and practices rather than disagreements about how to manipulate the easily manipulable terms of sex and gender.

Bigger and Better Disputes About Leave Policies

In response to conflicts between federal and state policies about pregnancy and maternity leave, many feminist lawyers have turned to Congress in the hope of broadening the policy debate and, more fundamentally, of remaking workplaces to accommodate persons with family obligations. Very quickly, however, woman's rights advocated discovered powerful opposition from employers and chambers of commerce. Like the courts, Congress operates within constraints. Advocates within these formal legal institutions learn to internalize these constraints and characterize their disagreements within the terms allowed by traditional institutional practices.[18]

In the context of considerable opposition, then, some women's rights advocates proposed the Family and Medical Leave Act, to require employers to grant leaves without pay to employees who satisfied specified criteria. Most dramatically, the bill expanded the pregnancy and maternity leave first to a parenting leave to cover fathers as well as mothers—and then to an even more general and functional definition of leaves based on the medical needs of the employee and the employee's needs to provide care for a close relative. Thus, one criterion involved medical needs of the individual employee; pregnancy-related medical needs would fall within this general category. An alternative criterion looked to the employee's relationship with a dependent person. Sons or daughters dependent upon the employee and the employee's own parents would be in sufficiently close relationship to entitle the employee to take an unpaid leave in order to be able to provide care.

However, even though limited to an unpaid leave, the bill elicited large opposition from employers and their representatives; it even drew criticism from its potential supporters. Despite the inclusion of fathers as potential beneficiaries of the bill, its provisions seemed effectively to exclude those without abilities to support themselves during an unpaid leave. Typically, single parents and members of the working poor would be unable to take advantage of the leave because they would lack adequate alternative sources of income. Although the bill's supporters hoped that it would provide a base-line of guarantees from which unionized workers could negotiate for wages during the leaves, the high proportion of non-unionized workers make this a very modest hope. In addition, the bill focuses on an archetypal nuclear family and neglects varieties of families and households whose lines of dependency and care do not fit its standard model. Family ties beyond the nuclear unit—ties between grandparents and grandchildren, aunts or uncles and nieces or nephews, and cousins, remain beyond the reach of the leave eligibility provisions even though these relationships may be crucial to family members. Lesbian and gay persons may be eligible to care for their children or parents, but not for anyone outside of these legally specified relationships. These problems of exclusion hobble the bill and expose it to charges of cultural, racial, and class myopia.

Moreover, by linking the leave policy to employment in a period of massive unemployment and underemployment especially for people of color, the bill defines the problems of accommodating child-care and economic security in terms appropriate to those who are already relatively well-off. The Family and Medical

Leave Act can be attacked as a trivial reform benefiting a small slice of the population while distracting attention from everyone else—especially when the Act is compared with simultaneous public policy reforms stressing obligations to seek and accept work outside the home for anyone seeking public income supports.

These larger issues suggest that there are better and bigger things to fight about than the sameness/difference argument. It is far from obvious what strategies could lead debates over leave policy out of the controversies in which they are embedded, but focusing on the larger questions may well promote a more effective coalition for reform. But selecting the issues that can marshall coalition support is itself potentially explosive, as recent efforts to regulate pornography suggest.

Pornography and Privacy

Catharine MacKinnon[19] has offered a powerful justification for characterizing the sexual comments, sexual touching, sexual demands, and sexual epithets familiar to a majority of women who work outside the home as impermissible sex discrimination.[20] Developing a theme pursued by many advocates for women's rights, MacKinnon argued that sexually harassing behavior is not only irritating but also subordinating. No feminist lawyers, to my knowledge, disagreed with this argument, even though it emphasized differences between men and women. Courts and ultimately employers have taken MacKinnon's claim seriously, and have developed rules against sexual harassment at the workplace. One kind of harassment encountered by women is their repeated exposure to pornography in posters and magazines displayed by their co-workers. In the 1980s, MacKinnon joined Andrea Dworkin in assisting first the city of Minneapolis, and then a series of other communities, in drafting ordinances that would permit individuals to seek legal relief for harms caused by pornography.[21] This time, MacKinnon encountered enormous opposition, and some of it specifically from feminists.[22]

As with her theory of sexual harassment, MacKinnon maintained that pornography is not merely irritating or offensive; it is actually subordinating to women. The subordination occurs as women are depicted in subjugated positions as objects of violence. These three elements, subjugation, objectification, and subjection to violence, could be occasions for direct harm to the women who are themselves the actresses hired to produce the pornography and to others who become harmed by these depictions. Thus, harms may be committed in the very production of pornography against the women used in the production; harms may be committed by viewers influenced to commit acts of sexual violence after continued exposure to eroticized violence, and harms may arise when both men and women absorb attitudes degrading to women.[23]

MacKinnon helped to draft a law defining pornography as "the graphic sexually explicit subordination of women, whether in pictures or in words."[24] The ordinance was not intended to give the government authority to ban or restrict pornography; instead, analogous to sex discrimination laws, it would set up an administrative body to receive and investigate complaints from individuals asserting injury. The administrative decisions would then be subject to review by courts at the instigation of either the complainant or the defending party. Besides civil penalties, the relief for a prevailing complainant would take the form of damages, much as a successful plaintiff in a suit for libel or defamation can obtain damages against a losing defendant.[25] There are no prior restraints of speech or in fact direct governmental suppressions of pornography; instead, the actions proceed against the individuals who produce or distribute it.[26]

Many feminists were inspired by such a challenge to rape and sexual assaults, to the social degradation of women, and to the exploitation of women in the marketplace.[27] Advocates of the anti-pornography ordinance marshalled evidence purporting to prove that exposure to violent pornography promotes contempt for women and eroticizes aggression against them.[28] Other feminists, however, joined the outcry by civil libertarians who opposed what they conceived to be a restriction on free speech. As the ordinance became the subject of debate in Minneapolis, and then in other cities, this argument produced bitter splits especially among feminists lawyers. For feminists struggling to work within a coalition of progressive lawyers, the fight often implicated relationships with organizations, such as the ACLU, which advocated feminist arguments in other contexts and which clearly opposed the anti-pornography ordinance on civil libertarian grounds. Restricting the government's powers to curb speech is so basic a principle among progressive lawyers, in part, because attacking governmental suppression of speech has been the continuous link connecting lawyering for the labor movement and for the civil rights movement throughout this century. Many of the feminists who began to oppose the ordinance expressed a more specific fear of unleashing governmental power in ways that could hurt women. If particular depictions of sexuality were to be judged harmful, whose depictions would be likely candidates for suppression? For those who prized the element of the women's movement that advocated sexual liberation for women, the pornography ordinance seemed a new guise for the repression of women's sexual expression. For those who sought room for the creation of sexuality defined by women, whether heterosexual or lesbian, the pornography ordinance seemed a tool of suppression.[29] Especially because the political coalitions behind anti-pornography regulations included social conservatives, some feminists viewed the initiatives as enemy tools. And for those who predicted hostility from city councils and local courts toward women's sexual freedom, the ever-present discretion of the government seemed most likely to fall on women-centered expression rather than on the materials women might define as violent and pornographic.

In answer to this specifically feminist opposition, MacKinnon argues that even what women find appealing and expressive of sexuality is already shaped by a society that devalues and harms women, that sexuality embedded in violence against women arouses women who grew up surrounded by these cultural forms and attitudes. MacKinnon thus responds that "the defense of lesbian sadomasochism would sacrifice all women's ability to walk down the street in safety for the freedom to torture a woman in the privacy of one's basement without fear of intervention, in the name of everyone's freedom of choice."[30] She also argues that the debate over pornography occurs in the context of lies that "got here first: Linda loved it,[31] we all do; feminist work against pornography is inherently right wing; the First Amendment is absolute and in constant danger; women are already legally inviolate and in no danger at all."[32] MacKinnon worked to reframe what had been a debate over obscenity and free speech; she persuaded many feminists but not others.

Feminist Divisions in Court and in Public

When Indianapolis adopted a version of the pornography ordinance, civil libertarians challenged it in court—and feminist lawyers lined up on opposing sides of the case. MacKinnon and others defended it; another group of self-identified feminists formed the "Feminist Anti-Censorship Taskforce" and filed a brief arguing that regulation of pornography would prevent the free development of women's sexuality which had so long been controlled and suppressed.[33]

This disagreement, specifically among feminists, took place within the larger legal and public debate. Lawyers wielded arguments about the scope of the First Amendment, the relationships between obscenity and pornography, issues of content and view-point regulation, analogies to group libel—but the feminists among them also specifically debated the relationship between pornography and women's sexual identities and values.[34]

Trying to sort out feminist and anti-feminist positions in the midst of the Commission report and the litigation over anti-pornography ordinances proved difficult for feminists themselves.

Whom Do You Distrust More?

Rather than face arguing about sameness or difference, the anti-pornography position starts with the premise that power and oppression are the underlying realities.[35] In the face of this domination, governmental agencies and courts provide some of the few avenues for change. Feminists opposed to the ordinance diverge in their responses. Some would claim that women in the past may have been sexually dominated by men, but that women's incipient freedom to explore would be jeopardized by any regulation. Others may agree that women today remain dominated and unable to claim their own sexuality, but for that very reason, the administrative agencies and courts hold no promise for relief. The patriarchal state is itself something to fear.

Thus, simply put, the feminists on opposite sides of the pornography debate seem fundamentally divided over whether to fear or to trust the state. For feminists on both sides, the alternative to the state authority in this context—the unregulated private pornography industry—is another source of power to fear. The question is whether to trust the state any more or any less than the private realm.

The distinction between the public and private realms is a familiar conundrum in contemporary legal thought. For example, in family law, practitioners and theorists alike constantly debate whether society should trust the state to protect children from child abuse or women from wife battery—or to instead fear the state as another source of potential abuse and neglect. Should private contractual arrangements about marital property be trusted more than judicial review of property settlements? Should families or state administrative committees be entrusted with decisions to provide or withhold treatment for severely disabled newborns or comatose adults? There are good reasons to distrust both private and public decisionmakers in each case.[36] A similar set of dilemmas arises with questions about which to distrust more: bargains made in the private marketplace or state officials given power to regulate economic transitions?[37]

However particular legal decisions have resolved these debates, they have maintained a picture of the world divided between a public and a private sphere. And yet, as theorists of many persuasions have argued, this picture neglects the mutual implication of public authority and private authority both in the family and in the commercial sphere.[38] Law and public authority control the very definition of the family. Law determines what counts as a contract or a property right. Private actors may comply with or resist legal rules and thereby challenge law's claims to have the ultimate authority. The preoccupation with maintaining the "public/private distinction" thus has united people who otherwise stand on opposite sides of particular debates over public regulation versus private control.[39]

The illusion of a sharp divide between public and private is strengthened by both sides of the pornography debate. The proponents of the ordinance seek to enlarge public power to protect individuals from private power; the opponents seek to preserve private power in order to defend against public power. What would happen if feminists resisted the framework of the public/private distinction altogether? Jean Bethke Elshtain offered a glimpse of this possibility in her essay, "Antigone's Daughters."[40] She warns feminists against putting faith in the State to challenge private patriarchal authority while also advocating action from the vantage point of a female subject. Each woman, like Antigone, is "excluded from legitimate statecraft unless she inherited a throne" and yet she is "an active historic agent, a participant in social life who located the heart of her identity in a world bounded by the demands of necessity, sustaining the values of life-giving and preserving."[41]

One way to avoid the public/private debate might be to organize private boycotts of merchandisers who participate in the production, sale, or distribution of pornography. This approach avoids the debate over whether to trust state officials as administrators or judges. A boycott also works against quiescence or complicity with the harms that pornography may well produce. As a private action organized to carry public weight, a boycott can remake the boundaries between public and private rather than line up competing political factions around the imagined divide between the two realms.

In an intriguing way, the very effort to use the public authority of city councils to adopt anti-pornography ordinances and courts to review could actually alter the significance of the public/private divide but only if more people view the effort as a use of public forums to challenge private attitudes. Rather than focusing on success within the terms of the public institutions—winning the adoption of an ordinance or sustaining it against litigation challenge—let us focus instead on how the effort brought the arguments about pornography's harms to the attention of millions of individuals. Prompting discussions among friends and families, this use of public settings to mobilize private attention and concern could by itself begin to alter attitudes that conjoin sexuality with violence. Consciousness-raising and boycotts are less direct and obvious but potentially more effective and enduring methods for change than the actual creation of a new administrative scheme. Creating public settings for debate rather than regulation may address the mutual implication of public and private spheres in the production and repro- duction of sexual desire framed by violence.

Deeper Divides

A question of priorities divides feminists about pornography just as it did in family law. Both proponents of anti-pornography ordinances and their opponents share the apparent view that the subject warrants a high priority in their attention and political work—but other feminists strongly disagree. Given issues of material deprivation—homelessness, women and children in poverty, AIDS—many femi- nists criticize the attention to pornography as a luxury. Supporters of the ordinance may well respond that the relationship between culture and material circumstances is close and significant. Opponents of the ordinance may respond that defending freedom of expression is a precondition for advocacy about any other issues, including housing policies, renovation of income maintenance programs, and AIDS prevention and treatment. Indeed, some might well charge that informal constraints on speech hamper communication about contraception and other precautions that could stem the spread of AIDS. This divide mirrors the charges of class, racial, and cultural myopia levied in the pregnancy and maternity leave debate. If feminists seek to challenge institutions that were designed without women in mind, and social practices that subordinate women, the construction of a feminist agenda must address all women. For feminist lawyers, this means talking with people beyond our own professional circles, and building a truly cooperative agenda for the future. As we struggle for new ways to struggle, we may begin to remake whom we mean by "we," and thus transform our most critical tool: ourselves.

Notes

1. I would like to thank Elizabeth Schneider, Joan Scott, and Elizabeth Spelman for comments on a previous draft.

2. Women started to enroll in law schools in large numbers during the 1970s after years of exclusion and then marginalization in the legal profession. See Karen Berger Morello, *The Invisible Bar: The Woman Lawyer in America: 1638 to the Present* (New York: Random House, 1986.

3. See Kristin Luker, *Abortion and the Politics of Motherhood* (Berkeley, CA: University of California Press, 1984). Some pro-life advocates have called themselves feminists; their disagreements with pro-choice advocates are beyond the scope of this chapter.

4. See, e.g., Nancy Cott's essay in this book; and Nancy Cott, *The Grounding of Modern Feminism* (New Haven: Yale Univ. Press, 1987).

5. See Geduldig v. Aiello, 417 U.S. 484 (1974) (constitutional challenge under equal protection clause); General Electric Co. v. Gilbert, 429 U.S. 125 (1976) (statutory challenge under Title VII).

6. 42 U.S.C. sec. 2000e(k) (1982) (amending Title VII).

7. See Wendy Williams, "Equality's Riddle: Pregnancy and the Equal Treatment/ Special Treatment Debate," *N.Y.U. Rev. of Law & Social Change*, 13 (1984–1985) 325; Lucinda Finley, "Transcending Equality Theory: A Way Out of the Maternity and the Workplace Debate," *Colum. L. Rev.*, 86 (1986) 1118; Sylvia Law, "Rethinking Sex and the Constitution," *U. Penn. L. Rev.*, 132 (1984) 1033; Nadine Taub, "From Parental Leaves to Nurturing Leaves," *N.Y.U. Rev. of Law & Social Change*, 13 (1984–1985) 381. For a thoughtful discussion of the tensions underlying these debates, see, Frances Olsen, "Statutory Rape: A Feminist Critique of Rights Analysis," *Tex. L. Rev.*, 63 (1984) 387.

8. Brief for Amicus Curiae Equal Rights Advocates, in California Federal Savings and Loan Association et al. v. Mark Guerra et al., U.S. Supreme Court. No. 85–494.

9. Brief for Amicus Curiae American Civil Liberties Union, in California Federal Savings and Loan Association et al., v. Mark Guerra et al., U.S. Supreme Court No. 85–494.

10. See Elisabeth Griffith, *In Her Own Right: The Life of Elizabeth Cady Stanton* (New York: Oxford Univ. Press, 1984) 54, 56, 100–01, 205. See also Aileen Kraditor, *The Ideas of the Woman Suffrage Movement, 1890–1920*, (New York: W.W. Norton, 1965) 52–53.

11. Indeed, this is the story told about the Yale Medical School.

12. See Lenore Weitzman, *The Divorce Revolution* (New York: Free Press, 1985).

13. See Alice Kessler-Harris, "Equal Opportunity Employment Commission v. Sears, Roebuck and Company: A Personal Account," *Radical History Review*, 35 (April

1986) 61; Offer of Proof Concerning the "Testimony of Dr. Rosalind Rosenberg," and Written Testimony of Alice Kessler-Harris, EEOC v. Sears, U.S. District Court for the Northern District of Illinois, Eastern Division, 79-C–4373; Ruth Milkman, "Women's History and the Sears Case," *Feminist Studies*, 12 (Summer 1986) 375; Joan Williams, "Deconstructing Gender," *Mich. L. Rev.*, 87 (1989) 797. See also, Joan Scott, this volume.

14. See Kathryn Abrams, "Gender Discrimination and the Transformation of Workplace Norms," *Vanderbilt L. Rev.*, 42 (1989) 1183.

15. See Lucinda Finley, "Transcending Equality Theory"; Christine Littleton, "Reconstruction Sexual Equality," *Calif. L. Rev.*, 75 (1987) 1279.

16. 107 S.Ct., p. 694

17. For a similar analysis of ways to avoid recreating socially assigned differences based on religion or physical disability, see Martha Minow, "The Supreme Court, 1986 Term—Foreword: Justice Engendered," *Harv. L. Rev.*, 101 (1987) 10. And for a similar analysis in the context of the Sears case, see Joan Scott, this volume.

18. It is often difficult then for an advocate to remember to ask, "How little will we settle for, and at that point, is it worth it?" Wendy Williams articulated this question effectively in a speech on work and family at Sarah Lawrence College, June 16, 1989, Conference on Women's History and Public Policy.

19. Catharine A. MacKinnon, *Sexual Harassment of Working Women*, (New Haven: Yale Univ. Press, 1979).

20. See Abrams, supra, p. 1198 (53 percent of women have experienced behavior that they describe as sexual harassment).

21. See Andrea Dworkin, *Pornography: Men Possessing Women* (New York: Perigeen, 1981).

22. For MacKinnon's own accounts, see *Feminism Unmodified—Discourses on Life and Law* (Cambridge: Harvard Univ. Press, 1987).

23. See Catharine MacKinnon, *Feminism Unmodified*, pp. 171–174.

24. Ibid., p. 262.

25. See, e.g., Indianapolis and Marion County, Ind., Ordinance 35, sec. 2, § 16–3(g).

26. See Catharine MacKinnon, "Pornography, Civil Rights, and Speech," *Harv.C.R.-C.L. Rev.*, 20 (1985) 1, 38–39, reprinted in *Feminism Unmodified*, 183–191.

27. See Susan Gubar and Joan Hoff, *For Adults Only: The Dilemma of Violent Pornography* (Bloomington: Indiana Univ. Press, 1989).

28. See Neil M. Malamuth and Edward Donnerstein, eds., *Pornography and Sexual Aggression* (Orlando, Fla.: Academic Press, 1984). See generally Note, Anti-Pornography Laws and First Amendment Values, *Harv. L. Rev.*, 98 (1984) 460, 479 (citing studies).

29. See Lisa Duggan, Nan Hunter, and Carole Vance, "False Promises: Feminist Legislation in the U.S.," in Varda Burstyn, ed., *Women against Censorship 145*(Toronto: Douglas and McIntyre, 1985).

30. Catharine MacKinnon, *Feminism Unmodified*, p. 15. See also pp. 200–201, 205 (arguing that women lawyers and feminists who side with pornographers have incorporated law's hostility to new ideas and historic rules keeping women out and down). Cass Sunstein puts the point this way: "In light of the harmful effects of pornography as defined here—with its focus on violence—the fact that some women enjoy it is not a reason to do nothing about it." "Feminism and Legal Theory: Book Review of Catharine MacKinnon, *Feminism Unmodified*," *Harv. L. Rev.*, 101 (1988) 826, 843.

31. This is a reference to the woman (Linda Marchiano) depicted in a notorious pornography film (*Deep Throat*) who later explained she had been coerced into performing in the film and joined MacKinnon and Dworkin in the campaign against pornography.

32. *Feminism Unmodified*, p. 224.

33. See Brief Amici Curiae of the Feminist Anti-Censorship Taskforce, in American Booksellers Ass'n v. Hudnut (7th Cir. 1985).

34. A similar fight surrounded the Attorney General Meese's Commission on Pornography which held hearings and produced a report finding a positive correlation between pornography and sex offenses. Dissenting from the Commission's report were two women members—a behavioral scientist and a journalist—who objected to the Commission's methodologies and to its right-wing politics and paternalist treatment of women as helpless victims.

35. See Sunstein, supra p. 827–835.

36. See Martha Minow, "Beyond State Intervention in the Family: For Baby Jane Doe", *U. Mich. J.L. Ref.*, 18 (1985) 933; Elizabeth Pleck, *Domestic Tyranny: The Making of American Social Policy Against Family Violence from Colonial Times to the Present* (New York: Oxford Univ. Press, 1987) (discussing historic state interests in shoring up the family rather than in strengthening victims in the context of domestic violence).

37. See Joseph William Singer, "Legal Realism Now: Book Review of Laura Kalman, *Legal Realism at Yale 1927–1960*," *Cal. L. Rev.*, 76 (1988) 465, 528–532, 534.

38. See Frances Olsen, "The Family and the Market: A Study of Ideology and Legal Reform," *Harv. L. Ref.*, 96 (1983) 1497; Singer, supra, pp. 477–495 (discussing the Legal Realists).

39. See Symposium on the Public/Private Distinction, *U. Penn. L. Rev.*, 130 (June, 1982) 1289.

40. Jean Bethke Elshtain, "Antigone's Daughters," in Wendy McElroy, ed., *Freedom, Feminism, and the State* (Washington, D.C.: The Cato Institute, 1982) 61.

41. Ibid., p. 70. For Elshtain, this is not an argument for confining women to a private sphere instead of a public one; instead, she urges recognition of a social location, grounded in family imagery as an entry point into the wider social world. See also p. 71.

10

Conflicts and Tensions in the Feminist Study of Gender and Science

Helen E. Longino and Evelynn Hammonds

Feminist thinking about the sciences in the last 15 years has produced an exciting proliferation of critical ideas and analytic approaches. The natural sciences have drawn our attention because of their multi-faceted participation in the subordination of women. In spite of gains in some areas, notably biology, they remain bastions of masculinity: the percentage of physicists who are women has hovered around 4%, of chemists 8%, of engineers 2%, of biologists 20%. The content of science is also hostile to women, from the biological research programs that suggest gender inequality is the ultimate outcome of genetic and physiological differences to the metaphorical identification of scientific inquiry with male sexual conquest. Finally, the procedures of science have been lauded as the very apex of human rationality—a height of human intellectual achievement of which women, stereotyped as incapable of detaching from our emotions, are believed incapable. Because the sciences are intimately embroiled with the structures of power in industrial (and post-industrial) societies, understanding their cognitive and social structure is high on the feminist scholarly agenda.

Accordingly, there are historical studies of the career patterns of women attempting to do science, studies of the history of exclusion of women, studies of the content of particular sciences both in their formative periods and in their contemporary manifestations. There is work appealing to science itself, rebutting the methods and conclusions of determinist research programs in biology. There are examinations of objectivity and rationality, of the affective dimensions of scientific practice. There are activist programs to increase the participation of women in the sciences. It should not be too surprising that this variety would generate conflicting analytical approaches. Science studies is in general host to wildly incompatible research programs. The conflicts that have developed among feminist scholars in this field, however, have a particular sharpness, sometimes evident in published work, but more often in interpersonal encounters harder to document. One scholar told one of us that she was leaving the field to get out of the crossfire.

When agreeing to contribute an essay to this volume, we hoped to uncover the intellectual roots of difference in this domain of feminist analysis and activism.

Our different backgrounds suited us to different aspects of this task and so we have made separate contributions. Helen Longino, an academic philosopher, undertook to review the philosophical differences between a set of representative feminist theorists. Evelynn Hammonds, a physicist now studying the history of science, undertook to analyze the reception of feminist critiques of science by practicing women scientists. Our results were, to us, surprising and sobering. We offer them in the hope of furthering existing dialogues and sparking new ones.

Part 1:
Political Dimensions of Epistemological Critiques (Helen E. Longino)

I approached the task of analyzing conflict from my location as a philosopher concerned with the implications of the current feminist critique of the sciences for the philosophy of science and as a participant in the development of that critique. I have been reading and listening to my colleagues in that endeavor as they write and speak about our common subject and about each other (in books and articles, public lectures and private conversation) for over ten years. I expected, on the basis of that experience, that a systematic comparison of central figures in our field would reveal three primary and related points of contention. From a metaphysical point of view, I expected no consensus on the nature of reality. Is reality one or many? Can we speak of a reality existing independently of our beliefs about it? Does it even make sense to speak of reality? Is reality knowable or will it constantly elude our attempts to find the appropriate description for what we can observe and the correct articulation of the orderly or lawful processes underlying the observable? From an epistemological point of view, I expected no consensus on the possibility and criteria of knowledge. Knowledge has traditionally been defined as justified true belief in philosophical circles. All of these defining terms are called into question in contemporary feminist thinking about the sciences. The desirability of justification is questioned by the claim that rationality is masculine or that rationality has been defined and appropriated in a way that privileges masculinity. The ideal of truth is undermined by perspectival accounts of knowledge and belief, which themselves draw some support from the wholist tradition in contemporary philosophy of science. Finally, even belief is rejected by those who join Foucault in proclaiming the death of the subject and is replaced by authorless and subjectless discourse in which individuals may be positioned but for which they are not responsible. I hoped to locate our theorists in those various oppositions.

The third point of contention is rarely directly raised but gives the epistemological and metaphysical debates their urgency. Which philosophical position is most likely to promote social change? Clearly answers to this question depend a great deal on the kind of change one wants. A list could include: expanding the community of scientists; increasing access for women; producing a biology whose contents do not diminish, neglect, or pathologize women; producing an alternative science; changing the priorities of science; releasing the grip of contemporary scientific theories on our imaginations. How one sets priorities among these desiderata depends in turn on a more comprehensive social and political analysis. Because of the connection between knowledge and politics, someone urging a view about scientific inquiry may be understood and read as supporting a political analysis, even when that is not her intent. We all care deeply about politics, hence there is more than enough room for misunderstanding and hurt.

I will outline the approaches of four principal writers in the feminist critique whose work illustrates the discrepancies and conflicts I have just mentioned.

Anne Fausto-Sterling

Anne Fausto-Sterling is a developmental biologist, still teaching and conducting research in biology. She is one of a number of biologists, including Ruth Bleier, Ruth Hubbard, Sue Rosser, Ruth Doell, Linda Birke[1] who have drawn attention to the invidious treatment of women and the feminine in much biological research. Sociobiology, for example, claims in general that the social behavior of social species is biologically adaptive and genetically based—a favorite example being coyness in females, and sexual aggressiveness in males. Elaborate evolutionary arguments are developed and mechanisms invoked to support the claim that a given behavior, or set of social relations, is an adaptation. Many other branches of contemporary life sciences harbor comparable sorts of views. For example, fetal testosterone is also invoked to explain the supposed greater aggressivity of males than of females, and the development of other elements of masculine temperament. Recently, premenstrual syndrome and menopause have been medicalized with, in some cases, bizarre outcomes for women. While those outside the sciences tend to view such ideas as quaint relics of a discredited 19th-century tradition, women inside know how seriously these approaches are taken and how well they are received in related fields. A network of purported results develops which seems to support the biological determination of a number of characteristics crucial to the perpetuation of a male dominant society.

Fausto-Sterling succeeds in showing that many of the contemporary genetic and biological determinist theories are untenable on "internalist" scientific grounds. In her book, *Myths of Gender*, she reviews a number of research areas showing the deficiencies of particular studies and setting all the work in larger biological contexts, which suggest alternate ways of approaching the material.[2] For example, in connection with research by John Money and Anke Ehrhardt on the fetal gonadal hormone influences on "gender role behavior," Fausto-Sterling points to a number of problems. The controls used were inadequate: the patients with adrenogenital syndrome who were the focus of the study differed from their control populations in many other ways besides hormonal exposures that could produce the behavior studied. The observational data regarding the patients' behavior was obtained from parents and others who knew of their condition and whose assessment may have been biased by that knowledge. And alternate explanations of the phenomena were not ruled out. So, by the rules of science itself, this research fails. It has succeeded in spite of this in attracting adherents, researchers, and supporters because it reinforces sexist attitudes in the culture.

Fausto-Sterling's vision of good science is work that is methodologically sound, but methodological soundness in a limiting or conventional framework is not enough. Her interest in criticizing the androcentric and sexist work is both to discredit it and to make room for more complex views of natural processes to emerge. Given our culture's longstanding misogyny, conventional science will inevitably derogate women and femininity. Good science about women, gender, and gender-linked processes can only begin to emerge in the context of a political women's movement which undercuts old stereotypes and provides a constituency for new research. In later work she is interested less in using science against itself than in showing the socio-political dimensions of a variety of biological research programs.[3] For example, she analyzes the way conventional ideas about sex and gender limit and frame research on embryonic sex determination. She contrasts this work with results of research on embryonic development informed by more egalitarian views of sexual difference.

Many thinkers about the sciences, while not disputing Fausto-Sterling's particular arguments, are impatient with this method of demonstrating masculine bias in the sciences. They argue that there is something tainted about science itself which this approach does not reveal. In particular they claim that the approach of Fausto-Sterling and other scientists critiquing the androcentric biases in their fields leaves scientific method and the culture's glorification of rationality and objectivity untouched: Science is still master. As Audre Lorde has said, "One cannot use the master's tools to tear down the master's house."

Critics of the master's tools approach have gone outside of the natural sciences for a more adequate theoretical fulcrum—looking to psychology, sociology, history, literary theory, and even philosophy. Radical and feminist work in these disciplines offers ways to think about the sciences as a whole rather than engaging in the dismantling of one (or several) offending part(s).

Evelyn Fox Keller

Evelyn Fox Keller has straddled the boundaries between science and meta-science in both the research and teaching aspects of her professional career. A mathematical biologist with an earlier training in physics, she has become internationally known for her biography of geneticist Barbara McClintock and even more for her attempt to grapple with the masculinity of science in her book *Reflections on Gender and Science*.[4] This is not an idle academic problem for Keller. The kinds of analyses developed in both these books help make sense of her own experience as a scientist—the personal distancing by fellow (but male) graduate students and the resistance to some of her ideas when a practicing theoretical biologist. Why are the natural sciences a male and a masculine preserve? Why are the sciences seemingly committed to linear causal analysis even when interactionist views generate equal if not better analyses? Keller argues that these are two sides of the same question. Her contributions to feminist science studies are multiple. She draws attention to contemporary research programs that inscribe domination in natural processes—searches for "the master molecule" governing any given biochemical process. She outlines alternative approaches actually pursued in the sciences—McClintock's work on genetic transposition and on the interaction of chromosomes and the cellular environment, Keller's own work with Lee Segel on slime mold aggregation. She offers an account, drawing on the object relations school of psychoanalysis, of the interaction of cognitive and affective processes. She argues, along with others like Carolyn Merchant and Brian Easlea, that the sciences were appropriated (or re-appropriated) during the 17th century as a masculine domain, in terms congenial not only to the new experimental science but also to new ideals of gender.[5]

In all of this Keller is committed to the importance of science, and seemingly to the power of scientific inquiry to reveal the character of real processes in the real world. At least this is what one might conclude on the basis of her very strong suggestion that a static objectivity (one which emphasizes the differences between the inquiring self and the known or knowable world) provides a familiar but distorted representation of natural processes while an objectivity she characterizes as dynamic has the capacity to provide a (different but) better or more reliable representation of these processes. This latter representation reveals a world characterized by interaction, interdependence, diversity, and self-organization. As Keller's own work and her commentary on McClintock's work indicate, she is herself more partial to models with these characteristics. To the extent that certain methodologies of the modern and contemporary sciences are incapable of revealing these aspects of nature, such methodologies, and the presuppositions from which they arise, are inadequate to the task of science. As Jane Martin and Ian Hacking have pointed out, one of Keller's contributions here is to draw us (philosophers) away from our obsession with propositional knowledge and the theoretical dimension of science to focus on the interactions of the scientist with her (material) subject matter.[6] Keller engages in multiple analytic tasks—substantive, epistemological, moral—that are integrated through their ultimate grounding in psychoanalytic theory. But while the concepts of psychoanalysis act as a sort of discovery tool, readers can respond to (and have responded to) the ideas about the sciences—to ideas about causality, knowledge, discovery, and our relationship to nature—without adopting the psychoanalytic perspective.

In more recent work, Keller has approached these metascientific issues from a slightly different vantage point.[7] In particular, her implicit judgments of the adequacy or inadequacy of a theory are (apart from issues of empirical adequacy) driven not by a commitment to a particular philosophy of nature but by views of human needs. Her view here is that the sciences provide models of nature with the aim of facilitating certain sorts of interventions, i.e. inducing changes in the real which affect our own relation to the real in certain desired ways. That we have any unmediated experience of the real, or that there could be a single correct model is not presupposed here. "We have proven that we are smart enough to learn what we need to know to get much of what we want; perhaps it's time we thought more about what we want."[8] Rather than the correct method, this work seems to set its audience the task of finding, choosing, or articulating the correct values from which will emerge a different science. As the paragraph ends, it becomes clear that Keller wants the sciences and those engaged in them to make a commitment to a particular value—survival. If we do think more about what we want, we will discover that this is the point "where the convergence of our [diverse] interests might be said to be obligatory."[9] Keller's essay is among other things a call to reorient scientific inquiry in the understanding that such reorientation cannot but change the character of scientific knowledge as well as the uses to which it can be put. Where in the earlier work she looked to the sources whence inquiry sprang, here she looks to the goals inquiry can help to fulfill.

While Keller's work has been taken up by feminist scholars and by historians and philosophers of science, her intended audience is scientists and her goal is the reform of the sciences. These intentions explain the rhetorical and argumentative strategies she has adopted throughout these discussions. Even as they have evolved they evince the desire for some invariant—whether it is a better developed cognitive attitude or a set of values—on which change can be grounded. These invariants are or could be characteristics of the practitioners of science. To the extent they recognize themselves in her portrayals they can find a rallying point and ground for effecting change in their specific fields of inquiry.

Donna Haraway

Donna Haraway, although herself trained as a biologist, seeks to distance herself from the sciences, at the very moment that she discusses them. She accomplishes this distancing through her choice of analytical tool—narrative theory. Rather than regard the sciences as a means of developing true representations or even instruments of prediction and thereby getting trapped by the epistemological quandaries this presents both for the scientist and for the critic of science, she treats scientific texts as stories, using the techniques of literary analysis to extract their meaning. The sciences she examines are the sciences of primatology—which tell stories of human origins and purportedly reveal what is natural about human nature. Haraway's readings of these stories are complex, intertextual, and socially and politically situated.[10] She examines the institutional contexts in which they were and are produced, the networks of instruction and affiliation in which their producers are enmeshed, and the multiple layers of meaning encoded and created in the texts. Such meanings come into being quite independently of the aims and intentions of individuals, and are a function both of the preoccupations of the social and institutional contexts in which the texts of primatology are produced and read and of the metaphors made current by such preoccupations. Haraway reads and encourages us to read primatological texts, therefore, not for what they tell us about human nature, or about the various primate species, but for what they tell us about their authors, not as individuals, but as spokespersons for their cultures.

The stories told—of sexual relations, of social dominance, of stress, and of choice—are produced according to strict rules (scientific method). Primatology has always been ostensibly about the members of certain ape and monkey societies and as it has been professionalized it has developed explicit (if changing) rules about how to extract or elicit information from and about these societies. Nevertheless, primatology has also been about production, social management, communication, control, and investment strategies; about the conditions for managing social relations among inherently cooperative organisms and about the conditions for establishing order among inherently aggressive, mutually antagonistic organisms. By showing the mutability of primatological visions in response to different human social and economic preoccupations, Haraway invites us to cast away our own preoccupation with objectivity, truth, and getting it right.

Her joyfully deconstructive approach to traditional boundaries between nature and culture, human and animal, organism and machine, and her dismissive attitude towards traditional epistemological concerns may lead readers to ascribe to Haraway an anti-realism that licenses any claim so long as it is in opposition to accepted mainstream discourses. Such a reading is itself too mired in the epistemological. Haraway is not telling us how to do science or how to create new knowledge. She is telling us how to read science—"primatology is politics" proclaims one of her titles—and telling us, if anything, how *not* to create knowledge of human society and human justice. The primatological texts she analyzes are produced from social positions reflecting certain interests. Many are produced as the basis for manuals of social manipulation and control, while others are produced with one hand extended to contemporary liberation movements. One of primatology's self-appointed explanatory goals is to develop some account of a transition from nature to culture. To speak of a transition must assume some distinction between the two, at a juncture inevitably constructed by the very socio-political preoccupations which the texts are meant to inform. Haraway's aims and audience are thus quite different from those of the authors previously considered. She is not contesting (though she does expose) androcentric or masculinist representations in science nor is she trying to recruit scientists to an alternative or oppositional scientific practice. While hoping to be read by her subjects she writes primarily for a lay-reader—a left-wing intellectual at least sympathetic to feminism and concerned with contesting the hegemony of scientism. Surely one hoped-for outcome would be the ejection of science, not from its role as representer of natural processes, but from its role as arbiter of politics. The sciences can tell us about the chemistry of immunity, even in highly politicized metaphors. They cannot tell us about justice; that is for us to define and realize.

Haraway's claims that a new social order will evoke a new biology may be read as a suggestion that science is just ideology. Haraway is not a simple relativist, nor can she be read as anti-realist in any metaphysical sense. In an essay that explores the metaphors of militarism, difference, and integrity constructing the meaning of selfhood in contemporary immunology, Haraway stops briefly to answer an imagined question about the facticity of biological entities as opposed to the ficticity of science fiction's fantasies.[11] Bodies, by which I understand "entities," are "material semiotic actors." They are not simply ideological constructions, but actively participate (as do the chimps of *Primate Visions*) in the construction of knowledge about them. What Haraway denies is only that bodies (from amino acids to you and me) uniquely and solely determine what counts as knowledge about them. Bodies certainly impose constraints on what can be said about them. These are just not the constraints Haraway is interested in exposing. The constraints which interest her are those imposed by politics, by the play of power among those who seek knowledge.

Sandra Harding

Unlike the previous three thinkers, Sandra Harding is an academic philosopher—explicitly concerned with epistemological questions and their convergence with issues in social and political theory. Empiricism, which she identifies with positivism, has failed, in Harding's view, as an account of human knowledge—scientific or otherwise. Harding endorses and extends the arguments of philosophers such as Quine against positivism by foregrounding aspects of positivism that work against an understanding of the operation of gender in science. Much of her book, *The Science Question in Feminism,* can be read as a canvas of feminist theory for an adequate replacement to positivism.[12]

The rejection of positivism is for Harding not just the rejection of a normative view about the forms of justification appropriate to the sciences. Harding implicitly treats positivism as correctly reflecting the methodology of mainstream science. The rejection of positivism is, thus, simultaneously a rejection of mainstream science. Harding concludes *The Science Question in Feminism* with a new vision of the unity of science, a vision in which reflexive and self-critical social sciences occupy the foundational place occupied by physics in the positivists' vision. She offers the promise of a science transformed in her reversal of the traditional unity of science, but it is also a science made unrecognizable. Part of the problem is the identification of scientific inquiry with the logical positivists' image of science. This is a misreading of the endorsement of logical positivism by some scientists. Such endorsement was really directed at positivism's privileging of scientific over other forms of knowledge rather than at its account of scientific practice. It is the positivists' image of scientific inquiry that must be rejected.

Harding locates her work within the feminist project to remake knowledge. It seems to be Harding's view that an adequate epistemology is a prerequisite for an adequate science. Her strategy in developing such an epistemology has been to look to the argumentative and rhetorical practices of self-identified feminists working in sociology and in biology. It is here that she has found the theories she identifies as feminist empiricism and feminist standpoint theory. She draws out the philosophical commitments and implications of these views partly by tracing the connections among their various feminist exponents and partly by reviewing their philosophical ancestry—classical empiricism, logical positivism, and Marxism. And surely there are elements of empiricism in the biologists' critique of sexist science, as well as elements of standpoint theory in Keller's account of objectivity. The women primatologists studied by Haraway include exponents of empiricism as well as claimants to a special access to the lives of other female primates or to the workings of primate societies. What has most occupied Harding are the conflicts between "empiricism" and "standpoint theory," which she is never able to resolve in favor of one or the other.[13] Even during her flirtation with a version of postmodernist anti-epistemology, she claimed that it could not displace empiricism and standpoint theory, both of which were still necessary. Given her explications of empiricism and standpoint theory, this has left her seemingly in the grip of a contradiction. In *The Science Question in Feminism,* Harding constructs an epistemological dialectic in which the internal contradictions of feminist empiricism give way, in turn, to feminist postmodernism. Nevertheless, the projects of feminist empiricism and of feminist standpoint theory must be carried on.

This position seems paradoxical, at best. Here, too, considerations of audience are useful. Harding writes for several audiences. One is the ever increasing multidisciplinary group of Women's Studies teachers and scholars. For these, she provides a guide to the literature about science, a way to see its various aspects in relation to each other. Both scholars identified as feminist empiricists and those identified as feminist standpoint theorists have made distinctive and crucial contributions to feminist scholarship. She may think, therefore, that it would be perverse to claim that either approach was based on so fatally flawed a philosophical view that it ought not be pursued. Harding identifies another audience in a recent exchange with Dorothy Smith: administrators of universities and foundations, the people who sit on grant committees, tenure committees, and thesis committees.[14] Here she is the feminist activist, striving to make the value of feminist work evident to those with the power to choke it off or let it grow. Here again she would undermine her aims by judging between the positions she describes. But a segment of Harding's audience, certainly her internal audience, consists of philosophers and this audience requires attention to philosophical topics, hence she must acknowledge, even while she does not resolve, the conflict between positivist and Marxist theories of knowledge. She is respectful of the situated character of the feminist research programs whose tensions she explores. The philosopher's impulse to universality sits uneasily with that respect.

Reflections

Each of these thinkers, and we with her, confronts a scientific world shaped by the concerns and interests of Euro-American middle-class males. Each stands in a different relation to that world and to the political movements that challenge Euro-American middle-class male supremacy, and each engages in a different mediation between these two worlds. Neither the scientific world nor these political movements constitute exclusive monoliths. They are each composed of a complex of partially overlapping communities, some of which participate in both worlds.

Each of the positions in which our actors find themselves is a node in a force field that defines a different set of possibilities and political tasks. The developmental biologist practicing in the laboratory who is a woman and feminist challenges the representations of women and the use of gender stereotypes in contemporary biology. Is it possible to do better? She answers by citing an example of a scientist who works in a manner accountable to women. The theoretical biologist, edged out of physics because of her sex, advocate of non-standard models, speaks to and for other such advocates, speaking at times out of a shared form of non-standard, because non-masculinist, relationship to nature and at times out of hope of a shared value around which deviant scientists can rally to produce an alternative representation of natural processes. Another biologist leaves the discipline altogether, finding a new home in history and cultural studies. The analytical tools of these disciplines and her insider's knowledge of the world of biology are resources which she makes available to the political movement outside biology. Haraway's rhetoric presupposes a commitment to anti-colonialism, anti-capitalism, anti-sexism on the part of her readers. Her analysis seeks to demystify science for such readers. By contrast, Keller seems to seek a more common denominator—perhaps a wise decision given the already small size of the pool from which she can expect recruits/allies. And Fausto-Sterling, while empowering women outside of science, does so by enabling them to talk back to their definers in a language they understand. That is, she shows the inadequacies of the biological representations of the female by reference to the very standards the promoters of those representations endorse. Finally, Harding claims to make the activities of feminists in science intelligible and legitimate to the administrators who have power over their projects. If in the process she succeeds in nudging the scientists themselves into even more self-reflection on their practice and the philosophical reconstruction of their practice, so much the better.

As a philosopher, however, I want to ask what the real philosophical differences are here. On first reading, and, as I said, hearing the reflection of their views in the feminist debates about the sciences, we might anticipate deep and interesting metaphysical and epistemological differences. When we look for explicit arguments, however, and discount for rhetoric aimed at certain audiences, these anticipations turn to dust.

For example, we find statements in Fausto-Sterling's book to the effect that the biological determinist view does not do justice to the facts of biology. *"Facts,"* we might say, "this shows Fausto-Sterling thinks that there are facts—she's a realist—and that biology can find them. She believes scientific method can reveal the real as it is in itself." But this rhetoric can also be read more modestly. Set in the context of Fausto-Sterling's other statements, it can mean merely that among the methodologies and theories in contemporary biology there are resources to draw on in countering the ideas of the determinists. We can read her strategy as bringing out the diversity and richness of biological thinking rather than claiming any privileged access to truth when the scientific method is properly applied.

Similarly, as we follow Haraway treating the texts of primatology as stories, we may be tempted (as some of her readers have been) to read her as saying they are "just stories" or "just fictions." Hence, anything goes. This is to ignore her assertions elsewhere that the production of these accounts is rule-governed and that representations produced according to rules of inquiry in given fields have made it possible to interact with our material surroundings in reliable ways. This, too, is not to say that the rules provide a privileged access to the real, but it should warn us against interpreting Haraway as licensing any claims whatever in science since they are all fiction anyway. (And the novelists among us might remind us that if there is a fiction in the discourses of truth, so there is a truth in the discourses of fiction.)

While I read, therefore, no firm commitment to scientific realism in these authors, neither do I find a commitment to any of the current alternatives to scientific realism in post-positivist philosophy of science. (This is not to say that when pressed they might not make such a commitment.) An interesting philosophical project would involve determining which of the various alternatives is most compatible with the ontological commitments in the work of any of the feminist scientists I've discussed. But this is a job for philosophers. The scientists themselves aren't interested unless we can persuade them that it matters.

It is equally hard to find commitments to particular epistemological theories, where by an epistemological theory we mean a justificatory theory. Instead, we find recipes for inquiry, suggested procedures for deciphering nature, none of which amount to criteria of justification. One point of difference here does lie in attitudes toward the pursuit of alternative accounts within the sciences. Both Fausto-Sterling and Keller seem to urge this project, whereas the historian explores tensions and conflicts among the various alternatives pursued by women in primatology, and the philosopher explores tensions and conflicts between metascientific views. Here again, I think it a mistake to read these differences as metaphysical or epistemological. It might be possible to read commitments to partial, local knowledge on one side as against the hope for a new but comprehensive framework on the other. But, for reasons already explored, it would be difficult to construct stable alignments along these axes and, secondly, the grounds for the attitudes towards alternative scientific practices and research programs are not primarily metaphysical or epistemological, but political.

Each of these theorists would claim that the sciences are a central conceptual (as well as material) support of the structures of power feminists wish to change. Where they disagree is on how best to weaken this particular foundation—from within or from without. Fausto-Sterling and Keller believe that the supportive role of science is acquired at the cost of constricting the variety possible within science and falsifying its epistemic character. Their work is directed at loosening in different ways the external constraints imposed upon scientific activity and thereby cracking its positivist image. Scientific research deviating from the mainstream may be of use to those seeking political change. More immediately it weakens the support the sciences can give to established power, by challenging the hegemony of a privileged world picture. Keller also sometimes seems to suggest that the sciences can contribute to changing the world. Rather than trying to produce the diversity of which scientific activity is capable, Haraway reveals that diversity—by documenting the mutability of mainstream primatology which is capable of including Carpenter, Yerkes, and Washburn as well as feminist (or female-centered) accounts of primate behavior. While her coolly ironic presentation may seem an attack from outside the walls of science, it depends crucially on the diversity within science. She contests not Science, but certain claims on behalf of Science. Harding does locate the origin of her critique firmly outside the sciences. By identifying the sciences with their positivist image, she treats arguments against positivism as effective against the claims of science. From this perspective, attempts to do science differently than prescribed by the established modes are doomed reformism. The only value of such attempts is that they will result in alienation of those scientists from the sciences, i.e. in a withdrawal of allegiance that will destabilize the claim of the sciences upon our belief. Science entire, not just particular claims and theories, must be created anew in a new social order.

If I am correct in seeing these conflicts as differences in political analysis and strategy, why do they get read and expressed as epistemological and metaphysical? Part of the problem lies in the language available to analyze the sciences. Here, feminists are badly served by traditional philosophy of science. As feminists, we are concerned with the sciences as a set of institutions. The critical language provided by philosophy to analyze the sciences is an epistemological one. But the transition between a critique of epistemological presuppositions and a critique of institutions is very treacherous, not least because traditional epistemology is framed in individualist terms, while institutions must be analyzed with social categories.[15] Traditional philosophy of science and its categories are ill suited to the critical analysis that our own kind of critique of the sciences demands. Feminist work in and about the sciences raises *new* questions not confinable to traditional issues about rationality and objectivity. Such questions include, among others: Just what *is* the relation between social change and scientific change? Is it possible to engage in theorizing that does not intimately articulate with existing social distributions of power? What are the consequences of directing our philosophical attention away from propositional knowledge to the relationship between scientist and phenomena?

Why do we persist in framing our arguments within the traditional categories, thus magnifying our differences? Here are some suggestions. First, one unspoken tension in this field lies between psychoanalytically based theorists and theorists based in Marxism. Are epistemological questions carrying the weight of conflict over these analytic approaches? If so, we need more direct and comparative discussion of what can be accomplished within these intellectual frameworks. Second, unlike some other areas of feminist scholarship, there are relatively few central participants in the debates over gender and science, and the field of feminist science studies is, compared with areas such as women's history or feminist literary criticism, still very small. Does this lead us to see our potential audience as a scarce resource? or to think that there is room for only one correct line? Third, could it be that our construction of these differences is itself refracted through the father's eye, through *his* language, *his* questions, for *his* attention? If we could free ourselves from this internal bondage, our disagreements surely would not disappear, but they might generate more creative and productive difference. Such disagreements would expand our intellectual horizons, as well as the domain of science studies, rather than fostering competition over limited concepts.[16]

Part 2
The Matter of Women *in* Science (Evelynn Hammonds)

Feminist studies of science face many other, considerably more vexing areas of conflicts, that arise between working women scientists and feminists critical of contemporary science. In fact, the reception of the feminist critique of science by practicing women scientists has not been an altogether positive one. Some of the reasons lie with the perceived political project of the feminist critique (and in this post-Reagan era much of the public perception of feminism is negative) and others lie with the failure of this critique to offer examples of the gendered structure of the physical sciences and mathematics. The central conflict, however, is over the interpretation of "science," "gender," and "feminism." This conflict can be expressed in two questions: Working women scientists persist in asking: "What is it about women and women's lives that have kept them from doing science?" whereas feminist critics of science ask: "What is it about science that has limited the participation of women and, by extension, other marginalized groups?"

Many women scientists continue to perceive the feminist critique as putting forth a simple characterization of science that reinforces traditional stereotypes both of women and of science. While many of us engaged in feminist studies of science see this work as ultimately helpful to women scientists, far too many of these women (perhaps especially those who have made it into the enclaves of the "hard" sciences) do not see it that way. In their view, the feminist critiques of science hurt, rather than advance their cause.

Professional organizations of women scientists and engineers were established to "promote equal opportunities for women to enter the professions and to achieve their career goals."[17] They believe that the problems women face in science and engineering can be traced first and foremost to environmental issues—how women are treated in schools and in the workplace; if they just work harder, show that they are team players, don't drop out when they have children, develop more confidence in themselves, put aside their desire for emotional connectedness in their work, dismiss stereotypes that science and engineering are "thing-oriented" professions, increase the numbers of women in science, the environment will change and the problems will be solved. As one scientist reassuringly insists, "The reality about women is that there need be no conflict between being fully-fledged scientists and being fully female; we get to be both."[18]

In her Presidential Lecture to the AAAS, Sheila Widnall, MIT Aeronautical & Astronautical engineer,[19] notes that women and minorities are needed to fill the anticipated gaps in scientific personnel in the future. She discusses recent studies which show that graduate school environments have had an effect on the completion rates of women and minorities in the natural sciences and engineering. She asserts that the issue is not that women are not capable of doing science but that the environment they encounter in their education fails to enhance their self-esteem and provide positive professional experiences. Her charge to her colleagues is: treat women better, we need them, we will all benefit by the improvement in the educational environment. More importantly this can be accomplished ". . . while being no less insightful and scientifically critical . . . ."[20] Widnall, like many other women scientists and engineers, makes no connection between the problems women encounter and the structure of scientific knowledge and scientific education. They persist in arguing against the perception that women can't do science while never attempting to address the source of such perceptions.

Widnall does however see a potential problem in the future funding of science if it continues to be perceived as an activity solely for white males. "The years ahead may be troublesome for the support of science, and the image of science as a community accessible to all will be important to maintain public support,"[21] she concedes. It is clearly not Widnall's intent to portray the exclusion of women and minorities from science as merely an image problem, but her comments do suggest that the perception of exclusion lies with the excluded and not within the scientific professions.

To confront culturally defined stereotypes about women's nature and about what scientists do, women scientists tend to offer two strategies. The first is to expose the "private world" of scientific work. As one woman mathematician notes: "It would appear that there is a private and public world of mathematics. The private world is where struggle, failure, incomprehension, intuition, and creativity dominate . . . The public world is where the results of the private struggle make their appearance in a formal, conventional abstract formulation from which all evidence of false trails, inadequate reasoning or misunderstandings have been eliminated. Unfortunately for our pupils, the majority are given access to only the public world."[22] By exposing this private world where values more often associated with women are displayed, these women scientists hope to show how women can fit into science without changing themselves. The second strategy suggests that women do have to change their view of their own abilities in order to be successful in science. Admitting the truth of some culturally familiar notions about women's problems with science and technology, articles about women's relationships to physical objects encourage them to overcome their fears or alienation from technology by developing more aggressive behaviors and more confidence in themselves. Such articles reinforce the belief that there are behaviors and attitudes peculiar to women that hamper their progress within science. This is the very idea women scientists want to dispel.

Many of these women scientists focus on "fitting" women to science, while denouncing the idea that science is a necessarily male activity as merely a stereotype. They do not believe that gender has any bearing on scientific work. Gender is not itself a scientific issue, it is a purely social one. Science, they argue, as understood by those who really do it, is an activity devoid of any connections to social behaviors. It follows then that science cannot be implicated in the "legitimation of society's gendered beliefs and norms."[23]

As Widnall's remarks suggest, many of the professional women scientists neither hear nor understand the feminist critique. Their deep belief in the meritocratic ideology of science is unexamined and unshaken. For the most part, they are unfamiliar even with the history of women in science, except for the uncritical portraits of great women of the past, so often published in the professional journals. What tends to go especially unnoted is the important critical analyses of many of these women's careers. For example, a review of Anne Sayre's book on Rosalind Franklin (in *U.S. Woman Engineer*) reads: "today we can look at Franklin's story as a lesson to keep an open mind, to listen to others, to avoid being overly dogmatic; and most importantly, to speak out when one is sure of the facts—not an easy balancing act!"[24] The complicated circumstances which led to the suppression of Franklin's contribution to the discovery of the structure of DNA is clearly not known to this reviewer. Instead, Franklin's story is reduced to a lesson in assertiveness training for women who want to be successful scientists. Unmarked by the alternate narratives of feminists, the professional journals of women scientists and engineers continue to reinforce the notion that women can do science and do it well, even while doing all the other things that women do. They portray the many successful women in the field who juggle home life and work, and insist that being a successful woman scientist is not different than being a successful woman in any other profession. The "science" that they want to do is the "science" that men do. Even if they acknowledge that women might want to engage in scientific work more directly connected to human concerns, they suggest that this can be done within the wide range of scientific work available. It is not necessary to go outside of science to accommodate such goals. The literature argues, in fact, that the prevailing image of scientists as dispassionate human beings with no need for close human contact or nurturance are nothing but stereotypes, stereotypes most detrimental to women. "Then women scientists are told that we are not good at and do not need what is almost considered a defining characteristic of our sex. We get appreciated for being different from other women rather than recognized for the characteristics we have in common."[25]

Unlike those who would merely encourage more women to enter science, or those who envision some uniquely "feminine" way of doing science, some working women scientists have attempted to understand and sympathize with the feminist critique of science, though they often find it unfamiliar and disturbing. For example, a recent article in the *Notices of the American Mathematical Society*, raises a number of by now familiar points against the feminist critique of science. The main objection is that it might work to discourage women from entering mathematics and science ". . . because this literature perpetuates stereotypes and misconceptions about mathematics and science . . ."[26] The author argues that feminist critics present the nature of science in such a way that it alienates women and perpetuates a strong anti-science bias. Few, if any, distinctions are made between feminist critics of science; the critique is represented as a static unified body of work. More significantly, there seems to be no understanding of the questions that feminist critics of science have attempted to address. Women mathematicians cited see the feminist critics as *accepting* stereotypical notions about women rather than *questioning* them. This is a very curious reading of the feminist literature. Ideas about how gender is constructed within scientific discourses are constantly read as statements *about* women scientists. One mathematician writes: "They reiterate rather than question our society's belief that women are closer to nature, that they are more instinctive, intuitive."[27] Another claims, "One of the main objections to the critiques is their view of science and mathematics as inherently masculine. This view is based on stereotypes of science and mathematics: the problem is that some of these scholars have taken the stereotypes literally."[28]

A more problematic point of contention between feminist critics and these women mathematicians is the inference or claim that mathematics and other mathematized sciences are also gendered. In fact, feminist critics have made little headway in specifically articulating how gender is inscribed in these sciences. Many, if not most, of the examples used in feminist critiques have come from the biological sciences where gender bias in language and practice seem more easily described. Women in the mathematical sciences object to the practice of extending generalizations based on biology to their own disciplines. They argue that strict adherence to scientific method makes mathematical science gender-free.

For these women scientists, science simply works; the laws of physics are what they are, proven by their consistency with experiment, and by the great technological advances they have spurred. To them, science is *defined* as the product of scientific method—a method that self-corrects for all human biases—including any that could arise from biases of gender. As one mathematician put it, "One still wants to know whether feminists' airplanes would stay airborne for feminist engineers."[29] Discussions of science in any other terms is incomprehensible to these women scientists. To them, the only possible connection that feminism could have to science would be to make it possible for more women to do science under the most equitable circumstances.

Conclusion

Women scientists are educated, as men scientists are, with no self-critical perspective about their own disciplines. Reflexivity and self-criticism are neither valued nor encouraged. It is therefore not surprising that they find little commonality with a feminist critique premised on just such a perspective. What is more troubling, however, is that women scientists have so little sense of history. The strategies proposed by feminists and non-feminists to help women achieve their career goals and to bring more women into the scientific professions are virtually identical to those of women scientists before World War II. As Margaret Rossiter notes, the separate organizations of women scientists found that efforts to provide psychological self-help to their members or lobbying professional organizations for more recognition of women failed. These groups ". . . were not designed or able to change the established structure of scientific employment in a sexist society."[30] The feminist critique of science begins, in part, with the acknowledgment that these strategies have failed.

That science is in fact neither fully objective nor value-free, that it serves particular social, economic, and political interests, is in some cases not too difficult for many women scientists to accept—the "private world" of science has always revealed to them such flaws. Yet, the absence of a clearly articulated alternative to conventional practices remains a critical stumbling block to a rapprochement between even these women scientists and feminist critics. What options do practicing women scientists have, other than to apply the existing method more faithfully? Feminists critics have articulated a sophisticated argument about the inscription of gender in the language and norms of scientific practice, but they have been less successful in demonstrating, at least to the satisfaction of practicing scientists, how the scientific method, especially in the "exact" sciences, is itself inscribed by gender. Above all, we have yet to demonstrate how the scientific method can provide successful representations of the physical world while at the same time inscribing social structures of domination and control in its institutional, conceptual, and methodological core.

Notes

1. For an excellent bibliography, see Alison Wylie, Kathleen Okruhlik, Leslie Thielen-Wilson, Sandra Morton, "Feminist Critiques of Science: the Epistemological and Methodological Literature," *Women's Studies International Forum*, 12, 3 (1989): 379–388.

2. Anne Fausto-Sterling, *Myths of Gender* (New York, NY: Basic Books, 1985).

3. Anne Fausto-Sterling, "Life in the XY Corral," *Women's Studies International Forum*, 12, 3 (1989): 319–332.

4. Evelyn Fox Keller, *A Feeling for the Organism: The Life and Work of Barbara McClintock* (San Francisco, CA: W.H. Freeman, 1983) and *Reflections on Gender and Science* (New Haven, CT: Yale University Press, 1985).

5. Several writers have described a masculine appropriation of knowledge and science in the 16th and 17th centuries. Carolyn Merchant in *The Death of Nature: Women, Ecology and the Scientific Revolution* (San Francisco, CA: Harper and Row, 1980); Brian Easlea in *Witch Hunting, Magic and the New Philosophy* (Brighton, U.K.: Harvester Press, 1980); and Keller in *Reflections on Gender and Science* all describe a struggle between the hermetic/magical tradition in natural philosophy and the newer mechanical philosophy. This struggle is expressed in a rhetoric of gender and sexuality that eventually makes of nature a female to be conquered and the scientist her male conqueror (by charm, wile, or force). The triumph of the mechanical corpuscularist philosophy of matter deanimates nature and by extension woman—matter and the female become a metaphor each for the other. The legacy of this ancient struggle is a natural science preoccupied with power and domination, expressed vividly in this century in the quests for the secrets of the atom and later the secret of life—the gene.

6. Jane Martin, "Science in a Different Style," *American Philosophical Quarterly*, 25 (1988): 129–140; Ian Hacking, "Philosophers of Experiment" in *PSA 1988*, ed. Arthur Fine and Jarrett Leplin (East Lansing, MI: Philosophy of Science Association, 1989), pp. 147–156.

7. Evelyn Fox Keller, "Critical Silences in Scientific Discourse: Problems of Form and Reform," paper presented at the Institute for Advanced Study, Princeton, NJ,

February 4, 1988. This material is incorporated in Keller's chapter "Gender and Science," *The Great Ideas Today* (Chicago, IL: Encyclopedia Britannica, Inc. 1990).

8. Keller, "Critical Silences," p. 28.

9. *Idem.*

10. Donna Haraway, *Primate Visions: Gender, Race and Nature in the World of Modern Science* (New York, NY: Routledge, 1989).

11. Donna Haraway, "The Biopolitics of Postmodern Bodies: Determinations of Self in Immune System Discourse," *Differences* 1, 1 (Winter, 1989): 3–44.

12. Sandra Harding, *The Science Question in Feminism* (Ithaca, NY: Cornell University Press, 1986).

13. As well as *The Science Question,* see Sandra Harding, "How the Women's Movement Benefits Science: Two Views," *Women's Studies International Forum,* 12,3 (1989): 271–284.

14. Sandra Harding, "Response," *Newsletter on Feminism and Philosophy,* 88,3 (June, 1989): 46–49.

15. Harding's restrictive account of the sciences locates the exclusionary power of the sciences in epistemology, rather than in the social and political interactions of scientists and scientific institutions. While it seems to be a more radical critique of the sciences, it achieves its radicality at the price of denying evident features of scientific thought and practice even when we remove our positivist spectacles.

16. I am indebted for this vision to Valerie Miner's image of expanding the bookshelf rather than fighting for a designated space in it in her essay "Rumors from the Cauldron: Competition Among Feminist Writers," in Valerie Miner and Helen Longino, eds., *Competition: A Feminist Taboo?* (New York: The Feminist Press, 1987).

17. Motto of the Association for Women in Science.

18. Sheela Mierson, "We're Ok; Internalized Sexism: Issues for Women Scientists," *AWIS Newsletter,* 18, 3 (May/June, 1989).

19. Sheila Widnall, "AAAS Presidential Lecture: Voices from the Pipeline," *Science,* 241, 30 (September, 1988).

20. Ibid., p. 1745.

21. Ibid., p. 1741.

22. Leone Burton quoted in Allyn Jackson, "Feminist Critiques of Science," *Notices of the American Mathematical Society,* 36, 6 (July/August, 1989)): 672.

23. Ruth Bleier, "A Decade of Feminist Critiques in the Natural Sciences," *Signs,* 14, 1 (1988).

24. Evelyn M. E. Murray, Review of A. Sayre, *Rosalind Franklin and DNA,* (New York: Norton & Co., 1975) in *U.S. Woman Engineer,* (May/June, 1988): 33.

25. Mierson, "We're Ok," p. 13.

26. Jackson, "Feminist Critiques," p. 669.

27. Ibid., p. 671.

28. Ibid., p. 672.

29. Margarita Levin, "Caring New World: Feminism and Science," *The American Scholar* (Winter 1988): 105.

30. Margaret Rossiter, *Women Scientists in America: Struggles and Strategies to 1940* (Baltimore: Johns Hopkins University Press, 1982) p. 316.

11

Race, Class, and Psychoanalysis?
Opening Questions

Elizabeth Abel

Although psychoanalytic theory has done a great deal to improve our understanding of sexual difference, it has done little or nothing to change the concrete social conditions of sex-relations and of gender-stratification. The latter is precisely the target of feminist practice.

            Rosi Braidotti, "The Politics of Ontological Difference"

It would seem fairly obvious by now that feminism's struggle to infuse into psychoanalytical theory the breath of an efficacious politics has not been a major success. Feminist approaches in recent years to Lacanian psychoanalysis, for example . . . have been thwarted by the obstinacy of psychoanalytic universalist *theories of subjective construction.*

            Paul Smith, "Julia Kristeva Et Al.; or, Take Three or More"[1]

Repudiating psychoanalysis has become a familiar gesture of contemporary feminist discourse—and with some good reasons.[2] Seduced by psychoanalytic accounts of subjectivity, much feminist theory of the 1970s has come to seem, from the vantage point of the late 1980s, to have lost its material groundings and with them the possibility of interpreting (and thereby promoting) social change. The traditional indifference of psychoanalysis to racial, class, and cultural differences, and the tendency of psychoanalysis to insulate subjectivity from social practices and discourses all run contrary to a feminism increasingly attuned to the power of social exigencies and differences in the constitution of subjectivity. It is clear that a psychoanalysis useful for contemporary feminism needs some infusion of the social—whether the "social" is construed as the technologies that regulate desire or (in this essay's terms) as the roles of race and class in a diversified construction of subjectivity.[3] It is less clear whether the resistance of psychoanalysis to the social is adventitious or intrinsic. If we agree (as I do) with Paul Smith that psychoanalysis has no innate political desire, we nevertheless can ask how labile psychoanalysis is, how far its boundaries can expand to incorporate issues of social difference into a discourse useful, if not for changing the social order, at least for theorizing this order's intervention in the production of diversely gendered subjects.

Psychoanalysis, of course, is not a monolithic discourse and has no uniform relation to the social domain. Freud's resistance to a culturally inflected psychoanalysis is overt and infamous.[4] The recent revisions of Freud that have been more influential for feminism, however, have opened possibilities for new negotiations between the psychoanalytic and the social domains. Introducing the category of the social into Lacanian discourse requires a deliberate intervention, since this discourse collapses the social into a symbolic register that is always everywhere the same. While de-essentializing gender by relocating it in a cultural arena that is severed from biology, orthodox Lacanians essentialize a dehistoricized paternal law, derived from the symbolic Father, "the dead father of the law who . . . is there however weak or absent his real representative may be."[5] According to Jacqueline Rose, "the force of psychoanalysis is . . . precisely that it gives an account of patriarchal culture as a trans-historical and cross-cultural force. It therefore conforms to a feminist demand for a theory which can explain women's subordination across specific cultures and different historical moments."[6] By insisting that the Father's law is necessary and tantamount to culture, however, the official Lacanian account prohibits alternative conceptualizations of culture and renders variations within patriarchal social forms (and thus in the degree and kind of women's subordination) either inconsequential or invisible. Yet the very erasures accomplished by this discourse have pointed its most revisionist practitioners toward a reading of the ways that gender is diversely (de)constructed by the gaps between the social and symbolic domains.[7]

A less deliberate intervention is required within feminist object relations theory, which explicitly locates the production of gendered subjectivity in historically specific and socially variable caretaking arrangements. To foreground these diverse social arrangements would entail not a revision of this theory but, rather, a fulfillment of its claims to explain how the "inexorably social" self that is "constructed in a relational matrix" varies, along with that matrix, "by individual, culture, period, gender."[8] In principle, this matrix is not restricted to an invariant or insulated nuclear family; instead, it functions as a permeable membrane through which a wide range of changing social relations inform the evolution of the gendered subject. Jane Flax, for example, insists: "The caretaker brings to the relationship . . . the whole range of social experience—work, friends, interaction with political and economic institutions, and so on. The seemingly abstract and suprapersonal relations of class, race, and male dominance enter into the construction of 'individual' human development."[9] In practice, however, object relations discourse has confined itself to the Western middle-class nuclear family and has bracketed all variables other than gender; while avoiding the homogeneity of the Lacanian symbolic, this discourse has tended to homogenize gender by implying that children learn within the family a single uniform masculinity or femininity. Elizabeth Spelman has mounted a powerful critique of this homogenizing tendency by arguing that "children learn what it means to be men or women by learning what it is to be men or women of their race, class, ethnicity" since "women mother in a social and political context in which they not only are distinguished from men, but are, along with men of their same cultural background, distinguished from men and women of other cultural backgrounds."[10] But the inadequately textured accounts produced by object relations are not limitations intrinsic to the theory. In her response to a methodological debate on *The Reproduction of Mothering,* Nancy Chodorow invites further research into "class and ethnic differences, differences in family and household structure, differences in sexual orientation of parents, and historical and cross-cultural variations in these relationships" and claims that if she were to write a new *Reproduction of Mothering* she would "examine the link between what seems exclusively gender related and the construction of other aspects of society, politics, and culture."[11] This is not the direction her own work has pursued; but there is no intrinsic incompatibility between the governing principles of object relations theory and socially inflected qualifications of that theory.[12]

Posing the question of the social enables us to redraw the map of psychoanalytic feminism, so sharply and hierarchically split over the last decade between Lacan and object relations. Both psychoanalytic discourses now seem guilty, either in theory or in practice, of privileging a decontextualized gender as the constitutive factor in subjectivity; and both discourses are (diversely) subject to revision. When difference is interpreted within a social as well as a linguistic framework, moreover, the Lacanian critique of the unitary subject loses some of its special edge, and the heterogeneity of the Lacanian subject seems insufficiently textured and less radically different from the intersubjectively constituted self of object relations.[13] Most importantly, the urgency of theorizing subjectivity within a range of social contexts has made it less productive to reiterate the old oppositions within psychoanalytic feminism, or between psychoanalysis and contemporary feminism, than to imagine more fluid intersections.

Toward this end, I want to ground this essay in a reading of two dense and brilliant texts that address the intersections of gender with race or class from perspectives both indebted to and critical of psychoanalysis. Both published in this country in 1987, Hortense J. Spillers's "Mama's Baby, Papa's Maybe: An American Grammar Book," a psychoanalytically informed meditation on the devastations wrought by slavery on African-American kinship and gender structures, and Carolyn Kay Steedman's *Landscape for a Good Woman: A Story of Two Lives,* a reading of class analysis against and with psychoanalysis, are teasingly and deliberately polyphonic texts. Although Spillers works primarily with Lacan, and Steedman primarily with object relations, each asserts and subverts a range of psychoanalytic and social discourses and propels them into provocative and complicated play.

II

Is the Freudian landscape an applicable text (say nothing of appropriate) to social and historical situations that do not replicate moments of its own cultural origins and involvements?
Hortense J. Spillers, " 'The Permanent Obliquity of an In[pha]llibly Straight':
In the Time of the Daughters and the Fathers"[14]

"Mama's Baby, Papa's Maybe: An American Grammar Book" offers a quali-fied yes to the question of the applicability of psychoanalysis to the African-American social landscape, although, as the shift from the epigraph's spatial metaphor to the figure of the "grammar book" suggests, Lacanian rather than Freudian discourse is at issue here. The essay's title also offers an intertextual clue to one function of Lacanian theory in Spillers's own discourse. In "Interstices: A Small Drama of Words," an earlier essay, Spillers introduces the folksay "Mama's baby, papa's maybe" to signal the importance of the "hidden and impermissible" paternal origins of feminist analysis in the dominant culture's master discourses, whose boundaries feminism can explode while exploiting an extended heritage of discursive strategies.[15] In "Mama's Baby, Papa's Maybe: An American Grammar Book," a discourse on the "grammar" of the European-American eradication of African kinship structures serves to destabilize Anglo-American universalizations of gender difference, to ally black feminist analyses of degendering under slavery with the larger theoretical project of poststructural-ism, and to recast the Lacanian symbolic in the terms of cultural domination. Overtly, a Lacanian discourse politicized through the African-American context authorizes a critique of an Anglo-American feminism identified with object relations and dismissed as "the reproduction of mothering"—as an account, that is, of female gender transmission entirely irrelevant to the brutally disrupted kinship bonds of persons in captivity. Nevertheless, as the essay's title indicates, there is a contradictory (although largely disavowed) alliance with the mother—both with the biological mother whose determinative role in the social definition of the slave child complicates Spillers's allegiance to the paternal discourse and the Name of the Father it privileges, and, consequently, with the discursive mother (an Anglo-American feminism allied with object relations) that, despite its different social context, also underscores the mother's centrality. This discursive genealogy is both irreducibly heterogeneous and necessary to Spillers's project of specifying the complex (de)constructions of gender under slavery.

Spillers invokes the Lacanian divorce between biology and culture in order to subvert the assumption she ascribes to Anglo-American feminism that shared biology entails a common gender, that all biological females participate in a single womanhood reproduced across the generations. In quite an orthodox Lacan-ian claim, she asserts that " 'gendering' takes place within the confines of the domestic, an essential metaphor that then spreads its tentacles for male and female subjects over a wider ground of human and social purposes. Domesticity appears to gain its power by way of a common origin of cultural fictions that are grounded in the specificity of proper names, more exactly, a patronymic."[16] Violently dislocated from their own kinship (and consequently gender) structures and situated outside the domestic realm in the New World, captive persons in Spillers's account are deprived of gender. This pulverization is also played out on the body. It is not only that gender is severed from biology but also that "biology" shifts in this account from the arena of sexual difference to the Lacanian zone of the fragmented body imperfectly effaced by our illusions of coherence.[17] During both slavery and the Middle Passage (for Spillers, at once a horrific historical reality and a metaphor of the slave's perpetually suspended social definition), violent assaults deprived the captive person's body of any integrity and, consequently, of gender. Distinguishing the socially conceptualized "body" from the undifferentiated, ungendered "flesh" subtending it, Spillers argues that the European capture of African bodies constituted "high crimes against the *flesh*. . . . If we think of the 'flesh' as a primary narrative, then we mean its seared, divided, ripped-apartness, riveted to the ship's hole, fallen, or 'escaped' overboard," or with "eyes beaten out, arms, backs, skulls branded, a left jaw, a right ankle, punctured; teeth missing, as the calculated work of iron, whips, chains, knives, the canine patrol, the bullet" (67). Torture deliberately undoes, and thus exposes the factitiousness of, the integrated body.

Spillers reads the degendering of captive persons through Lacan, but she also politicizes Lacan by focusing on the sites of cultural domination at which kinship, gender, and bodies are deconstructed. Rather than detailing a universal law of culture to which all speaking beings are "subjected," she examines relations of power among cultures, the encounters between different symbolic orders instead of the passage from infancy to culture. By delineating the practices of cultural domination, she renders their violence palpable: the slave's abused flesh bears "the marks of a cultural text whose inside has been turned outside" (67). These inscriptions are in turn perpetuated across generations by the symbolic substitutions of language, as violent (in this account) as the slaveowner's branding iron: "Sticks and bricks *might* break our bones, but words will most certainly *kill* us" (68). It is not, as for Lacan, that "language" speaks "us" but that a dominant symbolic order marks the bodies of its captives. For the African-American female, seizing the power to name within this system is both an imperative of survival and the condition of possibility for a new social subject undetermined by either the dichotomy phallus/castration that has vexed the efforts of Lacan's feminist heirs to theorize the place of "the feminine" in "language" or by the conventions of domesticity that have produced the Anglo-American "gendered female."

Spillers also politicizes Lacan by highlighting the fissures between the social and symbolic realms within the culture of slavery, in which the Name of the Father establishes not gender but property. Since slavery prohibits the African-American male from participating in "the prevailing social fiction of the Father's name, the Father's law," slave children (and their heirs) in Spillers's argument have a distinctive relation to the patriarchal symbolic register, a relation in which masculinity, constituted through a "dual fatherhood . . . comprised of the African father's *banished* name and body and the captor father's mocking presence," is inevitably divided (80). Within this fractured configuration, moreover, the position of the enslaved mother acquires special prominence. Probing the gaps between the social and symbolic fields opens a space for the mother and the mode of feminism that orthodox Lacanian rhetoric critiques.

Overtly, the enslaved mother is the locus of Spillers's sharpest distinction between biology and gender, between ungendered black "female bodies in the raw" and the white "gendered female" defined preeminently in terms of a revered maternity (75). Reproduction under slavery is breeding, not maternity; denied all maternal claims to her children, the enslaved mother simply increases her owner's stock; " 'motherhood' as female blood-rite/right" is destroyed (75). Nevertheless, Spillers accords the slave mother a critical, albeit transient, role in the formation of her children's subjectivity. Working from Frederick Douglass's account of the impact of his enforced early separation from his mother, which he claims eventually dissolved his sense of kinship with his siblings, Spillers locates the experience of kinship in the presence of the mother: "If the child's humanity is mirrored initially in the eyes of its mother, or the maternal function, then we might be able to guess that the social subject grasps the whole dynamic of resemblance and kinship by way of the same source" (76). Using a language of mirroring reminiscent of D. W. Winnicott, Spillers relocates the origin of the social subject in the maternal rather than the paternal function.[18] To underscore the eradication of kinship under slavery, Spillers envisages a maternal function that slavery (imperfectly) destroys.

By the end of the essay, where the subversive matricentric discourse culminates, it is clear that some maternal imprint survives the master culture's attacks. Unmediated by a father empowered by the Father's name, the enslaved child's relation to the mother gains an almost tangible proximity. Spillers carefully differentiates this relationship from the pathological structure that the Moynihan Report ascribes to the black family, since the mother's absolute disempowerment precludes any presumption of matriarchy; but at the same time that "motherhood as female blood-rite is outraged, is denied . . . it becomes the founding term of a human and social enactment" (80). According to the American slave code, the "condition" of the mother determines that of " 'all her remotest posterity' " (79). But, Spillers asks, "What is the 'condition' of the mother? Is it the 'condition' of enslavement the writer means, or does he mean the 'mark' and the 'knowledge' of the *mother* upon the child that here translates into the culturally forbidden and impure?" (79). This culturally forbidden maternal mark is a redemptive antidote to the marks the patriarchal symbolic order inscribes on the bodies of its slaves. Spillers examines the consequences of this marking for the African-American male, who "has been touched, therefore, by the *mother, handed* by her in ways that he cannot escape, and in ways that the white American male is allowed to temporize by a fatherly reprieve. . . . It is the heritage of the *mother* that the African-American must regain as an aspect of his own personhood—the power of 'yes' to the 'female' within" (80).

This invocation of androgynous African-American masculinity—seemingly a regendering rather than a degendering—introduces at the end of Spillers's text an anomalously Anglo-American discourse of "personhood" and gender that raises some important unanswered questions. Does the African-American mother mark her son and her daughter identically? If the mother's mark on her son enables some access to the " 'female' within," what does it enable for the daughter? Why is the daughter so conspicuously absent from this text? Shrouded in silence, she enters only as a double of the delegitimated African-American father, the mirroring pair with which the essay begins, and in apposition to the mother, as if mother and daughter were indistinguishable: "the African-American woman, the mother, the daughter" (80).[19] Allowed, like the son, no "fatherly reprieve," does the daughter merge with the mother—as she does in Chodorow's account of female identity formation in mother-centered (i.e., normative Western) families? Does the context of slavery, with its enforced alienation of the father, undo the fluidity of mother-daughter boundaries that Chodorow represents as the "reproduction of mothering," or, as Toni Morrison's *Beloved* suggests, does it exaggerate this loss of boundaries? Must the daughter be banned from Spillers's text to ward off the threat that possible gender differences between son and daughter pose to a discourse on degendering?

Addressing these questions directly might have complicated in productive ways Spillers's already dazzlingly complex analysis. Perhaps the contradictions involved in representing both an undoing and a redoing of gender in a language informed by the Lacanian critique of the subject and by the Anglo-American valorization of the female—a language (dis)loyal to both the identity-subverting Name of the Father and to the boundary-transgressing body of the mother—should be asserted and analyzed more fully as the necessary heteroglossia of a discourse bridging race, gender, psychoanalysis, and history.

III

Class and gender, and their articulations, are the bits and pieces from which psychological selfhood is made.

Carolyn Kay Steedman, *Landscape for a Good Woman*[20]

More self-consciously polyphonic, *Landscape for a Good Woman: A Story of Two Lives* takes a different contradiction for its subject. Written from the perspective of the daughter, this extraordinary hybrid text splices a double biography (the narrator's and her working-class mother's) with a feminist psychoanalytic critique of cultural criticism and a class critique of feminist psychoanalysis. The text gains its power from dizzying reversals that undo its own neatly mapped social and discursive landscape, bifurcated by a gate dividing an affluent terrain of "bourgeois household[s] where doors shut along the corridor"—the landscape that generates, and thus is rendered normative by, our dominant narratives of childhood subjectivity (psychoanalysis and fairy tales, affiliated forms in Steedman's account)—from the working-class terrain of the narrator's own childhood, the council houses of South London's long streets, "the world outside the gate" that has been represented only in the discourses of class (77). Despite the construction of these clear oppositions, the boundaries of class and discourse frequently dissolve. There is no stable narrative perspective: the adult narrator's ambiguously classed voice both merges with and ironically echoes the working-class child's, which itself frequently mimics her mother's. No individual discourse can adequately represent the complexity of feeling and class positioning. Overtly repudiated for its class specificity, psychoanalysis re-enters through a carefully crafted subtext of fairy tales that disclose the unruly features of the narrator's subjectivity, and through the narrative structure of the text, which, like a case history (Steedman's own analogy for it), "presents the ebb and flow of memory, the structure of dreams, the stories that people tell to explain themselves to others" (21). More provocative than the text's articulated claims are its unstated but clearly signaled contradictions and self-critiques, which open a different narrative scene.

Direct feminist psychoanalytic challenges to class analysis are the least successful aspect of this text. Steedman's most emphatic project is to grant her mother the subjectivity denied by the conventions of a (masculine) cultural criticism that construct the working-class mother as " 'Mum, the formidable and eternal Mum, virago, domestic law giver, comforter and martyr' " (92).[21] Stereotyped and misdescribed (Steedman insists on her mother's nondomestic roles as worker and economic provider), the figure of "our mam" epitomizes the absence of individuality in (even sympathetic) representations of the working class. "When the sons of the working class, who have made their earlier escape from this landscape of psychological simplicity, put so much effort into accepting and celebrating it . . . then something important, and odd, and possibly promising of startling revelation, is actually going on. This refusal of a complicated psychology to those living in conditions of material distress is a central theme of this book" (12). Writing as a daughter of the working class, Steedman strives to articulate and to validate her mother's desires, to fill in the psychological content absent from the accounts of such cultural critics as Jeremy Seabrook and Richard Hoggart, to revise a canonical class perspective through the lenses of gender and psychoanalysis. But her portrait has its own monolithic features. By insisting on the overriding centrality and legitimacy of her mother's craving for "the things of the earth," on her unresigned response to material deprivation, Steedman circumscribes the subjectivity whose complexity she asserts but does not demonstrate. The metonymic series that characterizes her mother's desire tends to unfold within a single register. "From a Lancashire mill town and a working-class twenties childhood she came away wanting: fine clothes, glamour, money; to be what she wasn't" (6).[22] Sexuality, love, loneliness, and loss barely inflect this story of thwarted desire and legitimate envy. Psychological complexity reduces in this context to a more nuanced narrative of class consciousness.

Privileging the politics of envy constricts the psychoanalytic complication of working-class maternal subjectivity; class, however, powerfully and variously revises psychoanalysis, most succinctly in two "primal" scenes that crystallize the narrator's childhood relation to her parents. In both these scenes, as in Freud's primal scene, the narrator is an observer rather than a participant: watching from the sidelines is *the* working-class child's position in this text. What she sees, in contrast to the scenario witnessed by the Freudian child, however, is a class rather than a sexual encounter, for her developmental task entails negotiating subjectivity between class as well as gender positions. The first (chronologically) of these scenes revises Lacan's revision of Freud in a way that suggests a daughterly counterpart to Spillers's analysis of African-American fathers and sons. The narrator's father takes his three-year-old daughter for a walk in the bluebell wood. After gathering the flowers, they are suddenly accosted by an angry forest-keeper who reprimands the father for picking the flowers and, snatching them from his hands, scatters them on the ground, "their white roots glimmering, unprotected" (50). Recalling "the roots and their whiteness, and the way in which they had been pulled away, to wither exposed on the bank," the narrator remembers her father as "the loser, feminized, undone" by "the very solid and powerful" forest-keeper (50–51).

Recasting oedipal conflict in terms of class, the scene dramatizes the narrator's perception of her father's "castration" and her consequent disbelief in the equation of power with masculinity: "the iron of patriarchy didn't enter into my soul" (19). Like Spillers, and *contra* Lacan, Steedman argues that the disenfranchised father's difference from the Name of the Father critically shapes his child's gender and sexuality. (And like Spillers, Steedman depicts a situation of illegitimacy, in which the father can't legally transmit his family name.) If the African-American son, in Spillers's account, has access, through the gap between the African-American father and the Name of the (symbolic) Father, to an intimacy with the " 'female' within," the working-class daughter, in Steedman's account, under-goes a different form of gender blurring by identifying with, rather than desiring, a socially castrated father. The narrator is called by one of her father's names for her, Kay, which Steedman signs here (and in no other text) as her middle name. As a young girl, she identifies with her father's body rather than her mother's: "A little girl's body, its neat containment, seems much more like that of a man than it does of a woman. . . . His body was in some way mine" (94). Without power as a gender differential, without the phallus giving meaning to the penis, genital differences lose their significance. Defined through neither opposition nor attraction to masculinity, the narrator's working-class femininity positions her outside the dominant psychoanalytic narratives, and their affiliated fairy tales, of heterosexuality. "In the fairy-stories the daughters love their fathers because they are mighty princes, great rulers, and because such power seduces. The modern psychoanalytic myths posit the same plot, old tales are made manifest: secret longings, doors closing along the corridors of the bourgeois household. But daddy, you never knew me like this . . . the iron didn't enter into the soul" (61). In her own household the mother, not the father, is the potent presence behind closed doors; marginalized both outside the family and (partially as a consequence) within, the father is an object of the daughter's pity rather than desire.[23]

Through the other primal scene, given far more weight than the one with the father and preceding it in the narrative (although, chronologically, it occurs a few months later), the narrator's relation to her mother calls into question the construction of femininity within different psychoanalytic discourses. As in the scene in the bluebell wood, the child is a spectator rather than a participant; once again, she observes a class encounter between two same-sex adults, here, her mother (who has just given birth to the narrator's sister) and a health visitor who censors the mother's provision of physical—and, by implication, psychological—nurture: " 'This house isn't fit for a baby' " (2).[24] In both scenes, a disciplinary figure bearing class authority intervenes in the narrator's relation to a parent and introduces a difference within gender. Watching from the curtainless window as the health visitor recedes, the child makes a silent pact of class solidarity with her mother, articulated by the adult narrator's vow: "I will do everything and anything until the end of my days to stop anyone ever talking to me like that woman talked to my mother. . . . I read a [middle-class] woman's book, meet such a woman at a party (a woman now, like me) and think quite deliberately as we talk: we are divided. . . . I know this and you don't" (2). The interaction simultaneously revises and conflates oedipal and preoedipal scenarios, for it is the middle-class woman (rather than the father) who both interrupts and consolidates the mother-daughter bond. The daughter's identification with her mother is not produced in a dyadic sphere created by the mother's mirroring gaze but through a common position at the window and a shared perception of a third term. Identification with the mother is disidentification with the health visitor; it is triadic rather than dyadic and triangulated by class instead of patriarchy.

To defend her mother from the middle-class critique personified by the health visitor, the narrator must avoid participating in psychoanalytic discourses that might signal her complicity with this critique. As a child, she approvingly echoes her mother's class-appropriate definition of good mothering—"we'd never gone hungry; she went out to work for us; we had warm beds to lie in at night"—and insists on the sufficiency of a purely material mothering (1). As an adult, she both reiterates this definition, with some ironic distance, and displaces it with Winnicott's notion of good enough mothering (in her one eager unequivocal appropriation of psychoanalysis) to argue that her own childhood desire to have children demonstrates, as Winnicott suggests, her mother's adequacy; but her case is unconvincing, and perhaps intentionally so, since her childhood desire for two children, one resembling herself and the other her mother, just as plausibly attests to a longing to repair insufficient mothering by remothering both her mother and herself. What the class configuration consistently inhibits is the direct articulation of anger and the endorsement of psychoanalytic accounts of childhood ambivalence that might seem, through their contaminating association with the health visitor's judgment, to blame the (maternal) victim. The middle-class intervention thus shapes the mother-daughter bond both by disallowing ambivalence and by seemingly resolving it through providing an alternative focus for the daughter's anger, deflecting it away from the mother. This female triangle enables a version of the splitting that Melanie Klein attributes to the infant, who divides the inevitably frustrating mother into a "good" breast and "bad" breast: the "bad" breast, by drawing anger to itself, preserves the idealization of the mother.[25] But rather than overtly asserting her ambivalence (which she occasionally enacts indirectly through sudden unexplained outbursts of tears), Steedman's narrator represents ambivalence as the psychic property of the working-class mother who loves her children but simultaneously resents the hardships they impose. Steedman renders maternal ambivalence as a temporal structure produced by economic exigencies (although the imagery seems, as I shall argue later, to return ambivalence to the child): "What came free could be given freely, like her milk: loving a baby costs very little. But feeding us during our later childhood was a tense struggle between giving and denial. We never went hungry, we were well nourished, but fed in the cheapest possible way. I knew this, I think, when I conjured her under the kitchen table, the thin wounds across her breasts pouring forth blood, not milk" (93). In contrast to her apostrophe to her father, the narrator never blames or even retrospectively addresses her mother. The only overt sign of trouble is a brief unexplained allusion to a nine-year period when the adult narrator refused to see her mother.

Declining to theorize the daughter's ambivalence both invokes and revokes the discourse of Klein; insisting on the mother's ambivalence differentiates Steedman's account from that of Klein's most influential feminist descendant, Nancy Chodorow, whom Steedman faults for the middle-class assumption that mothers identify and merge with daughters, who themselves become mothers in order to reproduce the original merger with their own mothers. There is a primary identification with the mother in this text—"she, myself, walks my dreams"—but no normative reproduction of mothering, most obviously because the narrator deliberately does not become a mother (61). (Her sister, however, does become a mother, in an untold story that haunts the fringes of this text.) More importantly, this daughter internalizes from her mother not relationality and fluid ego boundaries but stoicism in the face of inequality. What she learns from her mother's response to the health visitor—"she [the mother] had cried. . . . And then she stopped crying, my mother, got by, the phrase that picks up after all difficulty"— she learns again through the story of her great-grandmother, sent from home at age eleven to work as a maid in a distant town: "She cried, because tears are cheap; and then she stopped, and got by, because no one gives you anything in this world" (1–2, 31). The femininity (re)produced through this working-class female genealogy has more to do with self-sufficiency than with relationality. Replacing the tears that figure fluid boundaries is a maternal voice commanding self-restraint; under her mother's tutelage, the narrator learns to dry her "sentimental" tears over nineteenth-century accounts of child labor, as well as any tears she might shed for herself. The withholding, not the offer, of empathic merger here structures female subjectivity. In her description of her final visit to her mother, two weeks before her mother's death, the narrator represents this withholding as an inevitable function of a class position that makes its members feel endangered and illegitimate, threatened by emotions that are perilous for victims and denied the self-esteem that enables mirroring: "I was really a ghost who came to call. That feeling, the sense of being absent in my mother's presence, was nothing to do with illness, was what it had always been like. We were truly illegitimate, outside any law of recognition: the mirror broken, a lump of ice for a heart" (142).

Steedman's metaphors, however, signal a different discourse, with a less forgiving account of broken mirroring. The disavowed story of daughterly ambivalence returns through the middle-class discourse of fairy tales, ingeniously manipulated to encode a subversive psychoanalytic subtext to the daughter's faithful narrative of class. Never represented as coherent narratives, but nonetheless evoked through recurrent allusions, two interwoven fairy tales, "The Snow Queen" and "The Little Mermaid," create a violent imaginary of glass, mirrors, ice, tears, milk, and blood. By depicting scenarios in which the mother, absent from the family, assumes a terrifying mythic guise (as the Snow Queen and the sea witch), these tales call into question the narrator's legitimatization of working-class mothering.

"The Snow Queen" offers the least threatening and most explicit counternarrative, in which the narrator openly identifies with the (male) protagonist who shares her name, Kay. In the opening section of the fairy tale, the devil makes a distorting mirror that transforms beauty into ugliness; it falls and breaks into hundreds of millions of billions of pieces which pierce people's eyes, distorting their vision, and penetrate their hearts, turning them to ice. During a snowstorm, Kay (who lives with his grandmother) is visited by the Snow Queen, whose power he has defied by boasting he would melt her on the stove. "She was delicately lovely, but all ice, glittering, dazzling ice. . . . her eyes shone like two bright stars, but there was no rest or peace in them."[26] After this visit, two splinters from the devil's mirror suddenly enter Kay's eyes and heart; his vision transformed and his heart frozen, he becomes the Snow Queen's icy subject. Only the empathic tears of his devoted playmate, Gerda, who travels to the Snow Queen's arctic palace in search of him, melt Kay's frozen heart, and his tears of gratitude wash the splinters from his eye. Steedman's recurrent allusions to this story—"the mirror breaks . . . and a lump of ice is lodged in the heart" (97)—

indict the mother she overtly justifies. The stoical voice, from this perspective, is a frozen voice; the repudiation of tears, a form of death rather than of strength. The fairy tale intimates the unstated cost of "getting by" without empathic mothering. What the broken mirror (re)produces is a frozen heart.

Through its story of chosen mutilation, "The Little Mermaid" introduces a more violent psychoanalytic discourse, which replaces the Winnicottian language of mirroring with a Kleinian language of passion and blood.[27] Although the story itself focuses on the heterosexual romance between the mermaid and the prince, Steedman's choice of images highlights the relationship of the mermaid and the sea witch, whom the mermaid begs to transform her fishtail into legs in order to win the prince's love. The witch warns her: "It hurts; it is as if a sharp sword were running through you. . . . Every step you take will be as if you were treading upon sharp knives, so sharp as to draw blood" (132). As payment for this service, to be rendered through a potion made with her own blood, the witch demands the mermaid's beautiful voice: "She [the witch] punctured her breast and let the black blood drop into the caldron . . . thereupon she cuts off the tongue of the little mermaid, who was dumb now and could neither sing nor speak" (133–34). Although these sacrifices prove futile in the fairy tale, they constitute the central symbolic episode of Steedman's text, which circulates the images of knives and sacrifice without specifying who is cutting whom. Whereas the mermaid elects her sacrifice to gain the love of the prince, the violent sacrificial relationships in Steedman's text bind mothers and daughters, not women and men: "Somehow the iron of patriarchy didn't enter into my soul. . . . in the dreams it is a woman who holds the knife, and only a woman can kill" (19). (Steedman's final description of her dying mother as looking "like a witch" [140]—thin, dark, gaunt—secures the connection to the fairy tale.) During her first reading of the two fairy tales, at age seven, the narrator imagines her parents naked under the kitchen table, holding sharp-edged knives with which they "cut each other, making thin surface wounds like lines drawn with a sharp red pencil, from which the blood poured. . . . Downstairs I thought, the thin blood falls in sheets from my mother's breasts; she was the most cut, but I knew it was she who did the cutting. I couldn't always see the knife in my father's hand" (54). By the time she is twelve, her father has dropped out of the picture and sexual warfare has become self-dramatizing maternal self-mutilation, as the narrator reimagines "the knife in my mother's hand, and the thin red lines of blood drawn across her breasts: displaying to my imagination the mutilation involved in keeping and feeding us" (82). Lacing milk with blood, the imagery reveals at once the narrator's guilty conviction that she has, however inadvertently, bloodied her mother's breasts, and her anger at her mother's self-display. Through the parallel scene from "The Little Mermaid," it is clear that the sacrifice is mutual: the witch/mother mutilates herself to enable the mermaid/daughter's upward mobility (to the land/to the middle class), and in exchange the daughter relinquishes her voice, parroting instead her mother's working-class discourse on good mothering. Instead of being mirrored by her mother, the daughter faithfully echoes her voice.

Through the fairy-tale subtext, then, Steedman launches a subversive psychoanalytic critique of her own class-based critique of psychoanalysis. Both discourses are necessary to represent the subjectivity produced by a position straddling the class divide, for the narrator (in contrast to the mother with whom she so strongly identifies) is not confined to the working-class world of her childhood: she gains continued access, through education, to the middle-class culture she began at age seven to consume through fairy tales. Steedman doesn't speculate whether a contemporary child rooted entirely in the working class feels anger at her mother; instead, she demonstrates the prohibitions on that child's recognition of her anger and subtly devises strategies for representing her own complex position on the boundary.

She figures this position most deftly through the contrast between two narratives: the story of the little watercress girl recounted by Henry Mayhew in *London Labour and the London Poor* and the story of "Dora" recounted by Freud, the story "we" know intimately because it is *"the* story . . . of the bourgeois household and the romances of the family and the fairy-tales that lie behind its closed doors" (137–39). These narratives mark the range of her contradictory identifications: between working-class femininity (defined by labor) and middle-class femininity (defined by sexuality), between harmonious and disharmonious mother-daughter relationships, between history and psychoanalysis, and between coherent and hysterical (contradictory, disrupted) narrative modes. Steedman valorizes the story of the little watercress girl for resisting our dominant cultural narratives and insists that she finds a mirror image in this "good and helpful child, who eased her mother's life" (141); but her own troubled story far more closely resembles Dora's inconclusive tale. (The narrator's childhood failure to come home from rehearsing a school play in time to buy the watercress her mother wants for tea underlines her distance from the dutiful watercress girl.) For all its incoherence, Dora's narrative is legible to the narrator, while the watercress girl's remains opaque. Insisting that lives "outside the gate" be allowed to preserve their inscrutability, Steedman refuses to recuperate the watercress girl's story to familiar (psychoanalytic) narratives. But her own heterogeneous narrative, as full as Dora's of gaps, contradictions, repetitions, and revisions that interrupt and interlard the exposition, unfolds within a psychoanalytic register that seemingly operates for the person on the boundary as well as the one inside the gate.

IV

However unfeasible and inefficient it may sound, I see no way to avoid insisting that there has to be a simultaneous other focus: not merely who am I? but who is the other woman? How am I naming her? How does she name me?

Gayatri Chakravorty Spivak, "French Feminism in an International Frame"[28]

Steedman's focus on the boundary affiliates her with a current trend in readings of class and psychoanalysis. The boundary is the critical position in these readings, for it both destabilizes and extends the psychoanalytic enclosure, as Jane Gallop and Mary Poovey suggest in their investigations of the threshold figure of the governess, who exists at once outside and inside the middle-class family.[29] As a duplicate mother who is "castrated" by passing through the circuit of money, the governess disrupts the imaginary wholeness of the middle-class family and of psychoanalytic theory. Yet psychoanalysis is well suited to describe this disruption, which Gallop represents as an intervention of the symbolic in the imaginary. Poovey depicts psychoanalysis as the most appropriate discourse for articulating the splits, identifications, and displacements that characterize both the person on the boundary and the current historical situation of feminist criticism itself, positioned "between the powerful guardians of culture, among whom we do and do not belong, and a vast, heterogeneous majority who feel excluded from what we say, and between an outdated ideology of individualism and an ideology of decentered subjects whose hour is not yet here."[30]

Poovey's account of feminism's double loyalties returns us to Spillers's representation of feminism's discursive genealogy. Like Steedman, Gallop, and Poovey, moreover, Spillers locates psychoanalysis (as well as feminism) at the boundaries, rather than exclusively on either side. When she explicitly invokes psychoanalysis (as opposed to the analogies she implies between the effects of the Lacanian symbolic and of cultural domination), it is in relation to negotiations across racial and gender boundaries. Spillers examines a specific discursive moment in the representation of slavery, Harriet Jacobs's *Incidents in the Life of a Slave Girl*. Written by an escaped female slave and dictated to a woman abolitionist, Jacobs's text succinctly embodies these negotiations through the representation of a triangulated scene between Linda Brent, the autobiographical protagonist, and Mr. and Mrs. Flint, the white couple that owns her. By acting out her husband's desire for the captive woman, Mrs. Flint dissolves the boundaries of gender on both sides of the racial divide, "degendering" both herself and Linda Brent by subjecting Brent to female as well as male sexual desire (and thereby contrasting her to the "gendered female," who is defined by a relation of vulnerability solely to the male). There is an identification, however, not only between the Anglo-American woman and man but also between the Anglo-American and African-American women, "twin actants on a common psychic landscape" created by the sovereignty of the Anglo-American male: "Neither could claim her body and its various productions—for quite different reasons, albeit—as her own . . . we cannot unravel one female's narrative from the other's, cannot decipher one without tripping over the other" (77). These multiple interwoven identifications make this scene resemble "casebook narratives from psychoanalysis" (76). It is less the experience of captive persons themselves than the " 'threads cable-strong' of an incestuous interracial genealogy [that] uncover slavery in the United

States as one of the richest displays of the psychoanalytic dimensions of culture before the science of European psychoanalysis takes hold" (77).

Spillers and Steedman share (along with Gallop and Poovey) a preference for delineating situations and figures at the boundary and a reticence about representing the subjectivity of persons entirely dominated by oppression. Steedman explores her own liminal position and refuses to interpret the watercress girl's story; Spillers details the positioning, but not the subjectivity, of persons in captivity and suggests that the twentieth-century "black woman," rather than the captive person, constitutes the "profoundest revelation" of the "split subject that psychoanalytic theory posits" (65). Their caution raises a critical question about the limits of psychoanalysis. How do we know when social and cultural boundaries should be crossed, when "naming" the "other woman," as Spivak and others have exhorted us to do, simply appropriates "her" to "us"?[31] Rather than groping after some definitive answer, I want to end by gesturing toward a countertext that crosses, instead of lingering at, a boundary, a text that has been a kind of subtext to my own. *Beloved* deliberately represents captive persons as subjects rather than as objects of oppression, and does so primarily in a discourse on the hunger, passion, and violence generated in the "too thick" mother-daughter bond produced by the conditions of slavery.[32] This extraordinary project has its attendant risks, of course, discernible perhaps in the novel's enormous popularity with women readers across racial lines. But the text circumvents any easy delimitation of the boundaries of psychoanalysis.

It is too early for feminism to foreclose on psychoanalysis. Vast cultural terrains unfold beyond the boundaries of this essay, and beyond those of psychoanalysis as well, undoubtedly. But rather than fixing those boundaries, my goal has been to forestall the sense that we know exactly where they lie and what they necessarily exclude. Psychoanalysis has been resistant to the social, but it need not always, uniformly, be. It is better for feminism to challenge that resistance than to renounce psychoanalysis entirely or succumb to its seductions.

Notes

1. Rosi Braidotti, "The Politics of Ontological Difference," in *Between Feminism and Psychoanalysis,* ed. Teresa Brennan (London: Routledge, 1989), pp. 97–98. Paul Smith, "Julia Kristeva Et Al.; or, Take Three or More," in *Feminism and Psychoanalysis,* ed. Richard Feldstein and Judith Roof (Ithaca: Cornell University Press, 1989), pp. 84–85.

    I am grateful to Marianne Hirsch and Evelyn Fox Keller for their boundless patience and support during the composition of this essay. I am also grateful for Mary M. Childers's helpful criticism, which I have been able only in part to incorporate into this version of the essay.

2. There are diverse reasons for the pervasive current disrepute of psychoanalysis, ranging from the politics of academic discourse, in which the hegemony of psycho-analysis within "theory" has been displaced by more historical and socially nuanced discourses, to the politics of public discourse on the family, in which psychoanalysis has been tainted by its alleged complicity in the cover-up of child abuse. The exemplary case of the latter charge is Jeffrey Moussaieff Masson, *The Assault on Truth: Freud's Suppression of the Seduction Theory* (New York: Farrar, Straus, and Giroux, 1984). See also Judith Lewis Herman, with Lisa Hirschman, *Father-Daughter Incest* (Cambridge, Mass.: Harvard University Press, 1981) and Louise DeSalvo, *Virginia Woolf: The Impact of Childhood Sexual Abuse on Her Life and Work* (Boston: Beacon Press, 1989). These diverse discursive arenas share a perception of the social irresponsibility of psychoanalysis. For a response to this charge, see Jacqueline Rose, "Where Does the Misery Come From? Psychoanalysis, Feminism, and the Event," in *Feminism and Psychoanalysis,* pp. 25–39. For a similar attempt to rescue psychoanalysis for feminism, see Rachel Bowlby on the gendered implications of "repudiation," in "Still Crazy After All These Years," in *Between Feminism and Psychoanalysis,* pp. 40–60.

3. For an integration of psychoanalysis and the social realm under the aegis of Foucault, see Julian Henriques, Wendy Hollway, Cathy Urwin, Couze Venn, Valerie Walker-dine, *Changing the Subject: Psychology, Social Regulation and Subjectivity* (London and New York: Methuen, 1984).

4. *Totem and Taboo* is devoted to demonstrating that all culture originates in patricide, which is universally preserved in the psyche as the oedipus complex. In "Mother-Right and the Sexual Ignorance of Savages" Freud's British representative Ernest Jones defends the universality of the oedipus complex against the cultural relativism of Bronislaw Malinowski by arguing that only "primordial Oedipus tendencies" could generate the denial of paternity enabling the matrilinear Melanesian societies Malinowski studied. See Sigmund Freud, *Totem and Taboo* [1913–14], *The Standard Edition of the Complete Psychological Works of Sigmund Freud,* trans. and ed. James Strachey (London: Hogarth Press, 1953–66), vol. 13; Ernest Jones, "Mother-Right and the Sexual Ignorance of Savages" [1924], in *Essays in Applied Psycho-Analysis,* 2 vols. (London: Hogarth Press and the Institute of Psycho-Analysis, 1951), 2:170; and Bronislaw Malinowski, *Sex and Repression in Savage Society* (1927; Chicago: University of Chicago Press, 1985).

5. Juliet Mitchell, *Psychoanalysis and Feminism: Freud, Reich, Laing, and Women* (New York: Random House, 1974), p. 395.

6. Jacqueline Rose, *Sexuality in the Field of Vision* (London: Verso, 1986), p. 90. Here, and in her essay "Where Does the Misery Come From?" (see n. 2 above), Rose mounts the most eloquent defenses of the utility of Lacanian psychoanalysis for feminism.

7. This revision has emerged only from theorists with primary commitments to questions of race and class. In the Lacanian anthology *Between Feminism and Psychoanalysis,* for example, the editor, Teresa Brennan, comments in her Introduction that "real changes in either parenting patterns or the social position of women and men must have consequences for the symbolic" (p. 3), but neither the Introduction nor the rest

of the anthology examines these changes or their consequences. Despite Brennan's claim that the anthology unsettles the "relation of psychical structures to the political realities of women's social conditions" (p. 12), all of the essays (except for Rosi Braidotti's overt critique of psychoanalysis) either define the "social," the "political," and the "historical" within the terms of psychoanalysis (so that the "social" is coterminous with the death drive, for example) or circumscribe them radically (the only social context analyzed, for example, is the academy). The anthology bears witness to Paul Smith's charge that psychoanalysis cannot generate political desire and has tended to deplete that of feminism—unless, I would argue, feminism demands that psychoanalysis address specific social configurations.

8. Nancy J. Chodorow, *Feminism and Psychoanalytic Theory* (Cambridge: Polity Press, 1989), pp. 157, 159. Object relations theory has consistently emphasized the social context of development, in opposition to the intrapsychic terrain of drive theory; some slippage between the "social" as the narrowly interpersonal and as a more inclusive historical field has bolstered the discourse's political claims. For a recent critique, from an entirely different perspective, of the place of the social in object relations, see Daniel N. Stern, *The Interpersonal World of the Infant: A View From Psychoanalysis and Developmental Psychology* (New York: Basic Books, 1985).

9. Jane Flax, *Thinking Fragments: Psychoanalysis, Feminism, and Postmodernism in the Contemporary West* (Berkeley and Los Angeles: University of California Press, 1989), p. 122. This position is also presented in various ways throughout Nancy Chodorow's *Feminism and Psychoanalytic Theory*.

10. Elizabeth V. Spelman, *Inessential Woman: Problems of Exclusion in Feminist Thought* (Boston: Beacon Press, 1988), pp. 95, 157. For a recent critique of Chodorow's "cultural essentialism" from a Lacanian perspective that faults the assumptions that gender is constant within the subject and that psychological differences between the sexes are universal, see Toril Moi, "Patriarchal Thought and the Drive for Knowledge," in *Between Feminism and Psychoanalysis*, pp. 189–205. For a related critique of Chodorow from a Foucauldian perspective, see Cathy Urwin's contribution to *Changing the Subject*, which insists on the ways that the mother's response to her child, and hence the child's perception and internalization of the mother's gender, is always mediated by the mother's own "positioning within particular discourses which enter into the constitution of her role" (p. 320).

11. Chodorow, "On *The Reproduction of Mothering*: A Methodological Debate," *Signs* 6, no. 3 (Spring 1981): 514. At the end of her early essay "Family Structure and Feminine Personality" (in *Woman, Culture, and Society*, ed. Michelle Zimbalist Rosaldo and Louise Lamphere [Stanford: Stanford University Press, 1974]), Chodorow launches this cross-cultural work by drawing from ethnographies of Java and East London to contrast the pathological dimension of the mother-daughter bond in Western middle-class families with the higher self-esteem transmitted from mother to daughter in cultures in which mothers have authority and important connections with other women both outside and within the home. The complaint that Chodorow privileges (rather than simply represents) Western middle-class femininity seems to me based on a misperception.

12. Hence the recurrent claim that object relations theory is intrinsically inapplicable to diverse social configurations seems misguided to me. Recent explorations of multiple mothering in extended African-American families, for example, seem perfectly congruent with Chodorow's emphasis on the psychological consequences of female caretakers. See, for example, Patricia Hill Collins, "The Meaning of Motherhood in Black Culture and Black Mother/Daughter Relationships," in *Sage: A Scholarly Journal on Black Women* 4, no. 2 (Fall 1987): 3–10.

13. On the insufficiency of the Lacanian subject for a feminist politics, see Teresa de Lauretis, "Feminist Studies/Critical Studies: Issues, Terms, and Contexts," in *Feminist Studies/Critical Studies,* ed. Teresa de Lauretis (Bloomington: Indiana University Press, 1986), pp. 1–19. In her Introduction to *Between Feminism and Psychoanalysis,* Teresa Brennan eloquently argues for undoing the hierarchalized polarization of object relations and Lacan. For a reading of object relations theory as incorporating, rather than opposing, some basic principles of deconstruction, see Leslie Wahl Rabine, "A Feminist Politics of Non-Identity," *Feminist Studies* 14, no. 1 (Spring 1988): 11–31. For a partially comparable project, in another arena, of undoing the opposition between Anglo-American and French feminisms, see Betsy Draine, "Refusing the Wisdom of Solomon: Some Recent Feminist Literary Theory," *Signs* 15, no. 1 (Autumn 1989): 144–70. Reworking the opposition sometimes generates reversals. In *Thinking Fragments,* Jane Flax argues surprisingly that "Object relations theory is more compatible with postmodernism that Freudian or Lacanian analysis because it does not require a fixed or essentialist view of 'human nature'. . . . As social relations and family structures change, so would human nature" (p. 110). This assertion is based on privileging history as the *only* form of difference and on overlooking the radically disruptive, de-essentializing function of the unconscious in Lacan; it is important to remember that the intersubjectively constituted and historically variable self of object relations remains more integrated than the split subject of Lacan. Nevertheless, Flax's assertion usefully calls into question the oversimplified opposition between the allegedly unitary self of object relations and the heterogeneous Lacanian subject.

14. Hortense J. Spillers, " 'The Permanent Obliquity of an In[pha]llibly Straight': In the Time of the Daughters and the Fathers," in *Daughters and Fathers,* ed. Lynda E. Boose and Betty S. Flowers (Baltimore: Johns Hopkins University Press, 1989), p. 158.

15. Hortense J. Spillers, "Interstices: A Small Drama of Words," in *Pleasure and Danger,* ed. Carol Vance (Boston: Routledge and Kegan Paul, 1984), p. 88.

16. Hortense J. Spillers, "Mama's Baby, Papa's Maybe: An American Grammar Book," *diacritics* 17, no. 2 (Summer 1987): 72; subsequent citations of this work will be placed in parentheses in the text. For a non-Lacanian account of the ways that slavery undoes the meaning of domesticity, see Hortense J. Spillers, "Changing the Letter: The Yokes, the Jokes of Discourse, or, Mrs. Stowe, Mr. Reed," in *Slavery and the Literary Imagination,* ed. Deborah E. McDowell and Arnold Rampersad (Baltimore: Johns Hopkins University Press, 1989), pp. 25–61.

17. See Jacques Lacan, "The Mirror Stage as Formative of the Function of the I," *Ecrits: A Selection,* trans. Alan Sheridan (New York: W. W. Norton, 1977), pp. 1–7.

18. See D. W. Winnicott, "Mirror-role of Mother and Family in Child Development," *Playing and Reality* (Harmondsworth, Middlesex: Penguin Books, 1971). I cite Winnicott rather than Lacan (whose essay on the mirror stage influenced Winnicott) because Spillers's emphasis on the child's humanity and the social implications of the mother's responsive gaze are much closer to the discourse of object relations than to Lacan's insistence on the alienating structure of the ego produced by the mirror stage. For Lacan, the social subject is produced by the symbolic.

19. In " 'The Permanent Obliquity of an In[pha]llibly Straight': In the Time of the Daughters and the Fathers," Spillers offers a detailed analysis of the African-American father-daughter relationship, which has captured her attention more fully than the mother-daughter relationship.

20. Carolyn Kay Steedman, *Landscape for a Good Woman: A Story of Two Lives* (London: Virago, 1986; New Brunswick: Rutgers University Press, 1987), p. 7; subsequent citations of this work will be to the American edition and will be placed in parentheses in the text. I am grateful to Tricia Moran for calling this text to my attention.

21. From Jeremy Seabrook, *What Went Wrong?* (London: Victor Gollancz, 1978), cited by Steedman.

22. Or note another characteristic example: "Born into 'the old working class,' she wanted: a New Look skirt, a timbered country cottage, to marry a prince" (p. 9). Rather than introducing a new direction, the last term in these series encompasses the others.

23. As Julie Abraham points out in her review of *Landscape for a Good Woman* in the *Women's Review of Books* 5, no. 9 (June 1988), Steedman is reticent about her own sexuality. Her story, however, puts her at a distance from the dominant narratives of heterosexuality. Although as a daughter she desires to be marked by the father, or by the law he (inadequately) represents, she expresses no desire for the person that he is.

24. Steedman represents the boundaries of the working-class home as more permeable than the locked doors of the middle-class houses behind the gate. Curtainless windows and unlocked doors characterize the narrator's family home, whose domestic boundaries are also subverted by the frequent presence of boarders. That the marginalized father, who sleeps in the attic, is sometimes mistaken for another border underlines the blurring of the inside/outside dichotomy. On the psychoanalytic fiction of the insular middle-class family, see Jane Gallop, *The Daughter's Seduction: Feminism and Psychoanalysis* (Ithaca: Cornell University Press, 1982), p. 144.

25. See Melanie Klein, *"Love, Guilt, and Reparation" and Other Works, 1921–45* (New York: Dell, 1975). Conspicuously absent (repressed?) from Steedman's text, Klein is mentioned only in relation to the pathologization of envy, never in relation to the mother-daughter bond.

26. *Dulac's "The Snow Queen" and Other Stories from Hans Andersen* (Garden City: Doubleday, 1976), p. 16; subsequent citations of "The Snow Queen" will be placed in parentheses in the text. Citations of "The Little Mermaid" will also be to this edition and will be placed in parentheses in the text.

27. On the evolution of object relations from the Kleinian emphasis on hunger and aggression to Winnicott's more benign accounts of mother-infant mirroring, see Jay R. Greenberg and Stephen A. Mitchell, *Object Relations in Psychoanalytic Theory* (Cambridge, Mass.: Harvard University Press, 1983); Judith M. Hughes, *Reshaping the Psychoanalytic Domain: The Work of Melanie Klein, W. R. D. Fairbairn, and D. W. Winnicott* (Berkeley and Los Angeles: University of California Press, 1989); and D. W. Winnicott, "A Personal View of the Kleinian Contribution," in *The Maturational Processes and the Facilitating Environment* (London: Hogarth Press, 1965), pp. 171–78.

28. Gayatri Chakravorty Spivak, "French Feminism in an International Frame," *Yale French Studies* 62 (1981): 179.

29. Jane Gallop, *The Daughter's Seduction: Feminism and Psychoanalysis* (Ithaca: Cornell University Press, 1982), pp. 141–48; Mary Poovey, "The Anathematized Race: The Governance and *Jane Eyre*," in *Feminism and Psychoanalysis*, pp. 230–54.

30. Poovey, "The Anathematized Race," p. 254.

31. Spivak's line has been cited in numerous places. See especially Jane Gallop, "The Monster in the Mirror: The Feminist Critic's Psychoanalysis," in *Feminism and Psychoanalysis*, pp. 13–24; Jane Gallop, "Annie Leclerc Writing a Letter, with Vermeer," in *The Poetics of Gender*, ed. Nancy K. Miller (New York: Columbia University Press, 1986), pp. 137–56; and Helena Michie's extremely interesting comparison and critique of these two essays in "Not One of the Family: The Repression of the Other Woman in Feminist Theory," in *Discontented Discourses: Feminism/Textual Intervention/Psychoanalysis*, ed. Marleen S. Barr and Richard Feldstein (Urbana: University of Illinois Press, 1989), pp. 15–28.

32. Toni Morrison, *Beloved* (New York: Knopf, 1987), p. 164. "Too thick" is the charge made by Paul D and does not, of course, represent Morrison's perspective. The whole question of *Beloved* and psychoanalysis is, obviously, the subject of another essay.

12

The Facts of Fatherhood

Thomas W. Laqueur

This essay puts forward a labor theory of parenthood in which emotional work counts. I want to say at the onset, however, that it is not intended as a nuanced, balanced academic account of fatherhood or its vicissitudes. I write it in a grumpy, polemical mood.

In the first place I am annoyed that we lack a history of fatherhood, a silence which I regard as a sign of a more systemic pathology in our understanding of what being a man and being a father entail. There has unfortunately been no movement comparable to modern feminism to spur the study of men. Or conversely, history has been written almost exclusively as the history of men and therefore man-as-father has been subsumed under the history of a pervasive patriarchy—the history of inheritance and legitimate descent, the history of public authority and its transmission over generations. Fatherhood, insofar as it has been thought about at all, has been regarded as a backwater of the dominant history of public power. The sources, of course, support this view. Fathers before the eighteenth century appear in prescriptive texts about the family largely in their public roles, as heads of families or clans, as governors of the "little commonwealth," of the state within the state.

The rule of the patriarchy waned, but historians have not studied the cultural consequences for fathers of its recession. Instead, they have largely adopted the perspective of nineteenth-century ideologues: men belong to the public sphere of the marketplace and women to the private sphere of the family. A vast prescriptive literature explains how to be a good mother: essentially how to exercise proper moral influence and display appropriate affections in the home, duties that in earlier centuries would have fallen to the father. But there is little in the era of "separate spheres" on how to be the new public man in private. A rich and poignant source material on the affective relationship between fathers and children in the nineteenth century—Gladstone's account of watching for days by the bedside of his dying daughter, for example—speaks to the power of emotional bonds, but historians have largely ignored it. They have instead taken some Victorians at their word and written the father out of the family except as a parody of the domestic autocrat or as the representative of all those forces which stood in the way of the equality of the sexes.

Second, I write in the wake of Baby M and am annoyed with the neo-essentialism it has spawned. Baby M was the case of the decade in my circles, a "representative anecdote" for ancient but ageless questions in the late twentieth century. Like most people, I saw some right on both sides and had little sympathy for the marketplace in babies that brought them together. On the one hand Mary Beth Whitehead this . . . ; on the other William Stern that . . . The baby broker who arranged the deal was manifestly an unsavory character, the twentieth-century avatar of the sweatshop owners who in ages past profited unconscionably from the flesh of women. It was difficult not to subscribe to the doctrine that the baby's best interests must come first and it was by no means consistently clear where these lay. Each day brought new emotional tugs as the narrative unfolded on the front pages of every paper.

I was surprised that, for so many people, this transaction between a working-class woman and a professional man (a biochemist) became an epic prism through which the evils of capitalism and class society were refracted. It did not seem newsworthy to me that the poor sold their bodies or that the rich exploited their willingness to do so. What else would they sell? Malthus had pointed out almost two centuries ago that those who labored physically gave of their flesh and in the long run earned just enough to maintain and replenish it. So had Marx, who also identified women as the agents of social re-production.

Admittedly, the contract entered into by Whitehead and Stern was stripped of all shreds of decency and aesthetic mystification, flatfootedly revealing the deal for what it was—not a womb rental but a baby sale. This is why the New Jersey Supreme Court ruled it unenforceable. Every account that one reads of the surrogate baby broker's operations, with its well-dressed couples sitting in little cubicles interviewing long lines of less well-dressed but hopeful, spiffed-up women seeking work as surrogates, conjures up distasteful reminders of depression labor exchanges, starlet casting couches, or academic hiring fairs. But there surely are no new horrors in this case. Basically the Baby M narratives are modern versions of the industrial novel and allied genres in which factory labor is portrayed as wage slavery; in which children's tiny thin fingers are metamorphosed into the pin wire they hour after hour produce; in which paupers, whose labor is worthless on the open market, are depicted pounding bones into meal so that they might remain just this side of starvation.[1] In short, I remain cynical when some commentators discover Mary Beth Whitehead as the anti-capitalist Everywoman. If "surrogate" mothers were as well organized as the doctors who perform the much more expensive *in vitro* fertilization or as unionized baseball players they would earn a decent wage—say $100,000 instead of the ludicrously low $10,000—and opposition to surrogacy as emblematic of the evils of a free market in labor might be considered muted. (Though of course then the story might shift to emphasize the power of money to dissolve the very fabric of social decency, another nineteenth-century trope.)

I am, however, primarily interested in this case as the occasion for a return to naturalism. Feminism has been the most powerful de-naturalizing theoretical force in my intellectual firmament and, more generally, a major influence in the academic and cultural affairs that concern me. I regard it as both true and liberating that "the idea that men and women are two mutually exclusive categories must arise out of something other than a nonexistent 'natural' opposition," and that "gender is a socially imposed division of the sexes."[2] A major strand of commentary on Baby M, however, rejects this tradition and instead insists that the category "mother" is natural, a given of the world outside culture. Phyllis Chesler, for example, in the major article of a special "Mothers" issue of *Ms* (May, 1988) argues that motherhood is a "fact," an ontologically different category than "fatherhood," which is an "idea." Thus, "in order for the *idea* [my emphasis] of fatherhood to triumph over the *fact* of motherhood," she says, "we had to see Bill as the 'birth father' and Mary Beth as the surrogate uterus." (Actually Chesler misstates the claims. Mary Beth has been, rightly or wrongly, called the "surrogate mother," not the "surrogate uterus." But since the point of the article seems to be that mother and uterus are more or less the same thing this may be an intentional prevarication.)

I resist this view for obvious emotional reasons: it assumes that being the "factual" parent entails a stronger connection to the child than being the "ideational" parent. (This assumption is widespread. During my daughter Hannah's five-week stay in the preemie nursery her caretakers, in the "social comments" column of her chart, routinely recorded my wife's visits to her incubator as "mother in to bond," whereas my appearances were usually noted with the affectively neutral "father visited.") While I do not want to argue against the primacy of material connection directly I do want to point out that it is not irrational to hold the opposite view and that, "in fact," the incorporeal quality of fatherhood has been the foundation of patriarchy's ideological edifice since the Greeks. In other words, simply stating that mothers have a greater material connection with the child is not to make an argument but to state a premise which historically has worked against Chesler's would-be conclusion. The Western philosophical tradition has generally valued idea over matter; manual labor for millennia was the great horizontal social divide. In other words, precisely because the mother's claim was "only" corporeal, because it was a matter of "fact," it was valued less.

I will recount some of the history of this discourse, but I also want to argue against its basic operating assumption: the unproblematic nature of fact especially in relation to such deeply cultural designations as mother or father and to the rights, emotions, or duties that are associated with them. The "facts" of motherhood—and of fatherhood for that matter—are not "given" but come into being as science progresses and as the adversaries in political struggles select what they need from the vast, ever-growing storehouses of knowledge. The idea that a child is of one's flesh and blood is very old while its biological correlatives and their cultural importance depend on the available supplies of fact and on their interpretation.

But the reason that the facts of motherhood and fatherhood are not "given" has less to do with what is known or not known than with the fundamental gap, recognized by David Hume, between facts and their meaning. *Is* does not imply *ought,* and more generally no fact or set of facts taken together entails or excludes a moral right or commitment. Laws, customs, and precepts, sentiments, emotion, and the power of the imagination make biological facts assume cultural significance. An Algonquin chief, confronted by a Jesuit in the seventeenth century with the standard European argument against women's promiscuity (how else would you know that a child is yours?), replied that he found it puzzling that whites could apparently only love "their" children, i.e., that only individual ownership entailed caring and affection.

Before proceeding I want to again warn my readers that some of my evidence and most of my passion arise from personal circumstance. I write as the father of a daughter to whom I am bound by the "facts" of a visceral love, not the molecular biology of reproduction. The fact of the matter is that from the instant the five-minute-old Hannah—a premature baby of 1430 grams who was born by Caesarean section—grasped my finger (I know this was due to reflex and not affection) I felt immensely powerful, and before the event, inconceivably strong bonds with her. Perhaps if practitioners of the various sub-specialties of endocrinology had been present they might have measured surges of neuro-transmitters and other hormones as strong as those that accompany parturition. But then what difference would that make—with what is one to feel if not with the body?

I also write as the would-be father, some sixteen months before Hannah came along, of a boy weighing something less than 800 grams who was aborted late one night—an induced stillbirth really—after twenty-four weeks of gestation because of a burst amniotic sac and the ensuing infection. I can recapture my sadness at his demise vividly and still regard the whole episode as one of the gloomiest of my life. Gail, my wife, was ambivalent about having the child— she was, she says, unprepared at age 40 for becoming pregnant the very first month at risk—and regards the abortion as a painful but not especially fraught episode which cleared the emotional ground to allow her to welcome Hannah's birth un-equivocally.

Finally I write as the male member of a family in which gender roles are topsy turvy. Hannah early on announced that she would prefer being a daddy to being a mommy because mommies had to go to work—hers is a lawyer—while daddies only had to go to their study. (As she has grown older and observed my not silent suffering as I finished a book begun the year she was born her views have been somewhat revised.) I am far guiltier of the stereotypical vices of motherhood— neurotic worry about Hannah's physical and mental well being, unfounded premonitions of danger, excessive emotional demands, and general nudginess—than is

Gail. In short, my experiences—ignoring for the moment a vast ethnographic and somewhat smaller historical literature—make me suspect of the naturalness of "mother" or "father" in any culturally meaningful sense.

The association of fatherhood with ideas and motherhood with facts is ancient; only its moral valences have been recently reversed by some feminists. The Marquis de Sade suggests that the "idea" of fatherhood—the notion that a child is "born of the father's blood" and only incidentally of a mother's body—means that it "owes filial tenderness to him alone, an assertion not without its appealing qualities. . . ."[3] Sade is the most rabid of anti-maternalists and his argument is made to induce a girl to sexually defile and humiliate her mother; but his relative valuation of fact and idea is standard. The "idea" of fatherhood gave, and displayed, the power of patriarchy for much of Western history since the Greeks.

Bolingbrooke in *Richard II* (1, 3, 69) addresses his father as

"Oh thou, the earthly author of my blood,
Whose youthful spirit, in me regenerate."

He is author and authority because, like the poet who has in his mind the design for the verses that subsequently appear, he has the conceit for the child in him. The physical act of writing, or of producing the child, matters little. Conceiving a child in this model is a man's sparking of an idea in the uterus which contains, like a block of marble, a form waiting to be liberated. It is like writing on a piece of paper awaiting inscription. The "generation of things in Nature and the generation of things in Art take place in the same way," argued the great seventeenth-century physician William Harvey, who discovered the circulation of the blood. "Now the brain is the instrument of conception of the one . . . and of the other the uterus or egg."[4] And being the instrument is less elevated than being the author: "He," speaking of God, "was the author, thou the instrument," says King Henry in offering pardon to Warwick (*3 Henry VI*, 4, 6, 18).

But the idea of "father" as bound to his child in the way a poet is to verse, i.e., its genitor, is much older than Shakespeare. It is, argues Freud, one of the cornerstones of culture; believing in fathers, like believing in the Hebrew God, reflects the power of abstract thought and hence of civilization itself.

The "Moses religion's" insistence that God cannot be seen—the graven image proscription—"means that a sensory perception was given second place to what may be called an abstract idea." This God represents "a triumph of intellectuality over sensuality [*Triumph der Geistigkeit uber de Sinnlichkeit*], or strictly speaking, an instinctual renunciation. . . ." Freud briefs precisely the same case for fathers as for God in his analysis of Aeschylus' *Eumenides,* which follows immediately his discussion of the Second Commandment. Orestes denies that he has killed his mother by denying that being born of her entails special bonds or obligation. Apollo makes the defense's case: appearances notwithstanding, no man has a mother. "The mother is no parent of that which is called her child, but only nurse of the new-planted seed that grows." She is but "a stranger." The only true parent is "he who mounts."[5]

Here is the founding myth of the Father. "Paternity" [*Vaterschaft*], Freud concludes, "is a supposition" and like belief in the Jewish God it is "based on an inference, a premise," while "maternity" [*Mutterschaft*], like the old gods, is based on evidence of the senses alone. The invention of paternity, like that of a transcendent God, was thus also "a momentous step"; it likewise—Freud repeats the phrase but with a more decisive military emphasis—was "a conquest [*einen Sieg*] of intellectuality over sensuality." It too represented a victory of the more elevated, the more refined, the more spiritual over the less refined, the sensory, the material. It too is a world-historical *"Kulturfortschritt,"* a great cultural stride forward.

Similarly, the great medieval encyclopedist Isidore of Seville could, without embarrassment, make three different claims about the nature of seed—that only men had *sperma*, that only women had *sperma*, and that both had *sperma*—which would be mutually contradictory if they were about the body but perfectly compatible if they were instead corporeal illustrations of cultural truths purer and more fundamental than biological "fact." Isidore's entire work is predicated on the belief that the origin of words informs one about the pristine, uncorrupted, essential nature of their referents, of a reality beyond the corrupt senses, beyond facts.

In the first case Isidore is explaining consanguinity and, as one would expect in a society in which inheritance and legitimacy pass through the father, he is at pains to emphasize the exclusive origins of the seed in the father's blood, in the purest, frothiest, white part of that blood shaken from the body as the foam is beaten from the sea as it crashes on the rocks.[6] For a child to have a father *means* that it is "from one blood," the father's; and conversely to be a father *is* to produce the substance, semen, through which blood is passed on to one's successors. Generation seems to happen without woman at all and there is no hint that blood—"that by which man is animated, and is sustained, and lives," as Isidore tells us elsewhere—could in any fashion be transmitted other than through the male.[7] Now case two, illegitimate descent. This presents a quite different biology: the child under these circumstances is from the *body* of the mother alone; it is "spurious," he explains, because "the ancients called the female genitalia the *spurium*" (9, 5, 24). So, while the legitimate child is from the froth of the father, the illegitimate child seems to come solely from factual flesh, from the seed of the mother's genitals, as if the father did not exist. And finally, when Isidore is explaining why children resemble their progenitors and is not interested in motherhood or fatherhood he remarks pragmatically that "newborns resemble fathers, if the semen of the father is potent, and resemble mothers if the mothers' semen is potent." Both parents, in this account, have seeds which engage in repeated combat for domination every time, and in each generation, a child is conceived (Isidore, 11, 1, 145).

These three distinct and mutually exclusive arguments are a dramatic illustration that much of the debate about the nature of the seed and of the bodies that produce it was in fact not about bodies at all but rather about power, legitimacy, and the politics of fatherhood. They are in principle not resolvable by recourse to the senses. One might of course argue that "just so" stories like Isidore's or Aeschylus' are simply no longer tenable given what has been known since the nineteenth century about conception. Modern biology makes perfectly clear what "mother" and "father" are. But science is relevant only if these stories are understood as reductionistic, as claiming to be true because of biology, which is, rightly, not the sort of claim Isidore and Aeschylus are making. The facts they adduce to illustrate essentially cultural claims may no longer be acceptable and we may persist in reading their cultural claims as based in a false biology. But the "fact" of women bearing children has never been in dispute and has nonetheless counted for relatively little historically in establishing their claims to recognition or authority over children or property.

Facts, as I suggested earlier, are but shifting sands for the construction of motherhood or fatherhood. They come and go and are ludicrously open to interpretation. Regnier de Graaf's discovery of the ovum in 1672 seemed to relegate the male/father to an unaccustomed and distinctly secondary role in reproduction. (Actually de Graaf discovered the follicle that bears his name but which he and others mistakenly took to be the egg. Karl Ernst von Baer in 1827 was the first to observe a mammalian egg and an unfertilized human egg was not seen until 1930.[8]) The female after de Graaf could be imagined to provide the matter for the fetus in a pre-formed if not immediately recognized form while the male "only serv'd to Actuate it." This, one contemporary observed, "derogates much from the dignity of the Male-Sex," which he thought was restored when "Mons. Leeuwenhoek by the Help of his Exquisite Microscope . . . detected Innumerable small *Animals* in the Masculine sperm, and by his Noble Discovery, at once removed that Difficulty. . . ."[9]

I hope by this egregious example to suggest that the form of the argument, and not just its factual premises, are flawed; both conclusions are silly. And, the discovery, still accepted, that neither egg nor sperm contains a pre-formed human but that the fetus develops epigenetically according to plans acquired from both parents does not settle the question of the comparative claims of mother or father, just as the mistaken notions of the past did not entail judgments of their comparative dignities.

Interpretations, not facts, are at issue. The Archbishop of Hartford announced in the *New York Times* on August 26, 1988, that he had quit the Democratic party because it supported abortion: "it is officially in favor of executing unborn babies whose only crime is that they temporarily occupy their mother's womb." No one would dispute that the "thing" in the mother's womb is, under some construction, an unborn baby. "Baby" is a common term for fetus as well as for a very young child and the phrase "the baby is kicking again" to refer to an intra-uterine action is generally acceptable; baby-as-fetus is indisputably only a temporary occupant. The Archbishop's interpretation is objectionable because he elides the difference between "baby-in-the-womb" and "baby-in-the-world," between the womb and any other space an infant might occupy, and therefore between abortion and execution. At issue here is meaning, not nature.

David Hume makes manifest the chasm between the two. A beautiful fish, a wild animal, a spectacular landscape, or indeed "anything that neither belongs, nor is related to us," he says, inspires in us no pride or vanity or sense of obligation. We might with perfect reason fear a minor injury to ourselves and care almost nothing about the deaths of millions of distant strangers. The fault is not with the objects themselves but with their relationship to us. They are too detached and distant to arouse passion. Only, Hume argues, when these "external objects acquire any particular relation to ourselves, and are associated or connected with us," do they engage the emotions.[10] Owning the "external object" seems for Hume to be the most obvious way for this to happen, although ownership itself is, of course, an immensely elastic notion. A biological parent, uncle, clan, "family" can "own" a child in such a fashion as to love and cherish it. But more generally Hume is suggesting that moral concern and action are engendered not by the logic of the relationship between human beings but by the degree to which the emotional and imaginative connections which entail love or obligation have been forged.

The "fact" of motherhood is precisely the psychic labor that goes into making these connections, into appropriating the fetus and then child into a mother's moral and emotional economy. The "fact" of fatherhood is of a like order. If a labor theory of value gives parents rights to a child, that labor is of the heart, not the hand. (The heart, of course, does its work through the hand; we feel through the body. But I will let the point stand in its polemical nakedness.)

While I was working as a volunteer in an old people's home I was attracted to, and ultimately became rather good friends with, a gay woman who was its director of activities. At lunch one day—she had alerted me that she wanted to discuss "something" and not just, as we usually did, schmooz—she asked whether I would consider donating sperm should she and her long-time lover decide, as they were on the verge of doing, to have a child. I was for her a generally appropriate donor—Jewish, fit, with no history of genetic disorders in my family. She was asking me also, she said, because she liked me. It was the first, and remains the only, time I had been asked by anyone, much less someone I liked, and so I was flattered and pleased.

I was also hesitant. My wife the lawyer raised serious legal difficulties with donating "owned" sperm, i.e., sperm that is not given or sold for anonymous distribution. I would remain legally liable for child-support for at least twenty-one years, not to speak of being generally entangled with the lives of a couple I liked but did not know well. (Anonymous sperm is alienated from its producer and loses its connection with him as if it were the jetsam and flotsam of the sea or an artisan's product in the marketplace. Semen, in other words, counts as one of these products of the body that can be alienated, like plasma and blood cells, and not like kidneys or eyes, whose marketing is forbidden.)

Legal issues, however, did not weigh heavily with me. The attractive part of the proposition—that I was being asked because of who I was and therefore that I was to be a father and not just a donor—also weighed mightily against it. A thought experiment with unpleasant results presented itself. I immediately imagined this would-be child as a version of Hannah, imagined that I could see her only occasionally and for short periods of time, imagined that her parents would take her back to their native Israel and that I would never see her again. Potential conflicts with my friend about this baby were almost palpable on the beautiful sunny afternoon of our lunch. In short, I was much too cathexed with this imaginary child to ever give up the sperm to produce her.

I recognize now, and did at the time, that my response was excessive. My reveries of fatherhood sprang from a fetishistic attachment to one among millions of rapidly replenished microscopic organisms—men make on the order of 400 billion sperm in a lifetime—swimming in an abundant, nondescript saline fluid. All that I was really being asked to do was to "produce" some semen—a not unpleasant process—and to give it to my friend so that *a* very, very tiny sperm— actually only its 4–5 micrometers long and 2.5 to 3.5 micrometers wide (c. 1/ 10,000 to 1/20,000 of an inch) head—might contribute the strands of DNA wafting about in it to her egg. Since we humans apparently share 95% of our genetic material with chimpanzees, the sperm in question must share a still higher percentage of base pairs with those of my fellow humans. In short, my unique contribution to the proposed engagement, that which I did not share with billions of other men and monkeys, was infinitesimally small. I was making a mountain out of much, much, much less than a molehill and not very much more than a molecule.

But this is as it should be. For much of history the problem has been to make men take responsibility for their children. Prince and pauper as circumstances required could easily deny the paternity that nature did so little to make evident. The double standard of sexual morality served to insure that however widely they sowed their wild oats the fruits of their wives' wombs would be unambiguously theirs. In fact, until very recently paternity was impossible to prove and much effort went into developing histo-immunological assays that could establish the biological link between a specific man and child. The state, of course, has an interest in making some male, generally the "biological father," responsible for supporting "his" children. In short, a great deal of cultural work has gone into giving meaning to a small bit of matter. Ironically, now that tests make it possible to identify the father with about 100% accuracy, women—those who want children *without* a father—have considerable difficulty obtaining sperm free of filiation. History, social policy, imagination, and culture continue to encumber this cell with its haploid of chromosomes.

In 1978, Mary K., a gay woman living in Sonoma County, California, decided that she wanted to have a child which she would "co-parent" with a close gay woman friend living nearby."[11] Mary wanted to find a sperm donor herself rather than use anonymous sperm for several reasons which she later more or less clearly articulated. She did not want to make the repeated trips to Berkeley, the location of the nearest sperm bank; she did not want to use a physician in her community who might be able to acquire sperm anonymously because she felt that as a nurse she could not be assured of confidentiality; and—this would come to haunt her—she wanted some vestige of an individual human being to be associated with the sperm and with the hoped-for baby. She wanted a "father" of some ill-defined sort, and after a month or so of looking around and after interviewing three potential donors, she was introduced one January evening to a young gay man, Jhordan C., who seemed to fit her needs. He would become the "father" of her child, despite the fact that he did not have the red hair that she had originally sought in a donor.

Neither Jhordan or Mary thought very rigorously about what they expected from their relationship or just what his paternal rights and obligations would be. Neither sought legal counsel; they signed no contract or other written understanding and resolved only the most basic practical details of the matter: Jhordan, upon being notified that Mary was ovulating, would journey to her house, and "produce" sperm, which she would introduce into herself. It took six months before Mary conceived and each of his visits was apparently attended by commonplace social intercourse—some chit chat, tea, and other pleasantries.

After Mary conceived she and Jhordan saw each other occasionally. She accepted his invitation to a small New Year's party at the home of one of his close friends. She testifies that he "reiterated" to her that "he wanted to be known as the father—and I told him I would let the child know who the biological father was—and that he wanted to travel with the child when the child was older." In all other respects she believed that they had an implicit understanding that she would be the child's guardian and primary parent; that Victoria T., Mary's friend, would be co-parent; and that Jhordan would play effectively no role in the life of *her* child.

On the basis of Jhordan's own testimony, he did not know precisely what he meant by wanting "to be known as the father." The court-appointed psychologist described him as a young man of unsettled plans and interests. But Jhordan knew that he wanted somehow to be acknowledged. He was upset when Mary informed him, some months before the birth, that his name would not be on the birth certificate and he became increasingly uneasy as he came to realize that he was being increasingly written out of the family drama that he had helped launch.

Mary admits that she too had been vague about what Jhordan's being her child's father meant to her and that he did have some grounds for his expectation that he would play some sort of paternal role. Language failed her when she tried to describe it:

I had thought about and I was considering whether or not I would tell Sean [not his real name] who the father was, but I didn't know if I would tell him as a father. Like he would know that Jhordan helped donate the sperm, but I did not know if he would ever know Jhordan—How do I say this? I didn't plan on Sean relating as a father. No.

The confusion of names and collapse of grammar here suggests precisely the underlying ambiguities of this case.

When Sean was born Mary felt increasingly threatened by Jhordan's insistence on seeing him, on displaying him to his family, on taking pictures to show to friends and relatives, and in general on acting like a parent, a role that Mary had thought was reserved for herself and Victoria. Jhordan, on the other hand, told the psychologist who interviewed him to determine his fitness as a parent that when "he looked into Sean's eyes, he 'saw his whole family there.' " Whatever uncertainties he might have felt before vanished in the face of his imagined flesh and blood.

Mary finally refused to allow Jhordan to see the baby at all and he eventually gave up trying. There matters might have rested had not, a year later, Mary applied for welfare. The state sued Jhordan for child support (it was after all his sperm) and he, of course, eagerly agreed to pay. Two years and two lawyers later he won visiting rights with Sean at the home of Mary's friend and co-parent, Victoria. These privileges were subsequently expanded. From here on the story is like that of countless divorced couples: quarrels about visitation hours and pick-up times, about where Sean would spend holidays and birthdays, about whether Jhordan allowed him to eat too much sugar, and about other of the many controversial niceties of child-raising that divide parents in even the tightest of families. A court promulgated guidelines and issued orders; an uneasy peace settled over all the parties.

The trial judge in this case was a rather old-fashioned sort who did not seem terribly interested in the subtleties of the law regarding the rights of sperm donors but believed that "blood is thicker than water" and that Sean both needed, and had "a right to," a father. Jhordan was the father and therefore ought, in the judge's view, to be given commensurate visitation rights.

Mary appealed (*Jhordan C. v Mary K.* [1986] 179 CA3d 386, 224 CR 530). The central question before the high court was how to interpret sections 7005(a) and (b) of the California Civil Code. These provide that if, under the supervision of a doctor, a married woman is inseminated by semen from a man who is not her husband, that man under certain circumstances is treated as if he were *not* the natural father while the husband is treated as if he were. Mary's lawyers argued that while their client's case did not quite fit under this statute it was close enough and that the only possible distinction was one of sexual orientation, which ought not to matter. Other California statutes provide that the law must not discriminate against unconventional parenting arrangements in adoption and other reproductive rights issues. If Mary had been married to someone and had acquired Jhordan's sperm in precisely the same circumstances—admittedly not meeting all the conditions of the statute—it would be ludicrous to suppose that the State would give him rights that infringed upon those of the husband. (A German court has held that a man has no claims on a child of a married woman even if he is acknowledged to be the "biological father." Today, as has been generally true for centuries, children born in wedlock are presumed to belong to the husband of the woman who bore them.)

Moreover, Mary's lawyers argued, section 7005a's reference to semen given "to a licensed physician" was not intended to limit the law's application only to such cases but reflected simply a legislative directive to insure proper health standards by recourse to a physician. Mary, because of her training as a nurse, was able to comply with this standard on her own. Her lawyers also cited another court case which held—admittedly in different circumstances—that

> A child conceived through heterologous artificial insemination [i.e. with semen from a man other than the woman's husband] does not have a "natural father." . . . The anonymous donor of sperm can not be considered the "natural father," as he is no more responsible for the use made of his sperm than is a donor of blood or a kidney.

Echoes of Isidore of Seville. Jhordan might not have been anonymous but he was certainly a stranger to Mary.

His lawyers naturally argued for a stricter construal of section 7005a-b and the appeals court sided with them. By not employing a physician, the court agreed, Mary had excluded herself from the law's protection. Moreover, the court viewed the case before it as being more like those in which artificial insemination occurred within the context of an established relationship and in which the sperm donor retained paternal rights than it was like cases of anonymous donation. Jhordan's lawyer cited a New Jersey Supreme Court case, for example, in which a man and a woman were dating and intended to marry. She wanted to bear his child but did not want to have pre-marital intercourse so they resorted to artificial insemination. Three months into the pregnancy they broke up and she declared that she wanted nothing more to do with him and that she certainly would not allow him to visit their child. He sued for paternity and won.

Mary and Jhordan were obviously not as intimately involved as this couple but, the court felt, neither were they the anonymous strangers envisaged by statute. Enough humanity remained in Jhordan's transaction with Mary to allow him to believe that his sperm, however introduced into Mary's body, retained some of him.

As this case and others like it suggest, the legal status of a sperm donor remains deeply problematic and, advises a National Lawyers Guild Handbook, those "consulted by a lesbian considering artificial insemination must be extremely careful to explain the ramifications of the various choices available to their clients."[12] Using a medically supervised sperm bank where the identify of the donor is unknown to the recipient is the most certain way to guarantee that the donor will not at some time in the future be construed as the father. Other possibilities include having a friend secure semen but keeping the source secret; using semen from multiple donors (not recommended because of possible immune reactions); using a known donor but having a physician as intermediary. Some lawyers recommend having the recipient pay the donor for his sperm and describing the transaction in an ordinary commercial contract of the sort with which the courts are familiar. And even if agreements between sperm donors and recipients are not predictably enforceable, lawyers suggest that the parties set down their understanding of their relationship as clearly as possible.

Any or all of these strategies might have stripped Jhordan's sperm of paternity, not just in the eyes of the law but more importantly in his heart, and might thus have saved Mary and her co-parent their struggles with the parental claims of a near stranger. Mary was wrong to eschew a doctor's mediation or at least underestimated the hold that a very small bit of matter can, in the right circumstances, have on a man's imagination.

In designating a physician as middleman the legislature did not blindly medicalize an essentially social transaction but sought rather to appropriate one of modern medicine's least attractive features—its lack of humanity—for a socially useful end. Everyone knows, even politicians, that artificial insemination does not require a physician. De-paternalizing sperm might. A strange doctor in a lab coat working amidst white formica furniture, high tech instruments, officious nurses, and harried receptionists in a boxy office in a nondescript glass and steel building set in a parking lot may offer cold comfort to the sick and needy; he or she might, however, be perfect at taking the sparkle off sperm.

Had Jhordan donated sperm not at Mary's house, where he was offered tea and conversation, but at a clinic; had he never spoken to her after the inseminations began but only to the doctor's nurse, who would have whisked away the vial of fresh semen; had he never seen Mary pregnant or celebrated New Year's Eve with her, the fetish of the sperm might have been broken. The doctor as broker would have performed his or her priestly function, de-blessed the sperm, and gotten rid of its "paternity." (This I imagine as the inversion of normal priestly work, providing extra emotional glue between the participants in weddings, funerals, and the like.) Similarly, selling sperm at a price fixed by contract—the lawyer or sperm bank owner as de-blessing agent—would take off some of its paternal blush. Without such rites, a father's material claim in his child is small but his imaginative claims can be as endless as a mother's. Great care must be taken to protect and not to squash them.

Because fatherhood is an "idea," it is not limited to men. In a recent case litigated in Alameda County, California (Lofton v. Flouroy), a woman was, rightly in my view, declared to be a child's father, if not its male parent. Ms. Lofton and Ms. Flouroy lived together and decided to have a child. Lofton's brother Larry donated the required sperm but expressed no interest in having any further role in the matter. Ms. Lofton introduced her brother's semen into Flouroy with a turkey baster, Flouroy became pregnant, and in due course a baby was born. The "birth mother" was listed on its birth certificate as "mother," and L. Loften—Linda, not Larry, but who was to know?—was listed as "father."

Everything went well and the women treated the child as theirs until, two years later, they split up. The mother kept the child and there matters might have rested had not, as in the case of Mary and Jhordan, the State intervened. Flouroy applied for welfare benefits, i.e., aid to dependent children, and when asked by the Family Support Bureau to identify the father she produced, in a moment of unabashed concreteness, the turkey baster. The Bureau, not amused, did what it was meant to do and went after the "father" on the birth certificate—Linda, it was surprised to learn, not Larry. Like Jhordan she welcomed the opportunity to claim paternity, did not dispute the claim and eagerly paid the judgment entered against her: child support, current and retroactive. She also demanded paternal visitation rights, which Ms. Flouroy resisted. Lofton then asked the court to compel mediation. It held that she was indeed a "psychological parent" and thus had standing to have her rights mediated. The other L. Lofton, Larry, makes no appearance in this drama.

Linda's claim is manifestly not biological nor even material. That she borrowed her brother's sperm or owned the turkey baster is irrelevant. What matters is that, in the emotional economy of her relationship with her lover and their child, she was the father, whatever that means, and enjoyed the rights and bore the obligations of that status. She invested the required emotional and imaginative capital in the impregnation, gestation, and subsequent life to make the child in some measure hers.

I hasten to add that I do not regard biology in all circumstances as counting for nothing. Women have claims with respect to the baby within them simply by virtue of spatial relations and rights to bodily integrity. These are not the right to be or not to be a mother as against the right to be or not to be a father, nor the claims of a person as against those of a non-person—the terms in which the abortion debate is usually put—but the right shared by all mentally competent adults to control and monitor corporeal boundaries, to maintain a body as theirs. Thus I would regard a court compelling a woman to bear a child against her will as a form of involuntary servitude however much its would-be father might wish for the child. And I would regard an enforced abortion as an even more egregious assault on her body. But this is not to acknowledge the "fact" of motherhood as much as the "fact" of flesh. History bears witness to the evils that ensue when the state abrogates a person's rights in her body.

The flesh does not make a mother's body an ahistorical font of motherhood and maternity. A writer who wants, but cannot herself have, a child and who finds surrogate motherhood morally unacceptable "can not imagine" that "there are plenty of women now, the huge majority of surrogates who have, to hear them tell it, not suffered such a loss [as Mary Beth Whitehead's]."[13] While her empathic instincts extend easily to Whitehead she cannot, despite testimony to the contrary, conceive of a mother *not* feeling an instant and apparently unmediated bond to her child. Ms. Fleming cannot accept that feelings do not follow from flesh so that "surrogate mothers" who feel otherwise than they supposedly should must suffer, like un-class-conscious workers, from false consciousness.

Ms's special "Mothers Issue," quite apart from Chesler's article, is striking by its very cover—an airbrushed, soft-toned picture of a 1950s young Ivory Soap woman, with straight blond hair of the sort that waves in shampoo commercials, holding a blue-eyed baby to her bare bosom and looking dreamily out of the frame of the picture—which would have been denounced by feminists as perpetuating an unacceptable stereotype of women had it appeared in *Family Circle* a decade ago. In 1988 it unashamedly represents the Mother in America's largest selling feminist magazine.

What exactly are the facts of motherhood and what of significance ought to follow from them? For advocates of Mrs. Whitehead's, like Phyllis Chesler, her egg and its genetic contents are not especially relevant. She shares with Bill, a.k.a. Dr. Stern, the provision of chromosomes. The critical fact is therefore her nine months of incubation, which would remain a fact even if the fertilized egg she was bringing to term were not hers. Her claim, it appears, rests on labor, on her physical intimacy with the child within her, and would be just as strong if a second woman sought a stake in the child on the basis of her contribution of half its chromosomes.

I am immensely sympathetic to this view but not because of a fact of nature. Capitalist societies, as I suggested earlier, are not usually friendly to the notion that putting labor into a product entitles one to ownership or even to much credit. It is the rare company that gives its workers shares of stock. We associate a new production of *The Magic Flute* with David Hockney and not with those who sawed, hammered, and painted the sets; everyone knows that Walt Disney produced *Bambi* but only the "cognoscenti" could name even one of the artists who actually made the pictures. Having the idea or the plan is what counts, which is why Judge Sokoloff told Dr. Stern that in getting Melissa he was only getting what was already his. (The Judge should, of course, have said, "half his.")

I became so exercised by Baby M because Dr. Stern's claims have been reduced in some circles to his ownership of his sperm which, as I said earlier, amounts to owning very little. This puts him—all fathers—at a distinct material disadvantage to Mrs. Whitehead—all women—who contribute so much more matter. But, this essay has suggested, his claims, like hers, arise from the intense and profound bonding with a child, unborn and born, that its biological kinship might spark in the moral and affective imagination but which it does not entail.

The problem, of course, is that emotional capital does not accumulate steadily, visibly, and predictably as in a psychic payroll deduction plan. That is why, for example, it is unreasonable to demand of a woman specific performance on a surrogate mothering contract as if the baby were a piece of land or a work of art whose attributes would be well known to their vendor. A "surrogate mother," like a mother who offers to give up her baby for adoption to a stranger, must be allowed a reasonable time to change her mind and if she does, in the case of a surrogacy arrangement, be prepared to argue for her rights against those of the father.

Each parent would bring to such a battle claims to have made another person emotionally part of themselves. "Facts" like bearing the child would obviously be significant evidence but would not be unimpeachable, would not be nature speaking unproblematically to culture. While we can continue to look forward to continuing conflict over the competing claims of parents I suggest that we abandon the notion that biology—facts—will somehow provide the resolution. Neither, of course, will ideas alone in a world in which persons exist corporeally. The way out of the fact/idea dichotomy is to recognize its irrelevance in these matters. The "facts" of such socially powerful and significant categories as mother and father come into being only as culture imbues things, actions, and flesh with meaning. This is the process that demands our continued attention.

Notes

1. For an account of these industrial narratives see Catherine Gallagher, *The Industrial Reformation of English Fiction, 1832–1867* (Chicago: University of Chicago Press, 1985).

2. Gayle Rubin, "The Traffic in Women: Notes on the 'Political Economy' of Sex," in Rayna Reiter, ed., *Toward an Anthropology of Women* (New York: Monthly Review Press, 1975) pp. 179–180.

3. *Philosophy in the Bedroom* (New York: Grove Press, 1965) p. 106.

4. William Harvey, *Disputation Touching the Generation of Animals,* trans. Gweneth Whitteridge (Oxford: Oxford University Press, 1981) pp. 182–183.

5. Sigmund Freud, *Moses and Monotheism* (1939), in *The Standard Edition of the Complete Psychoanalytical Works,* ed. James Strachey (London: Hogarth Press) vol. 23, pp. 113–114; I have altered the translation slightly based on the standard German edition. Aeschylus, *The Eumenides,* trans. Richmond Lattimore, in David Greene and Lattimore, eds., *Greek Tragedies,* vol. 3 (Chicago: University of Chicago Press, 1960) pp. 26–28.

6. Isidore, *Etimologias [Etymologiarum],* ed. and trans. with facing Latin text by J. O. Reta and M. A. Marcos (Madrid: Biblioteca de Autores Christianos, 1983) 6, 4.

7. *Ibid.* 5, 5, 4. On blood, see 4, 5, 4.

8. See Thomas W. Laqueur, *Making Sex: Body and Gender from the Greeks to Freud* (Cambridge: Harvard University Press, 1990), for more extensive discussion of these points.

9. William Cowper, *Anatomy,* introduction, n.p.

10. David Hume, *A Treatise of Human Nature,* ed. L. A. Selby-Bigge (Oxford: Oxford University Press, 1965) 2, 1, 9, p. 303.

11. Civil Case no. A-027810. I am grateful to Donna Hutchins, Esq., of San Francisco for making available the various depositions, briefs, and other court papers on which I base the following discussion.

12. Roberta Achtenberg, ed., *Sexual Orientation and the Law* (New York: Clark, Boardman, Co. Ltd, 1989) section 1–70.

13. Anne Taylor Fleming, "Our Fascination with Baby M," *New York Times Magazine,* March 29, 1987, p. 87. There were at the time of this article about one thousand known "surrogate mothers."

13

Thinking about Fathers

Sara Ruddick

"I am annoyed that we lack a history of fatherhood."

                                                            Thomas W. Laqueur

"For the first time in history . . . we are in a position to look around us at the Kingdom of the Fathers and take its measure."

                                                            Adrienne Rich

Recent feminist literature abounds in disputes over the epistemological possibility and political consequences of making claims about "women." By contrast, there is a noticeable skittishness when "men" enter into feminist discussion. Women's Studies students rush to rescue the few men in the room from attacks on their "masculinity," feminist teachers anxiously insist that only some men— usually ruling class, rich, white, "Western"—are intended by feminist talk of "men," and feminist writers cling to Great Male Thinkers and Presences (often white, "Western," rulers of their worlds, and rich). The very idea of "men" threatens inter-sex friendships, heterosexual relationships, political alliances, household arrangements, and race and class loyalties. Moreover, feminist women have to keep their jobs, advance their careers, take their sexual pleasures, engage in politics, and hold their families together in societies that are still male dominated and heterosexist.

Recently, however, the discomforting and oft-evaded "problem of men" has forced itself into feminist debate as a "problem of fathers." Most dramatically, feminists are struggling with a politics of birth. Some developing reproductive practices, notably "surrogate" mothering, increase the possibilities of male abuse. At the same time, a more open and efficient use of artificial insemination, combined with more flexible sexual mores and an insistent gay politics, allow women increasing control over the role of men in procreation and mothering.

Women's procreative fears and powers are inseparable from their beliefs about the effect of father-men in children's and women's lives.

In the official story fathers are necessary ingredients both of childhood and of good-enough mothering. Daughters, as much as sons, long for the blessing of a protective, providing, just Father. Heterosexual mothers willingly sacrifice ambition and pleasure in the hope of keeping even barely good-enough fathers—and their cash—in the house. This "wifely" choice is confirmed by an array of social critics who warn that "female-headed households" are symptomatic of—if not responsible for—misery and failure. Psychoanalysts weigh in with the claim that sons—and to a lesser extent daughters—must bond with a father against a powerful, engulfing mother; that children without a father are trapped within a pre-oedipal (pre-cultural, almost pre-linguistic) maternal dyad. Not surprisingly, even women who expect to mother alone or with other women often look for a male who is willing to become a "known and knowable" father.

But the official story cannot conceal the fact that, as Gertrude Stein remarked, "fathers are depressing." Barely known, scarcely knowable, the "absence" of fathers permeates feminist stories. Some fathers are literally lost or gone; others can be located but will not, except under rarely effective legal pressure, offer cash or services. Fathers who provide materially for their children as best they can rarely assume a full share of the emotional work and responsibility of childcare. In developed countries, where the "double shift" has become notorious, cultural traditions and personal training undergird masculine entitlement. Fathers neither apologize nor worry if their jobs, hobbies, sports, fatigue, or personal ambition keep them from their children. By contrast, whatever their work, pleasures, or ambitions, mothers can (almost always) be counted on to take up the responsibilities of "parenting." In some feminist stories, even fathers who are determined to share parental responsibilities find themselves hindered by an entrenched, only partly conscious, gendered, self-identity. According to this psychoanalytic tale, in societies where children are raised primarily by females, "men develop by contrast [with women] a self based more on a denial of relation and connection and on a more fixed and firmly split and repressed inner self-object world: 'the basic masculine sense of self is separate.' "[1] Hence the basically masculine son of a female mother will, as a father, unwittingly absent himself from his children in order to keep and defend the distance his sense of masculine/separateness requires.

If an absent father is depressingly disappointing, a present father can be dangerous to mothers and their children. The early childhood development that compels "masculine" men (and women) to keep a safe distance from others also requires them to control and, when necessary, to subjugate their children's disruptive, intrusive, unpredictable, needy wills. Hence the father with no time for the double shift may well have time enough to serve as a controlling judge of his children's lives. Whatever his personal tendencies, such a father's temptations toward excessive, judgmental control will be exacerbated by his sense that he is entitled to rule over women and children, a right accorded him by the sexual-social contract implicit in political understandings of (at least) Western-style democracies.[2]

A father who is authoritarian, capricious, intrusive, and controlling may none-theless act kindly toward his children. Unfortunately, as feminist inquiry of the last decade has confirmed, many fathers are not kind. Children are vulnerable and provocative; parents are often exhausted, harassed, isolated, underhoused, and multiply undersupported. It is not surprising that many children suffer vio-lence and neglect from desperate mothers and fathers. What is striking is the extent and variety of the psychological, sexual, and physical battery suffered by women and children of all classes and social groups, often (though by no means always) at the hands of fathers, their mothers' male lovers, or male relatives.

If putative fathers are absent or perpetually disappearing and actual present fathers are controlling or abusive, who needs a father? What mother would want to live with one or wish one on her children? Even social theorists who bewail the toll of divorce and the immiseration of female-headed households recognize that while a good father is good for his children, a bad father is worse than none at all.[3] Most mothers do not choose and cannot afford to raise children alone. But in a state that provided for its children's basic needs, women could raise children together as lesbian co-parents or as part of larger friendship circles or intergenera-tional households. Exceptional men who proved particularly responsible and responsive might be invited to contribute to maternal projects—that is to donate, as other mothers do, their cash, labor, and love. But these donations would not be predictably connected to the donation of sperm nor would they confer upon the donating men any Fatherly rights or privileges that mothering women did not enjoy.

Some feminists will descry utopian possibilities in the promise of such rela-tively Father-free households and families. Secure in near-exclusively female enclaves that are governed by ideals of gender justice, women could undertake a politico-spiritual journey in which they (almost all) relinquished heterosexuality though not (necessarily) mothering, overcame their dependence on fathers and fears of fatherlessness, and claimed for themselves personal autonomy and collec-tive political and cultural power. Their households and families could be seen as an aspect of, prelude to, preparation for, the more ambitious project of creating a "future that is female," a Herland in which men as well as women would live safely because women would govern.

Although this utopian vision is feminist, many feminists do not share the despairing (or imperious or oppressive?) judgment of fathers on which it appears to depend. Rather than attempting to free mothers from men, they (we) work to transform the institutions of fatherhood. Their (our) reasons are naive and familiar: many men, single and partnered, gay and heterosexual, prove themselves fully capable of responsible, responsive mothering; in a world short of love why do without them? Feminists cannot afford to distance themselves from the many heterosexually active women for whom heterosexual and birthing fantasies are intertwined and who want to share mothering with a sexual partner. Nor should feminists condescend to mothers, lesbian and heterosexual, who want their sons to want to care for children and to undertake protective and nurturant father-like relationships. Moreover, even in adverse social circumstances, mothering is often a deeply rewarding, life-structuring activity that tends to create in mothers distinctive capacities for responsibility, attentive care, and non-violence. Men are roughly half of the world's people; it would be self-destructive as well as unjust to exclude them (or *any* social group) from a work that so often has such beneficial psychological and social effects. In any case, only a minority of women can afford a fatherless world. Under current U.S. economic conditions increasing numbers of mothers are dependent on a (usually) male partner's wage as well as their own, and many are desperate for some measure of (usually his) economic support. And whatever their sexual persuasion, many women who have fought against oppression and tyranny find in their father-inclusive families a source of strength and resistance. Finally there are the facts of bodily life, in particular the existence, the necessity of "the male body" that is represented in the fatherhood debate by the inconveniently necessary, unpredictably potent, increasingly traceable and manipulable male sperm.

For all these familiar reasons, many feminists, and I among them, envision a world where many more men are more capable of participating fully in the responsibilities and pleasures of mothering. But I have only to open a newspaper, read the testimony of women, listen to students, or walk into or (more frequently) remember the father-dominated homes of friends and colleagues to find myself fantasizing about a world without Fathers. Because so many daughters, mothers, and wives, have lived a sorry history of fatherhood, a feminist who works for gender-free, gender-full, mothering needs to imagine and justify her confidence in new ways of fathering. For this task, the words, as well as the work, of good and thoughtful fathers are indispensable.

Thomas Laqueur is a good father. Like many not so good fathers, he is bound powerfully by the "facts" of love for his child. Like the good Fathers of fiction, he talks with his daughter, proudly repeats her remarks, and, we can assume, tells inventive, witty, and erudite tales in the traditionally paternal story hour. More importantly, Laqueur, unlike most fathers, assumes a full share of child-tending in a household where, he tells us proudly, "gender roles are topsy turvey" and, we assume, an easy fairness reigns. Although—or because—he never mentions money, it seems clear that Laqueur does not suffer from an often anguishing (and in cultural ideology a distinctly "fatherly") burden. He and his partner can support their child—she is a lawyer, he is a university teacher and writer with time left over to volunteer at an old people's home. It is understandable that a gay friend wants Laqueur to become the "known and knowable" sperm donor for her and her partner's child. Laqueur is utterly welcoming of his friend's enterprise and personally flattered. He refuses primarily because, to shorten his longer and complicated story, he would love the (her and his) child too much.

Yet this blessed and blessing, loving and liberal father is grumpy, and I, though convinced that he is a daughter's dream and wife's delight, find myself grumpy with him. He is annoyed that he lacks a history of fatherhood, that the story of "man-as-father" is not discernable in the patriarchal histories that treat of inheritance, "legitimacy," and public authority. I am annoyed that he lacks the history feminists have begun to create, a story of men as fathers that is inseparable from the economic and domestic powers—including the claims of inheritance, legitimacy, and authority—that "fathers" wield over women and their (women's and men's) children. While he worries about the "neo-essentialist" claims of female birthgivers, I am struck by the shrinking significance of female birthgiving in the story such a good father tells.

Laqueur rightfully criticizes historians' acceptance of a nineteenth-century ideology that places men in public and women at home. Such a story cannot tell a father what it means to be a "new public man in private." But he says nothing about the women in father-ruled households of old. Feminists have pondered over the question of the degree of freedom and power enjoyed by women of different classes working in their own or other people's homes. But there is general agreement that the ideological construction of distinctive domestic power glosses over the very real, legal, psycho-social, physical, and too often abusive control that many men have exercised within the domain allegedly governed by women. But Laqueur, who is so evidently not tyrannical or abusive, is not much interested in the analysis of domestic power.

Nor, despite his proposing a labor theory of parenting, does Laqueur really attend to fathering as a kind of work. The distinctions he sometimes endorses between hand, heart, and brain are decidedly ill-suited for a work that is done with and amidst bodies, provokes and requires distinctive kinds of thinking and involves the passionate emotions of both parent and child. Laqueur initially distinguishes between heart and hand (while ignoring mind) in order to count fatherly emotion as a kind of work. He then needlessly protests his own paternal love. Feminists have never disputed the "fact" that many men—even some who are abusive—are bound by love to their children and make them "emotionally part of themselves." Indeed father-love is often part of the father-problem precisely because this "love"—in addition to binding children to damaging fathers— serves to establish fathers' claims to authority over children whether or not they have actually participated in the work of caring for them.

Indeed Laqueur's distinctions can all too easily be bent to serve the purposes of "absent" and perhaps even damaging fathers (although this bending is clearly neither his intent nor his practice). As Laqueur amusingly relates in his tales of biological paternity, the totalizing dichotomies of the philosophers[4] associate masculinity, fatherhood, activity, and mind and set them against passive, female birthgiving. In the dichotomies I know best (for example Plato, Augustine, and

Hannah Arendt), "mind," and with it authority and power, is set sharply against emotion, domestic life, and bodily necessity. By breaking into the usual binary opposition Laqueur rescues emotion and—apparently—makes it the crucial, even defining element of parental labor. He rejects a conception of fatherhood as generative idea (opposed to the passive matter of maternity) but he does not make the even more helpful gesture of associating the work of mothering and fathering with distinctive kinds of thinking. And he explicitly identifies parental labor with "the heart *not* the hand" (ital. added). Hence Laqueur effectively leaves fathers with emotions no one doubted they had, without the physical labor such emotions might rightly entail, but (at least in Laqueur's circles) with their minds intact but elsewhere. Most mothers are thus left not only with emotions everyone takes for granted, but also with the physical labor that has been rightly thought to be theirs, and without the minds that no one thought they had anyway unless, like fathers, they "go to [intellectual] work."

I am very sympathetic with Laqueur's labor theory of parenting. Indeed, I believe that if Laqueur reflected upon his *work* as a father he would quickly relinquish his ill-fitting and potentially harmful distinctions. But Laqueur is far less preoccupied with parenting than with procreation, and in particular with a father's reproductive acts and feelings. A labor theory of *parenting* loosens the ["essentialist"] conceptual connections between *birthgiving* and the very different work of child-tending and thus provides a place of entrance for men and "adoptive" parents. But while a "labor theory" of parenting is gender inclusive, a labor theory of birthgiving, as Laqueur himself finally recognizes, must privilege the female who gestates and gives birth to a child. Any man or woman can assume the responsibilities and share in the pleasures of maternal work, whatever his or her relationship to the birthgivers of the children they tend. But the labor of the most emotion-ridden male progenitor*—no matter how anxiously, joyously, tenderly, and responsibly he prepares for birthgiving and assists the birthgiver— cannot equal the labor of nine months gestation and a body-encompassing, almost always painful birthgiving.

Suppose, however, we ignore, like some of Laqueur's predecessors, the active and complex physicality and the reflective consciousness that birthgiving requires. A man's or woman's *emotional* bonding with a fetus could then appear as the best kind of procreative work. Were he to adopt this conceptual construction of birthgiving as emotional labor, a man could compete with a female birthgiver for "best worker" and have a fighting chance of earning the prize. While he takes a proprietary interest in the child she carries, imagines dramas of fatherhood, dreams about his ancestors, and prepares to see "his whole family" in his baby's eyes, she, who may well have similar dreams and fantasies, also has other, often ambivalent emotional responses occasioned by the very physical activities and

---

*or the labor of a similarly emotional female egg donor, though donating eggs is a more complex and painful enterprise than donating sperm through sexual or artificial insemination.

reflective consciousness that we have denied. She is sick, pulled out of shape, moves clumsily and worries about falling. She is tested and then makes conscious choices in response to those tests. She ponders over the effects of the simplest drug that might relieve a headache, often enough struggles against possibly damaging addictive habits, and frequently worries and then feels guilty about what she eats, drinks, or smokes. She is apprehensive of the pain she will almost surely suffer, yet (if she has the time and money) selects anesthetics and labor practices conducive to her infant's health. Typically, she expects to take on the greater share of the child tending on which parental visions ultimately depend; anxiously she devises strategies for getting the services she and her child will require and imagines ways in which she might maintain her job or pursue her career and still enjoy the friendships, projects, and pleasures of her pre-maternal adult life.

It is not surprising if a female birthgiver sometimes feels more invaded by than possessor of the baby she "carries." Despite the pain and struggle—and partly because of the excitement and pleasure which are also part of gestation and birth—many birthgivers report a nearly mystical connection with their newborn infant. But many other birthgivers feel that they have failed to "bond" with their child, a relationship that is romantically identified with welcoming, unambivalent love. While the experience of bonding is considered obligatory for female birthgivers, it may indeed come more easily to eager and financially confident fathers.

Suppose, however, that we take seriously a labor theory of birthgiving but insist on measuring "labor" by the variety of intellectual reflection, conscious choice, physical effort, *and* complex, ambivalent emotional experience and discipline that the work of birthgiving requires. Despite centuries of social construction designed to obscure the stories and "facts" of flesh, it is clear that female birthgivers perform by far the greatest part of birthing labor. Laqueur realizes this: "all fathers [are] at a distinct material disadvantage to . . . all women [birthgivers] who contribute so much more matter" and—he should have added—at least as much emotional "investment," intellectual reflection, and choice.

Turning to history and to current legal cases, Laqueur makes abundantly clear that the links between biological procreation and "mothering" or "fathering" are constructed and complex. Unlike many social constructionists before him, including many feminists, Laqueur does not intend to trivialize the experience of female birthgivers. He wants to include men, not to insult women; he is wittily critical of theorists who deny women's pro*creativity*. Nonetheless, he manages to contribute to reductive accounts of a birthgiver's myriad, emotionally laden, self-shaping, thought-provoking physical experiences. By focusing on legal cases and therefore (at least in the United States) creating an atmosphere in which conflict is irresoluble, he sets up a contest between female birthgivers and male progenitors. While the cases are meant only to underline the complexity of men's feelings (as well as the conventionality of connections between birthgiving and parenting), Laqueur tips the scales to the father by highlighting his emotional response to a genetic offspring and the birthgiver's insensitive or muddled reactions to him. Meanwhile, Laqueur ignores, though he never denies and probably takes for granted, the birthgiver's response to the fetal-infant life she carries and delivers.

More directly, Laqueur assimilates the hiring of women as birthgivers to the sexual exploitation of aspiring "starlets," the forced labor exchanges of the poor, employers' abuse of children's bodies, and "academic hiring fairs." "There are no new horrors here." Although Laqueur's concern for the sexual and economic exploitation of women, children, the desperately poor, and needy academics is admirable, it does not touch upon many women's specific, deeply felt rejection of the practices of surrogacy. At the end, Laqueur invokes a liberal theory of the right to "control and monitor corporeal boundaries," again with no specific reference to birthgiving or to the distinctive breakdown—or revisioning—of bodily boundary—as "fact" and "idea"—that birthgiving entails. Indeed at his and my grumpiest moments, I felt that Laqueur, like many philosophers before him, was almost afraid—and anyhow failed—to look at, listen to, imagine his way into the social and intellectual complexities of the female birthgiving experience.

In rejecting easy, "essentialist," connections between birthgiving and parenting, and insisting that we attend to men's emotional and physical reproductive experience, Laqueur articulates crucial steps toward the necessary feminist enterprise of rethinking the social and metaphysical significance of birth. But for those feminists who wish to include fathers but recognize the necessity of transforming Fatherhood, the work—the emotional, intellectual, imaginative, and physical labor—of reconstruction is still to be done.

How then are feminists to think about fathers? I would begin as Laqueur does, not with birthgiving, but with the *work* of parenting. If we see or remember child-tending accurately, we will be rid of distinctions, or more optimistically reimagine connections, between so-called physical, intellectual, and emotional activities.* We can also avoid the exclusive heterosexual coupledom in which parenting has been conceptually and ideologically mired. The *work* of child-tending can be, and is being, undertaken by women and men, gay and straight, single, coupled, or in many kinds of social arrangements.

Unlike Laqueur, however, and like the feminists who envision a world without "fathers," I speak of "mothering" rather than "parenting" as the work in which child-tending men and women engage. This terminology acknowledges the "fact" that mothering has been—and still is—primarily the responsibility of women and

*Focusing upon the *work* that child-tending requires will prompt a more general metaphysical revision of the categories of mind, emotion, and "physical" labor. This revision is one of the philosophical rewards of attending to mothering as "work" or as a "practice."

that history has consequences. Also, by the slight if passing frisson of referring to men as mothers I hope to jar a listener into reflecting upon the distinctive rights and privileges of "fathers" and upon the heterosexist knot in which our ideas of mothering are tied. By contrast, the abstract notion of "parent" obscures the pervasive injustices suffered by women-mothers and, more generally, the myriad father problems that vex and divide feminists.

In making the case for "mothering" as a gender-inclusive and therefore gender-less activity, I have been struck by the resistance even of those men who fully engage in child-tending. As a feminist I am aware of the dangers of "saming" (to borrow a useful phrase from Naomi Schor),[5] that is, denying the objectified other—in this case the male parent—"the right to [his] difference, submitting the other to the laws of [maternity]." But I do not understand what men fear to lose. Leaving aside penis, sperm, [phallus?], and other "essentialist" and essentially unthreatened equipment, what makes a parent a "father"?

Consider Laqueur's gender-bending case of a lesbian parent separated from her birthgiving partner who is accorded the status of father, not because she inseminated her lover with her brother's sperm, but because she has invested the "emotional and imaginative capital," and, as it happens, the cash, "to make the child in some measure hers." Why don't these investments—most of which will have occurred after birth—make L. Lofton, as in my view they would make any man, in some measure a mother? Is L. Lofton called a "father" because she lives apart from her child, is therefore less a mother, but still an absent father? Does she, do we, grant rights to an absent *father,* when a similarly absent mother would be delinquent? If so, are we not conceptually embroiled in the very institutions of fatherhood we are trying to revision? Is L. Lofton a father because she was legally enjoined to contribute support? Despite the ideology of fatherly provision, countless mothers support their children and absent, wage-earning mothers might be legally compelled to do so. Equally important, when fathering is identified with economic support in a way that mothering is not, and when men cannot consider themselves mothers, unemployed, impoverished young men cannot take themselves to be "parents."[6] Material support is not a distinctly *paternal* obligation but, on the contrary, is a fact of most women-mothers' lives and a necessary condition of any effective childcare. To be sure, recognizing these facts of men's or women's mothering, unsustained by the myth of the Providing Father, requires both confronting the economic injustices women and poor men suffer and defining "child support" in terms of a *social* obligation to provide for children's needs. Troubles of transition aside, this is just the kind of change that talk of "mothering" is intended to abet.

Despite my refusal of the abstract "parent" and the different "father," I am as determined as Laqueur to disrupt the presumption that female birthgiving is either necessary or sufficient for good-enough mothering. I see all mothers, including women-mothers who have given birth, as "adoptive." A man or woman is a "mother," in my sense of the term, only if he or she acts upon a social commitment to nurture, protect, and train children. All mothering depends upon some woman's birthgiving but there are many possible birth-respecting relationships between mothers and birthgivers. Finally, however, my account of "adoptive" maternal work and thinking comes no closer than Laqueur's labor theory of parenting to articulating a social, political, and metaphysical understanding of birth. It was only after several years of writing about potentially genderless mothering that I began to consider female birthgiving as an active, socially complex, chosen project.[7] Belatedly realizing that I had neglected (and feared) the female body, I insisted on birthgiving *women's* distinctive experiences and responsibilities. Determined to avoid reinscribing the "spurious" and "illegitimate" child of "single" or lesbian mothers, I construed the birthgiver and her infant(s) as a complex and complete couple, albeit economically, emotionally, and medically dependent upon others' help. Now, having read Laqueur's impassioned insistence on his participation in birthgiving, I realize that in my first attempts at reconceptualization I wrote male bodies out of birth. Laqueur reminds me that any account of birth that respects human bodily life should include male as well as female procreative acts and desires.

Ultimately it is men who will have to tell the story of male procreative feelings and acts. But mothers of both sexes might help to tell one version of the story by beginning at the beginning, attending to or remembering children's intense and elaborately imagined bodily lives and their own maternal engagement with children's bodies. Children's bodies, though phantastically interpreted, are irreducibly, "factually," given: whoever tends a child tends a particular bodily life. Mothers are meant to protect those bodies rather than assault or neglect them; they are meant to adorn, soothe, and feed, to applaud, delight, and caress. Children's bodies, like the bodies of adults, are sexual; the distinctive pleasures and curiosities of sexuality make their appearance not as an exception to, but as an essential ingredient of childhood bodily life. To protect children's bodies means to protect rather than intrude upon, exploit, suppress, or unduly regiment children's desires and shifting sex/gender identities.

A welcoming response to bodily life is only an ideal, one that many mothers do not express or share. But when mothering is governed by this ideal, and when, as sometimes happens, mothers are fairly successful at enacting the ideal by which they are governed, a practice of welcoming and protecting bodies becomes part of children's heritage. When children have been protected and appreciated they have also been taught (at least implicitly) to protect—rather than to abuse or neglect—their own and each others' bodies. By the time "sperm" appears, along with excitements, nocturnal emissions, unpredictable erections, and other phenomena only males can speak of, there is a context in which young women and men can identify and protect young men's—as well as young women's—procreative capacities. To be sure, adolescents are dismally apt to abuse and endanger their own and others' bodies, flaunting the protective circumstances on which they have depended. My point is that "sperm" and its/his adventures emerge within those practices, whether benign or punishing, protective or neglectful, that have constructed bodily life. If "bodies" are constructed as unpredictably developing beings that are meant to be enjoyed and protected then it is more likely that male procreation—like female birthgiving—will be imagined as a chosen activity through which men create for themselves responsible, responsive ways and occasions for "donating sperm."

Still the most benign socio-political context cannot make male procreation "equal" in physical, intellectual, or emotional labor to female birthgiving. As feminists have learned, the differences we deny come back to haunt us. Birthgiving is a complex, demanding, and sometimes self-transforming activity and hitherto, as in the foreseeable future, only women can give birth. As Laqueur's history of procreative mythology (implicitly) documents, men have often written (and presumably acted) on behalf of men, inspired by the envy, fear, resentment, and guilt their "different" relationship to birth inspires. The task, as I see it, is to construct—really *construct,* socially, materially, and politically—birthgiving practices in which women and men can participate unequally but with realistic self-respect, mutual regard, and a commitment to the well-being of the children that they, or other mothers, will adopt.

This is of course utopian. As it is, young men's bodies are "thrown away"— neglected and assaulted, sacrificed to militarist endeavor, capitalist greed, and racist domination. In a society where male (as well as female) bodies are so abused, male sexuality and "sperm," and the absent and abusive fathers who embody them, have often proved to be the socially constructed enemy of women. In the midst of this unprotective, often cruel, society, a rough justice is arising. Women buy men's sperm but leave men out. A man's increasingly traceable sperm is used to bind him to economic relations he would not have chosen and often cannot sustain. Now, like a woman, a man can be made materially accountable for, yet socially alienated from, his sexual activities; he may therefore feel that, like a woman (though surely less painfully), he too is a victim of his procreative body.

Rough justice is an improvement upon the misogynist and male-dominated institutions in which women have had to give birth and undertake mothering. But the practices and rhetoric of rough justice *can* make a person grumpy. It is far more heartening to imagine feminist transformations that will prove protective of adult and child, male and female; far more gratifying to create the health care, nurseries, jobs, employment policies, and educational programs—the myriad social structures on which all good-enough mothering depends. Then women and men, whatever their personal couplings and connections, might join together in a collective commitment to nurture and cherish the procreative promise of their children.

Notes

1.   Nancy Chodorow, *Feminism and Psychoanalytic Theory* (New Haven: Yale University Press, 1989), chap. 9, p. 185.

2. See, for example, Carole Pateman, *The Sexual Contract* (Stanford: Stanford University Press, 1988).

3. For example, Frank J. Furstenberg, Jr. reported this "finding" at a conference on adolescent pregnancy held at Stanford University, April 1989.

4. Feminists and post-structuralist critics have presented many versions of these dichotomies. The dichotomies are never so simple within the actual texts—including those of the authors I cite—as they are in feminist readings and deconstructions.

5. Naomi Schor, "This essentialism which is not one: coming to grips with Irigaray," *differences,* vol. 1, #2 (Summer 1989), pp. 38–58.

6. The lethal connections between poverty, racial injustice, and the capacity to be or to experience oneself as a father are among the most anguishing "facts of fatherhood" in the contemporary United States. See, for example, Marion Wright Edelman, *Families in Peril* (Cambridge: Harvard University Press, 1987) and William Julius Wilson, *The Truly Disadvantaged: The Inner City, the Underclass, and Public Policy* (Chicago: University of Chicago Press, 1987).

7. Throughout this section, I am drawing on my *Maternal Thinking: Toward a Politics of Peace* (Boston: Beacon Press, 1989).

14

The Woman Warrior versus The Chinaman Pacific: Must a Chinese American Critic Choose between Feminism and Heroism?

King-Kok Cheung

The title of the anthology notwithstanding, I will primarily be speaking not about topics that divide feminists but about conflicting politics of gender, as reflected in the literary arena, between Chinese American women and men.[1] There are several reasons for my choice. First, I share the frustrations of many women of color that while we wish to engage in a dialogue with "mainstream" scholars, most of our potential readers are still unfamiliar with the historical and cultural contexts of various ethnic "minorities." Furthermore, whenever I encounter words such as "conflicts," "common differences," or "divisive issues" in feminist studies, the authors more often than not are addressing the divergences either between French and Anglo-American theorists or, more recently, between white and nonwhite women. Both tendencies have the effect of re-centering white feminism. In some instances, women of color are invited to participate chiefly because they take issue with white feminists and not because what they have to say is of inherent interest to the audience. Finally, I believe that in order to understand conflicts among diverse groups of women, we must look at the relations between women and men, especially where the problems of race and gender are closely intertwined.

It is impossible, for example, to tackle the gender issues in the Chinese American cultural terrain without delving into the historically enforced "feminization" of Chinese American men, without confronting the dialectics of racial stereotypes and nationalist reactions or, above all, without wrestling with die-hard notions of masculinity and femininity in both Asian and Western cultures. It is partly because these issues touch many sensitive nerves that the writings of Maxine Hong Kingston have generated such heated debates among Chinese American intellectuals. As a way into these intricate issues, I will structure my discussion around Kingston's work and the responses it has elicited from her Chinese American male critics, especially those who have themselves been influential in redefining both literary history and Asian American manhood.

Attempts at cultural reconstruction, whether in terms of "manhood" and "womanhood," or of "mainstream" versus "minority" heritage, are often inseparable from a wish for self-empowerment. Yet many writers and critics who have challenged the monolithic authority of white male literary historians remain in thrall to the norms and arguments of the dominant patriarchal culture, unwittingly upholding the criteria of those whom they assail. As a female immigrant of Cantonese descent, with the attendant sympathies and biases, I will survey and analyze what I construe to be the "feminist" and "heroic" impulses which have invigorated Chinese American literature but at the same time divided its authors and critics.

I

Sexual politics in Chinese America reflect complex cultural and historical legacies. The paramount importance of patrilineage in traditional Chinese culture predisposes many Chinese Americans of the older generations to favor male over female offspring (a preference even more overt than that which still underlies much of white America). At the same time Chinese American men, too, have been confronted with a history of inequality and of painful "emasculation." The fact that ninety percent of early Chinese immigrants were male, combined with anti-miscegenation laws and laws prohibiting Chinese laborers' wives from entering the U.S., forced these immigrants to congregate in the bachelor communities of various Chinatowns, unable to father a subsequent generation. While many built railroads, mined gold, and cultivated plantations, their strenuous activities and contributions in these areas were often overlooked by white historians. Chinamen were better known to the American public as restaurant cooks, laundry workers, and waiters, jobs traditionally considered "women's work."[2]

The same forms of social and economic oppression of Chinese American women and men, in conjunction with a longstanding Orientalist tradition that casts the Asian in the role of the silent and passive Other,[3] have in turn provided material for degrading sexual representations of the Chinese in American popular culture. Elaine H. Kim notes, for instance, that the stereotype of Asian women as submissive and dainty sex objects has given rise to an "enormous demand for X-rated films featuring Asian women and the emphasis on bondage in pornographic materials about Asian women," and that "the popular image of alluring and exotic 'dream girls of the mysterious East' has created a demand for 'Oriental' bath house workers in American cities as well as a booming business in mail order marriages."[4] No less insidious are the inscriptions of Chinese men in popular culture. Frank Chin, a well-known writer and one of the most outspoken revisionists of Asian American history, describes how the American silver screen casts doubts on Chinese American virility:

> The movies were teachers. In no uncertain terms they taught America that we were lovable for being a race of sissies . . . living to accommodate the whitemen. Unlike the white stereotype of the evil black stud, Indian rapist, Mexican macho, the evil of

the evil Dr. Fu Manchu was not sexual, but homosexual. . . . Dr. Fu, a man wearing a long dress, batting his eyelashes, surrounded by muscular black servants in loin clothes, and with his bad habit of caressingly touching white men on the leg, wrist, and face with his long fingernails is not so much a threat as he is a frivolous offense to white manhood. [Charlie] Chan's gestures are the same, except that he doesn't touch, and instead of being graceful like Fu in flowing robes, he is awkward in a baggy suit and clumsy. His sexuality is the source of a joke running through all of the forty-seven Chan films. The large family of the bovine detective isn't the product of sex, but animal husbandry. . . . *He never gets into violent things* [my emphasis].[5]

According to Chin and Jeffery Paul Chan, also a writer, "Each racial stereotype comes in two models, the acceptable model and the unacceptable model. . . . The unacceptable model is unacceptable because he cannot be controlled by whites. The acceptable model is acceptable because he is tractable. There is racist hate and racist love."[6] Chin and Chan believe that while the "masculine" stereotypes of blacks, Indians, and Mexicans are generated by "racist hate," "racist love" has been lavished on Chinese Americans, targets of "effeminate" stereotypes:

The Chinese, in the parlance of the Bible, were raw material for the "flock," pathologi-cal sheep for the shepherd. The adjectives applied to the Chinese ring with scriptural imagery. We are meek, timid, passive, docile, industrious. We have the patience of Job. We are humble. A race without sinful manhood, born to mortify our flesh. . . . The difference between [other minority groups] and the Chinese was that the Christians, taking Chinese hospitality for timidity and docility, weren't afraid of us as they were of other races. They loved us, protected us. Love conquered.[7]

If "racist love" denies "manhood" to Asian men, it endows Asian women with an excess of "womanhood." Elaine Kim argues that because "the characterization of Asian men is a reflection of a white male perspective that defines the white man's virility, it is possible for Asian men to be viewed as asexual and the Asian woman as only sexual, imbued with an innate understanding of how to please and serve." The putative gender difference among Asian Americans—exaggerated out of all proportion in the popular imagination—has, according to Kim, created "resentment and tensions" between the sexes within the ethnic community.[8]

Although both the Asian American and the feminist movements of the late sixties have attempted to counter extant stereotypes, the conflicts between Asian American men and women have been all the more pronounced in the wake of the two movements. In the last two decades many Chinese American men—especially such writers and editors as Chin and Chan—have begun to correct the distorted images of Asian males projected by the dominant culture. Astute, eloquent, and incisive as they are in debunking racist myths, they are often blind to the biases resulting from their own acceptance of the patriarchal construct of masculinity. In Chin's discussion of Fu Manchu and Charlie Chan and in the perceptive contrast he draws between the stock images of Asian men and those of other men of color, one can detect not only homophobia but perhaps also a sexist preference for stereotypes that imply predatory violence against women to "effeminate" ones. Granted that the position taken by Chin may be little more than a polemicist stance designed to combat white patronage, it is disturbing that he should lend credence to the conventional association of physical aggression with manly valor. The hold of patriarchal conventions becomes even more evident in the following passage:

The white stereotype of the Asian is unique in that it is the only racial stereotype completely devoid of manhood. Our nobility is that of an efficient housewife. At our worst we are contemptible because we are womanly, effeminate, devoid of all the traditionally masculine qualities of originality, daring, physical courage, creativity. We're neither straight talkin' or straight shootin'. The mere fact that four of the five American-born Chinese-American writers are women reinforces this aspect of the stereotype.[9]

In taking whites to task for demeaning Asians, these writers seem nevertheless to be buttressing patriarchy by invoking gender stereotypes, by disparaging domestic efficiency as "feminine," and by slotting desirable traits such as originality, daring, physical courage, and creativity under the rubric of masculinity.[10]

The impetus to reassert manhood also underlies the ongoing attempt by Chin, Chan, Lawson Inada, and Shawn Wong to reconstruct Asian American literary history. In their groundbreaking work *Aiiieeeee! An Anthology of Asian-American Writers,* these writers and co-editors deplored "the lack of a recognized style of Asian-American manhood." In a forthcoming sequel entitled *The Big Aiiieeeee! An Anthology of Asian American Writers,* they attempt to revive an Asian heroic tradition, celebrating Chinese and Japanese classics such as *The Art of War, Water Margin, Romance of the Three Kingdoms, Journey to the West,* and *Chushingura,* and honoring the renowned heroes and outlaws featured therein.[11]

The editors seem to be working in a opposite direction from that of an increasing number of feminists. While these Asian American spokesmen are recuperating a heroic tradition of their own, many women writers and scholars, building on existentialist and modernist insights, are reassessing the entire Western code of heroism. While feminists question such traditional values as competitive individualism and martial valor, the editors seize on selected maxims, purportedly derived from Chinese epics and war manuals, such as "I am the law," "life is war," "personal integrity and honor is the highest value," and affirm the "ethic of private revenge."[12]

The *Aiiieeeee!* editors and feminist critics also differ on the question of genre. According to Chin, the literary genre that is most antithetical to the heroic tradition is autobiography, which he categorically denounces as a form of Christian confession:

the fighter writer uses literary forms as weapons of war, not the expression of ego alone, and does not [waste] time with dandyish expressions of feeling and psychological attitudinizing. . . . A Chinese Christian is like a Nazi Jew. Confession and autobiography celebrate the process of conversion from an object of contempt to an object of acceptance. You love the personal experience of it, the oozings of viscous putrescence and luminous radiant guilt. . . . It's the quality of submission, not assertion that counts, in the confession and the autobiography. The autobiography combines the thrills and guilt of masturbation and the porno movie.[13]

Feminist critics, many of whom are skeptical of either/or dichotomies (in this instance fighting vs. feeling) and are impatient with normative definitions of genre (not that Chin's criteria are normative), believe that women have always appropriated autobiography as a vehicle for *asserting,* however tentatively, their subjectivity. Celeste Schenck writes:

the poetics of women's autobiography issues from its concern with constituting a female subject—a precarious operation, which . . . requires working on two fronts at once, *both* occupying a kind of center, assuming a subjectivity long denied, *and* maintaining the vigilant, disruptive stance that speaking from the postmodern margin provides—the autobiographical genre may be paradigmatic of all women's writing.[14]

Given these divergent views, the stage is set for a confrontation between "heroism" and "feminism" in Chinese American letters.

II

The advent of feminism, far from checking Asian American chauvinism, has in a sense fueled gender antagonism, at least in the literary realm. Nowhere is this antagonism reflected more clearly than in the controversy that has erupted over Maxine Hong Kingston's *The Woman Warrior.* Classified as autobiography, the work describes the protagonist's struggle for self-definition amid Cantonese sayings such as "Girls are maggots in the rice," "It is more profitable to raise geese than daughters," "Feeding girls is feeding cowbirds" (51, 54). While the book has received popular acclaim, especially among feminist critics, it has been censured by several Chinese American critics—mostly male but also some female—who tax Kingston for misrepresenting Chinese and Chinese American culture, and for passing fiction for autobiography. Chin (whose revulsion against autobiography we already know) wrote a satirical parody of *The Woman Warrior;* he casts aspersions on its historical status and places Kingston in the same company as the authors of Fu Manchu and Charlie Chan for confirming "the white fantasy that everything sick and sickening about the white self-image is really Chinese."[15] Jeffery Paul Chan castigates Knopf for publishing the book as "biography rather than fiction (which it obviously is)" and insinuates that a white female reviewer praises the book indiscriminately because it expresses "female anger."[16] Benjamin Tong openly calls it a "fashionably feminist work written with white acceptance in mind."[17] As Sau-ling Wong points out, "According to Kingston's critics, the most pernicious of the stereotypes which might be supported by *The Woman Warrior* is that of Chinese American men as sexist," and yet some Chinese American women "think highly of *The Woman Warrior* because it confirms their personal experiences with sexism."[18] In sum, Kingston is accused of falsifying culture and of reinforcing stereotype in the name of feminism.

At first glance the claim that Kingston should not have taken the liberty to infuse autobiography with fiction may seem to be merely a generic, gender-neutral criticism, but as Susan Stanford Friedman has pointed out, genre is all too often gendered.[19] Feminist scholars of autobiography have suggested that women writers often shy away from "objective" autobiography and prefer to use the form to reflect a private world, a subjective vision, and the life of the imagination. *The Woman Warrior,* though it departs from most "public" self-representations by men, is quite in line with such an autobiographical tradition. Yet for a "minority" author to exercise such artistic freedom is perilous business because white critics and reviewers persist in seeing creative expressions by her as no more than cultural history.[20] Members from the ethnic community are in turn upset if they feel that they have been "misrepresented" by one of their own. Thus where Kingston insists on shuttling between the world of facts and the world of fantasy, on giving multiple versions of "truth" as subjectively perceived, her Chinese American detractors demand generic purity and historical accuracy. Perhaps precisely because this author is female, writing amid discouraging realities, she can only forge a viable and expansive identity by refashioning patriarchal myths and invoking imaginative possibilities.[21] Kingston's autobiographical act, far from betokening submission, as Chin believes, turns the self into a "heroine" and is in a sense an act of "revenge" (a word represented in Chinese by two ideographs which Kingston loosely translates as "report a crime") against both the Chinese and the white cultures that undermine her self-esteem. Discrediting her for taking poetic licence is reminiscent of those white reviewers who reduce works of art by ethnic authors to sociohistorical documentary.

The second charge concerning stereotype is more overtly gender-based. It is hardly coincidental that the most unrelenting critics (whose grievance is not only against Kingston but also against feminists in general) have also been the most ardent champions of Chinese American "manhood." Their response is understandable. Asian American men have suffered deeply from racial oppression. When Asian American women seek to expose anti-female prejudices in their own ethnic community, the men are likely to feel betrayed.[22] Yet it is also undeniable that sexism still lingers as part of the Asian legacy in Chinese America and that many American-born daughters still feel its sting. Chinese American women may be at once sympathetic and angry toward the men in their ethnic community: sensitive to the marginality of these men but resentful of their male privilege.

III

Kingston herself seems to be in the grips of these conflicting emotions. The opening legend of *China Men* captures through myth some of the baffling intersections of gender and ethnicity in Chinese America and reveals the author's own double allegiance. The legend is borrowed and adapted from an eighteenth-century Chinese novel entitled *Flowers in the Mirror,* itself a fascinating work and probably one of the first "feminist" novels written by a man.[23] The male protagonist of this novel is Tang Ao, who in Kingston's version is captured in the Land of Women, where he is forced to have his feet bound, his ears pierced, his facial hair plucked, his cheeks and lips painted red—in short, to be transformed into an Oriental courtesan.

Since Kingston explicitly points out at the end of her legend that the Land of Women was in North America, critics familiar with Chinese American history will readily see that the ignominy suffered by Tang Ao in a foreign land symbolizes the emasculation of Chinamen by the dominant culture. Men of Chinese descent have encountered racial violence in the U.S., both in the past and even recently.[24] Kingston's myth is indeed intimating that the physical torment in their peculiar case is often tied to an affront to their manhood.

But in making women the captors of Tang Ao and in deliberately reversing masculine and feminine roles, Kingston also foregrounds constructions of gender. I cannot but see this legend as double-edged, pointing not only to the mortification of Chinese men in the new world but also to the subjugation of women both in old China and in America. Although the tortures suffered by Tang Ao seem palpably cruel, many Chinese women had for centuries been obliged to undergo similar mutilation. By having a man go through these ordeals instead, Kingston, following the author of *Flowers in the Mirror,* disrupts the familiar and common-place acceptance of Chinese women as sexual objects. Her myth deplores on the one hand the racist debasement of Chinese American men and on the other hand the sexist objectification of Chinese women. Although *China Men* mostly commemorates the founding fathers of Chinese America, this companion volume to *The Woman Warrior* is also suffused with "feminist anger." The opening myth suggests that the author objects as strenuously to the patriarchal practices of her ancestral culture as to the racist treatment of her forefathers in their adopted country.

Kingston reveals not only the similarities between Chinamen's and Chinese women's suffering but also the correlation between these men's umbrage at racism and their misogynist behavior. In one episode, the narrator's immigrant father, a laundryman who seldom opens his mouth except to utter obscenities about women, is cheated by a gypsy and harassed by a white policeman:

When the gypsy baggage and the police pig left, we were careful not to be bad or noisy so that you [father] would not turn on us. We knew that it was to feed us you had to endure demons and physical labor. You screamed wordless male screams that jolted the house upright . . . Worse than the swearing and the nightly screams were your silences when you punished us by not talking. You rendered us invisible, gone. (8)

Even as the daughter deplores the father's "male screams" and brooding silences, she attributes his bad temper to his sense of frustration and emasculation in a white society. As in analogous situations of Cholly Breedlove in Toni Morrison's *The Bluest Eye* and Grange Copeland in Alice Walker's *The Third Life of Grange Copeland,* what seems to be male tyranny must be viewed within the context of racial inequality. Men of color who have been abused in a white society are likely to attempt to restore their sense of masculinity by venting their anger at those who are even more powerless—the women and children in their families.

Kingston's attempt to write about the opposite sex in *China Men* is perhaps a tacit call for mutual empathy between Chinese American men and women. In an interview, the author likens herself to Tang Ao: just as Tang Ao enters the Land of Women and is made to feel what it means to be of the other gender, so Kingston, in writing *China Men,* enters the realm of men and, in her own words, becomes "the kind of woman who loves men and who can tell their stories." Perhaps, to extend the analogy further, she is trying to prompt her male readers to participate in and empathize with the experiences of women.[25] Where Tang Ao is made to feel what his female contemporaries felt, Chinese American men are urged to see parallels between their plight and that of Chinese American women. If Asian men have been emasculated in America, as the aforementioned male critics have themselves argued, they can best attest to the oppression of women who have long been denied male privilege.

IV

An ongoing effort to revamp Chinese American literary history will surely be more compelling if it is informed by mutual empathy between men and women. To return to an earlier point, I am of two minds about the ambitious attempt of the *Aiiieeeee!* editors to restore and espouse an Asian American heroic tradition. Born and raised in Hong Kong, I grew up reading many of the Chinese heroic epics—along with works of less heroic modes—and can appreciate the rigorous effort of the editors to introduce them to Asian American and non-Asian readers alike.[26] But the literary values they assign to the heroic canon also function as ideology. Having spoken out against the emasculation of Asian Americans in their introduction to *Aiiieeeee!,* they seem determined to show further that Chinese and Japanese Americans have a heroic—which is to say militant—heritage. Their propagation of the epic tradition appears inseparable from their earlier attempt to eradicate effeminate stereotypes and to emblazon Asian American manhood.[27] In this light, the special appeal held by the war heroes for the editors becomes rather obvious. Take, for example, Kwan Kung, in *Romance of the Three Kingdoms*:

loud, passionate, and vengeful, this "heroic embodiment of martial self-sufficiency" is antithetical in every way to the image of the quiet, passive, and subservient Oriental houseboy. Perhaps the editors hope that the icon of this imposing Chinese hero will dispel myths about Chinese American tractability.

While acquaintance with some of the Chinese folk heroes may induce the American public to acknowledge that Chinese culture too has its Robin Hood and John Wayne, I remain uneasy about the masculist orientation of the heroic tradition, especially as expounded by the editors who see loyalty, revenge, and individual honor as the overriding ethos which should be inculcated in (if not already absorbed by) Chinese Americans. If white media have chosen to highlight and applaud the submissive and nonthreatening characteristics of Asians, the Asian American editors are equally tendentious in underscoring the militant strain of their Asian literary heritage.[28] The refutation of effeminate stereotypes through the glorification of machismo merely perpetuates patriarchal terms and assumptions.

Is it not possible for Chinese American men to recover a cultural space without denigrating or erasing "the feminine"? Chin contends that "use of the heroic tradition in Chinese literature as the source of Chinese American moral, ethical and esthetic universals is not literary rhetoric and smartass cute tricks, not wishful thinking, not theory, not demagoguery and prescription, but simple history."[29] However, even history, which is also a form of social construct, is not exempt from critical scrutiny. The Asian heroic tradition, like its Western counterpart, must be re-evaluated so that both its strengths and limits can surface. The intellectual excitement and the emotional appeal of the tradition is indisputable: the strategic brilliance of characters such as Chou Yu and Chuko Liang in *Romance of the Three Kingdoms* rivals that of Odysseus, and the fraternal bond between the three sworn brothers—Liu Pei, Chang Fei, and Kuan Yu (Kwan Kung)—is no less moving than that between Achilles and Patrocles. But just as I no longer believe that Homer speaks for humanity (or even all mankind), I hesitate to subscribe wholeheartedly to the *Aiiieeeee!* editors' claim that the Asian heroic canon (composed entirely of work written by men though it contains a handful of heroines) encompasses "Asian universals."

Nor do I concur with the editors that a truculent mentality pervades the Chinese heroic tradition, which generally places a higher premium on benevolence than on force and stresses the primacy of kinship and friendship over personal power. By way of illustration I will turn to the prototype for Kingston's "woman warrior"—Fa Mu Lan (also known as Hua Mulan and Fa Muk Lan). According to the original "Ballad of Mulan" (which most Chinese children, including myself, had to learn by heart) the heroine in joining the army is prompted neither by revenge nor by personal honor but by filial piety. She enlists under male disguise to take the place of her aged father. Instead of celebrating the glory of war, the poem describes the bleakness of the battlefield and the loneliness of the daughter (who sorely misses her parents). The use of understatement in such lines as "the general was killed after hundreds of combats" and "the warriors returned in ten years" (my translation) connotes the cost and duration of battles. The "Ballad of Mulan," though it commits the filial and courageous daughter to public memory, also contains a pacifist subtext—much in the way that the *Iliad* conceals an anti-war message beneath its martial trappings. A re-examination of the Asian heroic tradition may actually reveal that it is richer and more sophisticated than the *Aiiieeeee!* editors, bent on finding belligerent models, would allow.[30]

Kingston's adaptation of the legend in *The Woman Warrior* is equally multivalent. Fa Mu Lan as re-created in the protagonist's fantasy does excel in martial arts, but her power is derived as much from the words carved on her back as from her military skills. And the transformed heroine still proves problematic as a model since she can only exercise her power when in male armor. As I have argued elsewhere, her military distinction, insofar as it valorizes the ability to be ruthless and violent—"to fight like a man"—affirms rather than subverts patriarchal mores.[31] In fact, Kingston discloses in an interview that the publisher is the one who entitled the book "The Woman Warrior" while she herself (who is a pacifist) resists complete identification with the war heroine:

> I don't really like warriors. I wish I had not had a metaphor of a warrior, a person who uses weapons and goes to war. I guess I always have in my style a doubt about wars as a way of solving things.[32]

Aside from the fantasy connected with Fa Mu Lan the book has little to do with actual fighting. The real battle that runs through the work is one against silence and invisibility. Forbidden by her mother to tell a secret, unable to read aloud in English while first attending American school, and later fired for protesting against racism, the protagonist eventually speaks with a vengeance through writing—through a heroic act of self-expression. At the end of the book her tutelary genius has changed from Fa Mu Lan to Ts'ai Yen—from warrior to poet.

Kingston's commitment to pacifism—through re-visioning and re-contextualizing ancient "heroic" material—is even more evident in her most recent book, *Tripmaster Monkey*. As though anticipating the editors of *The Big Aiiieeeee!*, the author alludes recurrently to the Chinese heroic tradition, but always with a feminist twist. The protagonist of this novel, Wittman Ah Sing, is a playwright who loves *Romance of the Three Kingdoms* (one of the aforementioned epics espoused by Chin). Kingston's novel culminates with Wittman directing a marathon show which he has written based on the *Romance*. At the end of the show he has a rather surprising illumination:

> He had made up his mind: he will not go to Viet Nam or to any war. He had staged the War of the Three Kingdoms as heroically as he could, which made him start to understand: The three brothers and Cho Cho were masters of the war; they had worked out strategies and justifications for war so brilliantly that their policies and their tactics

are used today, even by governments with nuclear-powered weapons. And they *lost*. The clanging and banging fooled us, but now we know—they lost. Studying the mightiest war epic of all time, Wittman changed—beeen!—into a pacifist. Dear American monkey, don't be afraid. Here, let us tweak your ear, and kiss your other ear.[33]

The seemingly easy transformation of Wittman—who is curiously evocative of Chin in speech and manner—is achieved through the pacifist author's sleight of hand. Nevertheless, the novel does show that it is possible to celebrate the ingenious strategies of the ancient warriors without embracing, wholesale, the heroic code that motivates their behavior and without endorsing violence as a positive expression of masculinity.[34]

Unfortunately, the ability to perform violent acts implied in the concepts of warrior and epic hero is still all too often mistaken for manly courage; and men who have been historically subjugated are all the more tempted to adopt a militant stance to manifest their masculinity. In the notorious Moynihan report on the black family, "military service for Negroes" was recommended as a means to potency:

Given the strains of the disorganized and matrifocal family life in which so many Negro youth come of age, the Armed Forces are a dramatic and desperately needed change: a world away from women, a world run by strong men of unquestioned authority.[35]

Moynihan believed that placing black men in an "utterly masculine world" will strengthen them. The black men in the sixties who worshipped figures that exploited and brutalized women likewise conflated might and masculinity. Toni Cade, who cautions against "equating black liberation with black men gaining access to male privilege," offers an alternative to patriarchal prescriptions for manhood:

Perhaps we need to let go of all notions of manhood and femininity and concentrate on Blackhood. . . . It perhaps takes less heart to pick up the gun than to face the task of creating a new identity, a self, perhaps an androgynous self. . . .[36]

If Chinese American men use the Asian heroic dispensation to promote male aggression, they may risk remaking themselves in the image of their oppressors—albeit under the guise of Asian panoply. Precisely because the racist treatment of Asians has taken the peculiar form of sexism—insofar as the indignities suffered by men of Chinese descent are analogous to those traditionally suffered by women—we must refrain from seeking antifeminist solutions to racism. To do otherwise reinforces not only patriarchy but also white supremacy.

Well worth heeding is Althusser's caveat that when a dominant ideology is integrated as common sense into the consciousness of the dominated, the dominant class will continue to prevail.[37] Instead of tailoring ourselves to white ideals, Asian Americans may insist on alternative habits and ways of seeing. Instead of drumming up support for Asian American "manhood," we may consider demystifying popular stereotypes while reappropriating what Stanford Lyman calls the "kernels of truth" in them that are indeed part of our ethnic heritage. For instance, we need not accept the Western association of Asian self-restraint with passivity and femininity. I, for one, believe that the respectful demeanor of many an Asian and Asian American indicates, among other things, a willingness to listen to others and to resolve conflict rationally or tactfully.[38] Such a collaborative disposition—be it Asian or non-Asian, feminine or masculine—is surely no less valid and viable than one that is vociferous and confrontational.

V

Although I have thus far concentrated on the gender issues in the Chinese American cultural domina, they do have provocative implications for feminist theory and criticism. As Elizabeth Spelman points out, "It is not easy to think about gender, race, and class in ways that don't obscure or underplay their effects on one another."[39] Still, the task is to develop paradigms that can admit these crosscurrents and that can reach out to women of color and perhaps also to men.

Women who value familial and ethnic solidarity may find it especially difficult to rally to the feminist cause without feeling divided or without being accused of betrayal, especially when the men in their ethnic groups also face social iniquities. Kingston, for instance, has tried throughout her work to mediate between affirming her ethnic heritage and undermining patriarchy. But she feels that identification with Asian men at times inhibits an equally strong feminist impulse. Such split loyalties apparently prompted her to publish *The Woman Warrior* and *China Men* separately, though they were conceived and written together as an "interlocking story." Lest the men's stories "undercut the feminist viewpoint," she separated the female and the male stories into two books. She says, "I care about men . . . as much as I care about women. . . . Given the present state of affairs, perhaps men's and women's experiences have to be dealt with separately for now, until more auspicious times are with us."[40]

Yet such separation has its dangers, particularly if it means that men and women will continue to work in opposing directions, as reflected in the divergences between the proponents of the Asian heroic tradition and Asian American feminists. Feminist ideas have made little inroad in the writing of the *Aiiieeeee!* editors, who continue to operate within patriarchal grids. White feminists, on the other hand, are often oblivious to the fact that there are other groups besides women who have been "feminized" and puzzled when women of color do not readily rally to their camp.

The recent shift from feminist studies to gender studies suggests that the time has come to look at women and men together. I hope that the shift will also entice both men and women to do the looking and, by so doing, strengthen the alliance between gender studies and ethnic studies. Lest feminist criticism remain in the wilderness, white scholars must reckon with race and class as integral experiences for both men and women, and acknowledge that not only female voices but the voices of many men of color have been historically silenced or dismissed. Expanding the feminist frame of reference will allow certain existing theories to be interrogated or reformulated.[41] Asian American men need to be wary of certain pitfalls in using what Foucault calls "reverse discourse," in demanding legitimacy "in the same vocabulary, using the same categories by which [they were] disqualified."[42] The ones who can be recruited into the field of gender studies may someday see feminists as allies rather than adversaries, and proceed to dismantle not just white but also male supremacy. Women of color should not have to undergo a self-division resulting from having to choose between female and ethnic identities. Chinese American women writers may find a way to negotiate the tangle of sexual and racial politics in all its intricacies, not just out of a desire for "revenge" but also out of a sense of "loyalty." If we ask them to write with a vigilant eye against possible misappropriation by white readers or against possible offense to "Asian American manhood," however, we will end up implicitly sustaining racial and sexual hierarchies. All of us need to be conscious of our "complicity with the gender ideologies" of patriarchy, whatever its origins, and to work toward notions of gender and ethnicity that are nonhierarchical, nonbinary, and nonprescriptive; that can embrace tensions rather than perpetuate divisions.[43] To reclaim cultural traditions without getting bogged down in the mire of traditional constraints, to attack stereotypes without falling prey to their binary opposites, to chart new topographies for manliness and womanliness, will surely demand genuine heroism.

Notes

1. Research for this essay is funded in part by an Academic Senate grant and a grant from the Institute of American Cultures and the Asian American Studies Center, UCLA. I wish to thank the many whose help, criticism, and encouragement have sustained me through the mentally embattled period of writing this essay: Kim Crenshaw, Donald Goellnicht, Marianne Hirsch, Evelyn Fox Keller, Elaine Kim, Elizabeth Kim, Ken Lincoln, Gerard Maré, Rosalind Melis, Jeff Spielberg, Sau-ling Wong, Richard Yarborough, and Stan Yogi.

A version of this article was delivered at the 1989 MLA Convention in Washington, DC. My title alludes not only to Maxine Hong Kingston's *The Woman Warrior* and *China Men* but also Frank Chin's *The Chickencoop Chinaman* and *The Chinaman Pacific & Frisco R. R. Co.* The term "Chinamen" has acquired divers connotations through time: "In the early days of Chinese American history, men called themselves 'Chinamen' just as other newcomers called themselves 'Englishmen' or 'Frenchmen': the term distinguished them from the 'Chinese' who remained citizens of

China, and also showed that they were not recognized as Americans. Later, of course, it became an insult. Young Chinese Americans today are reclaiming the word because of its political and historical precision, and are demanding that it be said with dignity and not for name-calling" (Kingston, "San Francisco's Chinatown: A View from the Other Side of Arnold Genthe's Camera," *American Heritage* [Dec. 1978]: 37). In my article the term refers exclusively to men.

2. The devaluation of daughters is a theme explored in *The Woman Warrior* (1976; New York: Vintage, 1977); as this book suggests, this aspect of patriarchy is upheld no less by women than by men. The "emasculation" of Chinese American men is addressed in *China Men* (1980; New York: Ballantine, 1981), in which Kingston attempts to reclaim the founders of Chinese America. Subsequent page references to these two books will appear in the text. Detailed accounts of early Chinese immigrant history can be found in Victor G. Nee and Brett De Bary Nee, *Longtime Californ': A Documentary Study of an American Chinatown* (1973; New York: Pantheon, 1981); and Ronald Takaki, *Strangers from a Different Shore: A History of Asian Americans* (Boston: Little Brown, 1989), 79–131.

3. See Edward Said, *Orientalism* (New York: Vintage, 1979). Although Said focuses on French and British representations of the Middle East, many of his insights also apply to American perceptions of the Far East.

4. "Asian American Writers: A Bibliographical Review," *American Studies International* 22.2 (Oct. 1984): 64.

5. "Confessions of the Chinatown Cowboy," *Bulletin of Concerned Asian Scholars* 4.3 (1972): 66.

6. "Racist Love," *Seeing through Shuck,* ed. Richard Kostelanetz (New York: Ballantine, 1972), 65, 79. Although the cinematic image of Bruce Lee as a Kung-fu master might have somewhat countered the feminine representations of Chinese American men, his role in the only one Hollywood film in which he appeared before he died was, in Elaine Kim's words, "less a human being than a fighting machine" ("Asian Americans and American popular Culture," *Dictionary of Asian American History,* ed. Hyung-Chan Kim [New York: Greenwood Press, 1986], 107).

7. "Racist Love," 69.

8. "Asian American Writers: A Bibliographical Review," 64.

9. "Racist Love," 68. The five writers under discussion are Pardee Lowe, Jade Snow Wong, Virginia Lee, Betty Lee Sung, and Diana Chang.

10. Similar objections to the passage have been raised by Merle Woo in "Letter to Ma," *This Bridge Called my Back: Writings by Radical Women of Color,* ed. Cherríe Moraga and Gloria Anzaldúa (1981; New York: Kitchen Table, 1983), 145; and Elaine Kim in *Asian American Literature: An Introduction to the Writings and Their Social Context* (Philadelphia: Temple UP, 1982), 189. Richard Yarborough delineates a somewhat parallel conundrum about manhood faced by African American writers in the nineteenth century and which, I believe, persists to some extent to this day; see "Race, Violence, and Manhood: The Masculine Ideal in Frederick Douglass's 'Heroic Slave,' " forthcoming in *Frederick Douglass: New Literary and Historical Essays,* ed. Eric J. Sundquist (Cambridge, MA: Cambridge UP). There

is, however, an important difference between the dilemma faced by the African American men and that faced by Asian American men. While writers such as William Wells Brown and Frederick Douglass tried to reconcile the white inscription of the militant and sensual Negro and the white ideal of heroic manhood, several Chinese American male writers are trying to disprove the white stereotype of the passive and effeminate Asian by invoking its binary opposite.

11. *Aiiieeeee! An Anthology of Asian-American Writers* (1974; Washington: Howard UP, 1983), xxxviii; *The Big Aiiieeeee! An Anthology of Asian American Writers* (New York: New American Library, forthcoming). All the Asian classics cited are available in English translations: Sun Tzu, *The Art of War,* trans. Samuel B. Griffith (London: Oxford UP, 1963); Shi Nai'an and Luo Guanzhong, *Outlaws of the Marsh [The Water Margin],* trans. Sidney Shapiro (jointly published by Beijing: Foreign Language P and Bloomington: Indiana UP, 1981); Luo Guan-Zhong, *Romance of the Three Kingdoms,* trans. C. H. Brewitt-Taylor (Singapore: Graham Brash, 1986), 2 vols.; Wu Ch'eng-en, *Journey to the West,* trans. Anthony Yu (Chicago: U of Chicago P, 1980), 4 vols.; Takeda Izumo, Miyoshi Shoraku, and Namiki Senryu, *Chushingura (The Treasury of Loyal Retainers),* trans. Donald Keene (New York: Columbia UP, 1971). I would like to thank Frank Chin for allowing me to see an early draft of *The Big Aiiieeeee!.* For a foretaste of his exposition of the Chinese heroic tradition, see "This is Not an Autobiography," *Genre* 18 (1985): 109–30.

12. The feminist works that come to mind include Paula Gunn Allen, *The Sacred Hoop: Recovering the Feminine in American Indian Traditions* (Boston: Beacon: 1986); Nina Auerbach, *Communities of Women: An Idea in Fiction* (Cambridge: Harvard UP, 1978); Zillah R. Eisenstein, *The Radical Future of Liberal Feminism* (New York: Longman, 1981); Carol Gilligan, *In a Different Voice: Psychological Theory and Women's Development* (Cambridge: Harvard UP, 1982); Christa Wolf, *Cassandra: A Novel and Four Essays,* trans. Jan van Heurck (New York: Farrar, 1984). The Chinese maxims appear in the introduction to *The Big Aiiieeeee!* (draft) and are quoted with the editors' permission. The same maxims are cited in Frank Chin, "This Is Not an Autobiography."

13. Chin, "This Is Not An Autobiography," 112, 122, 130.

14. "All of a Piece: Women's Poetry and Autobiography," *Life/Lines: Theorizing Women's Autobiography,* ed. Bella Brodzki and Celeste Schenck (Ithaca: Cornell UP, 1988), 286. See also Estelle Jelinek, ed., *Women's Autobiography: Essays in Criticism* (Bloomington: Indiana UP, 1980); Donna Stanton, *The Female Autograph* (New York: New York Literary Forum, 1984); Sidonie Smith, *Poetics of Women's Autobiography: Marginality and the Fictions of Self-Representation* (Bloomington: Indiana UP, 1987).

15. "The Most Popular Book in China," *Quilt 4,* ed. Ishmael Reed and Al Young (Berkeley: Quilt, 1984), 12. The essay is republished as the "Afterword" in *The Chinaman Pacific & Frisco R. R. Co.* The literary duel between Chin, a self-styled "Chinatown Cowboy," and Kingston, an undisguised feminist, closely parallels the paper war between Ishmael Reed and Alice Walker.

16. "The Mysterious West," *New York Review of Books,* 28 April 1977: 41.

17. "Critic of Admirer Sees Dumb Racist," *San Francisco Journal,* 11 May 1977: 20.

18. "Autobiography as Guided Chinatown Tour?," *American Lives: Essays in Multicultural American Autobiography,* ed. James Robert Payne (Knoxville: U of Tennessee P, forthcoming). See also Deborah Woo, "The Ethnic Writer and the Burden of 'Dual Authenticity': The Dilemma of Maxine Hong Kingston," forthcoming in *Amerasia Journal.* Reviews by Chinese American women who identify strongly with Kingston's protagonist include Nellie Wong, "The Woman Warrior," *Bridge* (Winter 1978): 46–48; and Suzi Wong, review of *The Woman Warrior, Amerasia Journal* 4.1 (1977): 165–67.

19. "Gender and Genre Anxiety: Elizabeth Barrett Browning and H. D. as Epic Poets," *Tulsa Studies in Women's Literature* 5.2 (Fall 1986): 203–28.

20. Furthermore, a work highlighting sexism within an ethnic community is generally more palatable to the reading public than a work that condemns racism. *The Woman Warrior* addresses both forms of oppression, but critics have focused almost exclusively on its feminist themes.

21. Susanne Juhasz argues that because women have traditionally lived a "kind of private life, that of the imagination, which has special significance due to the outright conflict between societal possibility and imaginative possibility, [Kingston] makes autobiography from fiction, from fantasy, from forms that have conventionally belonged to the novel" ("Towards a Theory of Form in Feminist Autobiography." *International Journal of Women's Studies* 2.1 [1979]: 62).

22. Cf. similar critical responses in the African American community provoked by Alice Walker's *The Color Purple* and Toni Morrison's *Beloved.*
    Although I limit my discussion to sexual politics in Chinese America, Asian American women are just as vulnerable to white sexism, as the denigrating stereotypes discussed by Kim earlier suggest.

23. Li Ju-Chen, *Flowers in the Mirror,* trans. and ed. Lin Tai-Yi (London: Peter Owen, 1965).

24. A recent case has been made into a powerful public television documentary: "Who Killed Vincent Chin?" (directed by Renee Tajima and Christine Choy, 1989). Chin, who punched a white auto-worker in Detroit in response to his racial slurs, was subsequently battered to death by the worker and his stepson with a baseball bat.

25. The interview was conducted by Kay Bonetti for the American Audio Prose Library (Columbia, MO, 1986).
    Jonathan Culler has discussed the various implications, for both sexes, of "Reading as a Woman" (*On Deconstruction: Theory and Criticism after Structuralism* [Ithaca: Cornell UP, 1982], 43–64); see also *Men in Feminism,* ed. Alice Jardine and Paul Smith (New York: Methuen, 1987).

26. The other modes are found in works as diverse as T'ao Ch'ien's poems (pastoral), Ch'u Yuan's *Li sao* (elegiac), selected writing by Lao Tzu and Chuang Tzu (metaphysical), and P'u Sung-ling's *Liao-Chai Chih I* (Gothic). (My thanks to Shu-mei Shih and Adam Schorr for helping me with part of the romanization.) One must bear

in mind, however, that Asian and Western generic terms often fail to correspond. For example, what the *Aiiieeeee!* editors call "epics" are loosely classified as "novels" in Chinese literature.

27. Epic heroes, according C. M. Bowra, are "the champions of man's ambitions" seeking to "win as far as possible a self-sufficient manhood" (*Heroic Poetry* [London: Macmillan, 1952], 14). Their Chinese counterparts are no exception.

28. Benjamin R. Tong argues that the uneducated Cantonese peasants who comprised the majority of early Chinese immigrants were not docile but venturesome and rebellious, that putative Chinese traits such as meekness and obedience to authority were in fact "reactivated" in America in response to white racism ("The Ghetto of the Mind," *Amerasia Journal* 1.3 [1971]: 1–31). Chin, who basically agrees with Tong, also attributes the submissive and "unheroic" traits of Chinese Americans to Christianity ("This Is Not An Autobiography"). While Tong and Chin are right in distinguishing the Cantonese folk culture of the early immigrants from the classical tradition of the literati, they underestimate the extent to which mainstream Chinese thought infiltrated Cantonese folk imagination, wherein the heroic ethos coexists with Buddhist beliefs and Confucian teachings (which do counsel self-restraint and obedience to parental and state authority). To attribute the "submissive" traits of Chinese Americans entirely to white racism or to Christianity is to discount the complexity and the rich contradictions of the Cantonese culture and the resourceful flexibility and adaptability of the early immigrants.

29. "This Is Not an Autobiography," 127.

30. Conflicting attitudes toward Homeric war heroes are discussed in Katherine Callen King, *Achilles: Paradigms of the War Hero from Homer to the Middle Ages* (Berkeley: U of California P, 1987). Pacifist or at least anti-killing sentiments can be found in the very works deemed "heroic" by Chin and the editors. *Romance of the Three Kingdoms* not only dramatizes the senseless deaths and the ravages of war but also betrays a wishful longing for peace and unity, impossible under the division of "three kingdoms." Even *The Art of War* sets benevolence above violence and discourages actual fighting and killing: "To subdue the enemy without fighting is the acme of skill" (77).

31. " 'Don't Tell': Imposed Silences in *The Color Purple* and *The Woman Warrior*." *PMLA* (March 1988): 166. I must add, however, that paradoxes about manhood inform Chinese as well as American cultures. The "contradictions inherent in the bourgeois male ideal" is pointed out by Yarborough: "the use of physical force is, at some levels, antithetical to the middle-class privileging of self-restraint and reason: yet an important component of conventional concepts of male courage is the willingness to use force" ("Race, Violence, and Manhood: The Masculine Ideal in Frederick Douglass's 'Heroic Slave' "). Similarly, two opposing ideals of manhood coexist in Chinese culture, that of a civil scholar who would never stoop to violence and that of a fearless warrior who would not brook insult or injustice. Popular Cantonese maxims such as "a superior man would only move his mouth but not his hands" (i.e. would never resort to physical combat) and "he who does not take revenge is not a superior man" exemplify the contradictions.

32. Interview conducted by Kay Bonetti.

33. *Tripmaster Monkey: His Fake Book* (New York: Knopf, 1989), 348.

34. I am aware that a forceful response to oppression is sometimes necessary, that it is much easier for those who have never encountered physical blows and gunshots to maintain faith in nonviolent resistance. My own faith was somewhat shaken while watching the tragedy of Tiananmen on television; on the other hand, the image of the lone Chinese man standing in front of army tanks reinforced my belief that there is another form of heroism that far excels brute force.

35. Lee Rainwater and William L. Yancey, *The Moynihan Report and the Politics of Controversy* (Cambridge: M.I.T. Press, 1967), 88 (p. 42) in the original report by Daniel Patrick Moynihan).

36. "On the Issue of Roles," *The Black Woman: An Anthology,* ed. Toni Cade (York, ON: Mentor-NAL, 1970), 103; see also Bell Hooks, *Ain't I a Woman: Black Women and Feminism* (Boston: South End Press, 1981), 87–117.

37. *Lenin and Philosophy and Other Essays* (New York: Monthly Review Press, 1971), 174–83.

38. Of course, Asians are not all alike, and most generalizations are ultimately misleading. Elaine Kim pointed out to me that "It's popularly thought that Japanese strive for peaceful resolution of conflict and achievement of consensus while Koreans— for material as much as metaphysical reasons—seem at times to encourage combativeness in one another" (personal correspondence, quoted with permission). Differences within each national group are no less pronounced.

39. *Inessential Woman: Problems of Exclusion in Feminist Thought* (Boston: Beacon, 1988), 115. I omitted class from my discussion only because it is not at the center of the literary debate.

40. Elaine Kim, *Asian American Literature: An Introduction to the Writings and Their Social Context* (Philadelphia: Temple UP, 1982), 209.

41. Donald Goellnicht, for instance, has argued that a girl from a racial minority "experiences not a single, but a double subject split; first, when she becomes aware of the gendered position constructed for her by the symbolic language of patriarchy; and second, when she recognizes that discursively and socially constructed positions of racial difference also obtain . . . [that] the 'fathers' of her racial and cultural group are silenced and degraded by the Laws of the Ruling Fathers" ("Father Land and/or Mother Tongue: The Divided Female Subject in *The Woman Warrior* and *Obasan,*" paper delivered at the MLA Convention, 1988).

42. *The History of Sexuality,* vol. 1, trans. Robert Hurley (New York: Vintage, 1980), 101.

43. Teresa de Lauretis, *Technologies of Gender: Essays on Theory, Film, and Fiction* (Bloomington: Indiana UP, 1987), 11.

III
Contested Sites

15

Upping the Anti (sic) in Feminist Theory

Teresa de Lauretis

I. Essentialism and Anti-Essentialism

Nowadays, the term *essentialism* covers a range of metacritical meanings and strategic uses that go the very short distance from convenient label to buzzword. Many who, like myself, have been involved with feminist critical theory for some time and who did use the term, initially, as a serious critical concept, have grown impatient with this word—essentialism—time and again repeated with its reductive ring, its self-righteous tone of superiority, its contempt for "them"— those guilty of it. Yet, few would deny that feminist theory is all about an essential difference, an irreducible difference, though not a difference between woman and man, nor a difference inherent in "woman's nature" (in woman as nature), but a difference in the feminist conception of woman, women, and the world.

Let us say, then, that there is an essential difference between a feminist and a non-feminist understanding of the subject and its relation to institutions; between feminist and non-feminist knowledges, discourses, and practices of cultural forms, social relations, and subjective processes; between a feminist and a non-feminist historical consciousness. That difference is essential in that it is constitutive of feminist thinking and thus of feminism: it is what makes the thinking feminist, and what constitutes certain ways of thinking, certain practices of writing, reading, imaging, relating, acting, etc., into the historically diverse and culturally heterogeneous social movement which, qualifiers and distinctions notwithstanding, we continue with good reasons to call feminism.[1] Another way to say this is that the essential difference of feminism lies in its historical specificity—the particular conditions of its emergence and development, which have shaped its object and field of analysis, its assumptions and forms of address; the constraints that have attended its conceptual and methodological struggles; the erotic component of its political self-awareness; the absolute novelty of its radical challenge to social life itself.

But even as the specific, essential difference of feminism may not be disputed, the question of the nature of its specificity or what is of the essence in feminist thought and self-representation has been an object of contention, an issue over which divisions, debates, and polarizations have occurred consistently, and without resolution, since the beginning of that self-conscious critical reflection that constitutes the theory of feminism. The currency of the term "essentialism" may be based on nothing more than its capacity to circumvent this very question—the nature of the specific difference of feminism—and thus to polarize feminist thought on what amounts to a red herring. I suggest that the current enterprise of "anti-essentialist" theorists engaged in typologizing, defining and branding various "feminisms" along an ascending scale of theoretico-political sophistication where "essentialism" weighs heavy at the lower end, may be seen in this perspective.[2]

Which is not to say that there should be no critique of feminist positions or no contest for the practical as well as the theoretical meanings of feminism, or even no appeal for hegemony by participants in a social movement which, after all, potentially involves all women. My polemical point here is that either too much or too little is made of the "essentialism" imputed to most feminist positions (notably those labeled cultural, separatist or radical, but others as well, whether labeled or not), so that the term serves less the purposes of effective criticism in the ongoing elaboration of feminist theory than those of convenience, conceptual simplification or academic legitimation. Taking a more discerning look at the *essence* that is in question in both *essentialism* and *essential difference,* therefore, seems like a very good idea.

Among the several acceptations of "essence" (from which "essentialism" is apparently derived) in the OED, the most pertinent to the context of use that is in question here are the following:

1. Absolute being, substance in the metaphysical sense; the reality underlying phenomena.
2. That which constitutes the being of a thing; that "by which it is what it is." In two different applications (distinguished by Locke as *nominal essence* and *real essence* respectively):
   a. of a conceptual entity: The totality of the properties, constituent elements, etc., without which it would cease to be the same thing; the indispensable and necessary attributes of a thing as opposed to those which it may have or not. . . .
   b. of a real entity: Objective character, intrinsic nature as a "thing-in-itself;" "that internal constitution, on which all the sensible properties depend."

Examples of a., dated from 1600 to 1870, include Locke's statement in the *Essay on Human Understanding:* "The Essence of a Triangle, lies in a very little compass . . . three Lines meeting at three Angles, make up that Essence"; and all the examples given for b., from 1667 to 1856, are to the effect that the essence of a real entity, the "thing-in-itself," is either unknown or unknowable.

Which of these "essences" are imputed to feminist "essentialists" by their critics? If most feminists, however one may classify trends and positions—

cultural, radical, liberal, socialist, poststructuralist, and so forth—agree that women are made, not born, that gender is not an innate feature (as sex may be) but a sociocultural construction (and precisely for that reason it is oppressive to women), that patriarchy is historical (especially so when it is believed to have superseded a previous matriarchal realm), then the "essence" of woman that is described in the writings of many so-called essentialists is not the *real essence,* in Locke's terms, but more likely a *nominal* one. It is a totality of qualities, properties, and attributes that such feminists define, envisage, or enact for themselves (and some in fact attempt to live out in "separatist" communities), and possibly also wish for other women. This is more a project, then, than a description of existent reality; it is an admittedly feminist project of "re-vision," where the specifications *feminist* and *re-*vision already signal its historical location, even as the (re)vision projects itself outward geographically and temporally (universally) to recover the past and to claim the future. This may be utopian, idealist, perhaps misguided or wishful thinking, it may be a project one does not want to be a part of, but it is not essentialist as is the belief in a God-given or otherwise immutable nature of woman.

In other words, barring the case in which woman's "essence" is taken as absolute being or substance in the traditional metaphysical sense (and this may actually be the case for a few, truly fundamentalist thinkers to whom the term essentialist would properly apply), for the great majority of feminists the "essence" of woman is more like the essence of the triangle than the essence of the thing-in-itself: it is the specific properties (e.g., a female-sexed body), qualities (a disposition to nurturance, a certain relation to the body, etc.), or necessary attributes (e.g., the experience of femaleness, of living in the world as female) that women have developed or have been bound to historically, in their differently patriarchal sociocultural contexts, which make them women, and not men. One may prefer one triangle, one definition of women and/or feminism, to another and, within her particular conditions and possibilities of existence, struggle to define the triangle she wants or wants to be—feminists do want differently. And in these very struggles, I suggest, consist the historical development and the specific difference of feminist theory, the essence of the triangle.

It would be difficult to explain, otherwise, why thinkers or writers with political and personal histories, projects, needs, and desires as different as those of white women and women of color, of lesbians and heterosexuals, of differently abled women, and of successive generations of women, would all claim feminism as a major—if not the only—ground of difference; why they would address both their critiques or accusations and their demands for recognition to other women, feminists in particular; why the emotional and political stakes in feminist theorizing should be so high, dialogue so charged, and confrontation so impassioned; why, indeed, the proliferation of typologies and the wide currency of "essentialism" on one hand, countered by the equally wide currency of the term "male theory" on the other.[3] It is one of the projects of this paper to up the *anti* in feminist theoretical debates, to shift the focus of the controversy from "feminist essentialism," as a category by which to classify feminists or feminisms, to the historical specificity, the essential difference of feminist theory itself. To this end I first turn to two essays which prompted my reflection on the uses of "essentialism" in current Anglo-American feminist critical writing, Chris Weedon's *Feminist Practice and Poststructuralist Theory,* published in London in 1987, and Linda Alcoff's "Cultural Feminism versus Post-Structuralism: The Identity Crisis in Feminist Theory," published in the Spring 1988 issue of *Signs.* Then I will go on to argue that the essential difference of feminist theory must be looked for in the form as well as the contents of its political, personal, critical, and textual practices, in the diverse oppositional stances feminism has taken vis-à-vis social and cultural formations, and in the resulting divisions, self-conscious reflection, and conceptual elaboration that constitute the effective history of feminism. And thus a division such as the one over the issue of "essentialism" only *seems* to be a purely "internal," intra-feminist one, a conflict within feminism. In fact, it is not.

The notion of an "essential womanhood, common to all women, suppressed or repressed by patriarchy" recurs in Weedon's book as the mark of "radical-feminist theory," whose cited representatives are Mary Daly, Susan Griffin, and Adrienne Rich. "Radical-feminist theory" is initially listed together with "socialist-feminist and psychoanalytic-feminist theories" as "various attempts to systematize individual insights about the oppression of women into relatively coherent theories of patriarchy," in spite of the author's statement, on the same page, that radical-feminist writers are hostile to theory because they see it as a form of male dominance which co-opts women and suppresses the feminine (p. 6). As one reads on, however, socialist feminism drops out altogether while psychoanalytic feminism is integrated into a new and more "politically" sophisticated discourse called "feminist poststructuralism." Thus, three-fourths of the way through the book, one finds this summary statement:

> For poststructuralist feminism, neither the liberal-feminist attempt to redefine the truth of women's nature within the terms of existing social relations and to establish women's full equality with men, nor the radical-feminist emphasis on fixed difference, realized in a separatist context, is politically adequate. Poststructuralist feminism requires attention to historical specificity in the production, for women, of subject positions and modes of femininity and their place in the overall network of social power relations. In this the meaning of biological sexual difference is never finally fixed. . . . An understanding of how discourses of biological sexual difference are mobilized, in a particular society, at a particular moment, is the first stage in intervening in order to initiate change. (p. 135)

There is more than simple irony in the claim that this late-comer, poststructuralist feminism, dark horse and winner of the feminist theory contest, is the "first stage" of feminist intervention. How can Weedon, at one and the same time, so strongly insist on attention to historical specificity and social—not merely individual—change, and yet disregard the actual historical changes in Western culture brought about in part, at least, by the women's movement and at least in some measure by feminist critical writing over the past twenty years?

One could surmise that Weedon does not like the changes that have taken place (even as they allow the very writing and publication of her book), or does not consider them sufficient, though that would hardly be reason enough to disregard them so blatantly. A more subtle answer may lie in the apologetic and militant project of her book, a defense of poststructuralism vis-à-vis both the academic establishment and the general educated reader, but with an eye to the women's studies corner of the publishing market; whence, one must infer, the lead position in the title of the other term of the couple, feminist practice. For, as the Preface states, "the aim of this book is to make poststructuralist theory accessible to readers to whom it is unfamiliar, to argue its political usefulness to feminism and to consider its implications for feminist critical practice" (p. vii). Somehow, however, in the course of the book, the Preface's modest claim "to point to a possible direction for future feminist cultural criticism" (p. vii) is escalated into a peroration for the new and much improved feminist theory called feminist poststructuralism or, indifferently, poststructural feminism.

In the concluding chapter on "Feminist Critical Practice" (strangely in the singular, as if among so many feminisms and feminist theories, only one practice could properly be called both feminist and critical), the academic contenders are narrowed down to two. The first is the poststructural criticism produced by British feminists (two are mentioned, E. Ann Kaplan and Rosalind Coward) looking "at the mechanisms through which meaning is constructed" mainly in popular culture and visual representation; the second is "the other influential branch of feminist criticism [that] looks to fiction as an expression of an already constituted gendered experience" (p. 152). Reappearing here, the word "experience," identified earlier on as the basis for radical-feminist politics ("many feminists assume that women's experience, unmediated by further theory, is the source of true knowledge," p. 8), links this second branch of feminist (literary) criticism to radical-feminist ideology. Its standard-bearers are Americans, Showalter's gynocritics and the "woman-centred criticism" of Gilbert and Gubar, whose reliance on the concept of authorship as a key to meaning and truth also links them with "liberal-humanist criticism" (pp. 154–55).

A particular subset of this—by now radical-liberal—feminist criticism "dedicated to constructing traditions" (p. 156) is the one concerned with "black and lesbian female experience"; here the problems and ideological traps appear most clearly, in Weedon's eyes, and are "most extreme in the case of lesbian writing and the construction of a lesbian aesthetic" (p. 158). The reference works for her analysis, rather surprisingly in view of the abundance of Black and lesbian feminist writings in the 1980s, are a couple of rather dated essays by Barbara

Smith and Bonnie Zimmerman reprinted in a collection edited by Elaine Showalter and, in fact, misnamed *The* New *Feminist Criticism.*[4] But even more surprisingly—or not at all so, depending on one's degree of optimism—it is again poststructuralist criticism that, with the help of Derridean deconstruction, can set all of these writers straight, as it were, as to the real, socially constructed and discursively produced nature of gender, race, class, and sexuality—as well as authorship and experience! Too bad for us that no exemplary poststructuralist feminist works or critics are discussed in this context (Cixous, Kristeva, and Irigaray figure prominently, but as psychoanalytic feminists earlier in the book).

Now, I should like to make it clear that I have no quarrel with poststructuralism as such, or with the fundamental importance for all critical thinking, feminist theory included, of many of the concepts admirably summarized by Weedon in passages such as the following:

> For a theoretical perspective to be politically useful to feminists, it should be able to recognize the importance of the *subjective* in constituting the meaning of women's lived reality. It should not deny subjective experience, since the ways in which people make sense of their lives is a necessary starting point for understanding how power relations structure society. Theory must be able to address women's experience by showing where it comes from and how it relates to material social practices and the power relations which structure them. . . . In this process subjectivity becomes available, offering the individual both a perspective and a choice, and opening up the possibility of political change. (pp. 8–9)

But while I am in complete agreement that experience is a difficult, ambiguous, and often oversimplified term, and that feminist theory needs to elaborate further "the relationship between experience, social power and resistance" (p. 8), I would insist that the notion of experience in relation both to social-material practices and to the formation and processes of subjectivity is a feminist concept, not a poststructuralist one (this is an instance of that essential difference of feminism which I want to reclaim from Weedon's all-encompassing "poststructuralism"), and would be still unthinkable were it not for specifically feminist practices, political, critical, and textual: consciousness raising, the rereading and revision of the canon, the critique of scientific discourses, and the imaging of new social spaces and forms of community. In short, the very practices of those feminist critics Weedom allocates to the "essentialist" camp. I would also add that "a theory of the relationship between experience, social power and resistance" is precisely one possible definition of feminist, not of poststructuralist, theory, as Weedon would have it, since the latter does not countenance the notion of experience within its conceptual horizon or philosophical presuppositions; and that, moreover, these issues have been posed and argued by several non-denominational feminist theories in the United States for quite some time: for example, in the works of Biddy Martin, Nancy K. Miller, Tania Modleski, Mary Russo,

Kaja Silverman, as well as myself, and even more forcefully in the works of feminist theorists and writers of color such as Gloria Anzaldúa, Audre Lorde, Chandra Mohanty, Cherríe Moraga, and Barbara Smith.

So my quarrel with Weedon's book is about its reductive opposition—all the more remarkable, coming from a proponent of deconstruction—of a *lumpen* feminist essentialism (radical-liberal-separatist and American) to a phantom feminist poststructuralism (critical-socialist-psychoanalytic and Franco-British), and with the by-products of such a *parti-pris:* the canonization of a few, (in)famous feminists as signposts of the convenient categories set up by the typology, the agonistic narrative structure of its account of "feminist theories," and finally its failure to contribute to the elaboration of feminist critical thought, however useful the book may be to its other intended readers, who can thus rest easy in the fantasy that poststructuralism is the theory and feminism is just a practice.

The title of Alcoff's essay, "Cultural Feminism versus Post-Structuralism: The Identity Crisis in Feminist Theory," bespeaks some of the same problems: a manner of thinking by mutually oppositional categories, an agonistic frame of argumentation, and a focus on division, a "crisis in feminist theory" that may be read not only as a crisis *over* identity, a metacritical doubt and a dispute among feminists as to the notion of identity, but also as a crisis *of* identity, of self-definition, implying a theoretical impasse for feminism as a whole. The essay, however, is more discerning, goes much further than its title suggests, and even contradicts it in the end, as the notion of identity, far from fixing the point of an impasse, becomes an active shifter in the feminist discourse of woman.[5]

Taking as its starting point "the concept of woman," or rather, its redefinition in feminist theory ("the dilemma facing feminist theorists today is that our very self-definition is grounded in a concept that we must deconstruct and de-essentialize in all of its aspects"), Alcoff finds two major categories of responses to the dilemma, or what I would call the paradox of woman (p. 406). Cultural feminists, she claims, "have not challenged the defining of woman but only that definition given by men" (p. 407), and have replaced it with what they believe a more accurate description and appraisal, "the concept of the essential female" (p. 408). On the other hand, the poststructuralist response has been to reject the possibility of defining woman altogether and to replace "the politics of gender or sexual difference . . . with a plurality of difference where gender loses its position of significance" (p. 407). A third category is suggested, but only indirectly, in Alcoff's unwillingness to include among cultural feminists certain writers of color such as Moraga and Lorde in spite of their emphasis on cultural identity, for in her view "their work has consistently rejected essentialist conceptions of gender" (p. 412). Why an emphasis on racial, ethnic, and/or sexual identity need not be seen as essentialist is discussed more fully later in the essay with regard to identity politics and in conjunction with a third trend in feminist theory which Alcoff sees as a new course for feminism, "a theory of the gendered subject that does not slide into essentialism" (p. 422).

Whereas the narrative structure underlying Weedon's account of feminist theories is that of a contest where one actor successively engages and defeats or conquers several rivals, Alcoff's develops as a dialectics. Both the culturalist and the poststructuralist positions display internal contradictions: for example, not all cultural feminists "give explicitly essentialist formulations of what it means to be a woman" (p. 411), and their emphasis on the affirmation of women's strength and positive cultural roles and attributes has done much to counter images of woman as victim or of woman as male when in a business suit; but insofar as it reinforces the essentialist explanations of those attributes that are part and parcel of the traditional notion of womanhood, cultural feminism may, and for some women does, foster another form of sexist oppression. Conversely, if the poststructuralist critique of the unified, authentic subject of humanism is more than compatible with the feminist project to "deconstruct and de-essentialize" woman (as Alcoff puts it, in clearly poststructuralist terms), its absolute rejection of gender and its negation of biological determinism in favor of a cultural-discursive determinism result, as concerns women, in a form of nominalism. If "woman" is a fiction, a locus of pure difference and resistance to logocentric power, and if there are no women as such, then the very issue of women's oppression would appear to be obsolete and feminism itself would have no reason to exist (which, it may be noted, is a corollary of poststructuralism and the stated position of those who call themselves "post-feminists"). "What can we demand in the name of women," Alcoff asks, "if 'women' do not exist and demands in their name simply reinforce the myth that they do?" (p. 420).

The way out—let me say, the sublation—of the contradictions in which are caught these two mainstream feminist views lies in "a theory of the subject that avoids both essentialism and nominalism" (p. 421), and Alcoff points to it in the work of a few theorists, "a few brave souls," whom she rejoins in developing her notion of "woman as positionality": "woman is a position from which a feminist politics can emerge rather than a set of attributes that are 'objectively identifiable'" (pp. 434–435). In becoming feminist, for instance, women take up a position, a point of perspective, from which to interpret or (re)construct values and meanings. That position is also a politically assumed identity, and one relative to their sociohistorical location, whereas essentialist definitions would have woman's identity or attributes independent of her external situation; however, the positions available to women in any sociohistorical location are neither arbitrary nor undecidable. Thus, Alcoff concludes,

> If we combine the concept of identity politics with a conception of the subject as positionality, we can conceive of the subject as nonessentialized and emergent from a historical experience and yet retain our political ability to take gender as an important point of departure. Thus we can say at one and the same time that gender is not

natural, biological, universal, ahistorical, or essential and yet still claim that gender
is relevant because we are taking gender as a position from which to act politically.
(p. 433)

I am, of course, in agreement with her emphases on issues and arguments that
have been central in my work, such as the necessity to theorize experience in
relation to practices, the understanding of gendered subjectivity as "an emergent
property of a historicized experience" (p. 431), and the notion that identity is an
active construction and a discursively mediated political interpretation of one's
history. What I must ask, and less as a criticism of Alcoff's essay than for the
purposes of my argument here, is: why is it still necessary to set up two opposing
categories, cultural feminism and poststructuralism, or essentialism and anti-
essentialism, thesis and antithesis, when one has already achieved the vantage
point of a theoretical position that overtakes them or sublates them?

Doesn't the insistence on the "essentialism" of cultural feminists reproduce
and keep in the foreground an image of "dominant" feminism that is at least
reductive, at best tautological or superseded, and at worst not in our interests?
Doesn't it feed the pernicious opposition of low versus high theory, a low-grade
type of critical thinking (feminism) that is contrasted with the high-test theoretical
grade of a poststructuralism from which some feminists would have been smart
enough to learn? As one feminist theorist who's been concurrently involved with
feminism, women's studies, psychoanalytic theory, structuralism, and film theory
from the beginning of my critical activity, I know that learning to be a feminist
has grounded, or embodied, all of my learning and so en-gendered thinking and
knowing itself. That engendered thinking and that embodied, situated knowledge
(in Donna Haraway's phrase)[6] are the stuff of feminist theory, whether by "feminist theory" is meant one of a growing number of feminist critical discourses—on
culture, science, subjectivity, writing, visual representation, social institutions,
etc.—or, more particularly, the critical elaboration of feminist thought itself and
the ongoing (re)definition of its specific difference. In either case, feminist theory
is not of a lower grade than that which some call "male theory," but different in
kind; and it is its essential difference, the essence of that triangle, that concerns
me here as a theorist of feminism.

Why then, I ask again, continue to constrain it in the terms of essentialism and
anti-essentialism even as they no longer serve (but did they ever?) to formulate
our questions? For example, in her discussion of cultural feminism, Alcoff accepts
another critic's characterization despite some doubt that the latter "makes it appear
too homogeneous and . . . the charge of essentialism is on shaky ground" (p.
411). Then she adds:

> In the absence of a clearly stated position on the ultimate source of gender difference,
> Echols *infers* from their emphasis on building a feminist free-space and woman-
> centered culture that cultural feminists hold some version of essentialism. I share

Echols's *suspicion.* Certainly, *it is difficult to render the views of Rich and Daly into a coherent whole without supplying a missing premise* that there is an innate female essence. (p. 412; emphasis added)

But why do it at all? What is the purpose, or the gain, of supplying a missing premise (innate female essence) in order to construct a coherent image of feminism which thus becomes available to charges (essentialism) based on the very premise that had to be supplied? What motivates such a project, the suspicion, and the inferences?

II. Theorizing Beyond Reconciliation

For a theorist of feminism, the answer to these questions should be looked for in the particular history of feminism, the debates, internal divisions, and polarizations that have resulted from its engagement with the various institutions, discourses, and practices that constitute the social, and from its self-conscious reflection on that engagement; that is to say, the divisions that have marked feminism as a result of the divisions (of gender, sex, race, class, ethnicity, sexuality, etc.) in the social itself, and the discursive boundaries and subjective limits that feminism has defined and redefined for itself contingently, historically, in the process of its engagement with social and cultural formations. The answer should be looked for, in other words, in the form as well as the contents that are specific to feminist political practices and conceptual elaboration, in the paradoxes and contradictions that constitute the effective history, the essential difference, of feminist thought.

In one account that can be given of that history, feminist theory has developed a series of oppositional stances not only vis-à-vis the wider, "external" context (the social constraints, legislation, ideological apparati, dominant discourses and representations against which feminism has pitched its critique and its political strategies in particular historical locations), but also, concurrently and interrelatedly, in its own "internal," self-critical processes.[7] For instance, in the seventies, the debates on academic feminism vs. activism in the United States defined an opposition between theory and practice which led, on the one hand, to a polarization of positions either *for* theory or *against* theory in nearly all cultural practices and, on the other, to a consistent, if never fully successful, effort to overcome the opposition itself.[8] Subsequently, the internal division of the movement over the issue of separatism or "mainstreaming," both in the academy and in other institutional contexts, recast the practice/theory opposition in terms of lesbian vs. heterosexual identification, and of women's studies vs. feminist cultural theory, among others. Here, too, the opposition led to both polarization (e.g., feminist criticism vs. feminist theory in literary studies) and efforts to overcome it by an expanded, extremely flexible, and ultimately unsatisfactory redefinition of the notion of "feminist theory" itself.

Another major division and the resulting crucial shift in feminist thought were prompted, at the turn of the decade into the eighties, by the wider dissemination of the writings of women of color and their critique of racism in the women's movement. The division over the issue of race vs. gender, and of the relative importance of each in defining the modes of women's oppression, resistance, and agency, also produced an opposition between a "white" or "Western feminism" and a "U.S. Third World feminism" articulated in several racial and ethnic hyphenations, or called by an altogether different name (e.g., black "woman-ism").[9] Because the oppositional stance of women of color was markedly, if not exclusively, addressed to white women in the context of feminism—that is to say, their critique addressed more directly white feminists than it did (white) patriarchal power structures, men of color, or even white women in general—once again that division on the issue of race vs. gender led to polarization as well as to concerted efforts to overcome it, at least internally to feminist theoretical and cultural practices. And once again those efforts met with mostly unsatisfactory or inadequate results, so that no actual resolution, no dialectic sublation has been achieved in this opposition either, as in the others. For even as the polarization may be muted or displaced by other issues that come to the fore, each of those oppositions remains present and active in feminist consciousness and, I want to argue, must so remain in a feminist theory of the female-sexed or female-embodied social subject that is based on its specific and emergent history.

Since the mid-eighties, the so-called feminist sex wars (Ruby Rich) have pitched "pro-sex" feminists vs. the anti-pornography movement in a conflict over representation that recast the sex/gender distinction into the form of a paradoxical opposition: sex and gender are either collapsed together, and rendered both analytically and politically indistinguishable (MacKinnon, Hartsock) or they are severed from each other and seen as endlessly recombinable in such figures of boundary crossing as transsexualism, transvestism, bisexualism, drag and impersonation (Butler), cyborgs (Haraway), etc. This last issue is especially central to the lesbian debate on sadomasochism (*Coming to Power, Against Sadomasochism*), which recasts the earlier division of lesbians between the women's liberation movement, with its more or less overt homophobia (Bearchell, Clark), and the gay liberation movement, with its more or less overt sexism (Frye), into the current opposition of radical S/M lesbianism to mainstream-cultural lesbian feminism (Rubin, Califia), an opposition whose mechanical binar-ism is tersely expressed by the recent magazine title *On Our Backs* punning on the long-established feminist periodical *Off Our Backs*. And here may be also mentioned the opposition pro and against psychoanalysis (e.g., Rose and Wilson) which, ironically, has been almost completely disregarded in these sexuality debates, even as it determined the conceptual elaboration of sexual difference in the seventies and has since been fundamental to the feminist critique of representa-tion in the media and the arts.[10]

This account of the history of feminism in relation to both "external" and "internal" events, discourses, and practices suggests that two concurrent drives, impulses or mechanisms, are at work in the production of its self-representation: *an erotic, narcissistic drive* that enhances images of feminism as difference, rebellion, daring, excess, subversion, disloyalty, agency, empowerment, pleasure and danger, and rejects all images of powerlessness, victimization, subjection, acquiescence, passivity, conformism, femininity; and *an ethical drive* that works toward community, accountability, entrustment, sisterhood, bonding, belonging to a common world of women or sharing what Adrienne Rich has poignantly called "the dream of a common language." Together, often in mutual contradiction, the erotic and ethical drives have fueled not only the various polarizations and the construction of oppositions but also the invention or conceptual imaging of a "continuum" of experience, a global feminism, a "house of difference," or a separate space where "safe words" can be trusted and "consent" be given uncoerced. And, as I suggest in my discussion of a recent text of Italian feminism by the Milan Women's Bookstore collective, an erotic and an ethical drive may be seen to underlie and sustain at once the possibility of, and the difficulties involved in, the project of articulating a female symbolic.[11] Are these two drives together, most often in mutual contradiction, what particularly distinguishes lesbian feminism, where the erotic is as necessary a condition as the ethical, if not more?

That the two drives often clash or bring about political stalemates and conceptual impasses is not surprising, for they have contradictory objects and aims, and are forced into open conflict in a culture where women are not supposed to be, know, or see themselves as subjects. And for this very reason perhaps, the two drives characterize the movement of feminism, and more emphatically lesbian feminism, its historically intrinsic, essential condition of contradiction, and the processes constitutive of feminist thought in its specificity. As I have written elsewhere, "the tension of a twofold pull in contrary directions—the critical negativity of its theory, and the affirmative positivity of its politics—is both the historical condition of existence of feminism and its theoretical condition of possibility."[12] That tension, as the condition of possibility and effective elaboration of feminist theory, is most productive in the kind of critical thinking that refuses to be pulled to either side of an opposition and seeks instead to deconstruct it, or better, to disengage it from the fixity of polarization in an "internal" feminist debate and to reconnect it to the "external" discursive and social context from which it finally cannot be severed except at the cost of repeatedly reducing a historical process, a movement, to an ideological stalemate. This may be the approach of those writers whom Alcoff would call "brave souls . . . attempting to map out a new course" (p. 407). But that course, I would argue, does not proceed in the manner of a dialectic, by resolving or reconciling the given terms of an opposition—say, essentialism/anti-essentialism or pro-sex/anti-pornography—whether the resolution is achieved discursively (for example, alleging a larger, tactical or political perspective on the issue) or by pointing to their actual sublation in existing material conditions (for example, adducing sociological data or statistical arguments). It proceeds, in my view, by what I call upping the "anti": by analyzing the undecidability, conceptual as well as pragmatic, of the alternative *as given,* such critical works release its terms from the fixity of meaning into which polarization has locked them, and reintroduce them into a larger contextual and conceptual frame of reference; the tension of positivity and negativity that marks feminist discourse in its engagement with the social can then displace the impasse of mere "internal" opposition to a more complex level of analysis.[13]

Seen in this larger, historical frame of reference, feminist theory is not merely a theory of gender oppression in culture, as both MacKinnon and Rubin maintain, from the respective poles of the sex/gender and pro-sex/anti-pornography debates, and as is too often reiterated in women's studies textbooks;[14] nor is it the essentialist theory of women's nature which Weedon opposes to an anti-essentialist, poststructuralist theory of culture. It is instead a developing theory of the female-sexed or female-embodied social subject, whose constitution and whose modes of social and subjective existence include most obviously sex and gender, but also race, class, and any other significant sociocultural divisions and representations; a developing theory of the female-embodied social subject that is based on its specific, emergent, and conflictual history.

Notes

Another version of this essay was published in *Differences: A Journal of Feminist Cultural Studies* 1, no. 2 (Fall 1989) with the title "The Essence of the Triangle or, Taking the Risk of Essentialism Seriously: Feminist Theory in Italy, the U.S., and Britain." The essay was initially written for the issue of *Differences* devoted to "The Essential Difference: Another Look at Essentialism," but then rethought in the context of the project of this book, addressing the problem of "conflicts in feminism." The two versions have in common the arguments set out in Part I, but then, in Parts II and III, present two quite distinct accounts of what I call the effective history of feminist theory and its specific, essential difference as a developing theory of the female-sexed or female-embodied social subject: there, an account, one possible history of feminist theory in Italy, here one account of feminist theory in North America.

1. For two very different historical views of feminism, see Rosalind Delmar, "What Is Feminism?," in *What Is Feminism: A Re-Examination.,* ed. Juliet Mitchell and Ann Oakley (New York: Pantheon Books, 1986), p. 8–33, and Karen Offen, "Defining Feminism: A Comparative Historical Approach," *Signs: Journal of Women in Culture and Society* 14, no. 1 (Autumn 1988): 119–57.

2. The typological project is central to, for example, Alice Echols, "The New Feminism of Yin and Yang," in *Powers of Desire: The Politics of Sexuality,* ed. Ann Snitow, Christine Stansell, and Sharon Thompson (New York: Monthly Review Press, 1983), 439–59, and "The Taming of the Id: Feminist Sexual Politics, 1968–83," in *Pleasure and Danger: Exploring Female Sexuality,* ed. Carole S. Vance (Boston: Routledge

& Kegan Paul, 1984), 50–72; Hester Eisenstein, *Contemporary Feminist Thought* (Boston: G. K. Hall, 1983); Zillah Eisenstein, *The Radical Future of Liberal Feminism* (New York: Longman, 1981); Alison M. Jaggar and Paula S. Rothenberg, *Feminist Frameworks: Alternative Theoretical Accounts of the Relations Between Women and Men* (New York: McGraw-Hill, 1984); and more recently Chris Weedon, *Feminist Practice and Poststructuralist Theory* (Oxford: Basil Blackwell, 1987). In this proliferation of typologies, essentialism as the belief in "female nature" is associated with cultural feminism, "separatist" (read: lesbian) feminism, radical feminism (with qualifications), and occasionally liberal feminism, while socialist feminism and now poststructuralist or deconstructive feminism come out at the top of the scale. Third World feminism is also widely used as a term but seldom given official type status in the typologies. A notable exception is Jaggar and Rothenberg's anthology which, in its 1984 revised edition, adds the new category "Feminism and Women of Color" to the five categories of the 1978 edition of *Feminist Frameworks:* conservatism, liberalism, traditional Marxism, radical feminism, and socialist feminism. On their part, Black, Latina, Asian, and other U.S. Third World feminists have not participated in the making of such typologies, possibly because of their ongoing argument with and ambivalence toward the larger category of "white feminism." And hence, perhaps, Jaggar and Rothenberg's respectful labeling of the new category "Feminism *and* Women of Color," suggesting a distance between the two terms and avoiding judgment on the latter.

3. María C. Lugones and Elizabeth V. Spelman, "Have We Got a Theory for You!: Feminist Theory, Cultural Imperialism and the Demand for 'the Woman's Voice,' " *Women's Studies International Forum* 6, no. 6 (1983): 573–81.

4. *The New Feminist Criticism: Essays on Women, Literature, and Theory,* ed. Elaine Showalter (New York: Pantheon Books, 1985) includes Barbara Smith, "Toward a Black Feminist Criticism," first published in 1977, and Bonnie Zimmerman, "What Has Never Been: An Overview of Lesbian Feminist Criticism," first published in 1981.

5. Since Alcoff refers extensively to my own work, this essay is in a sense a dialogue with her and with myself—that dialogue in feminist critical writing which often works as a variation of consciousness raising or better, its transformation into a significant form of feminist cultural practice, and one not always reducible to "academic" activity.

6. Donna Haraway, "Situated Knowledges: The Science Question in Feminism and the Privilege of Partial Perspective," *Feminist Studies* 14, no. 3 (Fall 1988): 575–99.

7. The quotation marks around "internal" and "external" are there to denaturalize any notion of boundary between feminism and what is thought of as its outside, its other, non-feminism. For, even as we must speak of divisions within feminism, of a feminist political thought, a feminist discourse, a feminist consciousness, etc., we nonetheless well know that no permanent or stable boundary insulates feminist discourse and practices from those which are not feminist. In fact, as Ernesto Laclau and Chantal Mouffe argue in *Hegemony and Socialist Strategy: Towards a Radical Democratic Politics* (London: Verso, 1985), "the irresoluble interiority/exteriority tension is the condition of any social practice. . . . It is in this terrain, where neither

a total interiority nor a total exteriority is possible, that the social is constituted" (p. 111). In thinking through the relation of feminism to other social discourses and practices, I find very useful their notion of *articulation*. If we abandon the notion of "*'society'* as a sutured and self-defined totality," Laclau and Mouffe state, we may instead conceive of the social as a field of differences, where no single underlying principle fixes, and hence constitutes, the whole field of differences (p. 111); but the "impossibility of an ultimate fixity of meaning implies that there have to be partial fixations—otherwise, the very flow of differences would be impossible. Even in order to differ, to subvert meaning, there has to be *a* meaning." Thus they define a "practice of articulation" as "the construction of nodal points which partially fix meaning," an attempt to arrest the flow of differences, to construct a center (pp. 112–13). In this sense, the history of feminist theory would be the history of a series of practices of articulation.

8. I am indebted to Kirstie McClure for pointing out to me that the opposition between theory and practice is a long-standing element of the Western intellectual tradition well before Marxism. One of the classic modern efforts to overcome that opposition, and an equally unsuccessful effort, is Kant's essay "On the Common Saying: 'This May be True in Theory, but it does not Apply in Practice,'" in *Kant's Political Writings,* ed. Hans Reiss (Cambridge: Cambridge University Press, 1970), 61–92.

9. See, for example, Alice Walker, *In Search of Our Mothers' Gardens: Womanist Prose* (San Diego, CA: Harcourt Brace Jovanovich, 1983); Bell Hooks, *Feminist Theory: From Margin to Center* (Boston: South End Press, 1984); Audre Lorde, "An Open Letter to Mary Daly," in *Sister Outsider: Essays and Speeches* (Trumansburg, NY: The Crossing Press, 1984), 66–71; and especially Chela Sandoval, "Oppositional Consciousness in the Postmodern World: U.S. Third World Feminism, Semiotics and New World Cinema," a dissertation in progress for the Ph.D. in History of Consciousness at the University of California, Santa Cruz.

10. See B. Ruby Rich, "Feminism and Sexuality in the 1980s," *Feminist Studies* 12, no. 3 (Fall 1988): 525–61; Catharine A. MacKinnon, *Feminism Unmodified: Discourses on Life and Law* (Cambridge: Harvard University Press, 1987); Nancy Hartsock, "The Feminist Standpoint: Developing the Ground for a Specifically Feminist Historical Materialism," in *Discovering Reality,* ed. Sandra Harding and Merrill B. Hintikka (Dordrecht: Reidel, 1983), 283–310; Judith Butler, "Gender Differences: Feminist Theory and Psychoanalytic Narrative," 1988 manuscript; Donna Haraway, "A Manifesto for Cyborgs: Science, Technology and Socialist Feminism in the 1980s," *Socialist Review* 80 (1985): 65–107; Samois, *Coming to Power: Writings and Graphics on Lesbian S/M* (Boston: Alyson Publications, 1982); *Against Sadomasochism: A Radical Feminist Analysis,* ed. Robin Ruth Linden, Darlene R. Pagano, Diana E.H. Russell, and Susan Leigh Star (East Palo Alto, CA: Frog in the Well Press, 1982); Chris Bearchell, "Why I am a gay liberationist: thoughts on sex, freedom, the family and the state," *Resources for Feminist Research/ Documentation sur la Recherche Féministe [RFR/DRF]* 12, no. 1 (March/Mars 1983): 57–60; Wendy Clark, "The Dyke, the Feminist and the Devil," in *Sexuality: A Reader,* ed. Feminist Review (London: Virago, 1987), 201–15; Marilyn Frye, "Lesbian Feminism and the Gay Rights Movement: Another View of Male Supremacy, Another Separatism," in *The Politics of Reality: Essays in Feminist Theory*

(Trumansburg, NY: The Crossing Press, 1983), 128–50; Pat Califia, "Introduction," in *Macho Sluts: Erotic Fiction* (Boston: Alyson Publications, 1988), 9–27; Gayle Rubin, "Thinking Sex: Notes for a Radical Theory of the Politics of Sexuality," in *Pleasure and Danger,* pp. 267–319; Jacqueline Rose, "Femininity and Its Discontents," *Feminist Review* 14 (Summer 1983); 5–21, a response to Elizabeth Wilson, "Psychoanalysis: Psychic Law and Order," *Feminist Review* 8 (Summer 1981).

11. Teresa de Lauretis, "The Essence of the Triangle or, Taking the Risk of Essentialism Seriously: Feminist Theory in Italy, the U.S., and Britain," *Differences: A Journal of Feminist Cultural Studies* 1, no. 2 (Summer 1989): 3–37. The text I discuss there is Libreria delle Donne di Milano, *Non credere di avere dei diritti: La generazione della libertà femminile nell'idea e nelle vicende di un gruppo di donne* ["Don't Think You Have Any Rights: The Engendering of Female Freedom in the Thought and Vicissitudes of a Women's Group"] (Turin: Rosenberg & Sellier, 1987). An English translation of this book is forthcoming by Indiana University Press with the title *Sexual Difference: A Theory of Social-Symbolic Practice* (1990).

12. Teresa de Lauretis, *Technologies of Gender: Essays on Theory, Film, and Fiction* (Bloomington: Indiana University Press, 1987), 26.

13. See, for example, Moira Gatens, "A Critique of the Sex/Gender Distinction," in *Beyond Marxism: Interventions After Marx,* ed. J. Allen and P. Patton (Sydney: Intervention Press, 1983), 143–60; B. Ruby Rich, "Anti-Porn: Soft Issue, Hard World," *The Village Voice,* July 20, 1982; Sue-Ellen Case, "Towards a Butch-Femme Aesthetic," *Discourse: Journal for Theoretical Studies in Media and Culture* 11, no. 1 (Fall–Winter 1988–89): 55–73; and Mariana Valverde, "Beyond Gender Dangers and Private Pleasures: Theory and Ethics in the Sex Debates," *Feminist Studies* 15, no. 2 (Summer 1989): 237–54.

14. For example, Jaggar and Rothenberg in *Feminist Frameworks:* "We believe that the feminist struggle must be guided by feminist theory, by a systematic analysis of the underlying nature and causes of women's oppression" (p. xii).

16

Split Affinities:
The Case of Interracial Rape

Valerie Smith

I

Black feminism, at once imaginative, critical, and theoretical, is simultaneously deconstructive and reconstructive, reactive and proactive. Historically it has revealed ways in which the lives and cultural productions of black women have been overlooked or misrepresented within Eurocentric and androcentric discourses, yet its aims are not as fully determined by these other modes of inquiry and bodies of literature as this formulation might seem to suggest. Black feminists seek not only to dismantle the assumptions of dominant cultures, and to recover and reclaim the lives and texts of black women, but also to develop methods of analysis for interpreting the ways in which race and gender are inscribed in cultural productions.

I have argued elsewhere that black feminist criticism might be seen to have evolved in relation to Afro-Americanist criticism and Anglo-American feminist criticism.[1] Both Afro-Americanist criticism and Anglo-American feminism rely on the notion of difference, exploring, respectively, the meanings of social constructions of race and of gender. Yet in establishing themselves in opposition to hegemonic culture, Afro-Americanists and Anglo-American feminists depended historically upon totalizing formulations of race on the one hand, gender on the other. Male-authored Afro-Americanist criticism assumed a conception of blackness that concealed its masculinist presuppositions; Anglo-or Euro-centered feminism relied upon a notion of gender that concealed its presumption of whiteness.[2] It has fallen to feminists whose work explicitly addresses issues of race, class, sexual preference, and nationality to confront the implications of difference within these modes of oppositional discourse.[3]

The critical stance that black feminism sometimes assumes in relation to other ideological modes of inquiry is from time to time regarded with disapprobation as being divisive.[4] However, it seems to me that the impetus for the development of Afro-Americanist, feminist, and other oppositional modes of inquiry depends inevitably upon our attempts to challenge and reassess our presuppositions.

In my own teaching and writing as a black feminist critic I have been drawn to those subjects around which differences both between black men and women, and between feminists are illuminated; these topics are precisely those that lend specificity to and justify the theoretical assumptions that inform my work. To borrow Mary Poovey's term, I am drawn to "border cases," issues that challenge the binary logic that governs the social and intellectual systems within which we live and work. As Poovey argues, border cases are "the site of intensive debates . . . because they [threaten] to challenge *the* opposition upon which all other oppositions are claimed to be based."[5] Poovey here refers to the centrality within culture of sexual difference; I would extend her point to include the putative centrality of racial difference as well.

"Border cases" are precisely those issues that problematize easy assumptions about racial and/or sexual difference, particularly insofar as they demonstrate the interactions between race and gender. Indeed, as Kimberlé Crenshaw has argued (drawing on work by Elizabeth V. Spelman, Barbara Smith, and others), within dominant discourses, race and gender are treated as if they are mutually exclusive categories of experience. In contrast, black feminism presumes the "intersectionality" of race and gender in the lives of black women, thereby rendering inapplicable to the lives of black women any "single-axis" theory about racism or sexism.[6]

The institution of slavery in the U.S. represents one such "border case." While feminist historians such as Catherine Clinton introduce the category of gender into the analysis of slavery, exploring the subordination of women within a system of racial oppression, they sometimes obscure the impact of race on the construction of women's place in the plantation economy. As Hazel Carby argues, the nature of the oppression of black women under slavery is vastly different from that experienced by white women within that institution. Carby shows that the primary duty of women in the planter class was to produce heirs, thereby providing the means of consolidating property through the marriages between plantation families. In contrast, black women's destiny was bound to capital accumulation; black women gave birth to property and, directly, to capital itself in the form of slaves.[7]

Given the profound and multifarious connections between racism and sexual exploitation throughout U.S. history, interracial rape constitutes another such "border case." Myths of black male and female sexual appetitiveness were constructed to enable certain white men during slavery to exert their rights over the bodies of black men and white and black women. The image of sexually inexhaustible black men was used to police relations between black men and white women and invoked in order to justify violence against black men. The myth of the promiscuity of slave women allowed white men to rape them and claim ownership of their offspring with impunity.

After slavery the slippage between racism and sexism assumed other forms and continued to victimize black men and women in related ways. Mobs of whites frequently raped black women in order to restrict the progress of black communities as a whole and black men in particular.[8] In addition, especially during the period from Reconstruction through World War II, accusations of interracial rape were used to legitimate lynching, a form of random, mob violence connected routinely to the alleged rape of a white woman by a black man, even when no evidence of sexual assault existed. Jacquelyn Dowd Hall has argued that the perceived connection between lynching and rape grows out of the construction of white women as "the forbidden fruit, the untouchable property, the ultimate symbol of white male power." This association in turn sets in motion a cultural narrative in which the rape of a frail white victim by a savage black male must be avenged by the chivalry of her white male protectors.[9]

The explosive coverage of actual or alleged cases of interracial rape (the Tawana Brawley case, the Central Park rape, the Willie Horton case, the Stuart murder case, to name but a few) and the political uses to which these incidents have been put, suggest the myriad ways in which the history of slavery and lynching informs the construction of racial and gender relations in contemporary United States culture. To explore the complex subtext of accusations of interracial rape in this essay, I consider within three contexts ways in which interracial rape operates as a site where ideologies of racial and gender difference come into tension with and interrogate each other. I analyze here representations of interracial rape in some examples of journalistic discourse and in a short story by Alice Walker entitled "Advancing Luna—and Ida B. Wells." The essay ends with a brief examination of some of the pedagogical issues that arose for me during my attempts to teach "Advancing Luna." In each context, I suggest that silences speak volumes, indicating the ways in which cultural anxieties about racial and gender differences are projected upon each other.

In her autobiography, *Crusade for Justice,* Ida B. Wells, a turn-of-the-century black woman journalist and political activist, argues that "[Lynching] really was . . . an excuse to get rid of Negroes who were acquiring wealth and property and thus 'keep the nigger down.'"[10] Wells's analysis acknowledges how the structure of gender relations and domination has been used to propel and facilitate racial oppression. Yet her opposition to lynching as a practice requires her effectively to deny the veracity of any white woman's testimony against a black man. Elsewhere in *Crusade* Wells discredits the testimony of an alleged rape victim even more directly. The classic situation she cites represents white women as willing participants in sexual relations with the black male victims of lynching. In one instance she argues that while white men assume the right to rape black women or consort with them, black men are killed for participating in any kind of sexual activity with white women: "these same white men lynched, burned, and tortured Negro men for doing the same thing with white women; even when the white women were willing victims" (71). The final clause, specifying the category of white women "willing victims," takes precedence over the implied "unwilling victims" to whom Wells alludes earlier in the sentence. The following sentence elaborates upon the logic of the previous one, effectively blaming white women for the lynching of black men: "It seemed horrible to me that death in its most terrible form should be meted out to the Negro who was weak enough to take chances when accepting the invitations of these white women" (71). Wells's focus on the unreliability of white rape victims may well have been strategic, if not accurate, given the structure of race relations from the mid-nineteenth until the mid-twentieth centuries; as an antecedent, however, it presents difficulties for feminist critiques of interracial rape in the late twentieth century.

Wells's formulations subordinate the sexual to the racial dimension of interracial rape, thereby dramatizing the fact that the crime can never be read solely as an offense against women's bodies. It is always represented and understood within the context of a variety of public issues, among them race, imperialism, and the law.[11] As the media coverage and public response to recent criminal cases involving the hint, the allegation, or the fact of interracial rape demonstrate, a variety of cultural narratives that historically have linked sexual violence with racial oppression continue to determine the nature of public response to them.

For example, instances of interracial rape constitute sites of struggle between black and white men that allow privileged white men to exercise their property rights over the bodies of white women. As Angela Davis has shown, in the United States and other capitalist countries, rape laws, as a rule, were framed originally for the protection of men of the upper classes whose daughters and wives might be assaulted. By this light, the bodies of women seem decidedly less significant than the interests of their male superordinates. As merely one example, this objectification of the white victim was dramatized powerfully in the recent Central Park rape case in which New York personalities and politicians issued threats against black men while the rape victim lay silent, comatose, and unnamed, in her hospital bed.[12]

The rise of feminism from the late sixties through the present has done much to construct woman-centered anti-rape positions, although these responses sometimes reveal a racist bias. In the 1970s and 1980s rape emerged as a feminist issue as control over one's body and sexuality became a major area for concern and activism. Women addressed the need to break the silence about a pervasive aspect of female experience. From that beginning derived analyses of the place and function of rape within patriarchal culture. Moreover, feminists began to develop strategies for changing the legal and medical treatment of rape victims and the prosecution of perpetrators.

Susan Brownmiller's early study of rape, *Against Our Will: Men, Women, and Rape,* contributes prominently to analyses of the historical and cultural function of rape. Yet often it risks resuscitating the myth of the black rapist. Brownmiller, for example, argues that the history of the oppression of black men makes legitimate expressions of male supremacy beyond their reach. They therefore resort to open sexual violence. In the context of her study, the wolf whistle that led to Emmett Till's lynching is read as a deliberate insult just short of physical assault.[13]

More recent feminist analyses improve upon Brownmiller's work by increasingly focusing on the interplay of issues of race and class within the context of gender relations. Susan Estrich, Angela Davis, and Catherine MacKinnon examine the implications of the fact that rape is the most underreported of all crimes and that the majority of rapes committed are intraracial.[14] Each shows in her respective argument how cultural assumptions about rapes and rapists protect privileged white men who rape white women and continue to fetishize the black male perpetrator. As MacKinnon writes:

> For every reported rape there are between two and ten unreported rapes; it is extremely important to ask not only why the ones that are reported are, but why the ones that are not reported are not.
>
> I think women report rapes when we feel we will be believed. The rapes that have been reported, as they have been reported, are the kinds of rapes women think will be believed when we report them. They have two qualities; they are by a stranger, and they are by a Black man. These two elements give you the white male archetype of rape. When the newspaper says that these rapes are unusual, they are right in a way. They are right because rapes by strangers are the least common rapes women experience. And to the extent that these are interracial, they are also the least common rapes women experience. Most rapes are by a man of the woman's race and by a man she knows: her husband, her boss, an acquaintance, or a date.[15]

Given their position within the racial and gender hierarchy in U.S. culture, it is not surprising that black Americans respond in a variety of different ways to instances of interracial rape. Within a context in which rape charges were often used to justify lynching or legal execution, black men and women often perceive an accusation of rape as a way to terrorize innocent black men. This kind of reasoning may lead to the denial of the fact that some black men do rape. To cite but one example, Alton Maddox, one of Tawana Brawley's attorneys, leaped immediately to the defense of the young men accused in the 1989 Central Park rape case and demanded proof that a rape had actually occurred.

Black women's positions in relation to cases of interracial rape are particularly vexed. As members of communities under siege, they may well sympathize with the black male who stands accused. At the same time, as women they share the victim's sense of violation. Yet that identification with white women is problematic, since black women represent the most vulnerable and least visible victims of rape. Their relative invisibility is to some degree rooted in the systematic sexual abuse to which they were subjected during slavery and upon which the institution of slavery depended. The same ideology that protected white male property rights by constructing black males as rapists, constructed black women as sexually voracious. If black women were understood always to be available and willing, then the rape of a black woman becomes a contradiction in terms.

The relative invisibility of black women victims of rape also reflects the differential value of women's bodies in capitalist societies. To the extent that rape is constructed as a crime against the property of privileged white men, crimes against less valuable women—women of color, working-class women, and lesbians, for example—mean less or mean differently than those against white women from the middle and upper classes.[16]

Given the nature of their history as rape victims, one might expect that black women would find common cause with white women in the anti-rape movement. Yet their own invisibility as victims within the movement, and a perceived indifference within the movement to the uses to which the fraudulent rape charge has been put, has qualified their support.

The reporting of and response to a variety of recent cases involving the hint, the allegation, or the fact of interracial rape demonstrate the persistent and competing claims of these various cultural narratives in the public imagination. I want here to comment briefly on the representation of the Stuart murder case and the Central Park rape, but certainly much remains to be said about many other cases, including the construction of the Tawana Brawley case, and the uses to which Willie Horton was put in the Bush-Quayle campaign.

The Stuart murder case merits consideration in the context of a discussion about race and rape precisely because no allegation of rape was made. Despite the nonsexual nature of the alleged crime, the fiction of a black male perpetrator automatically sexualized a nonsexual crime, thereby displaying the profound and unarticulated links between race and sexuality.

Initially ascribed to a black gunman in a jogging suit, the October 29, 1989 murder of Carol Stuart in Boston has subsequently been attributed to her husband, Charles, who committed suicide on January 4, 1990. The persistence and brutality of the Boston police, who terrorized working-class black communities in search of a suspect, recalls the vigilante justice of earlier decades. The specter of interracial rape hovers over this case even though no specific allegations were made; witness the sexualized ways in which at least certain black men were interrogated. As Andrew Kopkind writes: "Young black men were stopped, searched and detrousered on the street for no cause more reasonable than their skin color. The cops called the blacks "pussy" and "faggot," and sexual humiliation—white male power against black male impotence—became another disgusting tactic of the occupation."[17]

We must take note here of the sexism and homophobia inherent in the policemen's tactics for investigating a crime against a woman. In the name of the body of a woman, the white policemen sought to humiliate black men by effeminizing them. Clearly, in this case the existence and identity of the victim became secondary to the power struggle between men.

The narrative linking sexual violence to racism is evident perhaps even more powerfully in the rhetoric surrounding the incident that has come to be known as the Central Park rape. To review the details: on the night of Wednesday, April 19, 1989, a young white woman jogger was raped repeatedly and severely beaten in Central Park in Manhattan by a group of black and Puerto Rican adolescent males between the ages of 14 and 17. In the hour before they attacked the jogger, the young men were reported to have been involved in at least four other assaults: they are alleged to have robbed a 52-year-old man, obtaining a sandwich; thrown rocks at a taxicab; chased a man and a woman on a tandem bicycle; and attacked a 40-year-old male jogger, hitting him on the head with a lead pipe. The rape victim, a well-educated, 28-year-old investment banker who worked at Salomon Brothers, emerged from a coma after two weeks, but appears to have sustained some brain damage.

The inflammatory rhetoric of the journalistic accounts of the Central Park rape reveals the context within which the narrative was constructed. In and of itself the crime was certainly heinous. Yet the media coverage intensified and polarized responses in New York City and around the country, for it made the story of sexual victimization inseparable from the rhetoric of racism.

From the tabloids—*The New York Daily News* and *The New York Post*—to the putatively more respectable *New York Newsday* and *The New York Times,* journalists circulated and resuscitated myths of black male animalism and of the black male rapist. In terms that recalled lynch law at the turn of the century, a conservative Republican candidate for mayor ran prime-time television advertisements calling for the death penalty for rapists, along with cop-killers and serial murderers. Likewise, Donald Trump ran a full-page advertisement in *The New York Times* calling for the death penalty for the rapists.

News and feature stories were equally incendiary. On Friday, April 20, *The Daily News* headline announced: "Female jogger near death after savage attack by roving gang." The major story in that day's *Daily News* begins in the following manner: "A 28-year-old investment banker who regularly jogged in Central Park was repeatedly raped, viciously beaten and left for dead by a wolfpack of more than a dozen young teenagers who attacked her at the end of an escalating crime spree." The editorial in *The Daily News* that day begins:

> There was a full moon Wednesday night. A suitable backdrop for the howling of wolves. A vicious pack ran rampant through Central Park. They attacked at least five people. One is now fighting for her life. Perhaps by the time you read this, she will have lost that fight. . . . This was not shoplifting licorice sticks and bubble gum from a candy counter. This was bestial brutality. "Mischief" is not mugging. It is not gang rape. It is not beating someone's face to a pulp with fists and crushing someone's skull with a rock.

This imagery of the young males as subhuman is then recapitulated in articles and editorials in *The News* and the other New York dailies. Indeed, in even the ostensibly more sedate *New York Times,* an editorial dated April 26 is entitled "The Jogger and the Wolf Pack." The editorial itself is replete again with imagery of savagery and barbarity. Although the tone of the coverage is at one level appropriate for the severity of the crime, I wish to emphasize the fact that the press shaped the discourse around the event in ways that inflamed pervasive fears about the animality of black men. Further, the conventional journalistic practice of protecting the privacy of rape victims by concealing their identity—a practice that may well contribute to a climate that blames the victim—in addition to the inability of this particular woman to speak, contributed to the objectification of the victim. As a result, the young woman became a pawn in the struggle of empowered white men to seize control of their city.

The implications of the ways that journalists characterized the young men involved in the Central Park rape become powerfully clear when we juxtapose the reporting of this case with that involving the rape and sexual assault of a 17-year-old "mildly retarded" white middle-class young woman in northern New Jersey by five, middle-class white teen-age football players on March 1. This crime was first reported on March 22; formal charges were brought against the young men in mid-May. In this case, the young men were charged with having raped the young woman and penetrated her vaginally with a broomstick handle and a miniature baseball bat. Yet in this case, the rhetoric is about the effect of this crime on the community. Moreover, there is a marked emphasis on the victim's mental abilities.

My point here is not to compare the two incidents to determine which is the more savage. Rather, I mention this other case to suggest the difference that race and class make in the writing of rape. The reporting of these two cases must prompt us to ask why the rape of a brilliant, middle-class investment banker by a group of young black men is constructed to seem more heinous than the rape of a "mildly retarded" young white woman by a group of young white men. Rape here is clearly not represented as a violation of a woman's body alone. Rather, in the terms of interlocking issues of race, class, and gender, these crimes suggest that certain women's bodies are more valuable than others.

II

Unacknowledged cultural narratives such as those which link racial and gender oppression structure our lives as social subjects; the ability of some people to maintain dominance over others depends upon these narratives' remaining pervasive but unarticulated. In my teaching, both in courses that are explicitly about black feminism and those that are not, I take seriously the responsibility to teach texts by and about black women, and to develop strategies for discussing the ways in which interactions between race and gender are inscribed in narrative. However, it is to me equally important to work with my students toward the recognition of the kinds of silences that structure the social hierarchy in which we live.

The teaching of texts about "border cases" such as interracial rape, makes more explicit for students the theoretical principles of "intersectionality" that inform my courses. A story such as "Advancing Luna—and Ida B. Wells," by Alice

Walker, prompts students to speak from a variety of perspectives on the issue of interracial rape. To the extent that the story foregrounds the range of positions that different women assume around the subject, it requires readers to acknowledge as well the extent to which we keep secret our responses to such cases. My goal in teaching a work such as this one is to enable students to develop a vocabulary for addressing the differences between them that necessarily exist.

I return to this particular story because of the way it confronts the issue of difference. I teach it additionally because it is representative of Walker's less well-known, but to me more interesting fiction. *The Color Purple,* which continues to be one of the most widely read and frequently taught works written by a black woman, raises knotty questions about sexual violence, and the construction of race and sexuality. Yet for me, the utopian vision with which the novel ends disappoints and undermines the complexity of narration and characterization that has gone before. In contrast, "Advancing Luna" and the other stories included in Walker's 1981 collection of stories entitled *You Can't Keep a Good Woman Down,* individually and collectively confront the inadequacy of representation and eschew easy resolutions. This story calls attention to the unspeakability of interracial rape; others in the volume address issues having to do with the representation of, for example, the female body, or the relationship between racial and gender politics.[18]

Moreover, a discussion of "Advancing Luna" seems to me to be especially pertinent in a feminist classroom because it self-consciously participates in a variety of discourses, thereby problematizing the boundaries between literature and theory, literature and "real life." By thematizing one of the central paradoxes of the black feminist enterprise, it is simultaneously narrative and theory. It exemplifies the tendency that Barbara Christian identifies for writers of color "to theorize in narrative forms, in stories, riddles and proverbs, and in the play with language."[19] Moreover, to the extent that the narrator function breaks down and is replaced by an author figure or function who establishes a relation with narratives of the lives of "real people," the story presents itself as simultaneously fiction and fact/autobiography.

In the first two paragraphs of the story, the unnamed narrator/protagonist, a young black woman, establishes significant differences between herself and Luna, a young white woman with whom she worked in the movement and with whom she subsequently shared an apartment in New York. As the story develops, the space between them becomes increasingly resonant, charged with anger, betrayal, and the specter of sexual competitiveness.

"Advancing Luna" opens in the summer of 1965 in Atlanta at a political conference and rally. Within the context of the Civil Rights movement, the narrator is endowed with the advantages of both race and class—in this case her status as a black woman and a student. The narrator/protagonist is thus an insider among the high-spirited black people graced with a "sense of almost divine purpose."[20] An undergraduate at Sarah Lawrence College, she feels doubly at home in this "summery, student-studded" revolution (85). Luna is no doubt also a student, but the narrator represents her as an outsider, passive, and wan. While the narrator characterizes herself as bold and energetic, Luna tentatively awaits the graciousness of a Negro home. To emphasize the space between them, the narrator confidently strides through Atlanta instead of riding in the pickup truck with Luna.

The narrator's hostility to Luna is nowhere more evident than in her description of her. Here she inscribes her hostility on Luna's body in the process of anatomizing it. Moving from her breasts to the shape of her face to her acne to her asthmatic breathing, she renders Luna a configuration of inadequacies. Moreover, the idiosyncratic organization of the paragraphs of description makes it that much harder to conceive of Luna as a social or narrative subject:

> What first struck me about Luna when we later lived together was that she did not own a bra. This was curious to me, I suppose, because she also did not need one. Her chest was practically flat, her breasts like those of a child. Her face was round, and she suffered from acne. She carried with her always a tube of that "skin-colored" (if one's skin is pink or eggshell) medication designed to dry up pimples. At the oddest times—waiting for a light to change, listening to voter registration instructions, talking about her father's new girlfriend, she would apply the stuff, holding in her other hand a small brass mirror the size of a thumb, which she also carried for just this purpose. (86–87)

The narrator's hostility to Luna is evident not only in the way in which she anatomizes her, but also in less direct ways. For instance, by suggesting that Luna's skin is "skin-colored" she blames her for conforming to the image of the ideal Clearasil user. By means of the disruptive logic of the passage, the narrator caricatures her. She interrupts the order of a physical or spatial description to catch Luna, as if unawares, in the midst of the uncomplimentary, repeated activity, of applying her acne medication.

In the next paragraph, the narrator's hostility toward Luna takes the form of momentarily erasing her from her own description:

> We were assigned to work together in a small, rigidly segregated South Georgia town that the city fathers, incongruously and years ago, had named Freehold. Luna was slightly asthmatic and when overheated or nervous she breathed through her mouth. She wore her shoulderlength black hair with bangs to her eyebrows and the rest brushed behind her ears. Her eyes were brown and rather small. She was attractive, but just barely and with effort. Had she been the slightest bit overweight, for instance, she would have gone completely unnoticed, and would have faded into the background where, even in a revolution, fat people seemed destined to go. (87)

Although Luna is not fat, the narrator says she is the sort of person who would have faded into the background if she were.

During the summer of 1965, Luna and the narrator become friends through their shared work. The story focuses primarily on their life together in New York where they shared an apartment the following year.

The first exchange between the narrator and Luna that is actually dramatized in the text is one in which Luna admits to having been raped by a black man named Freddie Pye during her summer in the South. This conversation explains the source of the narrator's retrospective hostility to her. The narrator resents Luna for having spoken of the rape; her characterization is a way of punishing her for the admission. In addition, the description might be read as an attempt to undermine Luna' testimony by denying her desirability. By sexually denigrating Luna, the narrator indirectly blames her for her own victimization. This hostility points to a thinly-veiled sexual competitiveness between the black and the white woman which may more generally problematize the discourse of interracial rape.

Immediately after Luna's revelation, the story begins to break down. The narrator is unable to position herself in relation to Luna's testimony; as a result, the trajectory of the narrative disintegrates. The narrator's first reaction is to step out of the present of the text to historicize and censure the rape—she reads it in the context of Eldridge Cleaver's and Imamu Amiri Baraka's defenses of rape. Responding to Luna's position as a silenced victim, the narrator asks why she didn't scream and says she felt she would have screamed.

As the exchange continues, almost involuntarily the narrator links the rape to the lynching of Emmett Till and other black men. Then, instead of identifying with the silenced woman victim, she locates herself in relation to the silenced black male victim of lynching: "I had seen photographs of white folks standing in a circle roasting something that had talked to them in their own language before they tore out its tongue" (92–93). Forced to confront the implications of her split affinities, she who would have screamed her head off is now herself silenced. First embarrassed, then angry, she thinks, not says, "'How dare she tell me this!'" (93).

At this point, the narrative shifts to one of the first metatextual moments. Here it is no longer focused on the narrator/protagonist's and Luna's conversation about the rape, but rather the narrator/author's difficulty in thinking or writing about interracial rape. The narrator steps out of the story to speculate and theorize about the exclusion of black women from the discourse surrounding rape. The conversation at this juncture is not between Luna and the narrator, but between the narrator and Ida B. Wells—or rather, with an imaginary reconstruction of Wells's analysis of the relationship between rape and lynching.

The issue of rape thus forces a series of separations. Not only does it separate the narrator from Luna, but it also separates the narrator/protagonist from the narrator/author. Moreover, Luna's admission generates a series of silences. In an oddly and doubly counter-feminist move that recalls Wells's own discrediting of the testimony of white victims, the narrator wants to believe that Luna made up the rape; only Luna's failure to report the crime—her silence—convinces her that the white woman has spoken the truth. Indeed, in the final section of the main portion of the story, silences function as a refrain. Luna "never told [the narrator] what irked her" (97) the day the narrator had two male friends spend the night at their apartment, even though that event marked the ending of their relationship. The two women never discussed the rape again; they "never discussed Freddie Pye or Luna's remaining feelings about what had happened" (97). Perhaps most strikingly, they never mention Freddie Pye's subsequent visit to the apartment during which he spends the night in Luna's bedroom. It is as if the subject of interracial rape contains within itself so many unspeakable issues that it makes communication between the black and the white woman impossible.

Near the end of the main portion of the story, the narrator mentions Freddie Pye's return visit without explicit comment. By failing to explain the relation of his visit to Luna's story, the narrator suggests that Luna's word is unreliable. Luna's position is further undermined by the anecdote with which this section ends. This portion concludes with the story of Luna's visit to the narrator's home in the South several years later. On this occasion Luna brings a piece of pottery which is later broken by the narrator's daughter. The narrator remarks that in gluing the pot back together she "improves the beauty and fragility of the design" (98). This claim yet again bestows authority upon the narrator over and above Luna's power.

What follows are four other "endings" to the story. The narrator's inability to settle on one underscores the unnarratability of the story of interracial rape. Further, each ending absents the narrator from the story, absolving her of responsibility for the account and raising issues about the possibility of representation. It is as if the conflict between her racial and her gender identity has deconstructed the function of the narrator.

The first in this series of metatextual sections, entitled "Afterwords, Afterwards Second Thoughts" emphasizes again the unresolvability of the account. Told from the perspective of a voice that suggests that of the author, it discusses her inability to conclude the story.[21] On the one hand, she would have liked to have used a conclusion, appropriate for a text produced in a just society, in which Luna and Freddie Pye would have been forced to work toward a mutual understanding of the rape. Given the contradictions around race and gender in contemporary culture, however, she is left with an open ending followed by a series of sections that problematize even that one.

The second appended section, entitled "Luna: Ida B. Wells—Discarded Notes" continues this exploration of the relationship between narrative choices and ideological context. This section acknowledges the nature of the selections that the narrator/author has made in constructing the character of Luna. In "Imaginary Knowledge," the third appended section, the narrator creates a hypothetical meeting between Luna and Freddie Pye. This ending is the one that the author figure of the "Afterwords" section says would be appropriate for a story such as this were it published "in a country truly committed to justice" (98). In this cultural context, however, she can only employ such an ending by calling attention to its fictionality: she says that two people have become "'characters'" (101). This section is called "Imaginary," but the narrator will only imagine so much. She brings Luna and Freddie to the moment when they would talk about rape and then says that they must remove that stumbling block themselves.

The story ends with a section called "Postscript: Havana, Cuba, November 1976" in which the author figure speaks with a muralist/photographer from the U.S. about "Luna." The muralist offers a nationalist reading that supplants the narrator's racial and gender analysis. In this section it becomes clear that the attention has shifted away from the narrator and the significance of her interpretation, to Freddie Pye and his motivations. The lack of closure in the story, as well as the process by which the narrator recedes from the text, all suggest that the story is unwriting itself even as it is being written.

III

I last taught "Advancing Luna" in a seminar on Black Women Writers in the United States which was evenly divided between black and white women undergraduates. In this seminar students would occasionally argue about interpretations or dispute the ascendancy of racial or gender issues in the texts under discussion, but we seemed for the most part to arrive at consentaneous readings of the texts we discussed. This particular experience of teaching this text of interracial rape dramatized within the classroom the very divisions that operate at the level of narrative within the story itself. I found it to be a story that breaks various codes of silence even as its own narration breaks down.

The tendency toward unanimity that characterized this seminar may well have been a function of our collective response to the syllabus and to the composition of the class. As a teacher of Afro-American literature in integrated classrooms at elite white universities, I admit to foregrounding the accessibility of the texts to all students even as I articulate the strategies and components that reveal their cultural specificity. I further suspect that the students and I at some unexamined level assumed that our disagreements notwithstanding, as a community of women we would be able to contain differences within some provisional model of consensus. "Advancing Luna" forced us to confront the nature of differences that could not be resolved and to acknowledge the difficulty of speaking across them.

This story silenced a group of ordinarily talkative students in a number of ways. When I asked them where they positioned themselves in the story, no one would answer. My students then began to deconstruct the question, asking what it meant to "position" or "locate" oneself in a narrative. As our discussion progressed, they began to admit that, in fact, they did know where they positioned themselves. They were embarrassed or frightened by their affinities, however, and could not speak through that self-consciousness. For example, several white students finally admitted that they located themselves with Luna. I prompted them to discuss her motivations, and was struck by the extent to which students who are otherwise careful readers had manufactured an entire inner life for Luna. It was as if they were compensating unintentionally for the narrator's vicious representation of her character.

During the course of the conversation, it became clear that the black women students who spoke sided with Freddie Pye, the white women who spoke, with Luna.[22] Once this split became evident, then my project became to get the students to articulate their differences. My hope was that the black students would claim their divergent affinities with the black man on racial grounds and the white woman on the basis of gender, and that the students would recognize the cost of their respective identifications. For it was important to me that they acknowledge the implications of their discomfort, the extent to which they felt betrayed by their divisions from each other.

To my mind, within the space of a classroom students should be able to develop a vocabulary for speaking across differences that are initially the source of silences. Perhaps more importantly, I would hope that they would begin to develop a sense of respect for each other as the individual products of discrete cultural and historical experiences. Not surprisingly, however, I cannot claim that in my seminar I was able to achieve either of these goals. No doubt we only managed to enact the fraught and fragile nature of the issues that divide us.

The story forced the students to confront the circumstances of their own embodiment, the conditions that made them different. It perhaps also required them to confront my embodiment. The story might thus be seen as a "border case" in and of itself, for it illuminated the silences upon which our consensus depended.

The process of teaching (and then writing about the teaching) of this story has required me to confront the limits of what a class and a syllabus can accomplish. Not only were we unable to reach any kind of satisfactory closure in our discussion of "Advancing Luna," but moreover our discussions of subsequent texts did not seem to take place at a heightened level of consciousness. I can therefore only allow myself the guarded hope that in this instance, as is so often the case in teaching, a few students will comprehend the impact of our experience of this text at some point in the future.

Faced with the conundra of classroom and text, the only closure available to me (as is the case with Walker's author figure) is the metatextual. I would argue that what Walker and her narrator confront in writing "Advancing Luna" and what my students confront in discussing the story is the status of the text as a specific cultural formation that reflects and shapes their experience as social subjects. The issue of an incident of interracial rape (for our purposes here, one involving a black man and a white woman) sets in motion a variety of historical, cultural, and ideological narratives and associations. Mutually contradictory, and rooted deeply in cultural practice, these embedded narratives and associations interfere with the articulation of positions around an instance of interracial rape.

IV

During the summer of 1989 I overheard someone say that all of the talk about race and class in relation to the Central Park rape was beside the point. For this person, it was a crime about gender relations: in Central Park on April 19, a group of young men raped a young woman. Race and class had nothing to do with it.

To the extent that the crime seems not to have been racially motivated, this person's reading of the incident seems to be true at one level. Yet at another level, the comment seems strikingly naive, for neither the perpetrators nor the victim are purely gendered beings. To paraphrase Teresa de Lauretis, men and women are not purely sexual or merely racial, economic, or (sub)cultural, but all of these together and in conflict with another.[23]

From a sociological point of view, columnist Tom Wicker wrote in the April 28 issue of *The New York Times* that the crime was racial because the attackers lived surrounded by the social pathologies of the inner city and that these influences have had consequences on their attitudes and behavior. He also argued that the crime was racial to the extent that it exacerbated racial tensions in the metropolitan New York area.

I would add that to the extent that the discourses of race and rape are so deeply connected, cases of interracial rape are constituted simultaneously as crimes of race and of gender. The inescapability of cultural narratives means that instances of this sort participate in the ongoing cultural activity around ideologies of gender, race, and class. Rather than attempting to determine the primacy of race or class or gender, we ought to search for ways of articulating how these various categories of experience inflect and interrogate each other and how we as social subjects are constituted.

Notes

I wish to thank Marianne Hirsch and Evelyn Fox Keller for their advice and patience as I prepared this essay. I am grateful also to Ruth Wilson Gilmore, Craig Gilmore, and Agnes Jackson for carefully reading this paper and suggesting revisions.

1. See Valerie Smith, "Black Feminist Theory and the Representation of the 'Other,'" in Cheryl A. Wall, ed., *Changing Our Own Words: Essays on Criticism, Theory, and Writing by Black Women* (New Brunswick, NJ: Rutgers University Press, 1989), pp. 38–57.

2. See Michèle Barrett's discussion of the construction of difference in feminist theory, "The Concept of 'Difference'," *Feminist Review*, no. 26 (July 1987), pp. 29–41.

3. See, for example, Kimberlé Crenshaw, "Demarginalizing the Intersection of Race and Sex: A Black Feminist Critique of Antidiscrimination Doctrine, Feminist Theory and Antiracist Politics," *The University of Chicago Legal Forum*, 1989, pp. 139–67.

4. See for instance Deborah McDowell's account of black male responses to black feminism in "Reading Family Matters," in Cheryl A. Wall, ed., *Changing Our Own Words*, pp. 75–97.

5. Mary Poovey, *Uneven Developments: The Ideological Work of Gender in Mid-Victorian England* (Chicago: University of Chicago Press, 1988), p. 12.

6. See Crenshaw, "Demarginalizing the Intersection of Race and Sex," p. 140.

7. Hazel V. Carby, *Reconstructing Womanhood: The Emergence of the Afro-American Woman Novelist* (New York: Oxford University Press, 1987), pp. 20–39.

8. See Angela Y. Davis, "Rape, Racism and the Myth of the Black Rapist," in *Women, Race and Class* (New York: Random House, 1983), pp. 172–201.

9. Jacquelyn Dowd Hall, "'The Mind That Burns in Each Body': Women, Rape, and Racial Violence," in Ann Snitow, Christine Stansell, and Sharon Thompson, eds., *Powers of Desire: The Politics of Sexuality* (New York: Monthly Review Press, 1983), pp. 329–49.

10. Ida B. Wells, *Crusade for Justice: The Autobiography of Ida B. Wells* (Chicago: University of Chicago Press, 1970), p. 64.

11. Stephanie H. Jed discusses the relationship between the rape of Lucretia and the creation of republican Rome in *Chaste Thinking: The Rape of Lucretia and the Birth of Humanism* (Bloomington: Indiana University Press, 1989). See also Norman Bryson, "Two Narratives of Rape in the Visual Arts: Literature and the Visual Arts," in Sylvana Tomaselli and Roy Porter, eds., *Rape: An Historical and Social Enquiry* (New York: Basil Blackwell, 1986), pp. 152–73.

12. It seems to me that the journalistic practice of "protecting the identity" of rape victims needs to be reconsidered. I would argue that leaving victims unnamed objectifies them. Moreover, this silence contributes to the construction of rape as an experience of which the victim ought be ashamed.

13. For a systematic analysis of the ways in which Brownmiller and some other early feminist discussions of rape use the figure of the black male rapist see Angela Y. Davis, "Rape, Racism and the Myth of the Black Rapist," pp. 178–82.

14. See Susan Estrich, *Real Rape* (Cambridge: Harvard University Press, 1987); Davis, "Rape, Racism and the Myth of the Black Rapist"; and Catherine MacKinnon, "A Rally Against Rape," in *Feminism Unmodified: Discourses on Life and Law* (Cambridge: Harvard University Press, 1987), pp. 81–84.

15. MacKinnon, "A Rally Against Rape," p. 81.

16. During the week of the Central Park rape, twenty-eight other first-degree rapes or attempted rapes were reported in New York City. Nearly all the reported rapes involved black women or Latinas. Yet, as Don Terry wrote in *The New York Times*, most went unnoticed by the public. See "A Week of Rapes: The Jogger and 28 Not in the News," *The New York Times*, May 29, 1989, p. 25.

17. Andrew Kopkind, *The Nation*, vol. 250, no. 5 (February 5, 1990), 1, p. 153.

18. See, for instance Deborah McDowell's discussion of Walker's "Source," in her essay "Reading Family Matters" in Cheryl A. Wall, ed., pp. 75–97.

19. Barbara Christian, "The Race for Theory," in Linda Kauffman, ed., *Gender and Theory: Dialogues on Feminist Criticism* (New York: Basil Blackwell, 1989), p. 226.

20. Alice Walker, "Advancing Luna—and Ida B. Wells," in *You Can't Keep A Good Woman Down* (New York: Harcourt Brace Jovanovich, 1981), p. 85. Subsequent references will be to this edition and will be noted in the text by page number.

21. I problematize the figure of the author here to make clear that I do not intend to refer to Alice Walker, but rather to the multiplicity of narrative selves that is generated out of the disintegrating of the text.

22. This need not always be the case. See Mary Helen Washington's discussion of teaching this story in her essay "How Racial Differences Helped Us Discover Our Common Ground," in *Gendered Subjects: The Dynamics of Feminist Teaching,* ed. Margo Culley and Catherine Portuges (Boston: Routledge, Kegan Paul, 1985), pp. 221–29.

23. Teresa de Lauretis, "Feminist Studies/Critical Studies: Issues, Terms, and Contexts," in De Lauretis, ed., *Feminist Studies/Critical Studies* (Bloomington: Indiana University Press, 1986), p. 14.

17

Birth Pangs: Conceptive Technologies and the Threat to Motherhood

Michelle Stanworth

Introduction

Louise Brown celebrates her twelfth birthday in 1990; the world's first "test-tube baby" is not a baby any more. In the years since her birth, reproductive technologies that initially seemed bizarre have come to acquire a sense of the routine. Terms such as in vitro fertilization or surrogate motherhood have gained the status of household words. More and more people turn to the new reproductive technologies not as a last "desperate" pioneering option, but as a predictable stage in a reproductive career. If we judge by the number of women and men seeking their use, or by the flimsy evidence from opinion polls, reproductive technologies are increasingly popular. Yet within the feminist community, opposition to these technologies has become more coherent and more intense. In this essay, I would like to explore the reception of the new conceptive technologies, particularly in vitro fertilization and related techniques and, to a lesser extent, surrogacy.[1]

One basis for feminist hostility to the conceptive technologies is a powerful theoretical critique which sees in these new techniques a means for men to wrest "not only control of reproduction, but reproduction itself" from women.[2] It has been suggested that men's alienation from reproduction—men's sense of disconnection from their seed during the process of conception, pregnancy, and birth—has underpinned through the ages a relentless male desire to master nature, and to construct social institutions and cultural patterns that will not only subdue the waywardness of women but also give men an illusion of procreative power. New reproductive technologies are the vehicle that will turn men's illusions of reproductive control into a reality. By manipulating eggs and embryos, scientists will determine the sort of children who are born—will make themselves the fathers of humankind. By removing eggs and embryos from some women and implanting them in others, medical practitioners will gain unprecedented control over motherhood itself. Motherhood as a unified biological process will be effectively deconstructed: in place of "mother," there will be ovarian mothers who supply eggs, uterine mothers who give birth to children, and, presumably, social mothers who raise them. Through the eventual development of artificial wombs, the capacity may arise to make biological motherhood redundant. Whether or not women are reduced by this process to the level of "reproductive prostitutes," the object and the effect of the emergent technologies is to deconstruct motherhood and to destroy the claim to reproduction that is the foundation of women's identity.

While this theoretical account of the new technologies may be in some ways extremely radical, in other respects it ironically tends to echo positions that feminists have been keen to challenge. In the first place, this analysis entails an exaggerated view of the power of science and medicine, a mirror image of that which scientists and medical practitioners often try themselves to promote. Science may well be, as Emily Martin argues, a hegemonic system; but as she shows, that system does not go unchallenged.[3] The vigorous critique of science in this account needs to be tempered with a deeper understanding of the constraints within which science and medicine operate, and of the way these can be shaped for the greater protection of women and men. Second, in the urgent concern to protect infertile women from the sometimes unscrupulous attentions of medical science, infertile women are all too often portrayed as "desperate people," rendered incapable by pronatal pressures of making rational and ethical decisions.[4] This view of infertile women (and by implication, of all women) comes uncomfortably close to that espoused by some members of the medical profession. Third, this theoretical account sometimes seems to suggest that anything "less" than a natural process, from conception through to birth, represents the degradation of motherhood itself. But motherhood means different things to different women, and to identify motherhood so exclusively with nature, with the absence of technology, and indeed, with pregnancy and childbirth runs the risk of blunting the cutting edge of feminist critique.

The Case Against Reproductive Technology

Feminist opposition to conceptive technologies, like all oppositions, has a history. In the mid-1960s, I and many of my classmates at the University of British Columbia had no difficulty believing that we were emancipated because we had access to "the pill." The significance of the fact that the pill had to be obtained illegally, with fake identification that suggested we were married, seemed to escape us—technology was freedom, however sordidly obtained.

Today the honeymoon with technology is decisively over. Decades of involvement with technologies of fertility control, as well as with those directed at the "management" of labor and childbirth, have left most women somewhat sadder and a great deal wiser. The health risks and the side-effects of existing means of contraception, and the fact that we weren't informed of these dangers beforehand; the escalating use of aggressive medical intervention in childbirth; the tendency to relegate maternal welfare in the broadest sense to third place, after the safety of the fetus and the convenience of medical personnel; the linking of reproductive technology to medical models in which menstruation is seen as failed production and pregnancy as a pathological state; and, finally, the management of reproductive technologies in such a way that access depends powerfully on women's age, ethnicity, social class, sexual orientation, and physical abilities—so that black women, for example, have even less control over the experience of birthing than white women, or so that access to safe abortion depends on ability to pay: all these and more contribute to healthy scepticism among women about the potential effects of new forms of reproductive technology.[5]

This scepticism goes far beyond the simple dictum that medicine makes mistakes. After all, we all (even feminists) make mistakes. Instead, it has been recognized that far from being neutral artefacts or neutral ways of doing things that are independent of the societies they inhabit, reproductive technologies—like all technologies—bear the hallmark of the cultural context in which they emerge. Prevailing social relations are reflected in the nature of technologies, their particular strengths and weaknesses, the possibilities they open up, and the avenues they foreclose.[6] So, for example, the failure to develop safer and more acceptable means of birth control is not simply a technical problem; in part, it reflects the low priority given to women's health, and a tendency to disregard issues and symptoms that women themselves think are important.[7] Or, for instance, the fact that most obstetricians and gynecologists are male goes some way to account for the extensive use of technologies such as ultrasound which help to establish that medical practitioners "know more" about pregnancy and women's bodies than women do themselves.[8]

Against this background, it is not surprising that the detailed case against conceptive technologies, so forcefully and frequently articulated by feminist critics, has found a ready hearing within the feminist community. With the aid of Bryan Jennett's criteria for the evaluation of high-technology medicine (and the addition of a few of my own), I have organized the charges laid against the major conceptive technologies into seven discrete categories.[9] Conceptive technologies are accused of being:

Unsuccessful: Whatever the image of in vitro fertilization with embryo transfer, or of GIFT, as miracle cures for infertility, the miracle works in remarkably few cases.[10]

Unsafe: Risks are associated with the hormonal drugs used to stimulate ovulation for ivf patients, and those used to regulate cycles in some types of surrogacy. Where several embryos are transferred, infant and maternal health may suffer because of the frequency of multiple births. Women undergoing conceptive treatments are subject even more frequently than other women to procedures (e.g., ultrasound, caesarian deliveries) the routine use of which has been challenged by the women's health movement.[11]

Unkind: Whether treatment is "successful" or not, the pressure, emotional upheaval, disruption, and indignities involved do incommensurable damage to a woman's quality of life. The very existence of conceptive technologies makes it difficult for women to reconcile themselves to childlessness.[12]

Unnecessary: Infertility is a social condition, the seriousness of which depends entirely on the social evaluations attached to childlessness. Infertility does not require in vitro fertilization, or surrogacy, or any medical solution at all. If there were less hype about conceptive technologies, and if infertile people were less obsessed with securing their own biological child, then infertility might be resolved by the more satisfactory strategy of adoption.[13]

Unwanted: Women who expose their bodies to conceptive technologies or submit themselves as "surrogate" mothers have been coerced (1) by pressure from male partners, (2) by the limited economic opportunities for women and restricted avenues of self-esteem, which mean (especially in the case of "surrogate" mothers) that the "choice" isn't really a choice, (3) by pronatalist values and practices, which ensure that women who fail to bear children face constant reminders of the extent to which they fall short of hegemonic ideals. As Grundberg and Dowrick so clearly put it, none of us is free in our choices until it is possible to say aloud without fear of censure, "I don't wish to have children," (4) by unscrupulous and authoritarian doctors, who mislead them about the risks, intimidate them into "consent," or whose clinics offer "counseling into treatment" rather than counseling about treatment.[14]

Unsisterly: Women who use conceptive technologies harm other women, including women who don't (1) by seeking medical solutions to infertility, and thereby reinforcing the illusion that childbearing is a necessary component of femininity, (2) by providing doctors with experimental data and material to further their knowledge of the reproductive process and thus, by contributing to the expansion of a medical empire, the power of which is inimicable to women, (3) by taking advantage of a "surrogate" mother's poverty and powerlessness (or altruism) for their own benefit; this exploitation is potentially racist or imperialist, since women from subordinate ethnic communities and from poorer countries might be extensively used as "surrogate" mothers by privileged Western women in the future.[15]

Unwise: The low success rate of conceptive technologies as well as their many disadvantages make them an unwise focus for resources. Greater benefits would be derived if the resources currently being absorbed by in vitro fertilization and associated techniques were redeployed to fund research into the causes of infertility, or into preventative measures.[16]

The above charges constitute a powerful analysis of the impact of conceptive technologies, an analysis that goes beyond the unacceptably narrow terms of conventional medical assessment. But the strength of the feminist position we ultimately evolve depends upon the care with which these accusations are deployed and upon the implications for action that are drawn from them. Take, for example, the accusations that conceptive technologies are both *unwanted and unsisterly*. Underlying these charges is a telling critique of coercive pronatalism and of the place of medical practice in relation to it. But even this extremely useful analysis raises a number of questions.

While challenging the ways that coercive pronatalism shapes women's motivations to mother, we must be very clear that "shaped" is not the same as "determined." The battery of sanctions and rewards designed to entice women into motherhood indicates, not that conformity is guaranteed, but that childlessness is a genuine option, which efforts are made to contain. The most effective analyses of pronatalism are scrupulous about recognizing that even the pain of infertility does not prevent infertile women from making rational decisions about motherhood, and that the rejection of childbearing, while a difficult option for many women, is not necessarily a more authentic one.

As well as exposing pronatalist ideologies, we need also to articulate more convincing rationales for childlessness. For instance, in recent critiques of pronatalism (perhaps reacting against the fragile compromise involved in "having it all"?) it sometimes seems as if eschewing motherhood depends upon the compensation provided by a career. As one article says about protagonists in the Baby M surrogacy case:[17]

> the Sterns are not free either. . . . The Sterns, two people deeply committed to challenging professional careers, still feel the cultural imperative to "have" a child.

But why is it relevant to such a compulsion that people are committed to challenging professional careers? If it is assumed that a career can and should displace the wish for a child, then what type of economism does that bespeak? And what are we to make of the implied contrast: that professional women might be expected to have their minds on higher things, but that motherhood is the sensible course for women without rewarding careers? These interpretations may well not be what the authors of the above remarks on the Sterns had in mind, but they do signal how difficult it is for us to deal with the question of voluntary childlessness in a theoretically adequate way. To the extent that our discussions of pronatalism inadvertently justify childlessness in terms of career commitment, we run the risk of leaving no justification for childlessness—no refuge against pronatalist pressures—for the majority of women.

Finally, indignation at coercive pronatalism needs to be matched by an equally resolute opposition to the invidious distinctions that target some women as mothers and label others, on grounds that have little to do with their capacity to nurture a child, as unfit. As all participants in the debate are aware, pro-motherhood propaganda is not uniformly disseminated;[18] it coexists with disincentives and obstacles to motherhood for women from disempowered groups. According to ideologies of motherhood, all women want children; but single women and teenagers, women from ethnic minorities and those on state support, lesbian women and women with disabilities are often urged to forgo mothering "in the interests of the child." Do some feminists unintentionally endorse a similar pattern of invidious distinctions when it seems to be suggested that infertile women should not be mothers, or that their desire for children (and only theirs) is selfish, misguided, and potentially dangerous?

It seems to me that our critique of pronatalism and of reproductive technologies will be all the more persuasive when it ceases to distinguish so categorically between fertile women and infertile. The pressures which propel women into motherhood—the cultural imperative to have a child, the expectations of male partners, and the limited sources for women of fulfillment, security, and self-esteem—enter into the decision of any woman to be a mother, regardless of her fertility. There is no particular reason to challenge the authenticity of the desire for motherhood of women who are infertile. Nor is there any good reason to identify infertile women in particular as unsisterly for reinforcing the illusion that motherhood is inevitable; any desired pregnancy, presumably, could have that effect (just as any pregnancy *may* be interpreted as a rebuke to women who are childless). And is it only infertile women whose attendance at medical clinics validates medical power, or is this an unintended side-effect of the use of many contraceptive or abortion or birthing technologies as well as of conceptive ones? And if the latter, can we be justified in asking only infertile women to turn their backs on medical treatment—or should we be seeking ways of containing medical power that are more consistent across different groups of women? That doctors pressure women into treatment, for example, and fail to provide the data necessary for informed consent, is a problem against which we must make a stand, but it is a problem by no means confined to infertility treatment.[19]

One of the most politically sensitive elements of the case against conceptive technologies is the claim that these are "*unnecessary*"—that infertility does not dictate a medical solution, and that the condition of involuntary childlessness can be resolved satisfactorily by adoption. For some infertile women (and I count myself among them) this happy ending is indeed possible. But it is a long and implausible leap from there to the conclusion that conceptive technologies are in general unnecessary.

For one thing, the description of infertility as a social condition of involuntary childlessness doesn't hold for all women. For some women, pregnancy and childbirth are not only a route to a child, but a desired end in itself.[20] Our passionate concern as feminists to defend the integrity of the experience of childbirth (against intrusive obstetricians, for example) would sit uneasily with the view that the attachment to giving birth of some infertile women reflects a misguided commitment to biological motherhood.

For another, it would be naive to regard the adoption process as necessarily free of the drawbacks and risks that characterize medically assisted conception. Adoption and fostering are often subject to strict surveillance and regulation and that surveillance and regulation is not necessarily benign to women. Adoption agencies in many countries are (rightly) rigorous about who may exercise parental rights: but their policies and criteria of assessment are framed against a conventional notion of parenting—and particularly, of motherhood—which will deter many would-be mothers. Adoption agencies in Britain may (and often do) refuse single women or those aged over thirty; may (and usually do) refuse those who are not heterosexual, whether married or not; may (and sometimes do) refuse women who have jobs, women who have had psychiatric referrals, women with disabilities, women whose unconventional life-styles cast doubt—for the social workers at least—on their suitability as mothers. They are also likely to refuse, in spite of the long and uncertain waiting period for adoption, women who intend to continue trying to achieve a pregnancy. For many would-be mothers, particularly those who want their relationship with a child to begin while it is still in infancy or toddlerhood, the conceptive technologies are not so much about biological motherhood as about having a child at all. The tensions surrounding the adoption process, the raising and dashing of hopes, the rejection by adoption agencies of prospective mothers who would have endured no questions about their fitness had they been fertile—all of these mean that adoption may, like the conceptive technologies, sometimes be "unsuccessful," sometimes "unsafe" and often "unkind."

And there is, of course, another complication when we consider the adoption process from the point of view of the birthmother. To the same extent that surrogacy can be seen as *"unsisterly"*—as involving the exploitation of birthmothers by infertile women—adoption can be seen as unsisterly too. The pressures that lead some women to surrender their babies for adoption are very like those condemned in the case of surrogate mothers, right down to the possibility of exploitation of women from subordinate ethnic communities or from poorer nations. Indeed, in Britain, the potential for exploitation has been an element in a largely successful campaign to eliminate "trans-racial" adoptions of black children by white parents. It is ironic that while adoption is often presented in a positive light as a solution to infertility, the sometimes painful experiences of women who have surrendered their children to adoption are also invoked to demonstrate the dangers of surrogacy.[21]

In highlighting the difficulties of adoption, I am not arguing for an end to adoption, nor am I identifying it as an unsatisfactory practice. On the contrary, I think adoption is to be encouraged; it is often the basis for strong and joyful mother-child relationships, and it enables many birthmothers to find a secure and loving home for children whom they decide not to mother.[22] What I would like to emphasize is that the impact of adoption on women (like that of surrogacy or other conceptive technologies) depends upon the conditions we create for these practices. We cannot ensure that a birthmother's decision to surrender her child for adoption will be painless (any more than we can make abortion decisions easy). But what we can and must do is to try to create conditions—crucially, about freedom from restriction during pregnancy and about custody—that will preserve her autonomy and help to ensure that the decision is hers;[23] and we can commit ourselves with renewed vigor to efforts to secure forms of economic and social support for all mothers so that fewer such decisions are coerced by poverty and need.

The exaggerated and untruthful promises made by many infertility clinics in the 1980s for conceptive technologies as a safe and simple "cure" for infertility have been ruthlessly and rigorously exposed by feminist researchers. They have demonstrated beyond a doubt that while in vitro fertilization may be the only route to pregnancy for some women, it is by no means a certain route or a kind one. Because of the dearth of studies that compare treated and untreated women who are similar in terms of age, fertility problems, and so forth, lack of safety is harder to establish; but what is clear is that evidence of safety has not been a priority for clinicians, and that in the absence of such evidence, we are right to maintain a sceptical stance.

Feminist attempts to document the charges that conceptive technologies are *unsuccessful, unsafe, and unkind* have received a wide circulation. In Europe, for example, these views were prominently represented at the first WHO debate on reproductive technologies,[24] and have been influential in shaping policies within the Green movement. The success of this feminist critique is also reflected in its takeup in medical circles; articles sharply critical of current practice with regard to in vitro fertilization have recently appeared in major medical journals in several countries.[25]

But what is still at issue is the best way for feminists to respond to the data that has been so painstakingly brought to light. For it is a hallmark of critical discussions of science and medicine that technical knowledge (about efficacy, or safety, or anything else) should inform the choices we make, rather than dictate decisions.[26] It is important to remember this, because among other things the calculus of risks and benefits for reproductive technologies is different for different social groups, according to their circumstances and the resources they can command. For instance, it makes excellent sense for women to refuse contraceptives that carry health risks when they have better contraceptive options, or access to safe abortion, or are able to refuse intercourse; for women in less enviable circumstances the availability of such contraceptives can sometimes mean the different between life and death. Before we reject technologies that are relatively unsuccessful, unsafe, or unkind, we need always to remind ourselves that the rejection of reproductive technology can sometimes be a luxury that only relatively privileged women can realistically afford.[27]

With conceptive technologies, the central issue is slightly different. Before setting our minds against conceptive technologies, we have to consider whether this is really the best way to protect women who have sought (and will continue to seek) their use. An implacable opposition to conceptive technologies could mean that any chance of exerting pressure on those who organize infertility services—for example, pressure for better research and for disclosure of information; for more stringent conditions of consent; for means of access for poorer women, who are likely to be the majority of those with infertility problems—would be lost. Would it be wise to abandon infertile women to the untender mercies of infertility specialists, when a campaign, say, to limit the number of embryos that may be implanted (and thereby to reduce multiple pregnancies, pressures for selective reduction, and so forth), or to regulate the use of hormonal stimulation, might do a great deal to reduce the possible risks to women and to their infants?[28]

Perhaps in the light of these reflections, we might reconsider the claim that these technologies are *"unwise"*—that it would be better to divert resources to fund research into causes of infertility. Better for whom? Infertility services are often the poor cousin of health services—poorly funded, badly organized, extremely unequally distributed, and run in an authoritarian and insensitive fashion.[29] Do we really want to argue that resources be removed from the already inadequate provision for infertile people, and redeployed for the protection of those who are currently fertile? Surely this kind of divisive strategy runs counter to the feminist concern to improve health care provisions for all women, and to be sensitive to the needs of the infertile. On the other hand, a feminist campaign for a better range of services around infertility (research into causes, independent woman-staffed counseling services, and a range of treatments, high-tech and low) would make common cause with infertile women and men, who are often themselves very critical of the quality of help they are offered and the terms on which it is available.

Tensions Around Motherhood

The depth of feeling among feminists about conceptive technologies has partly to do with their links, not to medical technology, but to the difficult terrain of motherhood. In some accounts, conceptive technologies have been used to delineate a boundary between "good" motherhood and "bad." On one side of the boundary is empowering motherhood, the motherhood that represents a positive counterpole to masculinity. On the other side of the boundary, where creating or sustaining a pregnancy depends upon medical assistance, lies coercive motherhood that locks women into subordination.

The starkness of this contrast between "good" motherhood and "bad" may reflect the difficulty of juggling positive and negative interpretations of women as mothers, in the face of the paradox that motherhood is simultaneously women's weakness and women's strength.[30] On the one hand, maternal practices are increasingly acknowledged as a source of alternative values—as generating, in Sara Ruddick's terms, a discipline that orients mothers to distinctive themes and commitments, virtues and standards of achievement some of which stand in hopeful opposition to oppressive forms of thought.[31] On the other hand, feminists also recognize the pivotal role of motherhood in the subordination of women.

The material and social disadvantages that follow from childcare; the cultural associations with birth that condemn women to an inferior place in symbolic systems; the psychological effects on future adults of asymmetrical mothercare: all suggest that motherhood locks women into institutional and psychological structures of dependency and powerlessness, which render them vulnerable to men. In a sense, the debates around conceptive technologies are a way of talking about different cultural conceptions of motherhood—a way of expressing both a commitment to the positive experience of motherhood and an opposition to its sometimes debilitating effects on women.

These competing conceptions of motherhood resonate with tensions at the level of personal politics and over the difficult individual decision whether or not to have children. Political and economic developments in the past fifteen years (for example, the new right's vociferous insistence on self-sufficiency, and the growing view of children as a personal indulgence; the changing opportunity structure for women; or the failure to establish a rationale for childlessness, even among feminists, that can challenge the near-hegemonic appeal of maternity) have tended to sharpen the divisions between women with young children and those without. But the positive feminist understanding of motherhood makes it more difficult to challenge maternity, and as a result this conflict is rarely addressed. A focus on the degrading impact of conceptive technologies is attractive, perhaps, because it seems to make possible the impossible: to attack the coercive aspects of maternity, the way that motherhood makes victims of women—and to do so in the name of motherhood itself.

But beyond this, an apocalyptic reading of the impact of conceptive technologies speaks to our sense that motherhood is today endangered. Discussions of surrogacy and of in vitro fertilization ring with references to the commercialization of motherhood, to the potential to turn babies and motherhood itself into a commodity like any other, to the replacement of maternal love with the cold harsh flare of clinical lights. This makes me wonder whether it is not motherhood per se that we feel the need to preserve, but whether we are afraid instead (as Linda Gordon once said in a different context) "of a loss of mothering, in the symbolic sense"—of a society in which tenderness and caring are displaced by the ruthless pursuit of individual advantage.[32] As more and more women grapple with the endless pressure involved in combining commitments to career with children, this fear speaks to feelings that many feminist mothers have about their lives—that all too often there is less time for tenderness, less chance for closeness, than we might wish. The "eye of love" may be steadfast on our children but it often has not the time to be "patient"—and indeed there is less time than we need to mother even ourselves. The urgency of the "dangers to motherhood" we apprehend in the new conceptive technologies has something to do, I suspect, with our own sense of loss, our sense that in current circumstances some aspects of mothering are escaping our grasp.

And we feel motherhood to be threatened, too, in another respect. The escalating rate of divorce over recent decades, and the rapid rate of formation of step-families or reconstituted families, signify a markedly greater uncertainty in the 1980s and 1990s (compared with say the 1950s) about the ties that bind individual parents to individuals children. Legal battles over custody and access are only part of the story: alongside these run uncounted numbers of households in which uncontested custody or access arrangements are nevertheless a source of anxiety, in which one parent or both must be more self-conscious about the basis of their claims upon the child. And this experience is not confined to parents: grandmothers and grandfathers, uncles and aunts, friends or lovers who have shared in the upbringing of a child, discover in times of break-up new difficulties in negotiating a secure relationship with children whom they love. It seems to me that the concern about genetic and biological parenthood that has greeted the arrival of new technologies—the attention of commissions of inquiry to issues of inheritance and paternity, the huge public interest in court cases concerned with the custody not only of children born of surrogacy arrangements, but also of embryos—reflects in part these pre-existing uncertainties about claims on relationships to children. In the face of divorce and rising rates of remarriage, the pressure to rethink the moral and legal basis of claims upon children is clearly intense.

But if anxiety about claims on children has a wide purchase, it is particularly poignant for women. It is women who make the largest investment in children, in terms of daily, weekly, yearly care and commitment; and it is women who are held (and hold themselves) most responsible when something goes wrong. Women's worries are fueled by a political context where women are, indeed, at particular risk in the judicial process; where mothers' prerogatives over children are often represented as selfish and unjust; and where fathers and children "are increasingly depicted as the losers [of a judicial preference for mother custody] in emotional and material terms."[33] Thus women are, and know themselves to be, vulnerable as mothers;[34] the urge to protect biological motherhood stems partly from the desperate need to find a secure and defensible basis on which to reassert mothers' claims.

But while the anxiety and the vulnerability that triggers it is real, we need to address that vulnerability in the most effective way. While men cannot bear children, every child does have a "biological" father; and trends towards enhancing the legal rights that flow from biological parenthood, as opposed to purposive parental commitment and care, could work decisively to the detriment of women.[35] One of our concerns must be that, in the search for a secure incontestable basis for claims to children, the anxieties that conceptive technologies crystallize do not lead us to give even greater legal priority to biological claims.[36]

The fears generated by conceptive technologies may be a way not only for women to articulate perceived threats to motherhood, but also to keep those threats at bay, by projecting them onto one particular group of women (the infertile) who aren't "really" mothers anyway. But however appealing this solution, and whatever conclusions we come to in the final analysis about the impact of conceptive technologies, the tendency to foreground technology is risky not so much because of what it says as because of what it ignores.

It ignores, first, the strenuous and partly successful efforts of the women's movement to transcend the identification of women with nature. Conception, pregnancy, and childbirth (as we are forever reminding members of the medical profession) are not merely the biological rite of passage that signifies a woman's entry into motherhood. The thrust of feminist analysis since the mid-1970s has been to rescue childbearing from the status of the "natural," to insist more and more confidently upon seeing pregnancy and childbirth as part of a sphere of significant action as meaningful and as civilized as any of the accomplishments of men. But the attempt to reclaim motherhood as a female accomplishment need not mean giving the natural priority over the technological—that pregnancy is natural and good, technology unnatural and bad. As I have argued elsewhere, it is not at all clear what a "natural" relationship to our fertility, our reproductive capacity, would look like—and it is even less clear that it would be desirable.[37] The defense of motherhood that we ultimately construct will be stronger if we resist the temptation to use nature as a territory on which to stake our claims.[38]

Moreover, an emphasis upon conceptive technologies is problematic insofar as it overshadows a concern with other dimensions of the social context of motherhood. How important is medical intervention in conception compared with the institutional structures, for example, that make childcare for many women isolating and exhausting, rather than enriching? That give fathers control without responsibility over children they conceive? That burden mothers with expectations dictated by "experts," but fail to provide them with the resources necessary to meet those standards? How much space do we leave for a concern with the legal system that, for example, denies many lesbians custody of their children, or sends mothers to prison for refusing access to violent or abusive fathers? With the material conditions that force some women to choose between health care for themselves or medicine for their children? With the fundamental question of whether the woman who becomes pregnant by "natural" means wishes to be a mother or not?

We know now (or ought to know) that the balance of positive and negative elements in motherhood is historically and culturally specific—that the nature of motherhood and its impact, as well as the qualities evinced by those who mother, is not the same in any two societies; nor is the experience of motherhood identical across different groups of women within the same society.[39] Many feminists in the West can strongly identify with *Balancing Acts,* Katherine Gieve's collection of candid accounts of contemporary British women's often wistful relinquishment of fantasies of the "perfect mother," and of their struggles to combine politics, careers, and relationships with children.[40] But what a world of difference between these mothers and Toni Morrison's Baby Suggs, who had three children stolen from her by the slavemasters and who "could not or would not" love the rest.[41] Or between the European mothers in Jacklyn Cock's compelling study of South Africa, and the African nannies who look after the European children but are rarely enabled to spend time with their own daughters and sons.[42] While motherhood exacts sacrifices from most women and provides joy, only the blandest generalities are true in any universal sense. Attempts to understand and to influence the nature of motherhood must, it seems to me, come to terms with the range of conditions—social, legal, political, and economic, as well as medical— that sustain these differences. Only in this context will conceptive technology, and the impact of technology more generally, be allowed its proper place.

Notes

I would like to thank David Held, Marianne Hirsch and Evelyn Fox Keller for their encouragement and advice.

1. By in vitro fertilization I generally mean ivf with embryo transfer; related techniques include insemination, embryo transfer without ivf, lavage, and gamete intrafallopian transfer or GIFT. For descriptions of these techniques, see the glossary of Patricia Spallone, *Beyond Conception* (London: Macmillan, 1989).

2. Janice Raymond, "Preface," p. 12, in Gena Corea et al., eds., *Man-Made Women* (London, Hutchinson, 1985). This critique is associated with FINRRAGE, the Feminist International Network of Resistance to Genetic and Reproductive Engineering, whose views are elaborated in a number of books, including Jocelynne Scutt, ed., *The Baby Machine: the Commercialisation of Motherhood*, (Carlton, Australia: McCulloch Publishing, 1988).

3. Emily Martin, *The Woman in the Body* (Milton Keynes: Open U. Press, 1989). Feminists have been responsible for broadcasting alternative views of women and health, while the women's health movement has campaigned vigorously for the extension of health services and for their transformation, to make them more accountable to women and more responsive to women's needs.

4. Infertile women are far from being passive victims of medical technology, not only in the sense that they actively seek out infertility treatments (as Gerson rightly points out) but also (as Pfeffer argues) in the sense that they question those treatments, stop them, reject them in favor of others, or never present for treatment at all. Deborah Gerson, "Infertility and the construction of desperation," *Socialist Review*, vol. 19, no. 3 (July–September 1989) and Naomi Pfeffer, "Artificial insemination, in-vitro fertilisation and the stigma of infertility," in Michelle Stanworth, ed., *Reproductive Technologies: Gender, Motherhood, and Medicine* (Minneapolis: U. Of Minnesota Press, 1988).

5. Boston Women's Health Book Collective, *The New Our Bodies Ourselves*, 3rd edn (New York: Simon and Schuster, 1985); Ann Oakley, *The Captured Womb* (Oxford: Basil Blackwell, 1985); Lesley Doyal, *The Political Economy of Health* (London: Pluto Press, 1979); Janet Gallagher, "Eggs, embryos and foetuses: anxiety and the

law," in Michelle Stanworth, ed., *Reproductive Technologies;* Rosalind Pollack Petchesky, *Abortion and Woman's Choice* (Boston: Northeastern U. Press, 1986); Ruth Hubbard, "Personal courage is not enough: some hazards of childbearing in the 1980s," in Rita Arditti et al., eds., *Test-Tube Women* (London and Boston: Pandora Press, 1984); Jennifer Terry, "The body invaded: medical surveillance of women as reproducers," *Socialist Review,* vol. 19, no. 3 (July–September 1989), pp. 13–43.

6. Donald MacKenzie and Judy Wajcman, eds., *The Social Shaping of Technology* (Milton Keynes: Open U. Press, 1985); Judy Wajcman, *Women and Technology* (Cambridge: Polity Press, forthcoming, 1991).

7. Scarlett Pollock, "Refusing to take women seriously," in Rita Arditti et al. eds., *Test-Tube Women.*

8. Ann Oakley, "From walking wombs to test-tube babies"; Rosalind Pollack Petchesky, "Foetal images: the power of visual culture in the politics of reproduction"; both in Michelle Stanworth, ed., *Reproductive Technologies.*

9. Jennett's original five criteria were: unnecessary, unsuccessful, unsafe, unkind, unwise. Scambler suggested the addition of 'unwanted' in his discussion of childbirth. Bryan Jennett, *High Technology Medicine: Benefits and Burdens* (Oxford: Oxford U. Press, 1986), p. 174. Graham Scambler, "Habermas and the power of medical expertise," in Scambler, ed., *Sociological Theory and Medical Sociology* (London: Tavistock, 1987).

10. E.g., Gena Corea and Susan Ince, "Report of a survey of IVF clinics in the USA," in Patricia Spallone and Deborah Steinberg, eds., *Made to Order: the Myth of Reproductive and Genetic Progress* (Oxford: Pergamon Press, 1987).

11. E.g., Renate Duelli Klein and Robyn Rowland, "Women as test-sites for fertility drugs," *Reproductive and Genetic Engineering* vol. 1, no. 3 (1988), pp. 251–73.

12. E.g., Christine Crowe, "Bearing the consequences—women experiencing IVF," in Jocelynne Scutt, ed., *The Baby Machine.*

13. This has been argued most elegantly by Deborah Gerson, "Infertility and the construction of desperation"; also Mary Sue Henifin, "Introduction" to Elaine Hoffman Baruch et al. eds., *Embryos, Ethics and Women's Rights* (New York and London: Harrington Park Press, 1988).

14. E.g., Judith Lorber, "In vitro fertilization and gender politics," in Elaine Hoffman Baruch et al., eds., *Embryos, Ethics and Women's Rights,* for a very thoughtful analysis of the dominance of male partners in reproductive decisions. The restricted "choice" of women with regard to reproductive technologies is argued eloquently by Andrea Dworkin, *Right-Wing Women* (London: The Women's Press, 1983), pp. 181–82; and by various contributors to Renate Duelli Klein, ed., *Infertility: Women Speak Out* (London: Pandora Press, 1989), who also offer vivid illustration of the power of pronatalism. For the way that clinics may manipulate women into treatment, see e.g. Gena Corea, *The Mother Machine* (New York: Harper and Row, 1985). Stephanie Dowrick and Sibyl Grundberg's sensitive discussion of pronatalism is in their edited collection, *Why Children?* (London: The Women's Press, 1980).

15. E.g., Sultana Kamal, "Seizure of reproductive rights? A discussion on population control in the third world and the emergence of new reproductive technologies in the west," in Patricia Spallone and Deborah Steinberg, eds., *Made to Order*. In her extended discussion of surrogacy contracts, Carole Pateman makes the pertinent observation that the view of surrogacy as involving women in helping or exploiting other women conveniently obscures the part of men in surrogacy arrangements; Carole Pateman, *The Sexual Contract* (Cambridge: Polity Press, 1988).

16. E.g., Mary Sue Henifin, "Introduction: women's health and the new reproductive technologies," in Elaine Hoffman Baruch et al., eds., *Embryos, Ethics and Women's Rights;* or Marion Brown, Kay Fielden, and Jocelynne Scutt, "New frontiers or old recycled?" in Jocelynne Scutt, ed., *The Baby Machine*.

17. Janice Doane and Devon Hodges, "Risky business: familial ideology and the case of Baby M," *differences*, vol. 1, no. 1 (Winter 1989), pp. 67–81.

18. Linda Singer, "Bodies—pleasures—powers," *differences*, vol. 1, no. 1 (Winter 1989), pp. 45–65, writes tellingly of the "differential strategies" by which motherhood is currently marketed to particular segments of the female population.

19. For example, it was recently reported that 46% of medical students in the U.K. "gained their first experience of vaginal examinations on unconscious patients, some of whom may not have given their consent"; from "Shock survey sparks curb on medical tests," *Cambridge Evening News*, February 3, 1989. More generally, see Carolyn Faulder, *Whose Body is It?* (London: Virago, 1985).

20. Naomi Pfeffer and Anne Woollett, *The Experience of Infertility* (London: Virago, 1983).

21. Betty Jean Lifton urges us to consider also the psychological effects of surrogacy on children, in the light of the experiences of some adopted children; "Brave new baby in the brave new world," in Elaine Hoffman Baruch et al., eds., *Embryos, Ethics and Women's Rights*.

22. Feminist support for adoption rests, among other things, on the recognition that motherhood is not a unitary experience, to which all women have the same relationship (or to which any woman necessarily has the same relationship throughout her life). Different orientations to pregnancy and childbirth are discussed in, for example, Emily Martin, *The Woman in the Body*, pp. 104–5; Kristin Luker, *Abortion and the Politics of Motherhood* (Berkeley and London: U. of California Press, 1984); see esp. Sara Ruddick, *Maternal Thinking: Toward a Politics of Peace* (Boston: Beacon Press, 1989).

23. There have been encouraging calls in recent articles for the risks to be shared more equally by all parties to a surrogacy contract, rather than being all taken by the mother; this might entail no restrictions on behavior, diet, health, or even abortion during pregnancy, and full rights to change her mind for a period of time after the birth. Janice Doane and Devon Hodges, "Risky business: familial ideology and the case of Baby M," pp. 77–79; and Linda Singer, "Bodies—pleasures—powers," p. 63.

24. Margaret Stacey, "The manipulation of the birth process," paper prepared for the February 1988 meeting of the European Advisory Committee for Health Research, World Health Organization.

25. E.g., Marsden G. Wagner and Patricia St. Clair, "Are in-vitro fertilisation and embryo transfer of benefit to all?," *The Lancet* (October 28, 1989), pp. 1027–30; F. J. Stanley, "In vitro fertilization: a gift for the infertile or a cycle of despair?" *Medical Journal of Australia,* no. 148 (1988) pp. 425–26.

26. Hilary Rose, "Victorian values in the test-tube," in Michelle Stanworth, ed., *Reproductive Technologies.*

27. Rebecca Sarah, "Power, certainty and the fear of death," in Elaine Hoffman Baruch et al., eds., *Embryos, Ethics and Women's Rights.*

28. These are merely off-the-cuff examples of campaigns that might benefit women using infertility services; but it is the principle of feminist intervention to improve safety standards that interests me, and I am by no means committed to these particular campaigns.

29. Lesley Doyal, "Infertility—a life sentence? Women and the National Health Service," in Michelle Stanworth, ed., *Reproductive Technologies*; Naomi Pfeffer and Alison Quick, *Infertility Services: A Desperate Case* (London: GLACH, 1988); David Mathieson, *Infertility Services in the NHS—What's Going On?* Report prepared for Frank Dobson, M.P., Shadow Minister of Health, 1986.

30. Ann Oakley, "The woman's place," *New Society* (March 6, 1987) pp. 14–16; Ann Ferguson makes a similar point in *Blood at the Root: Motherhood, Sexuality and Male Dominance* (London: Pandora, 1989), pp. 171–72, but she also emphasizes that the impact of motherhood depends on the social context in which it takes place.

31. Sara Ruddick, "Maternal thinking," in Barrie Thorne and Marilyn Yalom, eds., *Rethinking the Family* (New York and London: Longman, 1982).

32. Linda Gordon makes this point in relation to opponents of abortion, in "Why nineteenth century feminists did not support birth control and twentieth century feminists do," in Barrie Thorne and Marilyn Yalom, eds., *Rethinking the Family.*

33. Carol Smart and Selma Sevenhuijsen, eds., *Child Custody and the Politics of Gender* (London: Routledge, 1989); the quotation is from the editors' preface, p. xvi.

34. Susan Suleiman's "On maternal splitting" is a stimulating discussion of the effect of mothers' vulnerability on their reluctance to relinquish the fantasy of the perfect mother. She locates surrogacy, alongside divorce and custody disputes, as one of the "causes" of mothers' vulnerability; I'm locating reactions to surrogacy and other conceptive technologies as part of the "effect." Suleiman, "On maternal splitting: a propos of Mary Gordon's *Men and Angels,*" *Signs,* vol. 14, no. 1 (Autumn 1988), pp. 25–41.

35. Carol Smart and Selma Sevenhuijsen, eds., *Child Custody and the Politics of Gender.*

36. "As a result of legislation on reproductive technology the legal concept of paternity could be extended" argues Juliette Zipper, in "What else is new? Reproductive technologies and custody politics," in Carol Smart and Selma Sevenhuijsen, *ibid.,* p. 266.

37. Michelle Stanworth, "Reproductive technologies and the deconstruction of motherhood," in Stanworth, ed., *Reproductive Technologies,* pp. 32–35.

38. The excellent and extensive literature on this issue includes: Rosalind Coward, *The Whole Truth: The Myth of Alternative Health* (London: Faber, 1989); Carol MacCormack and Marilyn Strathern, eds., *Nature, Culture and Gender* (Cambridge: Cambridge U. Press, 1980); Maureen McNeil, "Introduction" to her edited collection, *Gender and Expertise* (London: Free Association Books, 1987).

39. Henrietta Moore, *Feminism and Anthropology* (Minneapolis: U. of Minnesota Press, 1986); Felicity Edholm, "The unnatural family," in Elizabeth Whitelegg et al., eds., *The Changing Experience of Women* (Milton Keynes: Open U. Press, 1982).

40. Katherine Gieve, *Balancing Acts: On Being a Mother* (London: Virago, 1989).

41. From the novel *Beloved* by Toni Morrison (London: Picador, 1988). The experience of "Baby Suggs" is described on page 23.

42. Jacklyn Cock, *Maids and Madams: Domestic Workers under Apartheid* (London: The Women's Press, rev. edn 1989).

18

Notes of a Post-Sex Wars Theorizer

Carla Freccero

Origin stories about the women's movement are interested stories, all of them.
Katie King, "The situation of lesbianism as feminism's magical sign," *p. 65*

I do not believe that feminism is a matter, first or last, of sexuality.
June Jordan, *Civil Wars, p. 141*

I. Foreword

I transcribed at least three voices in this paper: the first voice would prefer to speak about this topic in a group of women.[1] The second voice is analytical and politically committed to comprehensive revolution, therefore somewhat impatient with the topic at hand. The third voice is that of a listener trying to paraphrase for the one who cannot speak within this text.

II. Introduction

ok, before i get started here i'm going to talk about porn, because i don't think any kind of academic article-style theoretical description will get us there. people say porn isn't violence, it's the representation of violence. but there is violence in representation. i feel it viscerally when i see the woman in the movie giving a blow-job to a black revolver, and there's a guy's hand on the trigger, and one on her head. it's my contention you can't draw the line between porn and any sexually explicit representation involving (at least one) human body, and while i do think that there's a sexist "regime of representation" out there, i agree with rosalind coward when she points out that porn is neither the sole nor the most serious offender.[2] for one thing there are ads, and a whole lot more people see, read, watch ads than they do porn. for another thing, porn is always considered bad or naughty or illicit or transgressive, whereas ads aren't. so basically i think porn's not the big issue here. and if we're going to do something about porn why not infiltrate the industry, set up competing systems of sexual representation, watch, read, see porn in groups and talk about it? and please, could we lighten up about fantasies? we haven't even begun to make inroads on what they are and already we want to say which ones are good and which ones are bad.

there's no way to decide in the abstract what are theoretically good thoughts and what are bad ones, politically i mean. that decision has to take place in context a group of people who are together struggling towards a goal, fighting for a cause. that's the only way theorizing should be happening to begin with; otherwise you get into all these undecidables (because there really are undecidables, theoretically) and you know that undecidables are not decided theoretically, they are decided. and the decision's not THE right one, THE best one, it's contingent, radically so, and hopefully subject to revision, modification, change, in other words, based on subsequent experience. whatever happened to theory/ praxis, experience/theory, the dialectic? this said, i'm about to launch into undialogical (and unself-deconstructive) theory and attempt to undialogically describe experience, taking katie king's sentence into account, meaning that i organize the conflicts around porn into a story, and a story constructs origins and ends, and is interested.[3] i don't want such storytelling to become a habit and i trust it won't if there are women's movements happening or, as bell hook says, if there is feminist movement, period.[4]

In *The Handmaid's Tale* (Boston: Houghton Mifflin, 1986), Margaret Atwood's masterful novel about a feminist dystopia, Aunt Lydia, rehabilitation instructor for the Handmaids, chillingly euphemizes female slavery in Gilead:

> There is more than one kind of freedom, . . . Freedom to and freedom from. In the days of anarchy, it was freedom to. Now you are being given freedom from. Don't underrate it. (p. 24)

Atwood depicts, here and throughout the novel, some of the consequences of the appeal to state protection that is a current and familiar dilemma in the struggle for "civil" or political rights. Women, under the old order, were jeopardized by rape, pornography, and ideological degradation; in Gilead they are protected from abuse by a strictly patriarchal state that claims total ownership of their bodies. They have become, literally, state property.

That Atwood chose the genre of utopia to explore some of the conflicts in North American feminism underscores the impasses of political theory in its attempt to address questions of sex and race discrimination within current legislative and political frameworks, for utopia is precisely that representational working out of what as yet has no theoretical solution.[5] Can the bourgeois political tradition, although constitutive of rights movements, ever adequately address systemic domination?

The United States has provided interesting laboratory conditions for the bourgeois political experiment. The civil rights movement of the early sixties sought to exploit contradictions between the interests of individual states and those of the federal government to achieve political rights for African Americans. Activists believed that federal interests were more inclusive because answerable to a wider and more disparate polis than that of the states or regions of the country. There was the hope that the acquisition of equal political rights would begin to impact upon white economic domination of African Americans. What began as an analysis of civil rights moved in the direction of a more radical class analysis, to which the Poor Peoples' March on Washington was to attest. Yet the achievement (however partial) of political rights has not rectified the enormous economic disparities that continue to subordinate Blacks to white power and render civil rights legislation vulnerable to changes in the political climate of the nation (as the recent Supreme Court rulings demonstrate).

The women's movement in the seventies proceeded in a somewhat analogous fashion, exploiting federal law to break the discriminatory policies of state legislation, as in the Roe v. Wade decision of the Supreme Court in 1973. It too, suffered from an initial focus on political rights as the means to economic empowerment, and its legacy is similar: statistics on the growing population of poor women and their children, as well as the rollback in Affirmative Action policies and abortion rights, attest to the limits of this strategy.

There are clearly limitations to a strategy of empowerment that chooses political rights as its privileged domain, particularly in the face of economic subordination. This does not mean that anyone can abandon rights or the political as fields of struggle, but it does mean that one can assess the limitations of certain rights disputes and establish priorities for action in movements for global human empowerment.[6]

III. The Movement

It seems astonishing, from the perspective of 1989, that pornography should have become so important in feminist movements and that it should have provoked such bitter animosities and deep divisions. Betty Friedan attested to its centrality in 1985, when she exclaimed in disgust, "Get off the pornography kick and face the real obscenity of poverty" (*New York Times Magazine,* November 3, 1985).

Atwood's novel not only criticizes the tactics of a branch of the North American women's movement, but also suggests a relation between tactical choices and philosophical positions. When the state oppresses a number of people by virtue of a certain commonality, it is on the basis of that commonality that people organize to become visible in their opposition to the state. But that does not necessarily mean that an all-encompassing "identity" exists among those people, though the legal identity produced may and often does (at least in the U.S.) become reified as it becomes totalizing. Identity politics may be an expedient means of acquiring rights (or unifying a "nation") but not necessarily descriptive of a metaphysical "essence" (as Frantz Fanon has argued in his studies of bourgeois, anti-colonial nationalism).[7] The identities or nations constructed in order to conduct a struggle for visibility and thus for rights or sovereignty produce the *appearance* of solid identity where none may (be thought to) exist. Thus, rather than claiming for pornography the central or most important oppression women suffer, the anti-pornography movement may have been an expedient means of attempting to unify women and create visibility at a time when women's movements were experiencing backlash from the dominant culture and when a conservative national administration was already eroding other gains.[8]

I understand one feminist anti-pornography movement of the late seventies and early eighties to have been, in part, an attempt to expose the systemic domination of women at a vulnerable point—vulnerable because there exists legislation already in place that facilitates anti-porn legislation, namely, obscenity laws, and because a significant portion of the U.S. population is already mobilized against this particular manifestation of misogyny, although for diverse and often contradictory reasons.

The most nationally visible political attempt to attack the pornography industry as agent of the sexual subordination of women was the anti-pornography ordinance co-authored by Andrea Dworkin and Catharine MacKinnon, acting as consultants to the Minneapolis City Attorney's Office in 1983.[9] The MacKinnon/Dworkin pornography ordinance sought to make damage by pornography actionable (by an individual woman claiming damage to herself or by an individual woman in the name of all women) in a civil procedure. One goal was thus to render economically costly what was perceived as a form of sex discrimination. Another goal was to create a gap in the legal system whereby women could insert themselves—their voices, their agencies—and thereby begin structurally to modify the patriarchal hegemony embodied in the U.S. law. An admirable strategy by any feminist account. But was the tactical decision to apply pressure in the particular area of female sexuality so clearly advisable?[10]

Proponents of the ordinance and others who denounced pornography, an industry that experienced significant growth in the late seventies and early eighties, heightened public consciousness of what had traditionally been a private matter, and in doing so exposed other "private" practices as matter for public politics: wife battering and violence against women generally, sexual abuse of women and children, sexual violence.[11] They also "deconstructed" the tenets of constitutional "freedom of expression" by exposing the collusion between a given social order and the forms of expression it is willing to protect, as well as the indeterminacy of the difference between representation and act.[12] The public circulation of hardcore and violent pornographic materials as objects of study also enabled many to understand the concept of systemic sexual subordination via its explicit representations. Finally, many (middle-class) women who had never been exposed to what was viewed by the dominant class as an all-male preserve got to "see" it and express their views about it, often in "mixed" company.[13]

Opposition to the ordinance was vociferous and intense within feminist movements. The Feminist Anti-Censorship Task Force (FACT) filed an *amicus* brief in the case, while Varda Burstyn edited a volume called *Women Against Censorship* that, among other things, critiques the ordinance itself. Dworkin and MacKinnon had already written extensively about their project, and their legislative efforts were accompanied by collections such as *Take Back The Night: Women on Pornography,* which, while not specifically directed at legislation, positions itself, principally through its contributors, "against" pornography.

Sex and its representations have a long non-feminist political history in the United States. The feminisms that situate themselves within the pornography debate perforce claim a certain commonality with the entire political tradition that frames the question. Thus no matter how carefully Andrew Dworkin and Catharine MacKinnon work to dissociate their ordinance from First Amendment issues, much of the debate about pornography and sexual practices moves between the poles of civil libertarianism (the "liberal" position) and moral absolutism (the anti-porn position of the New Right).[14] Neither position specifically addresses the interests of women conceived as a political category; each, rather, produces contradictions in its intersection with feminist theorizing. Civil libertarianism advocates the protection of the domain of the "private" from public intervention by the state, advocating therefore a minimum of state interference in personal liberties. But feminist sexual politics target precisely the domain of the "personal" or "private" as one in which much of women's oppression takes place. "The personal is political" undoes a masculinist libertarian view of the personal by identifying what was once an invisible site of oppression as the focus of a politics. Moral absolutism, on the other hand, seeks a single standard of morality for the polity, and while some feminisms indeed align themselves with such a position, it is historically opposed to the liberationist theories at the roots of most feminisms and sexual liberation movements. Although attempting to distance themselves from either of these traditional political positions, "cultural feminism" and Women Against Pornography (WAP) have a reputation for the latter, while the Feminist Anti-Censorship Task Force (FACT) has a reputation for the former.[15]

Much of the conflict within feminisms was produced around the theoretical assumptions underpinning legislative attempts to target pornography as sex discrimination (or sexual subordination) and denunciations of the genre as a whole.[16] Alice Echols describes, from a highly critical perspective, the branch of feminism whose philosophy, in her opinion, corresponds to the rhetoric deployed in the feminist anti-pornography movement. She calls this "cultural feminism," although those feminists call themselves "radical" feminists.[17] She argues that its ideology "mirrors dominant cultural assumptions about gender and sexuality" ("Cultural Feminism," p. 34). This mirroring may to some extent be necessary if one wishes to argue within the purview of the law in order to modify its treatment of the category in question. The difficulty arises when rhetorical positioning and ideology collapse into one.

I understand "cultural feminism" to have as its most basic assumption the belief that there is something that characterizes women which is fundamentally different from what characterizes men, whether the difference is initially constructed or not. This "difference" may in fact be "the common experience of oppression as women," and thus not biological or psychological, but in practice and in law it is often collapsed into an essential identity rather than a collection of experiences. Some of the assumptions in what is called "cultural feminism" or "essentialism" produce specific problems for feminist politics when this collapse occurs, the most common being that the identity equated with "women" will be that of women belonging to otherwise dominant groups in society: middle class, white, protestant or secular, heterosexual, over 18 and under 50.

The adoption of a dualistic, oppositional view of male and female whereby an aggressive, predatory, dehumanizing masculinity is opposed to a nurturant, humanizing, egalitarian, peaceful femininity (that is also, in an interesting twist, equated with lesbianism or its euphemistic, de-sexualized counterpart, "woman-identification") renders problematic the theorizing of female sexuality, particularly with regard to sexual desire and its relation to aggression. In many ways the feminist anti-pornography movement (although rightly critiquing the liberal notion of "consent") contributes to the suppression of female sexual desire and pleasure, as they are lived today, by positing a transcendent, non-aggressive, utopian sexuality that would exist in a non-partriarchal society.[18] Pornography, as that medium which sexualizes aggression (or, as Dworkin puts it, sexualizes domination and subordination), comes to be associated then with "masculine" sexuality, and, in the absence of a true feminine sexuality (because suppressed by patriarchy), women are thereby de-sexualized.

IV. Sex Wars

The dispute centered around a political tactic in the movement is thus only one aspect of the conflict, which also involved broader theoretical debates within feminism on (a feminist ethics or, some say, politics of) sexuality, debates which gave rise to a flurry of experimental, exciting, and creative writing as well as vituperation and insult. Public (and published) feminist discussions of sexuality reached their peak in the early eighties. A year after Ronald Reagan entered the Oval Office, *Heresies* published a sex issue; SAMOIS published its *Coming to Power: Writings and Graphics on Lesbian S/M;* Pat Califia's *Sapphistry* had just come out and was revised in 1983. In 1982 *Feminist Review* published a special issue on sexuality; and on April 24, 1982 Barnard College held its notorious conference, "Towards a Politics of Sexuality," published as *Pleasure and Danger*. *Feminist Review* subsequently published an issue with articles relating to that conference and the issues it raised. In 1983, the fledgling Kitchen Table Press published *Home Girls: A Black Feminist Anthology,* including discussions of sexuality among women of color.[19]

The conference and its Speakout on Politically Incorrect Sex (sponsored by the Lesbian Sex Mafia) exacerbated and publicized deep rifts among feminists, visible and documentable because the disputes were conducted in print. Position papers included the leaflet protesting the conference signed by the Coalition for a Feminist Sexuality and against Sadomasochism (accidentally published in *Feminist Studies* 9:1, spring 1983); the "Petition in Support of the Scholar and Feminist IX Conference" (published in *Pleasure and Danger*); letters to the Editor in *Feminist Studies;* debates in *The Village Voice* and *Gay Community News;* even entire volumes of collected essays, such as *Against Sadomasochism* and *Powers of Desire.* Reports from the press indicate that Barnard College confiscated the Diary of the conference (since published independently as *Diary of a Conference on Sexuality*), the Helena Rubenstein Foundation withdrew its financial support, and the independence of the Barnard Women's Center was curtailed, all as a result of the many "unorthodox" sexualities being discussed at the conference and the Speakout.[20]

> Represented at this conference are organizations that support and produce pornography, that promote sex roles and sadomasochism, and that have joined the straight and pedophile organizations in lobbying for an end to laws that protect children from sexual abuse by adults. Excluded from this conference are feminists who have developed the feminist analysis of sexual violence, who have organized a mass movement against pornography, who have fought media images that legitimize sexual violence, who believe that sadomasochism is reactionary, patriarchal sexuality, and who have worked to end the sexual abuse of children. (*Feminist Studies* 9:1, spring 1983; p. 180)

This statement of the leaflet by the Coalition for a Feminist Sexuality and against Sadomasochism (Women Against Violence Against Women [WAVAW], Women Against Pornography [WAP], New York Radical Feminists [NYRF] points to an exclusion in the conference (borne out by its publication, *Pleasure and Danger*) that is the primary source of discontent. Had the exclusion not occurred, the question of "a feminist sexuality" (for those excluded) might not have turned on the issue of lesbian sadomasochism alone, but on the strategic advisability or ideological necessity of a politics of feminist sexuality. As it is, while opening up a space within feminist theorizing for the discussion and analysis of women's actual sexual practices, the conference's exclusions (and the excluded's reactions) contributed to the alienation of what indeed looked like a mass movement (self-designated "radical feminists," generally the anti-pornography movement) that included many newly politicized feminists. This alienation, in turn, became such a focus of (predominantly middle-class white) feminist attention that, in my opinion, it obstructed other kinds of coalition building and organizing that would have been useful for the eighties. On the other hand, the rejection of sexual radicals or sexual "minorities" by mainstream feminism (NOW's 1980 resolution condemning S/M, cross-generational sex, pornography, and public sex, under the guise of a resolution for "gay and lesbian rights") facilitated alliances between feminist sexual radicals and gay (male) rights movements, which have become the strongest movements for sexual rights in the United States.[21]

Throughout this period of feminist sexual theorizing there appear writings by women across a broad spectrum of subject-positions. Yet the conference and ensuing sex wars alienated feminists for whom the politics of sexuality (as in sexual practices) was not the most important issue when framed in terms of the legitimacy of sadomasochistic sexual practices. Three voices from the conference point to theoretical issues obscured by the results of the event. Hortense Spillers's critique of the discourse of sexuality as a dominative mode interrogates the entire project of articulating such a discourse. Her essay concludes: "The goal is not an articulating of sexuality so much as it is a global restoration and dispersal of power. In such an act of restoration, sexuality is rendered one of several active predicates. So much depends on it" (*Pleasure and Danger*, p. 96). Gayle Rubin suggests that feminism is inadequate as the privileged site of a theory of sexuality: "Feminism is the theory of gender oppression. To automatically assume that this makes it the theory of sexual oppression is to fail to distinguish between gender, on the one hand, and erotic desire, on the other" (p. 307).

Cherríe Moraga's comments on the results of the Speakout still seem tactically and substantively relevant to the entire issue of a "politics of sexuality," whose political volatility has in fact preempted analysis. In "played between white hands," a letter to *off our backs* about the conference, she says, "The way the movement is breaking down around sex makes me feel like women of color are being played between two white (sector's) hands. And I don't like it" (*off our backs*, p. 23). The organizers downplayed S/M in soliciting some speakers for the event, then visually billed the Speakout as about S/M. Moraga argues that by not taking into account the already marginalized position of some women's movements within the dominant feminist community, the organizers may have rendered them all the more vulnerable. Finally, she asks a series of questions that have not, as yet, been analyzed in depth by feminists or by other movements whose politics include prescriptions for personal behavior.

> . . . Lesbian s/m has never been critically examined in any sensitive and realistic way, which could be useful to its feminist practitioners and to other feminists who simply want a right to their sexual desire, and at the same time, understand what that desire means in a racist/sexist and violent culture.
>
> So how does one build a sexual politic that incorporates this complexity? For example, what does it mean that some images and acts of s/m sex mirror actual acts

of violence visited upon people of color, Jews, and women as a group—and that some Jewish women and women of color are sexually stimulated by these? Do images mean anything in relation to life? Does sex influence non-sexual behavior? If so, what do we do about this, sexually? Can a class analysis provide us with any useful insights into the inefficacy of feminist sex theory to date? And finally, is sex separate from politics and if so, does it only become political when the "sex deviant" is denied his/her civil rights? (p. 23)

The right of lesbian feminist sadomasochists to call themselves feminists and to "come out" in feminist communities was part of what was at stake.[22] For radical ("cultural") feminists of the eighties (sometimes known as political lesbians), there is a connection between pornography and (lesbian) sadomasochism (heterosexuality being summarily regarded as reactionary sexual practice). If pornography sexualizes the subordination of women, then sadomasochism, by reenacting relations of domination and submission, celebrates that sexualization. The critique of compulsory heterosexuality (or marriage) as the dominant and repressive social institution for women seems justified, whereas the suggestion that the practice of sadomasochism (straight or otherwise) constitutes hegemonic practice does not. Sadomasochistic sexual practices are not "simply" a literalization of a metaphor for social relations; the dominant culture may indeed sanction metaphorically sadomasochistic relations, but at the same time it legislates against, stigmatizes, and condemns practicing sadomasochists.[23]

V. Good Girls/Bad Girls[24]

Gayle Rubin succinctly states why it is that the analysis of women's oppression should concern itself with sexuality at all: "Because sexuality is the nexus of the relationships between genders, much of the oppression of women is borne by, mediated through, and constituted within, sexuality" (*Pleasure and Danger,* pp. 300–301). However, historically sexuality has also been, in philosophic, political, economic, and social discourse, constitutive of women's identity prior to its identification as a mediator of oppression. Thus women's sexuality becomes a primary ground of contestation in the struggle for female emancipation. Cora Kaplan notes how the construction of women's subjectivity through sexual categories haunts the feminist appropriation of both radical and liberal humanist discourses.[25] She traces the genealogy of the disputes in contemporary feminist sexual ideologies to Rousseau's *Emile,* where "the possibility of women's civil, economic and psychological independence is rejected because it would also enable the independent and licentious exercise of her supposedly insatiable appetite" (p. 33) and notes that,

While most feminists have recognized that the regulation of female sexuality and the ideological mobilization of its threat to order are part of women's subordination, it is not surprising that they have too often accepted the paradigm that insists that desire is a regressive force in women's lives, and have called for a sublimation of women's sexual pleasure to meet a passionless and rational ideal. Rousseau's formulation has cast a long shadow that cannot be dispersed by simple inversions of his argument. As long as the idea survives that a reformed libidinal economy for women is the precondition for a successful feminist politics, women can always be seen as unready for emancipation. (*Sea Changes*, pp. 33–34)

Kaplan analyzes how Mary Wollstonecraft's *A Vindication of the Rights of Woman* accepts the negative description of female sexualty set forth by Rousseau (as that which undermines women's efforts to become rational political subjects on the one hand and, on the other, as that which threatens the social order with the possibility of infinite and uncontrollable circulation, or anarchy). Wollstonecraft seeks to redefine the causes of sexual degradation in order to argue for the political and social emancipation of women; she argues that emancipation will raise women above their corrupt anatomical destinies into sober and responsible bourgeois citizenship.[26] Kaplan demonstrates that Wollstonecraft, in suppressing female sexual desire, consolidated a class sexuality, whereby the middle-class woman is envisioned as sexually pure as a result of her education and sociopolitical emancipation, but lower-class women, exploited and living in squalor, are seen as sexually profligate. Once this division is made, it becomes easy to justify the denial of rights to subordinated classes of women.

This argument for emancipation is echoed throughout women's early suffrage struggles. The rhetoric is redeployed as a race/class distinction in the liberal racist discourses upholding a patriarchal "ideology of femininity" in order to argue for its moral and political purchase, during both the abolitionist and female suffrage struggles in the U.S. It appears in U.S. slave narratives (those written both by women and by men) where the "lesser virtue" of which the Black woman is accused is accepted in order to argue that the brutalization of slavery is the cause.[27] A modern version of this discourse informs the by-now-infamous 1965 Moynihan Report and its contemporary sequel, Bill Moyers's "The Vanishing Family: Crisis in Black America."[28]

The "good girl/bad girl" splits that persist within feminist mappings of sexuality, to distinguish between, for example, feminists and sex trade workers, lesbians and heterosexuals, vanillas and sadomasochists, also find their place solidly within this political tradition. Feminists employed in the production of sexually explicit entertainment (either in the pornography industry or as whores) thus argue that to exploit this moral distinction does not serve their interests in eliminating sexism or their oppression as women; many of them suggest a strategy familiar to U.S. labor movements of the twenties and thirties, mobilization of the workers themselves, rather than an appeal to statist paternalism to guarantee the political rights of sexually sublimated (coded "white") middle-class women.

VI. Exhibits and Capital

You were a hooker once, well, a lot actually, but formally only once. I mean before that you had used sex to get things from guys, traded sex for favors, presents, dinners, a kind of barter economy, he gets laid you get something else. That was high school, and all the bad girls you knew followed those rules, pretty informally but also pretty explicitly. In fact you often got criticized for taking "dudes" too seriously. Then there was the time, when you were working at a Pizza Parlor, that a middle-aged male customer gave you a ten dollar tip for a five dollar purchase, on purpose. Well, you knew what that meant. You already wore your uniform short-skirted and low-cut so you'd get big tips, but this was a proposition. You don't remember how you made contact the second time, but he used to take you out to the woods in his Harvester Scout, fuck you, and give you money. But that still wasn't formal. After a while you felt like you were getting screwed so you told him you were pregnant and needed three hundred dollars for an abortion and he gave them to you. And actually you got the money 'cause this boyfriend of yours needed money, and so you gave him the money. He was the same guy who became your pimp when you were a hooker for real for a week in Montreal. There you would dress up really nice and he'd take you to the bars he knew and approach some guy. You'd go with the guy to a hotel, ask for sixty bucks, get paid, get fucked, and get dropped off back at the bar where, stupid you, you gave your boyfriend/pimp the money. Now if you'd been a working girl would you have been that stupid with your money? And I think that's the point: you can't know what it would mean to be depending on this to live. Anyway, there was this one guy who wanted to fuck you in the ass, and though the idea really turns you on, the reality hurts a lot. You never get used to it. So you wouldn't let him and he figured out you weren't a real whore (though you denied it) and he only gave you forty bucks, but he asked if he could see you again, maybe meet you in Montreal once a month or so.

As you're saying this you're feeling a sense of revenge, that writing about these guys is getting back at them somehow. But you don't remember their names, not even your boyfriend (who, after that week, fed you LSD at his birthday party and while you were tripping and napping in his bed, invited all his friends to partake of you. You were vicious though, and kicked them out). Hey, you're no victim, ask anyone who knows you. You're glad you did it, it was exciting, if not altogether pleasant, and it makes a great story. But this event, and all the other stories you could tell, have fueled your feminist rage for years and years. You were sixteen when that guy tipped you, for chrissake, and seventeen when you were hooking. Sometimes you think it would have been nice to have the privilege of becoming an adult woman without becoming so damn tough, you know, staying sensitive, staying soft and vulnerable and all those things that feminine women are supposed to be. But that's your privilege too; as a middle-class white woman with her basic needs met, you experience sexual subordination as your most restraining, if not your sole, oppression. Thus, for you in this whole experience, the way the guys treated you was the worst part, not fear of arrest, not low pay, poor working conditions, inadequate health care, not general social stigmatization, or a host of other problems the sex workers in Good Girls/Bad Girls *talk about.*[29]

Sex workers provide an important corrective to the middle-class intellectual feminists' debates about pornography and sexuality in that they focus on the sex industry from the point of view of its labor force. The issue is thus no longer the commodity itself (pornography) nor the "private" sexual practices of individuals, but rather their convergence in the marketplace. Recent work has focused on this interaction between sex and capital and the relations of workers, consumers, and producers. The video, "Ecstasy Unlimited" (1985), directed by independent video artist Laura Kipnis, analyzes the commodification of sexuality. It cautions those who adopt an unproblematic language of liberation with regard to the visible proliferation of sexual identities and sexualities in the United States. Consumer capitalism profits from markets consolidated around these identities, permitting even greater extensions of social control.[30] In characteristic tragicomic mode, the video also suggests that sadomasochistic sexual practices are the inscription onto the "first world" body of the tragedies of the "third world," a return of the politically repressed as sexual symptom.

Capitalist challenges to the reigning patriarchal "regime of representation" have come into being, complicating the ways in which sexism operates in cultural representations of women. Andrew Ross describes the development of a porn industry that targets a female consumer, such as Femme Productions, which also produces porn films directed by famous female porn stars (*No Respect*, pp. 171–172). Socialist feminist porn actress Nina Hartley describes the extent to which feminist organizing has influenced the industry.[31] MTV, perhaps one of the most hetero male-dominated spheres of representation, has also had to contend with (albeit ambiguous) challenges to its semiotic codes by stars like Madonna, whose gender-bending code dressing (as in "Open Your Heart" and "Express Yourself") and self-construction as active desiring agent (as in "Like a Prayer" and "Express Yourself") have enormous influence on adolescent female self-construction.[32] Indeed, relationships between cultural forms and consumers are mediated in ways far more complex than the anti-porn movement suggests.

Ross, in his work on pornography as popular culture, advocates developing "a cultural politics which seeks to *learn from* the forms and discourses of popular pleasure, rather than adopting or supporting a legislative posture in the name of the popular" (*No Respect*, p. 207). Thus it is only by refusing to contend with popular culture that feminists risk losing the gains that might be made in "educating desire."[33] Ross argues that "It may be that sex will have to become fully capitalist before it can be anything else," and suggests a strategy of "exploit[ing] the short-term pragmatic benefits of libertarian principles" in order to "salvage any available gains, under circumstances that are never ideal, from the contradictions of a capitalist culture" (p. 189).

When you fantasize, you sometimes imagine that you belong to a man who offers your sexual services to his friends; when sex acts occur they involve multiple penetration: there's a penis in your mouth and one in your anus usually (you flip back and forth between vagina and anus, and lately you've needed someone's mouth doing things to your clit as well—and this is usually, though not always, a woman). There's quite a bit of s/m: I mean you get tied up or beaten or penetrated with objects that cause pain, etc., and lately, since the latest issue of On Our Backs, *there have been women wearing prophylactic penises fucking you). You've tried playing with the races of your captors/rapists, but you're a white middle-class anti-racist politically left woman, so I think that must be why it's so hard for you to imagine the men as Black. You said you did have a fantasy the other day where the guy was Native American and working class, but it was a romantic fantasy, with only one short strictly sexual sequence in it. And he was the only guy involved. (And you had a daughter by him . . . but you've been reading Michael Dorris's* Yellow Raft in Blue Water, *so it figures.)*

Your fantasies come from the pornographic stuff you've read and seen all your life. It started with finding your father's collection. You don't remember the names of the novels you found there, but they excited you. You've never been courageous about purchasing porn: you relied on friends, accidental discoveries, other peoples' porn videos. Hey, you never even went out and bought your own vibrator! You got your own because you bought it for a friend who later said her pussy was too small and it hurt so she gave it back to you. It had rubber covers, one that was like a French Tickler with nubs all over it, and one that was a lifelike white male penis. That's the one you put on the vibrator permanently, but lately it seems weird to have what used to be called a "flesh color" penis. You saw a movie once where the vibrator was glow-in-the-dark hot pink, not "life-like" at all, and it made you wonder whether the illusion was relevant for you.

Your favorite porn video so far is "Ginger's Girl-Girl Hits," with excerpts from all of Ginger's movies, and a between-sequence narration from Ginger introducing each sequence. I think it's interesting that you like the girl-girl scenes; you think it's partly because the straight porn always has such ugly-looking guys whose penises are never fully erect. That's one of the reasons you like gay male porn—there are erect penises in the visuals. Now, the only kind of porn you feel ok buying in a store is lesbian porn, and you love it, especially the rough stuff. "For the Adventurous Lesbian" says On Our Backs. *The stories are lousy, you like the pictures better. The reason you can buy that stuff is because it's sold in women's bookstores; men's porn shops intimidate you, and you still haven't been able to rent the porn videos from stores.*

So what do these fantasies say about you? You know there's comfort in such a densely peopled fantasy world; fantasies keep the loneliness at bay. They keep you young and open too, without having to go through the humiliation that awaits older women who dare to embark on sexual quests, like Maryse Holder in "A Winter Tan." They give you power: you are always at the center of the scene. And you can change them.

VIII. Political Agendas

The particular form that public political concern with sex has taken in the eighties results in part from the convergence of pressure from feminists and sexual rights groups with the rise of the New Right and its moral absolutism, in part from the AIDS crisis and the homophobic reverberations in the culture.[34] Senator Jesse Helms's proposed amendment to the Fiscal Year 1990 Interior and Related Agencies Appropriations Bill (approved in the senate by a voice vote) illustrates, in apocalyptic fashion, the degree zero of appeals to legislate against representations of sexuality (specifically, the gay sadomasochism of some of Robert Mapplethorpe's photographs):

> None of the funds authorized to be appropriated pursuant to this act may be used to promote, disseminate, or produce—(1) obscene or indecent materials, including but not limited to depictions of sadomasochism, homo-eroticism, the exploitation of children, or individuals engaged in sex acts; or (2) material which denigrates the objects or beliefs of the adherents of a particular religion or non-religion; or (3) material which denigrates, debases, or reviles a person, group, or class of citizens on the basis of race, creed, sex, handicap, age, or national origin. (*Modern Language Association Newsletter,* August 9, 1989)

The denial of state funding to all representations of sexuality involving human bodies would relinquish such representation to capital, which will continue to produce, not to satisfy but to increase, desire and demand. Ironically, legislation that targets principally non-profit efforts, such as funding of the arts and sex and AIDS education, would encourage those seeking to learn about sex to make even greater use of pornography.

Within feminism, some of the most informative and explicit information about sexuality and AIDS has been produced by precisely those "pornographic" publications that the anti-pornography movement condemns within feminism, such as *On Our Backs* and Pat Califia's *Macho Sluts*. Straights and vanillas can find clear, explicit, non-moralistic, practical descriptions of AIDS prevention measures and safer sex techniques here, couched in a manner designed to salvage pleasure, to increase rather than corral it.[35]

IX. Conclusion

Returning to the epigraph by June Jordan at the beginning of this paper, it must be said that many, if not most, of the women in the world today do not have the privilege of debating the issue of a feminist sexual praxis.[36] Rekha Basu, in "Sexual Imperialism: The Case of Indian Women in Britain," argues that the sexuality of "Third World" women has often been so scrutinized that the struggle is for privacy rather than publicity:

> As Third World women, our sexuality has been subject to public scrutiny and judgment. We are viewed as either oversexed or asexual, immoral or puritanical. We are denied the right to sexual privacy as well as the freedom to make our own sexual choices. Either way, we must struggle to make our sexuality exclusively our own domain. (*Heresies* 12 (1981): 71–73; p. 71)

Basu's statement is echoed by many "Third World" feminists both abroad and in the United States. Here, the "politics of sexuality" is about the sexual violence visited upon women and not, "first or last," about women's sexual practices.[37] For those who have experienced the full impact of imperialist sexual violence, state involvement in sexual practices hints of genocide, not protection; indeed, many middle-class women in the United States are belatedly coming to terms with a "Gileadean regime."

Feminist movement and feminist thinking have the potential to conceive action and analysis in staggeringly revolutionary terms, and there are tactical priorities: imperialism, class stratification, the conditions of the neediest women in the United States. Many of the current conflicts in feminism continue to evade these priorities. Why?

Notes

1. My title is taken from the term used by B. Ruby Rich in her review essay, "Feminism and Sexuality in the 1980s" in *Feminist Studies* 12:3 (fall 1986): 525–561. I would like to thank Katie King for her amazing bibliography, and Cirri Nottage, who was my research assistant for this paper and is a great friend.

2. Rosalind Coward, "Sexual Violence and Sexuality" in Feminist Review, ed., *Sexuality: A Reader* (London: Virago Press, 1987), pp. 307–325.

3. Katie King, "The situation of lesbianism as feminism's magical sign: contests for meaning and the U.S. women's movement, 1968–1972" in *Communication* 9 (1986): 65–91.

4. See Bell Hooks, *Talking Back: Thinking Feminist/Thinking Black* (Boston: South End Press, 1989), especially chapter four, "Feminism: A Transformational Politic," pp. 19–27.

5. For a political analysis of utopian discourse see Fredric Jameson, "Of Islands and Trenches: Neutralization and the Production of Utopian Discourse" in *Diacritics* 7:2 (summer 1977): 2–21; also Carla Freccero, "Rabelais's 'Abbaye de Thélème': Utopia as Supplement" in *L'esprit créateur* 25:1 (spring 1985): 73–87.

6. Interesting theoretical debates among legal scholars about constitutional rights have most recently come to the fore in the Critical Legal Studies movement and its critics. See the *Harvard Civil Rights/Civil Liberties Law Review* 22:2 (spring 1987), "Minority Critiques of the Critical Legal Studies Movement." For other discussions of this issue see Jules Lobel, ed., *A Less Than Perfect Union: Alternative perspectives on the U.S. Constitution* (New York: Monthly Review Press, 1988); and Patricia Williams, "On Being the Object of Property" in *Signs: Journal of Women in Culture and Society* 14:1 (autumn 1988): 5–24.

7. See, in particular, *The Wretched of the Earth,* trans. Constance Farrington (New York: Grove Press, 1966), the chapters on "Spontaneity" and "The Pitfalls of National Consciousness."

8. Ann Snitow makes this point in "Retrenchment Versus Transformation: The Politics of the Antipornography Movement," pp. 110–111, in Varda Burstyn, ed., *Women Against Censorship* (Vancouver: Douglas & McIntyre, 1985), pp. 107–120. See also Alice Echols, "Cultural Feminism: Feminist Capitalism and the Anti-Pornography Movement" in *Social Text* 7 (1983): 34–53. Two overviews of the anti-pornography movement in the U.S., in particular, offer interesting perspectives from outside the polarized oppositions: see Andrew Ross, *No Respect: Intellectuals and Popular Culture* (New York: Routledge, 1989) and Caroline Ramazanoglu, *Feminism and the Contradictions of Oppression* (New York: Routledge, 1989).

9. Margaret Baldwin, "The Sexuality of Inequality: The Minneapolis Pornography Ordinance" in *Law and Inequality* 2 (1984): 629–653. See also Andrea Dworkin, "Against the Male Flood: Censorship, Pornography, and Equality" in *Harvard Women's Law Journal* 8:1 (1985): 1–29. See also Catharine MacKinnon, "Pornography as Sex Discrimination" in *Law and Inequality* 4:17 (1986): 38–49; and Michael A. Gershel, "Evaluating A Proposed Civil Rights Approach to Pornography: Legal Analysis as if Women Mattered" in the *William Mitchell Law Review* 11 (1985): 41–80. On December 30, 1983, the Minneapolis City Council included pornography as a form of sex discrimination in its municipal civil rights ordinance. Mayor Donald Fraser vetoed the ordinance on January 5, 1984, on the grounds that it violated the constitutional right of free speech. On May 1st of that year, Indianapolis Mayor Donald Hudnut III signed a modified version of the ordinance into law. The ordinance was challenged by the American Booksellers Association, Inc. and other distributors, including Video Shack, Inc. In November of 1984, the District Court for the Southern Division of Indiana found in favor of the plaintiffs, ruling against the ordinance. In August 1985, the U.S. Court of Appeals for the Seventh Circuit upheld the lower court's ruling. On February 24, 1986, the Supreme Court declared the anti-pornography ordinance unconstitutional because it violated the First Amendment right of free speech. See *American Booksellers Association v. Hudnut,* 598 F.Supp. 1316 (S.D. Ind. 1984) and *American Booksellers Association v. Hudnut,* 771 F.2d 323 (7th Cir. 1985); see also Susan Gubar and Joan Hoff, eds., *For Adult Users Only: The*

Dilemma of Violent Pornography (Bloomington: Indiana Univ. Press, 1989), pp. 8–9.

10. For a description and critical analysis of the ordinance see Lisa Duggan, Nan Hunter, and Carole S. Vance, "False Promises: Feminist Antipornography Legislation in the U.S." in Varda Burstyn, ed., *Women Against Censorship*, pp. 130–151.

11. Rosalind Coward makes this point in "Sexual Violence and Sexuality"; see Andrew Ross, *No Respect*, pp. 171–208, and Jeffrey Weeks, *Sexuality* (Chichester: Ellis Horwood, 1986), p. 93, on the growth of the pornography industry in the seventies and eighties. The "Public Hearings on Ordinances to Add Pornography as Discrimination Against Women: Before the Minneapolis City Council Government Operations Committee," 1st Sess. 4–12 (December 12, 1983) is an astonishing document of testimony by women claiming damage as a result of pornography.

12. See, in particular, Andrea Dworkin, "Against The Male Flood" and *Pornography: Men Possessing Women* (New York: Perigee Books, 1979, repr. 1981); Catharine MacKinnon, *Feminism Unmodified: Discourses on Life and Law* (Cambridge, Ma.; Harvard Univ. Press, 1987), part III. For a greater diversity of views, with the broad goal of consciousness-raising, see Laura Lederer, ed. *Take Back the Night: Women on Pornography* (New York: William Morrow, 1980). Alice Walker's essay in this collection, "Coming Apart," brilliantly articulates relations between theory and praxis in the fiction of a consciousness-raising struggle between a husband and wife.

13. B. Ruby Rich makes this point in her incisive critique of the Canadian film, "Not A Love Story: A Motion Picture about Pornography"; see "Anti-Porn: Soft Issue, Hard World" in Feminist Review, ed., *Sexuality: A Reader*, 340–354. See also Andrew Ross's critique of the attitudes of intellectuals towards pornography conceived of as popular culture in *No Respect*.

14. Jeffrey Weeks, in *Sexuality*, p. 100, uses these terms, but talks about three stances: libertarian, liberal-pluralist, and moral absolutist. He also points out that, in their view of sexuality as "natural," "libertarianism and absolutism are mirror-images of one another: both are committed to a view of sexuality which transcends the bounds of mere history" (p. 101). Rosalind Coward argues in "Sexual Violence," p. 323: "I don't think that feminism can afford to get caught up in the major political positions which have hegemonized our thinking about pornography; that is, the liberal 'anything goes so long as it's in private, without offence to "reasonable" people' or the pro-familial, right-wing, anti-sex position."

15. Andrew Ross discusses feminism's critique of libertarianism and, citing Gayle Rubin, argues that "a politics of sexuality that is relatively autonomous from categories of gender may be needed to achieve and guarantee the full sexual rights of sexual minorities" (*No Respect*, p. 177). Ross wants to call this politics the "liberatory imagination" which, he writes, "sets the agenda of radical democracy beyond liberal pragmatism in pursuit of claims, actions, rights, desires, pleasures, and thoughts that are often still considered too illegitimate to be recognized as political" (p. 177).

16. Both MacKinnon and Dworkin have written extensively on the theoretical/philosophical/ideological positions informing their movement politics in ways consonant with the rhetoric of the ordinance and the anti-pornography movement. For an intelligent

and, I think, fair though very critical assessment of MacKinnon's analysis in *Feminism Unmodified*, see Mariana Valverde, "Beyond Gender Dangers and Private Pleasures: Theory and Ethics in the Sex Debates" in *Feminist Studies* 15:2 (summer 1989): 237–254. This issue of *Feminist Studies* is devoted to "the problematics of heterosexuality."

17. Alice Echols, "Cultural Feminism: Feminist Capitalism and the Anti-Pornography Movement." This is a wild and fascinating essay, linking the assumptions of WAP (Women Against Pornography) to those of the feminist capitalist projects such as FEN (Feminist Economic Network) that became, of course, more capitalist than feminist. Echols argues that "cultural" feminism is the current dominant strain of "radical" feminism. She wants to make a distinction between the earlier radical feminism, which "had sought the abolition of gender as a meaningful category" (p. 34) and the cultural feminism emerging in the mid-seventies, which "equates women's liberation with the development and preservation of a female counterculture" (p. 35). One question I have with regard to Echols's argument is whether she means to discuss cultural feminism as a white women's theory and, if so, why does she not theorize this aspect of the theory as well?

18. For a feminist critique of the notion of consent, see Catharine MacKinnon, *Feminism Unmodified*, introduction: "The Art of the Impossible." See also her excellent critique of objectivity as objectification and its critique: "Desire and Power: A Feminist Perspective" in Cary Nelson and Lawrence Grossberg, eds., *Marxism and the Interpretation of Culture* (Urbana: Univ. of Illinois Press, 1988): 105–121.

19. Pat Califia, *Sapphistry: The Book of Lesbian Sexuality* (n.a.: Naiad Press, 1980, repr. 1988); Catharine Stimpson and Ethel Spector Person, eds., *Women: Sex and Sexuality* (Chicago: Univ. of Chicago Press, 1980); *Heresies* 3:4, Issue 12, "Sex Issue" (1981); SAMOIS, ed., *Coming to Power: Writings and Graphics on Lesbian S/M* (Boston: Alyson Publications, 1981); *Feminist Review* 11 (1982); Ann Snitow, Christine Stansell, and Sharon Thompson, eds., *Powers of Desire: The Politics of Sexuality* (New York: Monthly Review Press, 1983); Barbara Smith, ed., *Home Girls: A Black Feminist Anthology* (New York: Kitchen Table: Women of Color Press, 1983); Carole S. Vance, ed., *Pleasure and Danger: Exploring Female Sexuality* (Boston: Routledge & Kegan Paul, 1984).

20. For an amusing account of the conference, see Lisa Orlando, "Lust at Last! Or Spandex Invades the Academy" in *Gay Community News,* May 15, 1982 (pp. 8–9); for responses to the conference, see *Feminist Review* 13 (spring 1983); *Feminist Studies* 9:1,3 (spring, fall 1983) in the "Notes and Letters" sections; Lisa Orlando, "Bad Girls and 'Good' Politics" and Ellen Willis, "Who is a Feminist? A Letter to Robin Morgan" in *Voice Literary Supplement* December 13, 1982; *GCN Book Review*, December 4, 1982; numerous letters in *GCN* 1982–1983; the *Village Voice*, Dec. 24–Jan. 4, 1983; and *off our backs* 12:7 (July 1982), 12:10 (November 1982), etc. The location of the conference and the presses in New York City contributed to the national visibility of this particular conference and these particular disputes; Cherríe Moraga makes reference to others in *off our backs* 12:7 (July 1982) but none had the visibility of the Barnard Conference.

Volumes published as part of the disputes included Robin Ruth Linden, Darlene R. Pagano, Diana E. H. Russell, Susan Leigh Star, eds., *Against Sadomasochism:*

A Radical Feminist Analysis (San Francisco: Frog in the Well 1982); and Varda Burstyn, ed., *Women Against Censorship*.

21. See Gayle Rubin's excellent article, "The Leather Menace: Comments on Politics and S/M" in SAMOIS, ed., *Coming to Power*, pp. 194–229.

22. For the somewhat similar configuration of these issues in the U.K., see Susan Ardill and Sue O'Sullivan, "Upsetting the Applecart: Difference, Desire and Lesbian Sadomasochism" in Feminist Review, ed., *Sexuality: A Reader*, pp. 277–304.

23. Of those who have tried to analyze heterosexual sadomasochism, see in particular Robert Stoller, *Sexual Excitement: The Dynamics of Erotic Life* (New York Pantheon Books, 1979), which focuses particularly on sadomasochistic fantasies as ways of working out aggression; and Linda Williams, "Power, Pleasure, and Perversion: Sadomasochistic Film Pornography" in *Representations* 27 (summer 1989): 37–65. Williams's work concentrates on the agency involved in masochism and goes so far as to suggest a subversive potential for sadomasochism: "The rise of sadomasochism in the full variety of its forms may very well indicate some partial, yet important, challenges to patriarchal power and pleasure. In the genre of video and film pornography, S/M's emphasis on oscillating positions over strict sexual identities, and its extension of sexual norms to include sadomasochistic play and fantasy, suggest a regime of relative differentiations over absolute difference" (p. 60).

24. Laurie Bell, ed., *Good Girls/Bad Girls: Sex Trade Workers and Feminists Face to Face* (Toronto: OPIRG, 1987).

25. *Sea Changes: Culture and Feminism* (London: Verso, 1986). See chapter two: "Wild Nights: Pleasure/Sexuality/Feminism," pp. 31–56.

26. For some interesting discussions of how "woman" and women's sexuality figure in political discourse see Neil Hertz, "Medusa's Head: Male Hysteria under Political Pressure" and the response from Catherine Gallagher in Neil Hertz, *The End of the Line* (New York: Columbia Univ. Press, 1985), pp. 161–196. For the deployment of "woman" and her sexual meanings in the political discourse around "liberty" see Kaja Silverman, "Liberty, Maternity, Commodification" in *New Formations* 5 (summer 1988): 69–89.

27. See Harriet Jacobs, *Incidents in the Life of a Slave Girl, Written by Herself*, ed. by Jean Fagan Yellin (Cambridge, Ma.: Harvard Univ. Press, 1987); Mary Helen Washington, *Invented Lives: Narratives of Black Women 1860–1960* (Garden City, N.Y.: Anchor Press, 1987), pp. 3–15; William Wells Brown, *Clotel, or The President's Daughter: A Narrative of Slave Life in the United States*, ed. by William Edward Farrison (New York: Carol Publishing Group, 1969); Harriet Wilson, *Our Nig; or, Sketches from the Life of a Free Black* (New York: Random House, 1983); on the white abolitionist argument see Barbara Andolsen, *"Daughters of Jefferson, Daughters of Bootblacks": Racism and American Feminism* (Macon, Ga.: Mercer Univ. Press, 1986); and Angela Davis, *Women, Race, and Class* (New York: Vintage Books, 1981).

28. Moynihan argued that the legacy of slavery created a pathology in the Black family, which he described as matriarchal, consisting of dominating maternal figures and emasculated men. Until recently, many of the critiques of the Moynihan Report

persisted in constructing the "Black woman" as deviating from a model of femininity assumed to be the norm. See William Ryan, *Blaming the Victim* (New York: Pantheon Books, 1971), chapter three: "Mammy Observed: Fixing the Negro Family," pp. 61–85. Angela Davis makes this point in *Woman, Race, and Class*. Brilliant correctives to the racist sexist analysis of Moynihan and Moyers can be found in *The Nation* (July 24/31, 1989), Special Issue: "Scapegoating the Black Family: Black Women Speak." See especially Jewell Handy Gresham, "The Politics of Family in America," pp. 116–122. See also Rennie Simson, "The Afro-American Female: The Historical Context of the Construction of Sexual Identity," pp. 229–235; and Barbara Omolade, "Hearts of Darkness," pp. 350–367; both in Snitow, Stansell, and Thompson, eds., *Powers of Desire*.

29. See also Frédérique Delacoste and Priscilla Alexander, eds., *Sex Work: Writings by Women in the Sex Industry* (Pittsburgh: Cleis Press, 1987).

30. Laura Kipnis, "Ecstasy Unlimited: The Interpenetrations of Sex and Capital" (1985). Andrew Ross also discusses this in *No Respect*, pp. 188–189.

31. *Shmate: A Journal of Progressive Jewish Thought* 21/22 (spring 1989), "Focus: Pornography" contains interviews with Nina Hartley, self-identified Jewish socialist feminist porn star, founder of the Pink Ladies Social Club, a rap-group for women in sex work that publishes a bi-monthly newsletter, including a *Health and Hygiene Report* column by Hartley.

32. See John Fiske's studies of adolescent female's responses to Madonna, "British Cultural Studies" in R. Allen, ed., *Channels of Discourse: Television and Contemporary Criticism* (Chapel Hill: Univ. of North Carolina Press, 1987), 254–289; also *Television Culture* (London: Methuen, 1987), especially chapter twelve, "Pleasure and Play," pp. 224–239.

33. Richard Dyer argues for this approach to gay male porn in "Male Gay Porn: Coming to Terms," *Jump Cut* 30 (1985): 27–29. Andrew Ross also makes the case, by analyzing the structural organization of pornography according to the market it targets. He writes, "What, then, is so different about pornography that it can be considered a respectful way to think about educating the popular body? One possible answer to that question is that the education of desire through pornography, however it is conceived and practices, would have to involve *producing* pleasure, rather than *reducing* or combating pleasure" (*No Respect*, p. 199).

34. See Jeffrey Weeks, *Sexuality,* and Andrew Ross, *No Respect,* for analyses of the political importance of sexuality in the United States in the 1980s.

35. Susie Bright's "Toys For Us" column in the July–August 1989 issue of *On Our Backs* includes an enlightening report of a conference of AIDS care-givers and HIV + women and their lovers about pleasure after positive diagnosis. Pat Califia's *Macho Sluts: Erotic Fiction* (Boston: Alyson Publications, 1988) contains a feisty and interesting introduction about lesbian pornography which raises various "sex wars" issues, as well as "A Note on AIDS, Lesbians, and Safer Sex" at the end of the book providing helpful and radically non-judgmental information about safer sex and safer shooting for all women. It is very difficult, in general, to get information about HIV and menstrual blood, HIV and sex toys, HIV and tatoos, to mention a few of the subjects covered in this section. One impressive aspect of Califia's work is that she

exposes the gap between people's actual sexual practices and their self-identifications as gay, lesbian, bi, straight, which may, but often do not correspond.

36. June Jordan, *Civil Wars* (Boston, Beacon Press, 1981). The essay is entitled "Where is the Love?" and was written in 1978.

37. See Rennie Simson, "The Afro-American Female: The Historical Context of the Construction of Sexual Identity"; Barbara Omolade, "Hearts of Darkness"; and Jacqueline Dowd Hall, " 'The Mind That Burns in Each Body,' " which is a brilliant psychoanalytic and historical analysis of the interconnections of racial and sexual violence. All three essays are in Snitow, Stansell, and Thompson, eds., *Powers of Desire*.

19

Feminism and Difference: The Perils of Writing as a Woman on Women in Algeria

Marnia Lazreg

At the heart of the feminist project, East and West, is a desire to dismantle the existing order of things and reconstruct it to fit one's own needs. This desire is best expressed in Omar Khayyam's cry:

Ah love! Could you and I with Him conspire
To grasp this sorry scheme of things entire
Would not we shatter it to bits—and then
Remould it in the heart's desire![1]

However, feminists, East and West, differ in the grasp they have on this "sorry scheme of things" and the tools they use to "shatter it to bits." They also differ as to whether the process of remolding things can take place at all. Indeed, Western academic feminists can rediscover their womanhood, attempt to redefine it, and produce their own knowledge of themselves hampered only by what many perceive as male domination.[2] Ultimately, Western feminists operate on their own social and intellectual ground and under the unstated assumption that their societies are perfectible. In this respect, feminist critical practice takes on an air of normalcy. It appears as part of a reasonable (even if difficult) project for greater gender equality.

By contrast, the Algerian and Middle Eastern feminist project unfolds within an external frame of reference and according to equally external standards. Under these circumstances the consciousness of one's womanhood coincides with the realization that it has already been appropriated in one form or another by outsiders, women as well as men, experts in things Middle Eastern. In this sense, the feminist project is warped and rarely brings with it the potential for personal liberation that it does in this country or in Europe. The forms of expression used by Algerian feminists are, in fact, caught between three overlapping discourses, namely, the male discourse on gender difference, social science discourse on the peoples of North Africa and the Middle East, and academic discourses (whether feminist or protofeminist) on women from these same societies.

This article initially grew out of a preliminary reflection on the nature and specificity of U.S. feminist theory and on the ongoing search for a feminist epistemology. My forays into the production of U.S. feminist knowledge, at a time when feminism appears to be undergoing a crisis, impressed upon me the fact that academic feminism has yet to break away from the philosophical and theoretical heritage it has so powerfully questioned.[3] Knowledge is produced not only within a socioeconomic and political framework but also within an intellectual tradition with stated and unstated assumptions. Although it questions traditional assumptions, academic feminism has often neglected to investigate its own premises. If it were to do so more often, it might become apparent that "traditional" social science categories have not yet been transformed but have been given a different sex instead.[4]

When I turned my attention away from the center of the debate over feminist theory and epistemology to its North African and Middle Eastern periphery, for example, I noticed three intriguing phenomena. First, the interest of U.S. feminists in women from these parts of the world has spurred a growing literature that is noteworthy for its relative lack of theoretical import. With a few exceptions, women who write about North African and Middle Eastern women do not identify themselves as feminist, yet their work finds its legitimacy in academic feminism's need for information about their subject matter.[5] Second, "Eastern" feminists writing for a Western audience about women in their home countries have done so with the generally unstated assumption that U.S. feminist knowledge can be expanded or accommodated but seldom questioned.[6] U.S. minority women, in contrast, have consistently challenged academic feminist projects in a variety of ways. In so doing they have pointed out problem areas that feminist knowledge must address and resolve before it can claim to be an alternative to "traditional" knowledge.[7] Third, although U.S. feminists (like their European counterparts) have sought to define and carve out a space in which to ground their criticism, "Eastern" feminists have simply adjusted their inquiry to fill the blanks in the geographical distribution made available to them by U.S. feminist liberalism.[8] These observations on feminist knowledge, East and West, led me to search for the connecting links between Western feminist knowledge writ large and constituted knowledge, through the study of the concrete case of Algeria. What I discovered was a continuity between the traditional social science modes of apprehending North African and Middle Eastern societies rooted as they are in French colonial epistemology and academic women's treatment from these societies.[9] One continuity, for example, is expressed in the predominance of a "religious paradigm" that gives religion a privileged explanatory power.[10] Most academic feminist practice takes place within this paradigm, thereby reproducing its presuppositions and reinforcing its dominant position. This process takes place even when feminists claim they are aware of the paradigm's flaws.[11]

I also discovered a temporal and conceptual continuity between female (often protofeminist) and feminist discourses.[12] What was written about Algerian women by women in the first part of this century is reproduced in one form or another in the writings of contemporary French women and U.S. feminists about the same subject matter. More importantly, the themes defined by the French colonial or neocolonial discourse as significant for understanding Algerian women are the ones found today in Eastern feminists' writings.[13]

In the pages that follow I will describe some of these continuities and will suggest some of the ways in which poststructuralism impacts upon them. I will also discuss the need for reevaluating the feminist project within a humanistic/ ethical framework.

The Social Science and Feminist Paradigms

The study of Middle Eastern and North African societies has been plagued by a number of conceptual and methodological problems that prompted the British sociologist Bryan S. Turner to say that it "lags behind other area studies in both theoretical and substantive terms." Indeed, it is "underdeveloped."[14] Scholarship on North African and Middle Eastern societies typically focuses on Islam as a privileged subject of inquiry whether it is dealt with as a religion or as a culture. Underlying the study of these societies are a number of problematical assumptions. First, Islam is seen as a self-contained and flawed belief system impervious to change. In sociology, this assumption finds its theoretical justification in the work of Max Weber.[15] Second, Islamic civilization is assumed to have been in decline and to continue to decline. The "decline thesis," best exemplified in the work of H.A.R. Gibb and Harold Bowen,[16] prompted David Waines to say that "the birth of Islam is also the genesis of its decline."[17] Attempts made by indigenous people to change their institutions are more often than not explained in terms of a return to Islam. This is well illustrated by the work of Clifford Geertz on what he calls "scripturalism."[18] Last but not least, it is assumed that "Islam cannot produce adequate, scientific knowledge of itself, since the political conditions of Islamic societies preclude critical, autonomous scholarship. Islam requires Western science to produce valid knowledge of the culture and social organization of the Islamic world."[19]

Such science has managed to keep the study of North Africa and the Middle East in a sort of intellectual ghetto where theoretical and methodological developments that take place in the mainstream of social science are somehow deemed inapplicable. For instance, up until recently, one could not talk about social classes in the Middle East but only of social hierarchies, or mosaics of people. One cannot speak about revolution but only of upheavals and coups. One still cannot talk about self-knowledge but only of "local knowledge" or "the native's point of view."[20]

Even when efforts are made by well-intentioned scholars to accommodate theoretical/methodological developments from other fields, they end up reinforcing the old problematical assumptions. For example, the recent focus on "popular culture" feeds into the view of Islam as divided up into the orthodox and the mystical. Similarly, the introduction of the concept of class in the study of the Middle East and North Africa has sometimes resulted in making proletarian rebels out of theologians and/or members of religious sects.[21]

A bird's-eye view of the literature by women, whether they are feminists or only have interests in women's questions, indicates that by and large they reproduce the problematical assumptions that underlie the area study of the Middle East and North Africa.

Academic women's work on Middle Eastern and North African women is dominated by the religion/tradition paradigm and is characterized by a variant of what the late C. Wright Mills called "abstracted empiricism."[22] That is, the problems selected for study are limited by the method chosen to study them. Once researchers have decided on a functionalist/culturalist method, for example, they are unable to address anything but religion and tradition. The overall result is a reductive, ahistorical conception of women. The emphasis on the religion/tradition paradigm, a combination of orientalist[23] and evolutionary assumptions, constrains its critics by compelling them either to ritually refer to its parameters or to submit to them. Tradition in this case is seen as exemplified by the veil, seclusion, clitoridectomy, and so on.

Historically, of course, the veil has held an obsessive interest for many a writer. In 1829, for example, Charles Forster wrote *Mohammedanism Unveiled*, and Frantz Fanon, the revolutionary, wrote in 1967 about Algerian women under the caption: "Algeria Unveiled."[24] Even angry responses to this abusive imagery could not escape its attraction as when a Moroccan feminist titled her book: *Beyond the Veil*.[25] The persistence of the veil as a symbol that essentially stands for women illustrates the difficulty researchers have in dealing with a reality with which they are unfamiliar. It also reveals an attitude of mistrust. A veil is a hiding device; it arouses suspicion. Besides, veiling is close to masquerading so that studying women from societies where veiling exists is a form of theater! Some native (for example, "Eastern") feminists have pushed the theatrical imagery to its extreme by making the veil an integral part of the woman's persona.[26]

The evolutionary bias that suffuses most thinking about women in the Middle East and North Africa is expressed in a definite prejudice against Islam as a religion. Although U.S. feminists have attempted to accommodate Christianity and feminism and Judaism and feminism, Islam is inevitably presented as antifeminist.[27] What is at work here is not merely a plausible rationalist bias against religion as an impediment to the progress and freedom of the mind but an acceptance of the idea that there is a hierarchy of religions, with some being more susceptible to change than others. Like tradition, religion must be abandoned if Middle Eastern women are to be like Western women. As the logic of the argument requires, there can be no change without reference to an external standard deemed to be perfect.

Although religion is seen in Western societies as one institution among many, it is perceived as the bedrock of the societies in which Islam is practiced. A ritual is established whereby the writer appeals to religion as *the* cause of gender inequality just as it is made the source of underdevelopment in much of modernization theory. In an uncanny way, the feminist discourse on women from the Middle East and North Africa mirrors that of theologians' own interpretation of women in Islam. Academic feminists have compounded this situation by adding their own problematical specifications. They reduce Islam to one or two *sura,* or injunctions, such as those related to gender hierarchy and the punishment meted out to adulterous women (which is also applied to men).[28]

The overall effect of this paradigm is to deprive women of self-presence, of being. Because women are subsumed under religion presented in fundamental terms, they are inevitably seen as evolving in nonhistorical time. They have virtually no history. Any analysis of change is therefore foreclosed. When feminists "do" history, they generally appear to engage in an antihistory, where progress is measured in terms of a countback to the time where it all began, and all began to come unraveled. This means the time of the Koran for the female writer, just as it is the time of the Koran and the Traditions for the male writer.[29] The tenacious focus on religion in the scholarship on women in the Middle East and North Africa makes it the functional equivalent of fire in mythology and early scientific thought. A similar obsession/fascination with the mysterious power of fire dominated the "primitive" *as well as* the "scientific" mind up until the end of the eighteenth century.[30]

The question to raise at this point is this: Why hasn't academic feminism exposed the weaknesses of the prevailing discourse on women in the Middle East and North Africa? There have been articles and prefaces to anthologies that have denounced what Elizabeth Fernea and B.Q. Bezirgan have aptly referred to as "astigmatic writing" about women in the Middle East and North Africa.[31] Some studies have also attempted to break away from—although they have not displaced—the prevailing paradigm. It is also worth remembering that competing paradigms are "incommensurable" in that the criteria for judging their relative merits are not determined by value-neutral rules but lie within the community of scholars whose "expertise" has *produced* North Africa and the Middle East as a field of knowledge.[32] Still, no sustained effort has been made to challenge systematically the epistemological and theoretical presuppositions of much of the scholarship on women.[33]

Difference, in general, whether cultural, ethnic, or racial, has been a stumbling block for Western social science from its very inception. Nineteenth-century European ethnology and anthropology were established precisely to study different peoples and their institutions. However, regardless of the conceptual, theoretical, and methodological inadequacies and uncertainties in the works of many classical anthropologists and ethnologists, their interest in "difference" was a function of their desire to understand their own institutions better. This was the case with Emile Durkheim's work on religion, Marcel Mauss on exchange, and Bronislaw Malinowski on the Oedipus complex to cite only a few. Although I do not wish to absolve Western anthropology of its Europocentrism, it showed, at least in its inception, some awareness of a common denominator between people of different cultures, a *human* bond. The notion of "cultural universals" or that of the "human mind," however problematic, are expressions of such a common link between various peoples.

Contemporary academic feminism appears to have forgotten this part of its intellectual heritage. Of course, counterposing feminist scholarship to social science may appear senseless. Aren't female social scientists part of the same society and intellectual milieu as males? Indeed they are. But, academic feminists have generally denounced conventional social science for its biases regarding women both in its theory and its practice. Specifically, they have shown that it has reduced women to one dimension of their lives (such as reproduction and housework) and failed to conceptualize their status in society as historically evolving. Academic feminism, therefore, has brought a breath of fresh air into social science discourse on women and held out the promise of a more even-handed, less-biased practice. It is surprising, then, when one sees that women in Algeria (or in any other part of the Third World) are dealt with precisely in the ways with which academic feminists do not wish to be dealt.

Women in Algeria are subsumed under the less-than-neutral label of "Islamic women" or "Arab women" or "Middle Eastern women." Because language produces the reality it names, "Islamic women" must by necessity be made to conform to the configuration of meanings associated with the concept of Islam. The label affirms what ought to be seen as problematical. Whether the "Islamic women" are truly devout or whether the societies in which they live are theocracies are questions that the label glosses over.

The one-sidedness of this discourse on difference becomes grotesque if we reverse the terms and suggest, for example, that women in contemporary Europe and North America should be studied as Christian women! Similarly, the label "Middle Eastern women," when counterposed with the label "European women," reveals its unwarranted generality. The Middle East is a geographical area covering no less than twenty countries (if it is confined to the "Arab" East) that display a few similarities and many differences. Feminists study women in Victorian England or under the French Revolution; few would dare subsume French or English women under all-encompassing label of "European women" or Caucasian women, as substantive categories of thought. Yet, a book on Egyptian women was subtitled "Women in the Arab World."[34] Michel Foucault may have been right when he asserted that "knowledge is not made for understanding; it is made for cutting."[35]

There is a great continuity in the U.S. feminist treatment of difference within gender whether the difference is within or outside of U.S. society. In each case an attribute, whether physical (race or color) or cultural (religion or ethnicity), is used in an ontological sense. There is, however, an added feature to feminist modes of representing women from the Middle East and North Africa, and these modes reflect the dynamics of global politics. The political attitudes of "center" states are mirrored in feminist attitudes toward women from "peripheral" states. Elly Bulkin rightly notes that "women's lives and women's oppression cannot be considered outside the bounds of regional conflicts." She points out that Arab women are represented as being so different that they are deemed unable to understand or develop any form of feminism. When Arab women speak for themselves they are accused of being "pawns of Arab men."[36] The implication is that an Arab woman cannot be a feminist (whatever the term means) prior to disassociating herself from Arab men and the culture that supports them! In the end, global politics joins hands with prejudice, thereby closing a Western gynocentric circle based on misapprehended difference.[37]

The political bias in these representations of difference is best illustrated by the search of many feminists for the sensational and the uncouth. This search for the disreputable, which reinforces the notion of difference as objectified otherness, is often carried out with the help of Middle Eastern and North African women themselves. Feminism has provided a forum for these women to express themselves and on occasion for them to vent their anger at their societies. The exercise of freedom of expression often has a dizzying effect and sometimes leads to personal confession in the guise of social criticism. Individual women from the Middle East and North Africa appear on the feminist stage as representatives of the millions of women in their own societies. To what extent they do violence to the women they claim authority to write and speak about is a question that is seldom raised.

In assessing the issue of writing about Third World women, Gayatri C. Spivak points out that First World women and Western-trained women are complicitous in contributing to the continued "degradation" of Third World women whose "micrology" they interpret without having access to it. Although well taken, this view obscures the fact that complicity is often a conscious act involving social class position, psychological identification, and material interests. Of course, to include all "Western-trained" women in the plural "we," which also encompasses "First World" women, is to simplify the reality of the feminist encounter between Western and non-Western women. Unfortunately, academic feminist practice, just like that of its intellectual predecessors, is not pure on either side of difference. I, for one, refuse to be identified, even metaphorically, with Senanayak, the Indian antihero character who lends his expert knowledge to crush the revolution exemplified by "Dopti," a female revolutionary.[38] Affirming the existence of complicity is not sufficient. Indeed, the very act of translating this particular Indian short story for a U.S. audience did not bridge the chasm of cultural difference. It fits in with what Gaston Bachelard called the "museum of horrors." It documents the villainous acts of Indian men and the victimization of Indian women. The association of the Western and non-Western female reader with the process of victimization is an imaginative way of reducing the differential divide, but it does not fill it. And therein lies the dilemma of Third World women writing about Third World women.

Women in Algeria

As I have suggested, Euro-American and/or academic feminist discourse on women in Algeria reproduces the major elements of the prevailing social science paradigm. In addition, it makes explicit the connection between feminist or protofeminist practice and traditional geopolitics, of which colonialism and the international division of intellectual labor are a significant part. There is also continuity between nineteenth- and twentieth-century feminist and protofeminists writing about Algerian women. By and large, nineteenth- and twentieth-century literature on women in Algeria betrays a great deal of ambivalence. Male authors searched for women wherever they could find them, and although they bemoaned what they perceived as seclusion, they also expressed contempt for the libertines they encountered and surprise (rather than approval) before the unveiled rural women. Women writing from a social scientific perspective expressed their ambivalence in a slightly different mode, ostensibly empathizing with Algerian women they perceived as inferior and displaying unabashed contempt for Algerian men.[39]

A model of the protofeminist discourse on Algerian women is provided by Hubertine Auclert's *Les Femmes Arabes en Algérie,* published in 1900.

Auclert sees that colonialism victimized women but even though she is aware of the excesses of the colonial order, she still advocates the Frenchification of women. She suggests, moreover, that French women should become the tools of such an endeavor! "Upon entering tents and bolted doors, they [French women] would familiarize Muslim women with our lifestyles and ways of thinking"! Their task would no doubt be easy, because, according to Auclert, Algerian women were at heart the daughters of the free-thinking women of pre-Islamic Arabia. The eloquence they displayed in court, writes the author, was such that "you would think you heard, resuscitated, the beautiful speakers of pagan Arabia." In other words, Islam, the obstacle to being French, was but a veneer for women. Through women, moreover, one can undo Islam. Religion is identified with men so that a step toward the Frenchification of women is the construction of a pre-Islamic female essence. That same religion was responsible for what Auclert felt was Algerian women's inability to experience passionate love as French women were assumed to do. Algerian women were also found to be lacking a certain sensitivity that the French displayed because the latter read novels and had a different religion! In the end, the Algerian woman was perceived as living in limbo. "The Arab woman neither is nor does she feel at home at her husband's."[40]

In 1929, another French woman, Mathea Gaudry, a lawyer turned anthropologist, accepted the fact that she could not change the Algerian women's religious beliefs but did not give up the overall colonial project of Frenchification. Working with women from the Aurès mountains, she stated that "her intelligence would make the Auressian woman worthy of some education; what I mean is that we could teach her French, how to sew and run a home." As for the Algerian men from the region, she wrote that "their mental faculties appear to be stunted in the prime of life." Besides, the men are "inveterate liars" and display a "congenital nonchalance."[41] She too pursued the nostalgic notion of Algerian women's pre-Islamic past, to wit: "By subjecting her [the woman from Ammour mountain] to the authority of a master whom she must fear, Islamic law profoundly separated her from those Berber and pre-Islamic women: Sadouk, Raytah and others whose independence is legendary."[42] Indeed, this is more a matter of legend than reality. The author adds that the nomadic woman's "more or less confused understanding of this legendary past" accounts for her flirtatious games with men. Why can't a woman be free to flirt without a rationale being found for her behavior in mythical time?

Throughout the 1950s and 1960s, various monographs on women appeared with the aim of "guiding" Algerian women toward the ideal of French womanhood and downgrading their religion and customs, even at a time [the 1950s] when women were displaying the kind of behavior French women should have commended. In this respect it is noteworthy that only one study was written by two French women of an Algerian female revolutionary who became a *cause célèbre* during the war (1954–62).[43]

Germaine Tillion's work (*The Republic of Cousins*), which appeared to break new ground in bringing Algerian women together with southern Mediterranean women in the same theoretical framework, was also unable in the end to transcend the stumbling block of Islam. Algerian women emerged from the book at the bottom of the hierarchy of sisterhood. After asserting that Islam had little to do directly with what she termed the "degradation of the female condition," Tillion was unable to keep religion analytically separate from her comparative evaluation of Algerian and European women living in the northern rim of the Mediterranean. Tillion also managed to neglect the colonial factor in her analysis of the dynamics of religion, political economy, and the reproduction of gender relations.[44]

In a book that purports to have been written in a spirit of sisterhood, Françoise Corrèze stated that "the donkey and the mule tied to a ring undoubtedly suffer less from man's [authority] than the women cloistered in the shed we entered." That she, a stranger, was allowed to penetrate the "cloisters" is a fact that she did not bother to ponder. Having apparently approached her study of rural women with a preconceived interpretative framework, she found herself compelled to explain away facts that did not conform to her ideas. For example, she wondered why a mother-in-law she met did not exhibit the signs of the mythical "powerful mother-in-law" and concluded that "perhaps she was once [powerful]."[45]

The author's gaze at the Algerian female Other dwelt on women's postures, gestures, and clothes, and it studiously noted whether women's clothes were clean or dirty. In the process, the reader is not always told about the nature of the social changes that have affected the rural communities studied, although signs of such changes abound almost in spite of the author's will.

In 1980, Juliette Minces produced an essay on women in Algeria (in a book that, naturally, covers "the Arab World") in which she denied women any selfhood or ability to think. Women's participation in the war is presented as the result of men's will and manipulation. Her contempt for women is revealed in her remark that Algerian women chose Islam over colonialism. She, the scientist, tells women that "they have no consciousness of the double alienation they underwent"! Yet, she adds, "they had access to French society and were open to new ideas"![46] Echoing Minces, U.S. feminist Judith Stiehm has written that "the French held the Muslim culture in disdain because of its treatment of women." Using as her main source a State Department area handbook for Algeria, Stiehm revealed her ignorance of her subject matter by making factually incorrect statements. For example, she wrote that "as Muslim women move out of seclusion they tend to enter segregated schools, offices and/or factories."[47] As a matter of fact, offices are not segregated and what single-sex schools remain were inherited from the French era. In addition, the state has been implementing a policy of coeducation.

In a book published in 1980 entitled *Femmes d'Islam, ou le Sexe Interdit* (Women of Islam or the forbidden sex), encompassing North Africa, Renée Pelletier and Autilio Gaudio engaged in another diatribe against Islam, blaming it for, among other things, the Algerian president's alleged unwillingness to "show his wife in public." In fact, the current president has appeared with his wife in public, although he may not "show" her! The authors' analysis of the Koran is based on one *sura,* just as the rest of their essay is based on anecdotal information gleaned from one book written in the 1960s supplemented by images from a short film. What is most noteworthy about this book, however, are the leading questions used in a questionnaire meant to elicit responses about women in Morocco. For example:

> Question #10: "Have you felt sexual attraction for boys?"
> Question #13: "Have you already kissed a boy on the lips who is not your fiancé or husband?"
> Question #2: "How did you perceive your mother's condition when you were a child?"
> Question #5: "When have you, for the first time, felt the weight of traditions and prohibitions?"

In conclusion, the authors assert that "this study could be applied to all three countries of the Maghreb."[48] On the other side of difference, they must be, they are, all alike.

Echoing Stiehm, another U.S. feminist political scientist, Kay Boals, has written that the nature of female/male relations in Algeria "elicited contempt and derision from the colonizer." Also of interest is the typology of forms of consciousness that Boals set up to explain the behavior of colonized people, blacks, women, and homosexuals. Such individuals exhibit a type of consciousness that falls in one of six categories, ranging from "traditional" to "traditionalist, reformist, assimilationist, revolutionary," and "transforming" (which an earlier draft of the article termed "modernizing"). The author asserted that Algerian males are definitely "traditionalist" but women are "transforming." Indeed, what women "aspire to corresponds more closely to patterns of male-female relations in European than in traditional Muslim culture." A problem arises, however, when one turns to the definitions of these types of consciousness. The "traditionalist" is the man who "continues to reaffirm the criteria of judgement of his own traditional culture or religion but he is unable to do so with internal conviction. There is thus a strong internal incoherence between emotion and thinking, between what one would like to believe and what one 'knows in one's bones.' "[49]

No such conflict should exist among women whose consciousness is transforming. Yet "Algerian women are eager to change the traditional patterns but are somewhat inhibited in doing so by the internal psychic ambivalence created by the desire to affirm the Algerian heritage and culture." The "transforming consciousness" is defined as that which feels "genuinely free to forge new combinations of personality traits . . . without the need . . . to imitate the model of the European." If this is the case then one wonders why Algerian culture or heritage would be an obstacle to acquiring such a consciousness unless it is deemed inadequate and therefore something that ought to be rejected. Indeed, the author has defined "traditional consciousness" as that which is characterized by "a calm conviction of superiority over others and a sense of being at the center of the cosmos." The ideal human type of this consciousness is found in the person of Al Khidr Husayn, the first editor of the journal of Al Azhar University in Cairo. This creature, "although writing in the 1930's apparently remained essentially unaffected by the British occupation!"[50] In other words, the colonial/European factor defines a catch–22 situation. If you fall prey to it you are an "anomaly" in the sense that you wish for change deemed impossible to obtain; if you don't you are still anomalous because you are defined as "traditional." It is worth noting that the author does not provide any information about having interviewed or observed the females and males whose psyches she has furnished with ambivalence, contradictions, inhibitions, and anomaly.

The repetitive nature of the prevailing paradigm stifles the mind and dulls the senses. At the very least, it has no aesthetic value; it is like wearing the same clothes all the time. However, its ultimate effect is to preclude any understanding of Algerian women *in their lived reality:* as subjects in their own right. Instead, they are reified, made into mere bearers of unexplained categories. Algerian women have no existence outside these categories; they have no individuality. What is true of one is true of all; just as what is true of Algerian women is also held to be true of all women deemed to be like them over the space generously defined as the "Muslim world" or the "Arab world." This "worlding" of the female world is another instance of the unquestioned practice of "abstracted empiricism."

How, then, can an Algerian woman write about women in Algeria when her space has already been defined, her history dissolved, her subjects objectified, her language chosen for her? How can she speak without saying the same things?[51] The Algerian case supports Foucault's contention about Western culture that "the most tenacious subjection of difference is undoubtedly that maintained by categories."[52] What is needed is a phenomenology of women's lived experience to explode the constraining power of categories. Such a phenomenology would not be a mere description of the subjective meaning of women's experience. Rather, it would be the search for the organizing principles of women's lived reality as it intersects with men's.[53] To study women from a phenomenological perspective is different from merely interviewing them to elicit from them information about their lives that *confirms our* conceptions of *them*.[54]

The fetishism of the concept, Islam, in particular, obscures the living reality of the women and men subsumed under it. North African and Middle Eastern societies are more complex and more diverse than is admitted, and cannot be understood in terms of monolithic, unitary concepts. Religion cannot be detached from the socioeconomic and political context within which it unfolds. And religion cannot be seen as having an existence independent of human activity. As the product of human activity, it is subject to change, if not in content at least in function. To understand the role of religion in women's lives, we must identify the conditions under which it emerges as a significant factor, as well as those that limit its scope. In addition, we must address the ways in which religious symbols are manipulated by both women and men in everyday life as well as in institutional settings. Finally, we should refrain from thinking in terms of a "Middle East" and realize that what is useful to geopolitics is not necessarily so to sociology. Concrete women (like men) live in concrete societies and *not* in an ideologically uniform space. There are Turkish women and Egyptian women and Algerian women. Subsuming some under others results in obscuring, rather than improving, our understanding of gender relations.

Conclusion

This bird's-eye view of feminist discourse on women in Algeria points to the necessity of asking anew a question that might sound embarrassing: What is the nature of the feminist project? What is its relation to women in other places? Is there something at the heart of academic feminism that is inescapably Western gynocentric; that is, must it inevitably lead to the exercise of discursive power by some women over others?

To subscribe to the notion that the metaphysics of difference-as-misrepresentation is inescapable is self-defeating and betrays resistance to changing the intellectual status quo. The French philosopher Jacques Derrida upholds the view (shared by some Third World feminists) that ethnocentrism is necessarily irrevocable on the grounds that ethnology is a European science. He also adds that deconstruction is inscribed in the very language of European social science.[55] Read in an unorthodox fashion, this means that the metaphysics that sustains ethnocentrism also sustains deconstruction, a destructuring activity. In spite of its honest recognition of the ethnocentric core of social science, this view appears to legitimate its own existence. For if ethnocentrism reproduces itself in an endless cycle, the language of ethnocentrism may not be superseded; it can only be deconstructed. What applies to ethnocentrism also applies to the Western gynocentric conception of difference.

If academic feminism cannot be allowed to hide behind a deconstructionist approach to legitimate its misapprehension of difference within gender, it should not be allowed to seek refuge in the Foucauldian conception of power and language either. Foucault's conception of power as being decentered has legitimized the view, among some academic feminists, according to which power over women-in-general is diffuse. In so doing, the actual instrumentality of power that some women (for example, academic women) exercise over other women (such as Third World women) is neglected. Similarly, subsuming all reality under discourse, as Foucault does, has resulted in a shift of focus from women's lived reality to endless discoursing about it. It is true that a feminist engaged in the act of representing women who belong to a different culture, ethnic group, race, or social class wields a form of power over them; a power of interpretation. However, this power is a peculiar one. It is borrowed from the society at large which is male-centered. It is borrowed power that gives academic feminists engaged in interpreting difference status and credibility. But, when the power of men over women is reproduced in the power of women over women, feminism as an intellectual movement presents a caricature of the very institutions it was meant to question. The misrepresentation of "different" women is a form of self-misrepresentation. It bespeaks a repression of one's femaleness and glosses over the fact that the representer is also engendered and remains far from having achieved the freedom and capacity to define herself.

Just as some men's inability (or reluctance) to accept sexual difference as the expression of modes of being human has led them to formulate a sociobiological conception of women, Western gynocentrism has led to an essentialism of otherhood. Both phenomena are products of a larger differentialist trend that has affected Western Europe and North America since the end of World War Two. The collapse of the colonial empires, the rise of consumer societies, and the crises of the late capitalist states have formed the context within which assertions of "difference" have emerged. The celebration of difference between women and men, homosexuals and heterosexuals, the mad and the sane, has since become the unquestioned norm.

What is problematical in this conception of difference is that it affirms a new form of reductionism. The rejection of humanism and its universalistic character in discourse analysis and deconstruction deprives the proponents of difference of any basis for understanding the relationship between the varieties of modes of being different in the world. Difference becomes essentialized. It is not accidental that Foucault, for example, contributed little to our understanding of what it means to be mad, female, or male. What he did was to explain the *category* of madness and of sexuality. The discourse and deconstruction approaches to difference obviate the crucial issue of *intersubjectivity*. Although Derrida warns against an ontological conception of difference, he is unable to avoid affirming difference as unmediated otherness. He locates difference in language, thus removing it from the realm of shared experiences that language may not necessarily capture.

The inability to address the intersubjective foundation of difference is clearly a significant problem in academic feminism. In the United States, this problem is not merely the result of some feminists being influenced by Foucault or Derrida. It is also related to an intellectual tradition marked by pragmatism, a byproduct of positivism, that has characterized U.S. institutions of higher learning since the nineteenth century. In feminist scholarship, this has meant giving the female *experience* (read U.S. or "Western") a privileged ontological status.

To take intersubjectivity into consideration when studying Algerian women or other Third World women means seeing their lives as meaningful, coherent, and understandable instead of being infused "by us" with doom and sorrow. It means that their lives like "ours" are structured by economic, political, and cultural factors. It means that these women, like "us," are engaged in the process of adjusting, often shaping, at times resisting and even transforming their environment. It means they have their own individuality; they are "for themselves" instead of being "for us." An appropriation of their singular individualities to fit the generalizing categories of "our" analyses is an assault on their integrity and on their identity. Intersubjectivity alerts us to the common bond that ties women and men of different cultures together. It is a relative safeguard against the objectification of others, a reminder that the other is just as entitled as I am to her/his humanity expressed in his/her cultural mode.[56]

For the intersubjective component of experience to become evident in the study of difference within and between genders, a certain form of humanism must be reaffirmed. But the rejection of humanistic philosophy, which subsumed woman under man while making claims to universalism, has so far been replaced with the essentialism of difference.

It is often argued, of course, that humanism erases individuality, difference; that any return to a humanistic thought is self-defeating. Yet, it appears that the essentializing of difference between women has resulted in the erasure of "other" women. When these are locked into the categories of religion, race, or color, their own individuality as women has already been erased. For example, a "Muslim woman" is no longer a concrete individual. She is not Algerian, or Yemeni; she is an abstraction in the same way as a "woman of color" is. Their assumed uniqueness dissolves their concrete reality. They cannot by definition be compared with "First World" women. Indeed, what distinguishes them from the latter is also what is seen as accounting for their very essence.

Antihumanism has not provided any authority higher than itself that could monitor its excesses. Old-style humanism, in contrast, and despite its shortcomings, makes itself vulnerable to criticism by appealing to its unfulfilled promise of a more reasonable rationalism or a more egalitarian universalism. Indeed, the universalistic claim to a supracultural human entity embodied in reason provided colonized societies with the tool necessary to regain their freedom. Colonized women and men were willing to give up their lives in order to capture their share of humanity celebrated but denied by colonial powers. But what does antihumanism offer "different" peoples? On what grounds (moral or otherwise) can powerless people struggle against their relegation to the prison house of race, color, and nationality into which antihumanism locks them?

There is a sense in which the antihumanist celebration of unmediated "difference" may denote resistance to accepting difference as the other side of sameness. It is not accidental that the rise of antihumanism coincided with the collapse of the French colonial empire, more specifically the end of the Algerian war (and it was at this time that both Foucault and Derrida began publishing). Yet, antihumanism, as a philosophy, holds a great attraction for some feminists because of its nihilistic questioning of all (including moral/ethical) constraints on action or on thought. This is, of course, the very reason it is fraught with dangers as soon as discoursing about others' (not only men's but women's) subjectivity is at stake. To what extent can Western feminism dispense with an ethics of responsibility when writing about "different" women? Is the subject "women" free of all constraints only because women are the researchers? The point is neither to subsume other women under one's own experience nor to uphold a separate truth for them. Rather, it is to allow them to *be* while recognizing that what they are is just as meaningful, valid, and comprehensible as what "we" are. They are not the antithesis of "ourselves" that justifies "our" studying them in ways we do not study "ourselves."

Heidegger's letter on humanism offers an example of the kinds of questions that might be posed in order to reorient our thinking on humanism. We need to ask what is the "humanitas of homo humanus?" What is woman's/man's place in history? Is woman/man "a specter, a spectator or a creator?" What would a "humanism in a new dimension" be like? A new humanism requires a more original reexperiencing of what it is to be human. This involves a process of "questioning, etymologizing, and historicizing." Although Heidegger's answers are ambiguous, they nevertheless point to the importance of history, language, and ethics in reexploring humanistic thought. When seen as a "process of coming to the word," humanism precludes the assumption of woman's/man's domination by the word, a tenet of the antihumanist discursive approach to history.[57]

Finally, being aware that woman/man plays a role in history that requires specification points to the ethical component of human activity and thought. Indeed, when feminists essentially deny other women the humanity they claim for themselves, they dispense with any ethical constraint. They engage in the act of splitting the social universe into "us" and "them," "subjects" and "objects." This propensity to apprehend social reality in terms of binary oppositions is a contradictory element in feminist thought. Feminists have criticized the social and natural sciences precisely because they use dichotomous categories that assign women one attribute or role, thereby simplifying the far more complex reality of women's lives.

The split vision of the world that relegates non-Western women to a residual category, where fancy more than fact rules, is a significant error in feminist scholarship as a whole. It can be corrected only if and when Western feminists are ready and willing to think differently about the variety of modes of being female, including their own. They must recognize that knowledge of North African/Third World women is not given all at once. It is, like knowledge of women in Western societies, a process of sifting the true from the false and making visible that which remains submerged. It is historical and has a rationality of its own which human reason *can* comprehend.

As it now stands, difference is seen as mere division. The danger of this undeveloped view lies in its verging on *indifference*.[58] In this sense, *anything* can be said about women from other cultures as long as it appears to document their differentness from "us." This bespeaks a lack of concern for the complexity of difference as well as a simplification of difference to mean "particularity," that is to say, unmediated singularity.[59] Because the North African and Middle Eastern cultures have long been stereotyped, because the feminist movement ought to be a movement toward human liberation from epistemological domination, women from these cultures cannot satisfy themselves with a mere act of negation when they write about themselves. They must shoulder a double burden, namely, to work toward an epistemological break with the prevailing paradigm *and* to reevaluate the structure of gender relations in their own societies.

History has dealt these women a hard blow. It held them hostage to colonial or imperial ventures and delivered them to travelers, chroniclers, painters, and anthropologists of both sexes who mused about their lives. Now, they are in a position from which they could recapture the dispersed fragments of their selves and put them back together in combinations that the motley crowd of their observers may not suspect. The task is enormous but necessary. If feminism is seen as a critical intellectual movement, "Eastern" feminism should attempt to bring about that intellectual renaissance that men have so far failed to carry out.

This requires reflecting on the roles that female intellectuals should play in effectively promoting women's needs. It is crucial here to ponder the adequacy of the means for achieving these ends. To think of feminism in the singular is sociologically inappropriate. Similarly, French or U.S. styles of feminisms may not be functional in different socioeconomic and political contexts. What form should women's effort to reach gender equality take in the various societies of North Africa and the Middle East? Is feminism, as understood in Western societies, women's only avenue toward social change? Such questions may not be answered if Eastern feminists think of their audience as residing here instead of in their societies of origin.

There is a sense in which the issue for North African and Middle Eastern academic women is not the applicability of U.S. or French feminist theories. That is a luxury one cannot afford. The question is to define a critical writing space within which women who are not making their careers in western universities, but who are the subjects of our writing, can identify. This requires resisting the temptation of seeing in U.S. or French women's present needs our ideals. It also calls for a comprehensive exploring and understanding of the body of knowledge produced by the indigenous peoples of these areas of the world. To selectively pinpoint instances of women's "victimization," as is often done, obscures the complexity of gender processes and presents a truncated image of an intellectual heritage whose existence is barely suspected by all but a few experts. If this means to reinvent the wheel, so be it! The old wheel has not worked too well. Perhaps a new one might be an improvement on the old.

A failure to do so will inevitably result in storytelling. That can be a rewarding endeavor. Having told his wonderful story several times, Othello remarked that Desdemona "devoured up my discourse," and "my story being done she gave me for my pains a world of kisses." However, Othello was also devoured by his own discourse. In the end he bade Lodovico tell his story:

And say besides that in Aleppo once,
Where a malignant and turbaned Turk
Beat a Venetian and traduced the State,
I took by th' throat the circumcised dog
And smote him—thus (He stabs himself)[60]

If discourse can be murderous, speech may never rise above mere talk. In the words of Dostoevsky, some people "may be able to live in dark cellars for forty years and never open their mouth(s), but the moment they get into the light of day and break out they talk and talk and talk." . . . Isn't the whole point to have a *voice*?[61]

Notes

1. Omar Khayyam, *Rubaiyat of Omar Khayyam* (Boston: Houghton Miffin, 1884), quatrain 99.

2. The term "Western" here implies no particular ontology and is essentially inadequate. It is used in this text to refer to women who are identified as belonging to what is geographically and culturally presented as the "West" or the "First World." It is as inadequate as the term "Eastern," which I will also use.

3. See Marnia Lazreg, "The Epistemological Obstacle of Experience: A Critical Neo-Rationalist Approach" (Paper presented at the Pembroke Center Conference on Feminism, Theory, Politics, Brown University, 14–16 Mar. 1985).

4. This issue is best illustrated in the debate over what constitutes feminist science. See Sandra Harding, *The Science Question in Feminism* (Ithaca: Cornell University Press, 1986); Myra Jehlen, "Archimedes and the Paradox of Feminist Criticism," *Signs 6* (Summer 1981).

5. Significantly, the intense current interest in "Middle Eastern women" is occurring at a time when the "Middle East" has been neutralized as a self-sustaining political and economic force.

6. For an example of accommodation, see Mervat Hatem. "The Politics of Sexuality and Gender in Segregated Patriarchal Systems: The Case of Eighteenth- and Nineteenth-Century Egypt," *Feminist Studies* 12 (Summer 1986): 251–74. The author displays no awareness of the criticism leveled at the concept of "patriarchy," using Egypt to bear out the universalistic claims of U.S. feminist theory of patriarchy.

7. Examples of minority women's questioning of academic feminism include *This Bridge Called My Back: Writings by Radical Women of Color*, ed. Cherríe Moraga and Gloria Anzaldúa (New York: Kitchen Table: Women of Color Press, 1983): and Bell Hooks, *Feminist Theory: From Margin to Center* (Boston: South End Press, 1984). See also María Lugones and Elizabeth Spelman. "Have We Got a Theory for You? Feminist Theory, Cultural Imperialism, and the Demand for the Woman's Voice," *Women's Studies International Forum 6,* no. 6 (1983): 573–89.

8. Up to now, attempts at defining a space from which to address the woman question have been reduced to accepting or rejecting Islam as a religion. Thus, "Eastern" feminist writing oscillates between adopting or rejecting Western feminist modes of analysis. For example, Aziza Al Hibri makes lists of the positive and distorted aspects of the Koran in "A Study of Islamic Herstory: Or How Did We Ever Get into This Mess?" in her edited *Women and Islam* (New York: Pergamon Press, 1982), 207–20. Historians of religion Yvonne Y. Haddad and Jane L. Smith have made similar attempts in "Eve: Islamic Image of Woman," in *Women and Islam,* 135–44. Azar Tabari's and Nahid Yeganeh's exchange on whether (Shi'a) Islam can accommodate gender equality must be understood within the context of contemporary Iran where Shi'ism is in power. They, too, yield to the prevailing paradigm pitting modernity against tradition in *In the Shadow of Islam: The Women's Movement in Iran* (London: Zed Press, 1982), esp. pt. 1, 1–75.

9. The connection between the colonial discourse and contemporary women's and/or feminist discourses on Third World women is explored in some detail by Chandra Talpade Mohanty's "Under Western Eyes: Feminist Scholarship and Colonial Discourses," *Boundary 2* 12 (Spring/Fall 1984): 333–58: Gayatri Chakravorty Spivak, "French Feminism in an International Frame," *Yale French Studies* 62 (1981): 154–84. For an exploration of the relationship between French and American orientalisms

see Edward W. Said, *Orientalism* (New York: Vintage Books, 1979), esp. chap. 3, pt. 3.

10. By "paradigm," I mean the "rules, empirical and theoretical laws, experimental techniques, methodological directives, and even metaphysical principles that are involved in any particular scientific achievement." See Gary Gutting, ed. *Paradigms and Revolutions: Appraisals and Applications of Thomas Kuhn's Philosophy of Science* (Notre Dame: University of Notre Dame Press, 1980), esp. introduction, 1–21. The rise and fall of paradigms in science is classically discussed in Thomas S. Kuhn's *The Structure of Scientific Revolutions* (Chicago: University of Chicago Press, 1962). Cf. Michel Foucault's use of "discourse." See Hubert L. Dreyfus and Paul Rabinow, *Michel Foucault: Beyond Structuralism and Hermeneurics,* 2d ed. (Chicago: University of Chicago Press, 1983), esp. 197–204.

11. Algeria may be seen as an "ideal type" in which colonial domination, social science, and interest in women display their intimate connections. Disclaiming traditional/ Europocentric conceptions of Islam has become part of a ritual among feminist writers who nonetheless use the very language denounced. See, for example, Fatima Mernissi's introduction to the first edition of *Beyond the Veil: Male-Female Dynamics in a Modern Muslim Society* (Cambridge, Mass.: Schenkman, 1975); and Leila Ahmed, "Western Ethnocentrism and Perceptions of the Harem," *Feminist Studies 8* (Fall 1982): 521–34.

12. Making a distinction as to who is and is not a feminist—among Western women writing about Algerian or "Middle Eastern" women—has become nearly futile. U.S. academic feminism's market for "Middle Eastern women" is such that even writers who do not profess to feminism feel free to borrow its language: "private sphere," "sexual segregation," and "women's subordination," for example. Here, "protofeminist" refers to women writers who, within the Algerian context, at the turn of the century undertook the study of women with the purpose of making social policy recommendations. Hubertine Auclert, for example, was active in petitioning colonial authorities to outlaw polygamy. She was also aware of the less-than-equal status of French women who lacked the right to vote. See Hubertine Auclert, *Les Femmes arabes en Algérie* (Paris: Société d'Editions, Littéraires, 1900).

13. Although U.S. women writing about Eastern women have no direct colonial involvement, their discourse still reflects the direct domination in *all* spheres of socioeconomic and intellectual life of subjugated peoples. Popular culture in the United States upholds a view of "Islamic" societies that bears strong resemblances to French colonial and postcolonial female writers' perspectives. Were it not for the entrenched prejudices against "Islam," certain critiques would not have been necessary. See Elizabeth Fernea and B.Q. Bezirgan, eds., *Middle Eastern Muslim Women Speak* (Austin: University of Texas Press, 1976), esp. the introduction, xvii–xxxvi: Cynthia Nelson, "Public and Private Politics: Women in the Middle Eastern World," *American Ethnologist* 1 (August 1974): 551–63. See also Susan Dorsky's *Women of Amran* (Salt Lake City: University of Utah Press, 1986), esp. the conclusion, for recent disclaimers of "Islamic" female victimization.

14. Bryan S. Turner, *Marx and the End of Orientalism* (London: George Allen & Unwin, 1978), 1.

15. See Max Weber's study of Islam in *Economy and Society,* esp. vol. 3: and Bryan S. Turner's critique of it in *Weber and Islam: A Critical Study* (London: Routlege & Kegan Paul 1974).

16. For a critique of H.A.R. Gibb and Harold Bowen's *Islamic Society and the West,* see Roger Owen, "The Middle East in the Eighteenth Century: An 'Islamic Society' in Decline?," *Review of Middle East Studies* 1 (1975): 101–12.

17. David Waines, quoted in Turner, *Weber and Islam,* 6.

18. Clifford Geertz, *Islam Observed: Religious Development in Morocco and Indonesia* (New Haven: Yale University Press, 1968), esp. 56–89.

19. Turner, *Weber and Islam,* 6–7.

20. Clifford Geertz, *Local Knowledge: Further Essays in Interpretive Anthropology* (New York: Basic Books, 1983), chap. 8.

21. Jacques Berque wants "to give a privileged place, at least temporarily, to the marginal, the local, the peripheral" in Maghrebin history in order to discover, among other things, the "faults of the established order." See his *Ulemas, fondateurs, insurgés du Maghreb* (Paris: Sindbad, 1982), 16.

22. C. Wright Mills, *The Sociological Imagination* (New York: Oxford University Press, 1959), chap. 2.

23. Juliette Minces, *La Femme dans le monde arabe* (Woman in the Arab World) (Paris: Editions Mazarines, 1980). The recent English translation of the title was *The House of Obedience: Women in Arab Society* (London: Zed Press, 1980). This was apparently done in an effort to keep the orientalist conception of women alive. "Orientalism" refers to the view according to which the "Orient" is antithetical to and radically different from the "West." Thus, Minces is able to use the totalizing as well as reductive category of "obedience" to capture the essence of difference so conceived. A more recent example of this practice is provided by Camille Lacoste-Dujardin, *Des Mères Contre les Femmes* (Paris: Editions de la Découverte, 1986).

24. Cited in Edward W. Said, *The World, the Text, and the Critic* (Cambridge: Harvard University Press, 1983), 268; and see Frantz Fanon, *A Dying Colonialism* (New York: Grove Press, 1967), 34–67.

25. See Mernissi, *Beyond the Veil.*

26. See Leila Ahmed, "Islamic Women in Middle Eastern History" (Paper presented at the Mary Ingraham Bunting Institute, Radcliffe College, 12 Nov. 1985).

27. Feminist theology also suffers from a religious bias. Rosemary R. Reuther is eager to preserve the "Judeo-Christian affirmation that the divine is one," leaving out Islam's emphasis on the unity of the divine. See her *Sexism and God Talk: Toward a Feminist Theology* (Boston: Beacon Press, 1983).

28. See Eliz Sanasarian's *The Women's Rights Movement in Iran: Mutiny, Appeasement, and Repression* (New York: Praeger, 1982), 12, which studies feminism as a social movement. Even radicals who avoid religion still view women as hopeless victims of a reified culture where heterosexual love seems impossible. See Hatem, 258–62. Turkish feminists are proud of the state which secularized their society, but they are often unable to see the complex interaction between religion and state which might

play a role in structuring gender relations. For example, see Deniz Kandiyoti, "Sex-Roles and Social Change: A Comparative Appraisal of Turkey's Women," *Signs* 3 (Autumn 1977): 57–73; and Binnaz (Sayari) Toprak, "Religion and Turkish Women," in *Women in Turkish Society*, ed. Nermin Abadan-Unat (Leiden: The Netherlands: E.J. Brill, 1981), 281–93.

29. See Margaret Smith, *Rabi' a Al Adawiya and Her Fellow Saints in Islam* (Amsterdam: Philo Press, 1974). Smith's work on the Sufi mystic has been faithfully followed by Ahmed, who argues that Sufism provided women with a form of liberation from the constraints of what Smith perceived as "orthodox" Islam (see Ahmed's "Islamic Women in Middle Eastern History"). But Sufism finds its roots and justification in the Koran and cannot easily be placed in opposition to "Islam."

30. Gaston Bachelard, *La Psychanalyse du feu* (Paris: Gallimard, 1949).

31. See Fernea and Bezirgan, xvii–xxxvi.

32. There are works that consciously attempt to deviate from the prevailing paradigm as, for example, those cited in note 13. Among the most noteworthy are Andrea Rugh's *Family in Contemporary Egypt* (Syracuse: Syracuse University Press, 1984); and Judith Tucker's *Women in Nineteenth-Century Egypt* (Cambridge: Cambridge University Press, 1985). However, they have not constructed a competing paradigm.

33. Methodological/theoretical issues are discussed in some detail in Rosemary Sayigh, "Roles and Functions of Arab Women: A Reappraisal," *Arab Studies Quarterly* 3 (Autumn 1981): 258–74; Judith Tucker, "Problems in the Historiography of Women in the Middle East," *International Journal of Middle East Studies* 15 (1983): 324–36; and Nikki Keddie, "Problems in the Study of Middle Eastern Women," *International Journal of Middle Eastern Studies* 10 (1979): 225–40. Sayigh is the only author to have linked the practice of orientalism to the biases inherent in the study of "Arab women." The typical focus on religion in much of orientalist scholarship does not mean writers assert that ideas are the motor of Middle Eastern history. Rather, the argument is that *religious beliefs* keep women, men, and their institutions in the Middle East and in North Africa from evolving toward the Western type of secularization and "modernization."

34. See Nawal Saadawi, *The Hidden Face of Eve: Women in the Arab World* (Boston: Beacon Press, 1980).

35. Michel Foucault, *Language, Counter-Memory, Practice,* ed. D.B. Bouchard (Ithaca: Cornell University Press, 1977), 154.

36. Elly Bulkin, "Semite vs. Semite/Feminist vs. Feminist," in *Yours in Struggle: Three Feminist Perspectives on Anti-Seminism and Racism,* ed. Elly Bulkin, Minnie Bruce Pratt, and Barbara Smith (Brooklyn: Long Haul Press, 1984), 167, 168.

37. I am using the term "gynocentric," as suggested by Elizabeth Weed, associate director of the Pembroke Center, Brown University, to refer to the situation whereby some women as a group exercise discursive power over other women whom they exclude from their frame of reference.

38. Gayatri Chakravorty Spivak, "Darupadi by Mahasveta Devi," in *Writing and Sexual Difference,* ed. Elizabeth Abel (Chicago: University of Chicago Press, 1982), 261–

82, esp. translator's foreword. Senanayak's expertise is presumably similar to that of academic feminists' scholarship on Third World women: it can equally harm.

39. This article is not concerned with works of fiction on women in Algeria.

40. Hubertine Auclert, 26, 84, 91, 128. Even though Auclert was anticlerical, she shared with her contemporaries the view that Islam was inferior to Christianity.

41. Mathea Gaudry, *La Femme chaouia de l'Aurès* (Paris: Librarie Orientaliste Paul Geuthner, 1929), 287; 69, 84–85.

42. Mathea Gaudry, *La Société féminine du Djebel Amour et au Ksel* (Alger: Société Algérienne D'Impressions Diverses, 1961), 426.

43. See Simone de Beauvoir and Gisèle Halimi, *Djamila Boupacha* (New York: Macmillan, 1962).

44. Germaine Tillion, *Le Harem et les cousins* (Paris: Editions du Seuil, 1966), esp. 199–212. The book was translated as *The Republic of Cousins* (London: Al Saqui Books, 1983). Despite her mythic use of neolithic exigencies, Tillion was able to place Islam on a par with Christianity: "In Islam just as in Christianity, the Mediterranean woman was constantly deprived of her rights; here in spite of the French Revolution; there in spite of the Koran" (p. 175).

45. Françoise Corrèze, *Les Femmes des Mechtas* (Paris: Les Editeurs Français Réunis, 1976), 41, 42, 115.

46. Juliette Minces, 111–36, esp. 117, 118.

47. Judith Stiehm, "Algerian Women: Honor, Shame, and Islamic Socialism," in *Women in the World: A Comparative Study*, ed. Lynne B. Iglitzin and Ruth Ross (Santa Barbara, Calif.: Clio Books, 1976), 232, 240.

48. Autilio Gaudio and Renée Pelletier, *Femmes d'Islam ou le sexe interdit* (Paris: Denoël, 1980), 104, 105, 153.

49. Kay Boals, "The Politics of Cultural Liberation: Male-Female Relations in Algeria," in *Liberating Women's History: Theoretical and Critical Essays,* ed. Berenice A. Carroll (Urbana: University of Illinois Press, 1976), 203, 205.

50. Ibid., 196, 205, 201, 195.

51. Algerian academic feminist thought is an expression of the complex interaction between its colonial background, socialist ideals, and the continued French domination of Algerian universities. Examples of the range of their writings are Feriel Lalami Fates, "A corps perdu . . . ou des activités corporelles à caractère ludique des femmes travailleuses [Région d'Alger]," *Cahiers de la Méditerranée* 32 (June 1986): 91–99; Naziha Hamouda, "Les Femmes rurales et la production poétique," *Peuples Méditerranéens* 6, nos. 22–23 (1983): 267–79; and Fatiha Hakiki, "Le Travail féminin, emploi salarié et le travail domestique," *Actes des Journées d'Etudes et de Réflexion sur les Femmes Algériennes, 3–6 mai 1980, Cahiers du C.D.S.H.* no. 3 (1980): 35–107. See also Fatiha Hakiki and Claude Talahite, "Human Sciences Research on Women in Algeria," in *Social Science Research and Women in the Arab World* (Paris: UNESCO, 1984), 82–93.

52. Foucault, 186.

53. Fatima Mernissi's *Le Maroc raconté par ses femmes* (Rabat: Société Marocaine des Editeurs Réunis, 1984) purports to give a voice to illiterate women in Morocco. Yet the text reveals a narcissistic attempt to speak for other women while rising above them. Nayra Atiya's *Khul Khaal* (Syracuse: Syracuse University Press, 1982) constitutes another instance of "giving" a voice to illiterate or poor women. Both Mernissi and Atiyah raise highly problematic questions concerning representation of poor and illiterate women for both national and international audiences.

54. I am working on a methodology rooted in Husserlian phenomenology.

55. Jacques Derrida, *L'Écriture et la différence* (Paris: Editions du Seuil, 1967), 414.

56. This does not mean a return to a narrow-minded cultural functionalism. For example, to argue that the "veil" gives women a sense of selfhood is just as unacceptable as Patricia Jeffery's describing a veiled woman as "anonymous, a non-person, unapproachable, just a silent being skulking along, looking neither left nor right." See her *Frog in a Well* (London: Zed Press, 1979), 4. Veiling is a historical phenomenon that can be understood and explained. But, the meaning of the veil varies from individual to individual.

57. Robert Cousineau, *Heidegger, Humanism, and Ethics* (New York: Humanities Press, 1972), 9. This book reproduces substantial sections of Heidegger's letter. See also pp. 7, 9, 47.

58. See Henri Lefebvre, *Le Manifeste différentialiste* (Paris: Gallimard, 1976), esp. 93–145.

59. Cousineau, 48.

60. William Shakespeare, *The Tragedy of Othello* (New York: Signet, 1963), 56, 163.

61. Fyodor Dostoevsky, "Notes from the Underground," in *Great Short Stories of Fyodor Dostoevsky* (New York: Harper & Row, 1968), 293–94. This essay originally appeared in *Feminist Studies* 14, no. 1 (Spring 1988).

20

Criticizing Feminist Criticism

Jane Gallop, Marianne Hirsch, Nancy K. Miller

Editors' Note:

The aim of this informal conversation, which took place in October 1989, was to explore the issue of criticism among academic feminists in the United States in the late 1980s. The three participants belong to the same field (they are all edging out of French) and the same generation (they received their doctorates in the mid-1970s, when post-structuralism was on the rise, and were tenured in the early 1980s, when feminism began to be accepted in literary studies). Given the various controversies—more or less representative of the contemporary climate—in which they have been enmeshed, and given that climate, they felt it was important to discuss the style and practice of critique within feminism.

One particular project both provoked the conversation and ultimately shaped its course—Jane Gallop's "metacritical" book, a reading of anthologies of feminist literary criticism. One of her first protochapters, "The Monster in the Mirror," was a reading of a special feminist issue of Yale French Studies.[1] *Marianne Hirsch was one of the editors of that 1982 issue, the only editor to contribute an article to the issue. Gallop's reading focuses in particular on Hirsch's article and its relation to the editorial introduction. In the wake of their discussions of Gallop's reading of Hirsch, the two have become friends. Five years later, Gallop drafted a chapter, "The Coloration of Academic Feminism," which reads the anthology* The Poetics of Gender, *edited by Nancy K. Miller. The anthology is made up of papers from a colloquium at Columbia University, including one by Gallop. Gallop and Miller had been friends for more than a decade by the time Gallop sent Miller a copy of her reading. The fact that Gallop had both criticized Hirsch and Miller and had managed nevertheless to continue her friendship with them, gave this conversation its promise.*

The following has been edited—primarily cut and condensed—by all three participants. The disagreed about how much editing was needed. What you are reading represents a compromise.

Marianne: For me the idea for this conversation about feminist work that criticizes other feminist work came up at the School of Criticism and Theory this last summer. The only feminist speaker at the School insisted on talking "as a feminist," yet her paper was built on what appeared to me and others as the trashing of other feminists' work. The paper summarized, erroneously, and dismissed, as naive, a range of complex and influential feminist theoretical work for an audience that took these summaries to be "useful." All that to lead up to the "correct" answer which was Freud.[2] As I listened to that talk, I realized that this had become a pervasive move, that there is now a way of building a career on trashing feminist work. I feel like a lot of conversations are getting cut off by using the "club" words—essentialism or things like that. Even "race and class" are used as club words among white middle-class feminists. You say these words, people get defensive, and nothing happens further.

Jane: It's all about being right and wrong.

Nancy: What's the right feminist position? Who decides what's wrong or right and is that decision being made within feminism or outside of feminism?

Marianne: An example for me was set several years ago at the 1986 "Feminism and Psychoanalysis" Conference in Normal, Illinois, where I felt that the Lacanians and the object relations people just couldn't talk to each other.[3] The Lacanians acted dismissive and bored at the object relations papers because they found them to be so simple-minded, and the object relations people acted intimidated and angry because they couldn't and didn't want to understand the Lacanians. Even though the topic was the same, feminism and psychoanalysis, it meant two totally different things. And there was no mediating discourse.

Jane: That debate was just a repetition within feminism of a debate going on outside of feminism. It seems to me that a number of different debates going on within feminist criticism or feminist studies are versions of debates that exist outside of feminism, that have been taken on within feminism and what gets added is the question of which side is more feminist. I don't see them as intrinsically about feminism although they get expressed as such. Like, what is more feminist? Lacanianism or object relations? Neither. Whereas, in the seventies, embattled feminist scholarship was intellectually more separatist, and more suspicious of male systems, theories, etc., eighties feminist studies is much more full of other kinds of theories—psychoanalysis, deconstruction, or new historicism, or any number of different things.

Nancy: There are debates within feminism that are also taking place outside of feminism and there is a translated, transformed feminist version of them for feminist stakes.

Jane: It may be that these debates are so vehement and polarized because they are being fought out on the terrain of feminism by feminists, who think as feminists they should have a commonality but what is separating them did not arise within feminism so it can't be resolved within feminism. The only way they can get resolved would be to give up allegiance to these systems which include a polemic against each other.

Marianne: I'm not sure I agree with your historical narrative. I think that seventies feminism may have seemed more separate from these other theories because it was very set on theorizing difference—in the sense of attempting to define the specificity of women. From the mid to the end of the seventies, difference, in this sense, was the operative term. Because it seemed important to theorize the "feminine" and because there was somewhat of a separatist push to alter institutions and alter our way of running them, feminism seemed more separate, but I agree of course that feminism has always been embedded in other structures.

Jane: One of the big debates in the seventies was about whether to be intellectually separatist or not. That debate is no longer a major part of the discussion. I think that debate gets displaced onto debates in which *the other woman* is seen as very much tributary to some male system of thought. So then you can say "that's not feminist." It's a way of rejecting whatever doubts you have, as a feminist, about your relation to whatever male thought has been important to you.

Nancy: When discussions of separatism were going on in the seventies, I thought it was a bad idea. But now I think the most radical thought feminism ever had was separatism.

Jane: If you read male writing about feminism from the late seventies or early eighties, there is this hysteria about separatism. Talking about feminists who have never made a separatist move in their lives, men understood all feminism to be separatism whereas in fact academic feminism was only in a very minor form ever separatist. Perhaps we should take that as a sign that this was what was most powerful about the discourse because this was what was most scary. Not that we should go back to separatism because one can never simply go back to a position. But there are some unresolved questions about the relationship between feminism and institutions, feminism and other systems of thought.

Nancy: The masculinist reaction to feminist criticism is an anxiety over separatism. Separatism has been translated into "essentialism." The move from women's studies to gender studies which is everywhere around us keeps pushing us further and further away from anything separatist. In fact, it has become a positive embarrassment to talk about women. At the 1985 conference on feminist theory at the Pembroke Center I gave my paper "Changing the Subject," which ended with the words, "I hope we are becoming women."[4] Denise Riley, who has become one of the strongest voices of the current anti-essentialism, got up and declared—speaking, as I understand it, from a neo-Marxist position—that I was taking us backward into the past and that the worst thing we could be was women. I was completely thrown. Both because she misunderstood what I meant by the phrase—I explain in the published version—and because her response was cast as a denunciation (she read it out). Later in the conference Stephen Heath picked up her remarks, and I felt as though I was being publicly dismissed. It took me a *long* time to sort out, to recover from, to assimilate, and really to understand (I had a brief correspondence with Denise Riley on the subject). That was a turning point for me on many levels. I learned something important about my own work—what I absolutely believe—and the effect it can have on others. But I also learned to fear other women in a way I hadn't done until that point. If I was polemical, my polemic was with men. In my mind I was writing *for* women against some establishment—institution, theory—that was male. For the first time I thought, "I am now in a situation where *women* are not going to like what I'm saying." This had always been true to a degree of course, but Riley's reaction upped the ante. Now I have to deal with the fact that there are *always* going to be some women who *really* are not going to like my work—or me. (And vice-versa. This obviously is not a one-way street and I have been guilty of my own denunciations.)

Marianne: So what's at stake in these attacks and where does your fear come from? Certainly when one goes out and gives a talk, one expects some people will like it and others won't and we've also all been taught that polemic is great. But within feminism it is extraordinarily painful too.

Jane: There are at least two levels that always get mixed for me. Whether it's painful between women or whether it is painful between feminists. I think it is both and differently. I hate being attacked by other feminists. But I also find difference from or conflict with other women difficult. Conflict with men, I actually find somewhat pleasurable. There is an enormous fear of loss of something really important in irreparable conflict with another woman. But if the other woman can be categorized as "not-a-feminist," then that difference is easier to deal with. It makes it more like whatever pleasure is found in conflict with men. It is like the classic distinction between good and bad women, which is how a lot of this feels.

Also: I can't discount being attacked in the name of Marxism or historicism or racial difference, things that I recognize as serious political, as opposed to what I think of as high theoretical. I feel quite comfortable discounting the latter.

Nancy: You don't like to feel in a rank of things racist or classist.

Jane: Do they feel worse or better than being accused of being an essentialist?

Nancy: Well they go together. Because if you are an essentialist, the idea is that you don't see how different everybody is. You can be called an essentialist both from the side of deconstruction and from the side of neo-Marxism.

Jane: That's why the word is probably used so much.

Marianne: Those two sides may not agree at all about anything else.

Nancy: I would say that I also see a historical shift. In the early eighties, Marxist-feminist discourse was not neo-. It was more reconstructive than deconstructive. I'm thinking of work on "ideology and literature," for instance. The neo-Marxism of the late eighties is another matter; in some ways it has usurped the position of "French" deconstruction as the "left" of feminism. And as I just said, a critique from that position makes me feel pretty vulnerable.

In the early eighties, my own feminist rhetoric aligned me in what some people saw as a "materialist" position vis-à-vis deconstruction (that's not really a word I would use about myself): I cared about the signature of women writers, for instance, or for institutional acts—like creating women's studies programs, etc. (This is part of what is going on in my 1981 "dialogue" with Peggy Kamuf.) In those days I felt a certain anxiety about style, in the sense that it was considered more sophisticated, more elegant to be on the side of deconstruction than on the side of feminism. And I don't like to be thought of as a slob. I don't seem to take that problem to heart quite the way I used to—although the issues are still with us. I think that has a lot to do with the difference between 1981 and 1989. Now, the pressure on mainstream academic feminism comes from the side—if you can put it that way—of race. Which to me feels a lot more serious for all kinds of reasons.

May be the point is not why *now*, but why not *before*? It's as though race had to become a problem for *theory* before it could be taken seriously by white feminists.

Jane: I too, around 1981, experienced more anxiety about not being sophisticated enough whereas now my anxiety is about being bad, about having a white, middle-class outlook, stuff like that. But it strikes me that the discourse around me has changed. The anxiety about being a slob is an anxiety about not being high class enough, anxiety about being too low, whereas the other is anxiety about being too high. If you are looking up towards Derrida, Paris, sophistication, you feel like you're too low and you're anxious about not having something that comes from a higher class, to use the word metaphorically. Now the situation is the opposite. And one of the things that has happened clearly (for all three of us) is the change of status.

Nancy: A change of status in our positions?

Marianne: Like having tenure.

Nancy: Yes, there's been a change in our status but I don't think what that means is so simple. There is always a way in which as a tenured, published, feminist one necessarily becomes fair game.

Jane: In the Moglen-Keller piece on competition among academic feminists they talk about the fact that established feminists—feminists who are successful—continue to see themselves as powerless and victimized and this is very much resented by graduate students and assistant professors.[5] If I am giving a lecture and somebody stands up and attacks it, I feel deeply vulnerable. That subjective experience doesn't take into account that the person attacking is in fact a graduate student who is academically powerless and I am in front of that room by virtue of my authority. For me to respond as if I were a victim and that person was cruel would be not to take into account something like the symbolic as opposed to the imaginary. That is what you mean when you say "fair game."

Last spring I had a discussion with some graduate students who had read *Reading Lacan*. About half of them didn't like it because they saw my trying to talk about my vulnerability, given my position of authority, as a ruse to keep my authority because they couldn't figure out any way to "get" me. Whatever it might have meant for me, part of the meaning of my discourse when it reaches a graduate student is that it is the discourse of someone with authority. Feminists have a lot of trouble with our own authority because women are not in general in power. If we hold to a general feminist perspective we are still powerless victims oppressed as women. But if we talk about the world in which we operate, the small academic world of literary criticism, feminists do have power.

Marianne: And, of course, some have more power than others.

Nancy: When I give a lecture I feel not that *it's* being criticized but that *I'm* being attacked. I think this is something men are trained to do. I've seen Stanley Fish, for instance, go through an amazingly brutal exchange of assaults and then walk off, and it's as if he'd played a squash game and then went home to take a shower. That is something that most women don't know how to do. I certainly don't.

Jane: I think it is of very little use to us or our work to take any criticism of what we write as a personal attack. But I also wouldn't want to say that what we need to do is be socialized like men so that we see our work as a kind of product "out there."

Nancy: Whether or not you feel like you belong in there, you're the one getting the honorarium, you are the one invited and taken out to dinner. You are standing up there and they're not. It would be better for your health to realize that there is a separation between you and that.

Marianne: I think that the reason it is so hard to make that separation is that we never really *feel* in power. It is important for tenured feminists to articulate that, as difficult as it may be for younger feminists to hear. I don't know what it would mean to feel in power. Women—and feminists in particular, having tried to theorize or to think through some different ways of dealing with power and authority especially power and authority in relation to other women and to other feminists—find it extremely difficult actually to acknowledge that at times we are the powerful person, or in the powerful position. One of the effects of being in that place is getting attacked and disagreed with. There are a number of issues; there are institutional issues and there are personal, probably psychological issues and then there are the issues having to do with feminism's having had as a project trying to find a mode of knowing and operating that would not be based on trashing and attacking each other unfairly to score points. After all, we had hoped that when women had tenure, or were in power, things in the academy, in institutions, would look different.

Jane: In the world, women are not powerful and feminism isn't doing well and abortion is about to become illegal, etc. There is all this stuff to support one's sense that one is still simply oppressed. This makes me think of Linda Gordon's work on mothers and families and the classic evidence of the way that mothers who are powerless can be extremely abusive of the people they have power over because when you are powerless *and* have power over other people you can't use your power responsibly, you can't see it.[6] Not to say that we are literally abusing our children, but that there is some parallel in the inability to perceive oneself as both powerless and having power, at the same time in different contexts.

At a session sponsored by the Women's Caucus of the South Central MLA, I was the last of a panel of four to speak after Vivian Gornick, Rosellen Brown, and Sonia Saldivar-Hull. Each of them spoke from a position marginal to the academy. Saldivar-Hull was a Chicana graduate student, Brown had just given up her job as a university teacher, and Gornick was never an academic and spoke about it from outside. I got up and said I want to speak here as somebody who has an endowed chair, as somebody who is not marginal but centrally in the academy. I want to talk about how difficult it is as a feminist even to say that. Not that it is easier to be marginal, but it is easier to speak in a feminist context as from the margins. After I spoke, people got up and started to attack me for being successful, for saying I was powerful and also for saying that I didn't know how to use my power.

Marianne: This reminds me of your piece about *Yale French Studies* which, after all, we're here in part to talk about. In that piece, we were the editors of the issue, yet we set ourselves up as being very powerless. Here we were at Dartmouth in relation to Yale and a number of us were assistant professors. You read it very differently, you read it as our being Ivy League and blind about what that means. Your reading was coming from a different context.

Jane: I also read it as someone whose proposal had been rejected by the editorial collective so you had direct power over me. To talk about the specific context, I saw you as people who were editing this issue of *Yale French Studies*. I had always wanted to be published in *Yale French Studies* and saw this feminist issue as a way in.

Marianne: But then you gave your paper which was a critique of the issue at Yale. Where, even though we were editing a *Yale French Studies* issue, we were not giving talks. Where we had to force our way into the journal which really didn't want at the time to publish a feminist issue at all. So the reason it seemed politically problematic for you to be giving this talk was more *where* you were giving it. It's odd—every time we talk about this, the discussion revolves around this institutional pecking order. I guess it's an inevitable consequence of embedding feminism so firmly in the academy.

Nancy: Do you say in the piece on *Yale French Studies* that you were rejected?

Jane: No I don't.

Nancy: Did you consider saying it?

Jane: No, but I would consider saying it now.

Nancy: So what about that? Would that have made it any different for you [Marianne]?

Marianne: Yes, because it would have made Jane appear more vulnerable and less elevated than she now does in the piece; it would have given her critique a context.

Jane: Being invited to go to Yale was a big deal for me. When I was in graduate school, Yale was like "the" big place in French. That gesture was not just saying to Yale "you were right in not wanting to publish this feminist issue because this is what is wrong with the issue." It's basically saying this is what I think is worth talking about, this is what I consider an important talk.

Marianne: I felt both of those things. When I heard about it and read it, my first response was to feel totally exposed and criticized. And my second response was to feel incredibly flattered that you would read something I had written so carefully and reveal things to me about it, that you were reading me as a real writer. So it did have those two effects. But I know that the way the piece was heard and reported was that you were doing this incredibly anti-feminist thing.

Jane: I didn't know that until this moment. This is my ongoing problem with the book I am writing and may have to do with some bad thinking and naiveté on my part. I realize that what I all a "reading"—which involves a lot of attention to the text, trying to tease out what is going on there in order to interpret, describe, and observe it—is more often than not taken simply to be an attack. At first I complained that people just didn't understand, that they are so unused to anybody doing a reading of a critical text that they assume that if you are paying that much attention to a piece of criticism you must be attacking it. I still feel that. But it is clear to me that I need to take more responsibility for the way that my stuff is received, not just to say, "those fools don't get it."

Marianne: I was telling somebody that we were going to do this conversation about criticizing feminist work vs. trashing feminist work and she said "you are doing this with Jane Gallop? I thought Jane Gallop trashed you." I have read your piece many times and I have come to terms with it enough to see that you are not trashing me. But I think that this was somebody who had heard you give it as a talk where it does sound more hostile. This gesture of reading feminist work, reading criticism as text, can be heard/read as trashing.

Nancy: You established your method on male texts. Let's take the metonymy of that as calling Lacan a prick. Which made everybody very happy. Whereas it is certainly true that by calling him a prick, you say something important about Lacan which has explanatory value, it also has the merit of calling him a prick. It's not wholly negative; it has a critical edge but that could also be aimed toward bringing things to light.

Jane: In fact I was criticized for being too good a daughter of Lacan at the time I was writing that. So people understood that I was not just trashing Lacan.

Marianne: But in this scenario I think it's very different. My response to your piece has to do with power. I think reading as well as you do puts you in a position of power over me. So my first response was to try to do it back to you.

For about a month or two what I most wanted in life was to take a piece of yours and do the same thing to it. But that's not how I know how to read.

Jane: I do read like that as a means to power, empowerment as well as power. Whatever position or authority I have in the world, as well as money, comes from that. But also: when I read something that matters to me, I feel powerless until I "do a reading," write, and then I feel some power. It seems to me that part of my dilemma is having developed this as a style of reading in relation to men and French women.

Nancy: No one ever risked confusing you with them.

Jane: Having developed this style which was a very useful and powerful style of reading men, I was more and more uncomfortable spending all of this time reading men because that continues to give men a lot of power and importance. So I shifted toward women. You[Nancy]'ve asked me before, what happens when you turn that from men to women? But also: What happens if I turn from people who are clearly more powerful than I to people who are the same or less powerful?

Nancy: My way of looking at this is to see it as a question of positioning: are you the same as or different from? and how do you show this? So you with men have a David and Goliath thing, with little Jane Gallop from Duluth taking out her slingshot to use on the great man. But then what is her relationship to her cohort? This is really a question about writing—how you literally locate yourself in relation to these other people—who might be your equals, or your friends. . . .

So we come to *The Poetics of Gender*. I was shocked when I read that chapter; it really took me by surprise. My first reaction was that you were being unfair to me since you knew a lot about the scene at Columbia, the powers of the various players, and especially the limits of mine regarding the invitations. It seemed to me that you had to have known that my awkwardness in the preface about how to arrange the pieces, and finally settling on the "coloration" of the conference as an event, was a coded way of saying: "Look, this is what we have to work with, I'm doing the best I can under the circumstances." So I felt betrayed.

And of course your raising the issue of race the way you did got me very angry. I felt that you were holding me personally responsible for the fact that the conference, like the volume, was (as you said about its cover) white. The fact is that invitations were extended, but that they were late in being made, and of course they were too late altogether. I regretted this very much at the time—both the absence of the women and what I experienced as my powerlessness to do anything about it—but it's also true that I got so caught up in the thrill of a conference on gender at Columbia, at the Maison Française, with all those women (those feminists!), that it was only when I was putting the volume together and editing the papers that I began to measure seriously what the absence of women of color meant not only for an event, but for a poetics emerging from it. It seemed all wrong: not just politically and ethically, but intellectually. That was what I was trying to say in the wimpy footnote about a conference in the future that would be configured differently, etc.

Jane: But things had also changed between 1984 and 1986; it became a much more telling issue for white feminists.

Nancy: So that's why for me the date is 1985. Adrienne Rich wrote "Notes Toward a Politics of Location" in 1984, but I didn't see it until the book came out in 1986.[7]

Marianne: It has also provoked a turning point in your work.

Nancy: Yes, although as I just said, my own belatedness in trying to confront these issues is really not a subject of self-congratulation. In any event, by the time I received your piece, which was 1988, I was so far down the road in my own attempts—following Rich—to write about this that I dind't feel I was in need of a lesson from Jane Gallop about the inclusion of women of color in such an event.

Jane: Can I say that at no point did I say that what is wrong with this book is that women of color are not included? I was talking about what I felt to be the mark of their absence in people's discourse. I thought that there was a kind of subliminal consciousness about this absence. I was not talking about the fact that you did not invite anyone. I knew there was some attention to color at that conference because of my talk, among other things. I knew that this was a place in which there was a self-consciousness about the meaning of color.

Nancy: So you're saying what exactly?

Jane: Not that the text was racist, but that there was an awareness of that. That that was why these phrases kept coming up. I was basically putting color in the text not complaining it wasn't in the text.

Nancy: Monique Wittig uses the word "coloration" in her essay and it's interesting that Wittig doesn't talk about race in her work at all.

Jane: I got the "coloration" from her.

Nancy: I hadn't realized it was in both places until I was going back over the whole thing. I must have picked it up from her essay.

Jane: I only picked up yours because of hers. The two of them worked together; I was paying attention to color at this point. She uses "coloration" when she is saying that no other oppressed group bears their oppression in language. I thought her use of the word "coloration" in the paragraph was a mark of the repressed of her statement. Have you looked at it since I gave it to you?

Nancy: I looked at it quickly and I could feel myself still getting . . . .
I want to come back to a more general question about the difficulty of your project which has to do with positioning. Who are you in relation to the work of other feminist critics? You're not directly giving grades, saying "this is good work, this does not go far enough." You're not doing that, but I find it so hard to talk about the tone of doing the reading. Does it necessarily make you above or in the outside position of pointing things out? "Isn't it interesting how this is this and this?" It so quickly for me becomes a judgment, a negative judgment. I don't know whether that's me. There's a way in which it pulls your reader by the unpacking of it. In fact one winds up thinking these people aren't bright enough. You are showing them something that they've missed.

Marianne: About their own work. That is what I'm trying to say about the power. Reading people's work in that way puts you in a position of power that then puts others in the position of object in relation to it. Your revealing things to me about the unconscious of my writing places you in a position of superior knowledge.

Jane: In *The Poetics of Gender* piece it is at least marked as my own unconscious too, one that I shared. I see myself as very centrally a part of that anthology and not as somebody who knew better all along. I inscribe myself most in that essay called "The Coloration of Academic Feminism." Since this book represents my first major move out of French and my own francophilia, I was trying to think through what my own relation to France represents in terms of Eurocentrism. That essay thinks through my Eurocentrism, but in the larger context of race rather than in some kind of blinded context of just America and Europe.

Nancy: But somehow the fact. . . . I'm trying not to say this in a hostile way because I think it's really a difficult problem. Yes, you call yourself on it. I've done it myself: you say, "well, there I was. Little did I realize that I was being a—fill in the blank—at the time." The point is you can name yourself and still come out smelling like a rose (something else pink!).

Jane: But that doesn't solve the problem.

Nancy: It doesn't necessarily solve the problem to say "I was part of it" because you're out of it already. You are already one step out of it because you're naming it. Whereas the others are flailing around in it. They didn't notice.

Jane: They didn't notice then. I didn't notice then. This is a history problem: the fact that, of course, in 1988 I see things that other people didn't see in 1984, that I didn't see in 1984. Which is something that I want to try and talk about but I don't know how. The response that I am basically writing from a position of superiority is very widespread and I therefore cannot discount it. The other thing is that removing myself and saying "isn't this interesting and this is going on and this is going on" strikes me as the only way to get out of yelling at each other and polarizing and not seeing the reasons for the opposing person's position. When we read people to be either on their side or against them we just get locked in all these blindnesses. This is a method of understanding something better than we can when we're doing what we usually do: being for or against.

Nancy: Which is basically a deconstructive move. You show that on the one hand these oppositions are less solid than they appear; that on the other hand to insist upon them is in fact to install the very things you are trying to get rid of. If that isn't the horizon you want to emerge, then what is? It seems to me that what you need for the book that you haven't done yet in the individual pieces would require some other—more affirmative, less paradoxical?—kind of writing: in order to say what the end, the point of this project, might be. Or is your point finally some version of what you said earlier: that feminists are tearing each other apart over issues that are not necessarily their own and that maybe what we have to learn to see is exactly where the issues in feminism are? Or maybe, that's not possible, and that's the whole point. Which brings us back to deconstruction.

Marianne: For me it is still the question of context, of who's listening and who you are doing it for. I'd be interested for you to talk about where you think the audience of this book is. I see your gesture as very different when you are speaking in the auditorium at Harvard or Yale or when you're reading the paper at a feminist conference. I feel that "the men" get a tremendous amount of pleasure and reassurance out of hearing feminists criticize each other. At Dartmouth we had a Women's Studies Conference in 1982. Lots of very established colleagues came to this conference and one person actually stood up and said, "It is so gratifying to see that feminism has evolved to the point where feminists can criticize each other." This is like the mark of maturity. But you could also see that the real pleasure for "them" was to see that we are not a united front, that there are these splits, that in fact we're attackable.

Jane: The other aspect of separatism is that basically women are all bonded together.

Marianne: And so it is a relief to see that we are in fact not bonded. That we criticize each other. So I think all of these effects have to be taken into account by feminists who disagree with each other. As Adrienne Rich says, men are always overhearing and there are various ways to respond to that.[8] One of the responses we had to your piece on the *Yale French Studies* issue was precisely this feeling that you were exposing us to "them" in some way. You were exposing problems in the big arena out there where what we needed was protection and mutual support—the appearance, at least, of a united front.

Jane: This reminds me of books like *Sexual/Textual Politics*. It may have hurt people's feelings, but it doesn't seem to me that the people Moi was writing about who were very powerful in the scene are any less powerful because of her work.

Marianne: It is not that someone like Elaine Showalter is less powerful in the profession as a result of her critics, but it is that Showalter's work is now read by a lot of people through the critiques and therefore dismissed. For instance, I read a dissertation that starts with a long chapter on feminist criticism and its different positions, locating itself in relation to them. She quotes Toril Moi to characterize American feminism and Janet Todd's *Feminist Literary History* to characterize French feminism. At the defense we said to her "Why didn't you quote Showalter and Irigaray?" And she said, "Well, I read Showalter and Irigaray, but it would have just taken a lot longer for me to quote them." The way it came out in the thesis is that American feminism is totally bourgeois and simple-minded. So, this sort of dismissive critique does hurt people's work.

Jane: I assume my audience to be by and large feminist graduate students. It may be that, in fact, this whole project is a struggle not just about a relation to the fathers but a struggle over whose version of history is going to be told to the next generation.

Marianne: In that sense, you want to write the history.

Jane: Yes, I clearly am trying to write that history. Oddly enough, although maybe it makes me just the same, one of things I see myself trying to undo is the effect of books like *Sexual/Textual Politics* and the amount of influence that they've had for graduate students as a version of seventies feminist criticism. I see myself literally and directly trying to write, not the reverse of these books, but some other mode of looking at history as well as trying to demystify what I see as a reigning myth. I see this misconception of the seventies, for example, and all these received notions about French feminists and American feminists. It drives me up the wall and has actually given me something specific that I want to undo. Presumably we would then have something like quoting Gallop which would not be any better than quoting Moi or quoting Todd. I hope I am not doing the same thing, saying somebody is bad, somebody is good: this is the line, this is what they are. But rather insisting that these people be read in order to understand what they are saying. Moi's work represents to me what I hope I am not doing but also what I am writing to counter. But I'm not sure I'm not doing the same thing in perhaps some fancier way.

Marianne: Can you try to characterize the difference?

Jane: I get inside something and treat it as a text, understand as well as I can, and then try to make clear to people what I have understood. So I am trying not to give grades (although I am taking positions about certain things that are good or bad), but to understand why people are doing what they are. Mainly I am saying that feminist criticism has not been well enough understood. I am writing a history for people who already know a lot of the texts I am writing about rather than for somebody who doesn't know. I am writing a history of something that is too known in the sense that it is familiar, but that we don't really perceive anymore because we have our set notions and categories for what's going on. To try to defamiliarize in some mode . . . .

Marianne: How inclusive are you in this history? Are you including antholog-ies that foreground race, for example, and the intersections of race and gender?

Jane: I'm doing Pryse and Spillers's *Conjuring*.[9] Race only posed itself as an urgent issue to me in the last couple of years. Obviously there has been a larger shift in the valent feminist discourses in which I participated. I didn't feel the necessity of discussing race until I had moved myself out of a French post-structural orbit and began talking about American feminist literary criticism. . . .

I was telling this guy in Syracuse that I thought in writing *Reading Lacan* I had worked through my transference both onto Lacan and onto things French in general. And he asked, "So who do you transfer onto now?" My first thought was to say "no one." And then one of the things I thought of was a non-encounter with Deborah McDowell. I read work from my book last February at the University of Virginia. I had hoped Deborah McDowell would come to my talk: she was there, she was the one person in the audience that I was really hoping to please. Somebody in the audience asked me if I was writing about a black anthology. I answered no and tried to justify it, but my justifications rang false in my ears. Some weeks later a friend of mine showed me a letter from McDowell which mentioned my talk and said that I was just doing the same old thing, citing that I was not talking about any books edited by black women. I obsessed over McDowell's comment until I decided to add a chapter on Pryse and Spillers's *Conjuring*. I had already vowed not to add any more chapters out of fear that I would never finish the book. As powerful as my fear of not finishing is, it was not as strong as my wish for McDowell's approval. For McDowell, whom I do not know, read black feminist critic. I realize that the set of feelings that I used to have about French men I now have about African-American women. Those are the people I feel inadequate in relation to and try to please in my writing. It strikes me that this is not just idiosyncratic. This shift, for me, passed through a short stage when I felt like what I was saying was OK. The way McDowell has come to occupy the place of Lacan in my psyche does seem to correspond to the way that emphasis on race has replaced for me something like French vs. American feminism.

Nancy: Well, when I received your reading of *The Poetics of Gender,* I was working on "Dreaming, Dancing, and the Changing Locations of Feminist Criticism," my piece on the conflicts within feminism, including the question of race. When I finished (and gave!) the piece "on race"—let's just say it created more problems than it solved—I began to wonder whether there was any position from which a white middle-class feminist could say anything on the subject without sounding exactly like that. (I'm not sure that "coloration" doesn't fall into the same trap.) The rhetorical predictability of it all. The political correctness. Just like "men in feminism." In which case it might be better not to say anything. I had tried to circumvent the problem by a kind of montage of quotations. That didn't work any better. So now I'm thinking: just do the work—the reading, the institutional politics—and forget the rhetoric *about* doing it.

Marianne: I think this question about writing to please certain people comes back also to the question of what's the correct feminist way to write and what's more feminist. But I hope it does not mean that "the men" are no longer considered the enemy, and that feminists have become each other's principal censors and judges. Because I still believe that there is this larger scene in which feminists— and all feminists—feel vulnerable and in which our own struggles with one another are entangled. The question I really want to come back to, and that I think we disagree about, is whom does criticism, divisiveness, really hurt? What's the risk?

Jane: You keep on coming back to this question. I think you must have an answer.

Marianne: There is a certain generation of feminist theorists who have really gotten it from all sides: Elaine Showalter, Nancy Chodorow, Sandra Gilbert and Susan Gubar, Carol Gilligan.

Jane: I actually believe there is no direct relation between being trashed and having career difficulties, suffering in your career. There is a graduate student fantasy that if you stand up after a lecture and ask the devastating question you will get to take the place of the lecturer. They will lose everything they have and you will get it. I think that trashing poses a different problem. I am opposed to trashing not because I am opposed to criticizing but because I believe it falsifies issues and keeps us from thinking through or understanding anything.

Marianne: I agree with that, of course; there has been a great deal of bad faith and mutual appropriation. But in addition, I think that being trashed by other feminists actually has affected people's careers. I think that some people's work has gotten more careful and circumspect, some people have begun to write out of hurt and fear. One of the pleasures of working in feminism was the feeling of community. When you go to a conference and get attacked by other feminists— and I don't just mean criticized, I mean trashed—the whole tone and range of the project changes and certain work gets disallowed.

Jane: Feminists have been attacking feminists from the beginning. I think it's a myth that there was a moment feminists didn't attack feminists.

Marianne: When Carol Gilligan was *Ms.* "Woman of the Year," then people— feminists—felt free to just tear her work apart. I think at this point it is like a shorthand. All you have to say is Gilligan and it's like everything that's essential-ist, read bad. It's not "cool" to like, and more important, to use, to build on certain feminists' work, especially if it can be construed as essentialist. What are we afraid of?

Jane: I can't feel sorry for Carol Gilligan because despite it no longer being cool or sophisticated, Gilligan has an enormous impact. Her books have sold a lot. She's on the cover of the *New York Times Magazine*. All kinds of people who are not on the cutting edge of feminist theory continue to be influenced by her, to use and accept her.

Marianne: But you are saying not on the cutting edge.

Jane: Whatever that means and I'd like to put the phrase in quotation marks. Which is to say that "it is not 'cool' to like" Carol Gilligan. I'm using this phrase as synonymous. I think there is a problem in that there's been no attempt by people who consider themselves on the cutting edge or doing any other kinds of sophisticated feminist theory to grapple with Gilligan's work and in some ways it is dismissive. But I also think that despite this trashing, she has not been denied an enormous influence. Much more than I'll ever have.

Marianne: But, as you are saying, the hysteria around her work has prevented many from grappling with the radical potential it has in spite of its problems. I think it's a generational thing and I think that that generation has somehow not been able to raise a generation that builds on what came before. You're saying that maybe it was there in the beginning, but I guess I don't believe it was the same. In the seventies we were hungry for every new book and its discoveries. And, of course, there were disagreements and there was criticism. I think it again has very much to do with the issue of power and who is in power and how many of us there is room for in the academy. We are in an economy of scarcity and we know it much more clearly in the eighties. And so people try to establish their space by pushing out everyone else.

Jane: I see all these feminist graduate students whose first instinct is to trash some established feminist thinker.

Marianne: Why?

Jane: I don't know why but it doesn't seem very different than what I have already seen graduate students do, especially male graduate students. Take figures they perceive as powerful, who they are told to read in courses and find where they are wrong. There are now feminists who are perceived as powerful enough to be treated to the same kind of aggression as powerful figures have been for at least as long as I have been in this profession.

Nancy: One of the things that makes feminism particular is a self-consciousness about ways of knowing and the ways in which we believe what we know. Is it possible to try and think about some kind of pedagogy or some kind of way of being that would break the cycle of trashing the predecessor, killing the mother, and instead say, "here is what this opens and now we can go on from that" or "this gives us a ground, let's then go on to do other things that they haven't dealt with."

Jane: I think that is what is needed. I think it hasn't happened because, first of all, the reticence to recognize the power of the mothers has made it hard to talk about. In the attempt to have a different kind of pedagogy that would not repeat the killing the father model, with a mere change of gender, there has been too much assertion that women wouldn't do that because they are women. I think that assertion has operated as a kind of maternal super ego, a kind of idealism that produces the opposite. The only alternatives proposed are filial piety or killing the mother. The filial piety model actually reinforces the oedipal structure. Jane Marcus says that our job is to carry forward our mother's text.[10] The daughter graduate student trying to gain a voice for herself must kill the mother if that is the expectation. I think we need to make it all explicit and deal with it and then say, "wait a minute; this is a totally impossible alternative."

Marianne: So we seem to be operating in extremes: killing each other publicly or glossing over conflict altogether. But the middle course, which is obviously what is needed, is hard to find in the context of the academy as it is constituted.

There was a lot of conflict being suppressed in the Yale French Studies Collective. But I think we are really in a very difficult position because there is always that extra jury out there. Dartmouth, for example, had a very particular situation in those years which was that a number of women were hired at the same time. So the way the collective project even started was that five people were going to be up for tenure the same year (1982)—four of them women. So one of the ways to deal with the whole problem was to say, "OK we are going to work together." It was a way both to keep busy and to talk to each other (and obviously people had to write their own books at the same time). It was a way to bide the time until the tenure decisions came around and to do something together so it wouldn't be possible for "the system" to pit us against each other in every way. Now, three of the people in the collective were going to be voting on the other four. The only way to deal with the enormity of these contradictions was to suppress the whole thing, to suppress any conflict whatsoever because there was just too much at stake.

Jane: What I was troubled by in that introduction was not just the suppression of conflict but the celebration of no-conflict because I don't believe in no-conflict. And I found this celebration of no-conflict destructive because it basically means either repression of conflict or marginalization of those who can't bear to repress the conflict.

Marianne: But it wasn't a celebration of no-conflict. It as a celebration of a collective enterprise and I think that is different.

Jane: Maybe I misunderstood this because you were writing that introduction out of a very local context that I misperceived.

Marianne: It wasn't very local. The issue of tenure for feminists in the academy was not and is not at all a local issue. From conference to conference, people like Catharine Stimpson were saying, "the issue for feminists right now is tenure." People were saying, "Can you imagine that we've come to this, that women would vote against each other for tenure?" Something was broken when that happened. Some matter of trust and expectation and confidence was just ruptured. I guess the other thing I want to say about the Yale French Studies Collective is that, although some of those bonds are as tight as ever, some members of that group don't talk to each other any more. My sadness about that is enormous, but that collectivity did not turn out on the whole to be a success.

Jane: I never suspected that it was. Part of my response comes from my belief that collectivity is so difficult. I think it is deeply valuable but so difficult. I think the reigning discourse about collectivity so minimizes the difficulties that it makes it harder for collectivity to work. There is another issue which I think you feel really strongly. You ultimately feel a real danger in feminists criticizing each other in the earshot of men. I don't feel that it makes us more vulnerable and allows them to be able to get us.

Marianne: I guess danger is probably not the right word but I feel discomfort about it. I don't think we can stop criticizing each other, but we need to think through the implications. When I heard you give the talk at Harvard about Barthes and pleasure, I could just see the men's pleasure in hearing a powerful feminist criticizing other feminists' work. I could feel it in the room.[11]

Jane: The real problem with that piece is that I don't do any readings of the feminists; I do readings of Barthes. Maybe the difference between what I am now trying to do and trashing is that I was dismissing feminists based on "mythologies" of what feminist criticism was about. In that piece on Barthes and feminist criticism, there are no quotations from feminist criticism. I think that is much more dangerous than criticizing.

Nancy: That may be. You were playing the "men" to feminism—"they aren't reading our work, etc."—but that's really not the issue. The issue—and it's bound to become more acute with the arrival on the scene of a whole generation of younger feminists trained by us(!)—is the performance of a critique without the edge of violence that creeps into the tone. Maybe violence is too strong— without the contempt for other work that seems to come with the territory.

Jane: Maybe one has to distinguish between a criticism that actually attends to something and a criticism that's really dismissive. We've had too much of this debate about whether we should or shouldn't criticize. What we need is an ethics of criticism.

Notes

1. Jane Gallop, "The Monster in the Mirror: The Feminist Critic's Psychoanalysis," in Richard Feldstein and Judith Roof, eds., *Feminism and Psychoanalysis* (Ithaca: Cornell University Press, 1989).

2. A version of Toril Moi's talk has since been published as "Patriarchal Thought and the Drive for Knowledge," in Teresa Brennan, ed., *Between Feminism and Psychoanalysis* (New York: Routledge, 1989).

3. The keynote papers from that conference appeared in Richard Feldstein and Judith Roof, eds., *Feminism and Psychoanalysis*.

4. Published in Nancy K. Miller, *Subject to Change: Reading Feminist Writing* (New York: Columbia University Press, 1988).

5. Evelyn Fox Keller and Helene Moglen, "Competition: A Problem for Academic Women," in Helen E. Longino and Valerie Miner, eds., *Competition: A Feminist Taboo?* (New York: The Feminist Press, 1987).

6. Linda Gordon, *Heroes of Their Own Lives: The Politics and History of Family Violence: Boston: 1880–1960* (New York: Viking, 1988).

7. In Adrienne Rich, *Blood, Bread, and Poetry: Selected Prose, 1976–1985* (New York: Norton, 1986).

8. Adrienne Rich, "When We Dead Awaken: Writing as Re-Vision," in *On Lies, Secrets and Silence* (New York: Norton, 1979), p. 38.

9. Marjorie Pryse and Hortense Spillers, eds., *Conjuring: Black Women, Fiction, and Literary Tradition* (Bloomington: Indiana University Press, 1985).

10. Jane Marcus, "Still Practice, A/Wrested Alphabet: Toward a Feminist Aesthetic," in Shari Benstock, ed., *Feminist Issues in Literary Scholarship* (Bloomington: Indiana University Press, 1988).

11. "The Reverse Body," in *Thinking Through the Body* (New York: Columbia University Press, 1988).

Conclusion
Practicing Conflict in Feminist Theory

Marianne Hirsch and Evelyn Fox Keller

"What we need," Jane Gallop concludes, "is an ethics of criticism." That Gallop should end rather than begin her conversation with this plea is indicative of the difficulty of moving beyond that hopeful statement to a concrete formulation of what an ethics of criticism would indeed look like. In effect, she puts the question that faces us at the end of our own volume: Have the essays included here in fact brought us any closer to envisioning such an ethics? Have they helped provide "new models for a discourse of difference—models that would preserve the dynamic possibilities but defuse the explosive potential of enduring disagreements?" In this conclusion, we want to assess the strategies our contributors have chosen in response to the difficult assignment they accepted.

Feminists in the late 1980s have become exceedingly accomplished at articulating theoretical positions on the basis of disagreement and opposition; they have learned to define their own stance against other stances. But with this mastery of disputation, has come a corresponding difficulty in treating other positions with sympathy and respect. The task of clearing space for multiple agendas representing conflicting interests therefore poses a major challenge. Yet this is precisely what we enjoined our authors to do. Facing a vastly complex and often deeply embattled set of positions and views, with divergent and often contradictory claims, each had to choose an approach that would encourage dialogue and conversation among opposing factions.

To facilitate thinking about possible approaches to such a difficult task, we have re-sorted the essays, according to the principal strategies different authors have adopted, into four broad categories. It is interesting that many of the authors envision their task in spatial terms: the essays speak "from the place of feminism," they "map the terrain" of a given dispute, they look at "border cases" and "contested sites," they insist on "situating" knowledge and on describing "locations" and "relocations," they all analyze "positions." Yet, in the process of charting and mapping a field as complex and shifting as "feminism," in the process of charting the disputes over its "turf," each author finds the need for ever more intricate skills of cartography.

Some essays divide the map into two parts, focusing on the claims of opposing sides in order to represent the interests of women with the greatest force and success. A second group, rejecting polarities, remaps the terrain of the conflict, using various strategies to extricate it from the force of binary constructions. Still others focus on very particular "border cases," micro-moments which bring to the surface underlying differences and discordances and which demonstrate the precarious layout of any opposition. A fourth group confronts opposing sides more directly in conversation or dialogue. Here, the turf is not divided but openly disputed and ultimately, albeit uneasily, shared.

1. Representing Women's Interests: Opposing Views

A number of the essays in the volume begin by highlighting the oppositional nature of the conflicts they discuss, outlining the claims, often equally convincing, each side makes for its representation of women's interests. Yet as they proceed, giving rigorously fair descriptions of each side, confronting them with one another, pinpointing the assumptions, hopes, and fears on which they rest, each of these authors expresses increasing frustration at the way that disagreements lead to oppositional politics. Accordingly, each seeks, with more or less success, ways of extricating her essay from such narrow confines.

Nancy Cott exemplifies this approach as she locates the polarization of feminist politics in its historical repetition. The bitter ERA dispute in the 1920s was indeed a clearcut opposition between those who argued for equality and those who were firmly committed to the legal benefits of sex-based protective legislation. Both claimed ownership of the designation "feminist." In ending her narrative in the midst of the Depression, Cott asks a question that recurs throughout this volume: "What kind of group were women, when their occupational and social and other loyalties were varied, when not all women viewed 'women's' interests, or what constituted sex 'discrimination,' the same way?" From this vantage point, a dispute that looks like it has two sides, each representing "women's" interests, suddenly multiplies as both the group "women" and the notion of what constitutes "interests" splinters across economic and class divides.

Addressing two major disagreements among feminist lawyers—centering respectively on pregnancy and maternity leave policy and the regulation of pornography—Martha Minow chooses a strategy that resembles Cott's: she confronts opposing sides with one another, and demonstrates how each, even while believing it best serves the cause of women, interprets their interests differently in different situations. Her analysis of leave policies leads Minow back to "the sameness/difference conundrum," a construction she refuses because, she insists, when the ideology of gender difference rules our public policy choices, the variety of human experiences is obscured under facile either/or constructions. Starting from a different premise, the feminist debate about the regulation of pornography can move from the unresolvable question of sameness vs. difference into a critique of the structural relations of power and oppression. But here a different opposition emerges. Arguing over whether the state can be trusted to look out for women's interests, feminist lawyers fall into the "public/private debate," which is no less dichotomous, no less divisive. As she gives examples of decisions that reframe the way questions are posed, Minow begins to find a different way to think about the law, a situated decision-making that responds better to changing and competing needs. Yearning for a more thorough escape from dichotomous constructions, Minow concludes with the notion of a "deeper divide"—the divide that concerns "other women" who are poor, who are relegated to the margins of the social field, and who therefore may not have the luxury to benefit from the possibilities of a family leave, or to fight the degradation of pornography. Although in presenting the two sides of several different disputes, Minow can escape a simple binary, she succeeds only in gesturing toward the greater multiplicity which, she believes, will allow a thorough reconception of legal thought. Minow is not optimistic. As a lawyer, she is fully aware of the deep entrenchment of feminist lawyers in a system which, with its demands for precedent and justification, for "arguments that seem familiar and uncontroversial," wears down those who would dream of more radical change.

Michelle Stanworth similarly approaches her subject by articulating apparently clearcut, if virulently contested, "pro" and "contra" positions on reproductive technology. Stanworth discusses the case against conceptive technologies, identifies the assumptions about women's nature and the critique of medical treatment that underlie this antipathy, and reveals some of the ways it undermines itself and accordingly fails to serve, in her view, the very "interests of women," or even of mothers, to which it is committed. She locates the source of the dispute in conflicts inherent in competing constructions of motherhood—simultaneously empowering and disempowering—that feminists have elaborated but not resolved. The "apocalyptic reading" of conceptive technologies, she suggests, seeks to hold at bay perceived threats to motherhood that are real enough, but does so by misrepresenting that threat—focusing on a view of maternity too narrowly centered on the "natural" rather than the social dimensions of reproduction. Stanworth argues that a more adequate protection of mothers' claims requires the recognition of the great diversity of social and economic determinants of women's maternal experiences, as well as a more nuanced understanding of the relation between "natural" and "cultural." In this way, she echoes the moves out of the straightjacket of opposition already seen in Cott and Minow.

2. Mapping and Remapping

By far the greatest number of the essays in the volume begin with an attempt to displace "opposing views" by disputing their very delineations, and accordingly, to shift, or even refuse, the original ground of the discussion. Joan Scott's essay on the Sears case is not only a good example of this strategy, but an impassioned plea for a new history of feminism, beyond the familiar narratives of equality versus difference (too often rewritten as sameness versus difference). Her theoretical paradigm is deconstruction, and Scott appropriates an analytic strategy from literary and cultural analysis to dislodge a conflict in the very different arena of labor law. "It is surely not easy to formulate a 'deconstructive' political strategy in the face of powerful tendencies that construct the world in binary terms," she concedes. Yet it is precisely this strategy that she argues is necessary not only to displace the opposition between demands for equality and affirmations of difference in the recent Sears case, but also which continues to determine the ways in which feminists have been formulating their understandings of feminist movement.

Ann Snitow's argument that the history of feminism in its multiple manifestations (minimizers/maximizers; radical feminists/cultural feminists; essentialists/constructionists; motherists/feminists) does, in fact, come down to this same "recurring divide" between equality and difference might seem to place her approach in our first, "opposing views," category. Her actual presentation, however, and her sympathetic treatment of each side and each formulation, ultimately enables her to remap the terrain, presenting several interlocking and overlapping maps, illuminating the divide from the perspectives both of activist struggle and theoretical inquiry. Her "gender diary" embeds the analytic histories of feminism in a number of voices and stories which establish multiple dialogues. Her move from roman to italic print and her focus on particular locations of dispute, particular sites for the production of feminist theory—a consciousness raising group, a political meeting, an interdisciplinary study group—expand the range of the field and put local oppositions into dynamic play. Still, the fact that *one* fundamental and subsuming divide dominates her narrative means that even as some issues are illuminated, others will remain obscure. Cognizant of this inevitability, Snitow suggests that "perhaps the image works best as a place to start, not as a conclusion," and she ends her essay with a personal appeal for other maps to be placed alongside her own.

Carla Freccero's essay also takes the form of a dialogue with several voices. Freccero remaps one of the most intensely and passionately contested sites of feminist theory—namely, pornography. Like Snitow, Freccero needs to write from several places and in several voices precisely because she refuses to contain the "sex wars" in the discourse either of theory or of political strategy. First, redefining the question in terms of sexuality, and second, placing it in the context of a broader political agenda in which pornography finally cannot hope to play a central role, Freccero's essay enacts the contradictions raised in the sex wars. By interweaving the exacting voice of the theorist whose bibliography is impeccable, the oral voice of the feminist talking to friends in a study group, and the transgressive, repressed voice of female sexual fantasy (a second person voice, anonymous yet provocative and disturbing), she delineates a problematic with neither simple legal solutions, nor clearcut "sides."

For different reasons, King-Kok Cheung also refuses to engage in arguments with feminists: "[dichotomous] tendencies have the effect of re-centering white feminism," she charges. Instead, she asserts her belief that "in order to understand conflicts among diverse groups of women, we must look at the relations *between* women and men, especially where the problems of race and gender are closely intertwined." Cheung thus reframes the topic, looking at feminism itself as an agent of conflict among Chinese-American women and men. Although that conflict appears to take the form of a simple binary opposition—woman warrior versus chinaman pacific, feminist versus heroic—Cheung rejects this formulation, longing for redefinitions that would allow Chinese-American women to maintain their allegiance both to their ethnic and to their feminist causes. In this call for consolidation, she interestingly departs from the (by now) more familiar concluding call for multiplication.

The notion of remapping is itself one we have borrowed from Katie King's essay on gay/straight splits in feminism. King charts a historical narrative of these splits in the number of shifting, yet overlapping, forms they have taken in the last twenty years. All of them, King shows, are embedded in other splits—sometimes parallel, sometimes orthogonal—in the material, social, and political culture of which feminism is a part. Discussing the production of feminist theory and feminist culture, King can criticize academic feminism and its exclusions even as she advocates "coalitions among many differences." She does this in the name of feminist culture—a culture produced by an apparatus King deliberately calls "cultural feminism," thereby simultaneously reclaiming and redefining a label that (perhaps especially since the sex wars) itself has come to be used to silence and exclude. King's remappings have the effect of multiplying the points of contestation and the kinds of intersecting conversations in which she wants feminists to engage. Her essay also has two "voices": the dense, conflated preface to each section and the body of the texts that follow play off with and against each other to raise questions and stimulate reformulation. Yet other voices are introduced in her discussion and notes, where King identifies registers of feminist writings that are rarely heard in mainstream journals and presses, emerging from acentric and conventionally unacknowledged sites of theoretical production. The effect of the multiple lenses through which King looks at gay/straight divides is to reveal a diverse, multiply interconnected and forever shifting map which rejects all oppositional logic for feminism.

In her essay on essentialism, Teresa de Lauretis also seeks to shift the ground of the discussion and, thereby, to reclaim use of the term. Essence, she claims, is not to be found in the analysis of male/female difference or in women's nature, but rather, in the specificity of feminism itself. In fact, she writes, the very currency of the term "essentialism," "time and again repeated with its reductive ring, its self-righteous tone of superiority, its contempt for 'them'—those guilty of it," has only served to obscure the "specific difference of feminism—and thus to polarize feminist thought on what amounts to a red herring." Like others, De Lauretis also seeks to liberate feminist theory from conventional (and debilitating) dichotomies, but now in order to focus on another that she sees as more fundamental: the contradiction and tension between the erotic-narcissistic and the ethical impulses driving all feminist self-representation. At the end of her essay, she points toward intersections of the two drives in lesbian feminism, without, however, showing how a space beyond even this binary construction might be shaped. For this, her readers will have to turn to her fuller elaborations elsewhere.[1]

3. Border Cases

A "border case" in Mary Poovey's, and now Valerie Smith's, formulation is a site that reveals the cultural and historical specificity of perspectives and experiences conventionally contained in the category "women," and we would add, "feminist." Lying on the "border between two defining alternatives," such cases "mark the limits of ideological certainty."[2] A number of the essays in this volume focus on such "border cases"—i.e., on specific cases, moments, or personalities capable both of revealing more general conflicts and contradictions, and of calling into question the oppositional logic on which they rest. The Sears case is just such a "border case," for Joan Scott, the reception of Maxine Hong Kingston for King-Kok Cheung, the feminist peace movement for Ann Snitow, and the Baby M case for Tom Laqueur.

Elizabeth Abel refuses to validate the long-standing debate between feminism and psychoanalysis or even the competing claims of different psychoanalytic approaches. Instead, she looks at one area where psychoanalytic feminism seems particularly vulnerable—the analysis of race and class as they intersect with gender—and shows, unexpectedly, that psychoanalytic aims are not divergent from an analysis of race and class. On the contrary, Abel reveals extensive areas of convergence in aim and effect which demystify contradictions we have come to accept as givens in feminist theory (Lacanian versus object relations theory, psychoanalysis versus neo-Marxism). Her essay offers important insights into the processes by which differences become magnified and convergences erased.

Helen Longino and Evelynn Hammonds's essay on the particular tensions in feminist studies of science illustrates a combination of all three of these approaches. Longino begins with the common expectation of major disagreements among feminist contributors to this subject on fundamental philosophical issues, but ultimately she exposes such disagreements as curiously exaggerated. The consequence of her analysis is thus to shift our perception of the field. Her use of the "border case" approach is, however, distinctive. Unlike any of the other essays, hers focuses on individual personalities, following the evolution of the work of four scholars who have shaped the field. She provides an understanding of the differences among them by analyzing their different contexts of theoretical production, audiences addressed, and agendas aimed at. By so doing, Longino allows us to see convergences that are otherwise obscured. To understand why these different analyses have appeared so divergent, she points both to the inadequacy of existing categories of analysis, as well as to implicit competition for traditional male approval. Yet, as in all conflicts among feminists, there is also explicit competition for the approval of other feminists. In Part II of the essay, Evelynn Hammonds focuses not on the conflict among feminist theorists, but on the conflict between them and women scientists. In this, she provides a welcome enlargement of our concerns, pointing to the larger context in which feminists have sought to make a difference. Indeed, looking at these larger contexts provides one explanation of why differences among feminist critics of science tend to be so divisive. Especially for an endeavor that is so marginal, and the number of contributors so small, it is easy for "outsiders" to respond as if to a single unitary voice. In the face of this conflation, it may well be that feminists react by over-drawing their own differences, in the attempt to protect their different agendas and maintain communication with their different audiences.

Marnia Lazreg looks at a different kind of "border case" (feminist writing about Algerian women) in order to make manifest the contradictions she sees as implicit in Western feminism's discourse of difference. The call for a distinctive voice for every woman, she claims, is itself articulated in a voice that effects an inevitable erasure of some women. Post-structuralist approaches to ethnology, she finds, share the ethnocentrism of old-fashioned humanism, and Lazreg argues that feminist scholars, by participating in theoretical discourses that have become hegemonic in the academy, have thus far failed to resolve this impasse. In attempting to carve out space for the voice of the group she represents, in voicing her own anger at their exclusion, Lazreg points to "the murderous power of discourses," even if she herself cannot, yet, point the way beyond.

For Valerie Smith, interracial rape is a border case for the study of the connections between racism and sexual exploitation and, concomitantly, for the delineation of a black feminist praxis. Smith's texts—reports of the Central Park rape, Alice Walker's "Advancing Luna—and Ida B. Wells," and her own classroom—are as divergent in genre as possible, yet they allow her not only to suggest the ways in which race and class inflect the discourse of rape, but also to define the multiple and multiply disturbing silences that continue to dominate that discourse. Although Smith eloquently describes the "intersectionality" of race, class, and gender in the writing of rape—the writing of rape is always already the writing of race, she claims—her own meta-discourse of difference cannot yet break through those areas of silence. For this, the classroom may indeed offer a more promising arena.

4. Conversations across Differences

A complete history of feminist theory would have to include among its classic texts numerous dialogic encounters, ranging from conventional debates to dialogues, conversations, or collaborative pieces—some openly contentious, others aiming at the oral contrapuntal mode exemplified by the feminist acapella group

"Sweet Honey in the Rock." The dialogues between Carolyn Heilbrun and Catharine Stimpson; Elizabeth Spelman and María Lugones; Mary Helen Washington and Linda Dittmar; Gloria Joseph and Jill Lewis; Elly Bulkin, Minnie Bruce Pratt, and Barbara Smith to name just a few examples, have become classic texts in the Women's Studies canon. They have shaped a new form for stories of conflicts among feminists, suggesting new ways for feminists to confront divergent positions with one another, and to enact the dynamic of their disagreement.

We reprint here one of these dialogues, what has become known as the "Kamuf/Miller debate," published in 1982. In our retrospective view, this exchange illustrates both the productive potential and the pitfalls of staged dialogue. It has been used to exemplify and, as Miller and Kamuf themselves caution, in some ways to reify, what Donna Stanton termed the "Franco-American Dis-connection," later rewritten as feminism versus deconstruction. But Miller's response to Kamuf can be read very differently: as a dialogic performance that engages profound differences with mutual sympathy and respect. The correspondence Peggy Kamuf and Nancy Miller undertake at our request in the summer of 1989 rethinks both their original dialogue and its reception in light of more recent "dislocations" in feminist theory. Their meticulous effort to articulate agreement with disagreement in the traditionally feminine mode of the epistolary exchange provides an example of how dialogue can continue across and despite significant and enduring differences of view, of how the textual process of dialogue itself might refuse the work of polarization.

A very different "conversation" is staged in this volume between Thomas Laqueur and Sara Ruddick. We asked Sara Ruddick to respond to an essay Laqueur wrote for a different occasion, because we thought it important to allow the feminist engagement with/disengagement from fathers to be articulated both from the perspective of a father interested in the social and historical construction of gender, and in the voice of a scholar who has employed her own perspective as a mother and a philosopher to articulate a feminist reconception of mothering (and fathering). If the volume departs here from its practice of selecting modulated voices, eager to defuse polarization, it illustrates in the exchange between Laqueur and Ruddick a different mode of practicing conflict—a grumpyness that comes from disagreement but that provokes productive theoretical claims precisely because it is so deeply felt and so uncompromisingly stated. Laqueur's and Ruddick's claims originate in different places, and, clearly, aim at different goals and interests. Yet we are aware and also suspicious of our own greater willingness to let "grumpyness" stand in the one dispute that directly involves men and that is voiced by the only male contributor to the volume.

The last two pieces we discuss here are conversations actually taped and transcribed for the purposes of this volume. Mary Childers and Bell Hooks's "Conversation about Race and Class" is made possible by a friendship based on two common experiences: a working-class background and the resulting alienation from white middle-class feminism. Their cross-race dialogue about feminist theory, about languages allowed and disallowed in the academy and in feminism, about common and different personal histories, only begins to discover "the unknown terrain on which truly multi-racial politics can be developed." But the care with which both speak, the respect, friendship, and trust they show one another, the openness, even eagerness with which they discover convergences, bodes well for the future of other such engagements. As we read the "Conversation," however, we are invited also to listen to its own silences, and to contemplate the hard work it will take to approach those silences. In what it accomplishes, and in what it does not, this conversation can do much for feminists as they consider both future agendas and possibilities of future collaboration.

"Criticizing Feminist Criticism" is yet another kind of conversation. As a "border case" study for the practice of criticism among feminists, it uses the book Jane Gallop is in the process of completing—a series of readings of anthologies of feminist literary criticism. In this informal conversation, Marianne Hirsch and Nancy K. Miller, two friends/colleagues whose work Gallop has criticized, confront Gallop about the politics of her critical reading practice. In the process of discussing Gallop's work, the three address some of the feelings that underlie many of the other stories told in this volume—the angers, the cautions, the fears and anxieties that the current climate of feminist work seem to have fostered, along with the friendship, trust, and mutual recognition that persist. It is interesting that the conversation began as a discussion of disagreements between the three and ended up with an articulation of their *common* anxieties about race in feminism. Gallop, Hirsch, and Miller share similar racial, ethnic, class, and generational backgrounds, as well as academic status. The convergences and disagreements of their conversation articulate anxieties that preoccupy them as feminists who have been engaged in feminist theory since the late seventies. Among friends, certain angers, certain worries, certain wounds, certain frustrations can be spoken, even though they might not be politically or theoretically "correct." In allowing others to eavesdrop, Gallop, Hirsch, and Miller provide for their readers a less than usually censored narrative of the practice of conflict in the practice of feminism. It should be noted, however, that both of these conversations are taking place among feminist literary theorists, within a field, that is, where feminist concerns have moved to a central place in the profession. Perhaps it is the sheer fact that there are now so many feminist literary scholars that creates the space and the possibility for such dialogues in the first place.

Finally, all of these essays are informed by other, less visible, conversations that have taken place both between us and the authors and among the authors and their own colleagues. Each of them has gone through numerous readings and has benefited from the advice of others whose approach to feminist theory and whose ideological allegiances were markedly different. This more informal process of valuation and criticism that remains obscured beneath the surface of each text—acknowledged only in a footnote, if at all—may well come closest to the ethics of criticism we envision. Perhaps because they were informal and hence protected from public scrutiny, even harsh critiques were generally responded to with openness and respect. As such, *these* conversations have also come closest to the "new models for a discourse of difference" we had hoped to find.

CODA

As we look back and consider the ways in which the idealism and optimism of feminist theory in the late seventies were sustained by the "dream of a common language," we see also that that dream was in turn sustained, as all such dreams must be, by the illusion of a domain internally free of conflict. For the most part, feminists of the seventies wrote, and tried to think, of conflict as operating between feminism and its alternatives—be it marxism, militarism, racism, heterosexism, capitalism, or even the academy—not within. Those of us participating in the development of feminist theory at that time surely had to be aware that this was an illusion, for conflicts were everywhere among us, often explosively so. For the most part, however, we saw these conflicts as minor squabbles, and sought to contain them. Ever attentive to the hostilities without, we saw the primary need as one of keeping "feminism" together. Today, we have come to recognize those boundaries we wanted to think of as delineating "us" from "them" as conspicuous fault lines among "us": the "marxism" confronting feminists of the seventies has been superseded by feminist varieties of "neo-marxism"; feminists of color have revealed to white middle-class feminists the extent of their own racism; and perhaps especially significant, feminist theorists themselves have moved from the margins of the academy to its interior, in the process internalizing the pressures of that institution to conform, compete, and succeed. With these developments, the field of feminist theory has been dramatically reconfigured, its internal relations now fractured and its borders far more difficult to delineate.

The net effect is that feminists entering the 1990s require a new understanding of the meaning both of feminism and of feminist theory. Such an understanding needs to encompass the manifest contradictions between our recognition of "the disintegration of the representative subject of feminism," and the continuing need for a coherent voice with which to articulate political demands on behalf of the group called "women." Minimally, then, we face the task of learning, as Mary Childers puts it, "that practicing conflict is also practicing feminism." We face the task of learning how to use our own conflicts constructively, affiliatively, and pleasurably—as sources of pleasure precisely because they can be tools for forging new understanding and new forms of affiliation. In addition to an ethics of criticism, guiding us in the distinction between criticizing, censoring, and trashing, we may also need an aesthetic of conflict to help us redraw our maps of feminist movement. The constructive, even erotic, practice of conflict, however, appears to be an art in which many women, perhaps especially white American middle-class women, are poorly skilled. More commonly, it seems, feminists have learned to use conflict primarily as a shield, to cement internal ("lateral") bonds, rather than as a force for building new ("longitudinal") connections across lines of difference. Perhaps this is why the seventies' ideal of commonality had as much appeal as it did; it may also explain why the multiple conflicts amongst feminists—more and more overt as the eighties progressed—were, and often continue to be, experienced as so painful, so devoid of humor, irony, and possibility. But if some of us are poorly skilled in the art of conflict, we ought to be able to learn from others who are better skilled, who, from different kinds of experiences and even different traditions, can provide more useful models for practicing conflict constructively.

In our work on this volume, the two of us, closely placed as we are, found ourselves confronting surprising, sometimes upsetting, but always shifting areas of disagreement. At times, as we wrote the introduction and conclusion, one or the other of us felt uncomfortable with a formulation, a turn of phrase, the inflection of a sentence. At other moments, especially as we tried to pinpoint and delineate the extent of our disagreement, these differences magnified and we soon found ourselves polarized. Aware that we were acting out our own version of the practice of conflict in the practice of feminism, we came to see that no conclusion written under a single signature could do justice to the differences between the positions even we inhabit. Even though we are both invested in the possibility of a common voice, we value equally the integrity of each of our voices. We end, therefore, in a final "conversation."

EFK

A common refrain running through feminist theory these days, indeed through much of this volume, is that feminists of the seventies were able to maintain the illusion of commonality by their/our own exclusivity, because their/our eyes, and doors, were closed to the values and voices of women speaking different languages. There is indeed much truth to this charge, and the current preoccupation with multiplicity and specificity reflects a corrective movement that is accordingly both necessary and welcome. Feminists, like women in general, speak not only out of different perspectives and experiences, but also with different affiliations and different aims. Some of these differences derive from social, economic, and ethnic location, and it is

MH

In the conversation with Jane Gallop and Nancy Miller, I described what I saw to be the changes that had occurred in feminist theory in the 1980s in largely negative terms. I spoke primarily of what, from my perspective, has been lost. Here, I want to try to articulate, in very personal terms, a specific experience with the constructive face of conflict.

The story of my "coming-to-feminism" is a story of affiliations and collaborations. I remember 1970 as my first experience of genuine allegiance to any group, and I remember all too well the unexpected and for me utterly new exhilaration that came with this recognition of commonality. Having grown up in Eastern Europe as a member of a persecuted minority and having spent my primarily to such distinctions that recent feminist theory has become most attentive. But other kinds of differences—e.g., differences in theoretical aims and in intellectual and political affiliations—also cut through and across feminist allegiances. And while conflict has been undoubtedly productive for the enlargement of feminist consciousness and scholarly production with respect to some of these differences, it has been less productive with respect to others. Indeed, it appears that in the very effort to deconstruct some oppositions, others have been tacitly reinforced.

Take, for example, the division that has emerged between feminist critics of science and women working as scientists (discussed in this volume by Evelynn Hammonds). Along with Hammonds, my experience of this division has been personal, and for me, as for Hammonds, the course of my work has been accordingly affected. A decade ago, it was possible to articulate an intersection between the aims of feminist theory and those of the natural sciences thick enough for (some) women scientists to inhabit and even exploit; it was (albeit marginally) possible to be both a scientist and a feminist theorist. Today, that margin, and with it, that possibility, has vanished; feminists who began as scientists (like me and like Hammonds) increasingly feel obliged to choose between doing feminist theory and doing science.

When I first began writing about gender and science—a project I undertook in order to deconstruct the division between "woman" and "scientist"—one of the primary tasks I set myself was to teenage years as an immigrant, perpetually "wrong" in my tastes and behaviors, I knew little about affiliation. I came to feminism both unprepared and utterly open to the connections that consciousness-raising and feminist collaboration made possible.

In the mid-1970s, feminist literary studies provided a privileged field of inquiry which, unlike the feminist critique of science, would eventually touch and genuinely transform the larger discipline. It was through several collaborative writing projects and through repeated dialogic encounters with other feminist critics that I was able to develop a feminist reading practice and a feminist critical voice of my own. To see my ideas mirrored in those of others, to develop together a politics and a practice of mutual support, was not only to acquire professional confidence, but also to experience thinking as powerful and radical. I see now (and I appreciate the irony) that I learned in those years to fear conflict and disagreement. Was it my personal history that made consensus so precious? Or was it that our commonalities were made precarious by institutional pressures? Whichever, it seems clear to me that it was precisely the experience of affiliation that infused the theoretical project in which we were engaged with its radical and transformative potential.

By the late 1970s and early 1980s, several of the groups and programs I had helped to form, both personal and professional, faced serious and growing disagreements, disagreements so threatening as to require suppression. Major splits in feminist collective endeavors, conferences in particular, also began to come into focus. What I did find a way to talk about these issues that could be understood by other women scientists. The coalitions and affiliations that I sought were in the first place with others "like me"—i.e., other women who were both feminists and scientists. Indeed, I felt that the failure to reach these women would constitute a fundamental failure for my project. In this sense, my "we"—always more of a hope than a reality—reached tenuously in what became two very different directions. In place of the division between "woman" and "scientist," we now have a division between "feminist" and "scientist," ironically reinscribing the old conundrum of the "two cultures." The disruption of this particular "we"—by persistent, even insistent, misunderstandings fueled by familiar anxieties on both "sides"—is inevitably also, for me, an internal fracture. In part, then, this book proceeds from the same impulse that led me into feminist theory in the first place: for me, it is a dual protest against personally untenable divisions and against the erasure of the "difference" represented by my own particular concerns.

A focus on the supposed coherence of seventies feminism obscures the fact that, from its earliest days, feminist theory was in fact characterized by a marked multiplicity in its goals, and in its stated functions. For some, its purposes were largely representative—i.e., to give voice and space to that half of the human race that had been silenced and eliminated from dominant social institutions. To others, its primary purpose was explicitly epistemological, political in a different sense of the term, aimed not directly at changing

not then see was that the unwillingness or inability to confront openly differing agendas in large part caused the splintering I so tried to avoid. I could not see it because, at this point, my very theoretical work had become dependent on the belief in women's commonalities, on the analysis of "female experience," and of "feminine specificity," on the force that speaking on behalf of "women" could endow.

This is the history I brought to the Bunting Institute in 1984. I could not imagine a more conducive environment to the work of feminist theorizing than a community of forty women scholars and artists. But feminist community had changed by the mid-1980s. Not all the women at the Institute were feminists, which was a surprise in itself, but a feminist theory group—more diverse than any I had ever participated in—was nevertheless soon organized. As it became clear that diversity in membership also meant a diversity of perspective, diversity itself soon became the topic of reading, study, and discussion. Those often painful discussions produced a significant turning point in my feminist consciousness and in my theoretical work. More importantly, they provided the means by which I could come to participate in the shifts in theoretical direction from the analysis of "femininity" to an analysis of gender as it intersects with race and class.

The first discussion on race and feminism was chaired by a black and a Chicana member of the group. I had done my reading—I had read about the exclusion of women of color from mainstream feminism before and was prepared to work on that—and I was social institutions, but indirectly, at changing the intellectual canon to which these institutions appealed for justification. Still others set out to challenge the very meaning of "intellectual," of "knowledge," and of "ways of knowing." With multiple tools and visions, feminist theorists sought not just the enlargement of political, moral, and intellectual spaces, but also their reconfiguration.

By gaining access to the academy, some feminists, perhaps especially in history and literary criticism, have been notably successful in transforming the "language of the fathers"—largely by engaging in and with that language. Other feminists, in or out of the academy, in the same or in other disciplines, have been less successful. Some (e.g., Carol Gilligan) even appear to have been successful in the academy yet marginalized from feminist theory per se. As someone who has been involved with the production of feminist theory since the seventies, I feel compelled, before closing this volume, at least to call into question the absence from "the cutting edge" (as Jane Gallop calls it) of current theory of at least some of the aims that were initially so prominent. I am thinking in particular of early hopes to identify and restore, as intellectual resources, those "ways of knowing" that have traditionally been excluded from the cultural canon of the west precisely because they were labelled "female." Some of these early aims have been definitively blunted if not disabused altogether. I am not questioning the necessity of their recasting, only of their erasure. Many of the original efforts associated with these aims were

looking forward to a provocative discussion, even to action that would follow. But I was not in any way prepared for what happened. The two organizers started the meeting by questioning its very premise. "Why should we talk about this with you?" they asked. "What purpose will discussion serve? Wouldn't it be better to remain silent, to work and talk among ourselves?" I was shocked and silenced. Others reacted similarly and discussion almost came to a halt. But somehow we went on, for I remember the next shock: the Chicana woman's insistence that she felt more deeply connected to Hispanic men than to white women. There I knew what to say, I argued back, heatedly, passionately, terrified that if what she said was true I would lose what I had been building—personally and theoretically—for fifteen years. It took a long time for me to acknowledge that I was trying to argue her out of her experience. Her experience threatened me profoundly, and with my defensiveness I was only confirming her point.

We were fortunate to have a year to build up some trust and to work through, at least in part, some of the ruptures introduced at those first meetings. And we were fortunate to be in an institution which enabled such an endeavor by minimizing competition—after all we had already been awarded all it had to give. Although our meetings continued through the year, we didn't bridge those initial ruptures, and the "progress" made in those discussions was neither obvious nor easily measurable. Any consensus we reached, any coalitions we formed were acknowledged to be provisional marred by naive and simplistic expectations—among others, the expectations of ideological and cultural homogeneity that helped inform these questions. Today, feminists are vastly more careful, and more sophisticated, but it seems to me that we are also more fearful: made more fearful not only by the institutions we have come increasingly to inhabit, by the political conservatism of our times, but also (and surely relatedly) by our own eagerness to devalue, censor, and dismiss. It is almost as if we have sought to defuse the force of external censorship by becoming our own harshest critics. Too often, the work of exploring differences among commonalities, and commonalities within difference, has been displaced by a defensive and anxious need to "choose sides." As a result, we have divided along lines that often seem to me more illusory than real, that may have little, finally, to do with any of the political or intellectual tasks that lie ahead. If I were to name one feature of feminist theorizing in the seventies for which I am openly nostalgic, it is the conviction then widely held that there was important work to be done—work that could be supported in the name of feminism not because all feminists held the same priorities, but because that work had a radical thrust from which, we believed, feminists—and women— would generally gain some benefit. We have learned well the lesson that differences can be suppressed; I suggest we need also to learn that commonalities can be as facilely denied as they were once assumed.

Perhaps it is inevitable that, out of

and contingent. But through the silences I faced at those meetings, I did manage to understand something about my own assumptions, about feminism, and about the practice of conflict. As I allowed myself to look at the anger directed at me as the oppressor—a very different feeling than voicing my own anger at others—I had to relinquish something of the power of my theoretical voice. Finding myself positioned into the narrow identity of "white middle-class feminist," despite the contradictions of my own earlier experience, forced me to think beyond easy polarities and to question the boundaries of identity politics. I suspect that had those two women introduced that first meeting differently, less radically, less angrily, less conflictually, my resistance would have been stronger. In that context, conflict—openly confronted, voiced directly and clearly on all sides, in good faith—was utterly and searingly illuminating, even, in retrospect, a source of pleasure. It also enabled us to build powerful coalitions, even lasting bonds.

Still, that particular practice of conflict has not been easily translatable to other institutional contexts. It did not prepare me for the internal splintering that emerged among some of the feminists in my own field and my own institution—between junior women and senior women, between black women and white, between psychoanalytic critics and neo-Marxist critics, between "essentialists" and deconstructionists. But learning, through conflict, that my feminist experience is in so many respects different from others has cleared the very desire to create space within feminism for voices of all ranges, we have created new forms of occlusion and silencing. But an ethic of criticism ought to include a mandate to respect differences that cut across and along many kinds of axes. For the political as well as for the intellectual well-being of feminist theory, it needs, at the same time, to include as assiduous a search for, and recognition of, commonalities as we have mandated for differences. After all, the constructive and pleasurable practice of conflict presupposes both the existence and the possibility of connection—connections that are never either guaranteed or secure, but instead, motivating precisely because of their contingency.

the way for me to become part of theoretical work which seems to me truer, more honest, less idealistic—if more difficult to formulate and agree on—than the work of the 1970s. Placing differences among women so centrally in the project of feminist theorizing has its risks (obscuring commonalities, losing the power of consensus). Feminist movement is currently in a phase of reflectiveness; the essays in this book have described how many discussions have been repeated and recast without appearing to move ahead. My hope is that we might be able to agree about at least some of the work that lies ahead, perhaps even regain, around certain issues, the power that comes from solidarity.

But perhaps the main point that needs to be made in closing is that we leave this project with many questions unanswered. However illuminating the essays here may be about the nature of the conflicts that currently engage feminists, what remains unexplained is why feminist theorists find themselves with so little forward momentum at this particular moment in time. That question, however, would require a different kind of analysis, focusing less on internal issues and more on the power structures both in the academy and beyond. It would require, that is, an analysis of the impact the Reagan/Bush era has had on feminism as well as on other oppositional movements—in short, a history of feminism in its larger social and political context. But this is another book, and another project, one we hope will soon be forthcoming.

Notes

1. See Teresa de Lauretis, "The Essence of the Triangle or, Taking the Risk of Essentialism Seriously: Feminist Theory in Italy, the U.S., and Britain," *Differences* 1, no. 2 (Fall 1989).

2. See Mary Poovey, *Uneven Developments: The Ideological Work of Gender in Mid-Victorian England* (Chicago: University of Chicago Press, 1989), p. 12.

Index

Abbott, Sidney: 95
Abraham, Julie: 203n
Abrams, Kathryn: 162
Abzug, Bella: 12, 13, 37
Achtenberg, Robert: 221n
ACT UP: 89
Adam, Barry D.: 101
Ahmed, Leila: 344n, 345n
Al Hibri, Azia: 343n
Albister, Maite: 120
Alcoff, Linda: 16, 17, 18, 19, 38, 98, 258, 261-3, 266, 268n
Alexander, Priscilla: 97
Allen Pamela: 98
Allen, Paula Gunn: 248n
Allison, Dorothy: 96
Almaguer, Tomas: 96
Alpert, Jane: 15, 16
American Civil Liberties Union (ACLU): 151, 154, 157, 161
Anderson, Mary: 48, 50, 52, 54, 57, 58
Anzaldúa, Gloria: 96, 247n, 261, 343n
Archbishop of Hartford: 211-2
Arendt, Hanna: 227
Arguelles, Lourdes: 101
Armogathe, Daniel: 120
Armstrong, Nancy: 43
Atiya, Nayra: 348n
Atwood, Margaret: 306-7
Auclert, Hubertine: 333, 344n, 347n
Auerbach, Nina: 248n
Aury, Dominique ("Pauline Reage"): 119

Baby M Case: 3, 206-7, 219, 292
Bachelard, Gaston: 332, 246n
Baer, Judith A.: 57
Baer, Karl Ernst von: 211
Baker, Elizabeth F.: 57
Bamber, Linda: 18, 19, 38
Banks, Olive: 57
Barr, Marleen S.: 203n

Barrett, Michele: 19, 39, 81
Barry, Kathleen: 100
Barthes, Roland: 122, 125
Bartlett, Katharine T.: 41
Basu, Rekha: 319
Bearchell, Chris: 265, 269
Beauvoir, Simone de: 43, 116, 119, 347n
Becker, Susan: 56, 59
Beckett, Faith: 97
Bell, Laurie: 97, 100
Beneria, Lourdes: 37, 40
Benhabib, Seyla: 40
Berque, Jacques: 345n
Bertin, Joan E.: 40
Berzigan, B. Q.: 330, 344n, 346n
Bethel, Lorraine: 87, 99
Bhanavi, Kum-Kum: 81
Bird, Kai: 40
Birke, Linda: 166
Blackwell, Alice Stone: 58
Bleier, Ruth: 166
Boals, Kay: 335, 347n
Boose, Lynda: 202n
Bowlby, Rachel: 199n
Bradshaw-Camball, Pat: 81
Braidotti, Rosi: 184, 199-200n
Brawley, Tawana (case): 273, 275
Brennan, Teresa: 199-201n
Bree, Germaine: 119
Bridenthal, Renate: 39-40
Brodzki, Bella: 80, 98, 248n
Brontes, the: 117
Broughton, John: 40
Broun, Heywood: 57
Brown, Norman O.: 87
Brown, William Wells: 247n
Brownmiller, Susan: 274-5
Bulkin, Elly: 81, 96, 331, 346n
Burns, Lucy: 45
Burstyn, Varda: 163, 309, 320n
Butler, Judith: 265, 269n

Cade, Toni: 244, 251n
Califia, Pat: 96, 265, 269n, 310, 318, 322n, 324n
California Federal Savings & Loan Ass'n. v.
  Guerra: 153, 161
Cannon, Lynn Weber: 80
Carby, Hazel: 272
Carpenter, C. R.: 175
Casey, Josephine: 57
Catt, Carrie Chapman: 58
Central Park rape: 273, 276–78, 285, 286n
Ch'eng-en, Wu: 248n
Chafe, William: 56
Chan, Jeffrey Paul: 236–8
Chavkin, Wendy: 27, 40, 42
Chesler, Phyllis: 41n, 207, 219
Childress, Alice: 81
Chin, Frank: 235–7
Chodorow, Nancy: 74, 186, 190, 194, 200–1n,
  232n
Chow, Rey: 100
Christian, Barbara: 89, 99, 279, 287n
Christian, Shirley: 39
Chung, C.: 101
Cixous, Helene: 113, 115, 119, 260
Clark, Wendy: 265, 269n
Cliff, Michelle: 10
Clinton, Catherine: 272
Cock, Jacklyn: 300, 304n
Cohen, Rina: 81
Cohen, Sherrill: 41
Collins, Patricia Hill: 202n
Connolly, William: 146
Cornell, Drucilla: 40
Correze, Francoise: 334, 347n
Cory, T.K.: 57
Cott, Nancy F.: 55, 161
Coulson, Margaret: 81
Coursineau, Robert: 348n
Coward, Rosalind: 259, 304–5n, 319n, 321n
Cowper, William: 221
Crenshaw, Kimberle: 272, 285–6n
Crimp, Douglas: 98
Culler, Jonathan: 146, 249n

D'Emilio, John: 95, 101
Daly, Mary: 17, 26, 42, 258, 264
Davidoff, Leonore: 81
Davis, Angela: 80, 274–5, 286n, 323n
Davis, James: 57
Davis, Tonya Bolden: 97
Decarnin, Camilla: 96
Deforges, Regine: 119

DeKoven, Marianne: 18, 19, 38
Delacoste, Frederique: 97
Delmar, Rosalind: 267n
Deming, Barbara: 16, 38
Derrida, Jacques: 18, 111, 112, 137, 146, 260,
  338–40, 348n
DeSalvo, Louise: 199n
Dill, Bonnie Thornton: 80
Donnerstein, Edward: 162
Donovan, Josephine: 40, 109, 120
Dorsky, Susan: 344n
Dostoevsky, Fyodor: 342, 348n
Douglass, Frederick: 189, 247n, 250n
Draine, Betsy: 201n
Dreyfus, Hubert L.: 146
Dubois, Ellen C.: 25, 42, 55
Duggan, Lisa: 163
Durkheim, Emile: 330
Dworkin, Andrea: 16, 38, 156, 162, 308–10,
  320n, 321n
Dye, Nancy Schrom: 57

Easlea, Brian: 168
Echols, Alice: 14, 15, 16, 17, 38, 90, 96, 98,
  263, 267n, 309, 321n, 322n
Edelman, Marion Wright: 233n
Ehrhardt, Anke: 166
Eisenstein, Hester: 40, 96, 268n
Eisenstein, Zillah R.: 27, 40, 42, 65, 95, 248n,
  268n
Elshtain, Jean Bethke: 58, 159, 163
Equal Employment Opportunity Commission
  (EEOC): 138–44
Escarpit, Robert: 98
Espin, Oliva M.: 96
Estrich, Susan: 275, 286n
Evans, Sara M.: 42

Fanon, Frantz: 308, 329, 345n
Fates, Feriel Lalami: 347n
Feldstein, Richard: 199n, 203n
Ferguson, Ann: 39
Fernea, Elizabeth: 330, 344n, 346n
Finley, Lucinda M.: 58, 147, 161, 162
Firestone, Shulamith: 43
Flax, Jane: 185, 200–1n
Fleming, Anne Taylor: 221
Florenne, Yves: 113, 118, 120
Flowers, Betty S.: 202n
Forster, Charles: 329
Foucault, Michel: 18, 106–9, 117–8, 165, 120,

135, 146, 199n, 246, 331, 337–40, 344n, 346n, 348
Frankenberg, Ruth: 94, 96
Franklin, Rosalind: 178f
Freccero, Carla: 95
Frederickson, Mary: 58
Freud, Sigmund: 18, 65, 117, 185, 187, 191–2, 196, 200n, 209–10, 220n
Friedan, Betty: 40, 307
Friedman, Susan Stanford: 239
Frye, Marilyn: 265, 269n
Furstenberg Jr., Frank J.: 233n

Gallagher, Catherine: 220n, 323n
Gallop, Jane: 39, 197–8, 203n
Gatens, Moira: 270n
Gaudio, Autilio: 335, 347n
Gaudry, Mathea: 333, 347n
Geduldig v. Aiello, 417 U.S. 484 (1974): 161
Geertz, Clifford: 328, 345n
Geidel, Peter: 56
Gieve, Katherine: 299
Gilligan, Carol: 40
Gilman, Charlotte Perkins: 45
Goldsby, Jackie: 96
Graffigny, Francoise de: 133
Greenberg, Jay R.: 203n
Greeno, Catherine G.: 40
Greenwald, Maurine: 58
Griffin, Susan: 258
Griffith, Elisabeth: 161
Groneman, Carol: 81
Gross, Elizabeth: 146
Guanzhong, Luo: 248n
Gubar, Susan: 162
Gustavsson, B.: 40
Guttierrez, Ramon A.: 101

Hacking, Ian: 168
Hamilton, Dr. Alice: 49, 50, 57, 58
Haraway, Donna: 91, 95, 97, 98, 99, 129, 146, 169–71, 172, 173–5
Harding, Sandra: 91, 99, 171–5, 343n
Harris, Adrienne: 37
Hartsock, Nancy: 99, 265, 269n
Harvey, William: 209, 220n
Hatem, Mervat: 343n, 345n
Haug, Frigga: 101
Heilbrun, Carolyn: 63, 77, 80, 81
Henriques, Julian: 199n
Herman, Judith Lewis: 199n
Herrmann, Claudine: 112

Herron, Matt: 100
Hess, Thomas B.: 43
Higginbothan, Elizabeth: 80
Hirsch, Marianne: 95
Hirschman, Lisa: 199n
Hockney, David: 219
Hoggart, Richard: 191
Holland, Max: 41
Hollibaugh, Amber: 101
Hollway, Wendy: 199n
Holly, Marcia: 108
Hooker, Edith Houghton: 57
Hooks, Bell: 2, 26, 42, 85, 96, 99, 251n, 269n, 319n, 343n
Horton, Willie (case): 273, 276
Howard, June: 99
Hubbard, Ruth: 166
Hughes, Judith M.: 203n
Hull, Gloria: 96
Hume, David: 207, 212, 221n
Hunter, Nan: 163
Hutchins, Donna: 221

Illich, Ivan: 40
Inada, Lawson: 237
Irigaray, Luce: 233n, 260
Isidore of Seville: 210, 216, 220n

Jacobs, Harriet: 198, 323n
Jaggar, Alison: 27, 40, 42, 98, 99, 100, 268n, 270n
Jailer, Todd: 97
Janiewski, Dolores: 58
Jardine, Alice: 40
Jeffery, Patricia: 348n
Jehlen, Myra: 27, 40, 42, 343n
Jelinek, Estelle: 248n
Jhordan C. v. Mary K. [1968] 179 CA3d, 224 CR 530: 214–7
Joff, Joan: 162
Johnson, Barbara: 137–8, 147
Johnson, Guion G.: 58
Johnson, Sonia: 100
Jones, Ernest: 200n
Jones, Jacqueline: 81
Jordan, June: 305, 319, 325n
Joseph, Gloria I.: 81
Juhasz, Susanne: 249n

Kalman, Laura: 163
Kamuf, Peggy: 2, 112, 113, 114–5, 117, 118, 119

Kandiyoti, Deniz: 346n
Kaplan, Caren: 95, 97
Kaplan, Cora: 43, 313–4
Kaplan, E. Ann: 259
Kaplan, Temma: 20, 39, 40
Karlsson, J. C.: 40
Kay, Herma Hill: 41
Kazi, Hamida: 81
Kelber, Mim: 37
Keller, Evelyn Fox: 94, 167–9, 172, 173–5
Kelley, Florence: 47, 56, 58
Kelly (or Kelly-Gadol), Joan: 13, 37, 39
Kelly, Janis: 100
Kennedy, Florence: 72
Kerber, Linda K.: 40
Kessler-Harris, Alice: 56, 138-44, 147, 148, 153, 162
Kim, A.: 101
Kim, Elaine H.: 235–6, 247n, 251n
Kimmel, Michael S.: 39
King, Katherine Callen: 250n
King, Ynestra: 10, 11, 23, 37
Kingston, Maxine Hong: 234, 238–41, 245, 246–9n
Kirk, Marshall: 100
Kitchelt, Florence: 59
Klein, Melanie: 193–5, 203n, 313, 326n
Koedt, Anne: 38
Koonz, Claudia: 40
Kraditor, Aileen: 161
Kramarae, Cheris: 98
Kristeva, Julia: 39, 114, 260
Kuhn, Thomas S.: 344n

Lacan, Jacques: 18, 185–90, 192, 198, 201n, 200n, 202n, 325n
Laclau, Ernesto: 268n
Lamphere, Louise: 226n
Landry, Donna: 95
Laqueur, Thomas W.: 200n, 220, 222, 225–32
Lauretis, Teresa de: 5, 91, 95, 97, 98, 99, 124, 201n, 251n, 270n, 285, 287n
Law, Sylvia A.: 147, 161
Lees, Sue: 81
Leigh, Carol: 100
Lemeshewsky, A. K.: 101
Lemons, Stanley: 56, 59
Lessinger, Hannah: 41
Levine, Ellen: 38
Levinson, Sanford: 146, 147
Lewis, Jill: 81
Lofton v. Flouroy: 217–8

Lorde, Audre: 32, 43, 95, 96, 167, 261, 269n
Love, Barbara: 95
Lugones, Maria C.: 268n, 343n
Lukens, Edward Clark: 57
Luker, Kristin: 161
Luria, Zella: 40
Lyman, Stanford: 245

Maccoby, Eleanor E.: 40
Mack, Phyillis: 37
MacKinnon, Catherine: 89, 156–8, 162, 163, 265, 267, 269n, 275, 286n, 308–10, 320–2n
Madsen, Hunter: 100
Malamuth, Neil M.: 162
Malson, Micheline R.: 98
Mani, Lata: 87, 94, 97, 101
Mansbridge, Jane L.: 58
Marchiano, Linda (a.k.a. Linda Lovelace): 163
Marks, Elaine: 111, 113
Martin, Biddy: 94, 97, 98, 146, 260
Martin, Jane: 168
Masson, Jeffrey Moussaieff: 199n
Mayhew, Henry: 196
McClintock, Anne: 39
McClintock, Barbara: 167n
McDonald, Christie, V.: 120
McIntosh, Mary: 81
Meer, Theo van der: 38
Merchant, Carolyn: 168
Mernissi, Fatima: 344n, 348n
Michie, Helena: 203n
Miles, Angela: 39
Milkman, Ruth: 43, 57, 138, 142, 147, 148, 162
Miller, Nancy K.: 111, 119, 148, 203n, 260
Millett, Kate: 117, 120
Minces, Juliette: 200n
Minnich, Elizabeth: 80
Minow, Martha: 139, 147, 162, 163
Mirza, Heidi Safia: 81
Mitchell, Juliet: 27, 40, 42, 43, 200n
Mitchell, Stephen A.: 203n
Mitter, Swasti: 96–7
Modleski, Tania: 260
Mohanty, Chandra (Talpade): 78, 95, 97, 99, 100, 261, 343n
Moi, Toril: 98, 201n
Molyneux, Maxine: 39
Moraga, Cherrie: 95, 96, 101
Morales, Aurora Levins: 96
Morales, Rosario: 96
Morello, Karen Berger: 161
Morgan, Robin: 100

Morris, Meaghan: 77
Morrison, Toni: 190, 199, 204n, 241, 249n, 300, 304n
Mouffe, Chantal: 268n
Moynihan Report: 189, 244, 251n, 314, 323n
Mullen, Harriet: 94
Murray, Mary: 57

Nai'an, Shi: 248n
Navarro, Marysa: 21, 39
Nee, Brett de Bary: 247n
Nee, Victor G.: 247n
Nelson, Barbara J.: 42
Nelson, Cynthia: 344n
Nestle, Joan: 96
Newman, Pauline: 49, 57
Niekerk, Anja van Kooten: 38
Nochlin, Linda: 43
Norton, Mary Beth: 81

O'Barr, Jean F.: 80, 98
O'Neill, William N.: 56
Oakley, Ann: 40, 300–1n, 303n
Offen, Karen: 267n
Olsen, Frances: 161, 163
Olson, Ann: 100
Ong, Aihwa: 100, 101
Owen, Roger: 345n

Palmer, Phyllis: 81
Park, Maud Wood: 47, 56
Pateman, Carole: 233n
Patton, Cindy: 100
Paul, Alice: 45, 46, 47, 48, 55, 56, 57
Paulhan, Jean: 115
Pelletier, Renee: 335, 347n
Peterson, Richard A.: 98
Petrey, Sandy: 120
Pheterson, Gail: 97, 100
Philipson, Ilene: 39
Phillips, Anne: 43
Phillips, Lena Madesin: 59
Pickering, Andrew: 146
Pleck, Elizabeth: 163
Pollitzer, Anita L.: 56
Poovey, Mary: 198, 203n, 272, 286n
Ports, Suki: 100
Poston, Carol H.: 43
Pratt, Minnie Bruce: 81, 96
Putnam, Mabel Raef: 56

Rabine, Leslie Wahl: 201n
Rabinow, Paul: 146
Rafregard, C.: 40
Ramazanoglu, Caroline: 81
Rampersand, Arnold: 202n
Rapone, Anita: 38
Reagon, Bernice Johnson: 88, 92, 97
Register, Cherri: 120
Reiter, Rayna: 220
Reage, Pauline: 115, 119
Rhode, Deborah L.: 40
Rich, Adrienne: 24, 39, 40, 67, 117, 222, 258, 264–5
Rich, B. Ruby: 5, 84–5, 88, 96, 101, 265, 269–70n, 319, 321n
Riley, Denise: 13, 38
Robbe-Grillet, Alain: 119
Robbins, Bruce: 98
Roe v. Wade: 307
Rollins, Judith: 76, 81
Roof, Judith: 199n
Rosaldo, Michelle Zimbalist: 201n
Rose, Jacqueline: 185, 199n, 200n, 265
Rosenberg, Rosalind: 138–44, 147, 148, 153, 162
Rosenfeld, Rachel: 80
Rosenfelt, Deborah: 31, 43
Ross, Andrew: 316
Rosser, Sue: 166
Rossiter, Margaret: 180
Rothenberg, Paula S.: 268n, 270n
Rothman, Sheila: 56, 57
Rubin, Gayle: 84, 86, 87, 90, 95, 97, 100, 200, 220n, 265, 267, 269n, 312–3, 321n, 323n
Ruddick, Sara: 296, 303n
Rugh, Andrea: 346n
Ruskin, Cindy: 100
Russell, Diana: 99
Russo, Mary: 260

Saadawi, Nawal: 346n
Said, Edward: 97, 247n, 345n
Sandoval, Chela: 85, 90, 91, 92, 94, 95, 96, 98, 99, 101
Sansarian, Elizabeth: 345n
Sarachild, Kathie: 14
Saussure, Ferdinand de: 136
Sayigh, Rosemary: 346n
Sayre, Anne: 178
Scharf, Lois: 57
Schenck, Celeste: 80, 98, 238, 248n
Schiesari, Juliana: 95

Schneider, Elizabeth: 161
Schor, Naomi: 117, 120, 141, 148, 230, 233n
Schreiber, Tatiana: 101
Schulman, Mark: 98
Scott, Joan W.: 43, 161, 162
Seabrook, Jeremy: 191, 202n
Seager, Joni: 100
Sealander, Judith: 56
Sears Case: 3, 42, 139–44, 153, 162
Sedgwick, Eve Kosofsky: 81, 95
Segrest, Mab: 96
Sex Wars: 5, 84, 86, 89
Showalter, Elaine: 117, 259–60
Silverman, Kaja: 119, 261
Singer, Joseph William: 163
Sinha, Mrinalini: 22, 39
Smith, Barbara Herrnstein: 146
Smith, Barbara: 73, 81, 87, 95, 96, 99, 259–61,
    268n, 272
Smith, Dorothy: 172
Smith, Ethel M.: 52, 56, 58
Smith, Jane I.: 343n
Smith, Jane Norman: 55, 56
Smith, Margaret: 346n
Smith, Paul: 184–5, 199n, 200n
Snitow, Anne: 3, 98
Spacks, Patricia Meyer: 114
Spector, Judith: 105–6
Spelman, Elizabeth: 74, 161, 186, 201n, 245,
    268n, 272, 343n
Spillers, Hortense: 95, 97, 186–90, 192, 198,
    201n, 245, 312
Spivak, Gayatri Chakravorty: 99, 197–8, 203n,
    332, 343n, 346n
Stacey, Judith: 31, 43
Stack, Carol B.: 40, 41
Stallybrass, Peter: 81
Stansell, Christine: 42, 98
Stanton, Donna: 248n
Stanton, Elizabeth Cady: 47, 151, 161
Steedman, Carolyn (Kay): 75, 186, 190–98,
    202n
Steihm, Judith: 335, 347n
Stephen, Lynn: 101
Sterling, Anne Fausto: 166–7, 173–75
Stern, Daniel N.: 200n
Stern, William: 206, 219, 292
Stimpson, Catharine: 14, 38, 115–6, 119
Stuard, Susan, 40
Suleiman, Susan: 303n
Sunstein, Cass: 163
Swerdlow, Amy: 10, 23, 37, 43

Tabari, Azar: 343n
Taub, Nadine: 41, 58, 148, 161
Tax, Meredith: 20, 39
Tennenhouse, Leonard: 43
Tentler, Leslie Woodcock: 55
Thompson, Sharon: 98
Tillion, Germaine: 334, 347n
Tong, Benjamin: 239, 249n
Toprok, Binnaz (Sayari): 346n
Trinh, T. Minh-ha: 101
Tucker, Judith: 346n
Turner, Bryan S.: 328, 344
Tzu, Sun: 412n

Urwin, Cathy: 199n, 201n

Van de Ven, Nicole: 99
Vance, Carole: 16, 38, 85, 95, 96, 119, 163,
    202n, 267n, 321–2n
Venn, Couze: 199n
Vogel, Lise: 41

Waines, David: 328
Walker, Alice: 19, 39, 241, 249n, 269n, 273,
    279, 284, 287n, 321n
Walkerdine, Valerie: 199n
Walkowitz, Judy R.: 42
Walzer, Michael: 148
Wandersee, Winifred: 57, 58
Ware, Celestine: 76, 98
Watney, Simon: 100
Weed, Elizabeth: 124, 146
Weedon, Chris: 258–62, 267, 268n
Weitzman, Lenore J.: 41, 161
Wells, Julie: 23, 39, 40
Westpahl-Wihe, Sarah: 98
White, Allon: 81
Whitehead, Mary Beth: 35–6, 206–7, 219
Whittemore, Robin: 58
Widnall, Sheila: 177
Wiggins, Mary: 57
Wilcox, Emily: 81
Williams, Joan: 58, 162
Williams, Wendy: 41, 58, 161, 162
Willis, Ellen: 16, 38, 96
Willis, Sharon: 97, 101
Wilson, Elizabeth: 265, 269n
Wilson, William Julius: 233n, 265
Winnicott, D. W.: 189, 193, 195, 202n
Winnow, Jackie: 100
Witte, Edwin E.: 56
Wolf, Christa: 248n

Wollstonecraft, Mary: 28–29, 30, 43, 314

Wong, Sau-ling: 239

Wong, Shawn: 237

Woo, Merle: 247n

Woolf, Virginia: 110, 116, 119

Wye, Mary: 98

Yarborough, Richard: 247n, 250

Yeagar, Patricia: 43

Yeganeh, Nahid: 343n

Zemke, Deborah: 100

Zimmerman, Bonnie: 260, 268n

Zinn, Maxine Baca: 80

Notes on Contributors

Elizabeth Abel, Associate Professor of English at the University of California, Berkeley, is author of *Virginia Woolf and the Fictions of Psychoanalysis* (1989), editor of *Writing and Sexual Difference* (1982), and co-editor of *The Voyage In: Fictions of Female Development* (1983) and *The Signs Reader: Women, Gender, and Scholarship* (1983).

Mary M. Childers is Assistant Professor of English at Villanova University. She has published essays on feminism in world literature and the subject of work and gender in English novels. Currently she is working on a book on middle-class novelists and working-class autobiographers in England from 1848 to 1928.

Nancy F. Cott is Professor of History and American Studies at Yale University, and the author of *The Grounding of Modern Feminism* (1987) and *A Woman Making History: Mary Ritter Beard through Her Letters* (1990).

King Kok-Cheung is Assistant Professor of English and Asian American Studies at the University of California, Los Angeles. *Articulate Silences,* her book-in-progress, is forthcoming from Cornell University Press.

Teresa de Lauretis is Professor of the History of Consciousness at the University of California, Santa Cruz. The author of *Alice Doesn't* and *Technologies of Gender,* she is currently working on a book on sexual structuring and lesbian subjectivity in relation to social practices and representations.

Carla Freccero teaches in the departments of French and Italian, Comparative Literature, and Women's Studies at Dartmouth College. Her book on father figures in the text of François Rabelais is forthcoming, and she has published numerous articles, including feminist readings of Renaissance texts and literary and historical studies of Renaissance women writers.

Jane Gallop is Professor of English and Comparative Literature at the University of Wisconsin-Milwaukee. Her most recent book is *Thinking Through the Body*; her next book (forthcoming from Routledge) is *Around 1981: Academic Feminist Literary Theory.*

Evelynn Hammonds is currently a Visiting Scholar at Hampshire College and a doctoral candidate in the History of Science at Harvard University.

Marianne Hirsch is Professor of French and chair of Comparative Literature at Dartmouth College. She is the author of *Beyond the Single Vision: Henry James, Michel Butor, Uwe Johnson* (1981) and *The Mother/Daughter Plot: Narrative, Psychoanalysis, Feminism* (1989), and co-editor of *The Voyage In: Fictions of Female Development* (1983).

Bell Hooks is Associate Professor of English and Women's Studies at Oberlin College. She is the author of *Ain't I a Woman: Black Women and Feminism, Feminist Theory: From Margin to Center, Talking Back,* and the soon to be published collection of essays, *Yearning: Race and Gender in the Cultural Marketplace.*

Peggy Kamuf is Professor of French at the University of Southern California. She is the author of *Fictions of Feminine Desire: Disclosures of Heloise,* and *Signature Pieces: On the Institution of Authorship.* She has also edited *A Derrida Reader: Between the Blinds* which is soon to appear.

Evelyn Fox Keller is a professor at the University of California, Berkeley, where she teaches feminist theory and the history and philosophy of science. She is the author of *Reflections on Gender and Science* (1985) and *A Feeling for the Organism: The Life and Work of Barbara McClintock* (1983), and co-editor of *Body/Politics: Women and the Discourses of Science* (1989) and *Keywords in Evolutionary Biology* (forthcoming).

Katie King is Assistant Professor of Women's Studies at the University of Maryland, College Park. Her previous articles have been on gay studies, feminist theory and the apparatus of literary production. She is currently writing on what counts as feminist theory, and proselytizing a field she calls "feminism and writing technologies," which examines the politics of distinctions between the "oral" and the "written."

Tom Laqueur is Professor of History at the University of California, Berkeley. He is the father of Hannah Laqueur and author of *Making Sex: Body and Gender from the Greeks to Freud* (Harvard University Press, 1990).

Marnia Lazreg is an Algerian sociologist. She is interested in feminist theory and epistemology, development, and cultural studies. She is Associate Professor of Sociology and Women's Studies at Hunter College, CUNY, New York. Her latest publication, "Gender and Politics in Algeria: Unravelling the Religious Paradigm," will appear in the forthcoming issue of *Signs.* She is at present working on a book dealing with "Women and the Contradictions of Islamic Socialism."

Helen Longino teaches philosophy at Rice University. She is the author of *Science as Social Process* (Princeton, 1990), and co-editor of *Competition: A Feminist Taboo?* (1987).

Nancy K. Miller is Distinguished Professor of English at Lehman College and the Graduate Center, CUNY. She is the author of *The Heroine's Text: Readings in the French and English Novel, 1722–1782* (1980) and *Subject to Change: Reading Feminist Writing* (1988), and editor of *The Poetics of Gender* (1986). She co-edited with Joan DeJean *The Politics of Tradition: Placing Women in French Literature, Yale French Studies 75* (1988).

Martha Minow is Professor of Law at Harvard Law School, and author of *Making All the Difference: Inclusion, Exclusion, and American Law* (Cornell University Press, 1990).

Sara Ruddick teaches philosophy and women's studies at the Eugene Lang College of the New School for Social Research. She is the co-editor of *Working It Out* and *Between Women* and the author of *Maternal Thinking: Toward a Politics of Peace*.

Joan Scott is Professor of Social Science at The Institute for Advanced Study and author, most recently, of *Gender and the Politics of History*.

Valerie Smith is Associate Professor of English at the University of California, Los Angeles. The author of *Self-Discovery and Authority in Afro-American Narrative* (1987) and the editor of *New Essays on Toni Morrison's "Song of Solomon"* (forthcoming), she has written essays on black feminist criticism, Afro-American narrative, and black independent film. She is currently at work on two books, one on slavery and recent Afro-American writing, the other on black feminist theory.

Ann Snitow has been a feminist-activist since 1970, when she was one of the founding members of New York Radical Feminists. She is a professor of literature and women's studies at Eugene Lang College of the New School for Social Research, and coeditor of *Powers of Desire: The Politics of Sexuality* with Christine Stansell and Sharon Thompson. In another life she wrote a book about Ford Madox Ford, and her articles appear in such places as the *Village Voice*, *The Nation*, *Ms*, the *Women's Review of Books*, *Mother Jones*, and the *New York Times*.

Michelle Stanworth teaches sociology at Anglia Higher Education College, Cambridge, and edits the Feminist Perspectives series for Polity Press and the University of Minnesota. Her books include *Gender and Schooling* (1983), *Women and the Public Sphere* (with Janet Siltanen, 1984) and *Reproductive Technologies* (1988).